MW01623367

Language Arts and Literature

Course 2

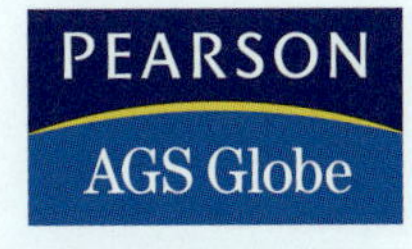

Shoreview, MN

Reading Consultant

Timothy Shanahan, Ph.D., Professor of Urban Education, Director of the Center for Literacy, University of Illinois Chicago, Author, *AMP™ Reading System*

Acknowledgments appear on pages 630–631, which constitutes an extension of this copyright page.

Reviewers

The publisher wishes to thank the following educators for their helpful comments during the review process for *Language Arts and Literature, Course 2.*

Sherie J. Campbell, ESE Teacher, Ben Hill Middle School, Tampa, FL; **Stephanie Fetterolf,** Vice Principal, Hilltop Middle School, Toronto, Ontario, Canada; **Jayne O'Gorman,** 6th Grade Reading Teacher, Clifford Crone Middle School, Naperville, IL; **Jane McKenney,** K–12 English Coordinator, Smith Middle School, Troy, MI; **Michelle Richards,** Instructional Coordinating Teacher, Cochrane Middle School, Charlotte, NC; **Mary Alice Ross,** Content Coordinator for English/Language Arts, Flint Community Schools, Flint, MI; **Ellen Smith De La Cruz,** Teacher, Balboa Park Academy—Juvenile Court and Community Schools, San Diego, CA; **Lori Wells,** M.Ed., LSSP, LPA, Educational Diagnostician, Harlingen High School South, Harlingen, TX; **Alicia Wingard,** Special Education Teacher, Mountain Brook Junior High School, Birmingham, AL

ISBN-13: 978-0-7854-6314-6

ISBN-10: 0-7854-6314-3

1 2 3 4 5 6 7 8 9 10 11 10 09 08 07

1-800-992-0244

www.agsglobe.com

Contents

How to Use This Book: A Study Guide

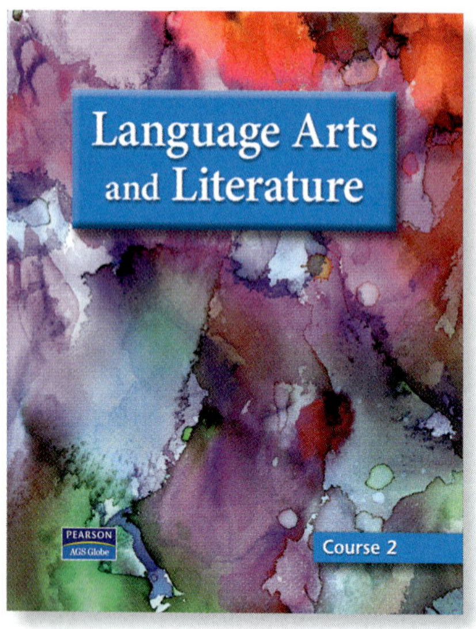

This book is an anthology of literature. An anthology is a collection of literature written by different authors. The literature can be poems, plays, short stories, essays, parts of novels, folktales, legends, or myths. Sometimes an anthology contains selections from a certain country or continent. For example, you might have an anthology with great literature from around the world. Sometimes anthologies are organized around different genres, or types of literature. Then, you might have sections on poems, short stories, plays, essays, or folktales.

Reading a Literature Anthology

This anthology contains much enjoyable literature. An anthology helps you understand yourself and other people. Sometimes you will read about people from other countries. Sometimes you will read about people who lived in the past. Try to relate what the author is saying to your own life. Ask yourself: Have I ever felt this way? Have I known anyone like this person? Have I seen anything like this?

A literature anthology can also help you appreciate the beauty of language. As you read, find phrases or sentences that you particularly like. You may want to start a notebook of these phrases and sentences. You may also want to include words that are difficult.

This anthology is also important because it introduces you to great works of literature. Many times, you will find references to these works in everyday life. Sometimes you will hear a quotation on TV or read it in the newspaper. Great literature can come in many forms. On the next page are definitions of some kinds of literature genres in an anthology.

Genre Definitions

autobiography a person's life story, written by that person

biography a person's life story told by someone else (you will find biographies of many famous authors in this book)

diary a daily record of personal events, thoughts, or private feelings

- A diary is like a journal, but a diary often expresses more of the writer's feelings.

drama a story told through the words and actions of characters, written to be performed as well as read; a play

essay a written work that shows a writer's opinions on some basic or current issue

fable a short story or poem with a moral (lesson about life), often with animals who act like humans

- Aesop was a famous author of fables.

fiction writing that is imaginative and designed to entertain

- In fiction, the author creates the events and characters.
- Short stories, novels, folktales, myths, legends, and most plays are works of fiction.

folktale a story that has been handed down from one generation to another

- The characters are usually either good or bad.
- Folktales make use of rhyme and repetitive phrases.
- Sometimes they are called tall tales, particularly if they are humorous and exaggerated.
- Folktales are also called folklore.

journal writing that expresses an author's feelings or first impressions about a subject

- Students may keep journals that record thoughts about what they have read.
- People also keep travel journals to remind themselves of interesting places they have seen.

legend a traditional story that at one time was told orally and was handed down from one generation to another

- Legends are like myths, but they do not have as many supernatural forces.
- Legends usually feature characters who actually lived, or real places or events.

myth an important story, often part of a culture's religion, that explains how the world came to be or why natural events happen

- A myth usually includes gods, goddesses, or unusually powerful human beings.
- Myths were first oral stories, and most early cultures have myths.

nonfiction writing about real people and events

- Essays, speeches, diaries, journals, autobiographies, and biographies are all usually nonfiction.

novel fiction that is book-length and has more plot and character details than a short story

poem a short piece of literature that usually has rhythm and paints powerful or beautiful impressions with words

- Often, poems have sound patterns such as rhyme.
- Songs are poetry set to music.

prose all writing that is not poetry

- short stories, novels, autobiographies, biographies, diaries, journals, and essays are examples of prose.

science fiction fiction that is based on real or imagined facts of science

- Most stories are set in the future.
- Jules Verne was one of the first science fiction authors.

short story a brief work of prose fiction that includes plot, setting, characters, point of view, and theme

- Edgar Allan Poe was a great writer of short stories.

How to Read This Book

Different works of literature should be read in different ways. However, there are some basic methods you should use to read all works of literature.

Great Wall of Books
William James

"'Tis strange, but true; for truth is always strange,— Stranger than fiction."
—Lord Byron
Don Juan (1823)

Unit 1 *Fiction and Nonfiction*

Sometimes we enjoy getting lost in the world of imagination. At those times, we read fiction—maybe a good adventure book or a mystery. Other times we want to learn about real people, places, or events. That is when we read nonfiction, like magazines articles, essays, biographies, or history books. There are times when fiction can seem very real and nonfiction very unreal. An imaginary character in a well-written story can seem like a real person. Yet newspapers often report on events that seem stranger than any fiction writer could imagine. Each way of telling a story can teach us something important about life.

In this unit, writers use both fiction and nonfiction to explore the world around us.

Fiction and Nonfiction Part 1 Unit 1 1

Before Beginning a Unit

- Read the unit title and selection titles.
- Read the paragraphs that introduce the unit.
- Look at the pictures and other artwork in the unit.
- Think about what you already know about the unit.
- Think about what you might want to learn.
- Develop questions in your mind that you think will be answered in this unit.

Before Reading a Selection

- Read the selection's title.
- Look at the pictures and other artwork.
- Read the background material included in About the Author and About the Selection.
- Read the Objectives and think about what you will learn by reading the selection.

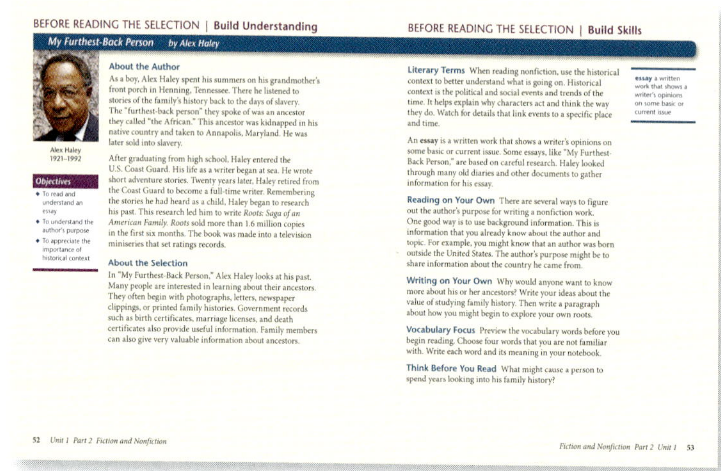

BEFORE READING THE SELECTION | **Build Understanding**

My Furthest-Back Person by Alex Haley

Alex Haley
1921–1992

Objectives
- To read and understand an essay
- To understand the author's purpose
- To appreciate the importance of historical context

About the Author

As a boy, Alex Haley spent his summers on his grandmother's front porch in Henning, Tennessee. There he listened to stories of the family's history back to the days of slavery. The "furthest-back person" they spoke of was an ancestor they called "the African." This ancestor was kidnapped in his native country and taken to Annapolis, Maryland. He was later sold into slavery.

After graduating from high school, Haley entered the U.S. Coast Guard. His life as a writer began at sea. He wrote short adventure stories. Twenty years later, Haley retired from the Coast Guard to become a full-time writer. Remembering the stories he had heard as a child, Haley began to research his past. This research led him to write *Roots: Saga of an American Family. Roots* sold more than 1.6 million copies in the first six months. The book was made into a television miniseries that set ratings records.

About the Selection

In "My Furthest-Back Person," Alex Haley looks at his past. Many people are interested in learning about their ancestors. They often begin with photographs, letters, newspaper clippings, or printed family histories. Government records such as birth certificates, marriage licenses, and death certificates also provide useful information. Family members can also give very valuable information about ancestors.

52 *Unit 1 Part 2 Fiction and Nonfiction*

BEFORE READING THE SELECTION | **Build Skills**

Literary Terms When reading nonfiction, use the historical context to better understand what is going on. Historical context is the political and social events and trends of the time. It helps explain why characters act and think the way they do. Watch for details that link events to a specific place and time.

An **essay** is a written work that shows a writer's opinions on some basic or current issue. Some essays, like "My Furthest-Back Person," are based on careful research. Haley looked through many old diaries and other documents to gather information for his essay.

essay a written work that shows a writer's opinions on some basic or current issue

Reading on Your Own There are several ways to figure out the author's purpose for writing a nonfiction work. One good way is to use background information. This is information that you already know about the author and topic. For example, you might know that an author was born outside the United States. The author's purpose might be to share information about the country he came from.

Writing on Your Own Why would anyone want to know more about his or her ancestors? Write your ideas about the value of studying family history. Then write a paragraph about how you might begin to explore your own roots.

Vocabulary Focus Preview the vocabulary words before you begin reading. Choose four words that you are not familiar with. Write each word and its meaning in your notebook.

Think Before You Read What might cause a person to spend years looking into his family history?

Fiction and Nonfiction Part 2 Unit 1 53

- Read the Literary Terms and their definitions.
- Complete the Before Reading the Selection activities. These activities will help you read the selection, understand vocabulary, and prepare for the reading.

As You Read a Selection

- Read the notes in the side margins. These will help you understand and think about the main ideas.
- Think of people or events in your own life that are similar to those described.
- Reread sentences or paragraphs that you do not understand.
- Predict what you think will happen next.
- Read the definitions at the bottom of the page for words that you do not know.
- Record words that you do not know. Also, write questions or comments you have about the text.

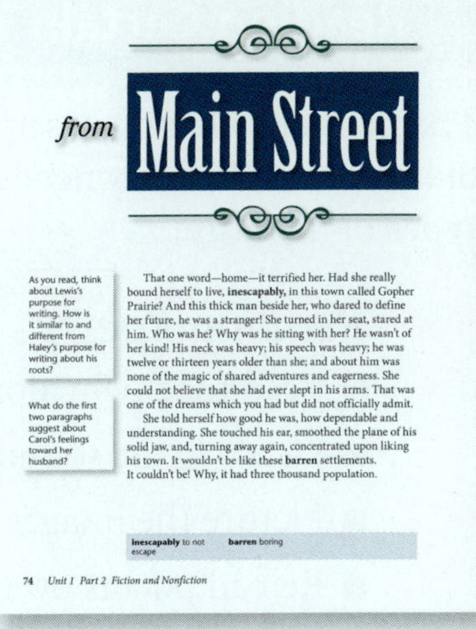

from **Main Street**

As you read, think about Lewis's purpose for writing. How is it similar to and different from Haley's purpose for writing about his roots?

What do the first two paragraphs suggest about Carol's feelings toward her husband?

That one word—home—it terrified her. Had she really bound herself to live, **inescapably,** in this town called Gopher Prairie? And this thick man beside her, who dared to define her future, he was a stranger! She turned in her seat, stared at him. Who was he? Why was he sitting with her? He wasn't of her kind! His neck was heavy; his speech was heavy; he was twelve or thirteen years older than she; and about him was none of the magic of shared adventures and eagerness. She could not believe that she had ever slept in his arms. That was one of the dreams which you had but did not officially admit.

She told herself how good he was, how dependable and understanding. She touched his ear, smoothed the plane of his solid jaw, and, turning away again, concentrated upon liking his town. It wouldn't be like these **barren** settlements. It couldn't be! Why, it had three thousand population.

inescapably to not escape   **barren** boring

74 *Unit 1 Part 2 Fiction and Nonfiction*

After Reading a Selection

- Reread interesting or difficult parts of the selection.
- Reflect on what you have learned by reading the selection.
- Complete the After Reading the Selection review questions and activities. The activities will help you develop your grammar, writing, speaking, listening, viewing, technology, media, and research skills.

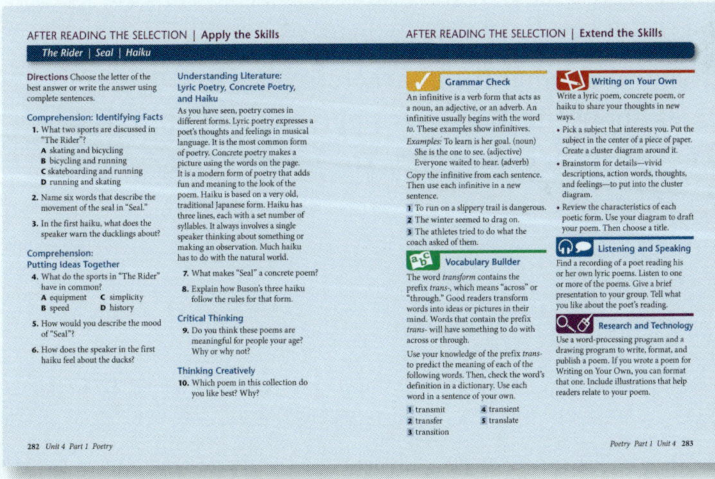

AFTER READING THE SELECTION | **Apply the Skills**

The Rider | Seal | Haiku

Directions Choose the letter of the best answer or write the answer using complete sentences.

Comprehension: Identifying Facts

1. What two sports are discussed in "The Rider"?
   - A skating and bicycling
   - B bicycling and running
   - C skateboarding and running
   - D running and skating
2. Name six words that describe the movement of the seal in "Seal."
3. In the first haiku, what does the speaker warn the ducklings about?

Comprehension: Putting Ideas Together

4. What do the sports in "The Rider" have in common?
   - A equipment
   - B speed
   - C simplicity
   - D history
5. How would you describe the mood of "Seal"?
6. How does the speaker in the first haiku feel about the ducks?

Understanding Literature: Lyric Poetry, Concrete Poetry, and Haiku

As you have seen, poetry comes in different forms. Lyric poetry expresses a poet's thoughts and feelings in musical language. It is the most common form of poetry. Concrete poetry makes a picture using the words on the page. It is a modern form of poetry that adds fun and meaning to the look of the poem. Haiku is based on a very old, traditional Japanese form. Haiku has three lines, each with a set number of syllables. It always involves a single speaker thinking about something or making an observation. Much haiku has to do with the natural world.

7. What makes "Seal" a concrete poem?
8. Explain how Buson's three haiku follow the rules for that form.

Critical Thinking

9. Do you think these poems are meaningful for people your age? Why or why not?

Thinking Creatively

10. Which poem in this collection do you like best? Why?

282 *Unit 4 Part 1 Poetry*

AFTER READING THE SELECTION | **Extend the Skills**

Grammar Check

An infinitive is a verb form that acts as a noun, an adjective, or an adverb. An infinitive usually begins with the word *to*. These examples show infinitives.

Examples: To learn is her goal. (noun)
She is the one to see. (adjective)
Everyone waited to hear. (adverb)

Copy the infinitive from each sentence. Then use each infinitive in a new sentence.

1 To run on a slippery trail is dangerous.
2 The winter seemed to drag on.
3 The athletes tried to do what the coach asked of them.

Vocabulary Builder

The word *transform* contains the prefix *trans-*, which means "across" or "through." Good readers transform words into ideas or pictures in their mind. Words that contain the prefix *trans-* will have something to do with across or through.

Use your knowledge of the prefix *trans-* to predict the meaning of each of the following words. Then, check the word's definition in a dictionary. Use each word in a sentence of your own.

1 transmit
2 transfer
3 transition
4 transient
5 translate

Writing on Your Own

Write a lyric poem, concrete poem, or haiku to share your thoughts in new ways.

- Pick a subject that interests you. Put the subject in the center of a piece of paper. Create a cluster diagram around it.
- Brainstorm for details—vivid descriptions, action words, thoughts, and feelings—to put into the cluster diagram.
- Review the characteristics of each poetic form. Use your diagram to draft your poem. Then choose a title.

Listening and Speaking

Find a recording of a poet reading his or her own lyric poems. Listen to one or more of the poems. Give a brief presentation to your group. Tell what you like about the poet's reading.

Research and Technology

Use a word-processing program and a drawing program to write, format, and publish a poem. If you wrote a poem for Writing on Your Own, you can format that one. Include illustrations that help readers relate to your poem.

Poetry Part 1 Unit 4 283

Reading Certain Types of Literature

The methods already described will help you understand all kinds of literature. You may need to use additional methods for specific types of literature.

Reading Poetry

- Read the poem aloud.
- Listen to the sounds of the words.
- Picture the images the author is describing.
- Reread poems over and over again to appreciate the author's use of language.

Reading Essays

- Review the questions in the After Reading the Selection before you begin reading.
- Use the questions to think about what you are reading.
- Remember that essays usually express an author's opinions. Try to understand why the author may have formed these opinions.

Reading Plays

- Picture the setting of the play. Since there usually is not much description given, try to relate the setting to something you have seen before.
- Pay attention to what the characters say. How does this give clues about the character's personality? Have you ever known anyone like this? Are you like this?

Tips for Better Reading

Literary Terms

Literary Terms are words or phrases that we use to study and discuss works of literature. These terms describe the ways an author helps to make us enjoy and understand what we are reading. Some of the terms also describe a genre, or specific type of literature. In this anthology, you will see white boxes on the side of the Before Reading the Selection pages. In these boxes are Literary Terms and their definitions. These terms are important in understanding and discussing the selection being read. By understanding these Literary Terms, readers can appreciate the author's craft. You can find the definitions for all of the Literary Terms used in this book in the Handbook of Literary Terms on page 598.

setting the place and time in a story

plot the series of events in a story

theme the main idea of a literary work

Using a Graphic Organizer

A graphic organizer is visual representation of information. It can help you see how ideas are related to each other. A graphic organizer can help you study for a test, organize information before writing an essay, or organize details in a literature selection. You will use graphic organizers for different activities throughout this textbook. There are 14 different graphic organizers listed below. You can read a description and see an example of each graphic organizer in Appendix A in the back of this textbook.

- Character Analysis Guide
- Story Map
- Main Idea Graphic (Umbrella)
- Main Idea Graphic (Table)
- Main Idea Graphic (Details)
- Venn Diagram
- Sequence Chain
- Concept Map
- Plot Mountain
- Structured Overview
- Semantic Table
- Prediction Guide
- Semantic Line
- KWL Chart

Six Traits of Writing

A *trait* is a quality or feature of something. Traits, or qualities, of good writing help students and teachers discuss writing using a common language. These traits will help you as you plan, draft, revise, and edit your writing. The Six Traits of Writing icons pictured below are used in the Writing Workshops at the end of each unit in this textbook. As you write, think about how you can use each trait to help make your writing better. You can also read more about each trait in Appendix C at the back of this book.

Ideas message, details, and purpose

Word Choice vivid words that "show, not tell"

Voice the writer's own language

Organization order, ideas tied together

Sentence Fluency smooth rhythm and flow

Conventions correct grammar, spelling, and mechanics

Taking Notes

You will read many selections in this literature anthology. As you read, you may want to take notes to help remember what you have read. You can use these notes to keep track of events and characters in a story. Your notes may also be helpful for recognizing common ideas among the selections in a unit. You can review your notes as you prepare to take a test. Here are some tips for taking notes:

- Write down only the most important information.
- Do not try to write every detail or every word.
- Write notes in your own words.
- Do not be concerned about writing in complete sentences. Use short phrases.

Using the Three-Column Chart

One good way to take notes is to use a three-column chart. Make your own three-column chart by dividing a sheet of notebook paper into three parts. In Column 1, write the topic you are reading about or studying. In Column 2, write what you learned about this topic as you read or listened to your teacher. In Column 3, write questions, observations, or opinions about the topic, or write a detail that will help you remember the topic. Here are some examples of different ways to take notes using the three-column chart.

The topic I am studying	What I learned from reading the text or class discussion	Questions, observations, or ideas I have about the topic
Fiction	• one genre of literature • many different types of fiction—science fiction, adventure, detective stories, romance, suspense	• The book I am reading right now is fiction. It is an adventure story. • I wonder if poetry is part of the fiction genre.

Vocabulary Word	Definition	Sentence with Vocabulary Word
Premises	a building or part of a building	Students are not allowed on the school **premises** during the weekend.

Character	Character Traits Found in the Selection	Page Number
John Krakauer	Conflict, person against self—Krakauer wonders if he will run out of oxygen before returning to camp.	p. 355
	Determined—Krakauer is determined to make it back to camp even though his oxygen has run out and it is snowing on the mountain.	p. 358
	Thankful—After reaching camp, Krakauer is thankful that he is safe.	p. 360

Reading Checklist

Good readers do not just read with their eyes. They read with their brains turned on. In other words, they are active readers. Good readers use strategies as they read to keep them on their toes. The following strategies will help you to check your understanding of what you read.

- **Summarizing** To summarize a text, stop often as you read. Notice these things: the topic, the main thing being said about the topic, important details that support the main idea. Try to sum up the author's message using your own words.
- **Questioning** Ask yourself questions about the text and read to answer them. Here are some useful questions to ask: Why did the author include this information? Is this like anything I have experienced? Am I learning what I hoped I would learn?
- **Predicting** As you read, think about what might come next. Add in what you already know about the topic. Predict what the text will say. Then, as you read, notice whether your prediction is right. If not, change your prediction.
- **Text Structure** Pay attention to how a text is organized. Find parts that stand out. They are probably the most important ideas or facts. Think about why the author organized ideas this way. Is the author showing a sequence of events? Is the author explaining a solution or the effect of something?
- **Visualizing** Picture what is happening in a text or what is being described. Make a movie out of it in your mind. If you can picture it clearly, then you know you understand it. Visualizing what you read will also help you remember it later.
- **Inferencing** The meaning of a text may not be stated. Instead, the author may give clues and hints. It is up to you to put them together with what you already know about the topic. Then you make an inference—you conclude what the author means.
- **Metacognition** Think about your thinking patterns as you read. Before reading a text, preview it. Think about what you can do to get the most out of it. Think about what you already know about the topic. Write down any questions you have. After you read, ask yourself: Did that make sense? If not, read it again.

What to Do About Words You Do Not Know

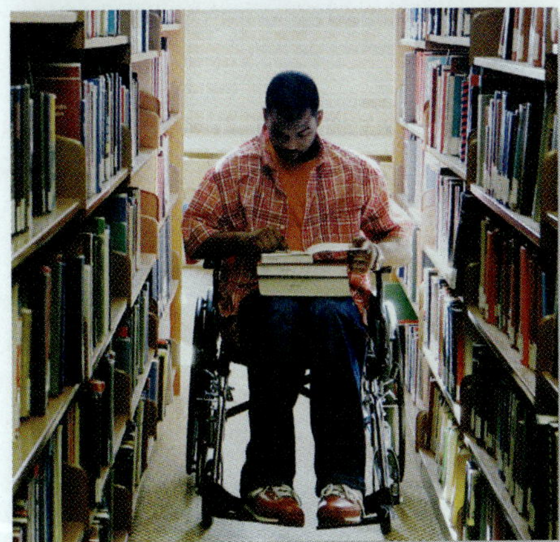

- If the word is in bold type, look for the definition of the word at the bottom of the page.
- If the word is not in bold type, read to the end of the sentence and maybe the next sentence. Can you determine the meaning now?
- Look at the beginning sound of the unknown word. Ask yourself, "What word begins with this sound and would make sense here?"
- Sound out the syllables of the word.
- If you still cannot determine the meaning, see if you know any parts of the word: prefixes, suffixes, or roots.
- If this does not work, write the word on a note card or in a vocabulary notebook. Then look up the word in a dictionary after you have finished reading the selection. Reread the passage containing the unknown word after you have looked up its definition.
- If the word is necessary to understand the passage, look it up in a dictionary or glossary immediately.

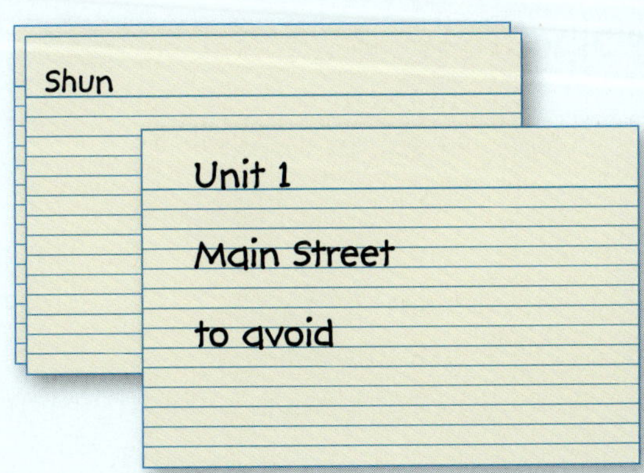

Word Study Tips

- Start a vocabulary file with note cards to use for review.
- Write one word on the front of each card. Write the unit number, selection title, and the definition on the back.
- You can use these cards as flash cards by yourself or with a study partner to test your knowledge.

Tips for Taking Tests

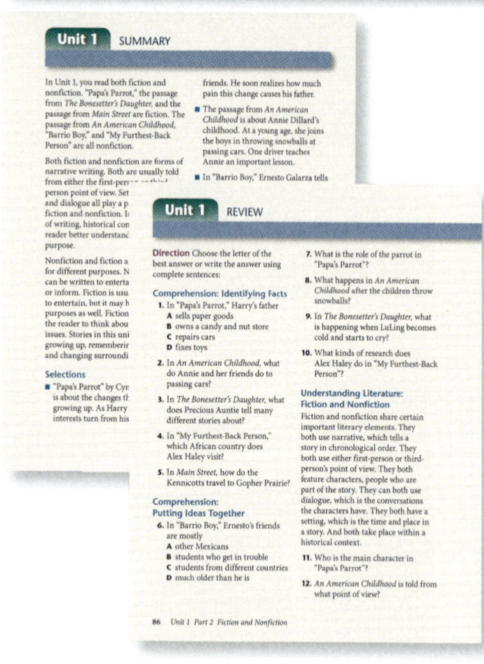

Unit 1 SUMMARY

In Unit 1, you read both fiction and nonfiction. "Papa's Parrot," the passage from *The Bonesetter's Daughter*, and the passage from *Main Street* are fiction. The passage from *An American Childhood*, "Barrio Boy," and "My Furthest-Back Person" are all nonfiction.

Both fiction and nonfiction are forms of narrative writing. Both are usually told from either the first-per

friends. He soon realizes how much pain this change causes his father.

- The passage from *An American Childhood* is about Annie Dillard's childhood. At a young age, she joins the boys in throwing snowballs at passing cars. One driver teaches Annie an important lesson.
- In "Barrio Boy," Ernesto Galarza tells

Unit 1 REVIEW

Direction Choose the letter of the best answer or write the answer using complete sentences.

Comprehension: Identifying Facts

1. In "Papa's Parrot," Harry's father
   - A sells paper goods
   - B owns a candy and nut store
   - C repairs cars
   - D fixes toys
2. In *An American Childhood*, what do Annie and her friends do to passing cars?
3. In *The Bonesetter's Daughter*, what does Precious Auntie tell many different stories about?
4. In "My Furthest-Back Person," which African country does Alex Haley visit?
5. In *Main Street*, how do the Kennicotts travel to Gopher Prairie?

Comprehension: Putting Ideas Together

6. In "Barrio Boy," Ernesto's friends are mostly
   - A other Mexicans
   - B students who get in trouble
   - C students from different countries
   - D much older than he is
7. What is the role of the parrot in "Papa's Parrot"?
8. What happens in *An American Childhood* after the children throw snowballs?
9. In *The Bonesetter's Daughter*, what is happening when LuLing becomes cold and starts to cry?
10. What kinds of research does Alex Haley do in "My Furthest-Back Person"?

Understanding Literature: Fiction and Nonfiction

Fiction and nonfiction share certain important literary elements. They both use narrative, which tells a story in chronological order. They both use either first-person or third-person's point of view. They both feature characters, people who are part of the story. They can both use dialogue, which is the conversations the characters have. They both have a setting, which is the time and place in a story. And both take place within a historical context.

11. Who is the main character in "Papa's Parrot"?
12. *An American Childhood* is told from what point of view?

86 *Unit 1 Part 2 Fiction and Nonfiction*

Before the Test Day

- Make sure you have read all of the selections assigned.
- Review the Literary Terms and definitions for each selection.
- Review your answers to the After Reading the Selection questions.
- Reread the Unit Summary and review your answers to the Unit Review.
- Review any notes that you have taken or graphic organizers you have developed.
- Ask your teacher what kinds of questions will be on the test.
- Try to predict what questions will be asked. Think of and write answers to those questions.
- Review the Test-Taking Tip at the bottom of each Unit Review page.

During the Test

- Come to the test with a positive attitude.
- Write your name on the paper.
- Preview the test and read the directions carefully.
- Plan your time.
- Answer the questions that you know first.
- Then go back and answer the more difficult questions.
- Allow time to reread all of the questions and your answers.

Great Wall of Books
William James

Unit 1 Fiction and Nonfiction

Sometimes we enjoy getting lost in the world of imagination. At those times, we read fiction—maybe a good adventure book or a mystery. Other times we want to learn about real people, places, or events. That is when we read nonfiction, like magazines articles, essays, biographies, or history books. There are times when fiction can seem very real and nonfiction very unreal. An imaginary character in a well-written story can seem like a real person. Yet newspapers often report on events that seem stranger than any fiction writer could imagine. Each way of telling a story can teach us something important about life.

In this unit, writers use both fiction and nonfiction to explore the world around us.

Unit 1 Selections **Page**

"'Tis strange, but true; for truth is always strange,— Stranger than fiction."

—Lord Byron
Don Juan (1823)

Unit 1 About Fiction and Nonfiction

Elements of Fiction

Fiction is writing that is imaginative and designed to entertain. The author creates the events and characters. All works of fiction share certain basic elements.

- They include people or animals called **characters.**
- The series of events in a story is called a **plot.**
- The time and place in a story is called the **setting.**
- The one that tells the story is the **narrator.**
- The main idea of the story is called the **theme.**

Fiction is told from a certain **point of view.** A point of view is the position from which the author tells the story. A **first-person point of view** is where the narrator is also a character, using the pronouns *I* and *we.* A **third-person point of view** is where the narrator is not a character, and refers to characters as *he* and *she.*

Types of Fiction

A **novel** is fiction that is book-length and has more plot and characters than a short story. Characters often face a problem in a certain time and place.

A **novella** is fiction that is longer than a short story but shorter than a novel.

A **short story** is a brief work of fiction. Like a novel, a short story has characters, a setting, and a plot. Unlike a novel, it has a single conflict and is meant to be read in one sitting.

Characteristics of Nonfiction

Nonfiction writing is different from fiction in a few important ways.

- Nonfiction writing is only about real people, events, or ideas.
- Nonfiction is told from the author's point of view.
- Nonfiction writing has facts or talks about ideas.
- It may show the historical context of the time period. Historical context may include information about the people, events, and culture of a certain time period.

"PEANUTS" reprinted by permission of United Feature Syndicate, Inc.

Types of Nonfiction

A **biography** is a person's life story told by someone else. A biography is usually told from the third-person point of view.

An **autobiography or memoir** is a person's life story, written by that person. An autobiography or memoir is told from the first-person point of view.

A **letter** is impressions or feelings written to a specific person. A letter might share information, thoughts, or feelings.

A **journal or diary** is writing that expresses an author's feelings or first impressions about a subject.

An **essay or article** is a written work that shows a writer's opinions on some basic or current issue.

Informational text is writing that we come across in everyday life, including instructions and newspaper articles.

Reading Strategy:
Context Clues

Looking at the boldfaced words is one way to understand how a text is organized. As you preview a text, you will likely notice some words that are unfamiliar to you. You can use context clues to help figure out the meanings of these difficult words. Context clues are the text around an unfamiliar word that helps you figure out the meaning. Use context clues to help you better understand what you are reading.

Literary Terms

narrator one who tells the story

narrative a story, usually told in chronological order

chronological order a plot that moves forward in order of time

style an author's way of writing

narration the act of telling a story or giving an account of something

point of view the position from which the author or storyteller tells the story

first person a point of view where the narrator is also a character, using the pronouns *I* and *we*

third person a point of view where the narrator is not a character, and refers to characters as *he* or *she*

autobiography a person's life story, written by that person

fiction writing that is imaginative and designed to entertain; the author creates the events and characters

nonfiction writing about real people and events

Papa's Parrot by Cynthia Rylant

Courtesy of Cynthia Rylant

Cynthia Rylant
1954–

About the Author

Cynthia Rylant grew up in a small mountain town in West Virginia. Growing up, she never thought about becoming a writer. Aside from comic books, she did not do much reading. The only writing she did was for school. A future career as an author was the farthest thing from her mind.

When Rylant entered college, her plan was to become a nurse. Then, in an English course, she read a story by Langston Hughes. The story "just knocked me off my feet," Rylant said. She decided to change her major to English. It was a good choice, because she has found great success as a writer.

Remembering her own childhood, Rylant wrote *When I Was Young in the Mountains* in 1982. She has since written picture books, novels, short stories, and biographies. An animal lover with many dogs at home, Rylant often includes animals in her stories.

Objectives

- To read and understand fiction
- To understand the use of time order in narrative writing

About the Selection

Harry Tillian's father owns and operates a nut and candy store. Harry once spent a good deal of his time there. As Harry gets older, he spends less time at the store. Harry's father falls ill, and Harry learns an important lesson from a pet parrot. He realizes how much his father misses him. He also realizes how much he has disappointed his father.

***Before Reading* continued on next page**

Papa's Parrot *by Cynthia Rylant*

narrator the one who tells the story

narrative a story, usually told in chronological order

chronological order a plot that moves forward in order of time

style an author's way of writing

narration the act of telling a story or giving an account of something

Literary Terms The **narrator** is the one who tells the story. A **narrative** is a story, usually told in chronological order. **Chronological order** is a plot that moves forward in order of time. A narrative may take the form of fiction, nonfiction, or poetry. An author may use a different **style** in each story. Style is an author's way of writing. The act of telling a story or giving an account of something is called **narration.**

Use a graphic organizer like this one shown to record events from the story.

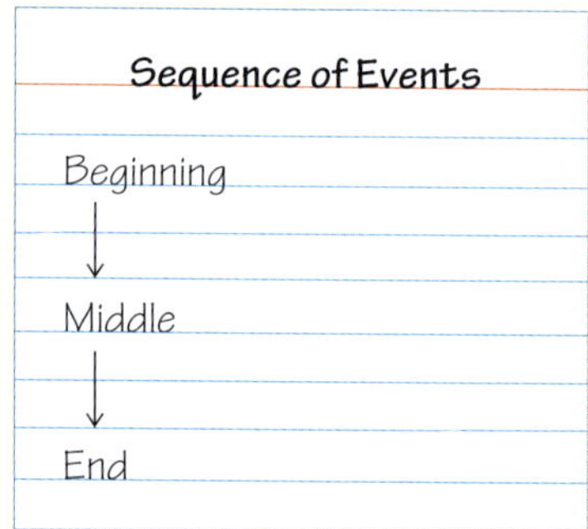

Reading on Your Own Context is the situation in which a word is used. Context clues are the words and phrases around an unfamiliar word. Use context clues to help you figure out the meaning of words you do not know. Words that mean the same or opposite can also help you figure out unfamiliar words.

Writing on Your Own In "Papa's Parrot," a boy's behavior changes when he enters middle school. Write several sentences about how behavior might change as one gets older.

Vocabulary Focus Preview the vocabulary words before you begin reading. Choose five words you are not familiar with. Write each word and its meaning in your notebook.

Think Before You Read Think about a friend or relative. Has your relationship with that person changed in any way recently? If so, how? As you read, compare your own changing relationship to that between Harry and his father.

Papa's Parrot

Though his father was fat and **merely** owned a candy and nut shop, Harry Tillian liked his papa. Harry stopped liking candy and nuts when he was around seven, but, in spite of this, he and Mr. Tillian had remained friends and were still friends the year Harry turned twelve.

As you read, think about how Harry's character continues to change as he gets older.

For years, after school, Harry had always stopped in to see his father at work. Many of Harry's friends stopped there, too, to spend a few cents choosing penny candy from the giant bins or to sample Mr. Tillian's latest batch of roasted peanuts. Mr. Tillian looked forward to seeing his son and his son's friends every day. He liked the company.

What details make this fictional narrative seem real?

When Harry entered junior high school, though, he didn't come by the candy and nut shop as often. Nor did his friends. They were older and they had more spending money. They went to a burger place. They played video games. They shopped for records. None of them were much interested in candy and nuts anymore.

Records are thin, grooved vinyl discs. They produce sound when played on a phonograph, or record player.

A new group of children came to Mr. Tillian's shop now. But not Harry Tillian and his friends.

The year Harry turned twelve was also the year Mr. Tillian got a parrot. He went to a pet store one day and bought one for more money than he could really afford. He brought the

How does Harry's behavior change after he enters junior high school?

merely only

parrot to his shop, set its cage near the sign for maple clusters, and named it Rocky.

Harry thought this was the strangest thing his father had ever done, and he told him so, but Mr. Tillian just **ignored** him.

Reading Strategy: **Context Clues**

Which context clue in the paragraph suggests what "romantic music" is?

Rocky was good company for Mr. Tillian. When business was slow, Mr. Tillian would turn on a small color television he had sitting in a corner, and he and Rocky would watch the soap operas. Rocky liked to scream when the romantic music came on, and Mr. Tillian would yell at him to shut up, but they seemed to enjoy themselves.

Why is Harry embarrassed by his father?

The more Mr. Tillian grew to like his parrot, and the more he talked to it instead of to people, the more embarrassed Harry became. Harry would stroll past the shop, on his way somewhere else, and he'd take a quick look inside to see what his dad was doing. Mr. Tillian was always talking to the bird. So Harry kept walking.

At home things were different. Harry and his father joked with each other at the dinner table as they always had—Mr. Tillian teasing Harry about his smelly socks; Harry teasing Mr. Tillian about his blubbery stomach. At home things seemed all right.

But one day, Mr. Tillian became ill. He had been at work, unpacking boxes of caramels, when he had grabbed his chest and fallen over on top of the candy. A customer had found him, and he was taken to the hospital in an ambulance.

Mr. Tillian couldn't leave the hospital. He lay in bed, tubes in his arms, and he worried about his shop. New shipments of candy and nuts would be arriving. Rocky would be hungry. Who would take care of things?

Harry said he would. Harry told his father that he would go to the store every day after school and unpack boxes. He would sort out all the candy and nuts. He would even feed Rocky.

ignored paid no attention to

© James Gritz / Robert Harding Picture Library Ltd / Alamy

So, the next morning, while Mr. Tillian lay in his hospital bed, Harry took the shop key to school with him. After school he left his friends and walked to the empty shop alone. In all the days of his life, Harry had never seen the shop closed after school. Harry didn't even remember what the CLOSED sign looked like. The key stuck in the lock three times, and inside he had to search all the walls for the light switch.

What does Harry do after school to help his father?

The shop was as his father had left it. Even the caramels were still spilled on the floor. Harry bent down and picked them up one by one, dropping them back in the boxes. The bird in its cage watched him silently.

Reading Strategy:
Context Clues
What clues suggest the meaning of the word *bin?*

Harry opened the new boxes his father hadn't gotten to. Peppermints. Jawbreakers. Toffee creams. Strawberry kisses. Harry traveled from bin to bin, putting the candies where they belonged.

"Hello!"

Harry jumped, spilling a box of jawbreakers.

"Hello, Rocky!"

Harry stared at the parrot. He had forgotten it was there. The bird had been so quiet, and Harry had been thinking only of the candy.

"Hello," Harry said.

"Hello, Rocky!" answered the parrot.

Harry walked slowly over to the cage. The parrot's food cup was empty. Its water was dirty. The bottom of the cage was a mess.

Harry carried the cage into the back room.

"Hello, Rocky!"

"Is that all you can say, you dumb bird?" Harry mumbled. The bird said nothing else.

Harry cleaned the bottom of the cage, refilled the food and water cups, and then put the cage back in its place and **resumed** sorting the candy.

"Where's Harry?"

Harry looked up.

"Where's Harry?"

Harry stared at the parrot.

"Where's Harry?"

Chills ran down Harry's back. What could the bird mean? It was something from "The Twilight Zone."

The Twilight Zone was a 1960s television show of fantasy and science fiction.

"Where's Harry?"

Harry swallowed and said, "I'm here. I'm here, you stupid bird."

resumed began again

"You stupid bird!" said the parrot.

Well, at least he's got one thing straight, thought Harry.

"Miss him! Miss him! Where's Harry? You stupid bird!"

Harry stood with a handful of peppermints.

"What?" he asked.

"Where's Harry?" said the parrot.

"I'm here, you stupid bird! I'm here!" Harry yelled. He threw the peppermints at the cage, and the bird screamed and **clung** to its perch.

Harry sobbed, "I'm here." The tears were coming.

Harry leaned over the glass counter.

"Papa." Harry buried his face in his arms.

"Where's Harry?" repeated the bird.

Harry sighed and wiped his face on his sleeve. He watched the parrot. He understood now: someone had been saying, for a long time, "Where's Harry? Miss him."

Harry finished his unpacking and then swept the floor of the shop. He checked the furnace so the bird wouldn't get cold. Then he left to go visit his papa.

clung held on tightly

AFTER READING THE SELECTION | Apply the Skills

Papa's Parrot *by Cynthia Rylant*

Directions Choose the letter of the best answer or write the answer using complete sentences.

Comprehension: Identifying Facts

1. Harry's visits to his father's candy store become less frequent when
- **A** Harry turns seven
- **B** Harry enters junior high
- **C** Mr. Tillian became ill
- **D** Mr. Tillian starts talking to his parrot

2. Harry agrees to take care of the candy store when
- **A** Mrs. Tillian becomes ill from eating too much candy
- **B** the parrot dies
- **C** the candy store is robbed
- **D** Mr. Tillian is taken to the hospital

3. Who is Rocky?

Comprehension: Putting Ideas Together

4. Why does Mr. Tillian buy a parrot?
- **A** He collects different kinds of birds.
- **B** He is starting a pet store.
- **C** He is lonely.
- **D** He thinks it will bring him closer to Harry.

5. Why have Harry and his friends stopped visiting Harry's father?

6. Why does Harry react so strongly to the words, "Where's Harry?" and "Miss him"?

Understanding Literature: Narrative

It is easier to understand this story if you follow the narrative. The narrative is in chronological order—the time order of events. Context clues can also help you better understand the narrative. Use context clues to figure out the meaning of unfamiliar words. To help with the order of a story, use a sequence chain. (described in Appendix A)

7. Did Mr. Tillian buy his parrot before or after Harry stopped coming to the store?

8. Tell the major events in "Papa's Parrot" in the order in which they happened.

Critical Thinking

9. Which character, Harry or his father, should be more understanding of the other?

Thinking Creatively

10. Should Harry tell his father the lesson he learned from Rocky? Explain.

Grammar Check

A common noun names a person, place, or thing. A proper noun names a specific person, place, or thing. Proper nouns are always capitalized. Common nouns are only capitalized in a title or when they begin a sentence.

Underline the common nouns and circle the proper nouns in each sentence.

1 Bethany drove to the store on Wednesday.

2 Will John feed the puppy in September?

3 The woman phoned Ralph on Tuesday.

Vocabulary Builder

The words *signify* and *significance* share a common Latin origin—*signum*, or sign. Words that have this origin have meanings related to showing or indicating, like a sign. For example, the significance of something is its meaning or importance.

Example The historian explained the *significance* of the ancient writing.

Using your dictionary, look up *signal* and *signify.* Explain how the meanings of the words are related to the origin they share with *significance.* Then, use each word in a sentence that shows the meaning of the word.

Writing on Your Own

Write an essay about how Harry's behavior changed after he entered junior high school. Before you write, list details from the story in a two-column chart:

Column 1: what Harry was like before junior high school.

Column 2: what Harry was like after entering junior high school.

Listening and Speaking

With a partner, present a reading of "Papa's Parrot." As you practice, remember to:

- speak slowly and clearly so that each word can be heard.
- use your voice to express the characters' feelings.
- look up at the audience from time to time.

Research and Technology

Use the Internet and library resources to learn about how parrots talk. Use the information to write a report. Your report should help you answer these questions: How is Rocky able to say "Where's Harry?" Why does he continue to ask for Harry when he is not there?

Reading Informational Materials

Encyclopedias

In Part 1 you are learning about context clues. Context clues help figure out a meaning of a word. Encyclopedias help you figure out the meaning of a subject. An *encyclopedia* is a book or set of books with facts on many subjects. It usually has a collection of articles in alphabetical order. Some encyclopedias include only one book, or volume. Others are made up of many volumes. Most encyclopedias have certain features in common. You can see some of these features in the diagram on the next page.

About Encyclopedias

Not all encyclopedias are printed books. You can also find encyclopedias on CD-ROMs and on the Internet. These electronic encyclopedias show information in ways that printed reference books cannot. An electronic encyclopedia can use sound and video as well as words and pictures. Some electronic encyclopedias let you listen to old speeches of U.S. presidents. Others allow you to view videos of sports events from many years ago.

Reading Skill

Encyclopedia articles often direct you to other articles on similar topics. These links between articles are called *cross-references.* Use cross-references to get as much as you can out of the encyclopedia. You might start out reading about one topic and end up reading about several others. You can find examples of cross-references on page 16.

Encyclopedia Features

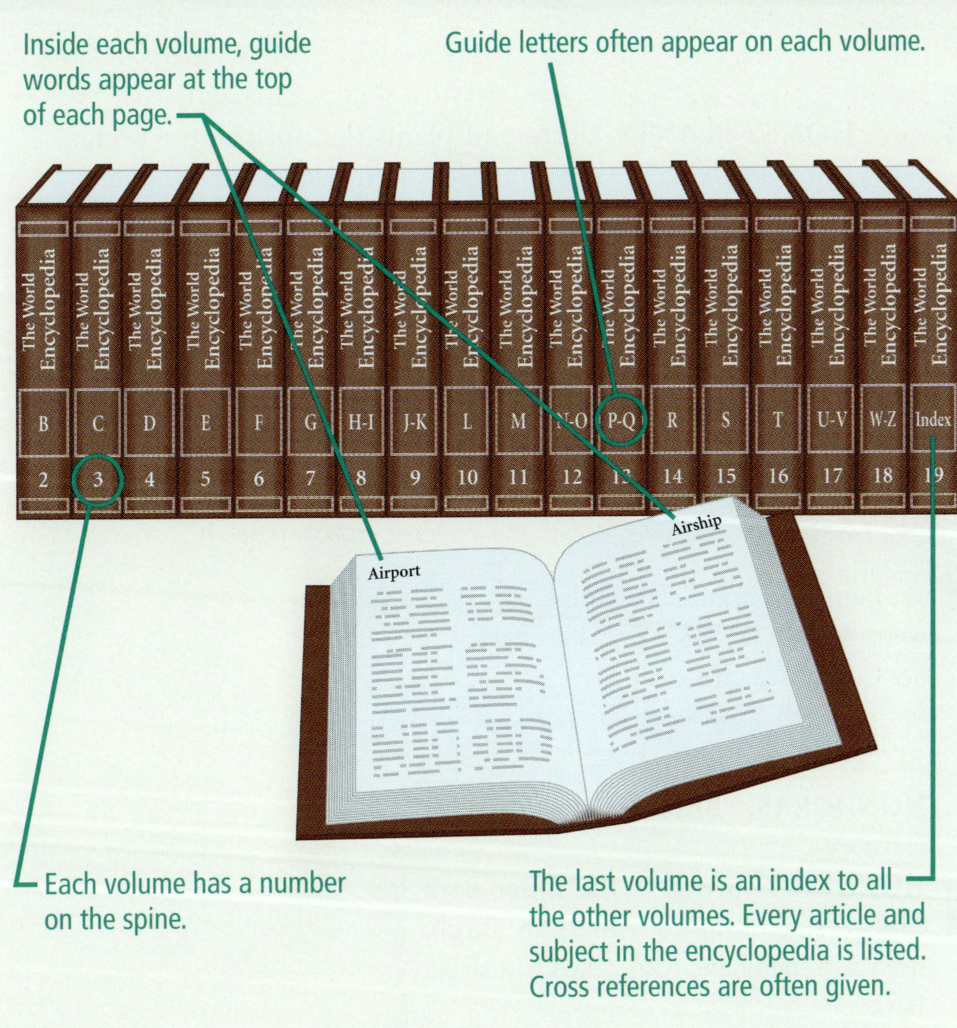

Examples of Encyclopedia Cross-References

Example 1

A

HONEY PLANTS, a group of plants that furnish the nectar from which bees make honey — often also called bee plants.

B

NECTAR is a sugary liquid produced by many flowers. Besides being the main source of honey, it is also very important in cross-pollination. *See also* **Pollination.**

Example 2

A

. . . Boundary arguments with Guatemala were settled in 1933. For Bibliography, *See* **Costa Rica** (History).

B

HONDURAS, BRITISH. *See* Belize (History).

HONDURAS BARK is the bitter bark from a small tropical American shrub, used as a medicine. Also called Cascarilla Bark.

Monitor Your Progress

Directions Choose the letter of the best answer or write the answer using complete sentences.

1. In which volume of an encyclopedia would you find facts about products of Spain?
   A 3
   B 7
   C 13
   D 15

2. What cross-reference is named in the article on nectar?
   A pollination
   B liquid
   C flowers
   D honey

3. What topic would you look up to learn more about Honduras bark?
   A Costa Rica
   B Belize (History)
   C medicine
   D cascarilla bark

4. What is the purpose of the guide words at the top of each page?

5. What is another name for honey plants?

Writing on Your Own

Think of a subject that you find interesting. It might be your favorite hobby, author, or style of music. It might even be something you learned in school. Make sure to pick a topic you really care about. Then write an encyclopedia article on the subject. Your article should be between 100 and 500 words in length. Use library resources or reliable Internet sources to do your research. Try to cover all the key facts about your subject. Be sure to list every source you used in a bibliography at the end of your article. Send your writing to an online dictionary to see if they will publish it.

from An American Childhood *by Annie Dillard*

Annie Dillard
1945–

Objectives

- To read and understand a memoir
- To understand point of view

About the Author

Growing up in Pittsburgh, Pennsylvania, Annie Dillard loved reading, drawing, and observing the natural world. During high school, Dillard began reading and writing poetry. Her favorite book is *The Field Book of Ponds and Streams.* She still reads this book once a year.

Dillard went to college in Virginia. While there, she lived near a creek in a valley of the Blue Ridge Mountains. Her book *Pilgrim at Tinker Creek* tells about the things she saw in that natural setting. She often sat for hours watching a praying mantis lay its eggs. Then she would return home and think about what she had seen. She wrote down her thoughts, mixing them with ideas from science and philosophy. Dillard gives this advice to young writers: "You have enough experience by the time you're five years old. What you need is the library. What you have to learn is the best of what is being thought and said."

About the Selection

The events in this nonfiction narrative take place in a suburban neighborhood. A suburb is a community just outside a city, or "urban" area. After World War II, more people had cars and were able to leave crowded cities. Many of them moved to the quieter suburbs while continuing to work in the city. In this passage, Dillard tells about an event she remembers from her childhood years in the suburbs.

Literary Terms This story is told from the **point of view** of the narrator. Point of view is the position from which the author or storyteller tells the story. In **first-person** point of view, the narrator is also a character, using the pronouns *I* and *we*. In **third-person** point of view, the narrator is not a character. The characters in the story are called *he, she, or they.*

Reading on Your Own Context clues are the words and phrases that surround a word you do not know. You can use context clues to figure out what an unfamiliar word means. For example: The doll had *minuscule* shoes on her tiny feet. You can tell that *minuscule* is an adjective describing the doll's shoes. Context clues tell you that the doll has tiny feet. You can guess from this clue that *minuscule* means "very small."

Writing on Your Own In this selection, Annie Dillard recalls how a childhood chase turned into an exciting adventure. Write a paragraph about a time when you put a lot of effort into doing something. Tell about how you felt before, during, and after. Try to make the reader feel what you were feeling at the time.

Vocabulary Focus Sometimes you can figure out a new word by looking for a smaller word in it. That smaller word is called the *root.* The word *describe,* for example, is based on the root *scrib,* which means "write." When you describe something, you write or tell about it. As you read, use roots and other word parts to figure out unfamiliar words.

Think Before You Read This passage is part of Annie Dillard's **autobiography.** In an autobiography, an author tells the story of his or her own life. In this story, the author tells about something that happened when she was seven years old. Do you think Annie Dillard remembers this event correctly? Or do you think she adds details to tell a good story? When you write an autobiography, do you have to stick to the facts?

point of view the position from which the author or storyteller tells the story

first person a point of view where the narrator is also a character, using the pronouns *I* and *we*

third person a point of view where the narrator is not a character, and refers to characters as *he* or *she*

autobiography a person's life story, written by that person

from An American Childhood

As you read, think about how point of view helps your understanding of the story.

Some boys taught me to play football. This was fine sport. You thought up a new **strategy** for every play and whispered it to the others. You went out for a pass, fooling everyone. Best, you got to throw yourself mightily at someone's running legs. Either you brought him down or you hit the ground flat out on your chin, with your arms empty before you. It was all or nothing. If you hesitated in fear, you would miss and get hurt: you would take a hard fall while the kid got away, or you would get kicked in the face while the kid got away. But if you flung yourself wholeheartedly at the back of his knees—if you gathered and joined body and soul and pointed them diving fearlessly—then you likely wouldn't get hurt, and you'd stop the ball. Your fate, and your team's score, depended on your concentration and courage. Nothing girls did could compare with it.

How can you tell the point of view from reading the first two paragraphs?

Boys welcomed me at baseball, too, for I had, through enthusiastic practice, what was weirdly known as a boy's arm. In winter, in the snow, there was neither baseball nor football, so the boys and I threw snowballs at passing cars. I got in trouble throwing snowballs, and have seldom been happier since.

On one weekday morning after Christmas, six inches of new snow had just fallen. We were standing up to our boot tops in snow on a front yard on trafficked Reynolds Street, waiting for cars. The cars traveled Reynolds Street slowly and evenly; they were targets all but wrapped in red ribbons, cream puffs. We couldn't miss.

strategy plan

I was seven; the boys were eight, nine, and ten. The oldest two Fahey boys were there—Mikey and Peter—polite blond boys who lived near me on Lloyd Street, and who already had four brothers and sisters. My parents approved Mikey and Peter Fahey. Chickie McBride was there, a tough kid, and Billy Paul and Mackie Kean too, from across Reynolds, where the boys grew up dark and furious, grew up skinny, knowing, and skilled. We had all drifted from our houses that morning looking for action, and had found it here on Reynolds Street.

What are Annie and her friends doing?

It was cloudy but cold. The cars' tires laid behind them on the snowy street a complex trail of beige chunks like crenellated castle walls. I had stepped on some earlier; they squeaked. We could have wished for more traffic. When a car came, we all popped it one. In the intervals between cars we **reverted** to the natural **solitude** of children.

Crenellated means notched. Castle walls often had spaces cut out for cannons.

reverted went back **solitude** being alone

I started making an iceball—a perfect iceball, from perfectly white snow, perfectly spherical, and squeezed perfectly translucent so no snow remained all the way through. (The Fahey boys and I considered it unfair actually to throw an iceball at somebody, but it had been known to happen.)

I had just embarked on the iceball project when we heard tire chains come clanking from afar. A black Buick was moving toward us down the street. We all spread out, banged together some regular snowballs, took aim, and, when the Buick drew nigh, fired.

A soft snowball hit the driver's windshield right before the driver's face. It made a smashed star with a hump in the middle.

Often, of course, we hit our target, but this time, the only time in all of life, the car pulled over and stopped. Its wide black door opened; a man got out of it, running. He didn't even close the car door.

Reading Strategy: **Context Clues**

What context clues help you understand the expression "gaining on us"?

He ran after us, and we ran away from him, up the snowy Reynolds sidewalk. At the corner, I looked back; incredibly, he was still after us. He was in city clothes: a suit and tie, street shoes. Any normal adult would have quit, having sprung us into flight and made his point. This man was gaining on us. He was a thin man, all action. All of a sudden, we were running for our lives.

Wordless, we split up. We were on our turf; we could lose ourselves in the neighborhood backyards, everyone for himself. I paused and considered. Everyone had vanished except Mikey Fahey, who was just rounding the corner of a yellow brick house. Poor Mikey, I trailed him. The driver of the Buick sensibly picked the two of us to follow. The man apparently had all day.

He chased Mikey and me around the yellow house and up a backyard path we knew by heart: under a low tree, up a bank, through a hedge, down some snowy steps, and across the grocery store's delivery driveway. We smashed through a gap in another hedge, entered a scruffy backyard and ran around its back porch and tight between houses to Edgerton Avenue; we ran across Edgerton to an alley and up our own

sliding woodpile to the Halls' front yard; he kept coming. We ran up Lloyd Street and wound through mazy backyards toward the steep hilltop at Willard and Lang.

He chased us silently, block after block. He chased us silently over picket fences, through thorny hedges, between houses, around garbage cans, and across streets. Every time I glanced back, choking for breath, I expected he would have quit. He must have been as breathless as we were. His jacket strained over his body. It was an **immense** discovery, pounding into my hot head with every sliding, joyous step, that this ordinary adult evidently knew what I thought only children who trained at football knew: that you have to fling yourself at what you're doing, you have to point yourself, forget yourself, aim, dive.

Why are Annie and her friends being chased?

Mikey and I had nowhere to go, in our own neighborhood or out of it, but away from this man who was chasing us. He impelled us forward; we **compelled** him to follow our

immense huge **compelled** forced

route. The air was cold; every breath tore my throat. We kept running, block after block; we kept **improvising,** backyard after backyard, running a frantic course and choosing it **simultaneously,** failing always to find small places or hard places to slow him down, and discovering always, **exhilarated, dismayed,** that only bare speed could save us—for he would never give up, this man—and we were losing speed.

He chased us through the backyard labyrinths of ten blocks before he caught us by our jackets. He caught us and we all stopped.

We three stood staggering, half blinded, coughing, in an obscure hilltop backyard: a man in his twenties, a boy, a girl. He had released our jackets, our pursuer, our captor, our hero: he knew we weren't going anywhere. We all played by the rules. Mikey and I unzipped our jackets. I pulled off my sopping mittens. Our tracks multiplied in the backyard's new snow. We had been breaking new snow all morning. We didn't look at each other. I was cherishing my excitement. The man's lower pants legs were wet; his cuffs were full of snow, and there was a prow of snow beneath them on his shoes and socks. Some trees bordered the little flat backyard, some messy winter trees. There was no one around: a clearing in a grove, and we the only players.

It was a long time before he could speak. I had some difficulty at first recalling why we were there. My lips felt swollen; I couldn't see out of the sides of my eyes; I kept coughing.

improvising making up on the spot

simultaneously at the same time

exhilarated excited

dismayed troubled

"You stupid kids," he began **perfunctorily.**

We listened perfunctorily indeed, if we listened at all, for the chewing out was redundant, a mere formality, and beside the point. The point was that he had chased us passionately without giving up, and so he had caught us. Now he came down to earth. I wanted the glory to last forever.

Reading Strategy: **Context Clues**

Which words in this paragraph restate the meaning of *redundant?*

But how could the glory have lasted forever? We could have run through every backyard in North America until we got to Panama. But when he trapped us at the lip of the Panama Canal, what precisely could he have done to prolong the drama of the chase and cap its glory? I **brooded** about this for the next few years. He could only have fried Mikey Fahey and me in boiling oil, say, or dismembered us piecemeal, or staked us to anthills. None of which I really wanted, and none of which any adult was likely to do, even in the spirit of fun. He could only chew us out there in the Panamanian jungle, after months or years of **exalting** pursuit. He could only begin, "You stupid kids," and continue in his ordinary Pittsburgh accent with his normal righteous anger and the usual common sense.

Why does the author not tell the reader what the man was thinking?

If in that snowy backyard the driver of the black Buick had cut off our heads, Mikey's and mine, I would have died happy, for nothing has required so much of me since as being chased all over Pittsburgh in the middle of winter—running terrified, exhausted—by this sainted, skinny, furious red-headed man who wished to have a word with us. I don't know how he found his way back to his car.

perfunctorily without interest

brooded worried

exalting joyful

AFTER READING THE SELECTION | **Apply the Skills**

from An American Childhood *by Annie Dillard*

Directions Choose the letter of the best answer or write the answer using complete sentences.

Comprehension: Identifying Facts

1. How old is Annie in this story?

A seven **C** nine
B eight **D** ten

2. Annie throws snowballs with

A five other girls
B five boys
C three other girls and two boys
D three girls and two other boys

3. What are Annie and her friends doing "one weekday morning after Christmas"?

4. What do most cars do when Annie and her friends throw snowballs at them?

5. What sports did the boys welcome Annie to play?

6. What does the driver of the Buick do after a snowball hits his windshield?

7. What does the driver of the Buick forget to do when he leaves his car?

8. What do the kids do when the man begins to run after them?

9. Which two kids does the driver of the Buick chase?

10. What does the driver say to the two kids when he catches up to them?

Comprehension: Putting Ideas Together

11. The boys allow Annie to take part in their sports because

A she is pretty
B they are afraid of her
C she is good at throwing
D they like to make fun of her

12. Annie's parents like Mikey and Peter Fahey because they are

A polite **C** athletic
B strong **D** popular

13. How does the man chase Annie and her friend?

14. Why does Annie call the man who chased her "our hero"?

15. How do the man's actions cause this hero to come down to earth?

16. What does Annie think most about the man during the chase?

17. What lesson does Annie learn from the man's behavior during the chase?

18. Why does Annie have trouble remembering why she is there when the chase ends?

19. Why does Annie think about this chase for the next few years?

20. What words best describe the driver's feelings?

Understanding Literature: Point of View

Stories are almost always told from the first-person or third-person point of view. In this story, the first-person point of view centers the action on the narrator. The story is about an adventure that she herself took part in.

21. How do you know which point of view this story is told from?

22. Give two examples of the narrator directly expressing her own thoughts or feelings.

23. How might the story be different if the driver of the car was the narrator?

24. How would the story be different if it had been told in the third person?

25. Read this sentence: "He chased us through the backyard labyrinths of ten blocks before he caught us by our jackets." How is this sentence different from most other sentences in the story? (Hint: What pronouns are not being used?)

Critical Thinking

26. What does the young Annie Dillard admire in adults? What does she not admire?

27. What larger meaning can be found in this story from the author's early life?

28. Why does Annie think that the "chewing out" by the driver is "beside the point"?

Thinking Creatively

29. Would you want the young Annie Dillard to be your friend? Why or why not?

30. Think about the adventures you had as a child. Which one stands out the most in your mind? Why?

***After Reading* continued on next page**

from an American Childhood by Annie Dillard

Grammar Check

Possessive nouns show ownership. Possessives are formed in different ways for plural and singular nouns.

Singular noun: add an apostrophe and *-s:* driver's

Plural noun that ends in *-s:* add an apostrophe: cars'

Plural noun not ending in *-s:* children's

Examples: The windshield of the driver becomes *the driver's windshield.*

The tires of the cars becomes *the cars' tires.*

The joy of the children becomes *the children's joy.*

Vocabulary Builder

The English word *verify* comes from the Latin word *verus,* meaning "true." If you verify something, you prove whether it is true.

Example: He brought a doctor's note to *verify* that he had been sick.

Answer the following question in a complete sentence.

1 If you were asked to verify your identity, how would you do it?

Writing on Your Own

Hyperbole is using gross exaggeration to show that something is important. It is often used for comic effect. Annie Dillard uses hyperbole several times in her story. For example: "We could have run through every backyard in North America until we got to Panama." Imagine being very hungry, very tired, or very cold. Now write a few sentences that use hyperbole to express what those things feel like. You might begin: "I was so hungry that . . ."

Listening and Speaking

Write a speech about the dangers of throwing snowballs at cars. Give examples of the bad things that could happen. Look for facts and figures that support your opinion. After you practice delivering your speech out loud, present it to the class.

Research and Technology

Use the Internet and library resources to learn more about Annie Dillard's life. Gather information about her childhood, major events in her life, and her writing career. Look for pictures of the author and places she has lived in and written about. Present your findings in a report to the class.

from Barrio Boy *by Ernesto Galarza*

Courtesy of the Library of Congress

Ernesto Galarza
1905–1984

About the Author

When he was seven years old, Ernesto Galarza moved from Mexico to California. There, his family harvested crops. His family struggled to make ends meet. Galarza learned English quickly, studied hard, and won a college scholarship.

Galarza later headed the Division of Labor and Social Information for the Pan-American Union. In this job, he dealt with education and labor in Latin America. When he returned to California, he worked hard to gain rights for farm workers.

About the Selection

This selection comes from Galarza's book *Barrio Boy.* He tells what it was like to attend a new school in a different place. Getting used to new places and new people is a part of growing up. Galarza's story is a work of nonfiction. It is based on an experience he really lived through. "Papa's Parrot," on the other hand, is fiction. It tells a made-up story about another part of growing up. Authors have explored the problems of growing up in both fiction and nonfiction. Which selection reminds you more of your own experience of growing up?

Objectives

- To read and understand nonfiction
- To compare fiction and nonfiction
- To understand techniques of narrative writing

Comparing **continued on next page**

Barrio Boy by Ernesto Galarza

fiction writing that is imaginative and designed to entertain; the author creates the events and characters

nonfiction writing about real people and events

Literary Terms **Fiction** is writing that is imaginative and designed to entertain. Novels and short stories are examples of fiction. **Nonfiction** is writing about real people and events. News articles, essays, biographies, and histories are all examples of nonfiction.

"Papa's Parrot" is fiction and *Barrio Boy* is nonfiction. Both selections are examples of narrative writing. Each tells a story with a narrator, characters, dialogue, and story events.

But these selections are different in several important ways. *Barrio Boy* tells about a real event in the writer's life. "Papa's Parrot" tells about the problems of an imaginary boy. As you read, use a Venn diagram (described in Appendix A) to note similarities and differences between the stories.

Reading on Your Own If you do not know what a *barrio* is, look it up in a dictionary. Think about what these two words—*barrio* and *boy*—mean when used together. Based on the title, what do you think the story might be about?

Writing on Your Own Think of a new experience you had that seemed a little scary. Write a paragraph about how you felt at the time. Tell what you learned from the experience.

Vocabulary Focus An *adjective* is a word that describes a person, place, or thing. Adjectives make clearer the meaning of a noun or pronoun. Writers often use adjectives to spice up their writing. As you read, think about how the sentences would be different without the adjectives. Notice how much they add to your enjoyment of the story.

Think Before You Read As you read, notice how "Papa's Parrot" and *Barrio Boy* are alike and different. How much does it matter that one story is fiction and the other is nonfiction?

from Barrio Boy

My mother and I walked south on Fifth Street one morning to the corner of Q Street and turned right. Half of the block was occupied by the Lincoln School. It was a three-story wooden building, with two wings that gave it the shape of a double-T connected by a central hall. It was a new building, painted yellow, with a shingled roof that was not like the red tile of the school in Mazatlán. I noticed other differences, none of them very **reassuring.** We walked up the wide staircase hand in hand and through the door, which closed by itself. A mechanical **contraption** screwed to the top shut it behind us quietly.

Up to this point the adventure of enrolling me in the school had been carefully rehearsed. Mrs. Dodson had told us how to find it and we had circled it several times on our walks. Friends in the barrio explained that the director was called a principal, and that it was a lady and not a man. They assured us that there was always a person at the school who could speak Spanish.

Exactly as we had been told, there was a sign on the door in both Spanish and English: "Principal." We crossed the hall and entered the office of Miss Nettie Hopley.

As you read, compare the narrator to the main character in "Papa's Parrot."

***Reading Strategy:* Context Clues**
Which word helps you understand what *contraption* means?

A *barrio* is a Latino neighborhood.

Who is telling this story? How do you know?

Where do the narrator and his mother go?

reassuring comforting

contraption machine

Miss Hopley was at a roll-top desk to one side, sitting in a swivel chair that moved on wheels. There was a sofa against the opposite wall, **flanked** by two windows and a door that opened on a small balcony. Chairs were set around a table and framed pictures hung on the walls of a man with long white hair and another with a sad face and a black beard.

The principal half turned in the swivel chair to look at us over the pinch glasses crossed on the ridge of her nose. To do this she had to duck her head slightly as if she were about to step through a low doorway.

What Miss Hopley said to us we did not know but we saw in her eyes a warm welcome and when she took off her glasses and straightened up she smiled **wholeheartedly,** like Mrs. Dodson. We were, of course, saying nothing, only catching the friendliness of her voice and the sparkle in her eyes while she said words we did not understand. She signaled us to the table. Almost tiptoeing across the office, I maneuvered myself to keep my mother between me and the gringo lady. In a matter of seconds I had to decide whether she was a possible friend or a **menace.** We sat down.

Then Miss Hopley did a **formidable** thing. She stood up. Had she been standing when we entered she would have seemed tall. But rising from her chair she soared. And what she carried up and up with her was a buxom superstructure, firm shoulders, a straight sharp nose, full cheeks slightly molded by a curved line along the nostrils, thin lips that moved like steel springs, and a high forehead topped by hair gathered in a bun. Miss Hopley was not a giant in body but when she mobilized it to a standing position she seemed a match for giants. I decided I liked her.

Buxom superstructure is an amusing way of saying that Miss Hopley is a large woman. *Mobilized* means "put into motion."

flanked situated on both sides of

wholeheartedly with all one's energy, enthusiasm, etc.

menace a danger

formidable amazing

She strode to a door in the far corner of the office, opened it and called a name. A boy of about ten years appeared in the doorway. He sat down at one end of the table. He was brown like us, a plump kid with shiny black hair combed straight back, neat, cool, and faintly obnoxious.

Miss Hopley joined us with a large book and some papers in her hand. She, too, sat down and the questions and answers began by way of our interpreter. My name was Ernesto. My mother's name was Henriqueta. My birth certificate was in San Blas. Here was my last report card from the Escuela Municipal Numero 3 para Varones of Mazatlán, and so forth. Miss Hopley put things down in the book and my mother signed a card.

Escuela Municipal Numero 3 para Varones of Mazatlán means Municipal School Number 3 for Boys of Mazatlán.

Doña is a Spanish title of respect for a woman.

As long as the questions continued, Doña Henriqueta could stay and I was secure. Now that they were over, Miss Hopley saw her to the door, dismissed our interpreter and without further ado took me by the hand and strode down the hall to Miss Ryan's first grade. Miss Ryan took me to a seat at the front of the room, into which I shrank—the better to survey her. She was, to skinny, somewhat runty me, of a withering height when she patrolled the class. And when I least expected it, there she was, crouching by my desk, her blond **radiant** face level with mine, her voice patiently maneuvering me over the awful idiocies of the English language.

During the next few weeks Miss Ryan overcame my fears of tall, energetic teachers as she bent over my desk to help me with a word in the pre-primer. Step by step, she loosened me and my classmates from the safe anchorage of the desks for **recitations** at the blackboard and consultations at her desk. Frequently she burst into happy announcements to the whole class. "Ito can read a sentence," and small Japanese Ito, squint-eyed and shy, slowly read aloud while the class listened in wonder: "Come, Skipper, come. Come and run." The Korean, Portuguese, Italian, and Polish first graders had similar moments of glory, no less shining than mine the day I conquered "butterfly," which I had been persistently pronouncing in standard Spanish as boo-ter-flee. "Children," Miss Ryan called for attention. "Ernesto has learned how to pronounce *butterfly!*" And I proved it with a perfect imitation of Miss Ryan. From that celebrated success, I was soon able to match Ito's progress as a sentence reader with "Come, butterfly, come fly with me."

Which students get private lessons with Miss Ryan?

Like Ito and several other first graders who did not know English, I received private lessons from Miss Ryan in the closet, a narrow hall off the classroom with a door at each end. Next to one of these doors Miss Ryan placed a large chair

radiant shining

recitations oral presentations given from memory

for herself and a small one for me. Keeping an eye on the class through the open door she read with me about sheep in the meadow and a frightened chicken going to see the king, coaching me out of my **phonetic** ruts in words like *pasture, bow-wow-wow, hay,* and *pretty,* which to my Mexican ear and eye had so many unnecessary sounds and letters. She made me watch her lips and then close my eyes as she repeated words I found hard to read. When we came to know each other better, I tried interrupting to tell Miss Ryan how we said it in Spanish. It didn't work. She only said "oh" and went on with *pasture, bow-wow-wow,* and *pretty.* It was as if in that closet we were both discovering together the secrets of the English language and grieving together over the tragedies of

phonetic having to do with sounds

How can you tell that Miss Ryan is a good teacher?

Bo-Peep. The main reason I was graduated with honors from the first grade was that I had fallen in love with Miss Ryan. Her radiant, no-nonsense character made us either afraid not to love her or love her so we would not be afraid, I am not sure which. It was not only that we sensed she was with it, but also that she was with us. Like the first grade, the rest of the Lincoln School was a sampling of the lower part of town where many races made their home. My pals in the second grade were Kazushi, whose parents spoke only Japanese; Matti, a skinny Italian boy; and Manuel, a fat Portuguese who would never get into a fight but wrestled you to the ground and just sat on you. Our **assortment** of nationalities included Koreans, Yugoslavs, Poles, Irish, and home-grown Americans.

What context clue tells you that the word *tongue* here means "language"?

What does this paragraph tell you about the children in Ernesto's class?

At Lincoln, making us into Americans did not mean scrubbing away what made us originally foreign. The teachers called us as our parents did, or as close as they could pronounce our names in Spanish or Japanese. No one was ever scolded or punished for speaking in his native tongue on the playground. Matti told the class about his mother's down quilt, which she had made in Italy with the fine feathers of a thousand geese. Encarnación acted out how boys learned to fish in the Philippines. I astounded the third grade with the story of my travels on a stagecoach, which nobody else in the class had seen except in the museum at Sutter's Fort. After a visit to the Crocker Art Gallery and its collection of heroic paintings of the golden age of California, someone showed a silk scroll with a Chinese painting. Miss Hopley herself had a way of expressing wonder over these matters before a class, her eyes wide open until they popped slightly. It was easy for me to feel that becoming a proud American, as she said we should, did not mean feeling ashamed of being a Mexican.

assortment variety

COMPARING LITERARY WORKS | **Apply the Skills**

from Barrio Boy *by Ernesto Galarza*

Directions Choose the letter of the best answer or write the answer using complete sentences.

Comprehension: Identifying Facts

1. What is Ernesto's first language?
A English **C** Spanish
B Japanese **D** Portuguese

2. Who puts Ernesto's words into English for the principal?
A Miss Ryan
B Miss Hopley
C another student
D Ernesto's mother

3. What does the principal do that makes her seem like a giant to Ernesto?

4. How does Ernesto feel about having his mother with him in the principal's office?

5. What is Ernesto's first proud moment in his new class?

6. How does Miss Ryan encourage the students to leave the safety of their desks?

7. How does Miss Ryan help with the special learning needs of students from different countries?

8. How did most English words sound to Ernesto when he first heard them?

9. What story does Ernesto tell in class that surprised his classmates?

10. How does the school feel about students speaking other languages?

Comprehension: Putting Ideas Together

11. Ernesto can tell that the principal is a good person because of her
A gestures **C** words
B looks **D** reputation

12. Which word best describes Ernesto's feelings during his first days in his new class?
A confident **C** sad
B nervous **D** angry

13. Why is Ernesto afraid of Miss Ryan at first?

14. How does Miss Ryan help Ernesto get over his fears?

15. How does Ernesto feel about having classmates who also come from different countries?

16. Why does Ernesto want to tell Miss Ryan how words are pronounced in Spanish?

***Comparing* continued on next page**

from Barrio Boy *by Ernesto Galarza*

17. How does Ernesto feel about Miss Ryan?

18. How does Miss Hopley feel about the stories the students tell about their countries?

19. What do all of Ernesto's new friends have in common?

20. How do Ernesto's feelings about his new country change after the first grade?

Understanding Literature: Comparing Fiction and Nonfiction

Fiction tells about imaginary events. Nonfiction tells about events that really happened. Both fiction and nonfiction can touch the reader's heart and mind. Both forms of literature can tell important truths about human life.

21. Are the people and events in "Papa's Parrot" and *Barrio Boy* real or made up?

22. How did these writers make their stories seem real to the reader?

23. In what ways are Harry in "Papa's Parrot" and Ernesto in *Barrio Boy* alike?

24. How might "Papa's Parrot" be different if it were nonfiction?

25. How might *Barrio Boy* be different if it were not based on true events?

Critical Thinking

26. What does it mean that Miss Ryan was "with it" and "with us"?

27. Why do you think Ernesto falls in love with Miss Ryan?

28. Why do you think Rylant uses the parrot to convey the message that Harry's father misses him?

29. Why do you think Harry reacts so strongly to the words of the parrot?

Thinking Creatively

30. What could you do to help a new student feel safe and welcome at your school?

Grammar Check

Every verb has four main forms, or *principal parts.* These parts are used to form verb tenses that show time. The principal parts are the *present, present participle, past,* and *past participle.*

	Regular	Irregular
Present	Right now **I wait.**	He **speaks** clearly.
Present Participle	I am still **waiting** now.	He is **speaking** to us.
Past	Yesterday we **waited** a long time.	He **spoke** to us last week.
Past Participle	We have often **waited** in long lines.	He has **spoken** to us often.

Notice that *regular verbs* form their past tense and past participles by adding *-ed* or *-d. Irregular verbs* form their past tense and past participles in different ways.

Vocabulary Builder

Adjectives describe persons, places, or things. Adjectives add meaning to a noun or pronoun. Both "Papa's Parrot" and *Barrio Boy* use adjectives to spice up the sentences.

Use each word below in a sentence that shows its meaning.

formidable reassuring radiant

Writing on Your Own

Write an essay comparing the narrators of *Barrio Boy* and "Papa's Parrot." In your essay, be sure to answer these questions:

- Which story gives more information about the narrator?
- How do the narrator's thoughts and actions help express the main idea of the story?

Listening and Speaking

In *Barrio Boy,* Ernesto struggles to pronounce English words correctly. Pick five English words from *Barrio Boy* or "Papa's Parrot." Find out how to say the words you have chosen in a foreign language. Talk about the experience of trying to pronounce words correctly.

Research and Technology

Ernesto tells how he became a proud American. Each year, thousands of people from other countries become American citizens. To do so, they must take a test. Use the Internet to find questions from that test. See how many questions you can answer correctly. Have your classmates test their knowledge of the United States history and government, too. Compare your answers.

Reading Strategy:
Text Structure

Understanding how text is organized helps readers decide which information is most important. Before you begin reading this unit, look at how it is organized.

- Look at the title, headings, boldfaced words, and photographs.
- Ask yourself: Is the text a problem and solution, description, or sequence? Is it compare and contrast or cause and effect?
- Summarize the text by thinking about its structure.

Literary Terms

setting the time and place in a story

mood the feeling that writing creates

flashback a look into the past at some point in a story

author's purpose the reason(s) for which the author writes: to entertain, to inform, to express opinions, or to persuade

essay a written work that shows a writer's opinions on some basic or current issue

satire humorous writing that makes fun of foolishness or evil

characterization the way a writer develops character qualities and personality traits

from The Bonesetter's Daughter by Amy Tan

Amy Tan
1952–

Amy Tan's parents came to the United States from China. Tan grew up in Oakland, California. As a child starting school, Tan would answer her mother's Chinese questions in English. As she grew older, Tan was eager to leave her mother's Chinese background behind.

When Tan was 35, she visited China with her mother. After this trip, Tan understood more about her mother's background and customs. She also became more aware of her Chinese roots. During this period, Tan stopped working as a business writer and began to write fiction. Her first novel was *The Joy Luck Club* (1989). It tells a story about four Chinese-American women and their mothers. The book made Tan famous. Tan's fourth novel, *The Bonesetter's Daughter,* came out in 2001.

Objectives

- To read and understand a work of fiction
- To understand setting
- To recognize the use of flashback

About the Selection

This selection is taken from Amy Tan's novel *The Bonesetter's Daughter.* The book shows the relationship between a Chinese mother and her Chinese-American daughter. The family lives in San Francisco in the 1990s. Ruth is a successful, middle-aged writer of self-help books. But her relationships with her mother and husband are not happy.

Ruth's mother, LuLing, becomes more forgetful as she grows older. This leads Ruth to look more deeply into her mother's past. She discovers a Chinese diary and uncovers many secrets about LuLing's life. Ruth learns that LuLing's nursemaid, Precious Auntie, is really her grandmother.

In this part of the novel, LuLing remembers her childhood in China in the 1930s.

Before Reading continued on next page

from The Bonesetter's Daughter *by Amy Tan*

setting the time and place in a story

mood the feeling that writing creates

flashback a look into the past at some point in a story

author's purpose the reason(s) for which the author writes: to entertain, to inform, to express opinions, or to persuade

Literary Terms The **setting** is the time and place in a story. In some stories, setting is just a background for the action. In other stories, setting is very important. It helps create the **mood** of the story. A good way to understand the setting is to use *background information.* This is information that you already know or that has been provided to you. Sometimes the setting of a story shifts from one time period to another. A **flashback** is a look into the past at some point in a story.

Reading on Your Own The **author's purpose** is the reason for which the author writes. Fiction authors may write for many different purposes. They may write to entertain, to inform, to express opinions, or to persuade. To better understand a story, watch for details that suggest the author's purpose. Sometimes, these details are not clearly spelled out. You must draw conclusions based on the facts to figure out the author's purpose.

Writing on Your Own Amy Tan's own mother was raised in China during the 1930s. How much do you know about your parents' childhood? Talk to parents or older family members about the key experiences of their childhood. Filling in gaps with your imagination, write a story about one of those experiences.

Vocabulary Focus As you read, underline or write down any words you do not know. Stop for a minute and look up those words in a dictionary. This gives you a better sense of their meaning in the context of the story.

Think Before You Read A poet once wrote, "The child is father to the man." He meant that childhood experiences help to shape who we become later in life. Which childhood experiences most shaped your own sense of who you are?

from The Bonesetter's Daughter

真

TRUTH

These are the things I know are true:

My name is LuLing Liu Young. The names of my husbands were Pan Kai Jing and Edwin Young, both of them dead and our secrets gone with them. My daughter is Ruth Luyi Young. She was born in a Water Dragon Year and I in a Fire Dragon Year. So we are the same but for opposite reasons.

As you read, think about LuLing's purpose for telling this story about her life.

I know all this, yet there is one name I cannot remember. It is there in the oldest layer of my memory, and I cannot dig It out. A hundred times I have gone over that morning when Precious Auntie wrote it down. I was only six then, but very smart. I could count. I could read. I had a memory for everything, and here is my memory of that winter morning.

Which phrase in this paragraph signals the beginning of a flashback?

I was sleepy, still lying on the brick *k'ang* bed I shared with Precious Auntie. The **flue** to our little room was furthest from the stove in the common room, and the bricks beneath me had long turned cold. I felt my shoulder being shaken. When I opened my eyes, Precious Auntie began to write on a scrap of paper, then showed me what she had written. "I can't see," I complained. "It's too dark."

A *k'ang* is a long sleeping platform that could be heated in cold weather.

When she was a child, LuLing shared a bed with Precious Auntie. What does this suggest about her early life?

flue a shaft for the passage of hot air

A *brazier* is a metal container that holds burning coals.

She huffed, set the paper on the low cupboard, and motioned that I should get up. She lighted the teapot brazier, and tied a scarf over her nose and mouth when it started to smoke. She poured face-washing water into the teapot's **chamber,** and when it was cooked, she started our day. She scrubbed my face and ears. She patted my hair and combed my bangs. She wet down any strands that stuck out like spider legs. Then she gathered the long part of my hair into two bundles and braided them. She banded the top with red ribbon, the bottom with green. I wagged my head so that my braids swung like the happy ears of palace dogs. And Precious Auntie sniffed the air as if she, too, were a dog wondering, What's that good smell? That sniff was how she said my nickname, Doggie. That was how she talked.

She had no voice, just gasps and **wheezes,** the snorts of a ragged wind. She told me things with **grimaces** and groans, dancing eyebrows and darting eyes. She wrote about the world on my carry-around chalkboard. She also made pictures with her blackened hands. Hand-talk, face-talk, and chalk-talk were the languages I grew up with, soundless and strong.

As she wound her hair tight against her skull, I played with her box of treasures. I took out a pretty comb, ivory with a rooster carved at each end. Precious Auntie was born a Rooster. "You wear this," I demanded, holding it up. "Pretty." I was still young enough to believe that beauty came from things, and I wanted Mother to favor her more. But Precious Auntie shook her head.

chamber an enclosed space

wheezes hard, whistling breathing sounds

grimaces twisting of the face in pain or disgust

She pulled off her scarf and pointed to her face and bunched her brows. *What use do I have for prettiness?* she was saying.

Her bangs fell to her eyebrows like mine. The rest of her hair was bound into a knot and stabbed together with a silver prong. She had a sweet-peach forehead, wide-set eyes, full cheeks tapering to a small plump nose. That was the top of her face. Then there was the bottom.

She wiggled her blackened fingertips like hungry flames. *See what the fire did.*

I didn't think she was ugly, not in the way others in our family did. "Ai-ya, seeing her, even a demon would leap out of his skin," I once heard Mother remark. When I was small, I liked to trace my fingers around Precious Auntie's mouth. It was a puzzle. Half was bumpy, half was smooth and melted closed. The inside of her right cheek was stiff as leather, the left was moist and soft. Where the gums had burned, the teeth had fallen out. And her tongue was like a **parched** root. She could not taste the pleasures of life: salty and bitter, sour and sharp, spicy, sweet, and fat.

What can you tell about Precious Auntie's life from reading this paragraph?

***Reading Strategy:* Text Structure**

How does LuLing feel about Precious Auntie's face? What does this tell you about her?

No one else understood Precious Auntie's kind of talk, so I had to say aloud what she meant. Not everything, though, not our secret stories. She often told me about her father, the Famous Bonesetter from the Mouth of the Mountain, about the cave where they found the dragon bones, how the bones were divine and could cure any pain, except a grieving heart. "Tell me again," I said that morning, wishing for a story about how she burned her face and became my nursemaid.

I was a fire-eater, she said with her hands and eyes. *Hundreds of people came to see me in the market square. Into the burning pot of my mouth I dropped raw pork, added chilis and bean paste, stirred this up, then offered the morsels to people to taste. If they said, "Delicious!" I opened my mouth as a purse to catch their copper coins. One day, however, I ate the fire, and the fire came back, and it ate me. After that, I decided not to be a cook-pot anymore, so I became your nursemaid instead.*

parched dried out

I laughed and clapped my hands, liking this made-up story best. The day before, she told me she had stared at an unlucky star falling out of the sky and then it dropped into her open mouth and burned her face. The day before that, she said she had eaten what she thought was a spicy Hunan dish only to find that it was the coals used for cooking.

Why are so many different accounts given of Precious Auntie's accident?

No more stories, Precious Auntie now told me, her hands talking fast. *It's almost time for breakfast, and we must pray while we're still hungry.* She retrieved the scrap of paper from the cupboard, folded it in half, and tucked it into the lining of her shoe. We put on our padded winter clothes and walked into the cold **corridor.** The air smelled of coal fires in other wings of the compound. I saw Old Cook pumping his arm to turn the crank over the well. I heard a tenant yelling at her lazy daughter-in-law. I passed the room that my sister, GaoLing, shared with Mother, the two of them still asleep. We hurried to the south-facing small room, to our **ancestral** hall. At the threshold, Precious Auntie gave me a warning look. *Act humble. Take off your shoes.* In my stockings, I stepped onto cold gray tiles. Instantly, my feet were stabbed with an iciness that ran up my legs, through my body, and dripped out my nose. I began to shake.

***Reading Strategy:* Text Structure**

How does the mood change when Precious Auntie and LuLing enter the ancestral hall?

The wall facing me was lined with **overlapping** scrolls of couplets, gifts to our family from scholars who had used our ink over the last two hundred years. I had learned to read one, a poem-painting: "Fish shadows dart downstream," meaning our ink was dark, beautiful, and smooth-flowing. On the long altar table were two statues, the God of **Longevity** with his white-waterfall beard, and the Goddess of Mercy, her face smooth, free of worry. Her black eyes looked into mine. Only she listened to the woes and wishes of women, Precious Auntie said. Perched around the statues were spirit tablets of the Liu ancestors, their wooden faces carved with their

Couplets are two lines of poetry that go together.

corridor a long hall

ancestral having to do with ancestors

overlapping extending over a part of something so as to coincide with that part

longevity long life

names. Not all my ancestors were there, Precious Auntie told me, just the ones my family considered most important. The in-between ones and those belonging to women were stuck in trunks or forgotten.

Notice how the statues of women ancestors were stored. What does this suggest about how women were viewed in China at that time?

Precious Auntie lighted several joss sticks. She blew on them until they began to **smolder.** Soon more smoke rose—a **jumble** of our breath, our offerings, and hazy clouds that I thought were ghosts who would try to yank me down to wander with them in the World of Yin. Precious Auntie once told me that a body grows cold when it is dead. And since I was chilled to the bone that morning, I was afraid.

A *joss stick* is a kind of sweet-smelling incense.

"I'm cold," I whimpered, and tears leaked out.

What season of the year do you think it is?

Precious Auntie sat on a stool and drew me to her lap. *Stop that, Doggie,* she gently scolded, *or the tears will freeze into icicles and poke out your eyes.* She kneaded my feet fast, as if they were dumpling dough. *Better? How about now, better?*

After I stopped crying, Precious Auntie lighted more joss sticks. She went back to the **threshold** and picked up one of

smolder smoke

jumble a mixture or confused heap

threshold a length of wood, stone, etc., along the bottom of a doorway her shoes. I can still see it—the dusty blue cloth, the black piping, the tiny **embroidery** of an extra leaf where she had repaired the hole. I thought she was going to burn her shoe as a send-away gift to the dead. Instead, from the shoe's lining, she took out the scrap of paper with the writing she had showed me earlier. She nodded toward me and said with her hands: *My family name, the name of all the bonesetters.* She put the paper name in front of my face again and said, *Never forget this name,* then placed it carefully on the altar. We bowed and rose, bowed and rose. Each time my head bobbed up, I looked at that name. And the name was—

What can you tell about LuLing's future from the detail about the orphan school?

Why can't I see it now? I've pushed a hundred family names through my mouth, and none comes back with the belch of memory. Was the name uncommon? Did I lose it because I kept it a secret too long? Maybe I lost it the same way I lost all my favorite things—the jacket GaoLing gave me when I left for the orphan school, the dress my second husband said made me look like a movie star, the first baby dress that Luyi outgrew. Each time I loved something with a special ache, I put it in my trunk of best things. I hid those things for so long I almost forgot I had them.

What words signals the end of the flashback?

This morning I remembered the trunk. I went to put away the birthday present that Luyi gave me. Gray pearls from Hawaii, beautiful beyond belief. When I opened the lid, out rose a cloud of moths, a stream of silverfish. Inside I found a web of knitted holes, one after the other. The embroidered flowers, the bright colors, now gone. Almost all that mattered in my life has disappeared, and the worst is losing Precious Auntie's name.

Precious Auntie, what is our name? I always meant to claim it as my own. Come help me remember. I'm not a little girl anymore. I'm not afraid of ghosts. Are you still mad at me? Don't you recognize me? I am LuLing, your daughter.

embroidery a design made on fabric with needlework

AFTER READING THE SELECTION | Apply the Skills

from The Bonesetter's Daughter *by Amy Tan*

Directions Choose the letter of the best answer or write the answer using complete sentences.

Comprehension: Identifying Facts

1. How old was LuLing when Precious Auntie wrote her family name?

   A six **C** thirty-five
   B thirteen **D** seventy-five

2. How does Precious Auntie "talk" to LuLing?

3. What do other people in the family think of Precious Auntie's appearance?

Comprehension: Putting Ideas Together

4. Which word best describes Precious Auntie's feelings for LuLing?

   A fake **C** caring
   B unkind **D** cold

5. What evidence suggests that LuLing's family is not wealthy?

6. What can you tell about the religious practices of LuLing's family?

Understanding Literature: Setting

The setting is the time and place of a story. This story takes place in China in the 1930s. Knowing this helps you understand the way people in the story think, speak, and act.

7. What happens to LuLing when she enters the ancestral room?

8. What is the setting for Precious Auntie's story about being a fire eater?

Critical Thinking

9. How can you tell that Precious Auntie is lying about how her face was burned?

Thinking Creatively

10. Why do you think LuLing wants to remember the family name? How do you think you would feel if you were in LuLing's place?

After Reading **continued on next page**

from The Bonesetter's Daughter by Amy Tan

Grammar Check

A pronoun is a word that takes the place of a noun or another pronoun. A personal pronoun refers to another noun in the sentence or paragraph. Some personal pronouns take the place of the subject—the one who is acting. Other personal pronouns take the place of the object—the one affected by the action.

Subject Pronouns	Object Pronouns
I, we, you, he, she, it, they	me, us, you, him, her it, them

Vocabulary Builder

The word recall is made up of the word call with the prefix *re-* added. In this case, the prefix *re-* means "back." To recall is to "call something back" or "to remember."

The prefix *re-* has several meanings. These meanings can help you understand and remember words that begin with *re-*.

Meanings	Words
Do action again or bring back an earlier state of affairs	Review, recommend, research
Action to answer or undo a situation	Revise, remove, respond
Backward action	Return, recall, repel

Answer each question in a complete sentence. Use the underlined word in your answer.

1. Why can you not review something you have not read yet?
2. How do you respond to funny stories?
3. Why should you revise an essay before turning it in?
4. How can research help you learn more about an author?
5. What book would you recommend to someone else?

Writing on Your Own

Write a news article about the life of a Chinese family in the 1930s. Your article should answer the questions *who, what, when, where, why,* and *how.* Use details from the story to write your article.

Listening and Speaking

Talk about the message of this story in a small group. Use these questions to guide you:

- At the end of the story, did you feel sorrier for LuLing or Precious Auntie? Why?
- Why was it so important to LuLing to remember the family name?
- What did the story teach you?
- Did this part of the book make you want to read the rest of the story? Why or why not?

As a group, identify two lessons readers might learn from the story.

Research and Technology

Work in a group to write an *annotated bibliography* for a report. The topic is how Chinese religious customs and beliefs have changed since the 1930s. Use the Internet or other library resources to identify several good sources of information. Make a list of resources. Then, write a short description of each resource that you would use for a report.

My Furthest-Back Person *by Alex Haley*

Alex Haley
1921–1992

Objectives

- To read and understand an essay
- To understand the author's purpose
- To appreciate the importance of historical context

About the Author

As a boy, Alex Haley spent his summers on his grandmother's front porch in Henning, Tennessee. There he listened to stories of the family's history back to the days of slavery. The "furthest-back person" they spoke of was an ancestor they called "the African." This ancestor was kidnapped in his native country and taken to Annapolis, Maryland. He was later sold into slavery.

After graduating from high school, Haley entered the U.S. Coast Guard. His life as a writer began at sea. He wrote short adventure stories. Twenty years later, Haley retired from the Coast Guard to become a full-time writer. Remembering the stories he had heard as a child, Haley began to research his past. This research led him to write *Roots: Saga of an American Family. Roots* sold more than 1.6 million copies in the first six months. The book was made into a television miniseries that set ratings records.

About the Selection

In "My Furthest-Back Person," Alex Haley looks at his past. Many people are interested in learning about their ancestors. They often begin with photographs, letters, newspaper clippings, or printed family histories. Government records such as birth certificates, marriage licenses, and death certificates also provide useful information. Family members can also give very valuable information about ancestors.

Literary Terms When reading nonfiction, use the historical context to better understand what is going on. Historical context is the political and social events and trends of the time. It helps explain why characters act and think the way they do. Watch for details that link events to a specific place and time.

essay a written work that shows a writer's opinions on some basic or current issue

An **essay** is a written work that shows a writer's opinions on some basic or current issue. Some essays, like "My Furthest-Back Person," are based on careful research. Haley looked through many old diaries and other documents to gather information for his essay.

Reading on Your Own There are several ways to figure out the author's purpose for writing a nonfiction work. One good way is to use background information. This is information that you already know about the author and topic. For example, you might know that an author was born outside the United States. The author's purpose might be to share information about the country he came from.

Writing on Your Own Why would anyone want to know more about his or her ancestors? Write your ideas about the value of studying family history. Then write a paragraph about how you might begin to explore your own roots.

Vocabulary Focus Preview the vocabulary words before you begin reading. Choose four words that you are not familiar with. Write each word and its meaning in your notebook.

Think Before You Read What might cause a person to spend years looking into his family history?

My Furthest-Back Person

As you read, think about why Haley worked so hard to learn about his roots.

What details show that the author wants to tell about his personal experience?

***Reading Strategy:* Text Structure**

What two kinds of "historical records" does the author tell about here?

One Saturday in 1965 I happened to be walking past the National Archives building in Washington. Across the **interim** years I had thought of Grandma's old stories—otherwise I can't think what **diverted** me up the Archives' steps. And when a main reading room desk attendant asked if he could help me, I wouldn't have dreamed of admitting to him some curiosity hanging on from boyhood about my slave **forebears.** I kind of bumbled that I was interested in census records of Alamance County, North Carolina, just after the Civil War.

The microfilm rolls were delivered, and I turned them through the machine with a building sense of **intrigue,** viewing in different census takers' penmanship an endless parade of names. After about a dozen microfilmed rolls, I was beginning to tire, when in utter astonishment I looked upon the names of Grandma's parents: Tom Murray, Irene Murray . . . older sisters of Grandma's as well—every one of them a name that I'd heard countless times on her front porch.

It wasn't that I hadn't believed Grandma. You just *didn't* not believe my Grandma. It was simply so **uncanny** actually seeing those names in print and in official U.S. Government records.

interim time between
diverted caused to change direction
forebears ancestors
intrigue great interest
uncanny strange

During the next several months I was back in Washington whenever possible, in the Archives, the Library of Congress, the Daughters of the American Revolution Library. (Whenever black attendants understood the idea of my search, documents I requested reached me with miraculous speed.) In one source or another during 1966 I was able to document at least the highlights of the cherished family story. I would have given anything to have told Grandma, but, sadly, in 1949 she had gone. So I went and told the only survivor of those Henning front-porch storytellers: Cousin Georgia Anderson, now in her 80's in Kansas City, Kan. Wrinkled, bent, not well herself, she was so overjoyed, repeating to me the old stories and sounds; they were like Henning echoes: "Yeah, boy, that African say his name was '*Kin-tay*'; he say the banjo was 'ko,' an' the river '*Kamby Bolong*,' an' he was off choppin' some

According to Haley's cousin, what happened to the African called "Kintay"?

wood to make his drum when they grabbed 'im!" Cousin Georgia grew so excited we had to stop her, calm her down, "You go 'head, boy! Your grandma an' all of 'em—they up there watching what you do!"

That week I flew to London on a magazine assignment. Since by now I was steeped in the old, in the past, scarcely a tour guide missed me—I was awed at so many historical places and treasures I'd heard of and read of. I came upon the Rosetta stone in the British Museum, marveling anew at how Jean Champollion, the French archaeologist, had miraculously deciphered its ancient demotic and hieroglyphic texts . . .

Demotic and hieroglyphic texts are ancient Egyptian writings that used symbols to represent words.

The thrill of that just kept hanging around in my head. I was on a jet returning to New York when a thought hit me. Those strange, unknown-tongue sounds, always part of our family's old story . . . they were obviously bits of our original African "*Kin-tay's*" native tongue. What specific tongue? Could I somehow find out?

Back in New York, I began making visits to the United Nations Headquarters lobby; it wasn't hard to spot Africans. I'd stop any I could, asking if my bits of phonetic sounds held any meaning for them. A couple of dozen Africans quickly looked at me, listened, and took off—understandably dubious about some Tennesseean's accent alleging "African" sounds.

My research assistant, George Sims (we grew up together in Henning), brought me some names of ranking scholars of African linguistics. One was particularly intriguing: a Belgian and English-educated Dr. Jan Vansina; he had spent his early career living in West African villages, studying and tape-recording countless oral histories that were narrated by certain very old African men; he had written a standard textbook, "The Oral Tradition."

What details show that the author wanted to use humor in telling in his story?

So I flew to the University of Wisconsin to see Dr. Vansina. In his living room I told him every bit of the family story in the fullest detail that I could remember it. Then, intensely, he **queried** me about the story's relay across the generations, about the gibberish of "k" sounds Grandma had fiercely

queried asked

muttered to herself while doing her housework, with my brothers and me giggling beyond her hearing at what we had dubbed "Grandma's noises."

Dr. Vansina, his manner very serious, finally said, "These sounds your family has kept sound very probably of the tongue called 'Mandinka.'"

I'd never heard of any "Mandinka." Grandma just told of the African saying "*ko*" for banjo, or "*Kamby Bolong*" for a Virginia river.

Among Mandinka stringed instruments, Dr. Vansina said, one of the oldest was the "kora."

"*Bolong*," he said, was clearly Mandinka for "river." Preceded by "*Kamby*," it very likely meant "Gambia River."

Dr. Vansina telephoned an **eminent** Africanist colleague, Dr. Philip Curtin. He said that the phonetic "*Kin-tay*" was correctly spelled "*Kinte*," a very old clan that had originated in Old Mali. The Kinte men traditionally were blacksmiths, and the women were potters and weavers.

I knew I must get to the Gambia River.

The first native Gambian I could locate in the U.S. was named Ebou Manga, then a junior attending Hamilton College in upstate Clinton, N.Y. He and I flew to Dakar, Senegal, then took a smaller plane to Yundum Airport, and rode in a van to Gambia's capital, Bathurst. Ebou and his father assembled eight Gambia government officials. I told them Grandma's stories, every detail I could remember, as they listened intently, then reacted. "'*Kamby Bolong*' of course is Gambia River!" I heard. "But more clue is your fore-father's saying his name was 'Kinte.'" Then they told me something I would never ever

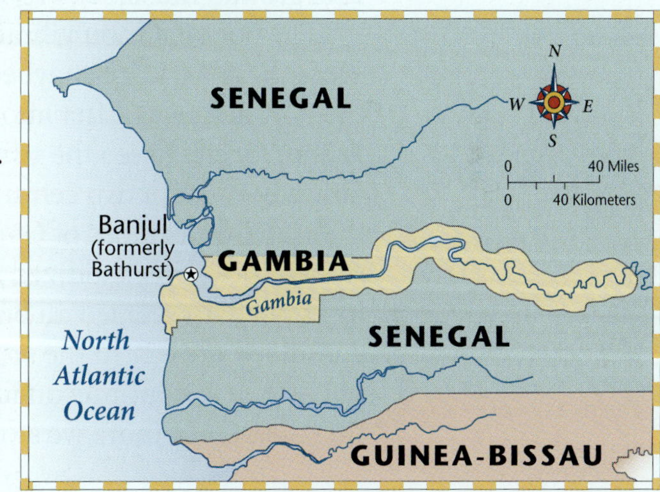

eminent outstanding

Reading Strategy: **Text Structure**
What effect does Haley's report of Grandma's stories have on the Gambian officials?

have fantasized—that in places in the back country lived very old men, commonly called *griots,* who could tell centuries of the histories of certain very old family clans. As for *Kintes,* they pointed out to me on a map some family villages, Kinte-Kundah, and Kinte-Kundah Janneh-Ya, for instance.

The Gambian officials said they would try to help me. I returned to New York dazed. It is embarrassing to me now, but despite Grandma's stories, I'd never been concerned much with Africa, and I had the routine images of African people living mostly in exotic jungles. But a compulsion now laid hold of me to learn all I could, and I began devouring books about Africa, especially about the slave trade. Then one Thursday's mail contained a letter from one of the Gambian officials, inviting me to return there.

Why do you think Haley had to travel by boat to visit the *griot?*

Monday I was back in Bathurst. It **galvanized** me when the officials said that a *griot* had been located who told the *Kinte* clan history—his name was Kebba Kanga Fofana. To reach him, I discovered, required a modified safari: renting a launch to get upriver, two land vehicles to carry supplies by a roundabout land route, and employing finally 14 people, including three interpreters and four musicians, since a *griot* would not speak the revered clan histories without background music.

Pith-helmets are hard hats often worn by tourists or hunters on safari.

What do the crumbling stones, cannons, and chains tell you about the fort?

The boat Baddibu vibrated upriver, with me acutely tense: Were these Africans maybe viewing me as but another of the pith-helmets? After about two hours, we put in at James Island, for me to see the ruins of the once British-operated James Fort. Here two centuries of slave ships had loaded thousands of cargoes of Gambian tribespeople. The crumbling stones, the deeply oxidized swivel cannon, even some remnant links of chain seemed all but impossible to believe. Then we continued upriver to the left-bank village of Albreda, and there put ashore to continue on foot to Juffure [jo͞o´ fo͞o rā], village of the *griot.* Once more we stopped, for me to see *toubob kolong,*

galvanized excited

the "white man's well," now almost filled in, in a swampy area with abundant, tall, saw-toothed grass. It was dug two centuries ago to "17 men's height deep" to insure survival drinking water for long-driven, famishing coffles of slaves.

How do these details remind readers of a particular time in history?

Walking on, I kept wishing that Grandma could hear how her stories had led me to the "*Kamby Bolong.*" (Our surviving storyteller Cousin Georgia died in a Kansas City hospital during this same morning, I would learn later.) Finally, Juffure village's playing children, sighting us, flashed an alert. The 70-odd people came rushing from their circular, thatch-roofed, mud-walled huts, with goats bounding up and about, and parrots squawking from up in the palms. I sensed him in advance somehow, the small man **amid** them, wearing a pillbox cap and an off-white robe—the *griot.* Then the interpreters went to him, as the villagers **thronged** around me.

And it hit me like a gale wind: every one of them, the whole crowd, was *jet black.* An enormous sense of guilt swept me—a sense of being some kind of hybrid . . . a sense of being impure among the pure. It was an awful sensation.

The old *griot* stepped away from my interpreters and the crowd quickly swarmed around him—all of them buzzing. An interpreter named A.B.C. Salla came to me; he whispered: "Why they stare at you so, they have never seen here a black American." And that hit me: I was symbolizing for them twenty-five millions of us they had never seen. What did they think of me—of us?

Then abruptly the old *griot* was briskly walking toward me. His eyes boring into mine, he spoke in Mandinka, as if instinctively I should understand—and A.B.C. Salla translated:

"Yes . . . we have been told by the forefathers . . . that many of us from this place are in exile . . . in that place called America . . . and in other places."

What do the *griot's* words suggest about the villagers' view of America and many Americans?

I suppose I physically wavered, and they thought it was the heat; rustling whispers went through the crowd, and a man brought me a low stool. Now the whispering hushed—the musicians had softly begun playing *kora* and *balafon,* and a canvas sling lawn seat was taken by the *griot,* Kebba Kanga Fofana, aged 73 "rains" (one rainy season each year). He seemed to gather himself into a physical rigidity, and he began speaking the Kinte clan's ancestral oral history; it came rolling from his mouth across the next hours . . . 17th- and 18th-century *Kinte* lineage details, **predominantly** what men took wives; the children they "begot," in the order of their births; those children's mates and children.

amid with

thronged circled around

predominantly mostly

Events frequently were dated by some proximate singular physical occurrence. It was as if some ancient scroll were printed **indelibly** within the *griot's* brain. Each few sentences or so, he would pause for an interpreter's translation to me. I distill here the essence:

The *Kinte* clan began in Old Mali, the men generally blacksmiths ". . . who conquered fire," and the women potters and weavers. One large branch of the clan moved to Mauretania from where one son of the clan, Kairaba Kunta Kinte, a Moslem Marabout holy man, entered Gambia. He lived first in the village of Pakali N'Ding; he moved next to Jiffarong village; ". . . and then he came here, into our own village of Juffure."

What do the quotation marks around many of these sentences show?

In Juffure, Kairaba Kunta Kinte took his first wife, ". . . a Mandinka maiden, whose name was Sireng. By her, he begot two sons, whose names were Janneh and Saloum. Then he got a second wife, Yaisa. By her, he begot a son, Omoro."

The three sons became men in Juffure. Janneh and Saloum went off and found a new village, Kinte-Kundah Janneh-Ya. "And then Omoro, the youngest son, when he had 30 rains, took as a wife a maiden, Binta Kebba.

"And by her, he begot four sons—Kunta, Lamin, Suwadu, and Madi . . . "

Sometimes, a "begotten," after his naming, would be accompanied by some later-occurring detail, perhaps as ". . . in time of big water (flood), he slew a water buffalo." Having named those four sons, now the *griot* stated such a detail.

"About the time the king's soldiers came, the **eldest** of these four sons, Kunta, when he had about 16 rains, went away from his village, to chop wood to make a drum . . . and he was never seen again . . . "

Goose-pimples the size of lemons seemed to pop all over me. In my knapsack were my **cumulative** notebooks, the

indelibly unable to be erased

eldest oldest

cumulative collection

first of them including how in my boyhood, my Grandma, Cousin Georgia and the others told of the African "*Kin-tay*" who always said he was kidnapped near his village—while chopping wood to make a drum . . .

I showed the interpreter, he showed and told the *griot,* who excitedly told the people; they grew very **agitated. Abruptly** then they formed a human ring, encircling me, dancing and chanting. Perhaps a dozen of the women carrying their infant babies rushed in toward me, **thrusting** the infants into my arms conveying, I would later learn, "the laying on of hands. . . through this flesh which is us, we are you, and you are us." The men hurried me into their mosque, their Arabic praying later being translated outside: "Thanks be to Allah for returning the long lost from among us." Direct descendants of Kunta Kinte's blood brothers were hastened, some of them from nearby villages, for a family portrait to be taken with

How are several different kinds of histories coming together?

agitated angry **abruptly** suddenly **thrusting** pushing me, surrounded by actual ancestral sixth cousins. More symbolic acts filled the remaining day.

When they would let me leave, for some reason I wanted to go away over the African land. Dazed, silent in the bumping Land Rover, I heard the cutting **staccato** of talking drums. Then when we sighted the next village, its people came **thronging** to meet us. They were all—little naked ones to wizened elders—waving, beaming; amid a **cacophony** of crying out; and then my ears identified their words: "*Meester Kinte! Meester Kinte!*"

Let me tell you something: I am a man. But I remember the sob surging up from my feet, flinging up my hands before my face and bawling as I had not done since I was a baby . . . the jet-black Africans were jostling, staring . . . I didn't care, with the feelings surging. If you really knew the odyssey of us millions of black Americans, if you really knew how we came in the seeds of our forefathers, captured, driven, beaten, inspected, bought, branded, chained in foul ships, if you really knew, you needed weeping . . .

Back home, I knew that what I must write, really, was our black saga, where any individual's past is the essence of the millions'. Now flat broke, I went to some editors I knew, describing the Gambian miracle, and my desire to pursue the research; Doubleday contracted to publish, and Reader's Digest to condense the projected book; then I had advances to travel further.

What do you learn about Haley's reason for writing this story? Why do you think he calls his experience a miracle?

What ship brought Kinte to Grandma's "'Naplis" (Annapolis, Md., obviously)? The old *griot's* time reference to "king's soldiers" sent me flying to London. Feverish searching at last identified, in British Parliament records, "Colonel O'Hare's Forces," **dispatched** in mid-1767 to protect the then British-held James Fort whose ruins I'd visited. So Kunta Kinte was down in some ship probably sailing later that summer from the Gambia River to Annapolis.

staccato short, quick beat

thronging rushing

cacophony noise

dispatched sent offshore

Now I feel it was fated that I had taught myself to write in the U.S. Coast Guard. For the sea dramas I had concentrated on had given me years of experience searching among yellowing old U.S. maritime records. So now in English 18th Century marine records I finally tracked ships reporting themselves in and out to the Commandant of the Gambia River's James Fort. And then early one afternoon I found that a Lord Ligonier under a Captain Thomas Davies had sailed on the Sabbath of July 5, 1767. Her cargo: 3,265 elephants' teeth, 3,700 pounds of beeswax, 800 pounds of cotton, 32 ounces of Gambian gold and 140 slaves; her destination: "Annapolis."

That night I recrossed the Atlantic. In the Library of Congress the Lord Ligonier's arrival was one brief line in "Shipping In The Port Of Annapolis—1748–1775." I located the author, Vaughan W. Brown, in his Baltimore brokerage office. He drove to Historic Annapolis, the city's historical society, and found me further documentation of her arrival on Sept. 29, 1767. (Exactly two centuries later, Sept. 29, 1967, standing, staring seaward from an Annapolis pier, again I knew tears.) More help came in the Maryland Hall of Records.

Archivist Phebe Jacobsen found the Lord Ligonier's arriving customs declaration listing, "98 Negroes"—so in her 86-day crossing, 42 Gambians had died, one among the survivors being 16-year-old Kunta Kinte. Then the microfilmed Oct. 1, 1767, Maryland Gazette contained, on page two, an announcement to prospective buyers from the ship's agents, Daniel of St. Thos. Jenifer and John Ridout (the Governor's secretary): "from the River GAMBIA, in AFRICA . . . a cargo of choice, healthy SLAVES . . ."

AFTER READING THE SELECTION | Apply the Skills

My Furthest-Back Person *by Alex Haley*

Directions Choose the letter of the best answer or write the answer using complete sentences.

Comprehension: Identifying Facts

1. In what year did Haley begin his research?

A 1955 **C** 1975

B 1965 **D** 1985

2. Where did Haley first go to speak to Africans?

A Africa

B the United Nations

C Washington, D.C.

D the University of Wisconsin

3. What did Haley find in the National Archives in Washington, D.C.?

4. How did the Rosetta stone make Haley feel?

5. What does the *griot* tell Haley about Kunta Kinte?

6. How does Haley feel when the villagers call out "Meester Kinte"?

7. What does Haley learn about the strange sounds his Grandma used to make?

8. How does Haley find out what part of Africa his family came from?

9. What do the villagers do when they recognize Haley as "one of them"?

10. What happens after Haley shows his notebooks about his ancestor?

Comprehension: Putting Ideas Together

11. Haley's main reason for going to the National Archives the first time was

A a long-time interest in African history

B general curiosity

C to research a magazine article

D to find out about Grandma's old stories

12. Why is Haley so interested in the historical treasures in London?

A His research into Grandma's past has awakened his interest in history.

B The magazine will pay him extra to find out about historical treasures.

C He hopes to find clues about his ancestors in London.

D He is doing research on the role of England in the African slave trade.

13. How does Haley's visit to the National Archives affect his view of Grandma's stories?

14. Why does Haley visit Georgia Anderson?

***After Reading* continued on next page**

My Furthest-Back Person by Alex Haley

15. How does Haley respond when he finds information about his family in the government documents?

16. Why is Dr. Vansina "intensely" interested in the "gibberish" that made Haley laugh as a child?

17. How is the Rosetta stone linked to the African sounds in Haley's family stories?

18. Why does the *griot* know about Kunta Kinte?

19. Look at *About the Author* and *About the Selection* on page 52. How does this information help you understand the author's purpose for writing this story?

20. What other purposes might Haley have had for writing this story?

Understanding Literature: Historical Context

Your knowledge of historical context increases your understanding and enjoyment of both fiction and nonfiction. Knowing the history of Africa and the slave trade helps you better understand Haley's story.

21. Which two countries are most talked about in this story?

22. Kunta Kinte was brought to Maryland because of what event in history?

23. Why did Haley have to travel by boat to visit the *griot?*

24. What chain of events leads Haley to learning the truth about his roots?

25. What details show how slaves were treated at James Fort?

Critical Thinking

26. How do the tales of the *griot* complete those told by Haley's family?

27. Why does Haley respond as he does when the villagers call out "Meester Kinte"?

28. Why do you think Haley ends his story with the word *slaves?*

Thinking Creatively

29. In his research, Haley uses both written and human sources of information. Which kind of research do you think is more important? Why?

30. What questions would you like to ask Alex Haley about his experience?

Grammar Check

A pronoun is a word that takes the place of a noun or another pronoun. A *possessive pronoun* is a pronoun that shows ownership. Possessive pronouns act as adjectives. They also answer the question *whose?*

Pronouns	Possessive Pronouns	Example
I, we	my, mine, our, ours	I wore *my* hat. The hat is *mine.* We took *our* car.
you	your, yours	You ate *your* plum. The plum is *yours.*
he, she, it	his, her, hers, its	He wore *his* jersey. The gloves are *hers.*
they	their, theirs	They rode *their* horses. The horses are *theirs.*

Vocabulary Builder

The word *previous* contains the prefix *pre-*, meaning "before." *Previous* means "taking place before."

Example: We had prepared during the previous week.

Answer each question in a complete sentence. Use the underlined word in your answer. You can use a dictionary to look up the underlined words.

1 Why can you not predict something that happened yesterday?

2 Why would you preview a book before buying it?

3 What precaution should you take when riding a bike?

Writing on Your Own

A *letter of proposal* is a letter that describes a new project. It is usually written to ask for money or other support. Write a letter of proposal that Alex Haley might have written to his publisher. Think about Haley's reason for writing the book. What kind of support might he want from the publisher?

Listening and Speaking

Interview an older person to learn how people lived in an earlier time period. Start by writing a list of questions to guide the interview. Listen carefully to what the older person says, and ask good follow-up questions. If possible, tape the interview. Present your findings to the class.

Media and Viewing

Work in a small group. Create a timeline of key events in the American slave trade. Use the Internet and library resources to gather information. Be sure to include the most important people and events on your timeline.

Memos

The Reading Strategy in Part 2 is Text Structure. Informational writing takes many different forms. People today share information in text messages, emails, letters, instant messages, and handwritten notes.

Some writing structures are more formal than others. The *memo* falls somewhere between formal and informal. A memo is used in offices and usually follows a standard format. At the same time, it is a quick and informal way to share information. In offices, memos sometimes are sent back and forth all day long. They offer a simple way to put ideas and opinions "on the record."

About Memos

The word *memo* comes from the Latin *memoria,* meaning "memory." Memos are often sent as reminders. They can also be used to inform, persuade, suggest, or announce. Most memos feature these basic parts:

- Header: This tells the date, whom it is from, whom it is for, and the subject. A typical header looks like this:

  Date: April 24, 2007

  To: Sander McFadden in Accounting Dept.

  From: Timon Juarez in Supply Dept.

  Subject: Suggested Ways of Saving Money on Paper Clips

- Purpose: This is where you state the purpose of the memo. Explain why you are writing and what you are writing about.
- Summary: This is where you state your main points.
- Action/Conclusion: Here you tell what needs to be done. This part of the memo may be a list of numbered or bulleted suggestions.

Reading Skill

Context clues can be very useful when writing or reading a memo. As a reader, you can use context clues to figure out the writer's purpose. A formal memo from your boss is probably an order rather than a suggestion. A memo from a coworker that uses informal language is a very different thing. "I urge workers to arrive at 9:00 A.M. sharp" sounds like an order. "Let's all try to get here around nine" sounds more like a suggestion. Look for context clues such as tone, word choice, and purpose. They will help you to send and receive the correct message.

Memos are used not only in businesses, but also in government offices. Sometimes they are big news. A memo written by a government employee might even make the front page of a newspaper.

These memos can become a big part of history. Imagine memos being written in the late third century. That's over 1,700 years ago! What would the memo have been about then? At that time the vast and powerful Roman Empire was having big problems. The emperor Diocletian (284–304) helped save the Empire with a program of reform. Imagine that, before he acted on these reforms, he suggested them in a memo. He might have sent a memo that looked something like this:

Date: 284

To: Maximian
From: Diocletian, Emperor of Rome
Subject: Proposed Plan to Save the Empire

As you know, our empire is stretched over too great a distance. Our army is not able to defend the vast reaches of our lands. Our money is nearly worthless. The Germanic tribes are pouring into our territories almost at will. The same old timid measures will not serve us in these times of crisis. Such grave threats to our Empire require big, bold measures. Therefore, I propose the following plan of action:

- We face different military threats in the East than in the West. Therefore, I suggest that we divide the Empire in two. You will rule the West, and I will rule the East.
- We should take the 50 provinces and combine them into 13 districts. This will make it easier to govern and collect taxes.
- We cannot defend our frontiers with our current army. I suggest doubling its size from 300,000 to 600,000. We can do this by ordering that sons must follow their father into the army.
- I further suggest that we start a military draft throughout the Empire.
- We must revive our worthless money. To this end, I propose that we issue a new currency. It will consist of gold and silver coins. There will be no cheating on gold or silver content.
- To raise money for these plans, I suggest a new land tax.
- We need a better system of tax collection. I suggest that businessmen in the cities be ordered to help us collect taxes.
- We must bring prices and wages under control. To do so, I suggest that the state set limits on wages and prices across the Empire.

If the gods give us the strength and will, these measures can save our Empire. Please let me know what you think.

Usually memos are concerned with matters more modest than saving an empire. Here's a more typical example of an everyday office memo. It might not make the front page of the newspaper. But it is no doubt very important to the author—and maybe to the readers.

Date: April 7, 2007
To: All Employees
From: Jo Otero, Human Resources Director, Spiffy Cleaning Products
Subject: Pet Policy

As you know, many companies now allow employees to bring their pets to work. Pets can make for a happier workplace. Spiffy Cleaning Products has discussed this issue for close to a year now. The management team has decided to allow pets into the office as of May 1, 2007. We have come up with some suggested guidelines. We welcome your feedback and ideas on these points.

After much debate, we think it is best to limit this privilege to dog owners. We know that cat owners love their pets just as much. But cats tend to be less comfortable in unfamiliar places than dogs. Most cannot be trained to sit and stay. Many will run for cover under desks and behind cabinets. This will require a major search effort to find the missing cat. We cannot spare this much time from work.

Assuming that we will limit this policy to dogs, here are some suggested guidelines:

- ✦ Dogs brought to the office must be trained not to bark at strangers or at one another.
- ✦ You must bring your own bowls and food.
- ✦ You are welcome to fill the dogs' water bowls at the water cooler. But please clean it with Spiffy cleanser afterward.
- ✦ Please keep your dog at your own desk. People like to pet dogs, but we all have a lot to do. We cannot risk turning the office into a petting zoo.
- ✦ Make sure you walk your dog at least twice during the work day. A sweet-smelling office is a productive office.
- ✦ Please bring an area rug for your dog to lie on. This will save on cleanup time.
- ✦ If someone in the neighboring space has a dog allergy, please ask to be moved.
- ✦ Please keep your dog food tightly sealed in the dog refrigerator.

This policy applies to the offices only. We cannot have pets in or near the Spiffy factory.

We hope to hear back from all employees with suggestions and ideas.

Monitor Your Progress

Directions Choose the letter of the best answer or write the answer using complete sentences.

1. Diocletian plans to pay for his reforms by
   A selling the emperor's jewels
   B conquering more territory
   C collecting a new land tax
   D setting up a policy of free trade

2. The Spiffy Human Resources Director suggests that employees with pets bring an area rug
   A to save on cleanup time
   B to make their work spaces more attractive
   C to make the pet feel more at home
   D to give the pet a familiar space to stay

3. How would you describe the situation faced by Emperor Diocletian as described in his memo?

4. Compare and contrast the main purpose of each memo.

5. Which memo is likely to be of interest to the largest number of people?

Writing on Your Own

Think of a current problem that people are talking about in your school or community. Write a memo to your principal or mayor with your ideas for fixing the problem. Be sure to follow the correct form for a memo.

COMPARING LITERARY WORKS | **Build Understanding**

from Main Street *by Sinclair Lewis*

Sinclair Lewis
1885–1951

Objectives

- To read and understand satire
- To identify the author's purpose
- To understand characterization

About the Author

Sinclair Lewis was a son of the American Midwest. His education and travels, however, took him far from his Midwestern roots. In fact, he is famous for criticizing the Middle American way of life. While Alex Haley wrote proudly about Africa, Lewis was not proud of his own roots.

Lewis's first major novel was *Main Street* (1920). It painted a gloomy picture of the emptiness of small-town life. His next few novels also made fun of American life in the early 20th century. Lewis received the Nobel Prize for literature in 1930. He was the first American writer to receive this honor. He died in Rome in 1951.

About the Selection

This story is taken from Lewis's novel *Main Street*. The book pokes fun at life in the small town of Gopher Prairie, Minnesota. It is an imaginary place modeled on Lewis's real Minnesota hometown, Sauk Centre. This story—and the entire novel—centers on the thoughts and feelings of Carol Kennicott. An Easterner, she has come to the Midwest to settle down with her doctor husband. Through her eyes, Lewis shows just how small life in a small town can be.

As you read, think about the similarities and differences of this story with "My Furthest-Back Person." How do both stories show the author's purpose?

Literary Terms **Satire** is humorous writing that makes fun of foolishness or evil. Lewis makes many of the residents of Gopher Prairie seem small-minded or silly. By contrast, in "My Furthest-Back Person," Haley clearly admires the people of Juffure.

In satire, historical context is often used to explain why characters do what they do. **Characterization** is the way a writer develops character qualities and personality traits.

satire humorous writing that makes fun of foolishness or evil

characterization the way a writer develops character qualities and personality traits

Reading on Your Own The author's purpose is the reason for which the author writes. An author may have more than one purpose for writing. One purpose of the novel *Main Street* is to entertain the reader. But Lewis also wants us to think about the limits of small-town life. Like many nonfiction works, "My Furthest-Back Person" seeks mainly to inform. But Haley also wants people to think about the importance of family roots.

Writing on Your Own Think about the image of roots. Like plants, people have roots—the people, places, and situations that shaped who they are. Roots in the soil provide food and water that help a plant grow. But they also root the plant to one place. Write a paragraph about your own family roots. Have they helped you grow, tied you down, or both?

Vocabulary Focus A *prefix* is added to the beginning of a word to change the word's meaning. The prefix *dis-* means "not." *Embarking* means "getting on a ship or train." *Disembarking* means "getting off a ship or train." Other examples include *distrust* and *dishonest.*

Think Before You Read Have you ever moved to a different city or home? How did the move make you feel? As you read, compare your feelings with Carol's feelings.

from Main Street

As you read, think about Lewis's purpose for writing. How is it similar to and different from Haley's purpose for writing about his roots?

What do the first two paragraphs suggest about Carol's feelings toward her husband?

That one word—home—it terrified her. Had she really bound herself to live, **inescapably,** in this town called Gopher Prairie? And this thick man beside her, who dared to define her future, he was a stranger! She turned in her seat, stared at him. Who was he? Why was he sitting with her? He wasn't of her kind! His neck was heavy; his speech was heavy; he was twelve or thirteen years older than she; and about him was none of the magic of shared adventures and eagerness. She could not believe that she had ever slept in his arms. That was one of the dreams which you had but did not officially admit.

She told herself how good he was, how dependable and understanding. She touched his ear, smoothed the plane of his solid jaw, and, turning away again, concentrated upon liking his town. It wouldn't be like these **barren** settlements. It couldn't be! Why, it had three thousand population.

inescapably to not escape

barren boring

That was a great many people. There would be six hundred houses or more. And—— The lakes near it would be so lovely. She'd seen them in the photographs. They had looked charming . . . hadn't they?

As the train left Wahkeenyan she began nervously to watch for the—lakes—the entrance to all her future life. But when she discovered them, to the left of the track, her only impression of them was that they resembled the photographs.

A mile from Gopher Prairie the track mounts a curving low ridge, and she could see the town as a whole. With a passionate jerk she pushed up the window, looked out, the arched fingers of her left hand trembling on the sill, her right hand at her breast.

And she saw that Gopher Prairie was merely an enlargement of all the hamlets which they had been passing. Only to the eyes of a Kennicott was it **exceptional.** The huddled low wooden houses broke the plains **scarcely** more than would a hazel thicket. The fields swept up to it, past it. It was unprotected and unprotecting; there was no dignity in it nor any hope of greatness. Only the tall red grain-elevator and a few tinny church-steeples rose from the mass. It was a frontier camp. It was not a place to live in, not possibly, not **conceivably.**

Hamlets are small villages

What is the author's purpose in describing Gopher Prairie in this way?

The people—they'd be as drab as their houses, as flat as their fields. She couldn't stay here. She would have to wrench loose from this man, and flee.

She peeped at him. She was at once helpless before his mature **fixity,** and touched by his excitement as he sent his magazine **skittering** along the aisle, stooped for their bags, came up with flushed face, and **gloated,** "Here we are!"

exceptional unusual

scarcely hardly

conceivably understandably

fixity steadiness

skittering skipping lightly

gloated observed with glee

Which phrase lends a satirical feeling to this description?

Reading Strategy:
Text Structure
What word or phrase in this paragraph best summarizes Carol's feelings?

She smiled loyally, and looked away. The train was entering town. The houses on the outskirts were dusky old red mansions with wooden frills, or **gaunt** frame shelters like grocery boxes, or new **bungalows** with concrete foundations imitating stone.

Now the train was passing the elevator, the grim storage-tanks for oil, a creamery, a lumber-yard, a stock-yard muddy and trampled and stinking. Now they were stopping at a squat red frame station, the platform crowded with unshaven farmers and with loafers—unadventurous people with dead eyes. She was here. She could not go on. It was the end—the end of the world. She sat with closed eyes, longing to push past Kennicott, hide somewhere in the train, flee on toward the Pacific.

gaunt thin and bony **bungalows** houses

Something large arose in her soul and commanded, "Stop it! Stop being a whining baby!" She stood up quickly; she said, "Isn't it wonderful to be here at last!"

He trusted her so. She would make herself like the place. And she was going to do tremendous things—

What kind of person do you think Carol is? Why?

She followed Kennicott and the bobbing ends of the two bags which he carried. They were held back by the slow line of **disembarking** passengers. She reminded herself that she was actually at the dramatic moment of the bride's homecoming. She ought to feel exalted. She felt nothing at all except irritation at their slow progress toward the door.

Kennicott stooped to peer through the windows. He shyly **exulted:**

"Look! Look! There's a bunch come down to welcome us! Sam Clark and the missus and Dave Dyer and Jack Elder, and, yes sir, Harry Haydock and Juanita, and a whole crowd! I guess they see us now. Yuh, yuh sure, they see us! See 'em waving!"

She obediently bent her head to look out at them. She had hold of herself. She was ready to love them. But she was embarrassed by the heartiness of the cheering group. From the vestibule she waved to them, but she clung a second to the sleeve of the brakeman who helped her down before she had the courage to dive into the cataract of hand-shaking people, people whom she could not tell apart. She had the impression that all the men had coarse voices, large damp hands, toothbrush mustaches, bald spots, and Masonic watch-charms.

A *cataract* is a waterfall or flood.

How does Lewis make fun of the people at the station?

She knew that they were welcoming her. Their hands, their smiles, their shouts, their affectionate eyes overcame her. She stammered, "Thank you, oh, thank you!"

One of the men was **clamoring** at Kennicott, "I brought my machine down to take you home, doc."

disembarking getting off a ship or train

exulted rejoiced

clamoring crying out

Paiges and *Marmons* were expensive automobiles built in the early part of the 20th century.

What phrase lends a note of satire to this paragraph?

"Fine business, Sam!" cried Kennicott; and, to Carol, "Let's jump in. That big Paige over there. Some boat, too, believe me! Sam can show speed to any of these Marmons from Minneapolis!"

Only when she was in the motor car did she distinguish the three people who were to accompany them. The owner, now at the wheel, was the essence of decent self-satisfaction; a baldish, largish, level-eyed man, rugged of neck but sleek round of face—face like the back of a spoon bowl. He was chuckling at her, "Have you got us all straight yet?"

"Course she has! Trust Carrie to get things straight and get 'em darn quick! I bet she could tell you every date in history!" boasted her husband.

But the man looked at her reassuringly and with a certainty that he was a person whom she could trust she confessed, "As a matter of fact I haven't got anybody straight."

"Course you haven't, child. Well, I'm Sam Clark, dealer in hardware, sporting goods, cream separators, and almost any kind of heavy junk you can think of. You can call me Sam—anyway, I'm going to call you Carrie, seein' 's you've been and gone and married this poor fish of a bum medic that we keep round here." Carol smiled **lavishly,** and wished that she called people by their given names more easily. "The fat cranky lady back there beside you, who is pretending that she can't hear me giving her away, is Mrs. Sam'l Clark; and this hungry-looking squirt up here beside me is Dave Dyer, who keeps his drug store running by not filling your hubby's prescriptions right—fact you might say he's the guy that put the '**shun**' in 'prescription.' So! Well, leave us take the bonny bride home. Say, doc, I'll sell you the Candersen place for three thousand plunks. Better be thinking about building a new home for Carrie. Prettiest *Frau* in G. P., if you asks me!"

lavishly generously **shun** to avoid

Contentedly Sam Clark drove off, in the heavy traffic of three Fords and the Minniemashie House Free 'Bus.

"I shall like Mr. Clark . . . I can't call him 'Sam'! They're all so friendly." She glanced at the houses; tried not to see what she saw; gave way in: "Why do these stories lie so? They always make the bride's home-coming a bower of roses. Complete trust in noble spouse. Lies about marriage. I'm not changed. And this town—Oh my God! I can't go through with it. This junk-heap!"

Her husband bent over her. "You look like you were in a brown study. Scared? I don't expect you to think Gopher Prairie is a paradise, after St. Paul. I don't expect you to be crazy about it, at first. But you'll come to like it so much—life's so free here and best people on earth."

She whispered to him (while Mrs. Clark considerately turned away), "I love you for understanding. I'm just—I'm beastly over-sensitive. Too many books. It's my lack of shoulder-muscles and sense. Give me time, dear."

Reading Strategy:
Text Structure
How does the phrase "too many books" contrast Carol with the people of Gopher Prairie?

"You bet! All the time you want!"

She laid the back of his hand against her cheek, snuggled near him. She was ready for her new home.

Kennicott had told her that, with his widowed mother as housekeeper, he had occupied an old house, "but nice and roomy, and well-heated, best furnace I could find on the market." His mother had left Carol her love, and gone back to Lac-qui-Meurt.

It would be wonderful, she exulted, not to have to live in Other People's Houses, but to make her own **shrine.** She held his hand tightly and stared ahead as the car swung round a corner and stopped in the street before a **prosaic** frame house in a small parched lawn.

Reading Strategy:
Text Structure
Why does the writer use the words "shrine" and "prosaic frame house" in the same paragraph?

shrine a holy place **prosaic** ordinary

from Main Street *by Sinclair Lewis*

Directions Choose the letter of the best answer or write the answer using complete sentences.

Comprehension: Identifying Facts

1. Kennicott and Carol are
- **A** newlyweds
- **B** brother and sister
- **C** old friends
- **D** recently divorced

2. What is Kennicott and Carol's destination?
- **A** St. Paul
- **B** Sauk Centre
- **C** Gopher Prairie
- **D** Wahkeenyan

3. What words best describe the scenes Carol sees from the train window?

4. What does Carol feel like doing as the train pulls into the station?

5. What does Carol feel as she steps off the train?

6. How do the people at the train station appear to Carol at first?

7. Who drives the Kennicotts from the train station to their house?

8. What does Sam Clark do for a living?

9. What does Carol's husband do for a living?

10. What feature of his old house does Kennicott boast about to Carol?

Comprehension: Putting Ideas Together

11. The word *home* terrified Carol because
- **A** she had been unhappy as a child
- **B** it reminds her of a town and man she does not like
- **C** she is not sure they can afford to buy a house
- **D** her husband has not told her what kind of place they are moving to

12. On first seeing Gopher Prairie, Carol is disappointed because
- **A** it is too large
- **B** it is not much larger than the nearby villages
- **C** there is no one waiting for them at the station
- **D** there are no lakes there

13. How would you compare the purpose of Carol's journey to that of Haley's journey?

14. What forms of transportation did Carol and Haley use in their journeys?

15. How are the people that Carol and Haley met similar and different?

16. Compare Gopher Prairie to the village of Juffure.

***Comparing* continued on next page**

COMPARING LITERARY WORKS | Apply the Skills *(cont.)*

from Main Street *by Sinclair Lewis*

17. What kind of welcomes do Carol and Haley receive when they arrive?

18. Explain how Carol and Haley change their views of another person.

19. Who seems the more satisfied character to you—Carol or Haley? Explain.

20. How are the overall feelings of Carol and Haley different as they set out on their journeys?

Understanding Literature: Satire

Main Street is a satire about a small town in Minnesota in the 1920s. Knowing this helps the reader understand Lewis's handling of tone and characterization.

21. What does Carol's long train ride show about the historical context of *Main Street?*

22. In what way is Lewis's story a satire?

23. Why would Haley be less likely than Lewis to use satire in a story?

24. What evidence suggests that both Carol and Haley are well-educated people?

25. How does the historical context of these two stories affect the main characters?

Critical Thinking

26. In what ways are both Carol and Haley outsiders?

27. Carol wants to make her house into her own shrine. How is Juffure also a shrine for Haley? Which place is more truly a shrine?

28. What unpleasant truths do Carol and Haley each learn from their journeys?

Thinking Creatively

29. In *Main Street*, Sinclair Lewis mostly points out the bad parts of small-town life. What do you think the good parts of living in a small town might be?

30. What do you think is likely to happen to Carol later on in Lewis's novel?

Grammar Check

An adjective is a word that describes a person, place, or thing. An adjective answers one of the following questions: *What kind? Which one? How many? How much?*

Identify each adjective in the sentences below. Then, write a new sentence replacing each adjective with a different adjective.

1 The cool air was a clear sign that fall had arrived.

2 In the early morning, I heard the distant squawks of geese.

3 Red and brown leaves crackled beneath my feet.

Vocabulary Builder

A *prefix* is added to the beginning of a word to change the word's meaning. Each story features words with prefixes, such as disembarking and indelibly. Answer each question to show your understanding of these and some other vocabulary words from these selections.

1 If an event was recorded indelibly in your memory, would it be a lasting memory?

2 Why might a movie be called prosaic?

3 What kinds of foods should you shun?

Writing on Your Own

Tone is the attitude an author takes toward a subject. It shows how the writer feels about the characters and the story. The author's purpose for writing often sets the tone of the work. Write a brief essay comparing the tone of Lewis's story and the tone of "My Furthest-Back Person." Mention each author's purpose and the words each author uses to create the tone.

Listening and Speaking

"It is better to grow up in a small town than in a big city." Give a speech in which you argue for or against this idea. Start by writing an outline. Then think of examples that support your idea. Practice your speech before presenting it to your classmates.

Media and Viewing

The American artist Edward Hopper (1882–1967) did many paintings of small-town scenes. Look on the Internet to find pictures of Hopper's work. Learn as much as you can about Hopper and his paintings. Look for similarities between Hopper's work and Lewis's view of small town life. Prepare a slide show to share your findings with classmates.

Unit 1 SPELLING WORKSHOP

Tricky or Difficult Words

A homophone is a word that sounds exactly like another word. However, it has a different spelling and meaning.

Two or Too?

One of the most common "spelling" errors occurs when a writer uses the wrong homophone. Spell-checker software will not find this kind of error, so proofread your work carefully. Use mnemonic devices, or memory aids, to help you remember which spelling to use. For example, the words *there* and *their* are often confused. Notice that the word meaning the opposite of *here* also contains the word *here.*

Practice

Write the word from the Word List that matches each mnemonic clue. Use different-color pens to show the letters that the clue helps you to remember.

1. If it is nice, you can **eat** outside.
2. The _____ is your **pal.**
3. **They** are in this word.
4. You get this number by putting one **with** one.
5. Decision words: **when,** _____, **why.** (They all begin with the same two letters.)
6. This word contains its opposite. Not **here** but _____.

Word List

- to
- too
- two
- weather
- whether
- they're
- their
- there
- principal
- principle

Unit 1 SUMMARY

In Unit 1, you read both fiction and nonfiction. "Papa's Parrot," the passage from *The Bonesetter's Daughter,* and the passage from *Main Street* are fiction. The passage from *An American Childhood,* "Barrio Boy," and "My Furthest-Back Person" are all nonfiction.

Both fiction and nonfiction are forms of narrative writing. Both are usually told from either the first-person or third-person point of view. Setting, characters, and dialogue all play a part in both fiction and nonfiction. In both kinds of writing, historical context helps the reader better understand the author's purpose.

Nonfiction and fiction are written for different purposes. Nonfiction can be written to entertain, persuade, or inform. Fiction is usually written to entertain, but it may have other purposes as well. Fiction may try to get the reader to think about important issues. Stories in this unit were about growing up, remembering the past, and changing surroundings.

Selections

- "Papa's Parrot" by Cynthia Rylant is about the changes that are part of growing up. As Harry turns 12, his interests turn from his father to his friends. He soon realizes how much pain this change causes his father.
- The passage from *An American Childhood* is about Annie Dillard's childhood. At a young age, she joins the boys in throwing snowballs at passing cars. One driver teaches Annie an important lesson.
- In "Barrio Boy," Ernesto Galarza tells of moving from Mexico to America as a child. He tells of going to school without knowing how to speak English. A kind teacher helps him to feel pride in being an American.
- The passage from Amy Tan's *The Bonesetter's Daughter* is about China in the 1930s. LuLing struggles to understand things that happened to her in her childhood long ago.
- "My Furthest-Back Person" was the inspiration for *Roots.* Author Alex Haley travels to Africa to learn more about where his family came from.
- The passage from *Main Street* by Sinclair Lewis is set in an imaginary small town. Carol Kennicott struggles to find her place in a town full of small-minded people.

Unit 1 REVIEW

Direction Choose the letter of the best answer or write the answer using complete sentences:

Comprehension: Identifying Facts

1. In "Papa's Parrot," Harry's father
- **A** sells paper goods
- **B** owns a candy and nut store
- **C** repairs cars
- **D** fixes toys

2. In *An American Childhood,* what do Annie and her friends do to passing cars?

3. In *The Bonesetter's Daughter,* what does Precious Auntie tell many different stories about?

4. In "My Furthest-Back Person," which African country does Alex Haley visit?

5. In *Main Street,* how do the Kennicotts travel to Gopher Prairie?

Comprehension: Putting Ideas Together

6. In "Barrio Boy," Ernesto's friends are mostly
- **A** other Mexicans
- **B** students who get in trouble
- **C** students from different countries
- **D** much older than he is

7. What is the role of the parrot in "Papa's Parrot"?

8. What happens in *An American Childhood* after the children throw snowballs?

9. In *The Bonesetter's Daughter,* what is happening when LuLing becomes cold and starts to cry?

10. What kinds of research does Alex Haley do in "My Furthest-Back Person"?

Understanding Literature: Fiction and Nonfiction

Fiction and nonfiction share certain important literary elements. They both use narrative, which tells a story in chronological order. They both use either first-person or third-person's point of view. They both feature characters, people who are part of the story. They can both use dialogue, which is the conversations the characters have. They both have a setting, which is the time and place in a story. And both take place within a historical context.

11. Who is the main character in "Papa's Parrot"?

12. *An American Childhood* is told from what point of view?

13. What is the setting of *Main Street?*

14. Which two countries provide the historical context of "My Furthest-Back Person"?

15. Which work of fiction in this unit uses almost no dialogue?

Critical Thinking

16. What are Harry's feelings at the end of "Papa's Parrot"?

17. In *An American Childhood,* how does Annie feel about the man who chases her?

18. Why is Alex Haley so interested in finding out about his family's past?

19. How does Carol Kennicott feel about her husband?

Thinking Creatively

20. Which story in this unit did you find the most interesting? Explain.

Speak and Listen

Hold a group discussion. Talk about the good and bad parts of living in your community. Listen closely to the ideas of others and give examples to support them. Be sure that everyone gets a chance to voice his or her opinion.

Writing on Your Own

Write an essay about characterization. Choose either Carol from *Main Street* or Harry from "Papa's Parrot." Tell about the character's main traits. Give examples of events in the story that show these traits.

Beyond Words

Work in a group. Use timelines, maps, and pictures to tell the story of the slave trade in America. Look for pictures and maps on the Internet or draw your own. When you are done, share your work with the class.

Test-Taking Tip

When you have vocabulary words to learn, make flash cards. Write each word on the front of a card. Write its definition on the back. Use the flash cards in a game to test your vocabulary skills.

Narration: Autobiographical Narrative

Some of the best stories you may read are not made up. They tell of real events in the writer's life. Such stories are called autobiographical narratives. Follow the steps outlined in this workshop to write your own autobiographical narrative.

Assignment Write an autobiographical narrative about an event in your life. It should be an event that helped you grow or changed your point of view.

Using the Form
You may use elements of this form in these writing situations:
- letters
- reflective essays
- journals
- persuasive essays

What to Include To succeed, your narrative should include the following:

- a clear ordering of events involving you, the writer
- a problem or conflict
- pacing that builds the action
- details that help readers to clearly imagine the events
- error-free writing, including correct use of pronouns

Prewriting

Choosing Your Topic

To choose the right event from your life to narrate, use one of these strategies:

- **Freewriting:** Write for five minutes about anything. Here are some suggestions: funny times, sad times, and lessons learned. When you are finished, review what you have written. Circle any ideas that could make a good topic.
- **Listing:** Make a chart with four columns. Label the first column *People,* the second *Places,* the third *Things,* the last *Events.* In each column, list names or descriptions of interesting people and things that you know. Draw on your experiences from home, school, or travel. Next, review your chart to find connections. For each connection you find, circle the two items and draw an arrow between them. Finally, review the connections you have found. Write ideas for stories they suggest.

Narrowing Your Topic

You now should have a general idea of the story you will tell. You now might want to get a better idea of its size and shape. For example, let's say you have decided to write about a friend named Carlos. Write notes on events involving him. Then select just one event on which to focus your attention.

Gathering Details

Make a timeline. Once you have a topic, begin gathering details to use in your narrative. You might find it useful to fill out a timeline like the one shown.

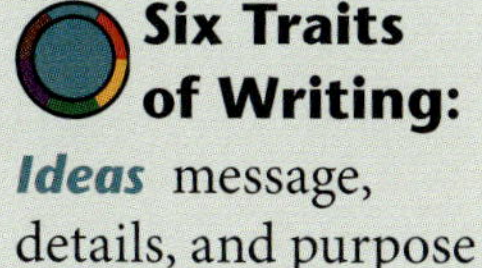

Ideas message, details, and purpose

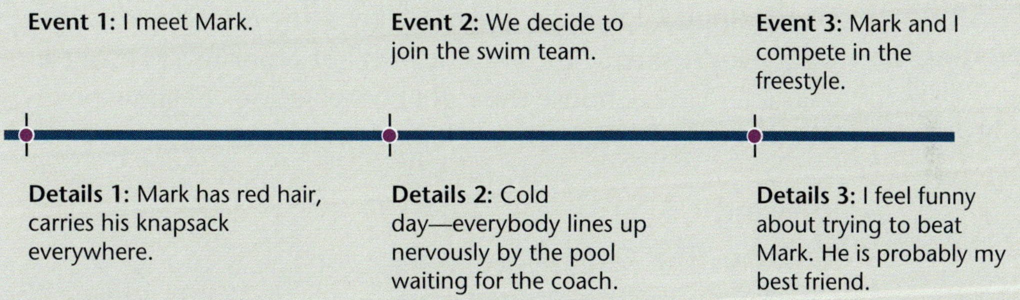

Writing Your Draft

Shaping Your Writing

Understand your conflict. Review your prewriting notes. Make a conflict chart like the one shown. In the center, describe the conflict. Fill in linked circles with narrative action related to the conflict. As you draft, look at your chart to connect details to your central conflict.

Make a story map. Use the conflict chart to map out the events of your story in order. Make sure to pace your story to build suspense. Review your map and add any details a reader might need to follow your story. (For a different type of story map, see Appendix A.)

Providing Elaboration

Show, do not tell. As you write, show readers what happened, do not just tell them. Add life to your story with clear descriptions of places, people, and events.

Tells: It was the first day of school. Ryan and I took our seats in our third-grade classroom.

Shows: The first day of school was the first true day of autumn. There was a rich blue sky and a nip in the air. Ryan and I took our seats in the third-grade classroom. You could hear the noisy excitement of all the other students.

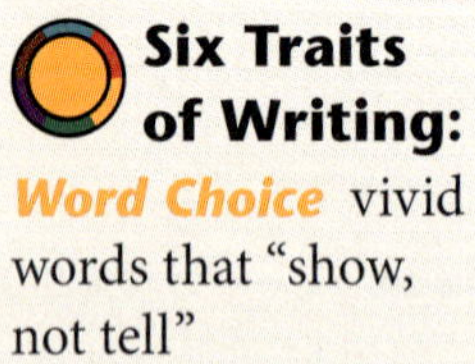

Six Traits of Writing: **Word Choice** vivid words that "show, not tell"

Use dialogue. Bring people to life by using dialogue. Quote what people said as they said it. Do not report everything a character says. Choose the right conversations to show how characters feel about what is happening.

Revising

Revising Your Overall Structure

Check your pacing. A good story builds to a single most exciting moment, called the climax. The secret of building to a climax is pacing. Pacing is the speed at which your story moves along. To improve the pacing of your story, use the following strategies:

- Cut details and events that do not build suspense or reader interest
- Rewrite or cut any paragraph not clearly linked to the central conflict
- Make it clear to readers how events are connected.

Peer Review: Give your draft to one or two classmates to read. Ask them to look for details that slow the story down. Also have them point out ideas that are not connected to the central conflict. Then get rid of any unnecessary details in your draft.

Revising Your Word Choice

Use specific nouns. Look for nouns that are too general and leave the reader wondering *what kind.* Replace general nouns with more exact ones. Then review your draft. Circle any nouns that do not answer the questions *What exactly?* and *What kind?* Replace these nouns with more specific nouns that paint a lively picture.

Six Traits of Writing:
Sentence Fluency smooth rhythm and flow

Editing and Proofreading

Once you have finished your draft, read it over. Make sure to correct errors in spelling, grammar, and punctuation.

Six Traits of Writing:
Conventions correct grammar, spelling, and mechanics

Focus on Dialogue: As you proofread your story, make sure to use the correct punctuation of dialogue. Dialogue is the actual words spoken by the character. All dialogue should be enclosed in quotation marks.

Publishing and Presenting

Choose one of the following ways to share your writing:

Present an oral narrative. Practice reading your story using note cards instead of reading from your draft. Keep practicing until you can read the story smoothly and naturally. Practice using gestures to show key points.

Make a poster. Arrange photos, artwork, or small souvenirs, along with a neat copy of your narrative. Display your work on a poster board. Show the completed poster to the class.

Reflecting on Your Writing

Writer's Journal Write your thoughts about writing an autobiographical narrative. Begin by answering these questions:

- Which strategies in this chapter did you use for revising? How would you rate them?
- As you wrote, what new thoughts about your story did you have?

Bear in Cave
Nicholas Wilton

Unit 2 Short Stories

Short stories are brief works of fiction. Fictional stories are made up by the person who writes them. Because short stories are brief, they usually take place over a short time period. Their plots include only the most important details. They usually have only a few characters. Readers enjoy the variety of characters, plots, and themes in short stories.

In this unit, you will read short stories that show how different this form of fiction can be.

Unit 2 Selections — Page

"Something that can be read in an hour and remembered in a lifetime."

—Stephen Vincent Benét, talking about his definition of a short story.

Unit 2 About Short Stories

Elements of Short Stories

A **short story** is a brief work of prose fiction that includes plot, setting, characters, point of view, and theme. The only limit a short story has is the writer's imagination. Although all short stories are different, they all share the same basic elements.

Characters are the people or animals in a story, poem, or play. Characters are directed by **motivation**—the reason or reasons that explain why characters act as they do.

Characterization is the way a writer develops character qualities and personality traits.

- In **direct characterization,** the writer explains the characters.
- In **indirect characterization,** the writer shows the character through speech and actions.

Theme is the main idea of a story. A **universal theme** is a message about life that is common to all different cultures and time periods. Some common universal themes are the following:

- Hard work always pays off in the end.
- Kids can often see what adults cannot.

Themes such as the ones listed above will show up in stories in all places and time periods, even though the people writing the stories are very different.

A **plot** is the series of events in a story. It is usually divided into five parts:

- **Exposition** introduces the **setting**—the time and place in a story.
- **Rising action** introduces the **conflict**—the struggle of the main character against himself or herself, another person, or nature.
- **Climax** is the high point of interest or suspense in a story.
- **Falling action** is the part of a story when there is less conflict.
- **Resolution** is the act of solving the conflict in a story.

Literary Devices

Literary devices are the tools that writers often use to make their writing more interesting. Some common literary devices you will see when reading short stories are listed here.

- **Foreshadowing** is clues or hints that a writer gives about something that has not yet happened.
- **Flashback** is a look into the past at some point in a story.
- **Irony** is the use of words that seem to say one thing and mean the opposite. When a story includes irony, something surprising happens.
- **Dialect** is the speech of a particular part of a country, or of a certain group of people. The use of dialect helps a character's words sound more realistic.

Reading Strategy:
Predicting

Previewing a text helps readers think about what they already know about a subject. It also prepares readers to look for new information—to predict what will come next. Keep this in mind as you make predictions:

- Make your best guess about what might happen next.
- Add details about why you think certain things will happen.
- Check your predictions. You may have to change your predictions as you learn more information.

Literary Terms

short story a brief work of prose fiction that includes plot, setting, characters, point of view, and theme

characters the people or animals in a story

setting the time and place in a story

conflict the struggle of the main character against himself or herself, another person, or nature

plot the series of events in a story

exposition the part of the story that introduces the setting, characters, and conflict

rising action the buildup of excitement in a story

climax the high point of interest or suspense in a story

falling action the events following the climax

resolution the act of solving the conflict in a story

suspense a quality that makes a reader uncertain or nervous about what will happen next

foreshadowing the clues or hints that a writer gives about something that has not yet happened

flashback a look into the past at some point in the story

mood the feeling that writing creates

character traits a character's way of thinking, behaving, or speaking

motive a reason a character does something

The Bear Boy *by Joseph Bruchac*

Joseph Bruchac
1942–

About the Author

Joseph Bruchac was raised by his grandparents in the Adirondack Mountains of New York State. His grandfather, an Abenaki Indian, taught Bruchac to appreciate the forest. His grandmother, a law school graduate, taught him to love books and writing. He has written more than 70 books for children and adults. He travels the world as a storyteller.

Storytelling plays an important role in American Indian cultures. Like "The Bear Boy," many of Bruchac's stories are based on traditional folktales. They often describe old ways of life. Bruchac describes his writing style in simple terms. "I always go back to what I have heard, what I have seen, what I have experienced. And whatever I imagine or create new always comes out of that life experience."

Objectives

- To read and understand a short story
- To identify plot elements
- To make predictions while reading
- To read and understand characters, setting, and conflict

About the Selection

In "The Bear Boy," a man ignores his son. He does not teach him the ways of Pueblo life. One day, the boy follows some bear tracks. He meets and becomes friends with bear cubs and is adopted by their mother. The bears teach the boy how to be sure of himself and live in a community. When the boy's father tries to rescue the boy, the father learns several lessons. Both learn to appreciate the bears and the importance of caring for one's own family.

In early times, American Indians depended on animals for food, clothing, and shelter. They showed their appreciation by including animals in their storytelling. "The Bear Boy" is an American Indian story that features a mother bear and her cubs.

***Before Reading* continued on next page**

The Bear Boy *by Joseph Bruchac*

short story a brief work of prose fiction that includes plot, setting, characters, point of view, and theme

characters the people or animals in a story

setting the time and place in a story

conflict the struggle of the main character against himself or herself, another person, or nature

plot the series of events in a story

exposition the part of the story that introduces the setting, characters, and conflict

rising action the buildup of excitement in a story

climax the high point of interest or suspense in a story

falling action the events following the climax

resolution the act of solving the conflict in a story

Literary Terms A **short story** is a brief work of prose fiction that includes plot, setting, characters, point of view, and theme. **Characters** are the people or animals in the story. **Setting** is the time and place. The **conflict** is the struggle of the main character. The main character can struggle against himself or herself, another person, or nature.

Plot is the series of events in a story. The **exposition** tells what the story is about. It introduces the characters, setting, and conflict. The **rising action** is the buildup of excitement to the **climax.** The climax is the high point of interest in the story. The story winds down in the **falling action.** The conflict is solved in the **resolution** as the story ends.

Reading on Your Own Predicting means guessing about what will happen next. Readers use details, as well as what they already know, to make predictions. For example, if a character in a story sees dark clouds, what might happen next? Based on what you already know about dark clouds, you might predict a rainstorm.

Writing on Your Own Most people believe animals are not very smart, and that people have much to teach them. However, many American Indians believe animals have a lot to teach us. Make a list of lessons that people might learn from animals. Use at least three of the following words: defend, respect, rescue, survive, honesty, and ancestor.

Vocabulary Focus Writers use special words to describe different kinds of settings. *Arroyo, desert,* and *plain* are words that tell about the land in the southwestern United States, the setting of this story. Write a list of words that describe the place where you live. Use a map or a dictionary for ideas.

Think Before You Read Young bears are called cubs, not boys. Predict what a story with the title "The Bear Boy" will be about.

THE BEAR BOY

Long ago, in a Pueblo village, a boy named Kuo-Haya lived with his father. But his father did not treat him well. In his heart he still mourned the death of his wife, Kuo-Haya's mother, and did not enjoy doing things with his son. He did not teach his boy how to run. He did not show him how to wrestle. He was always too busy.

As you read, notice how the plot builds to a climax.

As a result, Kuo-Haya was a timid boy and walked about stooped over all of the time. When the other boys raced or wrestled, Kuo-Haya slipped away. He spent much of his time alone.

The Pueblo Indians are one of the oldest living cultures in the United States.

Time passed, and the boy reached the age when his father should have been helping him get ready for his **initiation** into manhood. Still Kuo-Haya's father paid no attention at all to his son.

How are initiations used in our culture today?

One day Kuo-Haya was out walking far from the village, toward the cliffs where the bears lived. Now the people of the

initiation process by which one becomes a member of a group

village always knew they must stay away from these cliffs, for the bear was a very powerful animal. It was said that if someone saw a bear's tracks and followed them, he might never come back. But Kuo-Haya had never been told about this. When he came upon the tracks of a bear, Kuo-Haya followed them along an arroyo, a small canyon cut by a winding stream, up into the mesas. The tracks led into a little box canyon below some caves. There, he came upon some bear cubs.

An *arroyo* is a small streambed that is dry much of the time. It is commonly found in the southwestern United States.

When they saw Kuo-Haya, the little bears ran away. But Kuo-Haya sat down and called to them in a friendly voice.

"I will not hurt you," he said to the bear cubs. "Come and play with me." The bears walked back out of the bushes. Soon the boy and the bears were playing together. As they played, however, a shadow came over them. Kuo-Haya looked up and saw the mother bear standing above him.

Reading Strategy: **Predicting**

Based on what you know about bears, what do you think will happen to Kuo-Haya?

"Where is Kuo-Haya?" the people asked his father.

"I do not know," the father said.

"Then you must find him!"

So the father and other people of the pueblo began to search for the missing boy. They went through the canyons calling his name. But they found no sign of the boy there. Finally, when they reached the cliffs, the best trackers found his footsteps and the path of the bears. They followed the tracks along the arroyo and up into the mesas to the box canyon. In front of a cave, they saw the boy playing with the bear cubs as the mother bear watched them approvingly, nudging Kuo-Haya now and then to encourage him.

The trackers crept close, hoping to grab the boy and run. But as soon as the mother bear caught their scent, she growled and pushed her cubs and the boy back into the cave.

Reading Strategy: **Predicting**

How do you think the father will get his boy back?

"The boy is with the bears," the trackers said when they returned to the village.

"What shall we do?" the people asked.

"It is the responsibility of the boy's father," said the medicine man. Then he called Kuo-Haya's father to him.

A *medicine man* is a wise man and is greatly respected. He is like a teacher, a doctor, and a priest all in one.

"You have not done well," said the medicine man. "You are the one who must guide your boy to manhood, but you have neglected him. Now the mother bear is caring for your boy as you should have done all along. She is teaching him to be strong as a young man must be strong. If you love your son, only you can get him back."

Every one of the medicine man's words went into the father's heart like an arrow. He began to realize that he had been blind to his son's needs because of his own sorrow.

"You are right," he said. "I will go and bring back my son."

Kuo-Haya's father went along the arroyo and climbed the cliffs. When he came to the bears' cave, he found Kuo-Haya wrestling with the little bears. As the father watched, he saw that his son seemed more sure of himself than ever before.

"Kuo-Haya," he shouted. "Come to me."

The boy looked at him and then just walked into the cave. Although the father tried to follow, the big mother bear stood up on her hind legs and growled. She would not allow the father to come any closer.

So Kuo-Haya's father went back to his home. He was angry now. He began to gather together his weapons, and brought out his bow and his arrows and his lance. But the medicine man came to his lodge and showed him the bear claw that he wore around his neck.

"Those bears are my relatives!" the medicine man said. "You must not harm them. They are teaching your boy how we should care for each other, so you must not be cruel to them. You must get your son back with love, not violence."

Kuo-Haya's father prayed for guidance. He went outside and sat on the ground. As he sat there, a bee flew up to him, right by his face. Then it flew away. The father stood up. Now he knew what to do!

"Thank you, Little Brother," he said. He began to make his preparations. The medicine man watched what he was doing and smiled.

Kuo-Haya's father went to the place where the bees had their hives. He made a fire and put green branches on it so that it made smoke. Then he blew the smoke into the tree where the bees were. The bees soon went to sleep.

What is the climax of the story? How do you know?

Carefully Kuo-Haya's father took out some honey from their hive. When he was done, he placed pollen and some small pieces of **turquoise** at the foot of the tree to thank the bees for their gift. The medicine man, who was watching all this, smiled again. Truly the father was beginning to learn.

Kuo-Haya's father traveled again to the cliffs where the bears lived. He hid behind a tree and saw how the mother bear treated Kuo-Haya and the cubs with love. He saw that Kuo-Haya was able to hold his own as he wrestled with the bears.

He came out from his hiding place, put the honey on the ground, and stepped back. "My friends," he said, "I have brought you something sweet."

The mother bear and her cubs came over and began to eat the honey. While they ate, Kuo-Haya's father went to the boy. He saw that his little boy was now a young man.

Is this scene part of the rising action? Explain your answer.

"Kuo-Haya," he said, putting his hands on his son's shoulders, "I have come to take you home. The bears have taught me a lesson. I shall treat you as a father should treat his son."

Which details in this paragraph show how the story's conflict is resolved?

"I will go with you, Father," said the boy. "But I, too, have learned things from the bears. They have shown me how we must care for one another. I will come with you only if you promise you will always be friends with the bears." The father promised, and that promise was kept. Not only was he friends with the bears, but he showed his boy the love a son deserves. And he taught him all the things a son should be taught.

Everyone in the village soon saw that Kuo-Haya, the bear boy, was no longer the timid little boy he had been. Because of what the bears had taught him, he was the best wrestler among the boys. With his father's help, Kuo-Haya quickly became the greatest runner of all. To this day, his story is told to remind all parents that they must always show as much love for their children as there is in the heart of a bear.

turquoise a greenish-blue gemstone

AFTER READING THE SELECTION | **Apply the Skills**

The Bear Boy *by Joseph Bruchac*

Directions Choose the letter of the best answer or write the answer using complete sentences.

Comprehension: Identifying Facts

1. What kind of relationship does Kuo-Haya have with his father when the story begins?
A his father is helpful
B they are very close
C his father has neglected him
D they are always together

2. What does Kuo-Haya do when he first sees the bear cubs?

3. What advice does the medicine man give the father?

Comprehension: Putting Ideas Together

4. Why does Kuo-Haya choose to spend so much time alone?
A he is preparing for his initiation
B he is timid and feels like he doesn't fit in
C he prefers to be alone
D he doesn't like his father

5. How is Kuo-Haya's life with the bears different from his life in the village?

6. What did the father learn from the bee?

Understanding Literature: Plot Elements

You can keep track of the five parts in a story's plot by drawing a Plot Mountain (described in Appendix A). This picture can help you predict what will happen in the story.

To use: First, draw a mountain. Write the exposition at the left base of the mountain. Second, write the rising action events that lead to the climax on the left side of the mountain. Start at the base. Third, at the top of the mountain, write the climax. Fourth, list the falling action events that happen after the climax. Finally, write the resolution at the right base of the mountain.

7. In which part of the story does Kuo-Haya first meet the bear cubs? What did you predict would happen next?

8. Kuo-Haya's father discovers him living with the bears in which part of the story? What did you predict the climax would be at this point?

Critical Thinking

9. What lesson does this story teach? Do you think the lesson applies to all people? Why or why not?

Thinking Creatively

10. Do you think Kuo-Haya did the right thing by returning to live with his father? Why or why not?

***After Reading* continued on next page**

The Bear Boy *by Joseph Bruchac*

Grammar Check

A simile is a figure of speech in which two things are compared using a phrase that includes the words like or as. Writers use similes to bring descriptions to life. Sometimes similes compare two things that do not seem related. This can lead to creating a new and interesting description.

Example: The medicine man's words entered his heart like an arrow. We understand that the medicine man's message was painful to hear.

Create vivid descriptions by completing these similes:

- The thunder cracked like
- This whistle was as loud as

Vocabulary Builder

Guess the meanings of unfamiliar words using what you already know. Have you seen the word in other sentences? Look at the sentence where the word appears this time. What word or words in the sentence does the unfamiliar word relate to? Check with the dictionary to see if your guess was correct.

Answer each question. Explain your answer.

1 Would a fox be described as timid?

2 If you neglected a houseplant, what would happen to it?

Writing on Your Own

Write an informative article on how a mother bear raises her cubs. Use details from the story. Start with an exciting title to grab your readers' interest.

An informative article usually contains an introduction, a body, and a conclusion. It also has details that tell *when, how much, how often,* or *how long.*

Listening and Speaking

With a partner, have an informal debate on the training of wild animals. Think about some subjects to discuss. For example, consider the purpose of animals training in farming, security, and entertainment. Each of you should pick a different viewpoint to present.

To convince your partner to agree with your ideas, back them up with facts you have read or heard. You can also use examples from your own experience.

- Remember to respect your partner's time to talk.
- Do not interrupt.

Research and Technology

The bears in this story like honey. Use books and magazines to find out how bees make honey. Present your findings in a diagram to show how honey is made.

Rikki-tikki-tavi by Rudyard Kipling

Rudyard Kipling
1865–1936

About the Author

Rudyard Kipling was born in Bombay, India, in 1865. His parents were English. He moved to England when he was five, but remained strongly attached to his homeland. In 1882, he returned to India as a newspaper writer. He began writing the stories that would make him famous.

Kipling's stories became popular right away. Readers were excited to learn details about life in India. Soon his books were being read all over the world. Kipling traveled a lot. He wrote stories and poems about exotic places and adventure, including *The Jungle Book* and *Captains Courageous.* In 1907, Kipling became the first English writer to win the Nobel Prize in Literature.

Objectives

- To read and understand a short story
- To identify plot elements
- To make predictions while reading
- To recognize suspense

About the Selection

In this story, a brave mongoose battles a family of snakes known as Indian cobras. Cobras feed on small animals. The mongoose is small, brown, and furry—and the perfect size for a cobra's meal. However, the fast, fierce mongoose usually wins a battle with a cobra.

Teddy and his family, living in India, adopt a young mongoose. The mongoose, Rikki-tikki-tavi, is the natural enemy of a snake. With the help of Teddy's father and the other animals, Rikki-tikki-tavi kills two dangerous cobras. He also destroys their eggs. Through his triumph, Rikki-tikki-tavi earns respect.

***Before Reading* continued on next page**

Rikki-tikki-tavi *by Rudyard Kipling*

suspense
a quality that makes a reader uncertain or nervous about what will happen next

Literary Terms There are many different kinds of short stories. Each one has a plot, but no two are exactly alike. In some stories, there are no big surprises. Details in the story tell you how it will end ahead of time. In other stories, the details may add up in unexpected ways. A story is more exciting when it includes **suspense.** Writers use suspense to make the reader uncertain or nervous about what will happen next.

Reading on Your Own Writers give hints about what will happen next in stories. Careful readers watch for these clues. As you read, notice details. Add them to what you already know. This information will help you guess what is going to happen next. You might change your predictions as you learn more.

Writing on Your Own Animals and people naturally want to protect children. Some animals help human parents keep their children safe from harm. Write a list of ways that animals help people. Write a second list of ways that people help animals. What do the lists have in common?

Vocabulary Focus When you come across a word that you do not understand, do detective work. Details in the story can help you guess the meaning. When Rikki-tikki-tavi eats a small piece of meat he goes out into the *veranda* to sit in the sun. Where does he go? A veranda must be a part of the house that is sunny. It could be a porch or sunroom. The definition agrees. A veranda is an open porch. After you guess what a word means, check with a dictionary to see if you are right.

Think Before You Read This story has both human characters and animal characters. What do you know about how animals express themselves? What kinds of sounds do they make? If animals could speak in words, what do you predict they might say?

Rikki-tikki-tavi

This is the story of the great war that Rikki-tikki-tavi fought, single-handed, through the bathrooms of the big **bungalow** in Segowlee cantonment. Darzee, the tailorbird bird, helped him, and Chuchundra the muskrat, who never comes out into the middle of the floor, but always creeps round by the wall, gave him advice; but Rikki-tikki did the real fighting.

He was a mongoose, rather like a little cat in his fur and his tail, but quite like a weasel in his head and his habits. His eyes and the end of his restless nose were pink; he could scratch himself anywhere he pleased, with any leg, front or back, that he chose to use; he could fluff up his tail till it looked like a bottle brush, and his war cry as he scuttled through the long grass, was: "*Rikk-tikk-tikki-tikki-tchk!*"

As you read, notice important details about the mongoose that are revealed in the story.

Segowlee cantonment was the living quarters for British troops in Segowlee, India.

bungalow a cottage

One day, a high summer flood washed him out of the burrow where he lived with his father and mother, and carried him, kicking and clucking, down a roadside ditch. He found a little wisp of grass floating there, and clung to it till he lost his senses. When he **revived,** he was lying in the hot sun on the middle of a garden path, very **draggled** indeed, and a small boy was saying: "Here's a dead mongoose. Let's have a funeral."

"No," said his mother; "let's take him in and dry him. Perhaps he isn't really dead."

They took him into the house, and a big man picked him up between his finger and thumb and said he was not dead but half choked; so they wrapped him in cotton wool, and warmed him, and he opened his eyes and sneezed.

"Now," said the big man (he was an Englishman who had just moved into the bungalow); "don't frighten him, and we'll see what he'll do."

It is the hardest thing in the world to frighten a mongoose, because he is eaten up from nose to tail with curiosity. The motto of all the mongoose family is, "Run and find out"; and Rikki-tikki was a true mongoose. He looked at the cotton wool, decided that it was not good to eat, ran all round the table, sat up and put his fur in order, scratched himself, and jumped on the small boy's shoulder.

"Don't be frightened, Teddy," said his father. "That's his way of making friends."

"Ouch! He's tickling under my chin," said Teddy.

Rikki-tikki looked down between the boy's collar and neck, snuffed at his ear, and climbed down to the floor, where he sat rubbing his nose.

"Good gracious," said Teddy's mother, "and that's a wild creature! I suppose he's so tame because we've been kind to him."

"All mongooses are like that," said her husband. "If Teddy doesn't pick him up by the tail, or try to put him in a cage,

revived came back to consciousness

draggled wet and dirty

he'll run in and out of the house all day long. Let's give him something to eat."

They gave him a little piece of raw meat. Rikki-tikki liked it immensely, and when it was finished he went out into the **veranda** and sat in the sunshine and fluffed up his fur to make it dry to the roots. Then he felt better.

"There are more things to find out about in this house," he said to himself, "than all my family could find out in all their lives. I shall certainly stay and find out."

He spent all that day roaming over the house. He nearly drowned himself in the bathtubs, put his nose into the ink on a writing table, and burned it on the end of the big man's cigar, for he climbed up in the big man's lap to see how writing was done. At nightfall he ran into Teddy's nursery to watch how **kerosene lamps** were lighted, and when Teddy went to bed Rikki-tikki climbed up too; but he was a restless companion, because he had to get up and attend to every noise all through the night, and find out what made it. Teddy's mother and father came in, the last thing, to look at their boy, and Rikki-tikki was awake on the pillow. "I don't like that," said Teddy's mother; "he may bite the child." "He'll do no such thing," said the father. "Teddy's safer with that little beast than if he had a **bloodhound** to watch him. If a snake came into the nursery now—"

But Teddy's mother wouldn't think of anything so awful.

Early in the morning Rikki-tikki came to early breakfast in the veranda riding on Teddy's shoulder, and they gave him banana and some boiled egg; and he sat on all their laps one after the other, because every well-brought-up mongoose always hopes to be a house mongoose some day and have rooms to run about in, and Rikki-tikki's mother (she used to live in the General's house at Segowlee) had carefully told Rikki what to do if ever he came across Englishmen.

***Reading Strategy:* Predicting**

What might happen between Teddy and the mongoose? Think about what the father said and earlier details.

***Reading Strategy:* Predicting**

Based on the parents' thoughts about Rikki-tikki, what do you predict will happen in the story?

veranda an open porch

kerosene lamps oil-burning lamps

bloodhound a dog with a keen sense of smell

A garden in India might include native plants and plants from other lands. Bamboo, thornbushes, and wild grass are combined with English roses and fruit trees here.

Then Rikki-tikki went out into the garden to see what was to be seen. It was a large garden, only half **cultivated,** with bushes as big as summer houses of Marshal Niel roses, lime and orange trees, clumps of bamboos, and **thickets** of high grass. Rikki-tikki licked his lips. "This is a splendid hunting ground," he said, and his tail grew bottlebrushy at the thought of it, and he scuttled up and down the garden, snuffing here and there till he heard very sorrowful voices in a thornbush.

It was Darzee, the tailorbird, and his wife. They had made a beautiful nest by pulling two big leaves together and stitching them up the edges with fibers, and had filled the hollow with cotton and downy fluff. The nest swayed to and fro, as they sat on the rim and cried.

"What is the matter?" asked Rikki-tikki.

"We are very miserable," said Darzee.

"One of our babies fell out of the nest yesterday and Nag ate him."

"H'm!" said Rikki-tikki, "that is very sad—but I am a stranger here. Who is Nag?"

Darzee and his wife only **cowered** down in the nest without answering, for from the thick grass at the foot of the bush there came a low hiss—a horrid cold sound that made Rikki-tikki jump back two clear feet. Then inch by inch out of the grass rose up the head and spread hood of Nag, the big black cobra, and he was five feet long from tongue to tail. When he had lifted one third of himself clear of the ground, he stayed balancing to and fro exactly as a dandelion **tuft** balances in the wind, and he looked at Rikki-tikki with the wicked snake's eyes that never change their expression, whatever the snake may be thinking of.

Brahm is short for *Brahma*, the name of the chief god in the Hindu religion, a popular religion in India.

"Who is Nag?" he said. "*I* am Nag. The great god *Brahm* put his mark upon all our people when the first cobra spread his hood to keep the sun off Brahm . . . as he slept. Look, and be afraid!"

cultivated planted by man

thickets dense bushes

cowered crouched fearfully

tuft a tiny bunch

He spread out his hood more than ever, and Rikki-tikki saw the spectacle mark on the back of it that looks exactly like the eye part of a hook-and-eye fastening. He was afraid for the minute; but it is impossible for a mongoose to stay frightened for any length of time, and though Rikki-tikki had never met a live cobra before, his mother had fed him on dead ones, and he knew that all a grown mongoose's business in life was to fight and eat snakes. Nag knew that too, and at the bottom of his cold heart he was afraid.

"Well," said Rikki-tikki, and his tail began to fluff up again, "marks or no marks, do you think it is right for you to eat **fledglings** out of a nest?"

Nag was thinking to himself, and watching the least little movement in the grass behind Rikki-tikki. He knew that mongooses in the garden meant death sooner or later for him and his family; but he wanted to get Rikki-tikki off his guard. So he dropped his head a little, and put it on one side.

"Let us talk," he said. "You eat eggs. Why should not I eat birds?"

fledglings baby birds

"Behind you! Look behind you!" sang Darzee.

Rikki-tikki knew better than to waste time in staring. He jumped up in the air as high as he could go, and just under him whizzed by the head of Nagaina, Nag's wicked wife. She had crept up behind him as he was talking, to make an end of him; and he heard her savage hiss as the stroke missed. He came down almost across her back, and if he had been an old mongoose he would have known that then was the time to break her back with one bite; but he was afraid of the terrible lashing return stroke of the cobra. He bit, indeed, but did not bite long enough, and he jumped clear of the whisking tail, leaving Nagaina torn and angry.

What details build suspense here?

"Wicked, wicked Darzee!" said Nag, lashing up high as he could reach toward the nest in the thornbush; but Darzee had built it out of reach of snakes; and it only swayed to and fro.

Rikki-tikki felt his eyes growing red and hot (when a mongoose's eyes grow red, he is angry), and he sat back on his tail and hind legs like a little kangaroo, and looked all around him, and chattered with rage. But Nag and Nagaina had disappeared into the grass. When a snake misses its stroke, it never says anything or gives any sign of what it means to do next. Rikki-tikki did not care to follow them, for he did not feel sure that he could manage two snakes at once. So he trotted off to the gravel path near the house, and sat down to think. It was a serious matter for him.

***Reading Strategy:* Predicting**

What do you predict will be the outcome of the conflict? What do you already know that helps you make that prediction?

If you read the old books of natural history, you will find they say that when the mongoose fights the snake and happens to get bitten, he runs off and eats some herb that cures him. That is not true. The victory is only a matter of quickness of eye and quickness of foot—snake's blow against mongoose's jump—and as no eye can follow the motion of a snake's head when it strikes, that makes things much more wonderful than any magic herb. Rikki-tikki knew he was a young mongoose, and it made him all the more pleased to think that he had managed to escape a blow from behind. It gave him confidence in himself, and when Teddy came running down the path, Rikki-tikki was ready to be petted.

But just as Teddy was stooping, something flinched a little in the dust, and a tiny voice said: "Be careful. I am death!" It was Karait, the dusty brown snakeling that lies for choice on the dusty earth; and his bite is as dangerous as the cobra's. But he is so small that nobody thinks of him, and so he does the more harm to people.

Rikki-tikki's eyes grew red again, and he danced up to Karait with the peculiar rocking, swaying motion that he had inherited from his family. It looks very funny, but it is so perfectly balanced a **gait** that you can fly off from it at any angle you please; and in dealing with snakes this is an advantage. If Rikki-tikki had only known, he was doing a much more dangerous thing than fighting Nag, for Karait is so small, and can turn so quickly, that unless Rikki bit him close to the back of the head, he would get the return stroke in his eye or lip. But Rikki did not know: his eyes were all red, and he rocked back and forth, looking for a good place to hold. Karait struck out. Rikki jumped sideways and tried to run in, but the wicked little dusty gray head lashed within a fraction of his shoulder, and he had to jump over the body, and the head followed his heels close.

What details in this section build suspense in the story?

Teddy shouted to the house: "Oh, look here! Our mongoose is killing a snake"; and Rikki-tikki heard a scream from Teddy's mother. His father ran out with a stick, but by the time he came up, Karait had lunged out once too far, and Rikki-tikki had sprung, jumped on the snake's back, dropped his head far between his fore legs, bitten as high up the back as he could get hold, and rolled away. That bite **paralyzed** Karait, and Rikki-tikki was just going to eat him up from the tail, after the custom of his family at dinner, when he remembered that a full meal makes a slow mongoose, and if he wanted all his strength and quickness ready, he must keep himself thin.

He went away for a dust bath under the castor-oil bushes, while Teddy's father beat the dead Karait. "What is the use of that?" thought Rikki-tikki. "I have settled it all"; and then

gait pace of walking

paralyzed made unable to move

Teddy's mother picked him up from the dust and hugged him, crying that he had saved Teddy from death, and Teddy's father said that he was a **providence,** and Teddy looked on with big scared eyes. Rikki-tikki was rather amused at all the fuss, which, of course, he did not understand. Teddy's mother might just as well have petted Teddy for playing in the dust. Rikki was thoroughly enjoying himself.

That night, at dinner, walking to and fro among the wineglasses on the table, he could have stuffed himself three times over with nice things; but he remembered Nag and Nagaina, and though it was very pleasant to be patted and petted by Teddy's mother, and to sit on Teddy's shoulder, his eyes would get red from time to time, and he would go off into his long war cry of "*Rikk-tikk-tikki-tikki-tchk!*"

Teddy carried him off to bed, and insisted on Rikki-tikki sleeping under his chin. Rikki-tikki was too well bred to bite or scratch, but as soon as Teddy was asleep he went off for his nightly walk round the house, and in the dark he ran up against Chuchundra the Muskrat, creeping round by the wall. Chuchundra is a broken-hearted little beast. He whimpers and cheeps all the night, trying to make up his mind to run into the middle of the room, but he never gets there.

"Don't kill me," said Chuchundra, almost weeping. "Rikki-tikki don't kill me."

"Do you think a snake-killer kills muskrats?" said Rikki-tikki scornfully.

"Those who kill snakes get killed by snakes," said Chuchundra, more sorrowfully than ever. "And how am I to be sure that Nag won't mistake me for you some dark night?"

"There's not the least danger," said Rikki-tikki; "but Nag is in the garden, and I know you don't go there."

"My cousin Chua, the rat, told me—" said Chuchundra, and then he stopped.

"Told you what?"

providence a valuable gift

"H'sh! Nag is everywhere, Rikki-tikki. You should have talked to Chua in the garden."

"I didn't—so you must tell me. Quick, Chuchundra, or I'll bite you!"

Chuchundra sat down and cried till the tears rolled off his whiskers. "I am a very poor man," he sobbed. "I never had spirit enough to run out into the middle of the room. H'sh! I mustn't tell you anything. Can't you *hear*, Rikki-tikki?"

Rikki-tikki listened. The house was as still as still, but he thought he could just catch the faintest scratch-scratch in the world—a noise as faint as that of a wasp walking on a windowpane—the dry scratch of a snake's scales on brickwork.

"That's Nag or Nagaina," he said to himself; "and he is crawling into the bathroom **sluice.** You're right, Chuchundra; I should have talked to Chua."

He stole off to Teddy's bathroom, but there was nothing there, and then to Teddy's mother's bathroom. At the bottom of the smooth plaster wall there was a brick pulled out to make a sluice for the bath water, and as Rikki-tikki stole in by the **masonry** curb where the bath is put, he heard Nag and Nagaina whispering together outside in the moonlight.

"When the house is emptied of people," said Nagaina to her husband, "He will have to go away, and then the garden will be our own again. Go in quietly, and remember that the big man who killed Karait is the first one to bite. Then come out and tell me, and we will hunt for Rikki-tikki together."

"But are you sure that there is anything to be gained by killing the people?" said Nag.

"Everything. When there were no people in the bungalow, did we have any mongoose in the garden? So long as the bungalow is empty, we are king and queen of the garden; and remember that as soon as our eggs in the melon bed hatch (as they may tomorrow), our children will need room and quiet."

What details add to the conflict as Rikki-tikki overhears this conversation?

sluice a drain

masonry stonework

"I had not thought of that," said Nag. "I will go, but there is no need that we should hunt for Rikki-tikki afterward. I will kill the big man and his wife, and the child if I can, and come away quietly. Then the bungalow will be empty, and Rikki-tikki will go."

Rikki-tikki tingled all over with rage and hatred at this, and then Nag's head came through the sluice, and his five feet of cold body followed it. Angry as he was, Rikki-tikki was very frightened as he saw the size of the big cobra. Nag coiled himself up, raised his head, and looked into the bathroom in the dark, and Rikki could see his eyes glitter.

"Now, if I kill him here, Nagaina will know;—and if I fight him on the open floor, the odds are in his favor. What am I to do?" said Rikki-tikki-tavi.

Nag waved to and fro, and then Rikki-tikki-tikki heard him drinking from the biggest water jar that was used to fill the bath. "That is good," said the snake. "Now, when Karait was killed, the big man had a stick. He may have that stick still, but when he comes in to bathe in the morning he will not have a stick. I shall wait here till he comes. Nagaina—do you hear me?—I shall wait here in the cool till daytime."

There was no answer from outside, so Rikki-tikki knew Nagaina had gone away. Nag coiled himself down, coil by coil, round the bulge at the bottom of the waterjar, and Rikki-tikki stayed still as death. After an hour he began to move, muscle by muscle, toward the jar. Nag was asleep, and Rikki-tikki looked at his big back, wondering which would be the best place for a good hold. "If I don't break his back at the first jump," said Rikki, "he can still fight; and if he fights—O Rikki!" He looked at the thickness of the neck below the hood, but that was too much for him; and a bite near the tail would only make Nag savage.

***Reading Strategy:* Predicting**

What do you predict will be the outcome of this fight between Rikki and Nag? What makes you think this?

"It must be the head," he said at last; "the head above the hood; and, when I am once there, I must not let go."

Then he jumped. The head was lying a little clear of the water jar, under the curve of it; and, as his teeth met, Rikki braced his back against the bulge of the red earthenware to hold down the head. This gave him just one second's **purchase,** and he made the most of it. Then he was battered to and fro as a rat is shaken by a dog—to and fro on the floor, up and down, and round in great circles: but his eyes were red, and he held on as the body cart-whipped over the floor, upsetting the tin dipper and the soap dish and the fleshbrush, and banged against the tin side of the bath. As he held he closed his jaws tighter and tighter, for he made sure he would be banged to death, and, for the honor of his family, he preferred to be found with his teeth locked. He was dizzy, aching, and felt shaken to pieces when something went off like a thunderclap just behind him; a hot wind knocked him senseless and red fire singed his fur. The big man had been wakened by the noise, and had fired both barrels of a shotgun into Nag just behind the hood.

Rikki-tikki held on with his eyes shut, for now he was quite sure he was dead; but the head did not move, and the big man picked him up and said: "It's the mongoose again, Alice; the little chap has saved our lives now." Then Teddy's mother came in with a very white face, and saw what was left of Nag, and Rikki-tikki dragged himself to Teddy's bedroom and spent half the rest of the night shaking himself tenderly to find out whether he really was broken into forty pieces, as he fancied.

When morning came he was very stiff, but well pleased with his doings. "Now I have Nagaina to settle with, and she will be worse than five Nags, and there's no knowing when the eggs she spoke of will hatch. Goodness! I must go and see Darzee," he said.

Why is the death of Nag part of the rising action and not the resolution?

Without waiting for breakfast, Rikki-tikki ran to the thornbush where Darzee was singing a song of triumph at the top of his voice. The news of Nag's death was all over the garden, for the sweeper had thrown the body on the rubbish heap.

"Oh, you stupid tuft of feathers!" said Rikki-tikki, angrily. "Is this the time to sing?"

purchase a firm hold

"Nag is dead—is dead—is dead!" sang Darzee. "The valiant Rikki-tikki caught him by the head and held fast. The big man brought the bang-stick and Nag fell in two pieces! He will never eat my babies again."

"All that's true enough; but where's Nagaina?" said Rikki-tikki, looking carefully round him.

"Nagaina came to the bathroom sluice and called for Nag," Darzee went on; "and Nag came out on the end of a stick—the sweeper picked him up on the end of a stick and threw him upon the rubbish heap. Let us sing about the great, the red-eyed Rikki-tikki!" and Darzee filled his throat and sang.

"If I could get up to your nest, I'd roll all your babies out!" said Rikki-tikki. "You don't know when to do the right thing at the right time. You're safe enough in your nest there, but it's war for me down here. Stop singing a minute, Darzee."

"For the great, the beautiful Rikki-tikki's sake, I will stop," said Darzee. "What is it, O Killer of the terrible Nag!"

"Where is Nagaina, for the third time?"

"On the rubbish heap by the stables, mourning for Nag. Great is Rikki-tikki with the white teeth."

"Bother my white teeth! Have you ever heard where she keeps her eggs?"

"In the melon bed, on the end nearest the wall, where the sun strikes nearly all day. She had them there weeks ago."

"And you never thought it worthwhile to tell me? The end nearest the wall, you said?"

"Rikki-tikki, you are not going to eat her eggs?"

"Not eat exactly; no. Darzee, if you have a grain of sense you will fly off to the stables and pretend that your wing is broken, and let Nagaina chase you away to this bush! I must get to the melon bed, and if I went there now she'd see me."

Darzee was a featherbrained little fellow who could never hold more than one idea at a time in his head; and just because he knew that Nagaina's children were born in eggs like his own, he didn't think at first that it was fair to kill them. But his wife was a sensible bird, and she knew that cobra's eggs meant young cobras later on; so she flew off from the nest, and left Darzee to keep the babies warm, and continue his song about the death of Nag. Darzee was very like a man in some ways.

What role does Darzee play in the conflict between Rikki-tikki-tavi and the cobras?

She fluttered in front of Nagaina by the rubbish heap, and cried out, "Oh, my wing is broken! The boy in the house threw a stone at me and broke it." Then she fluttered more desperately than ever.

Nagaina lifted up her head and hissed, "You warned Rikki-tikki when I would have killed him. Indeed and truly, you've chosen a bad place to be lame in." And she moved toward Darzee's wife, slipping along over the dust.

"The boy broke it with a stone!" shrieked Darzee's wife.

"Well! It may be some **consolation** to you when you're dead to know that I shall settle accounts with the boy. My husband lies on the rubbish heap this morning, but before night the boy in the house will lie very still. What is the use of running away? I am sure to catch you. Little fool, look at me!"

***Reading Strategy:* Predicting**

What do you think Rikki is going to do with Nagaina's eggs? Why do you think so?

Darzee's wife knew better than to do *that*, for a bird who looks at a snake's eyes gets so frightened that she cannot move. Darzee's wife fluttered on, **piping** sorrowfully, and never leaving the ground, and Nagaina quickened her pace.

Rikki-tikki heard them going up the path from the stables, and he raced for the end of the melon patch near the wall. There, in the warm **litter** about the melons, very cunningly hidden, he found twenty-five eggs, about the size of a **bantam's eggs,** but with whitish skin instead of shell.

consolation something that comforts a disappointed person

piping singing

litter a straw covering

bantam's eggs eggs of a small chicken

"I was not a day too soon," he said; for he could see the baby cobras curled up inside the skin, and he knew that the minute they were hatched they could each kill a man or a mongoose. He bit off the tops of the eggs as fast as he could, taking care to crush the young cobras, and turned over the litter from time to time to see whether he had missed any. At last there were only three eggs left, and Rikki-tikki began to chuckle to himself, when he heard Darzee's wife screaming:

"Rikki-tikki, I led Nagaina toward the house, and she has gone into the veranda, and—oh, come quickly—she means killing!"

Rikki-tikki smashed two eggs, and tumbled backward down the melon bed with the third egg in his mouth, and scuttled to the veranda as hard as he could put foot to the ground. Teddy and his mother and father were there at early breakfast; but Rikki-tikki saw that they were not eating anything. They sat stone-still, and their faces were white. Nagaina was coiled up on the matting by Teddy's chair, within easy striking distance of Teddy's bare leg, and she was swaying to and fro singing a song of triumph.

Do you think this scene is the climax or part of the rising action? Why?

"Son of the big man that killed Nag," she hissed, "stay still. I am not ready yet. Wait a little. Keep very still, all you three. If you move I strike, and if you do not move I strike, Oh, foolish people, who killed my Nag!"

Teddy's eyes were fixed on his father, and all his father could do was to whisper, "Sit still, Teddy. You mustn't move. Teddy, keep still."

Then Rikki-tikki came up and cried: "Turn round, Nagaina; turn and fight!"

"All in good time," said she, without moving her eyes. "I will settle my account with *you* **presently.** Look at your friends, Rikki-tikki. They are still and white; they are afraid. They dare not move, and if you come a step nearer I strike."

"Look at your eggs," said Rikki-tikki, "in the melon bed near the wall. Go and look, Nagaina."

presently right away

The big snake turned half round, and saw the egg on the veranda. "Ah-h! Give it to me," she said.

Rikki-tikki put his paws one on each side of the egg, and his eyes were blood-red. "What price for a snake's egg? For a young cobra? For a young king cobra? For the last—the very last of the brood? The ants are eating all the others down by the melon bed."

Nagaina spun clear round, forgetting everything for the sake of the one egg; and Rikki-tikki saw Teddy's father shoot out a big hand, catch Teddy by the shoulder, and drag him across the little table with the teacups, safe and out of reach of Nagaina.

"Tricked! Tricked! Tricked! *Rikk-tck-tck!*" chuckled Rikki-tikki."The boy is safe, and it was I—I—I that caught Nag by the hood last night in the bathroom." Then he began to jump up and down, all four feet together, his head close to the floor. "He threw me to and fro, but he could not shake me off. He was dead before the big man blew him in two. I did it. *Rikki-tikki-tck-tck!* Come then, Nagaina. Come and fight with me. You shall not be a widow long."

What details increase the suspense in the story at this point?

Nagaina saw that she had lost her chance of killing Teddy, and the egg lay between Rikki-tikki's paws. "Give me the egg, Rikki-tikki. Give me the last of my eggs, and I will go away and never come back," she said, lowering her hood.

"Yes, you will go away, and you will never come back; for you will go to the rubbish heap with Nag. Fight, widow! The big man has gone for his gun! Fight!"

Rikki-tikki was bounding all round Nagaina, keeping just out of reach of her stroke, his little eyes like hot coals. Nagaina gathered herself together, and flung out at him. Rikki-tikki jumped up and backward. Again and again and again she struck, and each time her head came with a **whack** on the matting of the veranda and she gathered herself together like a watchspring. Then Rikki-tikki danced in a circle to get behind her, and Nagaina spun round to keep her head to his

whack a sharp hit

Reading Strategy: **Predicting**
What do you predict will be the outcome of Rikki-tikki's fight with Nagaina? Explain.

head, so that the rustle of her tail on the matting sounded like dry leaves blown along by the wind.

He had forgotten the egg. It still lay on the veranda, and Nagaina came nearer and nearer to it, till at last, while Rikki-tikki was drawing breath, she caught it in her mouth, turned to the veranda steps, and flew like an arrow down the path, with Rikki-tikki behind her. When the cobra runs for her life, she goes like a whiplash flicked across a horse's neck.

Rikki-tikki knew that he must catch her, or all the trouble would begin again. She headed straight for the long grass by the thornbush, and as he was running Rikki-tikki heard Darzee still singing his foolish little song of triumph. But Darzee's wife was wiser. She flew off her nest as Nagaina came along, and flapped her wings about Nagaina's head. If Darzee had helped they might have turned her; but Nagaina only lowered her hood and went on. Still, the instant's delay brought Rikki-tikki up to her, and as she plunged into the rat

hole where she and Nag used to live, his little white teeth were clenched on her tail, and he went down with her—and very few mongooses, however wise and old they may be, care to follow a cobra into its hole. It was dark in the hole; and Rikki-tikki never knew when it might open out and give Nagaina room to turn and strike at him. He held on savagely, and struck out his feet to act as brakes on the dark slope of the hot, moist earth.

Then the grass by the mouth of the hole stopped waving, and Darzee said: "It is all over with Rikki-tikki! We must sing his death song. **Valiant** Rikki-tikki is dead! For Nagaina will surely kill him underground."

How does Darzee's comment add to the suspense?

So he sang a very mournful song that he made up all on the spur of the minute, and just as he got to the most touching part the grass quivered again, and Rikki-tikki, covered with dirt, dragged himself out of the hole leg by leg, licking his whiskers. Darzee stopped with a little shout. Rikki-tikki shook some of the dust out of his fur and sneezed. "It is all over," he said. "The widow will never come out again." And the red ants that live between the grass stems heard him, and began to troop down one after another to see if he had spoken the truth.

What part of the plot does Rikki's comment fit into? Why do you think so?

Rikki-tikki curled himself up in the grass and slept where he was—slept and slept till it was late in the afternoon, for he had done a hard day's work.

"Now," he said, when he awoke, "I will go back to the house. Tell the Coppersmith, Darzee, and he will tell the garden that Nagaina is dead."

The Coppersmith is a bird who makes a noise exactly like the beating of a little hammer on a copper pot; and the reason he is always making it is because he is the town crier to every Indian garden, and tells all the news to everybody who cares to listen. As Rikki-tikki went up the path, he heard his "attention" notes like a tiny dinner gong; and then the steady

valiant brave

"*Ding-dong-tock!* Nag is dead—*dong!* Nagaina is dead! *Ding-dong-tock!*" That set all the birds in the garden singing, and the frogs croaking; for Nag and Nagaina used to eat frogs as well as little birds.

When Rikki got to the house, Teddy and Teddy's mother and Teddy's father came out and almost cried over him; and that night he ate all that was given him till he could eat no more, and went to bed on Teddy's shoulder, where Teddy's mother saw him when she came to look late at night.

"He saved our lives and Teddy's life," she said to her husband. "Just think, he saved all our lives."

Rikki-tikki woke up with a jump, for all the mongooses are light sleepers.

"Oh, it's you," said he. "What are you bothering for? All the cobras are dead; and if they weren't, I'm here."

How has Rikki changed, based on the events of the story?

Rikki-tikki had a right to be proud of himself; but he did not grow too proud, and he kept that garden as a mongoose should keep it, with tooth and jump and spring and bite, till never a cobra dared show its head inside the walls.

AFTER READING THE SELECTION | Apply the Skills

Rikki-tikki-tavi *by Rudyard Kipling*

Directions Choose the letter of the best answer or write the answer using complete sentences.

Comprehension: Identifying Facts

1. How does Rikki-tikki feel about the cobras?

A bored
B amused
C great dislike
D curious

2. What is Rikki-tikki's war cry?

A Stand back!
B Rikki-tikki-rikki-tikki!
C I rule the garden!
D Rikk-tikk-tikki-tikki-tchk!

3. How did Teddy's mother feel about Rikki-tikki at first?

4. How does Teddy's father feel about Rikki-tikki at first?

5. How are Nag and Nagaina related?

6. Who is the big man?

7. Who does Rikki-tikki call a stupid tuft of feathers?

8. What does Darzee think when Rikki-tikki follows Nagaina into the dark hole?

9. What does Rikki-tikki do to protect Teddy's family from future danger?

10. Where does the final battle take place?

Comprehension: Putting Ideas Together

11. Which phrase best describes Rikki-tikki?

A lazy as a dog
B eaten up from nose to tail with curiosity
C crazy as a loon
D could not care less

12. What does Nagaina do to make matters worse for Nag and herself?

A She steals food from the bungalow.
B She makes enemies of the other snakes.
C She plans to attack the family and angers Rikki-tikki.
D She pretends to be friendly with Rikki-tikki.

13. Why is Karait more dangerous than the cobras?

14. Why is Darzee miserable?

15. Who is Chuchundra and why is he afraid for his life?

16. What does a cobra look like when it is angry?

17. What does a mongoose look like when it is angry?

After Reading **continued on next page**

Rikki-tikki-tavi ***by Rudyard Kipling***

18. How are Rikki-tikki and the cobras alike?

19. Who killed Nag?

20. What prevents Rikki from celebrating Nag's death?

Understanding Literature: Suspense

Writers make stories more exciting by adding details. They may give clues that don't tell exactly what is going to happen. There may be hints of danger. Suspense and excitement build during the rising action. The climax is the high point of suspense. Here the characters take action, sometimes in surprising ways. During the falling action, characters solve the conflict. Suspense may rise or fall here.

21. What does Rikki-tikki mean when he says "It is all over. The widow will never come out again."

22. What helped you predict the outcome of the story before you read it?

23. Did you find the story suspenseful? Explain.

24. How did suspense affect the way you read the story?

25. Why does Rikki-tikki feel that he must find the cobras' eggs?

Critical Thinking

26. Why doesn't Rikki-tikki eat the eggs?

27. Why does Nagaina plead with Rikki-tikki to spare her last egg?

28. How do Teddy's mother's feelings change toward Rikki-tikki over the course of the story?

29. How did Rikki-tikki feel at the end of the story? Was his work finished?

Thinking Creatively

30. "Rikki-tikki-tavi" is one of the most widely read short stories ever written. Explain why you think the story has been so popular all over the world.

Grammar Check

Verbs are words that express an action (action verbs) or a state of being (linking verbs). Linking verbs join the subject of a sentence with a word or phrase that describes or renames the subject.

Action Verbs: Jake *rode* his bike.
Let's *skate* in the park.

Linking Verbs: James *is* a member of the club.
Her voice *sounds* beautiful.

Practice Underline the action verbs and linking verbs in the following sentences.

1 Thomas seems happy about his team's record.

2 Jen is always eager for a field trip.

3 Mr. Tan teaches history and science.

4 Gran waved at the children by the fence.

5 Sam joined the club and was a good member.

Vocabulary Builder

The root *-dict,* means "speak." Words that contain this root have meanings related to saying or speaking. When you predict, you make a guess based on what you already know.

Use your knowledge of the root *-dict* to predict the meaning of each of the following words. Then, check the word's definition in a dictionary. Use each word in a sentence of your own.

1 dictator

2 indict

3 verdict

4 diction

Writing on Your Own

How did Rikki-tikki get his name? Think of people you know whose names or nicknames are related to some special quality. Invent some characters for a play. Give each character a name. Write sentences to describe the characters and tell how they got their names.

Listening and Speaking

With a partner, choose an exciting scene from the story. Take turns reading the scene out loud. Imagine that your voice will be broadcast on the radio. Your audience will only be able to hear your voice. Bring each character to life with different tones and speech patterns.

Media and Viewing

The cobras in this story are based on real snakes. They also act like humans. The author combined fact and fiction to make up these characters. Draw a comic strip about the cobras. Include details about how cobras look when they fight. Write speech balloons for the characters. Look for facts about cobras in books and on the Internet to get you started.

Reading Informational Materials

Magazine Articles

In Part 1, you learned how to make predictions. When you look through a magazine, you can guess what the article will be about. The title and pictures can give you clues. If you read "Rikki-tikki-tavi," you may be interested in this magazine article. It gives more information about mongooses.

About Magazine Articles

A magazine is a form of print media that is usually smaller than a book. It is published at regular intervals—weekly, monthly, or quarterly (four times a year). Many people work together to create magazines, including writers, photographers, editors, and artists. Magazines usually contain photographs, advertisements, comics, and articles. Articles are short pieces of nonfiction writing. Magazines usually have a theme. Some news magazines are of interest to many readers. Other magazines have a special theme in mind such as runners, artists, or animal lovers.

Reading Skill

Will this article be useful or interesting to you? Preview the text. Look for clues that can help you guess what the article is about. Read it over quickly, but do not read every word. This will give you a general idea. Notice the following features that can help you make predictions.

- title
- subheads
- charts and graphs
- photos
- captions
- quotations

Use a graphic organizer like the one shown to predict what the article is about.

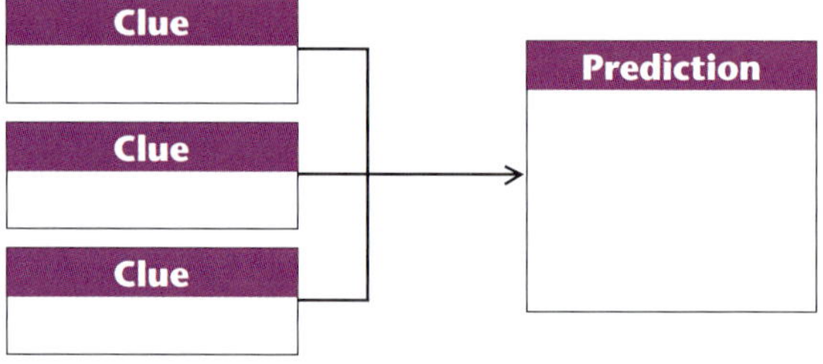

Mongoose on the Loose

Larry Luxner

The title and photo help you predict what the article will be about.

Boldface subtitles break up the text for easier reading.

In 1872 a Jamaican sugar planter imported nine furry little mongooses from India to eat the rats which were devouring his crops. They did such a good job, the planter started breeding his exotic animals and selling them to eager farmers on neighboring islands.

Population Explodes

With no natural predators—like wolves, coyotes, or poisonous snakes—the mongoose population exploded, and within a few years, they were killing not just rats but pigs, lambs, chickens, puppies, and kittens. Dr. G. Roy Horst, a U.S. expert on mongooses, says that today mongooses live on seventeen Caribbean islands as well as Hawaii and Fiji, where they have attacked small animals, threatened endangered species, and have even spread minor rabies epidemics. In Puerto Rico there are from 800,000 to one million of them. That is about one mongoose for every four humans. In St. Croix, there are 100,000 mongooses, about twice as many as the human population. "It's impossible to eliminate the mongoose population, short of nuclear war," says Horst. "You can't poison them, because cats, dogs, and chickens get poisoned, too. I'm not a prophet crying in the wilderness, but the potential for real trouble is there," says Horst.

According to Horst, great efforts have been made to rid the islands of mongooses, which have killed off a number of species including the Amevializard on St. Croix, presumed extinct for several decades. On Hawaii, the combination of mongooses and sports hunting has reduced the Hawaiian goose, or nene, to less than two dozen individuals.

Scientist Studies Problem

The fifty-nine-year-old biology professor, who teaches at Potsdam College in upstate New York, recently finished his third season at the 500-acre Cabo Rojo National Wildlife Refuge in southwestern Puerto Rico, using microchips to study the life cycle and reproductive habits of the Caribbean mongoose. (He is also doing similar work at the Sandy Point Fish and Wildlife Refuge on St. Croix in the U.S. Virgin Islands.) "I want to know what happens when you take a small animal and put him in an area with no competition. This is a model that doesn't exist anywhere else in the world."

Horst's five-year, $60,000 study is being sponsored by Earthwatch Incorporated, a non-profit group that has funded some 1,300 research projects in eighty-seven countries. Volunteers pay $1,500 each (not including airfare) to come to Puerto Rico for ten days and help Horst set out mongoose traps, study the animals, and keep records. Often he and his volunteers spend a sweaty day walking about ten miles while setting out mongoose traps in the wilderness. Later, they perform surgery on their unwilling subjects to implant the electronic devices that will allow them to track the animal's habits.

Horst has tagged more than 400 mongooses with PITs (permanently implanted transponders), a new microchip technology, which he says has changed his work dramatically. "You couldn't do this with ear tags. It was very hard to permanently mark these animals until this technology came along," he said.

This is a model that doesn't exist anywhere else in the world.

This quotation highlights an idea talked about in the article.

Horst has caught thousands of mongooses and has reached some interesting conclusions. Among them: mongooses have a life expectancy of six to ten years, much longer than the previously accepted figure of three years. Horst says his research will provide local and federal health officials with extremely valuable information if they ever decide to launch a campaign against rabies in Puerto Rico or the U.S. Virgin Islands.

Pictures and captions tell more about the content of the article.

A mongoose gets tagged.

Monitor Your Progress

Directions Choose the letter of the best answer or write the answer using complete sentences.

1. Which of the following clues does not help you predict what this article is about?
   A photos and captions
   B subheads
   C charts and graphs
   D title

2. Which clue tells where you will find information about changes in the number of mongooses?
   A the title "Mongoose on the Loose"
   B the subhead "Population Explodes"
   C the subhead "Scientist Studies Problem"
   D the caption "A mongoose gets tagged."

3. Which clue hints at the work being done by volunteers to help with the project?
   A the title "Mongoose on the Loose"
   B the subhead "Population Explodes"
   C the subhead "Scientist Studies Problem"
   D the caption "A mongoose gets tagged."

4. How were mongooses first introduced to the islands?

5. Explain how Roy Horst tracks mongooses and learns about their habits.

6. There are too many mongooses. How can their numbers be limited? Use details from the story to explain your answer.

Writing on Your Own

Write a short description of a mongoose. Tell how the animal looks and behaves. Include details from the magazine article. Choose words that give the reader a clear picture of the animal.

BEFORE READING THE SELECTION | **Build Understanding**

Train Time *by D'Arcy McNickle*

D'Arcy McNickle
1904–1977

Objectives

- To read and understand a short story
- To identify foreshadowing and flashback
- To make and verify predictions while reading
- To recognize mood in a short story

About the Author

D'Arcy McNickle was born in 1904 on the Flathead Reservation in St. Ignatius, Montana. After attending mission schools, he was sent away to boarding school in Oregon. He wrote stories, novels, articles, poems, and books of history. His early writing was praised but not widely popular. When "Train Time" was published in 1936, many readers were unfamiliar with American Indian culture. His stories helped to change that. His audience grew as readers came to understand more. He is one of the best-known American Indian fiction writers.

McNickle devoted his life to American Indian affairs. He co-founded the National Congress of American Indians. He was a professor of anthropology. The Newberry Library Center for the History of the American Indian was renamed in his honor.

About the Selection

The thoughts and memories of cavalry officer Major Miles tell the story in "Train Time." His duty is clear, but he is confused. Rounding up a group of children and putting them on a train should be easy. Boarding school will be a great opportunity, even if it is far from the Reservation. But nobody wants to go, and it is not just because they will be homesick. Although Major Miles usually follows orders without question, this time his heart tells him otherwise. Getting to know Eneas Lamartine, one of the boys, has shaken his beliefs.

Literary Terms Story events do not always happen in time order. In real life, time goes by. Writers can rearrange time. **Foreshadowing** is the clues or hints that a writer gives about something that has not yet happened. **Flashback** is a look into the past at some point in the story. **Mood** is the feeling that writing creates. You might feel nervous, sad, or silly when reading a story.

foreshadowing the clues or hints that a writer gives about something that has not yet happened

flashback a look into the past at some point in the story

mood the feeling that writing creates

Reading on Your Own A prediction is an informed guess about what will happen. Use details from the text to make predictions as you read. Ask yourself whether new details support your predictions. If they do not, change your predictions. Use a prediction guide to help organize your predictions (described in Appendix A).

- If the predictions you make are wrong, review the text to find details you might have missed.

Writing on Your Own Write a sentence describing something you believed in when you were very young. Write a list of reasons why you changed your mind.

Vocabulary Focus Reservations are parcels of land "reserved" for American Indians by the U.S. government. The children are being sent to a boarding school far from home. Here they will eat and sleep, or "board," as well as study. In the late 1800s–1920s, many American Indian children were forced to attend these schools. The purpose was to train children to fit in with society outside of the reservation. Children were required give up their native language and speak only English. They were also encouraged to give up the customs of their tribe.

Think Before You Read The characters in this story are about to take a long trip away from home. How do you feel about leaving home? You can use your own experiences to predict what will happen in the story.

Train Time

As you read, notice details that foreshadow the future.

On the depot platform everybody stood waiting, listening. The train has just whistled, somebody said. They stood listening and gazing eastward, where railroad tracks and creek emerged together from a tree-choked canyon.

Twenty-five boys, five girls, Major Miles—all stood waiting and gazing eastward. Was it true that the train had whistled?

"That was no train!" a boy's voice explained.

"It was a steer **bellowing.**"

"It was the train!"

Reading Strategy: **Predicting**

How do the children feel about the arrival of the train?

Girls crowded backward against the station building, heads hanging, tears starting; boys pushed forward to the edge of the platform. An older boy with a voice already turning heavy stepped off the weather-shredded boardwalk and stood widelegged in the middle of the track. He was the doubter. He had heard no train.

Major Miles boomed, "You! What's your name? Get back here! Want to get killed! All of you, stand back!"

The Major strode about, soldierlike, and waved commands. He was **exasperated.** He was tired. A man driving cattle through timber had it easy, he was thinking. An animal trainer had no idea of trouble. Let anyone try **corralling** twenty to thirty Indian kids, dragging them out of hiding places, getting them away from relatives and together in one place, then holding them, without tying them, until train time! Even now, at the last moment, when his worries were almost over, they were trying to get themselves killed!

What is the mood of the story?

bellowing roaring

exasperated extremely annoyed

corralling gathering

Major Miles was a man of conscience. Whatever he did, he did earnestly. On this hot end-of-summer day he perspired and frowned and wore his soldier bearing. He removed his hat from his wet brow and thoughtfully passed his hand from the hair line backward. Words tumbled about in his mind. Somehow, he realized, he had to **vivify** the moment. These children were about to go out from the **Reservation** and get a new start. Life would change. They ought to realize it, somehow—

"Boys—and girls—" there were five girls he remembered. He had got them all lined up against the building, safely away from the edge of the platform. The air was **stifling** with end-of-summer-heat. It was time to say something, never mind the heat. Yes, he would have to make the moment real. He stood soldierlike and thought that.

"Boys and girls—" The train whistled, dully, but unmistakably. Then it repeated more clearly. The rails came

vivify to bring to life

Reservation tribal land

stifling smothering

to life, something was running through them and making them sing.

Just then the Major's eye fell upon little Eneas and his sure voice **faltered.** He knew about little Eneas. Most of the boys and girls were mere names; he had seen them around the **Agency** with their parents, or had caught sight of them scurrying behind tipis and barns when he visited their homes. But little Eneas he knew. With him before his eyes, he paused.

He remembered so clearly the winter day, six months ago, when he first saw Eneas. It was the boy's grandfather, Michel Lamartine, he had gone to see. Michel had contracted to cut wood for the Agency but had not started work. The Major had gone to discover why not.

It was the coldest day of the winter, late in February, and the cabin, sheltered as it was among the pine and cottonwood of a creek bottom, was shot through by frosty drafts. There was wood all about them. Lamartine was a woodcutter besides, yet there was no wood in the house. The fire in the flat-topped cast-iron stove burned weakly. The reason was **apparent**. The Major had but to look at the bed where Lamartine lay, twisted and shrunken by **rheumatism.** Only his black eyes burned with life. He tried to wave a hand as the Major entered.

"You see how I am!" the gesture indicated. Then a nerve-strung voice faltered. "We have it bad here. My old woman, she's not much good."

Clearly she wasn't, not for wood-chopping. She sat close by the fire, trying with a good-natured grin to lift her **ponderous** body from a low seated rocking chair. The Major had to motion her back to her ease. She breathed with an **asthmatic** roar. Wood-chopping was not within her range. With only a squaw's hatchet to work with, she could scarcely have come within striking distance of a stick of wood. Two blows, if she had struck them, might have put a stop to her **laboring** heart.

faltered stumbled

Agency a tribal office

apparent easy to understand

rheumatism a painful disease of the muscles, joints, and nerves

ponderous large and very heavy

asthmatic gasping

laboring moving with great effort

"You see how it is," Lamartine's eyes flashed.

The Major saw clearly. Sitting there in the frosty cabin, he pondered their **plight** and at the same time wondered if he would get away without coming down with **pneumonia.** A stream of wind seemed to be hitting him in the back of the neck. Of course, there was nothing to do. One saw too many such situations. If one undertook to provide **sustenance** out of one's own pocket there would be no end to the demands. Government salaries were small, resources were limited. He could do no more than shake his head sadly, offer some vague hope, some small sympathy. He would have to get away at once.

Then a hand fumbled at the door; it opened. After a moment's struggle, little Eneas appeared, staggering under a full armload of pine limbs hacked into short lengths. The boy was no taller than an ax handle, his nose was running, and he had a **croupy** cough. He dropped the wood into the empty box near the old woman's chair, then straightened himself.

A soft chuckling came from the bed. Lamartine was full of pride. "A good boy, that. He keeps the old folks warm."

Something about the boy made the Major forget his determination to depart. Perhaps it was his wordlessness, his uncomplaining wordlessness. Or possibly it was his loyalty to the old people. Something drew his eyes to the boy and set him to thinking. Eneas was handing sticks of wood to the old woman and she was feeding them into the stove. When the firebox was full a good part of the boy's armload was gone. He would have to cut more, and more, to keep the old people warm.

The Major heard himself saying suddenly: "Sonny, show me your woodpile. Let's cut a lot of wood for the old folks."

It happened just like that, **inexplicably.** He went even farther. Not only did he cut enough wood to last through several days, but when he had finished he put the boy in

plight a bad situation

pneumonia a lung disease

sustenance aid

croupy hoarse

inexplicably in a way that cannot be explained

the Agency car and drove him to town, five miles there and back. Against his own principles, he bought a week's store of groceries, and excused himself by telling the boy, as they drove homeward, "Your grandfather won't be able to get to town for a few days yet. Tell him to come see me when he gets well."

That was the beginning of the Major's interest in Eneas. He had decided that day that he would help the boy in any way possible, because he was a boy of quality. You would be **shirking** your duty if you failed to recognize and to help a boy of his sort. The only question was, how to help?

When he saw the boy again, some weeks later, his mind saw the problem clearly. "Eneas," he said, "I'm going to help you. I'll see that the old folks are taken care of, so you won't have to think about them. Maybe the old man won't have rheumatism next year, anyhow. If he does, I'll find a family where he and the old lady can move in and be looked after. Don't worry about them. Just think about yourself and what I'm going to do for you. Eneas, when it comes school time, I'm going to send you away. How do you like that?" The Major smiled at his own happy idea.

There was silence. No shy smiling, no look of gratitude, only silence. Probably he had not understood.

"You understand, Eneas? Your grandparents will be taken care of. You'll go away and learn things. You'll go on a train."

The boy looked here and there and scratched at the ground with his foot. "Why do I have to go away?"

"You don't have to, Eneas. Nobody will make you. I thought you'd like to. I thought—" The Major paused, confused.

"You won't make me go away, will you?" There was fear in the voice, tears threatened.

"Why, no Eneas. If you don't want to go. I thought—"

What do you learn about Eneas in this flashback?

The Major dropped the subject. He didn't see the boy again through spring and summer, but he thought of him. In

shirking avoiding

fact, he couldn't forget the picture he had of him that first day. He couldn't forget either that he wanted to help him. Whether the boy understood what was good for him or not, he meant to see to it that the right thing was done. And that was why, when he made up a **quota** of children to be sent to the school in Oregon, the name of Eneas Lamartine was included. The Major did not discuss it with him again but he set the wheels in motion. The boy would go with the others. In time to come, he would understand. Possibly he would be grateful.

Thirty children were included in the quota, and of them all Eneas was the only one the Major had actual knowledge of, the only one in whom he was personally interested. With each of them, it was true, he had had difficulties. None had wanted to go. They said they "liked it at home," or they were "afraid" to go away, or they would "get sick" in a strange country; and the parents were no help. They, too, were frightened and uneasy. It was a tiresome, hard kind of duty, but the Major knew what was required of him and never hesitated. The difference was, that in the cases of all these others, the problem was **routine**. He met it, and passed over it. But in the

quota a group

routine regular

case of Eneas, he was bothered. He wanted to make clear what this moment of going away meant. It was a breaking away from fear and doubt and ignorance. Here began the new. Mark it, remember it.

His eyes lingered on Eneas. There he stood, drooping, his nose running as on that first day, his stockings coming down, his jacket in need of buttons. But under that shabbiness, the Major knew, was real quality. There was a boy who, with the right help, would blossom and grow strong. It was important that he should not go away hurt and resentful.

The Major called back his straying thoughts and cleared his throat. The moment was important.

"Boys and girls—"

The train was near. Already it had emerged from the canyon, and **momentarily** the headlong flying locomotive loomed blacker and larger. A white plume flew upward—*Whoo-oo, whoo-oo.*

The Major realized in sudden sharp remorse that he had waited too long. The **vital** moment had come, and he had paused, looked for words, and lost it. The roar of rolling steel was upon them.

Lifting his voice in desperate haste, his eyes fastened on Eneas, he bellowed: "Boys and girls—be good—"

That was all anyone heard.

momentarily briefly **vital** very important

AFTER READING THE SELECTION | Apply the Skills

Train Time by D'Arcy McNickle

Directions Choose the letter of the best answer or write the answer using complete sentences.

Comprehension: Identifying Facts

1. Where was the train headed?
   A to the east
   B to Washington, D.C.
   C to the desert
   D to a boarding school in Oregon
2. What signs showed that the train was coming?
3. What did "the doubter" do and why was it dangerous?

Comprehension: Putting Ideas Together

4. What did Major Miles mean when he said "Mark it. Remember it."?
   A There's no place like home.
   B This moment is a turning point in your life.
   C Label everything before you travel.
   D Take my advice.
5. How is driving cattle like corralling children?
6. How did Eneas feel when the Major offered to "send him away"?

Understanding Literature: Flashback and Foreshadowing

A flashback is a look into the past at some point in a story. It can help us get to know a character better. We can learn about old habits and fears, as well as joys. A flashback can teach us a lot about what is happening now in the story. A flashback to childhood can tell why a character makes choices as an adult. We can use information learned in flashbacks to think like the character. We can guess what they will do or choose. Foreshadowing helps build suspense and excitement in a story. Hints of what is coming make us interested in what will happen next.

7. What did the flashback in the story tell you about Major Miles? Did it explain his confusion at the depot?
8. Why were the children upset at the train station? What were they waiting for? Why were they afraid?

Critical Thinking

9. Predict what might have happened if the train had arrived one hour later. How would Major Miles have finished his final sentence?

Thinking Creatively

10. "Help someone and you help yourself." Can you think of times when it is best not to help someone?

Grammar Check

A sentence fragment is not a complete sentence. It may have a subject and a verb, but does not express a complete thought. Characters do not always think and speak in complete sentences.

Punctuation can be a clue to character traits. A character may be hesitant, undecided, shy, or puzzled. A dash can show a pause or a break in thought.

Major Miles repeats two phrases in the story: "Boys and girls—" "I thought—"

Sometimes writers use a series of periods to show an unfinished thought:

"I wonder..." "Did you ever...?"

Vocabulary Builder

The root *–ver* means *truth*. Words that contain this root have meanings related to truth. For example, to *verify* something is to prove that it is true.

Use your knowledge of the root *–ver* to predict the meaning of each of the following words. Then use a dictionary to see if you were right.

1 aver

2 very

3 verdict

4 version

Writing on Your Own

Write the journal entry Major Miles may have written the evening after the train left the station.

- Write as if you were Major Miles by using the word *I*.
- Include his thoughts and feelings.
- Use details from the story.

Listening and Speaking

With a partner, practice telling stories out loud. Take turns starting a story, then stopping and telling a flashback. Return to the story. For example:

I passed a German Shepherd. He was tied up, but . . .

I remember being bitten on the hand by a dog when I was five years old.

Media and Viewing

Screenwriters and directors make storyboards to plan a movie. A storyboard is a set of drawings. It shows the order of each scene. Think of a movie or television show that has a flashback in the plot. Make a simple drawing of each scene on a separate piece of paper. Put the pages in order. Then try putting the scenes in a different order. How does the change affect the story?

My Self, Myself *by René Saldaña, Jr.*

René Saldaña, Jr.

Objectives

- To read and understand a short story
- To identify character motives
- To compare character traits

About the Author

René Saldaña, Jr. was born in McAllen, Texas. He grew up in Texas and Georgia, the settings of many of his stories. He has taught English and writing in middle schools, high schools, and universities. His first book, *The Jumping Tree,* was one of the Top Ten Youth First Novels by *Booklist.*

René Saldaña's stories take a close look at Latino teens. He writes about things that teenagers care about. Not still children, not quite adults, everything feels super-sized.

About the Selection

Missy of "My Self, Myself" is a tomboy and a tender bully. She is jealous of her spoiled little brother, but would never say so out loud. She mostly just picks on him. This story comes from a collection published in 2003 called *Finding Our Way.* The story is told in the many voices of one teenaged girl. Missy is angry, tender, and sweet—all at the same time.

Major Miles in "Train Time" is also tough and tender. He keeps his feelings to himself, but for different reasons.

Literary Terms Details in a story can tell us what a character looks like. Writers include other details to bring characters to life. **Character traits** are a character's way of thinking, behaving, or speaking. **Motive** is a reason a character does something. This helps us to understand the character and ourselves. We can draw on our own personal experience and notice how we like or dislike the character.

character traits a character's way of thinking, behaving, or speaking

motive a reason a character does something

Reading on Your Own In "My Self, Myself," the author never tells us what the characters look like. We get our picture of Missy's character by the way she thinks and how she talks. Notice as you read how you can almost hear her speaking. Who does she remind you of? As you read the story, map out a character reference guide for Missy to help better understand her (described in Appendix A).

Writing on Your Own Newspapers feature shocking headlines. Think of four ideas for headlines. Use exciting words and write them in bold letters. For each one, write a sentence telling the motive behind what happened. Make headlines that you think will sell the most papers.

Vocabulary Focus Dialect is the speech of a particular part of a country or of a certain group of people. An author may show the way the character speaks by writing the words the way they sound. *Gonna, ooh,* and *duh* are examples from this story. *Nah, nope,* and *nyah-nyahnyah-nyah-nyah* are others. Make a list of other examples.

Think Before You Read Does the title "My Self, Myself" give you any idea what the story is about? Look for clues as you read.

My Self, Myself

As you read, imagine the sound of the character's voices.

Reading Strategy: **Predicting**

Who do you think was hurt? Why do you think this? What do you think happened?

They're punks—the both of them, always hugging him cozy and patting his back like when he actually was a baby, and whispering in his ear, "Ooh, poor baby, poor thing, are you okay, did she hurt you?"

"I didn't do anything. He did it to himself. Ask him: I didn't even touch the big crybaby," I say to them. I'm on the old, creaky swing set in our backyard. They're sitting on the patio.

My poor excuse for a mother glares at me. My father shakes his head. They think they're doing right by him, but here he is, middle-school age and they treat him like a baby. He'll be a sissyboy if they keep that up.

My way, he'll know what's what in this world and how to deal with it.

"Hush up, Missy!" my mother says. "You hush up. You've done enough harm already. Just shut it."

You shut it, Mabel, I think, but I don't say it. I know if I do Mabel'll let go of Deuce (that's what my dad calls my brother, not Leonard Junior for being named the same). Then she'll jump up and snag me off the swings; so instead I just think it and keep swinging. She won't hold me in her arms. Dad sometimes does, but not in a good long while. So I've learned my own way. Who needs hugs anyway?

What a baby Dewey is. That's what I call him, and he used to cry about it to Mom and Dad—"Missy's not calling me by my right name, Mommy." So I'd get a good talking-to, Mom sometimes shaking me by the arm and saying, "How can you not get it through your thick skull? Be nice to him. Stop teasing. He's only a boy." So, after our "talk" I'd go back to calling him Deuce, but within a week I'd forget the talking-to and the shaking by the arms and call him Dewey. He'd cry again, and again my parents would call me to their room.

Why does Dewey cry so much?

You'd think he wasn't in middle school and a starter on the football team, with his constant whimpering. He just now tried getting into Mom's lap, but he's so heavy that even Mom tells him, "Get off me and sit on the floor, baby, you're too big to be sitting on your mommy." But then she rubs his forehead like he likes, and they go inside to watch TV. I stay outside, swinging. The **lightning bugs** sparkling.

These last couple of weeks he hasn't complained about me calling him Dewey because some of the guys at school, Franky the quarterback for one, also called him Dewey one day at practice. And now the name is cool, and that's supposed to make Dewey cool too because the guys know his name.

Today, right before he went crying to Mabel and Dad, he and I were in the backyard. I was hammering anthills with a **croquet mallet,** and he was piddling around with his latest invention—a pulley, rigged up to the tree, that's connected to his bedroom window. Dewey's always trying to invent

lightning bugs fireflies

croquet a game using wooden balls and mallets

mallet a long-handled wooden hammer

stuff, but his ideas, even though he makes them work, serve zero purpose, I mean none whatsoever. This one seemed it could be good for something, but what kind of a sister would I be, telling him that? Still, I couldn't help looking at it and thinking it would be perfect for sending up secret notes, or food, if he were ever grounded and sent to his room. Like that would ever happen.

What does Missy's question reveal about her character?

This pulley system could only work, though, with two people operating it. One at the bottom pulling on the ropes and the other jailed in my brother's room waiting for the secret goods: a plate of food, a treasure map, or instructions for an escape. So Dewey said to me, "Hey, Missy, come here, will you? Let's see if this works. Come on."

I dropped the mallet and walked over.

"Okay," he said, "I'm gonna go upstairs, and when I say the word, you start pulling."

"What are you going to do?"

"I said, I'm going upstairs, and wait."

"Why don't I go upstairs, and you stay down here and do all the work?"

"It's not work. It's a pulley, duh. It keeps you from having to work. You would think you'd like a tool like this, that lets you be all lazy like you are." He laughed. When he wanted to, he could be a cool kid, like just then, making a crack like he did, but mostly he whimpered. I had my work cut out.

"Sure, whatever, jerk."

He started for the sliding door, then I asked, "You want me to pull on it this way?" And I pulled on it.

He ran toward me. "No no no. The other way, stupid. Like this." You see, a few months ago, he wouldn't've dared call me stupid. Now it's part of his daily "insult my sister" **vocabulary.**

***Reading Strategy:* Predicting**

Based on what you know about the characters, what do you predict will happen now?

I must have jammed the pulley somehow because it wasn't working now that Dewey was pulling on it hard. "You broke it," he said, then I heard a snap, looked up, the pulley came loose, and bonked Dewey on the shoulder.

vocabulary a group of words

He looked at me, then grabbed his shoulder, and I said, "You'll be okay. It was only a bump. You're not going to be a sissy and go crying to Mabel, are you?"

Then he screamed out and started crying. That's when my parents came out to the patio, hugged on him, and said, "Ooh, poor baby."

When Dewey settled down, they went in and turned on the TV.

I'm on the swing now, and I can hear the phony TV people talking, that's how loud my family likes it. Through the window at the kitchen and the sliding door I see the light of the TV shining on and off.

For the past two weeks, since Dewey went from being a nobody to a somebody because now he's okay with the name Dewey, I've been trying to come up with another name for him that'll bother him like before. But nothing. Earlier he gave me an idea, though. Right before he got hit with the pulley.

In French class, first thing we learned was the numbers: in French, two is deux, pronounced "dew," or even "doo," as in "doo-doo," but other people might misunderstand and think I'm calling him Dew and say, "What a nice thing to call your brother. You must really like him." But I don't; okay, I do, but so what?

I've got a better idea. He'd said, "It's a pulley, duh!" So that's it: Duh.

The sliding door opens, and there he is. "Hey, Sis, Mom and Dad want you to come inside."

"Hey, you know, in French the number two is pronounced 'dew,' but we're not in France, we're in Georgia, which means we're rednecks. I was going to call you Dew, but it just doesn't sound right, being redneck and all, so I'm gonna call you Duh instead."

He thinks about it for a moment, and I can't see the lights coming on in his head like people say they can see, just a blank stare. Then, "Maw, Missy's calling me names again."

"Grow up," I tell him.

He leaves the door open, and then I hear it. Mabel's screaming for me to come inside.

Then I say, "But I'm just putting to good use all the stuff I'm learning at school. You should be proud of me like you are of Duh when he invents one of his good-for-nothing contraptions and says he learned it in science class."

"I'll have none of that." Like always, she shakes me by the arm and tells me, "Deuce is young and **impressionable.** He's at a stage in his life where he could go good or bad depending on all kinds of stuff. I don't even want to think of him doing drugs, failing class, or quitting school. Listen, Missy, you're the grown-up here. You can take care of yourself. Your brother's still, you know, so can you help us out a bit?"

Why does her mother say that Missy is the grown-up?

Duh doesn't look at me like he used to when he was little, smiling because I was getting in trouble. He stares at the TV instead, then walks out of the room to the kitchen.

"But, Mom," I say.

"No buts, young lady. Apologize to your brother and go up to your room," she says.

And I scream, "I'm sorry for everything, Deuce," then go to my room.

I'll call him that, but when the shaking wears off it'll be back to Duh. I close the door behind me. I lie down on the bed and wonder, looking up at my blank ceiling, Who's worried about what path I take? What about my **self-esteem?**

I'll worry about my self myself.

There's a knock at the door. It's Duh, and he says, "Hey, sorry about that. Duh's good, from the pulley comment, right? But I'm getting older now and how do you think it looks a guy being poked fun at by his sister, so would you mind it too much going back to Dewey? I'll stop telling on you." He stands at the door, holding the knob, biting his bottom lip. "So?" he says.

I make like I'm thinking. But it's already been decided. I think all my bugging's finally paid off. "Don't stop whining

impressionable easily influenced

self-esteem a sense of worth

on my account. Do it for yourself, because I'll tell you what makes you look even stupider than I can is you crying on Momma's shoulder for any and every little thing. What you think those boys on the team would think if they knew that side of you?"

"Yeah, that's cool."

"Then it's settled, Dewey."

He gives me a **lopsided** smile, cuts the light, then shuts the door, and I'm looking up at the little glow-in-the-dark stars and moon on my ceiling. To see them, I can't look right at them, but sideways. Kind of like how I saw Dewey just now, saw him **insignificant** and little when looking right at him, and then the next minute all big and bright on a sidewise glance.

The last paragraph reveals something new about Missy. What is it?

There's stars on my ceiling, and I can't stop looking. It's an entire universe up there.

lopsided crooked

insignificant not important

My Self, Myself by René Saldaña, Jr.

Directions Choose the letter of the best answer or write the answer using complete sentences.

1. Think about "Train Time" and "My Self, Myself." Who does the main character talk about in both stories?
   A a pet
   B a priest
   C a schoolteacher
   D a young boy
2. What was Missy doing with a croquet mallet?
   A piddling around
   B hammering anthills
   C inventing stuff
   D playing croquet
3. Why does Missy call Mabel "a poor excuse for a mother"?
4. Why does Major Miles say that Eneas is "a boy of quality"?
5. How old is Missy's brother?
6. Where do Missy and her family live?
7. What is Dewey's most common complaint about Missy?
8. What is Missy's biggest complaint about Dewey?
9. What is Dewey's daily "insult my sister" vocabulary?
10. What is the origin of the nickname Duh?

Comprehension: Putting Ideas Together

11. Why do Major Miles and Missy keep a lot of thoughts to themselves?
    A They have a hard time putting their thoughts into words.
    B They are shy.
    C They do not want to make anybody mad.
    D They think they understand more than other people.
12. What does Missy mean when she says "I'll worry about my self myself."
    A Leave me alone, everyone.
    B I'm worried and confused.
    C Since no one else pays attention to me, I'll take care of myself.
    D I don't want help from anyone.
13. Missy wants her brother to change. Why?
14. Major Miles wants to send Eneas to school. What is his motive?
15. Why did Major Miles say that most of the boys and girls were mere names?
16. Does Dewey get along with his friends?

Comparing continued on next page

My Self, Myself by René Saldaña, Jr.

17. What happened when Missy helped with the pulley?

18. What happened when Major Miles started helping Eneas's family?

19. How does Missy's mother discipline her?

20. How does Major Miles talk to the children?

Understanding Literature: Character Traits

No character has just one character trait. A character might be funny and tough but also sneaky. It is the combination of traits that makes each character interesting. Sometimes characters have traits in common. Two characters might live in different parts of the world and share special qualities. Missy is a teenager living with her family. Major Miles is in charge of a group of children with lives very different from his.

21. How are Missy and Major Miles different?

22. How are they similar? What character traits do they share?

23. How is Missy like her brother Dewey?

24. Why does Missy spend so much time on the swing?

25. Why doesn't Missy tell her brother when he impresses her?

Critical Thinking

26. Imagine a meeting between Missy and Major Miles. Where would they meet? What would they talk about? What would they think of each other?

27. Does Missy always think that her brother acts like a baby?

28. Why does Missy look for a new insulting nickname for her brother?

29. What is Missy thinking about at the end of the story, looking up at the stars?

Thinking Creatively

30. Do you share any character traits with either Missy or Major Miles? Does this surprise you? Why or why not?

Grammar Check

Quotation marks show when a character is speaking out loud. They also bring attention to words that were spoken out loud in the past. Look at these examples from the stories:

They said they "liked it at home," or they were "afraid" to go away, or they would "get sick" in a strange country.

So, after our "talk" I'd go back to calling him Deuce.

Do not use quotation marks with a character's thoughts. These words are not heard out loud.

Vocabulary Builder

A hyphen is a short dash. It can be used to divide the words in a compound word. Look at these examples from the stories. Examine each part of the compound word and guess its meaning.

1 self-esteem
2 glow-in-the-dark
3 wide-legged
4 end-of-summer
5 talking-to

Writing on Your Own

Fashion magazines feature crazy descriptions of clothing. Write a short but interesting description of something you are wearing now. Combine words in unusual ways. Choose words that do not usually go together. You may be surprised by the results.

Listening and Speaking

Write a campaign speech highlighting your character traits that would help you win an election. These traits may be good or bad. Get started by making a list of your good and bad character traits. Which ones will voters like? Take turns delivering a speech to the group. Practice speaking without a fully written script. Use only your notes.

Media and Viewing

Magazines and newspapers are filled with stories about famous people. Why are people so interested in them? Do you think that everything you read about what they say and do is true?

Reading Strategy:
Inferencing

Sometimes the meaning of a text is not directly stated. You have to make an inference to figure out what the text means.

What You Know + What You Read = Inference

To make inferences, you have to think "beyond the text." Predicting what will happen next and explaining cause and effect are helpful strategies for making inferences.

Literary Terms

fairy tale an imaginary story with magical deeds and characters such as fairies, elves, and giants

external conflict a character's struggle with an outside force such as another character or nature

internal conflict a character's struggle with himself or herself to overcome opposing feelings, beliefs, needs, or desires

theme the main idea of a literary work

irony the difference between what is expected to happen in a story and what does happen

BEFORE READING THE SELECTION | Build Understanding

The Third Wish *by Joan Aiken*

Joan Aiken
1924–2004

About the Author

As a child, Joan Aiken often walked in the fields near her home in England. She made up stories to amuse herself, taking notes as she walked. She was inspired by her father and stepfather, both well-known writers. By age five, Aiken was writing her own stories. "Writing is just a family trade," she once said.

Aiken wrote for both children and adults. She wrote 92 novels in her lifetime, along with many plays, poems, and short stories. Her writing often combines parts of traditional tales and horror stories. Mystery and fantasy are woven together in surprising ways. "The Third Wish" comes from a collection of short stories published in 1974. The book has a title that sums up much of Aiken's writing—*Not What You Expected.*

About the Selection

"The Third Wish" is a **fairy tale.** A fairy tale is an imaginary story with magical deeds and characters such as fairies, elves, and giants. This tale includes magic and spells. In it, Mr. Peters frees a swan caught in the brush. It turns out that the swan is the King of the Forest. Mr. Peters receives three wishes for saving him. As in other tales, Mr. Peters must use his third wish to undo some choices he has made. Almost every culture in the world has a story like this that teaches a similar lesson.

Objectives

- To read and understand a fairy tale
- To identify conflict
- To make inferences while reading

Before Reading **continued on next page**

The Third Wish *by Joan Aiken*

fairy tale an imaginary story with magical deeds and characters such as fairies, elves, and giants

external conflict a character's struggle with an outside force such as another character or nature

internal conflict a character's struggle with himself or herself to overcome opposing feelings, beliefs, needs, or desires

Literary Terms Most fictional stories center on a conflict. A conflict is the struggle of the main character against himself or herself. It may also involve another person or nature. There are two kinds of conflict:

- **external conflict:** a chracter's struggle with an outside force such as another character or nature
- **internal conflict:** a charcter's struggle with himself or herself to overcome opposing feelings, beliefs, needs, or desires.

The resolution, or outcome of the conflict, often comes toward the end of the story. The resolution solves the problem in some way.

Reading on Your Own An inference means making a guess and judgment based on what you know. Short story writers do not directly tell you everything about the characters, setting, and events. Instead, they leave it to you to make inferences, or logical guesses, about unstated information.

- To form inferences, you must recognize details in the story and consider their importance.

Writing on Your Own In the following story, a man is granted three wishes. Make a list of three wishes that you think any person might request. Use at least three of the following words: improve, reduce, grant, obtain.

Vocabulary Focus Words sometimes have two or more meanings. Look for clues to decide which meaning makes sense. Use a dictionary to check your guesses.

In this story *account* is used twice. It has a different meaning each time.

Think Before You Read Keep in mind the warning "Be careful what you wish for" as you read. How does a solution to one conflict turn into another conflict?

The Third Wish

As you read, notice how Mr. Peters's character is revealed in details.

Once there was a man who was driving in his car at dusk on a spring evening through part of the forest of Savernake. His name was Mr. Peters. The **primroses** were just beginning but the trees were still bare, and it was cold; the birds had stopped singing an hour ago.

As Mr. Peters entered a straight, empty stretch of road he seemed to hear a faint crying, and a struggling and thrashing, as if somebody was in trouble far away in the trees. He left his car and climbed the mossy bank beside the road. Beyond the bank was an open slope of beech trees leading down to thorn bushes through which he saw the gleam of water. He stood a moment waiting to try and discover where the noise was coming from, and presently heard a rustling and some strange cries in a voice which was almost human—and yet there was something too hoarse about it at one time and too clear and sweet at another. Mr. Peters ran down the hill and as he neared the bushes he saw something white among them which was trying to **extricate** itself; coming closer he found that it was a swan that had become **entangled** in the thorns growing on the bank of the canal.

primroses small flowers

extricate to untangle

entangled tangled up

What problem does Mr. Peters face after he finds the swan?

The bird struggled all the more frantically as he approached, looking at him with hate in its yellow eyes, and when he took hold of it to free it, it hissed at him, pecked him, and thrashed dangerously with its wings which were powerful enough to break his arm. Nevertheless he managed to release it from the thorns, and carrying it tightly with one arm, holding the snaky head well away with the other hand (for he did not wish his eyes pecked out), he took it to the **verge** of the canal and dropped it in.

The swan instantly assumed great dignity and sailed out to the middle of the water, where it put itself to rights with much dabbling and **preening**, smoothing its feathers with little showers of drops. Mr. Peters waited, to make sure that it was all right and had suffered no damage in its struggles. Presently the swan, when it was satisfied with its appearance, floated in to the bank once more, and in a moment, instead of the great white bird, there was a little man all in green with a golden crown and long beard, standing by the water. He had fierce glittering eyes and looked by no means friendly.

"Well, Sir," he said threateningly, "I see you are **presumptuous** enough to know some of the laws of magic. You think that because you have rescued—by pure good fortune—the King of the Forest from a difficulty, you should have some fabulous reward."

"I expect three wishes, no more and no less," answered Mr. Peters, looking at him steadily and with **composure**.

"Three wishes, he wants, the clever man! Well, I have yet to hear of the human being who made any good use of his three wishes—they mostly end up worse off than they started. Take your three wishes then"—he flung three dead leaves in the air—"don't blame me if you spend the last wish in undoing the work of the other two."

Mr. Peters caught the leaves and put two of them carefully in his briefcase. When he looked up, the swan was sailing

verge edge

preening cleaning by licking

presumptuous overconfident

composure calmness

about in the middle of the water again, flicking the drops angrily down its long neck.

Mr. Peters stood for some minutes reflecting on how he should use his reward. He knew very well that the gift of three magic wishes was one which brought trouble more often than not, and he had no **intention** of being like the **forester** who first wished by mistake for a sausage, and then in a rage wished it on the end of his wife's nose, and then had to use his last wish in getting it off again. Mr. Peters had most of the things which he wanted and was very content with his life. The only thing that troubled him was that he was a little lonely, and had no companion for his old age. He decided to use his first wish and to keep the other two in case of an emergency. Taking a thorn he pricked his tongue with it, to remind himself not to utter **rash** wishes aloud. Then holding the third leaf and gazing round him at the dusky undergrowth, the primroses, great beeches and the blue-green water of the canal, he said:

"I wish I had a wife as beautiful as the forest."

What conflict is resolved for Mr. Peters when he gets a wife?

A tremendous quacking and splashing broke out on the surface of the water. He thought that it was the swan laughing at him. Taking no notice he made his way through the darkening woods to his car, wrapped himself up in the rug and went to sleep.

When he awoke it was morning and the birds were beginning to call. Coming along the track towards him was the most beautiful creature he had ever seen, with eyes as bluegreen as the canal, hair as **dusky** as the bushes, and skin as white as the feathers of swans.

"Are you the wife that I wished for?" asked Mr. Peters.

"Yes, I am," she replied. "My name is Leita."

She stepped into the car beside him and they drove off to the church on the outskirts of the forest, where they were married. Then he took her to his house in a remote and lovely

intention plan

forester someone who works in a forest

rash foolishly bold

dusky dark

valley and showed her all his treasures—the bees in their white hives, the Jersey cows, the **hyacinths**, the silver candlesticks, the blue cups and the **luster bowl** for putting primroses in. She admired everything, but what pleased her most was the river which ran by the foot of his garden.

"Do swans come up there?" she asked.

"Yes, I have often seen swans there on the river," he told her, and she smiled.

Leita made him a good wife. But as time went by Mr. Peters began to feel that she was not happy. She seemed restless, wandered much in the garden, and sometimes when he came back from the fields he would find the house empty and she would return after half an hour or so with no explanation of where she had been. On these occasions she was always especially tender and would put out his slippers to warm and cook his favorite dish—**Welsh rarebit** with wild strawberries—for supper.

One evening he was returning home along the river path when he saw Leita in front of him, down by the water. A swan had sailed up to the verge and she had her arms round its neck and the swan's head rested against her cheek. She was weeping, and as he came nearer he saw that tears were rolling, too, from the swan's eyes.

***Reading Strategy:* Inferencing**

Why were Leita and the swan crying?

"Leita, what is it?" he asked, very troubled.

"This is my sister," she answered. "I can't bear being separated from her."

hyacinths fragrant flowers

luster bowl a low vase for flowers

Welsh rarebit a dish of melted cheese served on crackers or toast

Now he understood that Leita was really a swan from the forest, and this made him very sad because when a human being marries a bird it always leads to sorrow.

"I could use my second wish to give your sister human shape, so that she could be a companion to you," he suggested.

"No, no," she cried, "I couldn't ask that of her."

"Is it so very hard to be a human being?" asked Mr. Peters sadly.

"Very, very hard," she answered.

"Don't you love me at all, Leita?"

"Yes, I do, I do love you," she said, and there were tears in her eyes again. "But I missed the old life in the forest, the cool grass and the mist rising off the river at sunrise and the feel of the water sliding over my feathers as my sister and I drifted along the stream."

"Then shall I use my second wish to turn you back into a swan again?" he asked, and his tongue pricked to remind him of the old King's words, and his heart swelled with grief inside him.

"Who will take care of you?"

"I'd do it myself as I did before I married you," he said, trying to sound cheerful.

She shook her head. "No, I could not be as unkind to you as that. I am partly a swan, but I am also partly a human being now. I will stay with you."

Poor Mr. Peters was very distressed on his wife's account and did his best to make her life happier, taking her for drives in the car, finding beautiful music for her to listen to on the radio, buying clothes for her and even suggesting a trip round the world. But she said no to that; she would prefer to stay in their own house near the river.

He noticed that she spent more and more time baking wonderful cakes—jam puffs, petits fours, eclairs and meringues. One day he saw her take a basketful down to the river and he guessed that she was giving them to her sister.

He built a seat for her by the river, and the two sisters spent hours together there, communicating in some wordless

Jam puffs, petits fours, éclairs, and *meringues* are small pastries. They are often filled with jam, frosting, or pastry cream.

manner. For a time he thought that all would be well, but then he saw how thin and pale she was growing.

One night when he had been late doing the account he came up to bed and found her weeping in her sleep and calling:

"Rhea! Rhea! I can't understand what you say! Oh, wait for me, take me with you!"

Then he knew that it was hopeless and she would never be happy as a human. He stooped down and kissed her goodbye, then took another leaf from his notecase, blew it out of the window, and used up his second wish.

Next moment instead of Leita there was a sleeping swan lying across the bed with its head under its wing. He carried it out of the house and down to the brink of the river, and then he said, "Leita! Leita!" to waken her, and gently put her into the water. She gazed round her in astonishment for a moment, and then came up to him and rested her head lightly against his hand; next instant she was flying away over the trees towards the heart of the forest.

He heard a harsh laugh behind him, and turning round saw the old King looking at him with a **malicious** expression.

"Well, my friend! You don't seem to have managed so wonderfully with your first two wishes, do you? What will you do with the last? Turn yourself into a swan? Or turn Leita back into a girl?"

"I shall do neither," said Mr. Peters calmly. "Human beings and swans are better in their own shapes."

But for all that he looked sadly over towards the forest where Leita had flown, and walked slowly back to his house.

Next day he saw two swans swimming at the bottom of the garden, and one of them wore the gold

malicious hateful

chain he had given Leita after their marriage; she came up and rubbed her head against his hand.

Mr. Peters and his two swans came to be well known in that part of the country; people used to say that he talked to swans and they understood him as well as his neighbors. Many people were a little frightened of him. There was a story that once when thieves tried to break into his house they were set upon by two huge white birds which carried them off **bodily** and dropped them into the river.

As Mr. Peters grew old everyone wondered at his **contentment**. Even when he was bent with **rheumatism** he would not think of moving to a drier spot, but went slowly about his work, with the two swans always somewhere close at hand.

Sometimes people who knew his story would say to him:

"Mr. Peters, why don't you wish for another wife?"

"Not likely," he would answer serenely. "Two wishes were enough for me, I reckon. I've learned that even if your wishes are granted they don't always better you. I'll stay faithful to Leita."

One autumn night, passers-by along the road heard the mournful sound of two swans singing. All night the song went on, sweet and harsh, sharp and clear. In the morning Mr. Peters was found peacefully dead in his bed with a smile of great happiness on his face. In his hands, which lay clasped on his breast, were a withered leaf and a white feather.

***Reading Strategy:* Inferencing**

What inferences can you make from knowing what Mr. Peters held in his hands when he died?

bodily physically

contentment calm happiness

rheumatism a painful disease of the muscles, joints, and nerves

AFTER READING THE SELECTION | Apply the Skills

The Third Wish *by Joan Aiken*

Directions Choose the letter of the best answer or write the answer using complete sentences.

Comprehension: Identifying Facts

1. What was the swan's reaction when it first saw Mr. Peters?

A It ignored him.

B It hissed at him, pecked him, and thrashed dangerously.

C It swam away gracefully.

D It preened.

2. How does Mr. Peters get the chance to ask for three wishes?

A He rescues a swan.

B He meets a magical king walking down a country lane.

C He has a dream.

D He finds white feathers.

3. What does the king predict that Mr. Peters will do with his wishes?

4. How does the king give Mr. Peters the wishes?

5. What was the forester's first wish?

6. Why did Mr. Peters prick his tongue with a thorn?

7. How does Mr. Peters use his second wish?

8. Why didn't Mr. Peters want to use one wish to turn himself into a swan?

9. What was the swan wearing at the end of the story?

10. What happened the night Mr. Peters died?

Comprehension: Putting Ideas Together

11. How do you know Mr. Peters loves Leita more than himself?

A He gives her fancy pastries as a gift.

B He takes a second wife so he will not be lonely.

C He gives her all of his riches.

D He uses the second wish on her.

12. Why did Mr. Peters's tongue prick when he offered to turn Leita back into a swan with his second wish?

A He bit his tongue because he was upset.

B He knew that someone was thinking about him at the same time.

C He remembered the old king's words.

D That was part of a spell the old king had cast.

13. How do you know that Leita still loves Mr. Peters even after changing back into a swan?

14. How does Mr. Peters know that Leita is unhappy?

15. How did Leita show that she loved her husband?

16. How did Mr. Peters try and make Leita happy?

17. Why didn't Leita want her sister transformed into human form?

18. Why did Leita seem to love her husband more after being away from him?

19. What finally proved to Mr. Peters that his wife was a swan?

20. What did Leita admire most about Mr. Peters's house and treasures?

Understanding Literature: Conflict

The way that a character struggles with conflict tells a lot about the character. You can make predictions using what you know about the way a character thinks and feels. Not knowing the outcome of a conflict draws readers in and holds their interest. The details in the story add up into a clearer picture of what might happen. Characters do not always think about the results of choices before they make them. Sometimes the way one conflict is solved leads to another conflict.

21. What conflict does Mr. Peters's first wish introduce?

22. How does he solve this conflict?

23. What did Leita miss about her previous life?

24. What was Leita's conflict?

25. After Mr. Peters became sick with rheumatism, why didn't he move to a drier climate?

Critical Thinking

26. Why do you think Mr. Peters didn't wish for riches?

27. Which details suggest that Mr. Peters was not afraid to die?

28. How did Mr. Peters spend his last wish? What proof do you have?

29. What advice would you have given Mr. Peters on how to use his third wish? Did he make a good choice? Explain your answer.

Thinking Creatively

30. Many cultures have traditional tales about wishes that do not work out. Why do you think this kind of story is so common?

After Reading continued on next page

The Third Wish *by Joan Aiken*

Grammar Check

An adjective modifies or describes a noun or pronoun. An adjective may answer the questions *What kind? How many? Which one? or Whose?*

Identify the adjective in each sentence. Then, tell which question the adjective answers. Use each adjective in a sentence of your own.

1 You have a beautiful house.

2 It has six rooms in all.

3 Would you like to see David's room?

Vocabulary Builder

The prefix *ob-* generally means "against" or "blocking." An object is a thing that can be seen or touched. It would block you from moving forward if it were placed in your way. With a different pronunciation, object is a verb that means "speak out against." Words beginning with the prefix *ob-* have meanings related to being blocked. Another meaning is "not able to continue."

Rewrite each sentence replacing a word or words with *obstructed* or *obstacle.* Your new sentence should have the same meaning as the original sentence.

1 The mudslide blocked the road.

2 The boulders in the path were a block that kept us from moving forward.

Writing on Your Own

Write an anecdote, or short story, using the three-wish pattern that Aiken's story follows. End the anecdote by writing a sentence that tells the lesson that your character learns. Use these ideas to help you write:

- First, think of a problem that could result from a wish.
- Then, think of ways that the character could try to solve the problem.
- Next, decide on one resolution to the conflict.

Listening and Speaking

Write a news story that announces the death of Mr. Peters and hails him as a local hero. Give examples of Mr. Peters's good deeds and good nature. Organize your story to give details in the best order. For instance, you might give your examples from weakest to strongest. Practice reading your news story aloud before reading it to the class.

Research and Technology

Use library search resources to find another story about wishes. Subject listings in the card catalog and the electronic catalog are good resources. Read the story you locate. Compare it to "The Three Wishes."

Reading Maps

The Reading Strategy in Part 2 is inferencing. Reading for clues and adding to what you know is also useful when reading maps. A map represents a place in the form of drawings, symbols, and words. To understand a map, you make inferences. Inferences are made based on what you know and what the map shows. To get a picture of a place, you must "think beyond the map."

About Maps

A map is a drawing of a place, usually as seen from above. There can be several maps of the same place. They might show different details. Maps usually feature important landmarks, such as roads and rivers. Schools and hospitals or national forests might also be highlighted. A map of the sky would show the positions of stars and planets.

You will recognize landmarks on a map of a place you have visited. You may learn about other things to see there. The relative location of objects is clearly shown on a map. When you study a map, you will learn about how the place is laid out. You will be able to imagine what it looks like, based on the details shown.

Maps have been drawn since early times. Some old maps are still accurate. Others need to be updated with new information. When countries are renamed, stars discovered, and buildings and roads built, maps reflect these changes.

On these pages you will read a map of Forestville Park Zoo.

Reading Skill

Maps contain many different kinds of information. They describe the features of a place. They show where things are located, and how far it is between them. Look at all of the information. Look at where things are located. Compare clues given in the form of words, symbols, and pictures to get an overall picture of a place.

N
P
FORESTVILLE
PARK
ZOO
Butterfly House
Eastern Trail
Tropical Rain Forest
Family Farm
ENTRANCE
W
African Savannah
Tropical Asia
P
S
ENTRANCE

When you study a map, you see many kinds of information. Symbols, text, and drawings all describe details about a place.

- Symbols represent objects on the ground, such as buildings and other landmarks. The legend, or map key, tells what the symbols mean.
- Names of important landmarks are included.
- Drawings show the general outlines of a place, including borders and roads.

Maps show a smaller picture of their subject. Scale is the relationship between distance on a map and distance on the ground. A large-scale map shows a small area of land in great detail. A small-scale map shows a large area with less detail.

Maps show the relative location of objects—what they are next to, or near. North, south, east, and west are used to describe direction. One location may be north or south of another place.

The compass rose has been used on maps and charts since the 1300s. It is named after the common flower. Originally it showed the directions of the four winds. The placement of this symbol on a map points to the north. This direction was originally indicated by a spearhead above the letter T, pointing north. The T referred to *tramontana*—the North wind. Now a bold arrow is used. Some compass roses are more decorated, but all contain the same directions. They must be clearly visible, even in a stormy sea. Captains of ships depend on maps to navigate, along with information provided by the stars. A ship captain needs to be sure that the map is facing the right direction.

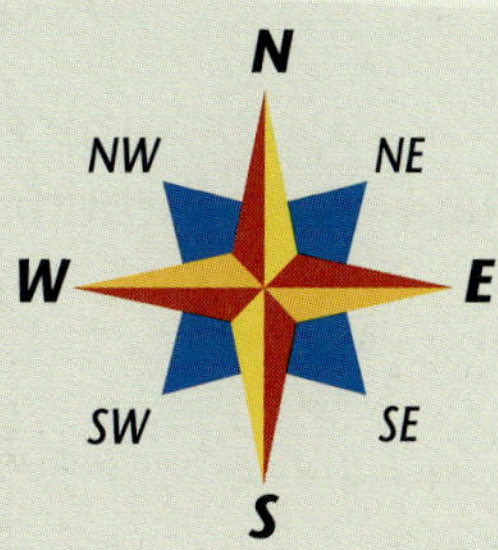

Legend

information   restroom

parking   restaurant

handicapped accessible   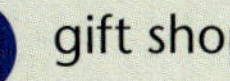 gift shop

first aid   concert stage

Monitor Your Progress

Directions Choose the letter of the best answer or write the answer using complete sentences.

1. Which information is included in the legend?
   A symbols and their meaning
   B the name of the zoo
   C the compass rose
   D zoo hours of operation

2. Where is the restaurant located?
   A south of Tropical Asia
   B east of the Butterfly House
   C south of the Family Farm
   D near the west entrance

3. What is NOT close to the south entrance?
   A gift shop **C** restaurant
   B concert stage **D** bathroom

4. Is the zoo accessible to handicapped visitors? How do you know?

5. Imagine you are walking from the Family Farm to the end of the Eastern Trail. Which animals would you pass?

Writing on Your Own

Write a description of a walking tour of the Forestville Park Zoo for a brochure. Describe the sights a visitor would see, using clear language and vivid details. Which places would children enjoy? Where are the most unusual exhibits located? Where can you stop for a snack?

BEFORE READING THE SELECTION | Build Understanding

Zoo *by Edward D. Hoch*

About the Author

When writing mystery stories, Edward Hoch stays away from fast-paced scenes with lots of action. Instead, he prefers to build suspense by making his readers guess what will happen next. Hoch creates stories that have unusual plots and carefully selected clues for readers to follow.

Although he has written several novels, Hoch is best known for his short stories. He was a research librarian before becoming a full-time writer. His first mystery story appeared in 1955 in the magazine *Famous Detective Stories.* A few years later, he began writing for *Ellery Queen's Mystery Magazine.* This popular magazine has been publishing mystery fiction longer than any other magazine. For more than 31 years, it featured a new story by Hoch every month.

Edward D. Hoch
1930–

About the Selection

Since early times, people have studied wild animals. In fact, experts believe that the first zoos were developed as far back as 4500 B.C. Until modern times, animals in zoos lived mostly in cages. However, many of today's zoos house animals in natural habitats. Filled with native plants and other animals, these environments let the animals feel more at home. In this story, you will read about a zoo that is unlike any other.

Objectives

- To read and understand a short story
- To recognize the theme
- To make inferences while reading

Before Reading **continued on next page**

Zoo *by Edward D. Hoch*

theme the main idea of a literary work

Literary Terms The **theme** is the main idea of a literary work. It may contain a message or an insight into life. Occasionally, the author states the theme directly. More often, however, the theme is implied.

As you read, look at what the characters say and do. Identify where the story takes place. There may be objects that seem important. All of these are clues to help you determine the theme—what the author wants to teach you about life.

Reading on Your Own An inference is an intelligent guess or judgment. It is based on what the story tells you about things *not* stated directly. For example, suppose that a man in a story is running down a dark alley. He is looking over his shoulder as he runs. You can infer that the man is trying to get away from someone or something.

- One way to make inferences is to read between the lines by asking questions. "Why does the writer include certain details? Why does the writer leave out other information?"

Writing on Your Own In your notebook, write sentences that describe a zoo you have visited or seen in pictures. Write from the perspective, or point of view, of an animal that lives there. Use at least three of the following words in your sentences: benefit, establish, comfortable, reduce.

Vocabulary Focus This story includes several examples of compound words. These words are formed from two words and are separated by a hyphen or dash. Some compound words do not include a hyphen. Use what you already know to define or describe each of these terms: she-creature, horse-like, three-legged, horse-spider.

Think Before You Read Think of a time in your life when you felt tired or sick. Another person may have thought you were acting cranky, stubborn, or mean. Consider how two people might see the same thing differently.

Zoo

The children were always good during the month of August, especially when it began to get near the twenty-third. It was on this day that the great silver spaceship carrying Professor Hugo's **Interplanetary** Zoo settled down for its annual six-hour visit to the Chicago area.

As you read, look for details that point to the time of the story.

Before daybreak the crowds would form, long lines of children and adults both, each one clutching his or her dollar and waiting with **wonderment** to see what race of strange creatures the Professor had brought this year.

In the past they had sometimes been treated to three-legged creatures from Venus, or tall, thin men from Mars, or even snakelike horrors from somewhere more distant. This year, as the great round ship settled slowly to earth in the huge tri-city parking area just outside of Chicago, they watched with **awe** as the sides slowly slid up to reveal the familiar barred cages. In them were some wild breed of nightmare—small, horse-like animals that moved with quick, jerking motions and constantly chattered in a high-pitched tongue. The citizens of Earth clustered around as Professor Hugo's crew quickly collected the waiting dollars, and soon the good Professor himself made an appearance, wearing his many-colored rainbow cape and top hat. "Peoples of Earth," he called into his microphone. The crowd's noise died down and he continued. "Peoples of Earth, this year you see a real treat for your single dollar—the little-known horse-spider people of Kaan—brought to you across

interplanetary between planets	**wonderment** astonishment	**awe** mixed feelings of fear and wonder

Why are the people so eager to see the horse-like animals?

a million miles of space at great expense. Gather around, see them, study them, listen to them, tell your friends about them. But hurry! My ship can remain here only six hours!"

And the crowds slowly filed by, at once horrified and fascinated by these strange creatures that looked like horses but ran up the walls of their cages like spiders. "This is certainly worth a dollar," one man remarked, hurrying away. "I'm going home to get the wife."

Reading Strategy: **Inferencing**

Based on the details in this paragraph, what can you infer about Professor Hugo's life?

All day long it went like that, until ten thousand people had filed by the barred cages set into the side of the spaceship. Then, as the six-hour limit ran out, Professor Hugo once more took the microphone in hand. "We must go now, but we will return next year on this date. And if you enjoyed our zoo this year, telephone your friends in other cities about it. We will land in New York tomorrow, and next week on to London, Paris, Rome, Hong Kong, and Tokyo. Then on to other worlds!"

He waved farewell to them, and as the ship rose from the ground, the Earth peoples agreed that this had been the very best Zoo yet . . . .

Some two months and three planets later, the silver ship of Professor Hugo settled at last onto the familiar jagged rocks of Kaan, and the odd horse-spider creatures filed quickly out of their cages. Professor Hugo was there to say a few parting words, and then they scurried away in a hundred different directions, seeking their homes among the rocks.

In one house, the she-creature was happy to see the return of her mate and offspring. She babbled a greeting in the strange tongue and hurried to embrace them. "It was a long time you were gone. Was it good?"

And the he-creature nodded. "The little one enjoyed it especially. We visited eight worlds and saw many things."

The little one ran up the wall of the cave. "On the place called Earth it was the best. The creatures there wear garments over their skins, and they walk on two legs."

A *commoc* is a form of money on the planet Kaan.

"But isn't it dangerous?" asked the she-creature.

"No," her mate answered. "There are bars to protect us from them. We remain right in the ship. Next time you must come with us. It is well worth the nineteen commocs it costs."

After reading the ending of the story, has your idea of the theme changed?

And the little one nodded. "It was the very best Zoo ever . . . ."

AFTER READING THE SELECTION | Apply the Skills

Zoo *by Edward D. Hoch*

Directions Choose the letter of the best answer or write the answer using complete sentences.

Comprehension: Identifying Facts

1. What creatures did Professor Hugo bring to Earth?

A alien children
B she-creatures
C flying monkeys
D horse-spider creatures

2. How often does Professor Hugo's Interplanetary Zoo visit Chicago?

3. Why did the horse-spider creatures feel safe on their trip?

Comprehension: Putting Ideas Together

4. Why does the crowd view the horse-spider creatures as "some wild breed of nightmare"?

A The creatures are totally unfamiliar.
B The creatures are untamed.
C The creatures are fragile.
D They have been dreaming of these same creatures.

5. How are people from Kaan like people from Earth?

6. How do you think Hoch wants readers to react at the end of the story?

Understanding Literature: Theme

A lesson is often part of the theme of a story. In many cultures around the world, lessons are shared in the form of stories. Wisdom is passed down through the ages from old to young. What theme does this story convey about people and their differences?

In a graphic organizer like this one, give details about the setting and characters that support the theme.

7. How do humans on Earth react to the horse-spider creatures from Kaan?

8. How do the residents of Kaan react to Earth people?

Critical Thinking

9. Would you like to visit Hoch's Interplanetary Zoo? Why or why not?

Thinking Creatively

10. What does this story say about how humans view things that look different from them?

After Reading **continued on next page**

Zoo *by Edward D. Hoch*

Grammar Check

An adverb is a word that modifies or describes a verb, an adjective, or another adverb. Adverbs provide information by answering the question *how? when? where? how often?* or *to what extent?* Many adverbs end in the suffix *-ly*.

Identify each adverb and the word it modifies. Tell what question it answers.

1 He proudly held the team's trophy.

2 I have the magazine here.

3 Dave filled the jar completely.

4 Juan never runs in a race.

5 I will visit my aunt tomorrow.

Vocabulary Builder

The word *conclude* begins with the prefix *con-*, which means "together" or "the same." The prefix *sub-* means "under" or "below" and is the prefix in the word *subject*. One meaning of subject is "a topic under study."

Guess the meaning of each word. Base your guess on the meaning of the prefix and the context of the sentence. Check the meanings in a dictionary. Then, use each word in a sentence.

1 The king's subjects *obeyed* his commands.

2 We reached a *conclusion* based on the clues.

3 The children were *subjected* to a stern lecture.

4 Our plans are *subject* to change based on the weather.

5 The ceremony *concluded* with a song.

Writing on Your Own

Write a letter to the editor of a local newspaper. Take a position about whether zoo animals should live in natural habitats or in cages. Include reasons and details in your letter that will convince readers to take your side.

Listening and Speaking

In "Zoo," some characters say the trip to Earth was worth the expense. Many people worry about the safety of travel. Choose a faraway location you would like to visit. Prepare and present a short speech describing the benefits of traveling to this place. Talk about the challenges you will face.

Media and Viewing

Use the Internet, library, or community resources to learn about a zoo in your area. Create a poster that includes zoo hours, admission fees, and animals that live there. Display posters and compare them to those of your classmates.

COMPARING LITERARY WORKS | **Build Understanding**

A Dozen of Everything by Marion Zimmer Bradley

Marion Zimmer Bradley
1930–1999

About the Author

Marion Zimmer Bradley was born on a farm in Albany, New York, in 1930. She was a fan of science fiction and fantasy stories as a teenager. In 1952, she sold her first short story. Her most famous novel is *The Mists of Avalon,* set during King Arthur's time. Many of her stories are inspired by myths and legends. Sometimes they are set in space.

A writer for more than 40 years, she was also the editor of many magazines. She first published the stories of many young and unknown writers. She encouraged the writers to invent strong and unusual heroines. She was awarded the World Fantasy Award in 2000 to honor her life's work.

About the Selection

"A Dozen of Everything" is another story about wishes. It is also a tale of warning: Be careful what you wish for! It was published in 1984. Although it seems like a simple story, it includes a powerful lesson. Like the story "Zoo," it also has an unexpected ending.

Objectives

- To read and understand a short story
- To recognize and compare irony
- To make inferences while reading

***Comparing* continued on next page**

A Dozen of Everything by Marion Zimmer Bradley

irony the difference between what is expected to happen in a story and what does happen

Literary Terms **Irony** is the difference between what is expected to happen in a story and what does happen. Irony is also the use of words that seem to say one thing but mean the opposite. Irony is a contrast that can make stories more interesting.

- When a paperboy says "Oh, great. I have to deliver my papers in the rain!" he is saying the opposite of what he really means.

Reading on Your Own As you read "A Dozen of Everything," look for examples of irony. Ask yourself questions like these to help you understand the writer's use of irony:

- What details lead you to expect something to happen?
- What happens instead of the outcome you expected?
- What details may have been clues to the outcome?

Writing on Your Own The stories "Zoo" and "A Dozen of Everything" involve surprises. Think about a time when you were surprised by a person or an event. Write a paragraph telling about what happened.

Vocabulary Focus Writers choose vivid words to describe characters, settings, and action. When you find an unfamiliar word, ask yourself why the writer chose to use it. Look in the dictionary for clues.

Use each word pair in a sentence.

boarders/lumbered vulgar/jumble incoherent/letterhead

Think Before You Read Human and nonhuman characters are included in both "A Dozen of Everything" and "Zoo." Describe a famous character that is not a person. For example, it could be an animal such as the big, bad wolf in "Little Red Riding Hood" Include details about the famous character's appearance and traits.

A Dozen of Everything

"What counts is what you mean."

When Marcie unwrapped the cut-glass bottle, she thought it was perfume. "Oh, fine," she said to herself **sardonically,** "Here I am, being married in four days, and without a rag to wear, and Aunt Hepsibah sends me perfume!"

As you read, look for clues to explain this first line.

It wasn't that Marcie was **mercenary.** But Aunt Hepsibah was, as the **vulgar** expression puts it, rolling in dough; and she spent about forty dollars a year. She lived in Egypt, in a little mud hut, because, as she said, she wanted to Soak Up the Flavor of the East . . . in large capitals. She wrote Marcie, who was her only living relative, long **incoherent** letters about the Beauty of the Orient, and the Delights of **Contemplation;** letters which Marcie dutifully read and as dutifully answered with "Dear Aunt Hepsibah; I hope you are well . . ."

Reading Strategy:
Inferencing

How does Marcie feel about her Aunt Hepsibah?

She sighed, and examined the label. Printed in a careful, vague Arabic script, it read "Djinn Number Seven." Marcie shrugged.

Djinn means a spirit or genie.

sardonically mockingly

mercenary interested only in money

vulgar tasteless

incoherent rambling

contemplation deep thought

Oh well, she thought, it's probably very **chi-chi** and expensive. If I go without lunch this week, I can manage to get myself a fancy **negligee,** and maybe a pair of new gloves to wear to the church. Greg will like the perfume, and if I keep my job for a few months after we're married, we'll get along. Of course, Emily Post says that a bride should have a dozen of everything, but we can't *all* be lucky.

She started to put the perfume into her desk drawer—for her lunch hour was almost over—then, on an impulse, she began carefully to work the stopper loose. "I'll just take a tiny sniff—" she thought . . .

The stopper stuck; Marcie twitched, pulled—choked at the curious, **pervasive** fragrance which stole out. "It sure is strong—" she thought, holding the loosened stopper in her hand . . . then she blinked and dropped it to the floor, where the precious cut-glass shattered into a million pieces.

Reading Strategy: **Inferencing**

What does Marcie expect to happen next?

Marcie was a normal child of her generation, which is to say, she went to the movies regularly. She had seen *Sinbad the Sailor,* and *The Thief of Baghdad,* so, of course, she knew immediately what was happening, as the pervasive fragrance rolled out and **coalesced** into a huge, towering figure with a vaguely oriental face. "My gosh . . ." she breathed, then, as she noticed **imminent** peril to the office ceiling, directed "Hey, stick your head out the window—quick!"

"To hear is to obey," said the huge figure **sibilantly**, "but, O mistress, if I might venture to make a suggestion, that might attract attention. Permit me—" and he promptly shrank to a less generous proportion, "They don't make palaces as big these days, do they?" he asked **confidentially.**

chi-chi trendy

negligee a sheer nightgown

pervasive spread all over

coalesced grew together

imminent about to happen

sibilantly with a hissing sound

confidentially in a secretive manner

"They certainly do not," gulped Marcie, "Are you—are you a genie?"

"I am not," the figure said with **asperity.** "Can't you read? I am a djinn—Djinn Number Seven to be exact."

"Er—you mean you have to grant me my wish?"

The djinn scowled. "Now, there is a strange **point of ethics,**" he murmured. "Since the stopper on the bottle is broken, I can't ever be shut up again. At the same time, since you so generously let me out, I shall gladly grant you one wish. What will it be?"

Marcie didn't even hesitate. Here was a chance to make a good wedding present out of Aunt Hepsibah's nutty old bottle, and after all, she wasn't a greedy girl. She smiled brilliantly. "I'm being married in a few days—" she started.

"You want an **elixir** of love? Of **eternal** beauty?"

"No, sir-eee!" Marcie shuddered, she had read the Arabian Nights when she was a little girl; she knew you could not make a magical bargain with a genie—er—djinn. "No, as a matter of fact, I just want—well, a household **trousseau.** Nice things to be married in, and that kind of thing—just to start us off nicely."

> Why does Marcie refuse the djinn's offer?

"I'm afraid I don't quite understand." The djinn frowned, "Trousseau? That word has come in since my time. Remember, I haven't been out of this bottle since King Solomon was in diapers."

> King Solomon was the ruler of Israel from 960 B.C. to 922 B.C.

"Well—sheets, and towels, and slips, and nightgowns—" Marcie began, then dismissed it. "Oh well, just give me a dozen of everything," she told him.

"To hear is to obey," the djhn **intoned.** "Where shall I put it, O mistress?"

asperity anger

point of ethics a matter of right and wrong

elixir a magic potion

eternal everlasting

trousseau a bride's clothes and linens

intoned said in a monotone or singsong voice

"Oh, in my room," Marcie told him, then, remembering the five-dollar-a-week hall bedroom. "Maybe you'll have to **enlarge** the room a little, but you can do that, can't you?"

"Oh, sure," said the djinn casually. "A djinn, my dear mistress, can do anything. And now, farewell forever, and thank you for letting me out."

He vanished so swiftly that Marcie rubbed her eyes, and the little cut-glass bottle fell to the floor. After a moment, Marcie picked it up, sniffing at the empty bottle. A curious faint fragrance still clung to it, but it was otherwise empty.

"Did I dream this whole thing?" she asked herself dizzily.

The buzzer rang, and the other typists in the office came back to their desks. "Gosh," someone asked, "have you been sitting here all during lunch hour, Marcie?"

"I—I took a little nap—" Marcie answered, and carefully palmed the cut-glass bottle into her desk drawer.

That afternoon seemed incredibly long to Marcie. The hands of the clock lagged as they inched around the dial, and she found herself beginning one business letter "Dear Djinn—" She ripped it out angrily, typed the date on a second letterhead, and started over; "Djinntlemen; we wish to call your attention—"

Finally, the hands reached five, and Marcie, whisking a cover over her typewriter, clutched her handbag and **literally** ran from the office. "There won't be anything there—" she kept telling herself, as she walked rapidly down the block, "there won't be anything—but suppose there was, suppose . . . ?"

The hall of the rooming-house was **ominously** quiet. Marcie ascended the stairs, wondering at the absence of the landlady, the lack of noise from the other **boarders.** A curious reluctance dragged at her hands as she thrust her key into the lock.

enlarge to make larger

literally actually

ominously menacingly

boarders people who live in a rooming-house

"It's all nonsense," she said aloud. "Here goes—"

She shut her eyes and opened the door. She walked in . . .

There was a dozen of everything. The room extended into gray space, and Marcie, opening her eyes, caught her hands to her throat to stifle a scream. There were a dozen of her familiar bed; a dozen gray cats snoozing on the pillow; a dozen dainty negligees, piled carefully by it; a dozen delicate packages labelled "Nylon stockings," and a dozen red apples rolling slightly beside them. Before her staring eyes a dozen elephants **lumbered** through the gray space, and beyond, her terrified vision focused on a dozen white domes that faded into the dim spaces of the expanded room, and a dozen tall cathedrals as well.

A dozen of everything . . .

"Marcie, Marcie, where are you?" she heard a man's voice shouting from the hall. Marcie whirled. Greg! And he was outside—outside this nightmare! She fled blindly, stumbling over a dozen rolled-up Persian carpets, grazing the edge of one of a dozen grand pianos; she screamed, **visualizing** a dozen rattlesnakes somewhere . . .

"Greg!" she shrieked.

Twelve doors were flung violently open.

How is the ending an example of irony?

"Marcie, sweetheart, what's the matter?" pleaded a **jumble** of tender voices, and twelve of Greg, pushing angrily at one another, rushed into the room.

lumbered moved slowly and heavily

visualizing seeing or forming a mental vision of

jumble mixture or confused heap

COMPARING LITERARY WORKS | Apply the Skills

A Dozen of Everything by Marion Zimmer Bradley

Directions Choose the letter of the best answer or write the answer using complete sentences.

Comprehension: Identifying Facts

1. What did Aunt Hepsibah send Marcie?

A perfume **C** money
B clothes **D** a postcard

2. What did Marcie want as a gift from her aunt?

A perfume **C** money
B clothes **D** a postcard

3. Who is the magical character in "A Dozen of Everything"?

4. Who are the fantastic creatures in "Zoo" and where do they live?

5. What does the djinn offer Marcie?

6. What is Marcie's reaction to the djinn's offer?

7. What does Professor Hugo offer to the people who visit his Interplanetary Zoo?

8. How long could Professor Hugo's Interplanetary Zoo remain on Earth?

9. Where does Marcie work?

10. How far away is the planet Kaan?

Comprehension: Putting Ideas Together

11. Why did Marcie believe that she was not only interested in money?

A She was about to get married and did not want any more trinkets.
B She thought that her rich aunt could easily share her wealth.
C She already had all the money she needed.
D She believed that cash was the most elegant wedding gift.

12. Where did Marcie learn to be cautious about genies and djinns?

A her mother's advice
B her own experience
C movies and books
D a rumor

13. Where did the Interplanetary Zoo go after its visit to Chicago?

14. Was Earth the first planet the Interplanetary Zoo visited?

15. Describe the djinn's speaking voice.

16. When was the last time the djinn was out of the bottle?

17. Where do the horse-spider people live on the planet Kaan?

18. Why did Marcie think she had a dream?

Comparing **continued on next page**

A Dozen of Everything *by Marion Zimmer Bradley*

19. What did Marcie expect to see when she returned home?

20. Was Marcie happy at the end of the story?

Understanding Literature: Irony

Irony always involves something unexpected. A character may be surprised or the reader may be surprised—or both. Irony is a contrast that can make a story more interesting. It may be the difference between what is said and what is meant. It can also be the difference between what is expected to happen and what happens. Ironic endings can be entertaining or shocking.

21. Did you expect the ending in "Zoo" or "A Dozen of Everything"?

22. What was surprising about the ending of "Zoo"?

23. What is memorable about the ending to "A Dozen of Everything"?

24. Who was surprised by the ending in "Zoo"?

25. Who was surprised by the ending of "A Dozen of Everything"?

Critical Thinking

26. Which would you rather receive: the elixir of love or the gift of eternal beauty? Explain your answer.

27. Why were people cautious about Professor Hugo's Interplanetary Zoo?

28. What lesson does "Zoo" teach?

29. What lesson is taught by "A Dozen of Everything"?

Thinking Creatively

30. Marion Zimmer Bradley and Edward D. Hoch were both born in 1930. Think of events that happened during their lifetimes. How did the times they lived in influence their writing?

Grammar Check

Sometimes the same word can have several meanings. For example: *perfume* is a noun meaning *a fragrant liquid.* It is also a sweet smell. It is also a verb meaning *to scent.*

Synonyms are words that have almost the same meanings. A thesaurus is a great resource of synonyms and other information about words. You can find interesting and often funny connections between words there.

Match the synonyms from the two lists.

djinn	increase
literally	always
eternal	really
enlarge	genie

Vocabulary Builder

An interjection is a sound, word, or phrase showing a strong emotion. It often has no other meaning. Stories with surprise endings often include interjections. An exclamation mark follows an interjection for emphasis.

Here are some examples of interjections:

Zounds! Yikes! Wow!
Abracadabra! Ka-pow!

Invent some interjections of your own based on "Zoo" and "A Dozen of Everything." Share them with the class.

Writing on Your Own

Compare the surprise endings in the two stories. Which one seemed more believable? Which one was more shocking? Write a review of one story and tell why you think it has a better ending than the other.

Listening and Speaking

Discuss the endings of the two stories with a partner. Brainstorm ideas about what might happen next if each story were to continue. Make a list of your ideas and see which story interests you more. Consider whether it would be a good idea for a movie.

Research and Technology

Conduct a survey among students at your school. Ask the question, "If you could have anything you wished for, what would it be?" Collect their answers and review them. What were the most popular answers? Make a chart showing your findings.

Unit 2 SPELLING WORKSHOP

Tricky Syllables

A syllable is a part of a word that has a single vowel sound.

The syllables in some words are barely heard. These silent letters are often left out in spelling. Look at the Word List. Say each word aloud as you look at it. Notice the unstressed syllables or syllables where letters combine to spell a single sound.

Pay attention to the syllables. Look up each word in a dictionary. Notice how the word is broken into syllables. Say the word aloud while you look at it. As you speak, exaggerate your pronunciation of the sounds and syllables.

Practice

Write the word from the Word List that matches each clue.

Then write the word with syllable breaks. Circle any letters that combine to make a single sound. Finally, use each word in a sentence.

Example: extraordinary ex•traor•di•nar•y

We saw some extraordinary gems at the museum.

1. word used in the closing of a letter
2. great and unusual
3. something to keep you on time
4. place where experiments are done
5. opposite of *same*
6. how hot or cold something is
7. place to eat a meal
8. almost
9. neither too good nor too bad
10. mother, father, sisters, brothers

Word List

- different
- temperature
- extraordinary
- practically
- average
- restaurant
- family
- schedule
- sincerely
- laboratory

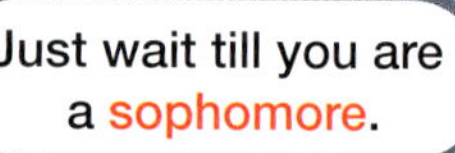

Unit 2 SUMMARY

Unit 2 introduced you to the wonderful world of short stories. You read stories that were set on an American Indian Reservation in the southwestern United States, in India, in a forest, and in outer space.

Although they share important elements, no two short stories are alike. They may be based on classic themes from the past or set in the future. They may tell a new story or tell an old story a different way. Animals may act and talk like humans.

Vivid details bring stories to life. Because short stories are brief, they often get to the point, or climax, quickly. Writers use literary devices to make plots more interesting. Foreshadowing builds suspense. Irony is found in the surprising twists a story can take. A flashback can give new meaning to a character's actions.

The characters you read about were humans, animals, and aliens. They often learned important lessons. Two different stories explored the lure of wishes and their hidden costs. We are drawn into a story by the details. How a character thinks and speaks tells us more about them than simply how they look. As we get to know them, we want to guess what they will do next. Stories do not tell everything that happens. Readers must read between the lines to get the full picture.

Selections

- "The Bear Boy" by Joseph Bruchac is a folktale. An important lesson about caring for one's own family is learned from bears.
- "Rikki-tikki-tavi" by Rudyard Kipling is an exciting story of a great battle in a garden in India.
- "Train Time" by D'Arcy McNickle is a quiet reflection on a difficult period of American history.
- "My Self, Myself" by René Saldaña, Jr. tells how the world looks to a teenaged girl.
- "The Third Wish" by Joan Aiken is a fairy tale based on the classic tale of three wishes.
- "Zoo" by Edward D. Hoch is a mystery story with a very surprising ending.
- "A Dozen of Everything" by Marion Zimmer Bradley shows what happens when a character does not say exactly what she means.

Unit 2 REVIEW

Directions Choose the letter of the best answer or write the answer using complete sentences.

Comprehension: Identifying Facts

1. A girl is the main character in which story?
   - **A** The Bear Boy
   - **B** Rikki-tikki-tavi
   - **C** Train Time
   - **D** My Self, Myself
2. Which stories feature talking animals?
3. What was Mr. Peters holding when he died?
4. Where do horse-spider creatures live?
5. Why does Marcie want a dozen of everything?

Comprehension: Putting Ideas Together

6. What is the climax in "Rikki-tikki-tavi"?
   - **A** Rikki almost dies
   - **B** Teddy adopts Rikki
   - **C** Rikki kills Nag and Nagaina
   - **D** the garden is peaceful again
7. What is the mood of "Train Time"?
8. What is meant by the title "My Self, Myself"?
9. Does Mr. Peters die a happy man?
10. What is the lesson in "A Dozen of Everything"?

Understanding Literature: Plot and Theme

The plot is the series of events in a story. The theme is the main idea. Short stories can be based on the same theme and have very different plots. The theme in a story might be a lesson. The plot can be a series of events set in the past, the present, or the future. Different characters can tell the same story. The same lesson can be illustrated in many ways.

Stories are often based on themes from the past. Folktales are stories that are passed down. They contain important lessons. Often, animals are the main characters. Fairy tales include human and magical characters. They can also include lessons about life. Many cultures have tales based on the same themes.

11. Who gives out the wishes in "The Third Wish"? What is his warning?
12. Who grants the wish in "A Dozen of Everything"? What does he say?
13. How are the horse-spider creatures like humans in "Zoo"?
14. Which creatures teach lessons in "The Bear Boy"?

15. Which human character traits are shared by the animals in "Rikki-tikki-tavi"?

Critical Thinking

16. Could "The Bear Boy" be told with all human characters?

17. What is memorable about the horse-spiders?

18. How does "Train Time" reflect a period of history?

Thinking Creatively

19. If Nag and Nagaina had won the battle in Rikki-tikki-tavi, how would the story be different?

20. Which do you prefer—stories with a lot of action or stories with a lot of suspense? Explain your answer.

Speak and Listen

Work with a partner. Review the stories in this unit and write a short phrase to describe each plot. Edit your phrases by adding exciting details and cutting unnecessary words. These phrases should be similar to the captions on posters describing movies. Pairs of students can read their captions to the class. If the captions are vivid, other students will be able to guess which story each describes.

Writing on Your Own

Write a different story for "A Dozen of Everything." Retell the story from the point of view of the djinn. Describe what it is like to be freed from the perfume bottle. What does the woman he meets look like? Is she yelling? How do her actions confuse the djinn? Include details to describe both characters.

Beyond Words

Draw a map of the bungalow and garden that make up the setting of "Rikki-tikki-tavi." Review the plot. Draw important landmarks on the map. Include places where the characters live and the sites of major battles. Create a legend that explains the symbols you use.

Test-Taking Tip

Do not wait until the night before a test to study. Plan your study time so that you can get a good night's sleep before a test.

WRITING WORKSHOP

Narration: Short Story

Sometimes a work of literature takes you to a place you have never been. It can introduce you to a whole new world of exciting characters. One type of writing that can do this is the short story. A short story is a brief work of prose. Follow the steps outlined in this workshop to write your own short story.

Assignment Write a short story about an interesting or original situation that will capture readers' attention.

What to Include Your short story should feature the following elements:

- one or more well-developed characters
- a conflict that keeps the reader asking, "What will happen next?"
- a plot
- effective pacing
- narrative that develops dialogue, suspense, and other literary elements and devices
- a title that catches the reader's attention
- effective word choice
- error-free writing

Using the Form
You may use elements of this form in these types of writing:
- autobiographical essays
- drama
- feature articles
- biographies

Prewriting

Choosing Your Topic

Use one of these strategies to get ready to write a short story:

- **Magazine Flip-Through** Review magazines, looking for photographs, articles, or ads that spark your interest. Use sticky notes to mark your finds. Later, review the flagged pages. Take notes on the most promising ideas for your story.
- **What If?** Try using a "What If?" strategy to get you started. Fill in the blanks of a sentence such as the one shown here. Try a number of situations and choose the one that interests you the most.

What if _____ (describe a person) suddenly _____ (describe a problem)?

Six Traits of Writing:
Ideas message, details, and purpose

Narrowing Your Topic

Identify the conflict. A conflict is the struggle of the main character against himself or herself, another person, or nature. A conflict may be with another character or an outside force, such as a storm. A character may struggle with his or her own powerful feelings of guilt or regret. To identify the conflict, answer these questions:

- Who is the main character of my story?
- What does the main character want?
- What is preventing him or her from getting it?

Gathering Details

Your next step is to gather details to include in your story. Follow these steps to focus your details.

1. Quickly write a list of everything that comes to mind about a general idea.
2. Circle the most interesting item on the list.
3. Focus on that detail. Create another list of everything that comes to mind about it.
4. Look for connections between the circled items on your lists. These connections will help you decide which details to include in your story.

Writing Your Draft

Shaping Your Writing

Create a plot. Begin by mapping your plot. A plot is a series of events in the story. In most stories, the plot follows this pattern:

- The exposition introduces the setting, characters, and conflict.
- The conflict builds during the rising action.
- The climax is the high point of interest or suspense.
- The story's falling action leads to the resolution, in which the conflict is resolved.

As you write, be sure to set the right pace so that your story does not drag or move too quickly.

Use literary elements and devices. A good story builds to a single exciting moment. To achieve this, writers use literary elements and devices. Foreshadowing is the use of clues hinting at future plot events. Suspense is the quality in a story that makes the reader wonder what will happen next. Flashback is a look into the past that may explain a character's actions.

Six Traits of Writing:

Organization order, ideas tied together

Providing Details

Use details to define character and setting. As you draft your story, add details that reveal what your characters look like. Include descriptions of how they act, what they think, and how others react to them. Make sure readers know when and where the action is taking place.

Revising

Revising Your Paragraphs

Improve Your Characterization. Cut a five-pointed star out of construction paper. Label the points dialogue, movement, gestures, feelings, and expressions. Slide the star down your draft as you read. Look for places where you can add details that tell more about your characters. Make notes in the margin as you review.

Dialogue: How does your character speak? Choose the words and phrasing he or she might use.

Movement: Describe a character's movements using words like rushed, timid, or excited.

Gestures: Do your characters use their hands when they talk? Do they stand tall or slouched? Insert details that show how characters look and act.

Feelings: How do events make your characters feel? Include words and details to reveal these emotions.

Expressions: What facial expressions do your characters make to show their ideas and feelings without words?

Peer Review: Give your draft to one or two classmates to read. Ask them to highlight places where you can include details that help develop stronger characters.

Revising Your Word Choice

Say exactly what you mean. Review your draft to find places where you can add details that will bring your ideas to life. Look for vague verbs that you can replace with exciting action verbs.

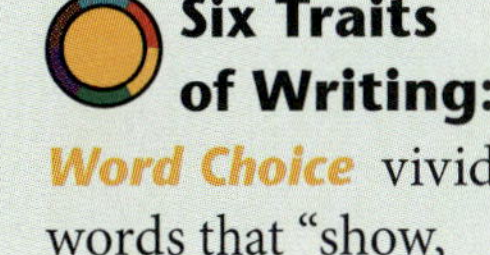

Six Traits of Writing:

Word Choice vivid words that "show, not tell"

Editing and Proofreading

Choose a strong title for your story. Check your writing to eliminate errors in grammar, spelling, and punctuation.

Focus on Dialogue: Enclose a character's exact words in quotation marks. If dialogue comes before the words announcing speech, choose the correct end punctuation. Use a comma, question mark, or exclamation point to end the quotation. A period will follow the words that announce, or tell about the quotation. If dialogue comes after the words announcing speech, use a comma before the quotation.

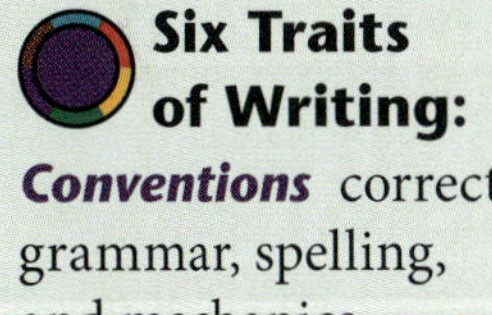

Six Traits of Writing:

Conventions correct grammar, spelling, and mechanics

Publishing and Presenting

Share your writing with a wider audience:

Submit your story. Submit your story to a school literary magazine, an online journal, or a contest.

Give a reading. Read your story aloud to your class or to a group of friends. Prepare posters announcing your reading. Pass out signed copies of your story at the event.

Reflecting on Your Writing

Writer's Journal Write your thoughts on the experience of writing a short story. Begin by answering these questions:

- What drafting advice would you give another student?
- How has your experience changed the way you read short stories?

Les Bougquinestes, Paris 2004
Isy Ochoa

Unit 3 Types of Nonfiction

Nonfiction is writing about real people and places. It is also about real ideas and events. This kind of writing has many uses. For example, the chapters in your science book tell you facts and ideas. A set of directions tells you how to do something or how something works. Emails are often nonfiction, too. They can entertain you, tell a true story, or give an opinion.

In this unit, you will read nonfiction. You will see how different writers express their ideas and feelings about the real world.

Unit 3 Selections — Page

"A good essay must . . . draw its curtain round us, but it must be a curtain that shuts us in, not out."

—Virginia Woolf
"The Modern Essay," 1925

Unit 3 About Types of Nonfiction

Common Forms of Nonfiction Writing

Nonfiction writing is about real people and events. Here are some common forms of nonfiction writing:

- **Letters** and **journals** express an author's feelings or first impressions about a subject.

Biographies and **autobiographies** tell life stories.

- A **biography** is a person's life story told by someone else.
- An **autobiography** is a person's life story, written by that person.

Media accounts are nonfiction stories written for newspapers, magazines, television, or radio.

Essays and **articles** show a writer's opinions on some basic or current issues. Essays and articles can be the following:

- **Expository writing** shows facts, talks about ideas, or explains something.
- **Persuasive writing** is meant to influence the reader.
- **Reflective writing** talks about an event in the writer's life and why it is important.
- **Humorous writing** is meant to be funny, to amuse.
- **Narrative writing** tells the story of real-life experiences.
- **Descriptive writing** uses the five senses.
- **Analytical writing** breaks a large idea into parts to help the reader see how they work together as a whole.

"PEANUTS" reprinted by permission of United Feature Syndicate, Inc.

Elements of Nonfiction Writing

Most nonfiction is **organized** in a way that shows information clearly.

- **Chronological organization** is a plot that moves forward in order of time.
- **Comparison-and-contrast organization** shows the ways in which two or more things are the same and different.
- **Cause-and-effect organization** shows the link between events.
- **Problem-and-solution organization** shows a problem and then offers a solution.

The **author's purpose** is the reason for which the author writes. The purpose can be to entertain, to inform, to express opinions, or to persuade.

Reading Strategy:
Summarizing

When readers summarize, they ask questions about what they are reading. As you read the text in this chapter, ask yourself the following questions:

- Who or what is this about?
- What is the main thing being said about this topic?
- What details are important to the main idea?

Literary Terms

essay a written work that shows a writer's opinions on some basic or current issue

expository essay an essay that informs or explains

main idea the most important thought or message in a written work

reflective essay a personal essay that explores an author's feelings

biography a person's life story, written by someone else

autobiography a person's life story, written by that person

character a person or animal in a story, poem, or play

character traits a character's way of thinking, behaving, or speaking

character analysis thinking carefully about a character's traits

idolized character a character that stands for a trait, such as honor or courage

idiom a phrase that has a different meaning than its words really mean

Life Without Gravity by Robert Zimmerman

Robert Zimmerman
1953–

Objectives

- To read and understand an expository essay
- To identify main ideas in an essay
- To summarize facts and ideas

About the Author

Robert Zimmerman has always wanted to know about space travel. As a boy in the 1960s, he liked science fiction. He read many stories about traveling into space. He knew these stories were pretend, but he liked their positive view of the future.

At that time, real space travel had just begun. Zimmerman watched the first flight of an American into space. Zimmerman was excited about seeing this event on television. He remembers thinking, "This is the United States. We can do anything if we put our minds to it!"

When Zimmerman grew up, he worked for 20 years in the movie business. He was a screenwriter and producer, among other jobs. As a hobby, he likes to explore caves. He says that exploring caves is like exploring outer space. He says that both are a hunt for the unknown.

About the Selection

In "Life Without Gravity," Robert Zimmerman tells how different life can be for people who are in space. On Earth, gravity is a force that most people do not even think about. Gravity holds people and objects down and helps gives them weight. In space, however, gravity is very weak. People and things weigh much less. Zimmerman explains how astronauts live with weak gravity. He shows that the weak gravity affects everything they do. It affects how they eat, drink, and move. It even can affect their bones and muscles.

***Before Reading* continued on next page**

Life Without Gravity *by Robert Zimmerman*

essay a written work that shows a writer's opinions on some basic or current issue

expository essay an essay that informs or explains

main idea the most important thought or message in a written work

Literary Terms An **essay** is a written work that shows a writer's opinions on some basic or current issue. "Life Without Gravity" is an **expository essay.** An expository essay is an essay that informs or explains. Every essay has a **main idea**—the most important thought or message in a written work. Every paragraph has a main idea, too. The main ideas in the paragraphs help you understand the main idea of the essay.

Reading on Your Own When readers summarize, they give the writer's main idea or most important ideas. To begin summarizing, read the title and opening sentences. Then, scan the selection. This means that you should look it over quickly, to see how it is organized. Then, read the selection closely. Look for topic sentences, key points, and supporting details.

Writing on Your Own "Life Without Gravity" tells about strange experiences. It tells how astronauts live when they are weightless in space. It describes what happens when they return to Earth. Write three sentences about gravity. Tell how it affects your life.

Vocabulary Focus Preview the vocabulary words in the story before reading. Choose five words that are unfamiliar and write them in your notebook. Then, as you read, look for clues for these words to help you with the meaning. You will find them close to the word or in nearby sentences. After reading, check your understanding by writing a sentence using each word. Use a dictionary if you need help.

Think Before You Read What do you know about space travel and astronauts? In a group, share what you have learned from books and films. Share your questions, too.

Life Without Gravity

Being weightless in space seems so exciting. Astronauts bounce about from wall to wall, flying! They float, they weave, they do somersaults and acrobatics without effort. Heavy objects can be lifted like feathers, and no one ever gets tired because nothing weighs anything. In fact, everything is fun, nothing is hard.

NOT! Since the first **manned** space missions in the 1960s, scientists have discovered that being weightless in space isn't just flying around like Superman. Zero gravity is **alien** stuff. As space tourist Dennis Tito said when he visited the international space station, "Living in space is like having a different life, living in a different world."

The *international space station* is a science station that orbits Earth.

Worse, **weightlessness** can sometimes be downright unpleasant. Your body gets upset and confused. Your face puffs up, your nose gets stuffy, your back hurts, your stomach gets upset, and you throw up. If astronauts are to survive a one-year journey to Mars—the shortest possible trip to the Red Planet—they will have to learn how to deal with this weird environment.

manned operated by astronauts

alien very different or strange

weightlessness being without weight

Our bodies are adapted to Earth's gravity. Our muscles are strong in order to **overcome** gravity as we walk and run. Our inner ears use gravity to keep us upright. And because gravity wants to pull all our blood down into our legs, our hearts are designed to pump hard to get blood up to our brains.

In space, the much weaker gravity makes the human body change in many unexpected ways. In **microgravity**, your blood is **rerouted,** flowing from the legs, which become thin and sticklike, to the head, which swells up. The extra liquid in your head also makes you feel like you're hanging upside down or have a stuffed-up nose.

The lack of gravity causes astronauts to **routinely** "grow" between one and three inches taller. Their spines straighten out. The bones in the spine and the disks between them spread apart and relax.

Disks are flat, round pieces of tissue that separate the bones in the spine.

But their bones also get thin and spongy. The body decides that if the muscles aren't going to push and pull on the bones, it doesn't need to lay down as much bone as it normally does. Astronauts who have been in space for several months can lose 10 percent or more of their bone tissue. If their bones got much weaker, they would snap once the astronauts returned to Earth.

***Reading Strategy:* Summarizing**

As you read, think about what weightlessness does to a person's bones.

And their muscles get weak and flabby. Floating about in space is too easy. If astronauts don't force themselves to exercise, their muscles become so **feeble** that when they return to Earth they can't even walk.

Worst of all is how their stomachs feel. During the first few days in space, the inner ear—which gives people their sense of balance—gets confused. Many astronauts become **nauseous.** They lose their appetites. Many throw up. Many throw up a lot!

overcome to defeat

microgravity very little gravity

rerouted sent in a different way

routinely naturally

feeble weak

nauseous sick to the stomach

Weightlessness isn't all bad, however. After about a week people usually get used to it. Their stomachs settle down. Appetites return (though astronauts always say that food tastes **blander** in space). The heart and spine adjust.

Then, flying around like a bird becomes fun! Rooms suddenly seem much bigger. Look around you: The space above your head is pretty useless on Earth. You can't get up there to work, and anything you attach to the ceiling is simply something you'll bump your head on.

In space, however, that area is useful. In fact, equipment can be **installed** on every inch of every wall. In weightlessness you choose to move up or down and left or right simply by pointing your head. If you turn yourself upside down, the ceiling becomes the floor.

And you can't drop anything! As you work you can let your tools float around you. But you'd better be organized and neat. If you don't put things back where they belong when you are finished, tying them down securely, they will float away. Air currents will then blow them into nooks and crannies, and it might take you days to find them again.

When the author says *nooks* and *crannies,* he means small or hidden places.

In microgravity, you have to learn new ways to eat. Don't try pouring a bowl of cornflakes. Not only will the flakes float all over the place, the milk won't pour. Instead, big balls of milk will form. You can drink these by taking big bites out of them, but you'd better finish them before they slam into a wall, splattering apart and covering everything with little tiny milk **globules**.

Reading Strategy: **Summarizing**

What is the main idea of this paragraph?

blander less tasty

installed put into place

globules small, round drops

Some meals on the space station are eaten with forks and knives, but scooping food with a spoon doesn't work. If the food isn't **gooey** enough to stick to the spoon, it will float away.

Everyone in space drinks through a straw, since liquid simply refuses to stay in a glass. The straw has to have a clamp at one end, or else when you stop drinking, the liquid will continue to flow out, spilling everywhere.

To prevent their muscles and bones from becoming too weak for life on Earth, astronauts have to follow a boring two-hour exercise routine every single day. Imagine having to run on a treadmill for one hour in the morning and then ride an exercise bicycle another hour before dinner. As Russian astronaut Valeri Ryumin once said, "Ye-ech!"

Even after all this exercise, astronauts who spend more than two months in space are usually weak and uncomfortable when they get back to Earth. Jerry Linenger, who spent more than four months on the Russian space station *Mir,* struggled to walk after he returned. "My body felt like a 500 pound **barbell,**" he said. He even had trouble lifting and holding his fifteen-month-old son, John.

Mir was the first long-term research station in space. Why do you think Jerry Linenger was willing to be uncomfortable?

When Linenger went to bed that first night, his body felt like it was being smashed into the mattress. He was constantly afraid that if he moved too much, he would float away and out of control.

***Reading Strategy:* Summarizing**

What is the main idea of this essay?

And yet, Linenger recovered quickly. In fact, almost two dozen astronauts have lived in space for more than six months, and four have stayed in orbit for more than a year. These men and women faced the **discomforts** of weightlessness and overcame them. And they all **readapted** to Earth gravity without problems, proving that voyages to Mars are possible . . . Even if it feels like you are hanging upside down the whole time!

gooey sticky and soft

barbell an exercise weight

discomforts difficulties

readapted got used to again

AFTER READING THE SELECTION | **Apply the Skills**

Life Without Gravity *by Robert Zimmerman*

Directions Choose the letter of the best answer or write the answer using complete sentences.

Comprehension: Identifying Facts

1. Which choice is NOT an effect of weightlessness?

A You can feel like you are flying like a bird.

B When you drop something, it lands on the ceiling.

C Milk floats around in globules.

D You can decide which direction is up.

2. How do someone's legs and head change in weightlessness?

3. Why do astronauts' bones become weak in space?

Comprehension: Putting Ideas Together

4. Which sentence best tells the main idea of the essay?

A Traveling in space seems exciting.

B In microgravity, you must learn new ways to eat.

C Astronauts can overcome problems with weightlessness.

D Astronauts should not travel in space.

5. What do you think is the most difficult thing about living in weightlessness?

6. What advice does Zimmerman give about space travel?

Understanding Literature: Expository Essay

An expository essay gives information and explanations. The main idea is the most important information. Details make the essay interesting. Details help you understand the main idea. When you put these details together, you can understand the author's main idea.

7. Why is "Life Without Gravity" called an expository essay? Explain your answer. Give two examples from the story.

8. In this essay, what are the problems of weightlessness? What is the main idea about the solution to those problems?

Critical Thinking

9. Think about the information in "Life Without Gravity." Would you like to experience weightlessness? Why or why not?

Thinking Creatively

10. Some of the experiences in space are difficult and strange. What does this tell you about astronauts? What kinds of people make good astronauts?

After Reading **continued on next page**

Life Without Gravity *by Robert Zimmerman*

Grammar Check

Coordinating conjunctions are words such as *and, but, or, nor, for, so,* and *yet*. They connect words or groups of words that are similar. Conjunctions show how parts of a sentence connect.

Look at these examples. The conjunctions are boldfaced. The words they connect are italicized.

Connecting nouns: Do the *pen* **and** *paper* contain fingerprints?

Connecting verbs: Please *slice* **or** *chop* these tomatoes.

Connecting groups of words: *He ran out the door,* **but** *the bus already had left.*

Write two sentences that follow each example. Be sure to use a comma in the sentences for the third example.

Vocabulary Builder

Weightless uses the suffix *-less*. Since *-less* means "without," *weightless* means "without weight." Words with the suffix *-less* will show that something is missing or not enough.

Use your knowledge of the suffix *-less* to predict the meaning of each of the following words. Then, check the word's definition in a dictionary. Use each word in a sentence of your own.

1 painless
2 homeless
3 priceless
4 ageless

Writing on Your Own

Think about "Life Without Gravity." Recall some of the problems with weightlessness and how they can be solved. Then write an essay about these ideas. In your own words, explain one problem and its solution. Use details from the essay in your writing.

Listening and Speaking

Work with a group to summarize Robert Zimmerman's essay. Then give a presentation to the class.

To prepare, outline the main ideas and details. Use a Main Idea Graphic (Table) (described in Appendix A) to organize your main idea and details. Collect photographs and make drawings and charts to aid your presentation. To present, speak clearly, show pictures to explain the information, and summarize the main idea again.

Research and Technology

In a group, talk about working in space and weightlessness; then list some topics that the group may be interested in. Next, find books and Web sites about each topic. List the sources you find. Finally, make a master list to share with the class. This is your bibliography. (See Appendix C for more information about bibliographies.)

BEFORE READING THE SELECTION | Build Understanding

I Am a Native of North America by Chief Dan George

Chief Dan George
1899–1981

Objectives

- To read and understand a reflective essay of an American Indian elder
- To summarize an author's feelings and thoughts

About the Author

Chief Dan George was born in 1899 in Canada. He was the son of a tribal chief and was given the birth name "Tes-wah-no." He also was known as Dan Slaholt. When he was five, he was sent to a mission boarding school. The teachers changed his last name to George.

When Dan George was 17, he left school to work. He became a bus driver. When he was more than 60 years old, he was offered an acting role. He had a natural talent for acting. First, he played an American Indian in a TV series. Next, he began to act in films.

Dan George won awards for his acting in Canada. Then he was given a role in *Little Big Man.* In this movie, he was a wise older Indian. George was nominated for an Academy Award.

George began to speak about his memories. He talked about the culture and the rights of his people. He spoke the truth for many American Indians.

About the Selection

Chief Dan George was a Coast Salish Indian. The Salish lived by the cycles of the seasons. During the winter, the people stayed in large villages near sheltered bays. In the spring, they moved to the beaches. There they fished, hunted, and gathered berries. Then, in the fall, groups met along the rivers to fish. This way of life connected them closely with the natural world. This story focuses on Chief Dan George sending children away from that natural world. He is sending 30 children on a train to Oregon for boarding school. The children do not want to go. We learn about Chief Dan George's thoughts and feelings throughout the story.

***Before Reading* continued on next page**

I Am a Native of North America *by Chief Dan George*

reflective essay
a personal essay that explores an author's feelings

Literary Terms A **reflective essay** is a personal essay that explores an author's feelings. It focuses on an experience or idea. Most important, this kind of writing is personal. This means that the main idea is the writer's most important thought or feeling. The author wants you to respond with your own feelings and thoughts. As you read, imagine that Chief Dan George is speaking directly to you.

Reading on Your Own Sometimes an author does not state the main idea. When this happens, you have to figure out the most important point. As you read, think about key points and details. Look for groups of related details. Look for sentences that pull details together. To understand the main idea, make connections between key points and supporting details. Then you can summarize what you read.

Writing on Your Own Chief Dan George was part of two cultures. He knew the American Indian culture. He also knew the Canadian culture in which he was raised. How might a person's background shape the person he or she becomes? List some ways.

Vocabulary Focus Preview the vocabulary words in the story before reading. Many of the vocabulary words refer to human values. Write what you think is the meaning of each word below. Write a sentence for each word. How does each word express something valuable to all people?

cultures	communal	acceptance	self-esteem
companionship	privacy	integration	

Think Before You Read You may have seen films or read books about American Indian culture. What do you know about American Indian customs and beliefs? Share your ideas in a group.

I Am a Native of North America

In the course of my lifetime I have lived in two distinct **cultures.** I was born into a culture that lived in **communal** houses. My grandfather's house was eighty feet long. It was called a smoke house, and it stood down by the beach along the **inlet.** All my grandfather's sons and their families lived in this large dwelling. Their sleeping apartments were separated by blankets made of bull rush reeds, but one open fire in the middle served the cooking needs of all. In houses like these, throughout the tribe, people learned to live with one another; learned to serve one another; learned to respect the rights of one another. And children shared the thoughts of the adult world and found themselves surrounded by aunts and uncles and cousins who loved them and did not threaten them. My father was born in such a house and learned from **infancy** how to love people and be at home with them.

And beyond this **acceptance** of one another there was a deep respect for everything in nature that surrounded them. My father loved the earth and all its creatures. The earth was his second mother. The earth and everything it contained was a gift from See-see-am . . . and the way to thank this great spirit was to use his gifts with respect.

See-see-am is the name of the Great Spirit, or "The Chief Above" in the Salishan language of Chief Dan George's people. As you read, think of the experience or idea the author reflects on here.

cultures organized societies

communal shared

inlet a narrow strip of water

infancy babyhood

acceptance thinking of something as good or right

I remember, as a little boy, fishing with him up Indian River and I can still see him as the sun rose above the mountain top in the early morning . . . I can see him standing by the water's edge with his arms raised above his head while he softly moaned . . . "Thank you, thank you." It left a deep impression on my young mind.

Gaffing means using a barbed spear to catch river fish.

And I shall never forget his disappointment when once he caught me gaffing for fish "just for the fun of it." "My Son," he said, "the Great Spirit gave you those fish to be your brothers, to feed you when you are hungry. You must respect them. You must not kill them just for the fun of it."

***Reading Strategy:* Summarizing**

What is the main idea of the essay so far?

This then was the culture I was born into and for some years the only one I really knew or tasted. This is why I find it hard to accept many of the things I see around me.

I see people living in smoke houses hundreds of times bigger than the one I knew. But the people in one apartment do not even know the people in the next and care less about them.

It is also difficult for me to understand the deep hate that exists among people. It is hard to understand a culture that **justifies** the killing of millions in past wars, and is at this very moment preparing bombs to kill even greater numbers. It is hard for me to understand a culture that spends more on wars and weapons to kill, than it does on education and **welfare** to help and develop.

In what two cultures has Chief Dan George lived?

It is hard for me to understand a culture that not only hates and fights its brothers but even attacks nature and abuses her. I see my white brother going about **blotting** out nature from his cities. I see him strip the hills bare, leaving ugly wounds on the face of mountains. I see him tearing things from the **bosom** of mother earth as though she were a monster, who refused to share her treasures with him. I see him throw poison in the waters, **indifferent** to the life he kills there; and he chokes the air with deadly **fumes.**

***Reading Strategy:* Summarizing**

What key words or sentences have helped you determine the essay's main idea?

justifies tries to prove that something is right

welfare support, especially for the poor

blotting remove

bosom a woman's chest

indifferent not caring

fumes gases

Jaune Quick-to-See-Smith, "Buffalo", 1992, oil, collage, mixed media on canvas, Diptyph 66" x 96".

Buffalo, **Jaune Smith**

My white brother does many things well for he is more clever than my people but I wonder if he knows how to love well. I wonder if he has ever really learned to love at all. Perhaps he only loves the things that are his own but never learned to love the things that are outside and beyond him. And this is, of course, not love at all, for man must love all **creation** or he will love none of it. Man must love fully or he will become the lowest of the animals. It is the power to love that makes him the greatest of them all . . . for he alone of all animals is capable of love.

Love is something you and I must have. We must have it because our spirit feeds upon it. We must have it because without it we become weak and faint. Without love our **self-esteem** weakens. Without it our courage fails. Without love we can no longer look out confidently at the world. Instead we turn inwardly and begin to feed upon our own personalities and little by little we destroy ourselves.

You and I need the strength and joy that comes from knowing that we are loved. With it we are creative. With it we march tirelessly. With it, and with it alone, we are able to sacrifice for others.

There have been times when we all wanted so desperately to feel a reassuring hand upon us . . . there have been lonely times when we so wanted a strong arm around us . . . I cannot tell you how deeply I miss my wife's presence when I return from a trip. Her love was my greatest joy, my strength, my greatest blessing.

What experiences does the author reflect on here?

creation life on Earth

self-esteem a sense of worth

I am afraid my culture has little to offer yours. But my culture did prize friendship and **companionship.** It did not look on **privacy** as a thing to be clung to, for privacy builds up walls and walls promote distrust. My culture lived in big family communities, and from infancy people learned to live with others.

My culture did not prize the **hoarding** of private possessions; in fact, to hoard was a shameful thing to do among my people. The Indian looked on all things in nature as belonging to him and he expected to share them with others and to take only what he needed.

Everyone likes to give as well as receive. No one wishes only to receive all the time. We have taken much from your culture . . . I wish you had taken something from our culture . . . for there were some beautiful and good things in it.

Soon it will be too late to know my culture, for **integration** is upon us and soon we will have no values but yours. Already many of our young people have forgotten the old ways. And many have been shamed of their Indian ways by scorn and **ridicule.** My culture is like a wounded deer that has crawled away into the forest to bleed and die alone.

***Reading Strategy:* Summarizing**

What key word is repeated in this paragraph and throughout the essay? How does that word help you summarize the author's feelings and thoughts?

The only thing that can truly help us is genuine love. You must truly love us, be patient with us and share with us. And we must love you—with a genuine love that forgives and forgets . . . a love that forgives the terrible sufferings your culture brought ours when it swept over us like a wave crashing along a beach . . . with a love that forgets and lifts up its head and sees in your eyes an answering love of trust and acceptance.

This is brotherhood . . . anything less is not worthy of the name.

I have spoken.

companionship the company of others

privacy secrecy or being alone

hoarding keeping too much

integration the mixing of people and ideas

ridicule making fun of something

AFTER READING THE SELECTION | **Apply the Skills**

I Am a Native of North America *by Chief Dan George*

Directions Choose the letter of the best answer or write the answer using complete sentences.

Comprehension: Identifying Facts

1. Chief Dan George says that many human needs are supported by love. Which of the following is NOT one of these?

A self-esteem **C** strength
B reassurance **D** privacy

2. Name three things that people learn growing up in communal homes.

3. What things puzzle Chief Dan George about his "white brothers"?

Comprehension: Putting Ideas Together

4. Chief Dan George lived in "two distinct cultures." Which sentence best explains how these cultures were different?

A One lived in harmony with nature; the other did not.
B One knew joy and happiness; the other was sad all the time.
C One was a group of actors; the other was an Indian tribe.
D One had communal houses; the other did not.

5. Chief Dan George says, "My white brother . . . is more clever than my people." What does he mean by *clever?*

6. What is the "brotherhood" that Chief Dan George talks about at the end of the essay? Is this brotherhood important? Why or why not?

Understanding Literature: Reflective Essay

In this reflective essay, Chief Dan George tells how people act and why they do so. He describes what he has seen. He shares his personal reasons for feeling a certain way. Then he writes reasons that are important to everyone. When we, as readers, add up the details, the main point becomes clear. We know why Chief Dan George wrote the essay and what he wanted to tell us.

7. How did Chief Dan George's father act toward nature? Use details from the essay in your answer.

8. What is the main idea of the essay?

Critical Thinking

9. Can people keep their old values and traditions when they move into a new culture? Explain your answer.

Thinking Creatively

10. Do you agree that "the power to love" is the most important human quality? Why or why not?

After Reading **continued on next page**

I Am a Native of North America *by Chief Dan George*

Grammar Check

A prepositional phrase begins with a preposition. It ends with the noun or pronoun that completes its meaning. These examples show prepositions and prepositional phrases.

Examples: Salish children learned the importance <u>of love</u>. They lived <u>in big family communities</u>.

Other common prepositions: above, around, behind, by, from, into, near, on, through, to, under, with

Copy the prepositional phrase from each sentence. Then change each sentence by using a new prepositional phrase.

1 Melissa quickly hid her diary under her bed.

2 In the distance, we saw an auto accident.

3 The field trip was canceled because of bad weather.

Vocabulary Builder

Part of the word *insignificant* is the prefix *in-*, which often means "not." The word *significant* means "important." Adding the prefix *in-* creates an antonym. So *insignificant* means "not important."

Add the prefix *in-* to create an antonym for each of the following words. Then, write a sentence that uses each new word correctly.

1 complete

2 sensitive

3 sufficient

4 visible

Writing on Your Own

Think about "I Am a Native of North America." Remember the author's message and the feelings that he shares. Then write a short reflective essay. Share thoughts or feelings about a memory or something that is important to you. Use your own experiences and ideas. Be sure to make your main idea clear.

Listening and Speaking

In a group, give a reaction to a short reflective essay written by another student. Explain what the essay made you think about and why. Use at least two examples from the essay. Also use some examples from your own experiences. At the end of your presentation, summarize your ideas.

Media and Viewing

Work with a group. Give a report on an American Indian group. Choose topics such as history, beliefs and values, and stories. Then, use the Internet and the library to find information. Bring in photos and maps. You also can use recordings, film clips, or other media to help with your report.

Problem-and-Solution Essay

In Part 1, you are learning about summarizing. In "I Am a Native of North America," you learned to find the main idea. You read details about American Indians. You read about the life of Chief Dan George. You will now summarize a problem-and-solution essay. "Keeping It Quiet" tells about a problem and a solution. As you read, think about the essay's main idea.

About Problem-and-Solution Essays

A problem-and-solution essay is organized in a logical manner. Usually, you will begin by learning what the problem is. Next, you will find facts that explain the problem. Then, you will learn about one or more solutions. The author will include facts, examples, and reasons to explain the solutions.

In this essay, you will learn about a problem with noise. You will learn some things people can do when there is too much noise.

Reading Skill

Writers have invented tools to help them understand what they read. One great tool is the outline. An outline will help you summarize. It shows how main ideas and details are connected. An outline is a good way to take notes on what you learn. It also can help you get organized before you write your own essay.

To begin an outline, identify the main ideas. Then, list the key points for each main idea. Finally, list the details. This example shows the structure of an outline. You can use it to take notes on "Keeping It Quiet." To make your outline longer, just keep adding main ideas, key points, and supporting details.

I. First Main Idea
- A. First key point
  - 1. supporting detail
  - 2. supporting detail
- B. Second key point
  - 1. supporting detail
  - 2. supporting detail

II. Second Main Idea
- A. First key point

Keeping It Quiet

As you read, notice how the writer states the main idea in the first paragraph. The main idea is the problem.

from *Prentice Hall Science Explorer*

A construction worker uses a jackhammer; a woman waits in a noisy airport; a spectator watches a car race. All three experience noise pollution. In the United States alone, 40 million people face danger to their health from noise pollution.

People start to feel pain at about 120 decibels. But noise that "doesn't hurt" can still damage your hearing. Exposure to 85 decibels (a kitchen blender) can slowly damage the hair cells in your cochlea. As many as 9 million Americans have hearing loss caused by noise. What can be done about noise pollution?

These facts are details about the dangers. They explain how big the problem really is.

The Issues

What Can Individuals Do?

These words are called *subheads*. How do the subheads tell you what to expect?

Some work conditions are noisier than others. Construction workers, airport employees, and truck drivers are all at risk. Workers in noisy environments can help themselves by using ear protectors, which can reduce noise levels by 35 decibels.

Many leisure activities also pose a risk. A listener at a rock concert or someone riding a motorbike can prevent damage by using ear protectors. People can also reduce noise at the source. They can buy quieter

The writer outlines some solutions to the problems.

machines and avoid using lawn mowers or power tools at quiet times of the day. Simply turning down the volume on headphones for radios and CD players can help prevent hearing loss in young people.

What Can Communities Do?

Transportation—planes, trains, trucks, and cars—is the largest source of noise pollution. About 15 million Americans live near airports or under airplane flight paths. Careful planning to locate airports away from dense populations can reduce noise. Cities can also prohibit late-night flights.

This statistic supports the idea that the problem is widespread.

Many communities have laws against noise that exceeds a certain decibel level, but these laws are hard to enforce. In some cities, "noise police" can give fines to people who use noisy equipment.

What Can the Government Do?

A National Office of Noise Abatement and Control was set up in the 1970s. It required labels on power tools to tell how much noise they made. But in 1982, this office lost its funding. In 1997, lawmakers proposed The Quiet Communities Act to bring the office back and set limits to many types of noise. But critics say that national laws have little effect. They want the federal government to encourage—and pay for—research into making quieter vehicles and machines.

The article outlines early attempts to solve the problem, as well as more recent solutions.

Monitor Your Progress

Directions Choose the letter of the best answer or write the answer using complete sentences.

1. Which sentence best states the main idea of this essay?
  A Large cities have the worst problem with noise pollution.
  B Noise pollution is one of the world's biggest problems.
  C Noise can be harmful, but there are ways to fix the problem.
  D The government should be doing more to limit noise pollution.

2. Which of the following details supports the main idea?
  A About nine million Americans have lost their hearing because of noise.
  B New laws would limit noise pollution.
  C Ear protectors are one solution because they lower noise levels.
  D All of the above.

3. Which idea is NOT supported by details in the essay?
  A The National Office of Noise Abatement and Control did not do its job well.
  B Communities are making laws to reduce noise pollution.
  C Lawmakers do not agree about noise pollution, so the problem remains.
  D There are many things that people can do to avoid loud noise.

4. Name the largest source of noise pollution. Explain your answer.

5. Why is pain not the best way to know if a noise is harming your ears?

6. Describe three ways you can reduce noise pollution in your own life.

Writing on Your Own

Write a summary of "Keeping It Quiet." First, explain the problem. Then, summarize the solutions. Remember to write your summary in just a few sentences. Use your own words. Tell only the main ideas and most important details.

For the Love of Country by Emma Trelles

Emma Trelles
1949–

About the Author

Emma Trelles is a journalist, and her essays have appeared in many publications. She also writes stories and poetry, and she teaches classes in writing.

Trelles likes to write about things in the world around her. "That can lead to anything," she explains. Some examples are "the wild landscapes of the Everglades," "what it's like to speak my Cuban Spanish in Mexico," "protest marches," and "rock bands." She gives writers this advice: "Pick a subject you care about, something that moves you. It will show in your work."

Objectives

- To read and understand a biography
- To analyze characters
- To compare and contrast characters in a biography and an autobiography

About the Selection

In "For the Love of Country," Trelles tells the stories of five women. Two were American Indian; three were Latin American. All of them struggled for freedom from Spain. The Spanish had come to America in 1492. They conquered Central America, Mexico, and most of South America. They also controlled areas in the southern United States. The Spanish brought diseases and guns to the New World. They killed many native people and brought a new culture. They ruled for more than 300 years.

These women lived in different times and places, but they had many things in common. Their lives were also similar to the life of Chief Dan George. Their countries were ruled by another culture. They all acted on their beliefs. They cared about their countries, and they gave great hope to others.

"For the Love of Country" is a group of biographies. A **biography** is a person's life story told by someone else. "I Am a Native of North America" is also a story about someone's life. However, it is an **autobiography**—a person's life story told by that person. Both kinds of life stories are true.

Comparing continued on next page

For the Love of Country by Emma Trelles

biography a person's life story, written by someone else

autobiography a person's life story, written by that person

character a person or animal in a story, poem, or play

character traits a character's way of thinking, behaving, or speaking

character analysis thinking carefully about a character's traits

idolized character a character that stands for a trait, such as honor or courage

idiom a phrase that has a different meaning than its words really mean

Literary Terms A life story tells about a **character.** A character is a person or animal in a story, poem, or play. **Character traits** are the way a person thinks, behaves, or speaks. **Character analysis** means thinking carefully about a character's qualities and traits. In an autobiography, a writer tells what really happened. His or her words and thoughts are clear. However, in a biography of someone who lived long ago, things are not as clear. Sometimes real people can seem bigger than life. They might stand for a character trait, such as courage or honor. A hero is an **idolized character.**

Reading on Your Own One way to summarize a character's traits is by comparing and contrasting. Think about how they are similar to and different from other people. As you read this essay, remember Chief Dan George, too. Think about how his life was like and unlike the lives of these women. You can compare and contrast ideas, events, and feelings. Also, notice each author's use of idioms in each story. An **idiom** is a phrase that has a different meaning than its words really mean. Both writers use idioms to make their stories more exciting.

Writing on Your Own "For the Love of Country" tells about five great women. Write about a woman who you think is a hero. Write a short biography. Then, tell why you admire the woman. Name the character trait you admire about her.

Vocabulary Focus The Spanish words in "For the Love of Country" give a sense of time and place. With a partner, learn their meaning. Use a Spanish dictionary or the Internet. Or, if you understand Spanish, translate for your classmates.

mujer, hija, tamales, Viva la patria!, patriota, novio, mercados, misa, conquistadores, enimigo, areito, una gran mujer, guerrara

Think Before You Read Heroes often do big things for all the world to see. What are some "small" ways of being a hero? In a group, compare your ideas.

For the Love of Country

They were soldiers and spies, rulers and revolutionaries. Now, in honor of Hispanic Heritage Month, we look at some of the legendary mujeres who, through their bravery and cunning, helped to shape the course of Latin American history.

Mujeres slinging guns alongside their husbands? Guerreras commanding **battalions** of men? That was the scene at the **onset** of the Mexican Revolution in 1910, when thousands of *mexicans* took up arms against the **federal** army in the fight for independence. Nicknamed las Adelitas after a folksong about a woman who joins her man in war, these fierce women included Margarita Neri, who led hundreds of men during a battle in Guerrero, and Colonel Petra Herrera, who **rallied** 200 rebel solders to help seize the city of Torreon.

As amazing as these feats were, however, what makes them all the more remarkable is knowing that they are simply examples of a greater truth: what throughout our history, women have repeatedly fought for the glory of their *patria* and the ideals of freedom and equality—women like the early **feminist** Ana Betancourt, the first mujer to address Cuba's Consitutional Assembly about women's rights; and the seductive *ecuatoriana* Manuela Sáenz, whose revolutionary **fervor** matched that of her lover, Simón Bolívar.

There's also the **regal** Anacaona, who kept her throne even after Spain claimed the island of Hispaniola, and Colombia's La Pola, whose spirit was so fierce that according to legend, it took six bullets to kill her. And then there's La Malinche, who—even though she is branded a traitor by some—is widely regarded as the mother of the mestizo culture.

This article was written originally for a magazine article to celebrate Hispanic Heritage Month.

In Spanish, *mujeres* means women, *patria* means country, and an *ecuatoriana* is a woman from Ecuador.

***Reading Strategy:* Summarizing**

As you read, you can think about the important idea. What is important about all of the women in this article?

Most people in Mexico are *mestizo.* This means that their ancestors were both Spanish and American Indian.

battalions groups of soldiers

onset beginning

federal national

rallied came together

feminist a person who fights for women's rights

fervor great feeling

regal royal

The *women's movement* was a movement to gain voting rights, equal pay, and respect for women.

Each of these women risked life and, by doing so, not only helped create the Latin America we see today but also lit the fires for the women's movement that would sweep across the Americas in the early 20th century. For that we owe these mujeres our gratitude—and this recognition.

Ana Betancourt

19th-century Cuba

Citizens: The Cuban woman, from the dark and ***tranquil*** *corner of her home, has waited patiently and with* ***resignation*** *for this* ***sublime*** *hour in which a just revolution will break her yoke, will untie her wings.*

These were the words spoken by Ana Betancourt, the first mujer to address Cuba's Constitutional Assembly on behalf of her countrywomen, during a **passionate** and poetic plea for Cuban women's rights. But this 1869 event was also notable for another reason: Ana's speech was the first to compare publicly the legal standing of women to that of slaves, arguing that for Cuba to be truly independent, it had to do more than overthrow the Spanish—it had to wipe out **discrimination.**

In Spanish, *hija* means daughter.

Feisty words for the well-mannered hija of Creoles from what is now Camagüey, but after marrying progressive thinker Ignacio Mora de la Pera when she was 22, Ana learned history, languages, and the power of her own ideas. She began **dictating** proindependence articles that her husband published in the local paper and encouraging public debates on women's issues; she and Ignacio also hid spies and stored guns in their home.

***Reading Strategy:* Summarizing**

Both Dan George and Ana Betancourt spoke for their people. How were their messages the same? How were they different?

Ana's courage had paid off by 1918, when Cuba finally gave its female citizens legal rights involving property and marriage. And although Cuba's colonial government exiled Ana twice because of her revolutionary activities (she died in Madrid in 1901), you can now find her name on the fronts of many hospitals and schools in her native country.

tranquil peaceful

resignation acceptance

sublime wonderful

passionate having strong feelings

discrimination unfair treatment and opinions

feisty lively

dictating speaking something to be written down by others

Policarpa "La Pola" Salavarrieta

19th-century Colombia

Policarpa Salavarrieta's unshakable courage during Colombia's War of Independence has inspired sonnets, songs—and a loyalty so strong that once, during a staging of a play about her, the theater audience flung tomatoes and **tamales** at the stage to try to prevent the scene of her 1817 execution. In real life, it is said, it took six bullets to stop the brave heart of this **seamstress**-turned-spy, and still the 20-year-old went down crying, "¡Viva la *patria*!" in front of 3,000 Spanish soldiers in Bogotá's main square.

Bogotá is the capital of Colombia.

Viva la patria! means long live this country! *Patriota* is a patriot, *mercados* are markets, *misa* is the Catholic mass, and a *peso* is Colombian money.

Nicknamed La Pola, Colombia's most famous *patriota* grew up poor in Guaduas, and like her novio and her younger brother, both of whom took up arms against Spain, she joined the **rebellion.** As a seamstress, La Pola often crossed paths with the Spanish **elite,** and she passed along any news she overheard—on city streets, at *mercados*, and even during *misa*—to the revolutionaries. She brought food to imprisoned Colombian soldiers so she could give them secret messages from the Colombian army, and opened her doors to soldiers in need of a safe place to hold meetings.

Within a year the Spanish authorities had learned of her activities, and after arresting La Pola, they sentenced her to death. As the story goes, she marched without hesitation toward the firing squad and refused both a blindfold and a sip of water—because the offers came from a Spaniard. Before **uttering** her famous last cry, she asked the crowd to save their tears for those she would leave behind, and today—some 180 years after Colombia won its independence—La Pola remains such an enduring figure of strength that her image is printed on the nation's 10,000-peso bill.

***Reading Strategy:* Summarizing**

What character traits did "La Pola" have?

tamales Latin American food made of meat wrapped in cornmeal

seamstress a woman who sews

rebellion a revolution

elite members of the leading class

uttering saying

La Malinche

16th-century Mexico

Was La Malinche a traitor who sold out her fellow Aztecs to the Spanish? Or did she save countless lives through her **shrewd negotiations** with the *conquistadores*? Historians today remain divided on exactly what La Malinche did, but they have no doubts about who she was: the mother of the mestizo race.

Born 500 years ago in the Yucatán to wealthy Aztec parents, La Malinche was a young girl when her father died; soon after his death, her mother sold her into slavery. Years later, when she was about 18, rulers of the defeated town of Tabasco presented La Malinche and 19 other women as a "gift" to Hernán Cortés, the leader of Spain's Mexican conquest—and history was forever changed. Because of her bright mind and **mastery** of the Spanish, Mayan, and Nahuatl languages, La Malinche became the married Cortés's mistress and one of his most trusted **aides, accompanying** him on every expedition and translating for him at his first meetings with the mighty Aztec emperor Montezuma. One historian notes that Cortés was so in love with La Malinche, he refused other women "won" in battle; and in a letter kept in **archives** in Spain, Cortés praises two forces for Spain's victory: God and La Malinche.

Because of such reports, Mexicans have long labeled her a sellout, and they still use the word *malinchista* to brand a traitor. But some historians credit her negotiating skills with saving thousands of Aztec people; in addition, the son La Malinche **conceived** with Cortés is the first known child born of a Spanish father and an Amerindian mother, marking the start of the mestizo people.

***Reading Strategy:* Summarizing**

How are the actions of Ana Betancourt, La Pola, and La Malinche similar? How are they different?

Hernán Cortés arrived in Mexico in 1519. He destroyed the Mexican/Aztec empire. He killed thousands of Aztec Indians.

shrewd clever

negotiations bargaining

mastery great skill

aides assistants

accompanying traveling with

archives old records and files

conceived created (a baby)

Anacaona

15th-century Hispaniola

As queen of the Tainos, an **indigenous** tribe that once thrived in the Caribbean, Anacaona ruled Jaraguá, the richest of five kingdoms on the lush green island of Hispaniola, which today is divided into the Dominican Republic and Haiti. And when Christopher Columbus turned up on her turf in 1492, Anacaona accomplished something few leaders in history were able to: She kept her land out of the hands of the Spanish.

With an **exquisite** beauty reflected by her name, which means "flower of gold," and a keen **intellect** she **nurtured** by writing poetry, Anacaona so charmed the arriving Spanish colonizers that even though they took over the island's other four kingdoms, she retained control of her throne for a remarkable 11 years. **Ultimately,** however, the **camaraderie** she shared with the *enemigo* proved her downfall. In 1503 after a new Spanish governor landed on the island with thousands of troops, he asked to meet the famous queen. Ever the generous hostess, Anacaona commanded her court to organize an *areito*, a great celebration to welcome her guests—but the Spanish believed the large gathering was nothing but a **ruse** for an uprising.

In the midst of the festivities, the governor's men turned on the crowd and murdered dozens of Taino leaders. Anacaona was arrested and taken to Santo Domingo, where, months later, she was hanged, but today she is remembered as *una gran mujer* who, if only briefly, kept the Spanish at bay.

Anacaona, Penny Slinger, 1989

Reading Strategy:
Summarizing
How are Anacaona's feelings like those of Chief Dan George? How is her life both similar to and different from his?

The Spanish wanted to explore and live in the Americas. They invaded American Indian kingdoms and claimed the land as their own.

indigenous native-born

exquisite beautiful in a delicate way

intellect the ability to think

nurtured took care of

ultimately finally

camaraderie friendship

ruse a plan to fool someone

Manuela Sáenz
19th-century Ecuador

Even before she fell in love with Simón Bolívar, the Venezuelan soldier and **statesman** who helped lead the South American revolution against Spain, Manuela Sáenz was a rebel. At a time when women were expected to keep their mouths shut and their minds empty, she smoked, wore low-cut gowns, and said whatever she pleased. And if anyone ever dared try to put her in her place, Manuela was ready to fight back, having learned how to handle a horse, swords, and pistols as skillfully as any man.

Simón Bolívar was a revolutionary. He vowed to fight until the Spanish left South America.

It was this fierceness that seduced Bolívar when the couple first met in 1822. While riding down the streets of Quito during a parade in his honor, Bolívar locked eyes with Manuela, who had thrown a wreath to him. For the next eight years, the couple's passion for each other would be matched only by their passion for freedom, as Manuela accompanied him in battle, eventually attaining the rank of colonel. She even saved his life more than once by thwarting **assassination** attempts, inspiring some to call her la Libertadora del Libertador.

Reading Strategy: **Summarizing**

What traits do all of these women share? How would you summarize the article?

Ultimately, however, Bolívar never saw his dream of a **unified** South America fulfilled, and in 1830 he went into **exile** in Colombia. Manuela stayed on in Colombia and continued to fight all those who had turned on the man she loved, inspiring historian Luis Augusto Cuervo to write, "Manuela was without doubt the soul of the revolution." By 1834, however, the Colombian government had lost all patience with Manuela and exiled her to Jamaica—although, true to form, she didn't go down without a fight: It took a squad of soldiers to force this proud *guerrera* from her home.

statesman a person in politics

assassination having to do with a planned murder

unified joined

exile being sent away from one's country or home

COMPARING LITERARY WORKS | Apply the Skills

For the Love of Country *by Emma Trelles*

Directions Choose the letter of the best answer or write the answer using complete sentences.

Comprehension: Identifying Facts

1. What was Ana Betancourt fighting for?
   A the rights of Cuban women
   B independence from Spain
   C the Constitutional Assembly
   D the rights of Creoles

2. What did "La Pola" ask people not to do?
   A throw tomatoes on stage
   B put her image on the 10,000-peso bill
   C weep for her when she died
   D love Simón Bolívar

3. Why was La Pola sentenced to death?

4. How did La Malinche help Cortés at meetings?

5. What are two opinions about La Malinche?

6. Who was Anacaona, and what did she do with her beauty and intelligence?

7. How did Anacaona lose her power?

8. Where was Manuela Sáenz from?

9. What two things did Manuela Sáenz feel very strongly about?

10. Which of these brave women lived in the 1400s?

Comprehension: Putting Ideas Together

11. Which character trait do all of the women share?
    A charm
    B courage
    C talent for poetry
    D a gift for languages

12. What kind of writing is "I am a Native of North America"? How does it differ from the stories in "For the Love of Country"?
    A autobiography: The writer tells what he thinks and feels.
    B biography: The writer tells readers what he thinks and feels.
    C autobiography: The writer tells what someone else thinks and feels.
    D biography: The writer tells the story of another person's life.

13. Think about when and where Chief Dan George lived. How did those facts make his life different from all of the women in this article?

14. Ana Betancourt says she waited for a revolution to untie her wings. What did she mean? What would Chief Dan George say about this idea?

Comparing **continued on next page**

For the Love of Country *by Emma Trelles*

15. What do Ana Betancourt, "La Pola," and Manuela Sáenz have in common?

16. Chief Dan George said, "This is why I find it hard to accept many of the things I see around me." Which woman from "For the Love of Country" would agree with this statement? Why?

17. Which people from these stories grew up poor and then became a leader?

18. Chief Dan George says that only with love are we are able to sacrifice for others. Would La Pola agree with this statement? How do you know?

19. What similar kinds of information do you learn from both stories? How is the writing different?

20. Chief Dan George was a movie star. Which woman in this essay do you think would be the best movie star?

Understanding Literature: Character Analysis; Comparing and Contrasting

When you compare and contrast two characters, you can learn more about each of them. To analyze traits, compare actions and words. You can also look for differences. Differences help you understand how each person is special.

21. How was Ana Betancourt like Chief Dan George?

22. How were Anacaona and La Malinche similar? How were they different?

23. How was La Pola idolized? How was Chief Dan George idolized?

24. Manuela Sáenz and Anacaona were very independent women. Compare and contrast their choices in life.

25. How were La Malinche and Ana Betancourt's choices limited by the times in which they lived?

Critical Thinking

26. If Anacaona wrote an autobiography, what would you want to learn from her words?

27. If Chief Dan George had been in Latin America during a revolution, what do you think he would have done?

28. Why do people remember the women in "For the Love of Country"?

29. What might Ana Betancourt and Chief Dan George have said about La Malinche being sold as a slave?

Thinking Creatively

30. Which character from these stories is most like you? Explain your answer.

Grammar Check

An idiom is a phrase that has a different meaning than its words really mean. Many idioms do not seem like correct usage or grammar. However, we have become used to using the sayings in everyday speech.

Look at these idioms from the essay:

1 She was a sellout.

2 She kept her land out of the hands of the Spanish

3 It was her downfall.

4 She kept the Spanish at bay.

5 They locked eyes.

6 He wanted to wipe out discrimination.

Write the meaning of each of the underlined idioms. If you do not know the meaning, ask your teacher or a classmate to explain.

Vocabulary Builder

The author's words make her characters seem bigger than life. Use at least five of these vocabulary words in a short paragraph. Describe someone you know. How do the words make the person seem interesting?

tranquil	sublime	passionate
notable	feisty	elite
shrewd	indigenous	exquisite

Writing on Your Own

Write a one-page essay. Compare and contrast one woman from "For the Love of Country" with Chief Dan George. Discuss the times and places in which they lived. Then write about their experiences, thoughts, and feelings. To decide how the characters felt, think about their actions and words.

Listening and Speaking

Work in a group to make characters come alive. One student can act the part of Chief Dan George, one can act as Ana Betancourt, and so forth. Choose a character and reread his or her story. Then, present a speech, acting as if you are that person. Tell what you have done and how you feel about it.

Media and Viewing

Draw a picture of a woman from "For the Love of Country." Use the picture in your book for an example, or research to find new pictures. Show the clothes each woman probably wore. Give a sense of place and time. Then compare and contrast your pictures with classmates' pictures.

Reading Strategy:
Asking Questions

As you read the selections in Part 2, ask yourself questions about what is happening. Also think about the facts and opinions that the author may use in the selections.

Ask yourself:

- Can this information be proven? If so, it is a fact.
- Is this information someone's belief that cannot be proven? If so, it is likely an opinion.
- Clue words such as *best*, *worst*, *always*, and *never* often suggest opinions.

Literary Terms

persuasive essay an essay meant to influence

fact something that actually happened or can be proven

opinion a belief or judgment

diction the proper choice of words, or saying words correctly

word choice words a writer uses and how they are put together

BEFORE READING THE SELECTION | Build Understanding

All Together Now by *Barbara Jordan*

Barbara Jordan
1936–1996

About the Author

Barbara Jordan fought for human rights all of her life. In 1990, the Women's Hall of Fame voted to honor her. They called her one of the most influential women of the century. Jordan grew up in Texas and was the daughter of a preacher. Jordan learned to speak in front of large groups. In high school, she argued in debates. She won awards for her speeches.

Jordan became a member of the Texas Senate in 1966. She was the first African American woman senator in Texas. In 1972, she joined the U.S. Congress. Then, in 1976, she was asked to give a speech. It was a speech at the Democratic National Convention. Jordan was the first African American to give such a speech. She knew that she was changing history. She said, ". . . there is something different about tonight. There is something special about tonight. What is different? What is special? I, Barbara Jordan, am a keynote speaker."

Objectives

- To read and understand a persuasive essay
- To ask questions to understand literature
- To understand the opinions of a well-known civil rights speaker

About the Selection

Until the 1960s, not all Americans had the same rights. Many African Americans suffered. They could not eat in many restaurants. They had to ride in certain sections of trains and buses. They did not have access to the same jobs and schools. In the 1960s, the U.S. government wrote new laws. Congress passed the Civil Rights Act, which gave the same rights to every American. In "All Together Now," Barbara Jordan talks about these laws. She tells how the laws fight racism. She also says that laws are not enough. She tells us to work together, with respect for people of every race.

***Before Reading* continued on next page**

All Together Now by Barbara Jordan

persuasive essay an essay meant to influence

fact something that actually happened or can be proven

opinion a belief or judgment

Literary Terms "All Together Now" is a **persuasive essay**. A persuasive essay means to influence. Its writer gives us **facts**, or something that can be proven. Its writer also shares **opinions**. Opinions are beliefs or judgments. Writers like Barbara Jordan use many ways to argue their points. They really want you to agree with them! Here are some of the best ways:

- using opinions of experts and well-known people
- repeating the words of an authority
- using logical arguments

Reading on Your Own As you read, ask yourself which ideas are opinions and which ideas can be proven. Look for words such as *I believe* or *In my opinion*. Also look for words such as *always, never, must, cannot, best, worst,* and *all*. These words may show where the writer shares a personal judgment.

Writing on Your Own Barbara Jordan writes about the civil rights movement in the 1960s. She tells how it changed many people's lives. How can people make sure that others are treated fairly? Make a list of things that people can do to work for equal rights. Share your ideas with the class.

Vocabulary Focus Make a word web to see how the vocabulary words are related. Draw three circles on your paper. Write *race relations* in the center circle. Write *feelings* under the left circle. Write *actions* under the right circle. Fill in the circles with the correct words from the list below. If you need help, use a dictionary to learn the meaning of the word.

tolerant	harmonious	segregation	discrimination	
culminated	ensured	diminished	compassion	fatigue
regained	excluded	nurture	prejudices	equality

Think Before You Read Talk with a group about ending racism. How would you convince someone to treat everyone fairly? Give reasons for your opinions.

All Together Now

When I look at race relations today I can see that some positive changes have come about. But much remains to be done, and the answer does not lie in more **legislation**. We *have* the legislation we need; we have the laws. Frankly, I don't believe that the task of bringing us all together can be accomplished by government. What we need now is soul force—the efforts of people working on a small scale to build a truly **tolerant, harmonious** society. And parents can do a great deal to create that tolerant society.

We all know that race relations in America have had a very rocky history. Think about the 1960s when Dr. Martin Luther King, Jr., was in his **heyday** and there were marches

Reading Strategy:
Asking Questions

As you read, ask yourself questions. Can these statements be proven? What clue words show that the author is giving an opinion?

legislation the making of laws

tolerant accepting

harmonious in agreement

heyday the best time for someone or something

and protests against **segregation** and discrimination. The movement **culminated** in 1963 with the March on Washington.

The Civil Rights Act stopped segregation in schools and businesses. It also ensured that all adults could vote.

Following that event, race relations reached an all-time peak. President Lyndon B. Johnson pushed through the Civil Rights Act of 1964, which remains the **fundamental** piece of civil rights legislation in this century. The Voting Rights Act of 1965 ensured that everyone in our country could vote. At last, black people and white people seemed ready to live together in peace.

But that is not what happened. By the 1990's the good feelings had diminished. Today the nation seems to be suffering from **compassion fatigue,** and issues such as race relations and civil rights have never regained **momentum.**

Those issues, however, remain crucial. As our society becomes more diverse, people of all races and backgrounds will have to learn to live together. If we don't think this is important, all we have to do is look at the situation in Bosnia today.

Bosnia is a country on the Balkan Peninsula in Europe. It was the site of a bloody war in the 1990s. Religious and ethnic groups fought each other. Think about the persuasive technique that Jordan uses by making this reference to Bosnia.

How do we create a harmonious society out of so many kinds of people? The key is tolerance—the one value that is **indispensable** in creating community.

If we are concerned about community, if it is important to us that people not feel excluded, then we have to do something. Each of us can decide to have one friend of a different race or background in our mix of friends. If we do this, we'll be working together to push things forward.

segregation the forced separation of racial groups

culminated had its greatest moment

fundamental basic

compassion feelings of love and understanding

fatigue tiredness

momentum the energy to move forward

indispensable absolutely necessary

One thing is clear to me: We, as human beings, must be willing to accept people who are different from ourselves. I must be willing to accept people who don't look as I do and don't talk as I do. It is crucial that I am open to their feelings, their inner reality.

What can parents do? We can put our faith in young people as a positive force. I have yet to find a racist baby. Babies come into the world as blank as slates and, with their beautiful innocence, see others not as different but as enjoyable companions. Children learn ideas and attitudes from the adults who **nurture** them. I absolutely believe that children do not adopt **prejudices** unless they absorb them from their parents or teachers.

***Reading Strategy:* Asking Questions**

Can the last statement in this paragraph be proven? Is it an opinion or a fact?

The best way to get this country faithful to the American dream of **tolerance** and equality is to start small. Parents can actively encourage their children to be in the company of people who are of other racial and ethnic backgrounds. If a child thinks, "Well, that person's color is not the same as mine, but she must be okay because she likes to play with the same things I like to play with," that child will grow up with a broader view of **humanity**.

I'm an **incurable optimist**. For the rest of the time that I have left on this planet I want to bring people together. You might think of this as a labor of love. Now, I know that love means different things to different people. But what I mean is this: I care about you because you are a fellow human being and I find it okay in my mind, in my heart, to simply say to you, I love you. And maybe that would encourage you to love me in return.

Why does the author say she loves the reader? How does this statement make you feel?

It is possible for all of us to work on this—at home, in our schools, at our jobs. It is possible to work on human relationships in every area of our lives.

nurture to care for

prejudices unfair feelings and ideas

tolerance respect for other people

humanity all people

incurable unable to change

optimist a very hopeful person

AFTER READING THE SELECTION | Apply the Skills

All Together Now by Barbara Jordan

Directions Choose the letter of the best answer or write the answer using complete sentences.

Comprehension: Identifying Facts

1. Which of the following statements is a fact?

- **A** Children learn ideas and attitudes from adults.
- **B** It is wrong to just accept the prejudices that other people have.
- **C** You should tolerate people who don't look or talk as you do.
- **D** I don't believe that this can be accomplished by government.

2. Jordan summarizes the history of race relations. What does she say has happened?

3. What does Jordan suggest that parents do?

Comprehension: Putting Ideas Together

4. Jordan tells about a problem and a solution. Which choice summarizes her solution?

- **A** People should make friends with people who are different from them.
- **B** New laws could prevent racism in jobs, homes, and schools.
- **C** People should be optimists and live together in peace.
- **D** People should remember the past.

5. Why does Jordan say that people should "start small"?

6. Jordan talks about "compassion fatigue." What does she mean? Use your own words.

Understanding Literature: Persuasive Essay

A persuasive essay tries to convince us to think, feel, or act in a certain way. Jordan expresses strong opinions. However, she thinks that most people already agree with her. Jordan keeps arguing because she wants us to think again about these ideas. Once we clarify our own opinions, we might agree to act in a different way.

7. What does Jordan ask us to think about? Give examples from the essay.

8. Jordan says, "I have yet to find a racist baby." What does she mean?

Critical Thinking

9. What is the strongest argument that Jordan makes? Why do you think so?

Thinking Creatively

10. Do you think that Jordan's ideas could work to bring more tolerance? Why or why not? Use an example from your own life.

Grammar Check

Every sentence has at least two parts: a subject and a predicate. The subject tells whom or what the sentence is about. The simple subject usually is a noun or pronoun. The predicate tells what the subject does or what is done to the subject. It can also tell what the condition of the subject is. The simple predicate is a verb or verb phrase.

Use each simple subject in a sentence with one of the simple predicates. Add other words to help each sentence make sense.

Subjects: child, mayor, gorilla, music
Predicates: gave, played, ate, ran

Vocabulary Builder

Barbara Jordan uses terms that are often heard in the context of politics and speeches. These words also have synonyms that we use every day. Rewrite each of the following sentences, using a word from the list. Be sure that the new sentences express the same meaning as before.

legislation	tolerant	fundamental
optimistic	racism	compassion

1 Freedom is a basic right.

2 The Congress passed new laws.

3 Joan is hopeful about the party's success.

4 Parents should teach their children to be free from bigotry.

5 Barbara Jordan felt love for all humanity.

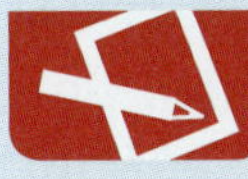

Writing on Your Own

Think about one of the author's opinions in "All Together Now." Do you agree with her opinions? Write your ideas. Support your view. Share an experience that explains your feelings and ideas. Also include ideas from Jordan's essay.

Listening and Speaking

In a small group, write a public service announcement (PSA). Explain why people should treat others fairly. Write an argument or slogan. Support it with good reasons and facts. Give everyone a turn, and listen well. Finally, share your PSA with the class.

Research and Technology

In a small group, research the civil rights movement. Use the Internet and other sources. Make a timeline to present your research. You might include topics like Martin Luther King, Jr., Rosa Parks, the March on Washington, or the Voting Rights Act of 1965.

The Real Story of a Cowboy's Life by Geoffrey C. Ward

Geoffrey C. Ward
1952–

Objectives

- To read and understand an essay about cowboy life in the 1800s
- To observe word choice and diction

About the Author

Geoffrey C. Ward writes about the past. He wants us to know what really happened. Ward is fascinated by the early days of America. He writes about the people who shaped our country. Two of his books are about Susan B. Anthony and Billy the Kid. He also wrote about the lives of writer Mark Twain and President Harry Truman. In 1989, he won the National Critics Circle Award. This was for *A First-Class Temperament: The Emergence of Franklin Roosevelt,* a biography of President Franklin D. Roosevelt.

Ward also writes scripts for films. He has worked on more than a dozen screenplays. Ward works well with a team. For example, he worked with filmmaker Ken Burns. They made documentaries about the Civil War and about baseball. These films were shown on PBS. Ward has also written about the tigers and jungles of India. In 1998 he worked with National Geographic photographer Michael Nichols. They created a book called *The Year of the Tiger.*

About the Selection

American cowboys were most active from the Civil War through the 1890s. After the Civil War, American cities grew. More people moved to America. Beef became a common source of food. Ranchers raised cattle in the open plains in the West. This wild land had few roads and trains. To get the cattle to market, cowboys drove them. That means that they made the cattle walk long distances. When people hear the word *cowboy* today, they think of a life of adventure and daring. As this essay shows, the life of a cowboy was not easy!

Literary Terms **Diction** means the proper choice of words, or saying words correctly. **Word choice** means the way that sentences are put together. Word choice is important because sometimes a writer wants to create a feeling. The right words can make writing funny or sad. In this essay, the writer's diction is different from the diction of the cowboys. The writer uses serious words. His diction sounds like a history book. The cowboys sound like real people. Their choice of words tells you about their personalities.

diction the proper choice of words, or saying words correctly

word choice words a writer uses and how they are put together

Reading on Your Own As you read, keep asking questions. For example, you can ask yourself if something is a fact. Then you can answer your question by trying to prove the fact. You can use resources like those below to check facts. As you read, you can list facts that the writer presents. Then you can write which resource could help you check the facts.

Resource	Statement in Text
almanac	
atlas or map	
biographical dictionary	
dictionary	
encyclopedia	
reliable Web site	

Writing on Your Own This essay describes what life was like for cowboys in the 1800s. Before reading the facts, write from your imagination. Imagine a day or night on a cattle drive. Write from the point of view of a cowboy. Describe the land and the animals. Describe the sounds, sights, and smells.

Vocabulary Focus Some words have more than one meaning. Compare the definition for each word below with the definitions in the selection. Then write two sentences for each word. Use all of the definitions.

discipline to train, sometimes by punishing
domestic related to the home
gauge a measuring tool, such as a yardstick

Think Before You Read Talk about cowboys with a group. What have you learned from television or movie westerns or from cowboy songs? What images do you have of the "Wild West"?

The Real Story of a Cowboy's Life

Here, *drive* means the long walk of the cattle to market.

Teddy Blue's real name was Edward C. Abbot. He was a cowboy who rode in a trail drive in the 1880s.

***Reading Strategy:* Asking Questions**

As you read, question facts and opinions. How could you check the size of Texas herds in the 19th century? What resource could you use?

A drive's success depended on **discipline** and planning. According to Teddy Blue, most Texas herds numbered about 2,000 head with a trail boss and about a dozen men in charge—though herds as large as 15,000 were also driven north with far larger escorts. The most experienced men rode "point" and "swing," at the head and sides of the long herd; the least experienced brought up the rear, riding "drag" and eating dust. At the end of the day, Teddy Blue remembered, they "would go to the water barrel . . . and rinse their mouths and cough and spit up . . . black stuff. But you couldn't get it up out of your lungs."

They had to learn to work as a team, keeping the herd moving during the day, resting peacefully at night. Twelve to fifteen miles a day was a good pace. But such steady progress could be interrupted at any time. A cowboy had to know how to **gauge** the **temperament** of his cattle, how to chase down a stray without alarming the rest of the herd, how to lasso a steer using the horn of his saddle as a tying post. His saddle was his most prized possession; it served as his chair, his workbench, his pillow at night. Being dragged to death was the most common death for a cowboy, and so the most feared occurrence on the trail was the nighttime stampede. As Teddy Blue recalled, a sound, a smell, or simply the sudden movement of a **jittery** cow could set off a whole herd.

If . . . the cattle started running—you'd hear that low rumbling noise along the ground and the men on herd wouldn't need to come in and tell you, you'd know—then you'd jump for your horse and get out there in the lead, trying

discipline order and control

gauge to measure

temperament mood

jittery nervous

to head them and get them into a mill before they scattered. It was riding at a dead run in the dark, with cut banks and prairie dog holes all around you, not knowing if the next jump would land you in a shallow grave.

A *mill* is a slow movement in a circle.

Most cowboys had guns, but rarely used them on the trail. Some outfits made them keep their weapons in the chuck wagon to **eliminate** any chance of gunplay. Charles Goodnight was still more **emphatic**: "Before starting on a trail drive, I made it a rule to draw up an article of agreement, setting forth what each man was to do. The main **clause** **stipulated** that if one shot another he was to be tried by the outfit and hanged on the spot, if found guilty. I never had a man shot on the trail."

An *outfit* is the team of cowboys who work together on the trail. Charles Goodnight was one of the most successful cattle ranchers of the 1800s.

Regardless of its **ultimate** destination, every herd had to ford a series of rivers—the Nueces, the Guadalupe, the Brazos, the Wichita, the Red.

To *ford* means to cross a river at a shallow point.

A big herd of longhorns swimming across a river, Goodnight remembered, "looked like a million floating rocking chairs," and crossing those rivers one after another, a cowboy recalled, was like climbing the rungs of a long ladder reaching north.

"After you crossed the Red River and got out on the open plains," Teddy Blue remembered, "it was sure a pretty sight to see them strung out for almost a mile, the sun shining on their horns." Initially, the land immediately north of the Red River was Indian territory, and some tribes charged tolls for herds crossing their land—payable in money or beef. But Teddy Blue remembered that the homesteaders, now pouring onto the Plains by railroad, were far more nettlesome:

> There was no love lost between settlers and cowboys on the trail. Those jay-hawkers would take up a claim right

eliminate to get rid of

emphatic forceful

clause a part of a law or contract

stipulated stated as a rule

ultimate final

Compare Teddy Blue's diction with the writer's diction.

***Reading Strategy:* Asking Questions**

Where could you find information about "Texas fever"?

Quarantine lines were marked boundaries. They were a way to try to keep disease from spreading.

A *Winchester* is a kind of rifle.

where the herds watered and charge us for water. They would plant a crop alongside the trail and plow a furrow around it for a fence, and then when the cattle got into their wheat or their garden patch, they would come **cussing** and waving a shotgun and yelling for damages. And the cattle had been coming through there when they were still raising punkins in Illinois.

The settlers' **hostility** was entirely understandable. The big herds ruined their crops, and they carried with them a disease, spread by ticks and called "Texas fever," that **devastated domestic** livestock. Kansas and other territories along the route soon established quarantine lines, called "deadlines," at the western fringe of settlement, and insisted that trail drives not cross them. Each year, as settlers continued to move in, those deadlines moved farther west.

Sometimes, farmers tried to **enforce** their own, as John Rumans, one of Charles Goodnight's hands, recalled:

Some men met us at the trail near Canyon City, and said we couldn't come in. There were fifteen or twenty of them, and they were not going to let us cross the Arkansas River. We didn't even stop. . . . Old man [Goodnight] had a shotgun loaded with buckshot and led the way, saying: "John, get over on that point with your Winchester and point these cattle in behind me." He slid his shotgun across the saddle in front of him and we did the same with our Winchesters. He rode right across, and as he rode up to them, he said: "I've monkeyed as long as I want to with you," and they fell back to the sides, and went home after we had passed.

There were few **diversions** on the trail. Most trail bosses banned liquor. Goodnight **prohibited** gambling, too. Even the songs for which cowboys became famous grew directly out of doing a job, remembered Teddy Blue:

cussing swearing

hostility not friendly

devastated ruined

domestic made of use to people

enforce to put into effect

diversions ways to have fun

prohibited refused to allow

The singing was supposed to soothe [the cattle] and it did; I don't know why, unless it was that a sound they was used to would keep them from spooking at other noises. I know that if you wasn't singing, any little sound in the night—it might be just a horse shaking himself—could make them leave the country; but if you were singing, they wouldn't notice it.

Which words give Teddy Blue's voice its personality?

The two men on guard would circle around with their horses on a walk, if it was a clear night and the cattle was bedded down and quiet, and one man would sing a verse of song, and his partner on the other side of the herd would sing another verse; and you'd go through a whole song that way. . . . "Bury Me Not on the Lone Prairie" was a great song for awhile, but . . . they sung it to death. It was a saying on the range that even the horses nickered it and the coyotes howled it; it got so they'd throw you in the creek if you sang it.

The number of cattle on the move was sometimes staggering: once, Teddy Blue rode to the top of a rise from which he could see seven herds strung out behind him; eight more up ahead; and the dust from an additional thirteen moving parallel to his. "All the cattle in the world," he remembered, "seemed to be coming up from Texas."

At last, the herds neared their destinations. After months in the saddle—often wearing the same clothes every day, eating nothing but biscuits and beef stew at the chuck wagon, drinking only water and coffee, his sole companions his fellow cowboys, his herd, and his horse—the cowboy was about to be paid for his work, and turned loose in town.

The Real Story of a Cowboy's Life by Geoffrey C. Ward

Directions Choose the letter of the best answer or write the answer using complete sentences.

Comprehension: Identifying Facts

1. Why did settlers not like cattle coming through?

A The settlers thought that the cowboys would take their land.
B The settlers were there first, long before the cowboys.
C The cattle ruined the settlers' farms and spread disease.
D The cowboys had guns and liked to gamble.

2. Describe two ways of keeping life on the trail from becoming violent.

3. How did the landscape make traveling hard for cowboys?

Comprehension: Putting Ideas Together

4. How do you know that Teddy Blue is a good source of facts?

A He was on the cattle drives himself.
B He had researched information in many books.
C He was a friend of Charles Goodnight.
D He loved his work on the trail.

5. How did people living along the cattle routes make a cowboy's life even harder?

6. The cowboys and people living along the routes disagreed. What solution would you suggest?

Understanding Literature: Diction and Word Choice

Geoffrey C. Ward uses two kinds of diction in this essay. He uses serious words. From him, you can expect mostly facts. Teddy Blue, however, has the diction of a cowboy. From him, you can expect personal memories, stories, and opinions.

7. How did Teddy Blue feel about his experiences on the trail? How do you know?

8. How do facts and opinions work together in this essay? How do they paint a full picture of the cowboy's life?

Critical Thinking

9. What feeling about cowboys did the writer want to express? Explain.

Thinking Creatively

10. Think about the description you wrote before reading the essay. How has your image of the cowboy changed?

Grammar Check

A compound subject contains two or more subjects that share a verb.

Example: Bob and I sat together at the rodeo.

A compound predicate contains two or more verbs that share a subject.

Example: The bull jumped and bucked.

Use a conjunction such as *and, as,* and *or* to join compound subjects or predicates.

Rewrite these sentences. First, find the compound subjects and compound predicates. Then replace them with subjects and predicates that are not compounds.

1 The horses and cattle slept throughout the night.

2 Many cowboys live or work near Austin, Texas.

3 The fire sizzled and crackled.

Vocabulary Builder

Practice makes perfect. Using a new word in your own writing will make you really think about the word's meaning. When you use a word often, it becomes a natural part of your own vocabulary.

For each item, write a sentence using all of the words and phrases indicated.

1 diversion; long train ride

2 gauge; progress

Writing on Your Own

Think about "The Real Story of a Cowboy's Life." Write a summary. Remember to include only the most important ideas in the essay.

Listening and Speaking

With a small group, write original lyrics to a cowboy song. You can write about a famous cowboy or about life on the trail. For examples, read the lyrics to old cowboy songs on the Internet. Write a rhyming poem with verses. Finally, read or sing your song to the class.

Research and Technology

Write a "help wanted" ad for a job working with cattle or horses. First, scan some ads in a newspaper or online. Notice the word choice in advertisements —vivid words and short phrases. Note the information that the ads list. In your ad, list the job responsibilities. Tell what education, experience, or skills are needed. Be sure to tell readers how to apply for the job, too!

Manuals

In Part 2, you are learning to ask questions as you read. This strategy can help you understand and use the information found in a manual. A manual usually asks you to follow steps. It also may use new language and terms. Here are some questions to ask as you read a manual:

- What does this unknown word mean?
- What tool do I need for this step?
- Which step did I just complete? Which one comes next?
- Did I do that step correctly? Does my work look like what the diagram shows?

About Manuals

A manual is a guide or book of instructions. Many manuals focus on how to do something. You might read about how to write a term paper or how to make a craft. Home manuals tell how to repair things around the home. Health manuals often give first-aid instructions. Many manuals include these features:

- a list of materials
- a bulleted or numbered list of steps to follow
- clearly labeled illustrations or diagrams
- safety warnings that describe "do's" and "don'ts"

On these pages, you will read pages from two different manuals. Both pages are sets of instructions. The first page is from a book about drawing. It will tell you how to draw a face. The second page is from a science textbook. It gives instructions for making an electromagnet.

Reading Skill

To use a manual, you need to understand technical terms. These words are related to the topic, but they are words you might not otherwise use. Usually, you can learn what a word means by thinking about its context. You can think about how a tool is used, or ask why a science term is mentioned. You also can look in nearby sentences for clues. Often a writer will give you definitions or context clues to help you learn a new word.

Drawing Made Easy

Chapter 6: How to Draw a Face

As you read, ask yourself questions. What does the word *proportions* mean? How do you know?

People's faces are all different. However, all faces have the same proportions, or measurements. This exercise shows how to plan and draw a face. The next time you draw a picture, use this exercise as a guide.

What You Will Need	
1 pencil	plain white paper
1 eraser	a ruler
markers	

1 Draw lightly. Draw a large oval on your paper. Imagine that this oval is a head.

2 Measure the distance from the top of the oval to the bottom. Mark the halfway point. At that point, draw a horizontal line across the oval. Mark it Line A.

3 Measure the distance from Line A to the bottom of the oval. Mark the halfway point of this measurement. Draw another horizontal line across the oval. Mark it Line B.

4 Measure the distance from Line B to the bottom of the oval. Mark this new halfway point. Draw a final horizontal line across the oval. Mark it Line C.

5 Divide Line A into five equal parts. Number the divisions, from left to right, 1 through 5. Your drawing should now look like diagram 1.

6 Now you are ready to use markers to draw your portrait. Take a minute to look at the diagram on this page. Note the placement of the features. Draw two eyes along Line A. Half of each eye should be above the line, and half below. The eyes should fit exactly in spaces 2 and 4. Spaces 1, 3, and 5 should be blank.

7 Draw the nose. Begin between the eyes, and end exactly at Line B.

8 Draw the lips. The line between the lips should be exactly on Line C.

9 Don't forget the ears! Their tops touch Line A, and their bottoms touch line B.

10 Erase any extra pencil lines. Now you can add hair, eyelashes, pupils, and eyebrows. Keep drawing until your diagram looks like a real face.

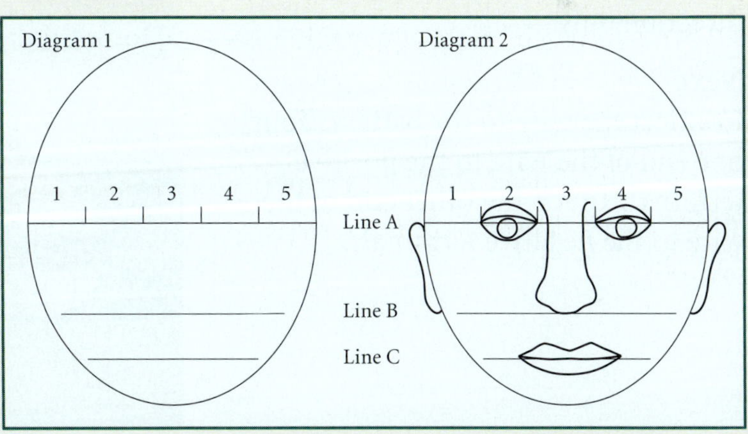

Science in the Classroom

Make an Electromagnet

Electricity and magnets are related. You can test this theory for yourself. You can turn a nail into an *electromagnet*. Before you begin, read all of the directions carefully. Collect your materials. Then follow the steps in order. You will need about 20 minutes for this experiment.

What do you think an electromagnet is? What context clues can you find?

You will need:

1 6-inch iron nail
1 "D" flashlight battery
2 feet of bendable copper wire
1 pile of paper clips and staples
1 pair needle-nosed pliers

Follow these steps.

First
Test the magnetic force of the nail. Try to pick up the paper clips and staples. Record the results.

Then
Wrap the copper wire around the nail. Leave at least five inches free on each end of the wire. When you wrap the wire, begin at one end. Wrap in one direction only.

Next
Connect the wire to the battery. Touch one end of the wire to the positive terminal. Touch the other end of the wire to the negative terminal.

Finally
Test the magnetic force of the nail. It should act as an electromagnet. It should attract metal, and pick up the staples and paper clips. Record the results.

Safety Tips
Do wear gloves when handling the wire.
Do not do this activity near water.

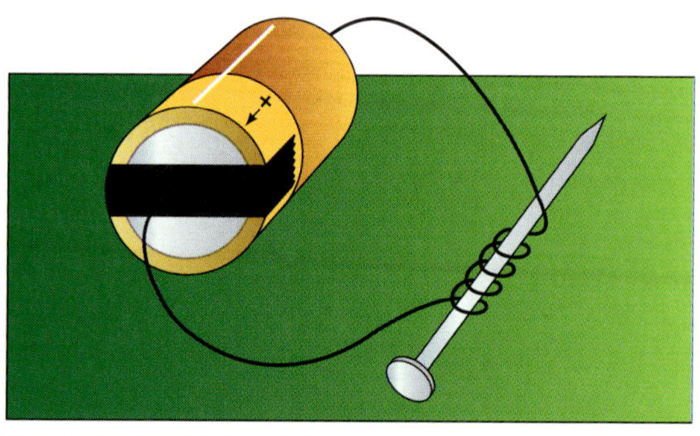

Monitor Your Progress

Directions Choose the letter of the best answer or write the answer using complete sentences.

1. What is a *portrait*?
 A a guide
 B a measurement
 C a diagram
 D a picture of a face

2. What is a *terminal*?
 A one end of a battery
 B a copper wire
 C a plug
 D the end of an experiment

3. Look at the context clues. Which choice is NOT a meaning of *magnetic force*?
 A the ability to attract metal objects
 B a force related to electricity
 C the natural force of all nails
 D a force that can pick up paper clips

4. When following instructions to draw a face, why would someone erase the pencil lines?

5. What are three questions you might ask before beginning the science experiment?

Writing on Your Own

Complete the steps in one of the manuals. Then write about the activity. Explain how the information in the manual is useful. Explain how the manual is organized, and why and when someone would want to read it. Answer any questions you think readers might have.

Walking *by Linda Hogan*

Linda Hogan
1947–

Objectives

- To read and understand a personal essay
- To compare and contrast writers' diction and ideas

About the Author

Linda Hogan, a Chickasaw Indian, grew up in Oklahoma. She is known as one of the finest American Indian poets. She has won several awards, as well. Linda is sometimes surprised by her success. She was the first person in her family to go to school. She never thought that she would be a writer or be published.

Hogan writes about issues that are important to her. She writes about the American Indian community. She writes about the lives of women. She also writes about plants and animals in nature. Hogan has written poetry, plays, stories, novels, and essays. In addition to writing, Hogan also teaches writing to college students and to groups within her tribe. Hogan is known for her understanding of nature. She helped write a book about swimming with dolphins. She talks with older members of the tribe about saving animals and plants. She even helped revise the Endangered Species Act. The government asked her to share her point of view.

About the Selection

In "Walking," Linda Hogan observes nature closely. She writes about her thoughts and feelings. Hogan has said, "I don't believe in such a thing as talent. It takes perseverance. I will do it over and over again until I get it right." In "Walking," to "get it right" meant to find music in the words. The style of this essay is close to poetry. She wants you to walk with her and to see the world through her eyes.

In "The Real Story of a Cowboy's Life," Geoffrey C. Ward writes about long cattle drives. He presents facts from history and comments from cowboys who worked on the trail. The stories convey a grand sense of space and land. They also tell about a specific time in history. Ward wants us to understand how real events affected people's lives.

Literary Terms In "The Real Story of a Cowboy's Life," cowboys used words such as *cussing* and *punkins*. Their diction showed their personalities. It showed when and where they lived. In "Walking," Linda Hogan also has unusual diction. She chooses words carefully—and sometimes she even invents words. Her words carefully describe nature. They express exact feelings. Diction also is the way that an author puts words together. Hogan writes long, poetic sentences. She does not complete every sentence.

Reading on Your Own In "The Real Story of a Cowboy's Life," most of the writer's statements were facts. The cowboys expressed most of the opinions. In "Walking," the facts and opinions are mixed together. Also, some of the facts may seem hard to believe. As you read, therefore, ask yourself:

- Does this word or phrase tell a fact, a feeling, or both?
- Can this fact be proven? How could I check it?

Writing on Your Own Hogan writes about a place where she likes to walk. Write a few sentences about a place where you like to walk. Write what you have seen, heard, felt, and thought in that place.

Vocabulary Focus Many of the vocabulary words describe the wonders of nature. Before you read, write a paragraph. Use four of the words below. Describe something you have seen in nature. If you do not know what a word means, read its definition in your text.

gully	aphids	subtle	elemental
diverse	immortal	emanating	audible

Think Before You Read In a group, review ideas from "The Real Story of a Cowboy's Life." (Remember, you will be comparing this essay to "Walking.") How did the cowboys view nature?

Reading Strategy:
Asking Questions

As you read, ask which ideas can be proven. Is this paragraph mostly fact, or mostly opinion?

When the author says "it," what is she referring to?

Reading Strategy:
Asking Questions

Where could you find information about why ants gather aphids?

It began in dark and underground weather, a slow hunger moving toward light. It grew in a dry **gully** beside the road where I live, a place where entire hillsides are sometimes yellow, windblown tides of sunflower plants. But this one was different. It was alone, and larger than the countless others who had established their lives further up the hill. This one was a traveler, a settler, and like a dream beginning in conflict, it grew where the land had been disturbed.

I saw it first in early summer. It was a green and sleeping bud, raising itself toward the sun. Ants worked around the unopened bloom, gathering **aphids** and sap. A few days later, it was a tender young flower, soft and new, with a pale green center and a troop of silver gray insects climbing up and down the stalk.

Over the summer this sunflower grew into a plant of incredible beauty, turning its face daily toward the sun in the most **subtle** of ways, the black center of it dark and alive with a deep blue light, as if flint had sparked an **elemental** fire there, in community with rain, mineral, mountain air, and sand.

gully a ditch

aphids tiny garden bugs

subtle hard to detect

elemental made of the elements

As summer changed from green to yellow there were new visitors daily: the late-winged insects, the bees whose legs were fat with pollen, and grasshoppers with their clattering wings and desperate hunger. There were other lives I missed, lives too small or hidden to see. It was as if this plant with its host of lives was a society, one in which moment by moment, depending on light and moisture, there was great and **diverse** change.

Compare the author's diction with Teddy Blue's diction.
The author invented the word *late-winged* to tell you that these insects just grew their wings.

There were changes in the next larger world around the plant as well. One day I rounded a bend in the road to find the disturbing sight of a dead horse, black and still against a hillside, eyes rolled back. Another day I was nearly lifted by a wind and sandstorm so fierce and hot that I had to wait for it to pass before I could return home. On this day the

***Reading Strategy:* Asking Questions**
Which word in this sentence shows the writer's opinion?

diverse varied

Birds eat sunflower seeds. Then they drop some seeds in new places, where they may grow.

faded dry petals of the sunflower were swept across the land. That was when the birds arrived to carry the new seeds to another future.

In this one plant, in one summer season, a drama of need and survival took place. Hungers were filled. Insects coupled. There was escape, exhaustion, and death. Lives touched down a moment and were gone.

How does the author's word choice show her personality?

I was an outsider. I only watched. I never learned the sunflower's golden language or the tongues of its citizens. I had a small understanding, nothing more than a shallow observation of the flower, insects, and birds. But they knew what to do, how to live. An old voice from somewhere, **gene** or cell, told the plant how to **evade** the pull of gravity and find its way upward, how to open. It was instinct, **intuition,** necessity. A certain knowing directed the seed-bearing birds on paths to ancestral homelands they had never seen. They believed it. They followed.

***Reading Strategy:* Asking Questions**

Where could you research these facts about bamboo?

There are other **summons** and calls, some even more mysterious than those commandments to birds or those survival journeys of insects. In bamboo plants, for instance, with their thin green canopy of light and golden stalks that creak in the wind. Once a century, all of a certain kind of bamboo flower on the same day. Whether they are in Malaysia or in a greenhouse in Minnesota makes no difference, nor does the age or size of the plant. They flower. Some current of an inner language passes between them, through space and separation, in ways we cannot explain in our language. They are all, somehow, one plant, each with a share of communal knowledge.

gene the part of living things that passes along traits

evade to avoid or escape

intuition knowledge that comes from feeling and sensing

summons a notice to appear in court

John Hay, in *The **Immortal** Wilderness*, has written: "There are occasions when you can hear the mysterious language of the Earth, in water, or coming through the trees, **emanating** from the mosses, seeping through the undercurrents of the soil, but you have to be willing to wait and receive."

John Hay is a well-known environmental writer.

Sometimes I hear it talking. The light of the sunflower was one language, but there are others, more **audible**. Once, in the redwood forest, I heard a beat, something like a drum or heart coming from the ground and trees and wind. That underground current stirred a kind of knowing inside me, a kinship and longing, a dream barely remembered that disappeared back to the body.

***Reading Strategy:* Asking Questions**

Is Hay's statement mostly fact, or mostly opinion?

immortal never dying

emanating coming out from a place

audible loud or clear enough to be heard

Another time, there was the booming voice of an ocean storm thundering from far out at sea, telling about what lived in the distance, about the rough water that would arrive, wave after wave revealing the disturbance at center.

Ancient stone sundials have been found in Greece, Rome, and Egypt.

Tonight I walk. I am watching the sky. I think of the people who came before me and how they knew the placement of stars in the sky, watched the moving sun long and hard enough to witness how a certain angle of light touched a stone only once a year. Without written records, they knew the gods of every night, the small, fine details of the world around them and of immensity above them.

Walking, I can almost hear the redwoods beating. And the oceans are above me here, rolling clouds, heavy and dark, considering snow. On the dry, red road, I pass the place of the sunflower, that dark and secret location where creation took place. I wonder if it will return this summer, if it will multiply and move up to the other stand of flowers in a territorial struggle.

It's winter and there is smoke from the fires. The square, lighted windows of houses are fogging over. It is a world of elemental attention, of all things working together, listening to what speaks in the blood. Whichever road I follow, I walk in the land of many gods, and they love and eat one another.

The author states this last opinion as if it is a fact. Why?

Walking, I am listening to a deeper way. Suddenly all my ancestors are behind me. Be still, they say. Watch and listen. You are the result of the love of thousands.

COMPARING LITERARY WORKS | **Apply the Skills**

Walking *by Linda Hogan*

Directions Choose the letter of the best answer or write the answer using complete sentences.

Comprehension: Identifying Facts

1. What kind of animal or plant does "Walking" focus on?
- **A** aphids
- **B** cattle
- **C** sunflowers
- **D** bamboo

2. What activity is Linda Hogan doing in this essay?
- **A** walking and thinking in wintertime
- **B** walking in the springtime beside a sunflower field
- **C** walking in her garden in early summer
- **D** researching sunflowers and bamboo

3. What society does Linda Hogan talk about? What society does Geoffrey C. Ward talk about?

4. What are four kinds of insects that gathered in the flower?

5. What surprising thing happens with certain bamboo plants?

6. What is one thing Linda Hogan wonders about? What is one thing a cowboy wonders about?

7. Why does Linda Hogan go walking?

8. Both cowboys and Linda Hogan found beauty in the land. Name one thing they each found beautiful.

9. What is the author's reason for writing "Walking"?

10. What is the author's reason for writing "The Real Story of a Cowboy's Life"?

Comprehension: Putting Ideas Together

11. Which sentence best states one of Linda Hogan's opinions about nature?
- **A** Nature has a language and wisdom that we cannot understand.
- **B** It was a pretty sight to see cattle strung out for almost a mile.
- **C** It is winter, and there is smoke from the fires.
- **D** There are as many stars as there are sunflowers.

12. Think about the writing in "The Real Story of a Cowboy's Life." How is the writing in "Walking" different?
- **A** It does not tell any facts or information.
- **B** It states more facts.
- **C** It is more poetic and personal.
- **D** It expresses mostly opinions.

***Comparing* continued on next page**

Walking by Linda Hogan

13. How might a cowboy feel about the way Linda Hogan talks about nature?

14. How did Geoffrey C. Ward use facts in his story?

15. Who talked in "Walking"? Who did the talking affect, and how?

16. In both essays, nature is compared to something else. Give an example from each essay.

17. How well does Linda Hogan know nature? How well did a cowboy know nature? Explain.

18. How far does Linda Hogan travel on her walk? How is her journey different from a cowboy's journey?

19. Which essay uses the word *spooking*? What do you think this word means?

20. How do both authors talk about wind and sandstorms?

Understanding Literature: Diction and Word Choice

Word choice is closely linked to what an author wants to say. As you compare "Walking" and "The Real Story of a Cowboy's Life," look carefully at the diction. They all use different styles.

21. How does diction from the first line of each story tell you about what you will read?

22. Teddy Blue said that something in nature "was sure a pretty sight." What words might Linda Hogan use to express this idea?

23. Why is *spooking* a good descriptive word?

24. When Linda Hogan writes about bamboo, she does not finish some sentences. Why?

25. Why do both writers not use the same diction?

Critical Thinking

26. How does it make you feel when Hogan doesn't finish her sentences?

27. What do you think Hogan would say about cowboys singing for their cattle?

28. How do these essays show *similar* ways of thinking?

Thinking Creatively

29. Think about both selections. What is one opinion you agree with? Why?

30. How would you like to travel in nature—like a cowboy, or like Linda Hogan? Why?

Grammar Check

A comma signals a brief pause. These examples show several uses of the comma. Use a comma these different ways:

between two clauses in a sentence:
The light of the sunflower was one language, but there are others.

after an introductory phrase or clause:
Once a century, all of a certain kind of bamboo flower on the same day.

between items in a series:
I had a small understanding of the flower, insects, and birds.

Write three sentences that use commas. Use commas in each of the ways above.

Vocabulary Builder

Some of the words in Linda Hogan's essay are technical terms. They are words used in science. Knowing more about them will increase your understanding of the essay. With a partner, look up the following words in an encyclopedia. Talk about them until you know what they mean.

aphids	sunflower	mineral
pollen	canopy	redwood
forest	elements	gene

Writing on Your Own

Write a one-page essay. Compare and contrast the essays "Walking" and "The Real Story of a Cowboy's Life." Answer these questions:

- How did each author choose words to explain and express their ideas?
- How were the opinions in the essays alike? How were the opinions different?

Listening and Speaking

In a small group, share your ideas about these two essays. Choose a paragraph from one of the essays. Tell your group why you like that paragraph. Talk about the facts and opinions in the writing. Also tell what you like about the author's choice of words.

Research and Technology

With your class, list some of the facts written by Geoffrey C. Ward and Linda Hogan. Then work with a partner. Research one of the facts. Use the Internet for your research. You can print out photos from Web sites. You even may find a short video clip to share with your class. Share what you have learned with your class.

Unit 3 SPELLING WORKSHOP

Tools for Checking Spelling

It can be hard to figure out whether you have spelled certain words correctly. There are reference tools that can help you.

Computer Spell-Checkers

Most word-processing programs contain a spell-checking feature. After you type a word incorrectly, the program will mark it. Here are a few things to remember about spell-checking programs, though:

- They cannot tell you if you used the wrong homophone (a word that sounds like another word).
- They cannot tell you if you typed the wrong word by mistake. (For example, they would call *in* correct, even if you meant *an, on, or it.*)

Dictionaries

Use a dictionary for spelling by following these steps:

- **Check the first letter of a word.** If you wrote *rench* and it looks wrong, think of other spellings of that *r* sound.
- **Check the other letters.** Once you spell the first sound right, sound out the rest of the word.

Sound	Some Ways to Spell It
"k"	**k**ennel, **c**arrot, **ch**aracter
"j"	**j**ump, **g**emstone, le**dge**
"g"	**g**o, **gu**est, **gh**ost
"s"	**s**even, **c**enter, **sc**ene
"f"	**f**orget, **ph**rase, tou**gh**
"n"	**n**ever, **kn**ife, **gn**aw

Practice

Match each phonetic spelling with one or more words from the Word List.

1. rēl
2. nōt
3. rēth
4. rông
5. rīt
6. no͞o

Word List
knew
new
note
knot
not
write
right
wrong
wreath
real

Unit 3 SUMMARY

Unit 3 introduced you to many forms of nonfiction. An expository essay explains facts. A reflective essay shares feelings and ideas. A persuasive essay asks you to think and respond. Biographies give you insight into people's lives.

The topics in this unit also were very different. You read about outer space, flowering bamboo, revolutions, and singing cattle to sleep. You read about the lives of American Indians, Latina heroines, astronauts, and cowboys.

The theme of Unit 3 may be best expressed by Barbara Jordan. She said, "I care about you because you are a fellow human being." The other essays showed how much people care. Robert Zimmerman shared his excitement about astronauts. Emma Trelles told you about women who fought—and sometimes died—for human rights. Alongside these real-life stories, you read writers' feelings and thoughts about caring. Chief Dan George asked you to love your brother. Geoffrey C. Ward and Linda Hogan told you how much they care about the world.

As you read these essays, you looked closely at writing and language. You learned how writers choose words and put them together. You thought about how words tell details and ideas, facts, and opinions. Now you know more about the different kinds of nonfiction writing.

Selections

- "Life Without Gravity" by Robert Zimmerman tells how astronauts live with low gravity in space. He explains how human bodies react to this strange environment.
- "I Am a Native of North America" by Chief Dan George argues for acceptance. The author compares his Salish culture to the modern world. Then he urges people to share a greater respect and love for each other.
- "For the Love of Country" by Emma Trelles tells about five strong women. These heroines lived in the Americas under Spanish rule. They wanted to make a difference, and they improved life for themselves and others.
- "All Together Now" by Barbara Jordan tells the history of the civil rights movement. Then she explains how we can end racism by starting at home.
- "The Real Story of a Cowboy's Life" by Geoffrey C. Ward tells about American cowboys in the 1800s. He describes the rules and hard times of the trail.
- "Walking" by Linda Hogan shares thoughts about nature as the writer looks at a sunflower.

Unit 3 REVIEW

Directions Choose the letter of the best answer or write the answer using complete sentences.

Comprehension: Identifying Facts

1. Which essay is a reflective essay?
- **A** "Life Without Gravity"
- **B** "All Together Now"
- **C** "I Am a Native of North America"
- **D** "For the Love of Country"

2. What did the five women in "For the Love of Country" have in common?

3. Which two authors expressed strong opinions about love and equality?

4. What are two problems you learned about in "Life Without Gravity"?

5. What are three things in nature that Linda Hogan discusses in her essay?

Comprehension: Putting Ideas Together

6. Which elements created hard times for a cowboy?
- **A** the cattle, weather, and horses
- **B** the landscape, weather, and settlers
- **C** ranchers, laws, and guns
- **D** other cowboys, rivers, and singing

7. Why is "Life Without Gravity" called an expository essay?

8. How are the messages from Chief Dan George and Linda Hogan alike?

9. Why are the women in "For the Love of Country" remembered?

10. How would you summarize Barbara Jordan's ideas?

Understanding Literature: Diction and Word Choice

In Part 2, you compared the diction and word choice in two selections. You saw how a manual and an expository essay differ in language and sentence length. You learned that every writer chooses words and sentences for his or her purpose.

11. How do the words and sentences in "Life Without Gravity" help you trust the writer?

12. Name three examples of poetic description in "Walking."

13. Which three authors speak the most personally?

14. Imagine that Teddy Blue wrote a speech against discrimination. What are two statements that he might use?

15. In which essay did you like the diction best? Why?

Critical Thinking

16. Which essay in this unit made you think carefully about your own ideas and opinions? Explain.

17. Why do people write essays? Use examples from the unit in your answer.

18. Choose two essays that talk about people's lives. How are the characters different? How are they alike?

Thinking Creatively

19. Which author from this unit would you have liked to meet? Why did you choose that author?

20. If you were asked to add another essay to this unit, what would it be about? Why?

Speak and Listen

Respond to one essay from this unit by writing a letter to its author. Talk about the main idea of the essay. Then write your own feelings and thoughts. You can tell him or her new information about the topic. Then read your letter aloud to the class.

Writing on Your Own

Write an essay on any topic. Try to copy the diction of one of the Unit 3 authors. You might use poetic descriptions, cowboy slang, or emotional arguments. Focus on putting the words together. Use the vocabulary list to remind you how the writer writes. Write and edit a draft. Ask a partner to review it; then rewrite the draft.

Beyond Words

Work with a group to create a pantomime based on one of the essays. A pantomime is a play without words. Begin by choosing a story to tell. You could act out one of the stories told in Unit 3. You could invent a story that shows a belief or idea from an essay. Create a five-minute play that shares the story without using words. Practice your pantomime and perform it for the class.

Test-Taking Tip

Always read test directions more than once. Underline words that tell how many examples or items you must provide.

Exposition: Comparison-and-Contrast Essay

A comparison-and-contrast essay tells how things are alike and different. It is about two or more related subjects. It can help you to decide which shoes to wear or which bicycle to buy. Follow these steps to write your own comparison-and-contrast essay.

Assignment Write a comparison-and-contrast essay. You can help readers make a decision. You can help them see old things in a fresh way.

What to Include Your expository essay should have these elements:

- a discussion of two or more things that are related but not the same
- details that show similarities and differences
- clear organization of details
- a snappy introduction and a strong, memorable conclusion
- error-free writing

Using the Form
You may use elements of this form in these types of writing:
- persuasive essays
- advertisements
- reviews
- journals

Prewriting

Choosing Your Topic

Use one of these strategies to list topics. Then, choose a topic from your list.

- **Quicklist** Make three columns. In the first column, list products you have bought or activities you decided to do. In the second column, describe each choice. In the third column, write another choice.
- **BUT Chart** Write the word BUT down the center of your paper. On the left, list items with something in common. On the right, list differences among the items.

Narrowing Your Topic

You can use these strategies to narrow your topic.

- Describe it to someone who is not familiar with it.
- Explain what you can do with it, on it, or to it.
- Analyze it by breaking it into parts.
- Argue for or against it, explaining good and bad points.

Six Traits of Writing:
Ideas message, details, and purpose

Gathering Details

Use a Venn diagram to organize your details. (See Appendix A for a description of this graphic organizer.) Draw two large circles that overlap in the middle. Write details about one subject on the left side. Write details about the other subject on the right side. Where the circles overlap, write details that the subjects have in common.

Writing Your Draft

Shaping Your Writing

Organize the body of your draft. There are two main ways to organize a comparison-and-contrast essay. Choose the one that works better for your topic and purpose.

- **Block Method** First, write all the details about one of your subjects. Then tell all the details about your next subject. Use this method when you write about more than two subjects. Use it if your topic is complicated.
- **Point-by-Point Method** Discuss one way in which both subjects are similar or different. Then discuss another point, and so on.

Block Method

A. Theater
 1. amount of variety
 2. intensity
 3. realism
B. Television
 1. amount of variety
 2. intensity
 3. realism

Point-by-Point Comparison

A. Amount of Variety
 1. Theater
 2. Television
B. Intensity
 1. Theater
 2. Television
C. Realism
 1. Theater
 2. Television

Providing Elaboration

One thing elaboration can mean is providing helpful details. Sometimes details are the most interesting parts! Use the SEE method to elaborate.

- State your main idea in every paragraph. This helps you stay on topic.

- Support the idea with a proof or explanation.
- Add examples where helpful.

Six Traits of Writing: ***Organization*** order, ideas tied together

Clarify relationships among details and ideas. Use words and phrases that make the transitions clear. To show comparisons, use *also, just as, like,* and *similarly.* To show contrasts, use *although, but, however, on the other hand, whereas,* and *while.*

Revising

Revising Your Overall Structure

Make your essay interesting. To grab and hold your reader's attention, use one or more of these strategies:

- Sharpen your introduction so that your readers will want to know more. Add a picture or a surprising comparison or question.
- Add details that are colorful and important.
- Add words that stress the similarities and differences.
- At the end of your essay, add a strong statement or ask a question. Remind your readers why your ideas are important.

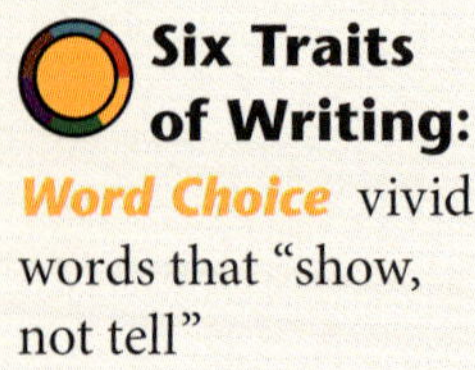

Six Traits of Writing: ***Word Choice*** vivid words that "show, not tell"

Revising Your Sentences

Avoid repetition. Perhaps you want to repeat a point but add something slightly different the second time. To do this, combine the two sentences. Then you can add ideas without repeating yourself.

Focus on empty language. Take out or change words that do not add value or meaning. You might cut words such as *very* and *really.* You might also cut clauses such as *I think, I said,* and *you know.*

Peer Review: Read your revised draft to a classmate. Ask your partner whether you repeated information. Together, look for ways to make the writing better.

Editing and Proofreading

Review your draft, and correct any errors.

Focus on Commas: Remember what you learned in Unit 3 about three uses of the comma:

- between two clauses in a sentence
- after an introductory phrase or clause
- between items in a series

Look for those uses in your writing; then check your use of commas.

Six Traits of Writing:
Conventions correct grammar, spelling, and mechanics

Publishing and Presenting

You might share your writing in one of these ways:

Be a consumer watchdog. Does your essay contain information useful to consumers? If so, form a Consumer Information Panel. Read your essays with a group, and use pictures in your presentation.

Submit your essay to a magazine that focuses on your topic. Look in the magazine to find out how and where to send your work.

Reflecting on Your Writing

Writer's Journal Write your thoughts about writing a comparison-and-contrast essay. Answer these questions:

- What was the most important improvement you made when revising?
- Did the writing process lead you to new ideas about your topic? Explain.

People Flying
Peter Sickles

Unit 4 Poetry

Poets express ideas, share memories, create images, or entertain. Poets must pay close attention to both the sound and the meaning of each word. They use writing tools that help them get the most out of every word. Poetry is known for creating powerful or beautiful impressions with words.

In this unit, you will meet poets from different lands and different eras.

Unit 4 Selections	Page

"I would define, in brief, the poetry of words as the rhythmical creation of Beauty."

—Edgar Allan Poe
The Poetic Principle, 1850

Unit 4 About Poetry

Characteristics of Poetry

Poems are usually divided into lines and then grouped into **stanzas.** A stanza is a group of lines that forms a unit and often has the same rhythm and rhyme pattern.

Figurative language is writing or speech not meant to be understood exactly as it is written. Writers use figurative language to express ideas in vivid or imaginative ways.

- A **metaphor** is a figure of speech that makes a comparison but does not use *like* or *as.* Metaphors often point to a likeness between two unlike things:

  The house was a zoo this morning!

- **Personification** is giving characters such as animals or objects the characteristics or qualities of humans.

  The cars growled in the traffic.

- A **simile** is a figure of speech in which two things are compared using a phrase that includes the words *like* or *as.*

  She is as slow as a turtle.

- A **symbol** is something that represents something else. For example, a dove is a common sign for peace.

Sound devices add a quality of music to poetry. Writers use these devices to add to a poem's mood and meaning.

- **Alliteration** is repeating sounds by using words whose beginning sounds are the same.
- **Repetition** is using a word, phrase, or image more than once, for emphasis.
- **Assonance** is repeating sounds by using words with the same vowel sounds.
- **Consonance** is the repetition of consonant sounds usually within the context of several words.
- **Onomatopoeia** is using words that sound like their meaning.
- **Rhyme** is words that end with the same or similar sound.
- **Meter** is the repetition of stressed and unstressed syllables in a line of poetry.

Forms of Poetry

Narrative poetry is a poem that tells a story. Narrative poems are like short stories because they often both have characters and a plot.

Haiku poetry is a form of Japanese poetry having three lines with five syllables in the first, seven in the second, and five in the third.

Free Verse poetry does not have a strict rhyming pattern or regular line length and uses actual speech patterns for the rhythms of sound.

Lyric poetry is a short poem that expresses a person's emotions or feelings.

A **ballad** is a simple song that often uses a refrain and sometimes uses rhyme and is passed from person to person.

Concrete poetry is a poem made to look like the writer's subject. The writer makes the lines of the poem into a picture on the page.

A **limerick** is a humorous five-line poem in which the first, second, and fifth lines, and third and fourth lines, rhyme.

A **rhyming couplet** is a pair of rhyming lines, usually the same meter and length.

Reading Strategy:
Inferencing

Readers use inferencing to find meaning in a text when the meaning is not directly stated. Another way to describe inferencing is "drawing conclusions." This is connecting details to make decisions or form opinions about a text—to make meaning of a text. Drawing conclusions is just another term for inferencing.

What You Know + What You Read =
Inference (Draw Conclusions)

Literary Terms

poetry literature in verse form that usually has rhythm and paints powerful or beautiful impressions with words

lyric poem a short poem that expresses a person's emotions or feelings

concrete poem a poem shaped to look like its subject

haiku a form of Japanese poetry having three lines with five syllables in the first, seven in the second, and five in the third

figurative language writing or speech not meant to be understood exactly as it is written

simile a figure of speech in which two things are compared using a phrase that includes the words *like* or *as*

metaphor a figure of speech that makes a comparison but does not use *like* or *as*

personification giving characters such as animals or objects the characteristics or qualities of humans

symbol something that represents something else

narrative poem a poem that tells a story

suspense a quality that makes a reader uncertain or nervous about what will happen next

The Rider | *Seal* | *Haiku*

About the Authors and Selections

Naomi Shihab Nye
1952–

William Jay Smith
1918–

As a teenager, Naomi Shihab Nye probably felt the loneliness she describes in this poem. She was born in St. Louis, Missouri, to a Palestinian father and an American mother. When Nye was 14, her family moved from Missouri to the Middle East. Though she now enjoys learning about her Arab background, the move was not easy. Nye has published books of poetry as well as books for children. In "The Rider," the speaker wonders if one can ride fast enough to escape loneliness.

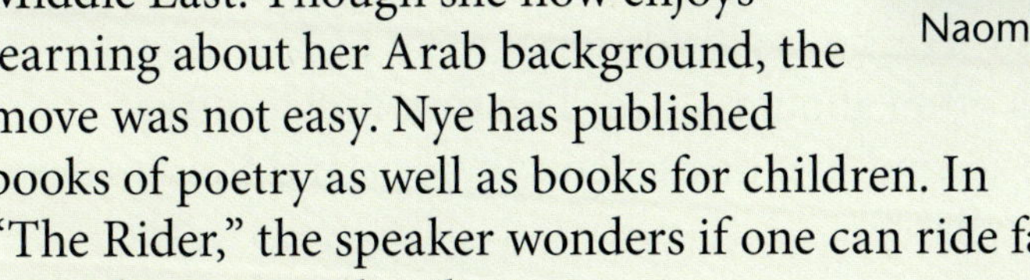

William Jay Smith was born in Winnfield, Louisiana. He has taught college students, written poetry and essays, and translated Russian and French poetry. He even served in the Vermont State Legislature for two years. In the poem "Seal," Smith uses a seal's shape to describe the animal as it dives and swims through the water. Like "Seal," many of Smith's poems show that poetry can be pure and simple—and fun.

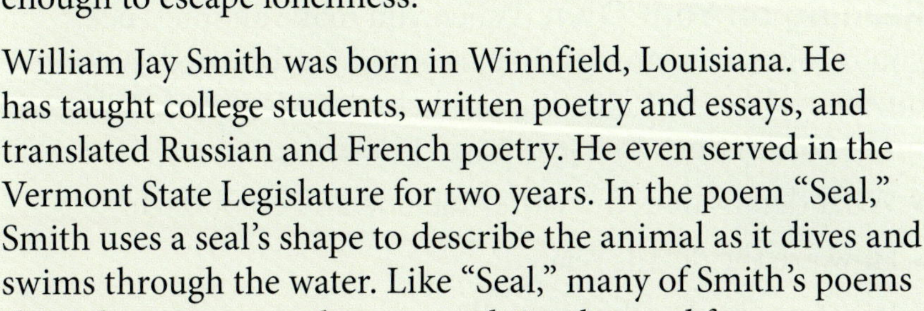

Buson
1716–1784

Japanese poet Buson was not only a skilled writer of haiku but also a talented painter. His poetry shows his love of color and interest in images. At age 36, Buson became the "master" at the haiku school in Kyoto, Japan. When a student asked him the secret of haiku, Buson answered, ["Use the commonplace to escape the commonplace."] The three haiku by Buson express different images and feelings: a pond with ducks, a forest, and a setting moon. In addition, the haiku express feelings of scorn, fear, and calm.

***Before Reading* continued on next page**

Objectives

- To read and understand a lyric poem
- To read and understand a concrete poem
- To read and understand haiku

The Rider | Seal | Haiku

poetry literature in verse form that usually has rhythm and paints powerful or beautiful impressions with words

lyric poem a short poem that expresses a person's emotions or feelings

concrete poem a poem shaped to look like its subject

haiku a form of Japanese poetry having three lines with five syllables in the first, seven in the second, and five in the third

Literary Terms There are many different forms of **poetry.** Poetry is a type of literature in verse form that usually has rhythm and paints powerful images or beautiful impressions with words. A poet will follow different rules depending on the structure of a poem. A **lyric poem** expresses the poet's thoughts and feelings about a single image or idea in vivid, musical language. In a **concrete poem,** the poet arranges the letters and lines to create a visual image that suggests the poem's subject. **Haiku** is a traditional form of Japanese poetry that is often about nature. The first line has five syllables, the second line has seven syllables, and the third line has five syllables.

Reading on Your Own When you make an inference, you recognize meanings that are not directly stated. Asking questions like the following can help you identify details and make connections that lead to an inference.

- What details does the writer include and emphasize?
- How are the details related?
- What do the details mean all together?

Writing on Your Own Each of these poems expresses a poet's observations or feelings in a creative way. Think about what you know about the way poems look and sound. Then, in a brief paragraph, tell why writers might choose to put their thoughts in a poem rather than in prose or drama.

Vocabulary Focus Poets use verbs that tell about precise movement. Use each of these verbs from the poems in a sentence that shows its meaning: *pedaling, darts, swerve, plunges, utter, drift.* Use a dictionary if it helps.

Think Before You Read How is reading a poem different from reading a story? Pay attention to how you read the poems in this section.

The Rider

A boy told me
if he rollerskated fast enough
his loneliness couldn't catch up to him,

the best reason I ever heard
for trying to be a champion.

What I wonder tonight
pedaling hard down King William Street
is if it translates to bicycles.

A victory! To leave your loneliness
panting behind you on some street corner
while you float free into a cloud of sudden **azaleas,**
luminous pink **petals** that have
never felt loneliness,
no matter how slowly they fell.

—Naomi Shihab Nye

As you read, think about the elements that make this a lyric poem.

***Reading Strategy:* Inferencing**

Who is the speaker? What is the speaker doing?

Notice the contrast between the speed of the rider and the slowness of the petals.

azaleas flowering shrubs or their flowers

luminous giving off light

petals colored parts of a flower

Seal

See how he dives
From the rocks with a zoom!
See how he darts
Through his watery room
Past crabs and eels
And green seaweed,
Past fluffs of sandy
Minnow feed!
See how he swims
With a **swerve** and a twist,
A flip of the flipper,
A flick of the wrist!
Quicksilver-quick,
Softer than spray,
Down he plunges
And sweeps away;
Before you can think,
Before you can **utter**
Words like "Dill pickle"
Or "Apple butter,"
Back up he swims
Past Sting Ray and Shark,
Out with a zoom,
A whoop, a bark;
Before you can say
Whatever you wish,
He plops at your side
With a mouthful of fish!

—William Jay Smith

Why might the poet have arranged the lines of the poem this way?

minnow a small fish

swerve to turn quickly

quicksilver a silver metal

utter to say

Haiku

O foolish ducklings,
you know my old green pond is
watched by a **weasel!**

Deep in a windless
wood, not one leaf dares to move. . . .
Something is afraid.

After the moon sets,
slow through the forest, shadows
drift and disappear.

—Buson

***Reading Strategy:* Inferencing**

What is the speaker in the first haiku worried about?

As you read, count the syllables. How does this poem conform to the rules of haiku?

weasel a small mammal that eats rats, mice, birds, and eggs

AFTER READING THE SELECTION | Apply the Skills

The Rider | Seal | Haiku

Directions Choose the letter of the best answer or write the answer using complete sentences.

Comprehension: Identifying Facts

1. What two sports are discussed in "The Rider"?

A skating and bicycling
B bicycling and running
C skateboarding and running
D running and skating

2. Name six words that describe the movement of the seal in "Seal."

3. In the first haiku, what does the speaker warn the ducklings about?

Comprehension: Putting Ideas Together

4. What do the sports in "The Rider" have in common?

A equipment
B speed
C simplicity
D history

5. How would you describe the mood of "Seal"?

6. How does the speaker in the first haiku feel about the ducks?

Understanding Literature: Lyric Poetry, Concrete Poetry, and Haiku

As you have seen, poetry comes in different forms. Lyric poetry expresses a poet's thoughts and feelings in musical language. It is the most common form of poetry. Concrete poetry makes a picture using the words on the page. It is a modern form of poetry that adds fun and meaning to the look of the poem. Haiku is based on a very old, traditional Japanese form. Haiku has three lines, each with a set number of syllables. It always involves a single speaker thinking about something or making an observation. Much haiku has to do with the natural world.

7. What makes "Seal" a concrete poem?

8. Explain how Buson's three haiku follow the rules for that form.

Critical Thinking

9. Do you think these poems are meaningful for people your age? Why or why not?

Thinking Creatively

10. Which poem in this collection do you like best? Why?

Grammar Check

An infinitive is a verb form that acts as a noun, an adjective, or an adverb. An infinitive usually begins with the word *to*. These examples show infinitives.

Examples: To learn is her goal. (noun)
She is the one to see. (adjective)
Everyone waited to hear. (adverb)

Copy the infinitive from each sentence. Then use each infinitive in a new sentence.

1 To run on a slippery trail is dangerous.

2 The winter seemed to drag on.

3 The athletes tried to do what the coach asked of them.

Vocabulary Builder

The word *transform* contains the prefix *trans-*, which means "across" or "through." Good readers transform words into ideas or pictures in their mind. Words that contain the prefix *trans-* will have something to do with across or through.

Use your knowledge of the prefix *trans-* to predict the meaning of each of the following words. Then, check the word's definition in a dictionary. Use each word in a sentence of your own.

1 transmit
2 transfer
3 transition
4 transient
5 translate

Writing on Your Own

Write a lyric poem, concrete poem, or haiku to share your thoughts in new ways.

- Pick a subject that interests you. Put the subject in the center of a piece of paper. Create a cluster diagram around it.
- Brainstorm for details—vivid descriptions, action words, thoughts, and feelings—to put into the cluster diagram.
- Review the characteristics of each poetic form. Use your diagram to draft your poem. Then choose a title.

Listening and Speaking

Find a recording of a poet reading his or her own lyric poems. Listen to one or more of the poems. Give a brief presentation to your group. Tell what you like about the poet's reading.

Research and Technology

Use a word-processing program and a drawing program to write, format, and publish a poem. If you wrote a poem for Writing on Your Own, you can format that one. Include illustrations that help readers relate to your poem.

Life | The Courage That My Mother Had | Loo-Wit

Naomi Long Madgett
1923–

Edna St. Vincent Millay
1892–1950

Wendy Rose
1948–

Objectives

- To read and understand a lyric poem
- To recognize and understand figurative language—simile, metaphor, personification, symbol

About the Authors and Selections

Naomi Long Madgett first discovered poetry at the age of seven or eight, while reading in her father's study. She was most inspired by poets Alfred, Lord Tennyson and Langston Hughes, though their styles are quite different. Madgett once said, "I would rather be a good poet than anything else." Her desire to write good poetry has led to nine collections of poems. In "Life," the speaker explains that life is like a pocket watch that entertains an infant and then winds down.

Edna St. Vincent Millay's mother was a hard-working nurse. She gave her daughters a sense of independence and a love for reading. Millay's mother had a powerful influence on young Edna. Edna grew up to be a widely published writer and political activist. Born in Rockland, Maine, Millay published her first poem at the age of 14. She was the first woman to win the Pulitzer Prize for poetry. In "The Courage That My Mother Had," Millay honors her late mother. She wishes that she had her mother's strength and courage.

Wendy Rose was born in Oakland, California, to a Hopi father and a Scots-Irish-Miwok mother. Rose has worked to protect American Indian burial sites from developers. She is also a painter, who illustrated some of her own books. "Loo-Wit" is based on legends of the Cowlitz people of Washington State. In "Loo-Wit," the eruption of Mount St. Helens is compared to an old woman's waking up. The sound of the eruption is described as her singing.

Literary Terms **Figurative language** is language that is not meant to be taken literally. Writers use figures of speech to express ideas in vivid and imaginative ways. Common figures of speech include the following: **simile, metaphor, personification,** and **symbol.** A simile is a figure of speech in which two things are compared using a phrase that includes the words *like* or *as: My love is like a red, red rose.* A metaphor makes a comparison but does not use *like* or *as: Life is a bowl of cherries.* Personification gives characters such as animals or objects the characteristics or qualities of humans: *The stars were dancing heel to toe.* A symbol is something that represents something else. For example, a dove is a symbol of peace.

Reading on Your Own An inference is a decision or opinion that you reach after considering the details in a literary work. Connecting the details can help you make inferences as you read. As you read, find important details. Then, look at the details together. Use them to make inferences about the poem or the speaker.

Writing on Your Own In “Loo-Wit,” poet Wendy Rose describes a volcano in an unusual way. Write several sentences of your own that describe a volcano. Try to express what a viewer might see, hear, and feel.

Vocabulary Focus Use your understanding of prefixes to help figure out the meaning of unfamiliar words. Think about the meaning of the prefix in each of these words: *unlock, undo.* That will help you understand unravel in “Loo-Wit.” Now think about the meaning of the prefix in these words: *disconnect, displace.* That will help you understand *dislodge.*

Think Before You Read Based on their titles, which poem do you expect to like best? Why?

figurative language writing or speech not meant to be understood exactly as it is written

simile a figure of speech in which two things are compared using a phrase that includes the words *like* or *as*

metaphor a figure of speech that makes a comparison but does not use *like* or *as*

personification giving characters such as animals or objects the characteristics or qualities of humans

symbol something that represents something else

Life

As you read, what type of figurative language does the poet use to describe life?

***Reading Strategy:* Inferencing**

How is a ticking watch like life?

Life is but a toy that swings on a bright gold chain
Ticking for a little while
To amuse a fascinated infant,
Until the keeper, a very old man,
Becomes tired of the game
And lets the watch run down.

—Naomi Long Madgett

The Courage That My Mother Had

The courage that my mother had
Went with her, and is with her still:
Rock from New England **quarried**;
Now granite in a granite hill.

The golden **brooch** my mother wore
She left behind for me to wear;
I have no thing I treasure more:
Yet, it is something I could spare.

Oh, if instead she'd left to me
The thing she took into the grave!—
That courage like a rock, which she
Has no more need of, and I have.

—Edna St. Vincent Millay

As you read, why might someone treasure an item that once belonged to a close relative?

Reading Strategy:
Inferencing

What detail in the third stanza shows how the speaker feels about her mother?

quarried carved out of the ground   **brooch** a large pin worn as jewelry

Loo-Wit

Loo-Wit is the name given by the Cowlitz people to Mount St. Helens, an active volcano in Washington State. It means "lady of fire."

As you read, which details does the writer use to compare the volcano to an old woman?

The way they do
this old woman
no longer cares
what others think
but spits her black tobacco
any which way
stretching full length
from her bumpy bed.
Finally up
she sprinkles ashes
on the snow,
cold **buttes**
promise nothing
but the walk
of winter.
Centuries of cedar
have bound her
to earth,
huckleberry ropes
lay prickly
on her neck.
Around her
machinery growls,
snarls and plows
great patches
of her skin.
She crouches
in the north,
her trembling

buttes steep hills standing alone in flat land

huckleberry a low bush bearing small blue-black berries

the source
of dawn.
Light appears
with the shudder
of her slopes,
the movement
of her arm.
Blackberries unravel,
stones **dislodge**;
it's not as if
they weren't warned.
She was sleeping
but she heard the boot scrape,
the creaking floor,
felt the pull of the blanket
from her thin
    shoulder.
With one free hand
she finds her weapons
and raises them high;
clearing the twigs from her
    throat
she sings, she
    sings,
shaking the sky
like a blanket about her
Loo-wit sings and sings and
    sings!

—*Wendy Rose*

***Reading Strategy:* Inferencing**

What are the "weapons" that the volcano-woman raises?

dislodge to come loose

AFTER READING THE SELECTION | Apply the Skills

Life | The Courage That My Mother Had | Loo-Wit

Directions Choose the letter of the best answer or write the answer using complete sentences.

Comprehension: Identifying Facts

1. In "Life," what image does Madgett use to describe life?

A an old man **C** a pocket watch
B an infant **D** a gamekeeper

2. What physical item did the mother leave behind for the speaker in "The Courage That My Mother Had"?

3. What details describe the eruption of the volcano in "Loo-Wit"?

Comprehension: Putting Ideas Together

4. What really happens when "the watch run(s) down" in "Life"?

A death **C** a new game
B adulthood **D** sleep

5. In "The Courage that My Mother Had," why would the speaker rather have her mother's character than the item her mother left her?

6. Which details from "Loo-Wit" support the idea that people are disturbing the mountain?

Understanding Literature: Figurative Language

Figurative language is not meant to be understood exactly as it is written. It works on a different level—the level of imagination. A poet may use a simile or metaphor to compare one thing to another, unlike thing. A poet may use personification to give human qualities to an animal or thing. A poet may use a symbol to stand for a concept or quality.

Poets can use figurative language to show how different parts of the world are connected. They can use it to express a deeper truth about the world.

7. What is a symbol for strength in "The Courage That My Mother Had"?

8. What human characteristics does the volcano in "Loo-Wit" have?

Critical Thinking

9. Which poem paints the most vivid pictures in your mind? Explain your answer by giving examples.

Thinking Creatively

10. Why do you think poets choose to write about real people and events?

Grammar Check

An appositive is a noun or pronoun placed after another noun or pronoun to identify, rename, or explain it.

An appositive phrase is a noun or pronoun with modifiers. It stands next to a noun or pronoun and adds information that identifies, names, or explains it.

Examples: The volcano, Loo-Wit, is ready to explode.
The keeper, a very old man, becomes tired of the game.

Write the appositive or appositive phrase in each sentence. Then, write the word each one modifies.

1 Ryan, the pitcher, reached the mound.

2 Ryan's mother, a great influence in his life, taught him to work hard.

Vocabulary Builder

The word part *-fer-* comes from the Latin root *-ferre-*, which means "to bring or to carry." When you infer, you read between the lines. You bring to your reading a meaning that is not directly stated.

Write the meaning of each word. Use a dictionary if you need one. Then, use each word in a sentence.

1 trans + fer = transfer, means ______

2 re + fer + ral = referral, means _____

Writing on Your Own

Write a metaphor about life. First, compare life to something else, such as an object, a place, or an animal. Then, extend the metaphor by making several connected comparisons.

Listening and Speaking

Have an in-class poetry reading. First, select a poet. Then, choose the poems that you will read aloud.

- Practice your readings alone or with a group.
- Practice reading slowly and with expression.
- Speak clearly, and make eye contact with your audience.

After you have finished practicing, hold a reading for the class.

Research and Technology

Work with two other students. Use library resources to find out more about volcanic eruptions. Present your findings in a science report. Use pictures, maps, or other visuals in your report. Make sure you put information from your research into your own words.

Reading Informational Materials

Book Review

In Part 1, you are learning about inferencing. Being able to make inferences can help you read a book review with understanding. A book review usually appears in a magazine or newspaper. It may also appear online. The review is meant for an audience of readers. Many readers use book reviews to determine what to read. For that reason, a book review may have a huge impact on book sales. A positive review may convince a large number of people to purchase the book. A negative review may turn readers off.

About Book Reviews

Book reviews are a form of literary criticism. The author of the review reads a book with a critical eye. The review itself includes facts and opinions. Both may help to influence a reader.

Facts

- author's name
- title of work
- information about content

Opinions

- how the book compares to others in its genre
- how the book compares to others by that author
- positive and negative comments
- overall opinion

The review you are about to read is of a book of poetry for young adults.

Reading Skill

To get the most from a book review, you must tell fact from opinion. Think about what is important to you as a reader. Are you interested in reading everything about one topic? In that case, you may not care about a reviewer's opinion. The facts in the review may be more important to you. Are you interested in reading books with strong characters and exciting action? In that case, the reviewer's opinion may be quite important. If the reviewer says the plot is thrilling, you may want to read the book. If the reviewer says the characters are weak, you may not want to read the book.

Remember that an opinion cannot be proved or checked. It only states what someone thinks or believes. To tell fact from opinion, look for loaded words. Adjectives such as *great, fascinating, dull, or poorly written* signal opinions.

You can use a graphic organizer to help you separate facts from opinions.

Reviewer's Facts	Reviewer's Opinions

Winter Thoughts: Selected Poems

by Rita Valero
238 pages
Gardner Press
reviewed by Kaitlyn Zaharis

A new collection by Rita Valero is always a cause for celebration. This one is no exception. Valero burst onto the scene a decade ago with *Spring Silence*. Since then, she has produced two more collections of poems for young adults. This one rounds out the year that includes *Summer Songs* and *Autumn Dreams*.

Notice the way Zaharis includes both facts and opinions in her paragraphs.

Valero teaches American literature at Westbrook Academy, a school for girls in upstate New York. Her work with young people has given her a voice that young adults will understand. It is a voice of rebellion and a voice of confusion. It is a swaggering voice and a serious voice. In her poetry, Valero explores the joys and sorrows of adolescence.

Consider the opening of this poem, which Valero calls "Spirit."

The decorations the holly the
fragrant pine boughs
the temporary gladness
all too soon lost
in shards of broken ornaments and
fragile brown needles. . .

The contrast is typical of Valero. She understands the lightning-fast switch between joy and sorrow that is part of being a teenager. The speaker then compares the death of the holiday spirit to the end of a friendship. The language is stark and clear. The feelings are familiar.

Often a review will include an excerpt from the book being reviewed.

Fans of Valero's may recall her most popular poem from *Spring Silence.* In "Awakening," she compared the opening of a leaf to the beginnings of young love. The poem has been translated into 15 languages. It seems to speak to young people worldwide. Now, in this collection, she includes a companion poem, "Retreat."

As the last leaves shrivel and die,
a young romance declines and ends,
Not suddenly
with loud words or wailing
But with a measured fading
Until one day we look, surprised
to see the leafless limbs.

Valero writes in the free-verse tradition. Her poems do not rhyme, and her lines differ in length. Often, her poems seem like diary entries written in poetic form. She speaks personally and confidingly to the reader.

There are some critics who consider Valero a writer for girls only. I have to disagree. Her poetry crosses gender lines, and her speaker is not always female. A high school teacher I know often asks her class to share favorite poems. She says that boys in her class nearly always pick Valero. This is hardly a scientific study, but I think it proves my point. Valero appeals to teenagers of all sorts.

Not every poem is a winner, of course. A few images fall flat, as in "Logsplitting," where Valero describes the "smiling, gap-toothed ax." A few rhythms are clunky, and a few metaphors seem strained.

Even a positive review may contain some negative opinions. A negative review can also have some positive comments.

On the whole, though, this is a fine addition to the genre. "Winter Thoughts" and its companion volumes are a wonderful introduction to poetry for any young adult.

The end of the review offers a final opinion and a recommendation.

Monitor Your Progress

Directions Choose the letter of the best answer or write the answer using complete sentences.

1. What is the author's primary purpose in writing this review?
   - **A** To compare and contrast four volumes of poetry
   - **B** To express an opinion about a book of poetry
   - **C** To explain the writing style of an American poet
   - **D** To reflect on experiences that can produce poetry
2. Which phrase from the review best summarizes Zaharis's opinion?
   - **A** This is a fine addition to the genre.
   - **B** Not every poem is a winner, of course.
   - **C** The contrast is typical of Valero.
   - **D** Her poetry crosses gender lines.
3. Which fact does Zaharis give to support her notion that Valero's poetry is not just for girls?
   - **A** Valero teaches at the Westbrook Academy for Girls.
   - **B** She explores the joys and sorrows of adolescence.
   - **C** Some critics consider Valero a writer for girls only.
   - **D** Boys in one class often choose Valero's poems to share.
4. Explain what Zaharis thinks about Valero's poetic voice.
5. Find three loaded words Zaharis uses to describe Valero's work.

Writing on Your Own

Choose one poem from Part 1. Imagine that you are a reviewer. Write a review of the poem. Include facts as well as opinions. Conclude with a final opinion and a recommendation.

How I Learned English *by Gregory Djanikian*

Gregory Djanikian
1949–

Objectives

- To read and understand a narrative poem
- To recognize suspense
- To compare narrative and lyric poetry

About the Author

When Gregory Djanikian was very young, he moved from Egypt to the United States with his family. He grew up in New York and Pennsylvania. Djanikian's experiences as an immigrant provided ideas for poems such as "How I Learned English." The collection *Falling Deeply into America* contains several poems about his first year in America.

Today Djanikian directs a creative writing program at the University of Pennsylvania and runs poetry workshops. He has won many awards for his poetry. He is known for his use of descriptive language to talk about ordinary things.

About the Selection

In "How I Learned English," Djanikian speaks in the voice of an immigrant boy who has just arrived in Williamsport, Pennsylvania. The boy is playing ball, even though he does not know the rules. A ball arcs through the air and hits him on the forehead. Dazed, he cries out, "Oh, my shin!" The other boys burst out laughing. Surprised, the boy laughs, too. His laughter helps him become "one of the boys." He plays with his new friends until night falls.

The poem is a narrative poem; it tells the story of something that happens. Unlike a lyric poem, it does not focus on thoughts and feelings. It focuses on actions and events. Look back at "The Rider" on page 279. Unlike "How I Learned English," that poem focuses on thoughts and feelings.

Literary Terms A **narrative poem** is a poem that tells a story. Just like a short story, it may have characters, a setting, and a plot. The plot may include a turning point. It may even include **suspense.** Suspense is a quality that makes a reader uncertain or nervous about what will happen next.

narrative poem a poem that tells a story

suspense a quality that makes a reader uncertain or nervous about what will happen next

Reading on Your Own Look at the title of the poem. What does the title tell you about the speaker? Remember that this is a narrative poem. Based on the title, make a prediction about the story the poem will tell.

Writing on Your Own Think about the difference between telling a story in prose and telling the story as a poem. Explain some pros and cons of using poetic form to tell a story. Think about the effect on the reader. Write a short paragraph.

Vocabulary Focus An idiom is a phrase that has a different meaning than its words really mean. For example, saying "I'll cross that bridge when I come to it" does not mean you are traveling. It means that you will deal with something whenever it happens. Idioms can be hard to understand, especially for English-language learners like the speaker in this poem. Work with a partner. Explain the meaning of each of these idioms from the poem.

- talking it up
- everybody peeled away
- his T-shirt riding up
- fit of laughter

Think Before You Read What would be most difficult about starting life in a new country? Why is learning the language important?

How I Learned English

It was in an empty lot
Ringed by elms and fir and **honeysuckle**.
Bill Corson was pitching in his **buckskin** jacket,
Chuck Keller, fat even as a boy, was on first,
His t-shirt riding up over his gut,
Ron O'Neill, Jim, Dennis, were talking it up
In the field, a blue sky above them
Tipped with **cirrus**.
And there I was,
Just off the plane and plopped in the middle
Of Williamsport, Pa., and a neighborhood game,
Unnatural and without any moves,
My notions of baseball and America
Growing **fuzzier** each time I **whiffed**.

As you read, use your own words to describe the setting of this poem.

honeysuckle a climbing shrub with sweet-smelling flowers

buckskin yellowish-gray leather made from the hide of a deer

cirrus high, thin clouds

fuzzier less clear

whiffed struck out

So it was not impossible that I,
Banished to the outfield and daydreaming
Of water, or a hotel in the mountains,
Would suddenly find myself in the path
Of a ball **stung** by Joe Barone.
I watched it closing in
Clean and untouched, transfixed
By its easy **arc** before it hit
My forehead with a thud.
I fell back.
Dazed, clutching my brow,
Groaning, "Oh my shin, oh my shin,"
And everybody peeled away from me
And dropped from laughter, and there we were,
All of us **writhing** on the ground for one reason
Or another.
Someone said "shin" again,
There was a wild stamping of hands on the ground,
A kicking of feet, and the fit
Of laughter overtook me too,
And that was important, as important
As Joe Barone asking me how I was
Through his tears, picking me up
And dusting me off with hands like swatters,
And though my head felt heavy,
I played on till dusk
Missing flies and pop-ups and grounders
And calling out in desperation things like
"Yours" and "take it," but doing all right,
Tugging at my cap in just the right way,
Crouching low, my feet set,
"Hum baby" sweetly on my lips.

What happens to the speaker, and how does he react?

Reading Strategy:
Inferencing
Why was the speaker's laughter "important"?

What is the turning point of the story? At what point are you in suspense about what might happen?

banished sent away
stung hit hard
arc a curved section of a circle
writhing twisting and turning, as if in pain

How I Learned English by Gregory Djanikian

Directions Choose the letter of the best answer or write the answer using complete sentences.

Comprehension: Identifying Facts

1. What are Bill and Chuck doing in lines 1–4?

A laughing **C** running
B playing ball **D** talking

2. What does the speaker do when he is hit in the head with the baseball?

3. What help does Joe Barone offer the speaker?

Comprehension: Putting Ideas Together

4. Suppose you included "The Rider" and "How I Learned English" in a book. In which chapter would both poems fit?

A "Love" **C** "Sports"
B "Going Fast" **D** "Immigrants"

5. What is the speaker's problem in "The Rider"? What is the speaker's problem in "How I Learned English"?

6. Think about "The Rider" and "How I Learned English." Which of the two poems has a more detailed setting? What is that setting?

Understanding Literature: Narrative Poetry

Unlike lyric poetry, narrative poetry tells a story. It is not written in paragraphs, but it has many of the features of a short story. It usually has a main character, who may or may not be the speaker. It often has a clear setting and a plot. Lyric poetry may tell about a person or a place, but it does not have a plot. It focuses more on thoughts and feelings. Narrative poetry focuses on action.

7. If you retold "How I Learned English" as a short story, who would the characters be?

8. Which poem, "The Rider" or "How I Learned English," uses suspense to interest the reader? How does the poet use suspense?

Critical Thinking

9. If "The Rider" were a narrative poem, what would have to change? Use "How I Learned English" to help you answer the question.

Thinking Creatively

10. Which poem, "The Rider" or "How I Learned English," would make a better TV episode? Why?

Grammar Check

The *-ing* form of a verb may be used in a modifying phrase.

Example: I watched it <u>closing in</u>.

The phrase must be as close as possible to the word it modifies. Otherwise, you end up with a dangling modifier, as here:

Dangling modifier: <u>Clutching my brow</u>, the ground rose to meet <u>me</u>.

Correct: <u>Clutching my brow</u>, <u>I</u> sank to the ground.

In "How I Learned English," find five phrases that contain *-ing* forms of verbs. Use each phrase in an original sentence. Avoid dangling modifiers.

Vocabulary Builder

Use each of these words from the poem in an original sentence. Use a dictionary if it helps.

writing banished arc

Writing on Your Own

Write a paragraph. Compare and contrast the speakers in "The Rider" and "How I Learned English." Think about what you know about them.

How old do they seem to be? What do they like or dislike? What are their joys and fears? Tell how they are alike and different.

Listening and Speaking

Work with a partner. Divide "How I Learned English" into these sections:

lines 1–8 lines 9–14 lines 15–23
lines 24–30 lines 31–46

Take turns reading sections aloud. Use the punctuation to help you. Work to make the words flow, just as if you were telling a story. Talk about the parts that are easy to read and the parts that give you trouble.

Media and Viewing

Go online to find a diagram of a baseball field. The diagram should show each player's position on the field. Use the diagram to draw your own picture of the field in "How I Learned English." Use clues from the poem to label the players with their names and positions.

Reading Strategy:
Visualizing

Visualizing is another strategy that helps readers understand what they are reading. It is like creating a movie in your mind. Use the following ways to visualize a text:

- Look at the photographs, illustrations, and descriptive words in the text.
- Think about experiences in your own life that may add to the images.
- Notice the order in which things are happening and what you think might happen next.

Literary Terms

onomatopoeia using words that sound like their meaning

alliteration repeating sounds by using words whose beginning sounds are the same

repetition using a word, phrase, or image more than once, for emphasis

rhythm a pattern created by the stressed and unstressed syllables in a line of poetry

rhyme words that end with the same or similar sounds

meter the repetition of stressed and unstressed syllables

imagery the use of words that appeal to the five senses

In an Iridescent Time | *Weather* | *One*

About the Authors and Selections

Ruth Stone
1915–

Eve Merriam
1916–1992

Ruth Stone is one of America's most honored poets. Accepting the National Book Award at age 87, she laughed. "I think you probably gave it to me because I'm old," she said. Stone writes about the countryside in Vermont, where she has lived for 50 years. She also writes about her family, who encouraged her to be creative. Her mother read her the poems of Tennyson when she was just a baby. Today Stone is called "Mother Poet" by many young poets who learned how to write from her. "In an Iridescent Time" is a look back at an earlier time. Stone describes a peaceful scene where girls do laundry by hand outdoors.

James Berry
1925–

Eve Merriam was born and raised in Philadelphia, Pennsylvania. Although she also wrote fiction, nonfiction, and drama, Merriam had a lifelong love of poetry. "I do think poetry is great fun," she said. "That's what I'd like to stress more than anything else: the joy of the sounds of language." The poem "Weather" describes rain from an indoor and outdoor perspective. The poem begins inside and moves outside, where the speaker splashes joyfully through the puddles.

James Berry grew up in Jamaica, in a small village by the sea. He learned to read before he was four years old. He began writing stories and poems when he got to school. In 1948, Berry moved to England, and soon after that, he began writing seriously. His poems include both English and Creole, the language he spoke growing up in Jamaica. "One" contrasts the ordinary and unique qualities of being human. The speaker talks about his unique traits, his moods, and his weaknesses.

Objectives

- To read and understand lyric poetry
- To recognize sound devices in poetry

***Before Reading* continued on next page**

In an Iridescent Time | Weather | One

onomatopoeia using words that sound like their meaning

alliteration repeating sounds by using words whose beginning sounds are the same

repetition using a word, phrase, or image more than once, for emphasis

Literary Terms

Sound devices create musical effects that appeal to the ear. Here are some common sound devices used in poetry:

- **Onomatopoeia** is the use of words whose sounds suggest their meanings. The *shooshing* of skis in the fresh fallen snow. . .
- **Alliteration** is the repetition of sounds at the beginning of words. *maggie* and *millie* and *molly* and *may*/Went down to the beach (to play one day)
- **Repetition** is the repeated use of words, phrases, or rhythms. To the swinging and the ringing/Of the *bells, bells, bells*. . .

Reading on Your Own

When you visualize, you picture a scene in your mind. You can use descriptive words and phrases to visualize a scene. As you read, ask yourself these questions.

- Where is the scene set?
- Who or what do I "see" in the scene?
- What descriptive words and phrases help me picture what is happening?

Writing on Your Own

All three poets in this collection use words to describe ordinary scenes. Make a list of 10 ordinary scenes from your own life that you might use to write a poem. Save your list to inspire you as you read the poems.

Vocabulary Focus

Compound words are words formed by combining two or more short words. Read these compound words from the poems. Divide each one into two short words. Explain how the meaning of the short words helps you understand the meaning of the compound words.

rainbow   bookmark   photocopy   fingerprints

Think Before You Read

The English poet Percy Bysshe Shelley wrote often about poetry. He once said that poetry "makes familiar objects be as if they were not familiar." What do you think this means? Why do you think poets often write about everyday things?

In an Iridescent Time

My mother, when young, scrubbed laundry in a tub,
She and her sisters on an old brick walk
Under the apple trees, sweet rub-a-dub.
The bees came round their heads, the wrens made talk.
Four young ladies each with a rainbow board
Honed their knuckles, wrung their wrists to red,
Tossed back their braids and wiped their aprons wet.
The Jersey calf beyond the back fence roared;
And all the soft day, swarms about their pet
Buzzed at his big brown eyes and bullish head.
Four times they rinsed, they said. Some things they starched,
Then shook them from the baskets two by two,
And pinned the fluttering **intimacies** of life
Between the lilac bushes and the **yew:**
Brown **gingham,** pink, and skirts of **Alice blue**.

—Ruth Stone

Which word names the sound the scrubbers make? This is an example of onomatopoeia. As you read, look for other words that tell about sounds.

Which words in line 10 begin with the letter b? This is an example of alliteration.

***Reading Strategy:* Visualizing**

What are the girls pinning up? Which words help you picture them?

honed sharpened by scraping

intimacies personal items; secrets

yew an evergreen

gingham a cotton fabric

Alice blue a steel blue color favored by Theodore Roosevelt's daughter Alice

Weather

As you read, think about how the poem makes you feel. How does repetition help create that feeling?

Dot a dot dot   dot a dot dot
Spotting the windowpane.
Spack a spack speck   flick a flack fleck
Freckling the windowpane.

A spatter a scatter   a wet cat a clatter
A splatter a rumble outside.
Umbrella umbrella umbrella umbrella
Bumbershoot barrel of rain.

Which sound devices does the poet use in the last stanza? Explain.

Slosh a galosh   slosh a galosh
Slither and slather and glide
A puddle a jump a puddle a jump
A puddle a jump puddle splosh
A juddle a pump a luddle a dump a
Puddmuddle jump in and slide!

—Eve Merriam

ONE

Only one of me
and nobody can get a second one
from a photocopy machine.

Nobody has the fingerprints I have.
Nobody can cry my tears, or laugh my laugh
or have my **expectancy** when I wait.

But anybody can **mimic** my dance with my dog.
Anybody can howl how I sing out of tune.
And mirrors can show me multiplied
many times, say, dressed up in red
or dressed up in grey.

Nobody can get into my clothes for me
or feel my fall for me, or do my running.
Nobody hears my music for me, either.

I am just this one.
Nobody else makes the words
I shape with sound, when I talk.

But anybody can act how I **stutter** in a rage.
Anybody can copy echoes I make.
And mirrors can show me multiplied
many times, say, dressed up in green
or dressed up in blue.

—James Berry

As you read, think about why the poet repeats the words *nobody* and *anybody.*

Reading Strategy:
Visualizing

What do you see when you read the words "mirrors can show me multiplied many times"?

expectancy a hopeful eagerness

mimic to copy

stutter to hesitate or stumble over words

AFTER READING THE SELECTION | **Apply the Skills**

In an Iridescent Time | Weather | One

Directions Choose the letter of the best answer or write the answer using complete sentences.

Comprehension: Identifying Facts

1. What are the girls wearing in "In an Iridescent Time"?
   A blue skirts
   B gingham dresses
   C aprons
   D fluttering gowns
2. Identify at least two made-up words in "Weather."
3. Name two things that the speaker of "One" says are unique about him.

Comprehension: Putting Ideas Together

4. Which clue tells you that "In an Iridescent Time" takes place in the past?
   A the "rainbow boards"
   B the wrens "talking"
   C the lilac bushes
   D the "old brick walk"
5. How does the speaker in "Weather" feel about the rain?
6. How do the mirrors in "One" challenge the speaker's feelings of being unique?

Understanding Literature: Sound Devices

Sound devices help a poet create a mood. They may also add to a poem's rhythm and make the poem seem musical. Onomatopoeia is the use of words that sound like their meaning. Alliteration is the use of words that begin with the same consonant sound. Repetition is the repeating of words, phrases, or images. Poets combine sound devices the way a composer might combine instruments. The result is a complete work that delights the listener with sound.

7. Find two examples of alliteration in "In an Iridescent Time."
8. List two examples of onomatopoeia in "Weather" that make the sound of water.

Critical Thinking

9. How does the repetition in "One" support the poet's message?

Thinking Creatively

10. Which poem in this collection gave you the clearest picture in your mind? How would you describe that picture?

Grammar Check

Most verbs form the past tense by adding *-ed.* The spelling may change first. Verbs that end in *e* drop the *e* and add *-ed.* Verbs that end in a vowel and a consonant double the consonant before adding *-ed.* Irregular verbs form the past tense in unusual ways.

For each verb, write the past-tense form. You can check your work by looking back at "In an Iridescent Time."

Regular Verbs: hone, scrub, toss, wipe

Irregular Verbs: come, make, wring, say

Vocabulary Builder

Choose one smaller word from each compound word below. Write a second compound word that contains that smaller word. Then write the meaning of your new word.

Examples: motorcycle ➜ motorboat
bookcase ➜ briefcase

photocopy windowpane rainbow

Writing on Your Own

Find your list of 10 ordinary scenes you made for Writing on Your Own on page 304. Choose one that you can easily visualize. Write a poem of eight or more lines. Describe the ordinary scene. Your poem does not need to rhyme, but it should use alliteration or repetition. Read your finished poem to your group.

Listening and Speaking

Work with a partner. Using "One" as a guide, tell your partner what you feel is unique about you. Then listen as your partner describes his or her own unique qualities. Finally, share with the class what you learned about your partner. Did you listen carefully and remember what he or she said?

Media and Viewing

Choose one of the poems from this collection. Use your visualizing skills to picture the scene described by the poet. Draw that scene. Give the scene a title. Compare and contrast your picture with your classmates' pictures. Did you see the scene the same way?

BEFORE READING THE SELECTION | **Build Understanding**

Annabel Lee | Martin Luther King | Sympathy

Edgar Allan Poe
1809–1849

Raymond Patterson
1929–2001

Paul Laurence Dunbar
1872–1906

Objectives

- To read and understand lyric poetry
- To recognize rhythm and meter in poetry
- To identify rhyme in poetry

About the Authors and Selections

Edgar Allan Poe was a very successful writer but suffered much personal loss in his life. His father left the family when Edgar was a baby. His mother died when he was just two years old. After serving in the army, he began to publish short stories and poems. He moved in with his aunt and married his young cousin, Virginia. In 1845, he finally achieved success with his poem, "The Raven." But Virginia died in 1847, and Poe's life went downhill. He died mysteriously in 1849. His writing is often chilling and disturbing. Poe finished "Annabel Lee" about two years after the death of his beloved wife. One Poe expert believes that Annabel Lee stands for all the women Poe loved and lost.

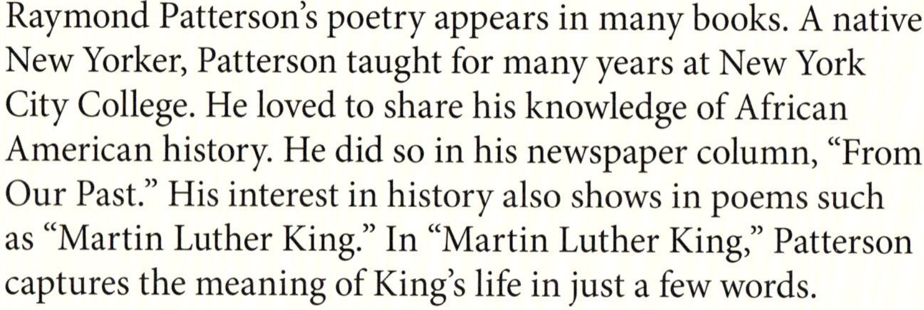

Raymond Patterson's poetry appears in many books. A native New Yorker, Patterson taught for many years at New York City College. He loved to share his knowledge of African American history. He did so in his newspaper column, "From Our Past." His interest in history also shows in poems such as "Martin Luther King." In "Martin Luther King," Patterson captures the meaning of King's life in just a few words.

Paul Laurence Dunbar grew up in Dayton, Ohio, the son of former slaves. Dunbar was the only African American student at his high school. When he was 17, he published a newspaper, which was printed by Orville Wright. He got a job as an elevator operator, but in his spare time, he wrote poetry. His first collection was published in 1893. Dunbar traveled a lot and gave many poetry readings before dying of lung disease at age 33. In "Sympathy," the speaker expresses understanding for the caged bird. As the son of slaves, the poet speaks from the heart.

Literary Terms **Rhythm** and **rhyme** make poetry musical. Rhythm is a poem's pattern of stressed (´) and unstressed (˘) syllables. **Meter** is a poem's rhythmic pattern. It is measured in feet, or single units of stressed and unstressed syllables. Rhyme is the repetition of sounds at the ends of words. In the example, the words *grass* and *glass* create a rhyme.

When the wind stirs soft through the springing grass
And the river flows like a stream of glass. . .

rhythm a pattern created by the stressed and unstressed syllables in a line of poetry

rhyme words that end with the same or similar sounds

meter the repetition of stressed and unstressed syllables

Reading on Your Own To visualize is to use your imagination to picture a scene. Poets use figurative language and imagery to help a reader see what they are describing. In the example above, the words "stirs soft" describe one kind of wind. "The springing grass" tells of grass moving down and up in the wind. As you read, let the poets' words create images in your mind.

Writing on Your Own The poems "Annabel Lee" and "Martin Luther King" each honor someone who is important to the speaker. Choose someone whom you would like to honor. Write three sentences that tell why that person is special.

Vocabulary Focus Words with nearly the same meaning are called synonyms. Usually, one synonym can replace the other in a sentence. Sometimes there are shades of meaning that make one synonym a bit different from the other. Talk over the differences in meaning of the synonyms in these pairs.

wind/breeze   caged/imprisoned   passion/obsession

Think Before You Read Why might it help to know a writer's history before reading his or her work? How can knowing a poet help you understand his or her meaning?

Annabel Lee

Reading Strategy:
Visualizing

As you read, think whether this photograph matches the scene you visualize.

It was many and many a year ago,
    In a kingdom by the sea.
That a maiden there lived whom you may know
    By the name of Annabel Lee;—
And this maiden she lived with no other thought
    Than to love and be loved by me.

She was a child and I was a child,
    In this kingdom by the sea.
But we loved with a love that was more than love—
    I and my Annabel Lee—
With a love that the wingèd **seraphs** of Heaven
    Coveted her and me.

Which syllables are stressed in the first two lines?

seraphs angels

coveted wanted; desired

And this was the reason that, long ago,
In this kingdom by the sea,
A wind blew out of a cloud by night
Chilling my Annabel Lee;
So that her highborn kinsmen came
And **bore** her away from me,
To shut her up in a sepulcher
In this kingdom by the sea.

Highborn means noble. *Kinsmen* means relatives. Poe is speaking of Annabel Lee's "noble relatives."

A *sepulcher* is a vault or chamber used for burial.

The angels, not half so happy in Heaven,
Went envying her and me:—
Yes! that was the reason (as all men know,
In this kingdom by the sea)
That the wind came out of a cloud, chilling
And killing my Annabel Lee.

But our love it was stronger by far than the love
Of those who were older than we—
Of many far wiser than we—
And neither the angels in Heaven above
Nor the demons down under the sea,
Can ever **dissever** my soul from the soul
Of the beautiful Annabel Lee:—

For the moon never beams without bringing
me dreams
Of the beautiful Annabel Lee;
And the stars never rise but I see the bright eyes
Of the beautiful Annabel Lee;
And so, all the nighttide, I lie down by the side
Of my darling, my darling, my life and my bride,
In her sepulcher there by the sea—
In her tomb by the side of the sea.

—Edgar Allan Poe

Why does the speaker repeat the name of his love so often in the poem?

bore carried

dissever to separate; divide

Martin Luther King

Martin Luther King, Jr. (1929–1968) was a civil rights leader. He used nonviolent ways to help end mistreatment of African Americans in the United States. In 1968, he was shot and killed at the age of 39.

As you read, identify the lines that rhyme in the poem.

He came upon an age
Beset by grief, by rage—

His love so deep, so wide,
He could not turn aside.

His **passion**, so **profound**,
He would not turn around.

He taught a suffering earth
The measure of man's worth.

For this he was slain,
But he will come again.

—Raymond Patterson

beset attacked from all sides

passion strong feeling

profound deeply felt

Sympathy

Bird Escaping Cage, Nadia Richie

I know what the caged bird feels, alas!
When the sun is bright on the **upland** slopes;
When the wind stirs soft through the springing grass
And the river flows like a stream of glass;
When the first bird sings and the first bud **opes**,
And the faint perfume from its **chalice** steals—
I know what the caged bird feels!

I know why the caged bird beats his wing
Till its blood is red on the cruel bars;
For he must fly back to his perch and cling
When he fain would be on the bough a-swing;
And a pain still throbs in the old, old scars
And they pulse again with a keener sting—
I know why he beats his wing!

I know why the caged bird sings, ah me,
When his wing is bruised and his **bosom** sore,—
When he beats his bars and he would be free;
It is not a carol of joy or glee,
But a prayer that he sends from his heart's deep core,
But a plea, that upward to Heaven he flings—
I know why the caged bird sings!

—Paul Laurence Dunbar

As you read, try to find the rhyming pattern of the poem.

***Reading Strategy:* Visualize**

Why is the scene in the first stanza so appealing to the caged bird?

To *fain would* means that he would prefer to.

How does repetition add to the rhythm of the poem?

upland high ground
chalice a large cup
bosom breast
opes opens

AFTER READING THE SELECTION | Apply the Skills

Annabel Lee | Martin Luther King | Sympathy

Directions Choose the letter of the best answer or write the answer using complete sentences.

Comprehension: Identifying Facts

1. In "Annabel Lee," with whom is the speaker in conflict?

A his beloved
B angels
C the moon and stars
D his kinsmen

2. According to the speaker in "Martin Luther King," what did King teach the world?

3. What kind of song does the caged bird in "Sympathy" sing?

Comprehension: Putting Ideas Together

4. What will prevent the speaker in "Annabel Lee" from losing his bride forever?

A their love
B angels and demons
C the sea
D the sepulcher

5. In "Martin Luther King," what does the poet mean by King's "passion, so profound"?

6. What does the title of "Sympathy" mean? Who has sympathy for whom?

Understanding Literature: Rhythm, Rhyme, and Meter

Rhythm is the pattern of stressed and unstressed syllables in a line. Rhyme is the repetition of ending sounds from line to line. Meter is the repetition of blocks of stressed and unstressed syllables. Rhythm, rhyme, and meter combine to make a poem musical. You can better understand all three if you think about songs you know. Sing part of your favorite song. What lines rhyme? Tap the rhythm. Do you see how it follows the stressed syllables in the words? Poets use rhythm, rhyme, and meter the same way songwriters do.

7. Which syllables are stressed in each line of "Martin Luther King"?

8. List the rhyming words in the first stanza of "Sympathy."

Critical Thinking

9. In your opinion, which poem has the most interesting rhythm? Why?

Thinking Creatively

10. Which of the three poems do you think would make the best song? Why?

Grammar Check

A simple sentence is one independent clause. It is a group of words that has a subject and verb. It can stand by itself as a complete thought. A compound sentence has two or more independent clauses. The clauses are linked by a word such as *and, but,* or *or.* A complex sentence contains one independent clause and one or more subordinate clauses. A subordinate clause has a subject and verb but is not a complete thought.

Write a sentence for each numbered item. Then, identify the structure of each sentence you wrote.

1 to tell a friend what time it is

2 to tell a friend what time practice is on Friday

3 to state what kind of homework you have

Vocabulary Builder

Use a word from the vocabulary list or notes on pages 312–315 to complete each analogy. Your choice should make a word pair that matches the relationship between the first two words.

1 DOGS are to TERRIERS as ___ are to uncles

2 CARESSED is to EMBRACED as attacked is to ___

3 PEAK is to VALLEY as ___ is to plain

Writing on Your Own

Use the rhyme pattern of "Martin Luther King" to write a short poem about a hero. Brainstorm a list of words that could describe the person. Use your list to write a poem. The poem should have pairs of rhymed lines.

Listening and Speaking

Good speakers vary their tone of voice to express emotions. Think about the tone of each poem. How is grief different from sympathy? How is praise different from grief? Work with a partner. Practice saying the lines from the poems with the proper tone of voice. Then choose one poem to read aloud.

Research and Technology

Conduct a survey in groups. Ask classmates to pick their favorite of the three poems in each of these categories:

- best character description
- best overall use of language
- best rhythm, rhyme, and meter

Count the number of votes that each poem receives for each category. Share your results with the rest of the class.

Reading Informational Materials

Résumés

In this unit, you are learning about visualizing. Poets use words to give you a picture of a scene. When you apply for a job, you must use words to give a picture of yourself. An employer reads a résumé to learn about a worker. In just a page, that worker must paint a picture that appeals to the employer.

About Résumés

The word *résumé* comes from the same root as *summarize*. A résumé is a short summary of a worker's experience. It usually includes these parts:

- personal information
- career goals
- education
- employment experience
- extracurricular and community activities
- awards and honors
- references

On these pages, you will read two different résumés. The writers are applying for the same job at a department store.

Reading Skill

As you read résumés, you must compare and contrast details. In other words, you must look at how the workers are alike and different. Any employer must learn to do this. It is one important way to decide which worker is better for the job.

You can use a Venn diagram (described in Appendix A) to compare and contrast the résumés that follow. Each circle shows details about the workers. The center shows the things both have in common.

Lucy Chen
424 Arden Drive
Encinitas, CA 92023
(760) 555-1280
lchen@email.net

CAREER GOALS
- to manage a retail store
- to oversee personnel and merchandise

EDUCATION
- High school diploma from Riverdale High School, June 2004
- Completing sophomore year at San Diego State with a major in Management

ACTIVITIES AND AWARDS
- Treasurer, Asian-American Society
- Winner, Fashion Institute Award, 2007

EXPERIENCE
- Retail clerk, Tim's Department Store, La Jolla (2005–2006)
- Part-time cashier, Jackson Foods, Encinitas (2003–2005)
- Mother's helper, Encinitas (summer of 2001 and 2002)

Chen placed the experience that best matches to her career goals first.

REFERENCES

Jennifer Rodel
Human Resources
Tim's Department Store
La Jolla, CA 92073
(858) 555-2340

Seymour Gleason
District Manager
Jackson Foods
Encinitas, CA 92023
(760) 555-2688

Professor Rita Muraca
School of Business Administration
San Diego State University
San Diego, CA 92182
(619) 555-1441

References include phone numbers so that employers can call and learn more.

The heading of a résumé must include ways for an employer to reach the worker.

Diana Monroe
22-12 Madison Street
Carlsbad, CA 92009
(760) 555-9876
dm24@message.com

CAREER GOAL: To design clothes for a major fashion house

EXPERIENCE

2005–present	Assistant Buyer Stacy's Department Store La Jolla, CA 92037
2004–2005	Student Intern Super Swimwear Carlsbad, CA 92008
2001–2004	Junior Lifeguard YMCA Carlsbad, CA 92008

COMMUNITY ACTIVITIES

2006	Representative, United Way Stacy's Department Store
2004–present	Big Sister Big Brother/Big Sister of Southern CA

EDUCATION

2005	Bachelor of Arts in Fashion Design Brooks College Long Beach, CA 90804
2001	High School Diploma La Costa Canyon High School Carlsbad, CA 92009

REFERENCES

Business
Jason Weir, Super Swimwear, 124 Marshall Ave., Carlsbad, CA 92008 (760) 555-3800
Mahar Khan, Stacy's Department Store, La Jolla, CA 92037 (858) 555-9000 x125

Personal
Risa Lafitte, 24-15 Prospect St., La Jolla, CA 92037 (858) 555-2776
Sharon Drake, 13 Roble Way, Long Beach, CA 90804 (310) 555-2210

Personal references may include family or friends.

Monitor Your Progress

Directions Choose the letter of the best answer or write the answer using complete sentences.

1. How could an employer learn more about Lucy Chen's work as a clerk?
   A call Jennifer Rodel
   B Visit the local grocery store
   C write to Seymour Gleason
   D call (619) 555-1441

2. Which detail on Diana Monroe's résumé has the least to do with her career goal?
   A her Bachelor of Arts degree
   B her work at Super Swimwear
   C her most recent job
   D her job at the YMCA

3. Based on both résumés, the job available is probably in
   A appliances.
   B sportswear.
   C housewares.
   D electronics.

4. Who appears to have more experience in retail work? Explain how you can tell.

5. Whose career goal seems like a better match for a job at a department store? Give reasons for your answer.

Writing on Your Own

Pretend you are a manager at the department store. Compare and contrast the two résumés. Then write a letter to the job seeker you prefer. Tell why you think she should come in for an interview. Use details from her résumé to explain why you want to meet her.

Miracles by *Walt Whitman*

Walt Whitman
1819–1892

Objectives

- To read and understand a lyric poem
- To compare imagery in poetry

About the Author

Walt Whitman grew up in Brooklyn, New York. He worked at many occupations during his life. He was a printer, carpenter, teacher, and newspaper reporter. During the Civil War, he nursed his wounded brother and other soldiers.

In 1855, Whitman published the first edition of *Leaves of Grass*. The book was made up of 12 long poems. In this book, Whitman left regular rhyme and rhythm behind. He turned to free verse, which followed no set pattern. At first, no one would publish it. Over the next 36 years, eight new editions of *Leaves of Grass* were published. The book led many critics to think of Whitman as the father of American poetry.

About the Selection

In "Miracles," the speaker states the belief that life is a miracle. He notes the small things that people take for granted. These things include elements of nature. The speaker finds the forests, oceans, and the cycle of day and night to be a miracle. As you read, compare this poem to "Annabel Lee" on page 312. Both authors look at nature in very different ways.

imagery the use of words that appeal to the five senses

Literary Terms In poetry, an image is a word or phrase that appeals to one or more of the five senses. Writers use **imagery** to bring poetry to life. They describe how their subjects look, sound, feel, taste, and smell.

Examples: "A wind blew out of a cloud by night
Chilling my Annabel Lee" (touch)
"And the stars never rise but I see the bright eyes
Of the beautiful Annabel Lee" (sight)

Reading on Your Own Free verse is written in uneven lines. The lines do not rhyme. They may not have a regular rhythm. How can you use punctuation to help you read free verse?

Writing on Your Own Take a moment to pay special attention to your surroundings. Write a few words that describe what you see, hear, feel, taste, and smell.

Vocabulary Focus Poets look for exact adjectives to create clear-cut images. Often, they choose synonyms that have an exact shade of meaning. Other times, they look for synonyms that fit their rhythm and rhyme pattern.

A thesaurus can help you find synonyms. Imagine you are writing a spine-chilling poem. Find a good synonym for each of these words. Use a thesaurus if you need help.

break smile colorful small odd

Think Before You Read What do you think of when you see the word miracles? Talk it over with a classmate. Then read the poem. Does Whitman write about the same kinds of miracles?

Miracles

Why, who makes much of a miracle?
As to me I know of nothing else but miracles,
Whether I walk the streets of Manhattan,
Or dart my sight over the roofs of houses toward the sky,

Or wade with naked feet along the beach just in the edge
of the water,
Or stand under trees in the woods,
Or talk by day with any one I love . . .
Or sit at table at dinner with the rest.
Or look at strangers opposite me riding in the car,
Or watch honeybees busy around the hive of a summer
forenoon
Or animals feeding in the fields,
Or birds, or the wonderfulness of insects in the air,
Or the wonderfulness of the sundown, or of stars shining
so quiet and bright,
Or the **exquisite** delicate thin curve of the new moon in
spring;
These with the rest, one and all, are to me miracles,
The whole **referring,** yet each **distinct** and in its place.

To me every hour of the light and dark is a miracle,
Every cubic inch of space is a miracle,
Every square yard of the surface of the earth is spread
with the same,
Every foot of the interior swarms with the same.

To me the sea is a continual miracle,
The fishes that swim—the rocks—the motion of the
waves—
the ships with men in them,
What stranger miracles are there?

As you read, look for images that appeal to the senses. Which image in the first seven lines appeals to the sense of touch?

***Reading Strategy:* Visualizing**
Identify a line in the poem that relates to this painting. Explain your choice.

forenoon late morning

exquisite beautiful in a delicate way

referring connecting

distinct different

COMPARING LITERARY WORKS | Apply the Skills

Miracles *by Walt Whitman*

Directions Choose the letter of the best answer or write the answer using complete sentences.

Comprehension: Identifying Facts

1. Think about "Annabel Lee" (page 312) and "Miracles." Which place do both Poe and Whitman describe?

A city streets **C** the woods
B a grave **D** the sea

2. Which word do both poets use to describe the stars?

3. Name some people that the speaker mentions in "Miracles."

Comprehension: Putting Ideas Together

4. Poe repeats the word *love* in "Annabel Lee." Which word or phrase does Whitman repeat in "Miracles"?

A cubic inch **C** wonderfulness
B the same **D** love

5. What draws the speaker in "Annabel Lee" to the sea?

6. Why is the sea "a continual miracle" to the speaker in "Miracles"?

Understanding Literature: Imagery

Writers use imagery to show a reader how things look, sound, feel, smell, and taste. It is imagery that lets you picture the "cloud of sudden azaleas" in "The Rider" (page 279). Imagery lets you hear the splashing of a child's boots in "Weather" (page 306). Imagery helps you feel the "soft day" in "In an Iridescent Time" (page 305). To create imagery, poets use adjectives and adverbs. They also use exact verbs, as in "Seal" (page 280). Word choice is important to good imagery. Choosing the right word can help a reader "see" what the poet sees.

7. What picture do you get of the moon in "Miracles"? How does that differ from the moon in "Annabel Lee"?

8. Poe's sea has "demons" in it. Does Whitman's sea have demons? Explain your answer.

Critical Thinking

9. What do the speakers in "Miracles" and "Annabel Lee" think about love?

Thinking Creatively

10. Whom would you like to meet more, the speaker in "Miracles" or the one in "Annabel Lee"? Why? How would you describe the speaker you prefer?

Grammar Check

The word *or* is a conjunction. Like the conjunctions *and* and *but,* it may connect words, subjects or predicates, or independent clauses. In "Miracles," the word *or* connects predicates in a long list. Tell what the word *or* connects in these examples.

1 You can read the poem aloud, or you might record it.

2 I prefer drama or short stories to poetry.

3 Sam, Rani, or I will collect the papers.

4 My teacher called on me or left me alone.

5 Any funny, scary, or sad poem will do.

Vocabulary Builder

Use a thesaurus to find a synonym for each of these words from "Miracles."

exquisite	distinct	swarms
dart	delicate	

Writing on Your Own

Write a short essay to compare and contrast the sea as described in "Miracles" and "Annabel Lee." Think about the following questions as you draft your essay: What does the sea look like? What happens in the sea? What is the sea a symbol of to the speakers?

Listening and Speaking

Poetry slams are competitions where poets perform their own work. There are places throughout the country where you can watch or take part in slams. Talk about how you might form a poetry slam at school. If enough students are interested, make a plan.

Media and Viewing

Choose "Annabel Lee" or "Miracles." Imagine that you are making a recording of the poem. You want to find sound effects to go with the reading in your recording. Read the poem carefully. Make a list of sound effects that might work. Write the line or lines where you would want each sound effect to be heard.

Unit 4 SPELLING WORKSHOP

Words with Prefixes and Suffixes

Prefixes are added in front of a word, and the spelling of the base word does not change. When you add certain suffixes, the spelling of some base words changes.

Watch for Spelling Changes

Prefixes should never cause you problems. They do not change the spelling of the base word. Suffixes can be a different story.

- Does the one-syllable word end in one vowel and one consonant? Double the consonant before adding *ed* or *est*.
- Does the word with more than one syllable end in one vowel followed by one consonant? Is the accent on the last syllable? Double the consonant before adding *ed* or *est*.
- Does the word end in a consonant followed by a silent *e*? Drop the *e* before adding *ing*.
- Does the word end in *y*? Change *y* to *i* before adding *es* or *ed*.

The words with suffixes on the Word List change their base spelling before the suffix is added.

Practice

Write the word from the Word List that is related to each word below. If the list word has a prefix, circle the prefix. If the list word has a suffix, circle the spelling change.

Word List
misspell
prearrange
reenlist
unnecessary
recognition
influential
suspension
abilities
description

1. recognize
2. influence
3. enlist
4. describe
5. suspend
6. ability
7. arrange
8. spell
9. necessary

Unit 4 SUMMARY

Unit 4 introduced you to many forms of poetry. You read lyric poetry that expressed the speaker's feelings. You read a concrete poem whose shape was an important element of its form. You read narrative poetry that told a story.

We often think of poetry as having rhythm and rhyme. You read many poems that had both, but you also read some that had neither. The free verse of Walt Whitman's "Miracles" contrasts with the sing-song rhyme of Edgar Allan Poe's "Annabel Lee."

One thing most poems share is a careful use of language. Poets create images with words. Their imagery may tell you how something looks, sounds, feels, smells, or tastes. Poets often use figurative language—similes, metaphors, or personification—to compare unlike things. They may use sound devices such as alliteration or onomatopoeia.

Selections

- "The Rider" by Naomi Shihab Nye is a free-verse poem. It tells of riding a bike fast to escape loneliness.
- "Seal" by William Jay Smith is a concrete poem that explores the actions of a seal.
- Three haiku by Buson provide snapshots of moments in nature.
- "Life" by Naomi Long Madgett is an extended metaphor. It compares life to a pocket watch.
- "The Courage That My Mother Had" by Edna St. Vincent Millay pays tribute to a strong woman.
- "Loo-Wit" by Wendy Rose compares a volcano to an old woman.
- "How I Learned English" by Gregory Djanikian tells the story of an immigrant. While playing baseball, he learns to be part of the gang.
- "In an Iridescent Time" by Ruth Stone paints a picture of four girls doing laundry.
- "Weather" by Eve Merriam explores the sounds of the rain.
- "One" by James Berry contrasts the ways the speaker is unique with the ways he is typical.
- "Annabel Lee" by Edgar Allan Poe mourns the loss of a young wife.
- "Martin Luther King" by Raymond R. Patterson honors a hero.
- "Sympathy" by Paul Laurence Dunbar tells why the speaker understands a caged bird.
- "Miracles" by Walt Whitman celebrates the small things in life.

Unit 4 REVIEW

Directions Choose the letter of the best answer or write the answer using complete sentences.

Comprehension: Identifying Facts

1. Which poem is a narrative poem?
   A "Martin Luther King"
   B "The Rider"
   C "How I Learned English"
   D "Miracles"
2. Which two poems from the unit tell about the poets' mothers?
3. What is "Loo-Wit"?
4. What kind of weather does the poet talk about in "Weather"?
5. For what does the speaker in "Sympathy" feel sympathy?

Comprehension: Putting Ideas Together

6. What makes "Seal" a concrete poem?
   A its shape
   B its imagery
   C its rhythm
   D its word choice
7. What happens when the watch "runs down" in "Life"?
8. In "In an Iridescent Time," why does the poet call the past *iridescent?*
9. What emotion does the speaker in "Annabel Lee" feel most strongly?
10. What is the poet's message in "Miracles"?

Understanding Literature: Figurative Language and Sound Devices

Poets use figurative language and sound devices to add interest to poetry. Similes and metaphors are comparisons that might not seem clear at first. Understanding how the things are alike can give us new insight into the poet's subject. Personification means giving human qualities to things that are not human. This kind of comparison can help us see things in new ways.

Many poems use rhythm and rhyme to create a musical feeling. Poets have other sound devices from which to choose. They may use alliteration, which is the repeating of beginning sounds. They may use onomatopoeia, the use of words that sound like their meanings. Repetition of words and phrases can add rhythm and stress important ideas.

11. In "The Rider," what idea is personified? What object is personified?
12. Find two examples of alliteration in the translated haiku by Buson.
13. Of the poems in this unit, which use rhyme? List them.
14. What simile does Edna St. Vincent Millay use to show her mother's courage? How are the two things alike?

15. What does Paul Laurence Dunbar stress through his use of repetition in "Sympathy"?

Critical Thinking

16. Which poem in this unit has the most cheerful mood? Explain your answer.

17. Choose two poems that have a young person as the speaker. How are the speakers alike? How are they different?

18. "The Courage That My Mother Had" and "Martin Luther King" honor real people. What qualities do the poets honor? How do the endings of the poems differ?

Thinking Creatively

19. Which poem in this unit can you imagine yourself writing? Why did you choose that poem?

20. Which three poems from this unit would you pick to read to the class? Why?

Writing on Your Own

Write a poem about a subject in one of the poems in this unit. Pick a topic. Use a concept map, described in Appendix A, to brainstorm ideas about the topic. Decide whether you want the poem to rhyme. Will it be a lyric poem? Will it be a concrete poem or a narrative poem? Write and edit a draft. Ask classmates to review it. Then rewrite the draft. You and your class can create a book of poems to share.

Beyond Words

Choose the poem from this unit that gives you the clearest mental picture. Search old magazines to find photographs or illustrations that fit the poem's mood or imagery. Cut them out and paste them on colored paper to create a collage. See whether your classmates can figure out which poem your collage illustrates.

Speak and Listen

Choose a poet from the unit whose poem you liked. In the library or online, find another poem by that poet. Practice reading the poem. Then read the new poem aloud to your classmates. For an extra challenge, try to read the poem from memory.

Test-Taking Tip

If you are having trouble answering a question on a test, go to the next question. Later, come back to any skipped questions.

WRITING WORKSHOP

Persuasion: Persuasive Essay

When you use words to influence others, you are using persuasion. A persuasive essay is a brief work in which a writer presents the case for or against a particular position. Follow the steps outlined in this workshop to write your own persuasive essay.

Assignment Write a persuasive essay that influences readers to share your point of view. Write about an issue about which you feel strongly.

What to Include Your persuasive essay should feature the following elements:

- a clear statement of your position on an issue that has more than one side
- persuasive evidence that supports your position
- language that appeals to both reason and emotion
- a clear structure for an argument
- statements that identify and address reader concerns and arguments
- error-free writing, including proper sentence structure

Using the Form
You may use elements of this form in these writing situations:
- editorials
- reviews
- advertisements
- problem-and-solution essays

Prewriting

Choosing Your Topic

Use one of these strategies to find an issue that matters to you:

- **Round Table** With a group, hold a roundtable discussion of problems in your school. Raise as many different issues as possible. Write topics that spark strong feelings in you. Choose from among these subjects for your essay topic.
- **Quicklist** Fold a piece of paper in thirds lengthwise. In the first column, write issues and ideas that interest you. In the second column, write a descriptive word for each. In the third column, give an example supporting that description. Make sure each issue has an opposing side. Choose the topic that interests you most.

Narrowing Your Topic

Once you have chosen an issue to write about, narrow your focus. For example, the topic "violence in the media" is broad. It includes violence on news reports, in movies, and on television. To write an effective persuasive essay, you might focus only on violence in television shows.

Six Traits of Writing:
Ideas message, details, and purpose

Gathering Details

Gather evidence to support your position. Do your research in the library, on the Internet, or by interviewing experts. Gather the following types of support:

Facts: statements that can be proved true
Statistics: facts presented in the form of numbers
Anecdotes: brief stories that illustrate a point
Quotes from authorities: statements of leading experts

Anticipate counterarguments. Make a list of the arguments people might have against your position. For each, think of a response. Use that response to address the issues in your essay.

Writing Your Draft

Shaping Your Writing

Develop and support your thesis statement. To keep your position clearly before your readers, review your notes and develop a thesis statement—one strong sentence that sums up your argument. Include this statement in your introduction.

Organize to stress your arguments. As you draft, present the supporting evidence you have gathered. Start with your least important points and build toward your most important ones. Address opposing concerns and counter-arguments directly. Do not avoid them. Consider organizing as shown in the pyramid.

Introduction and thesis

- First set of arguments
- Supporting details

- Concerns and counterarguments
- Statements proving opposition is weak or incorrect
- Strongest argument

- Supporting details

Conclusions

Providing Elaboration

Choose precise words. Forceful language helps make your point and builds support for your position. Use precise, lively words. Your goal is to stir readers' emotions and appeal to their sense of reason.

Six Traits of Writing:
Word Choice vivid words that "show, not tell"

Vague: a good candidate
Precise: a trustworthy or smart candidate

Appeal to your audience. Use words that your audience will know. If you are writing for teenagers, use informal language. If you are writing to a government official, use formal, serious language.

Revising

Revising Your Overall Structure

Highlight main points. To check your organization, first highlight each main point. Then, use one or more of these strategies:

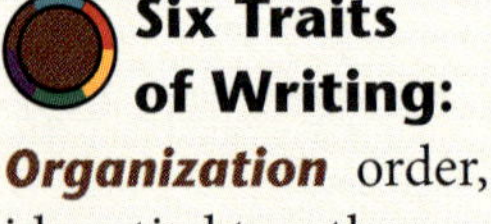

Six Traits of Writing:
Organization order, ideas tied together

- Does a reader need to know one main point to understand a second one? Make sure the first main point comes before the second.
- Does one main point mean the same as another? Combine them, or combine the paragraphs in which they appear.
- Is one main point stronger than the others? Move it to the end of your essay.

Peer Review: Read your draft to a group of peers. Ask whether the order of points was logical. Consider their responses as you revise.

Revising Your Sentences

Combine sentences to show connections. To improve your writing, combine short, choppy sentences to stress the connections you see.

Similar Ideas: The town permits skating on the lake.
We don't have the money to open a rink.

Combined: The town permits skating on the lake, and we don't have the money to open a rink.

Opposing Ideas: The food is better heated. Most classrooms do not have microwave ovens.

Combined: The food is better heated, but most classrooms do not have microwave ovens.

Editing and Proofreading

Check your writing to correct errors in spelling, grammar, and punctuation.

Focus on End Marks: Be sure to use the correct end mark for each kind of sentence in your essay. Use a period at the end of a statement or command. Use a question mark at the end of a question. Use an exclamation mark at the end of a statement that indicates strong feeling.

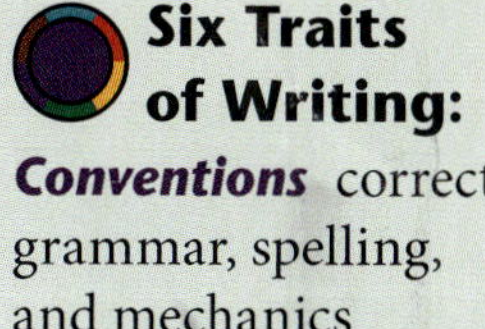

Conventions correct grammar, spelling, and mechanics

Publishing and Presenting

You might choose one of these ways to share your writing:

Give a speech. Use your persuasive essay as the basis for a speech for your classmates.

Submit a newspaper article. Many local newspapers will publish well-written persuasive compositions. Would your writing appeal to the newspaper's audience? Submit your writing and see what happens.

Reflecting on Your Writing

Writer's Journal Write your thoughts on the experience of writing a persuasive essay. Begin by answering these questions:

- What part of the writing process seemed difficult to you? Explain.
- What did you learn about your subject as you wrote?

Christmas Tree: Moonscape
Lou Wall

Unit 5 Drama

Drama comes from the Greek word *dran,* which means "to do" or "to act." Drama is the only type of literature that is not written only to be read. Instead, drama is meant to be performed. Plays, movies, and television shows are all dramas. Plays are usually done for live audiences. In many ways, plays are like poetry, stories, and novels. They all have characters, plots, settings, dialogue, and themes. Plays also have stage directions and certain theater words. These parts are only found in dramas. You will learn about stage directions and theater words in this unit.

"The stage but echoes back the public voice. The drama's laws the drama's patrons give, For we that live to please, must please to live."

—Ben Jonson
Prologue at the Opening of the Theatre in Drury Lane, 1747

Unit 5 Selections — Page

Unit 5 About Drama

Elements of Drama

Drama is a story told through the words and actions of characters, written to be performed as well as read.

The **playwright** is the author of a play. Actors are the people who perform the play.

An **act** is a major unit of action in a play. Acts are usually divided into **scenes.** A scene is a unit of action in a play that takes place in one setting.

Characterization is the way a writer develops character qualities and personality traits.

Dramatic speech is important in drama because it moves ahead the story's action. These are the most common types of speeches:

- **Dialogue** is the conversation among characters in a story; the words that characters in a play speak.
- **Monologue** is a longer speech told by one person.

Stage directions are notes by playwrights describing such things as setting, lighting, sound effects, and how the actors are to look, behave, move, and speak. Some writers use a code such as C, center stage; L, stage left; R, stage right; U, upstage or rear of stage; and D, downstage, or front of stage.

A **theater** is a place where plays are usually performed.

The **set** is the making of the stage that tells the time and place of the action. **Scenery** is another word for set.

A **prop** is a piece of equipment used on-stage during a play.

Types of Drama

Comedy is a form of drama that has a happy ending. The fun often comes out of the characters' dialogue. Comedies can be written for fun or to talk about something serious.

Tragedy is a play that ends with the suffering or death of one or more of the main characters.

Drama is a word used to tell that the play talks about something serious.

A drama is often written to be performed on a stage. However, a drama can be written for other reasons, too:

- **Screenplays** are scripts from which movies are made.
- **Teleplays** are types of screenplays written for television. Each of these has directions on where to put the camera. A teleplay usually has more scene changes than a stage play.
- **Radio plays** are written for radio. A radio play usually has sound effects, but not lighting or staging directions.

Reading Strategy:
Text Structure

The organization of a text helps readers figure out which parts are most important. Readers can also use text structure to help identify a purpose for reading. Two of the main reasons for reading a text are for entertainment and for information. As you read, ask yourself what is the purpose of the reading. Read each selection carefully so that you remember the information.

Literary Terms

drama a story told through the words and actions of characters, written to be performed as well as read

playwright the author of the play

act a major unit of action in a play

scene a unit of action in a play that takes place in one setting

dialogue the conversation among characters in a story; the words that characters in a play speak

character a person or animal in a story, poem, or play

stage directions what tells the actors how to perform their parts of a play; they describe movements, tone, use of props, lighting, and other details

motivation a reason a character does something

A Christmas Carol: Scrooge and Marley, Act I by Israel Horovitz

About the Authors

Charles Dickens
1812–1870

British writer Charles Dickens spent most of his life in London. The family was in debt, and Dickens lived through the problems of being poor. Dickens soon became a successful and popular writer. In his own day, he was a much-loved famous author.

Dickens wrote dozens of novels, short stories, and essays. He cared greatly about the suffering of poor people. Novels like *Oliver Twist* showed rich people what it was like to be poor. People who read Dickens's novel worked to change society.

A Christmas Carol is Dickens's most popular work. During his lifetime he was famous for giving public readings of the novel. Every Christmas, it is played on stages throughout the English-speaking world.

Israel Horovitz
1939–

Israel Horovitz was born in Wakefield, Massachusetts. He is the author of more than 50 plays and screenplays. As a teenager, Horovitz did not like books by Charles Dickens. As he grew older, however, he came to think of Dickens as "a masterful storyteller." Horovitz adapted the play you are about to read from the Dickens's novel *A Christmas Carol.*

About the Selection

Ebenezer Scrooge is a stingy old man who hates Christmas. One Christmas Eve, he receives a visit from Jacob Marley, his long-dead business partner. Marley's ghost warns Scrooge that his future looks terrible. He tells Scrooge that three more ghosts will come to visit him.

The first ghost arrives and shows him scenes of his past life. Scrooge sees himself as a boy and a young man. He begins to realize how important kindness and warmth are.

Objectives

- To read and understand a play
- To identify and understand dialogue in a play

Before Reading **continued on next page**

A Christmas Carol: Scrooge and Marley, Act I by Israel Horovitz

drama a story told through the words and actions of characters, written to be performed as well as read

playwright the author of the play

act a major unit of action in a play

scene a unit of action in a play that takes place in one setting

dialogue the conversation among characters in a story; the words that characters in a play speak

character a person or animal in a story, poem, or play

Literary Terms A **drama** is a story told through the words and actions of characters, written to be performed as well as read. The **playwright** is the author of the play. The author breaks the writing into **acts** and **scenes**. An act is a major unit of action in a play. A scene is a unit of action in a play that takes place in one setting. **Dialogue** is the conversation among characters in a story. In a play, the characters are developed largely through dialogue. A **character** is a person or animal in a story, poem, or play. Dialogue in prose looks somewhat different from dialogue in a play script. Look at the examples:

Dialogue in a Novel or Story	Dialogue in a Play
"Come on!" Ellen yelled.	Ellen: Come on!

Reading on Your Own To set a purpose for reading, follow these steps:

1. Preview the text. Glance through the pages. Look at the pictures and read a sentence here or a short passage there. Form an idea of what the text is like.
2. Think about what you might get out of reading this text. Ask questions as you preview the story.
3. Begin reading with your purpose in mind. Having a purpose makes reading interesting.

Writing on Your Own Have you ever heard someone called "a scrooge"? What kind of person is a scrooge? List some ideas that come to mind when you hear this word.

Vocabulary Focus *A Christmas Carol* includes dozens of words and expressions you may not know. Before you read, choose a partner. Together, go through the boldfaced vocabulary words at the bottom of each page.

Think Before You Read Have you ever been brought face to face with mistakes you made in the past? What did you learn from the experience?

A Christmas Carol: Scrooge and Marley

From A Christmas Carol by Charles Dickens

The People of the Play

JACOB MARLEY, a **specter**

EBENEZER SCROOGE, not yet dead, which is to say still alive

BOB CRATCHIT, Scrooge's clerk

FRED, Scrooge's nephew

THIN DO-GOODER

PORTLY DO-GOODER

SPECTERS (VARIOUS), carrying moneyboxes

THE GHOST OF CHRISTMAS PAST

FOUR **JOCUND** TRAVELERS

A BAND OF SINGERS

A BAND OF DANCERS

LITTLE BOY SCROOGE

YOUNG MAN SCROOGE

FAN, Scrooge's little sister

THE SCHOOLMASTER

SCHOOLMATES

FEZZIWIG, a fine and fair employer

DICK, young Scrooge's co-worker

YOUNG SCROOGE

A FIDDLER

MORE DANCERS

SCROOGE'S LOST LOVE

SCROOGE'S LOST LOVE'S DAUGHTER

SCROOGE'S LOST LOVE'S HUSBAND

THE GHOST OF CHRISTMAS PRESENT

SOME BAKERS

MRS. CRATCHIT, Bob Cratchit's wife

BELINDA CRATCHIT, a daughter

MARTHA CRATCHIT, another daughter

PETER CRATCHIT, a son

TINY TIM CRATCHIT, another son

SCROOGE'S NIECE, Fred's wife

THE GHOST OF CHRISTMAS FUTURE, a **mute Phantom**

THREE MEN OF BUSINESS

DRUNKS, **SCOUNDRELS**, WOMEN OF THE STREETS

A CHARWOMAN

MRS. DILBER

JOE, an old second-hand goods dealer

A CORPSE, very like Scrooge

AN **INDEBTED** FAMILY

ADAM, a young boy

A POULTERER

A GENTLEWOMAN

SOME MORE MEN OF BUSINESS

Charwoman is an old British word for a cleaning lady. A *poulterer* is like a butcher, but one who sells only poultry (turkey, chicken, ducks, geese). *Gentlewoman* is another term for a lady—someone wealthy and well-born.

specter a ghost

portly heavily built

jocund cheerful

mute silent

phantom a ghost

scoundrels criminals

indebted owing money

Act 1

As you read, make sure to read both the dialogue and the information in italics. Together, they will tell the whole story.

THE PLACE OF THE PLAY Various locations in and around the City of London, including Scrooge's Chambers and Offices; the Cratchit Home; Fred's Home; Scrooge's School; Fezziwig's Offices; Old Joe's Hide-a-Way.

THE TIME OF THE PLAY The entire action of the play takes place on Christmas Eve, Christmas Day, and the morning after Christmas, 1843.

Scene 1

Actors on stage often speak directly to the audience, as Marley does here. This is one way to give the audience important information.

[Ghostly music in ***auditorium.*** *A single spotlight on JACOB MARLEY, D.C. He is ancient; awful, dead-eyed. He speaks straight out to auditorium.]*

Marley *[Cackle-voiced]* My name is Jacob Marley and I am dead. *[He laughs.]* Oh, no, there's no doubt that I am dead. The **register** of my burial was signed by the clergyman, the clerk, the undertaker . . . and by my chief **mourner** . . . Ebenezer Scrooge . . . *[Pause; remembers]* I am dead as a doornail.

A *spotlight* literally creates a "spot of light" directly on an individual actor.

[A spotlight fades up, Stage Right, on SCROOGE, in his countinghouse, counting. Lettering on the window behind SCROOGE reads: "SCROOGE AND MARLEY, LTD." The spotlight is tight on SCROOGE's head and shoulders. We shall not yet see into the offices and setting. Ghostly music continues, under. MARLEY looks across at SCROOGE; ***pitifully.*** *After a moment's pause]*

I present him to you: Ebenezer Scrooge . . . England's most **tightfisted** hand at the grindstone, Scrooge! a squeezing, wrenching, grasping, scraping, clutching, **covetous,** old sinner! secret, and self-contained, and **solitary** as an oyster. The cold within him freezes his old features, nips his pointed

auditorium a theater

register a book of signatures

mourner one who grieves for a dead person

pitifully in a way that causes others to feel pity

tightfisted tight with money

covetous greedy

solitary alone, lonely

nose, shrivels his cheek, stiffens his **gait;** makes his eyes red, his thin lips blue; and speaks out shrewdly in his grating voice. Look at him. Look at him . . .

[SCROOGE counts and mumbles.]

Scrooge They owe me money and I will collect. I will have them jailed, if I have to. They owe me money and I will collect what is due me.

[MARLEY moves towards SCROOGE; two steps. The spotlight stays with him.]

Marley *[Disgusted]* He and I were partners for I don't know how many years. Scrooge was my sole executor, my sole administrator, my sole assign, my sole residuary legatee, my sole friend and my sole mourner.

But Scrooge was not so cut up by the sad event of my death, but that he was an excellent man of business on the very day of my funeral, and **solemnized** it with an undoubted bargain. *[Pauses again in disgust]* He never painted out my name from the window. There it stands, on the window and above the warehouse door: Scrooge and Marley. Sometimes people new to our business call him Scrooge and sometimes they call him Marley. He answers to both names. It's all the same to him. And it's cheaper than painting in a new sign, isn't it? *[Pauses; moves closer to SCROOGE]* Nobody has ever stopped him in the street to say, with gladsome looks, "My dear Scrooge, how are you? When will you come to see me?" No beggars **implored** him to **bestow** a

***Reading Strategy:* Text Structure**

What important information can you gather from the text on these first pages?

Executor, administrator, assign, and *residuary legatee* are legal terms. They mean that Scrooge handled Marley's remaining business affairs after Marley died.

What does the information in Marley's speech tell you about Scrooge? What kind of person does he seem to be?

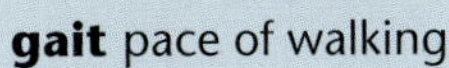

gait pace of walking

solemnized honored or remembered

implored begged

bestow to give

trifle, no children ever ask him what it is o'clock, no man or woman now, or ever in his life, not once, inquire the way to such and such a place. *[MARLEY stands next to SCROOGE now. They share, so it seems, a spotlight.]* But what does Scrooge care of any of this? It is the very thing he likes! To edge his way along the crowded paths of life, warning all human sympathy to keep its distance.

The abbreviation *D* stands for "downstage." It means "closer to the audience." *D.C.* means "downstage center," or in the middle of the stage.

*[A ghostly bell rings in the distance. MARLEY moves away from SCROOGE, now, heading D. again. As he does, he "takes" the light: SCROOGE has disappeared into the black **void** beyond. MARLEY walks D.C., talking directly to the audience. Pauses]*

The bell **tolls** and I must take my leave. You must stay a while with Scrooge and watch him play out his scroogey life. It is now the story: the once-upon-a-time. Scrooge is busy in his counting house. Where else? Christmas eve and Scrooge is busy in his counting-house. It is cold, **bleak,** biting weather outside: foggy withal: and, if you listen closely, you can hear the people in the court go **wheezing** up and down, beating their hands upon their breasts, and stamping their feet upon the pavement stones to warm them . . .

A *counting house* is an office. Scrooge is a moneylender. This means he lends money to people who would rather not deal with a bank. Moneylenders can charge very high rates of interest. The abbreviation Ltd. stands for "limited." In the United States, "Inc." means about the same as "Ltd."

[The clocks outside strike three.]

Only three! and quite dark outside already: it has not been light all day this day.

[This ghostly bell rings in the distance again. MARLEY looks about him. Music in. MARLEY flies away.]

trifle a little

void emptiness

tolls rings

bleak gray and cheerless

wheezing breathing heavily

Scene 2

[N.B. MARLEY's comings and goings should, from time to time, ***induce*** *the explosion of the odd flash-pot. I.H.]*

[Christmas music in, sung by a live chorus, full. At ***conclusion*** *of song, sound fades under and into the distance. Lights up in set: offices of Scrooge and Marley, Ltd. SCROOGE sits at his desk, at work. Near him is a tiny fire. His door is open and in his line of vision, we see SCROOGE's clerk, BOB CRATCHIT, who sits in a* ***dismal*** *tank of a cubicle, copying letters. Near CRATCHIT is a fire so tiny as to barely cast a light: perhaps it is one pitifully glowing coal? CRATCHIT rubs his hands together, puts on a white comforter and tries to heat his hands around his candle. SCROOGE's NEPHEW enters, unseen.]*

> A *flash-pot* is a special effect. It makes a small explosion.

> Cratchit's "comforter" is not a bedcover, but a scarf.

> Think about the time of year and what Marley has said about the weather. What do you think of Scrooge's reaction to Cratchit trying to warm his hands?

> *Humbug* means "false." *Bah! Humbug!* is Scrooge's most famous line of dialogue; something he says often.

Scrooge What are you doing, Cratchit? Acting cold, are you? Next, you'll be asking to **replenish** your coal from my coal-box, won't you? Well, save your breath, Cratchit! Unless you're prepared to find **employ** elsewhere!

Nephew *[Cheerfully; surprising SCROOGE]* A merry Christmas to you, Uncle! God save you!

Scrooge Bah! Humbug!

Nephew Christmas a "humbug," Uncle? I'm sure you don't mean that.

Scrooge I do! Merry Christmas? What right do you have to be merry? What reason have you to be merry? You're poor enough!

Nephew Come, then. What right have you to be dismal? What reason have you to be **morose?** You're rich enough.

Scrooge Bah! Humbug!

Nephew Don't be cross, Uncle.

induce persuade	**dismal** bare and ugly	**employ** a job
conclusion an ending	**replenish** to refill	**morose** gloomy and unhappy

Scrooge What else can I be? Eh? When I live in a world of fools such as this? Merry Christmas? What's Christmastime to you but a time of paying bills without any money; a time for finding yourself a year older, but not an hour richer. If I could work my will, every idiot who goes about with "Merry Christmas" on his lips, should be boiled with his own pudding, and buried with a stake of holly through his heart. He should!

Nephew Uncle!

Scrooge Nephew! You keep Christmas in your own way and let me keep it in mine.

Nephew Keep it! But you don't keep it, Uncle.

Scrooge Let me leave it alone, then. Much good it has ever done you!

What does this exchange of dialogue tell you about both Scrooge and his nephew?

Nephew There are many things from which I have **derived** good, by which I have not **profited,** I daresay. Christmas among the rest. But I am sure that I always thought of Christmas time, when it has come round—as a good time: the only time I know of, when men and women seem to open their shut-up hearts freely, and to think of people below them as if they really were fellow-passengers to the grave, and not another race of creatures bound on other journeys. And therefore, Uncle, though it has never put a scrap of gold or silver in my pocket, I believe that it has done me good, and that it will do me good; and I say, God bless it!

[The CLERK in the tank applauds, looks at the ***furious*** *SCROOGE and pokes out his tiny fire, as if in exchange for the moment of* ***impropriety.*** *SCROOGE yells at him.]*

Situation means "job." Scrooge threatens to fire Cratchit if he makes any more noise.

Scrooge *[To the clerk]* Let me hear another sound from you and you'll keep your Christmas by losing your situation.

Parliament is the lawmaking body of the British government. It is similar to the United States Congress.

[To the nephew] You're quite a powerful speaker, sir. I wonder you don't go into Parliament.

derived gotten

profited, made money on

furious very angry

impropriety bad behavior

Nephew Don't be angry, Uncle. Come! Dine with us tomorrow.

Scrooge I'd rather see myself dead than see myself with your family!

Nephew But, why? Why?

Scrooge Why did you get married?

Nephew Because I fell in love.

Scrooge That, sir, is the only thing that you have said to me in your entire lifetime which is even more ridiculous than "Merry Christmas"! *[Turns from NEPHEW]* Good afternoon.

Nephew Nay, Uncle, you never came to see me before I married either. Why give it as a reason for not coming now?

Scrooge Good afternoon, Nephew!

Nephew I want nothing from you; I ask nothing of you; why cannot we be friends?

Scrooge Good afternoon!

Nephew I am sorry with all my heart, to find you so **resolute.** But I have made the trial in **homage** to Christmas, and I'll keep my Christmas humor to the last. So A Merry Christmas, Uncle!

Scrooge Good afternoon!

Nephew And A Happy New Year!

Scrooge Good afternoon!

Nephew *[He stands facing SCROOGE.]* Uncle, you are the most . . . *[Pauses]* No, I shan't. My Christmas humor is **intact** . . . *[Pause]* God bless you, Uncle . . . *[NEPHEW turns and starts for the door; he stops at CRATCHIT's cage.]* Merry Christmas, Bob Cratchit . . .

Good afternoon means the same as "good-bye." Scrooge wants his nephew to leave.

resolute determined, not to be moved

homage respect

intact whole

Bedlam was a famous mental hospital in London. The basic unit of British money was (and is) a pound. 20 shillings = 1 pound. A half-crown, mentioned below, is worth 2½ shillings. In the nineteenth century, Saturday was a working day. Therefore Cratchit worked six days a week for his 15 shillings. This was very little money for a full-time job.

What does their conversation tell you about Scrooge's nephew and Cratchit?

Cratchit Merry Christmas to you sir, and a very, very happy New Year . . .

Scrooge *[Calling across to them]* Oh, fine, a perfection, just fine . . . to see the perfect pair of you: husbands, with wives and children to support . . . my clerk there earning fifteen shillings a week . . . and the perfect pair of you, talking about a Merry Christmas! *[Pauses]* I'll retire to Bedlam!

Nephew *[To CRATCHIT]* He's impossible!

Cratchit Oh, mind him not, sir. He's getting on in years, and he's alone. He's noticed your visit. I'll **wager** your visit has warmed him.

Nephew Him? Uncle Ebenezer Scrooge? Warmed? You are a better Christian than I am, sir.

Cratchit *[Opening the door for NEPHEW; two DO-GOODERS will enter, as NEPHEW exits]* Good day to you, sir, and God bless.

Nephew God bless . . . *[One man who enters is portly, the other is thin. Both are pleasant.]*

Cratchit Can I help you, gentlemen?

Thin Man *[Carrying papers and books; looks around CRATCHIT to SCROOGE]* Scrooge and Marley's, I believe. Have I the pleasure of addressing Mr. Scrooge, or Mr. Marley?

Scrooge Mr. Marley has been dead these seven years. He died seven years ago this very night.

Portly Man We have no doubt his **liberality** is well represented by his surviving partner . . . *[Offers his calling card]*

Scrooge *[Handing back the card; unlooked at]* . . . Good afternoon.

wager to bet

liberality generosity

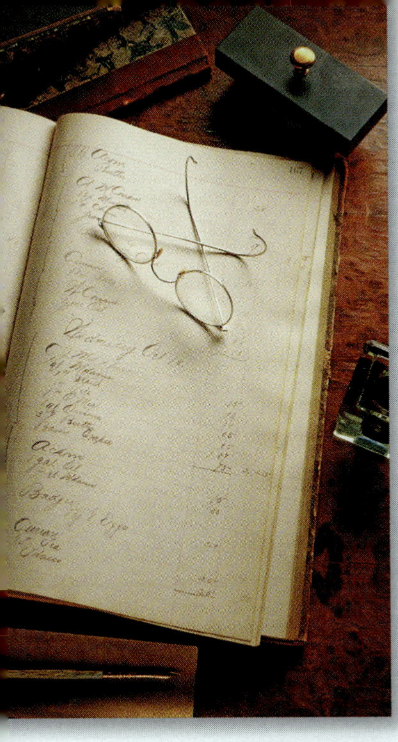

Thin Man This will take but a moment, sir . . .

Portly Man At this **festive** season of the year, Mr. Scrooge, it is more than usually **desirable** that we should make some slight **provision** for the poor and **destitute,** who suffer greatly at the present time. Many thousands are in want of common necessities; hundreds of thousands are in want of common comforts, sir.

Scrooge Are there no prisons?

Portly Man Plenty of prisons.

Scrooge And aren't the Union workhouses still in operation?

Thin Man They are. Still. I wish that I could say that they are not.

Scrooge The Treadmill and the Poor Law are in full **vigor,** then?

Thin Man Both very busy, sir.

Scrooge Ohhh, I see. I was afraid, from what you said at first, that something had occurred to stop them from their useful course. *[Pauses]* I'm glad to hear it.

Portly Man Under the impression that they scarcely furnish Christian cheer of mind or body to the **multitude,** a few of us are **endeavoring** to raise a fund to buy the Poor some meat and drink, and means of warmth. We choose this time, because it is a time, of all others, when Want is keenly felt, and Abundance rejoices. [*Pen in hand; as well as notepad*] What shall I put you down for, sir?

festive cheerful; like a party

desirable attractive

provision a gift

destitute people who have nothing

vigor strength

multitude the masses; the population

endeavoring trying

The *Treadmill* was a mill wheel turned by the weight of people. They continually climbed the steps of the wheel to turn it. The Treadmill was used to punish prisoners. The *Poor Law* of 1834 gave relief for the poor. The *Union Workhouses* were shelters that were started under the law. The shelters gave the poor homes, but they were a lot like prisons.

What does this dialogue tell you about Scrooge? Does it change your idea of him?

Abundance rejoices means "At this time of year there are many good things for people."

Scrooge Nothing!

Portly Man You wish to be left **anonymous?**

Scrooge I wish to be left alone! [*Pauses; turns away; turns back to them*] Since you ask me what I wish, gentlemen, that is my answer. I help to support the **establishments** that I have mentioned: they cost enough: and those who are badly off must go there.

Thin Man Many can't go there; and many would rather die.

Scrooge If they would rather die, they had better do it, and decrease the **surplus** population. Besides—excuse me—I don't know that.

Thin Man But you might know it!

Scrooge It's not my business. It's enough for a man to understand his own business, and not to **interfere** with other people's. Mine occupies me constantly. Good afternoon, gentlemen! [*SCROOGE turns his back on the gentlemen and returns to his desk.*]

Portly Man But, sir, Mr. Scrooge . . . think of the poor.

Scrooge [*Turns suddenly to them. Pauses*] Take your leave of my offices, sirs, while I am still smiling.

[The THIN MAN looks at the PORTLY MAN. They are undone. They shrug. They move to the door. CRATCHIT hops up to open it for them.]

Thin Man Good day, sir . . . [*To CRATCHIT*] A merry Christmas to you, sir . . .

Cratchit Yes. A Merry Christmas to both of you . . .

Portly Man Merry Christmas . . .

anonymous nameless

establishments companies, organizations, or businesses

surplus extra

interfere to involve oneself in

[CRATCHIT silently squeezes something into the hand of the THIN MAN.]

Thin Man What's this?

Cratchit Shhhh . . .

[CRATCHIT opens the door; wind and snow whistle into the room.]

Thin Man Thank you, sir, thank you.

[CRATCHIT closes the door and returns to his workplace. SCROOGE is at his own counting table. He talks to CRATCHIT without looking up.]

Scrooge It's less of a time of year for being merry, and more a time of year for being loony . . . if you ask me.

Cratchit Well, I don't know, sir . . . [*The clock's bell strikes six o'clock.*] Well, there it is, eh, six?

Scrooge Saved by six bells, are you?

Cratchit I must be going home . . . [*He snuffs out his candle and puts on his hat.*] I hope you have a . . . very very lovely day tomorrow, sir . . .

A candle snuffer is a small upside-down metal cone on the end of a long handle. When it is held on top of a candle flame, it puts out the flame.

Scrooge Hmmm. Oh, you'll be wanting the whole day tomorrow, I suppose?

Cratchit If quite convenient, sir.

Scrooge It's not convenient, and it's not fair. If I was to stop half-a-crown for it, you'd think yourself ill-used, I'll be bound?

Do you agree with Scrooge? Or do you think Cratchit deserves one paid holiday a year?

[CRATCHIT smiles faintly.]

Cratchit I don't know, sir . . .

Scrooge And yet, you don't think me ill-used when I pay a day's **wages** for no work . . .

wages salary

Cratchit It's only but once a year . . .

Scrooge A poor excuse for picking a man's pocket every 25th of December! But I suppose you must have the whole day. Be here all the earlier the next morning!

Cratchit Oh, I will, sir. I will. I promise you. And, sir . . .

Scrooge Don't say it, Cratchit.

Cratchit But let me wish you a . . .

Scrooge Don't say it, Cratchit. I warn you . . .

Cratchit Sir!

Scrooge Cratchit!

[CRATCHIT opens the door.]

Why do you think Cratchit insists on wishing Scrooge "Merry Christmas"?

Cratchit All right, then, sir . . . well . . . [*Suddenly*] Merry Christmas, Mr. Scrooge!

[And he runs out the door, shutting same behind him. SCROOGE moves to his desk; gathering his coat, hat, etc. A BOY appears at his window. . . .]

Boy *[Singing]* "Away in a manger . . ."

[SCROOGE seizes his ruler and whacks at the image of the BOY outside. The BOY leaves.]

Scrooge Bah! Humbug! Christmas! Bah! Humbug! *[He shuts out the light.]*

A note on the crossover, following Scene 2:

Why do you think Scrooge dislikes Christmas so much?

[SCROOGE will walk alone to his rooms from his offices. As he makes a long slow cross of the stage, the scenery should change. Christmas music will be heard, various people will cross by SCROOGE, often smiling happily.

There will be occasional pleasant greetings tossed at him.

SCROOGE, in contrast to all, will grump and mumble. He will snap at passing boys, as might a horrid old hound.

In short, SCROOGE's sounds and movements will define him in contrast from all other people who cross the stage: he is the ***misanthrope,*** *the* ***malcontent,*** *the* ***miser.*** *He is SCROOGE.*

This statement of SCROOGE's character, by contrast to all other characters, should seem comical to the audience.

During SCROOGE's crossover to his rooms, snow should begin to fall. All passers-by will hold their faces to the sky, smiling, allowing snow to shower them lightly. SCROOGE, by contrast, will bat at the flakes with his walking-stick, as might an ***insomniac*** *swat at a sleep-stopping, middle-of-the-night swarm of mosquitoes. He will comment on the blackness of the night, and, finally, reach his rooms and his* ***encounter*** *with the magical specter: MARLEY, his eternal mate.]*

***Reading Strategy:* Text Structure**

What does the look of the text have to do with your reading rate on this page? Does it change your purpose for reading?

Scene 3

Scrooge No light at all . . . no moon . . . that is what is at the center of a Christmas Eve: dead black: void . . .

[SCROOGE puts his key in the door's keyhole. He has reached his rooms now. The door knocker changes and is now MARLEY's face. A musical sound; quickly: ghostly. MARLEY's image is not at all angry, but looks at SCROOGE as did the old MARLEY look at SCROOGE. The hair is curiously stirred; eyes wide open, dead: absent of focus. SCROOGE stares wordlessly here. The face, before his very eyes, does ***deliquesce.*** *It is a knocker again. SCROOGE opens the door and checks the back of same, probably for MARLEY's pigtail. Seeing nothing but screws and nuts, SCROOGE refuses the memory.]*

By *stirred,* the playwright means that Marley's hair is blowing in the wind.

Pooh, pooh!

misanthrope someone who hates mankind

malcontent an unhappy person

miser one who hates to spend money

insomniac one who has trouble sleeping

encounter to meet or find

deliquesce to melt away; disappear

[The sound of the door closing ***resounds*** *throughout the house as thunder. Every room echoes the sound. SCROOGE fastens the door and walks across the hall to the stairs, trimming his candle as he goes; and then he goes slowly up the staircase. He checks each room: sitting room, bedrooms, slumber room. He looks under the sofa, under the table: nobody there. He fixes his evening gruel on the hob, changes his jacket. SCROOGE sits near the tiny low-flamed fire, sipping his gruel. There are* ***various*** *pictures on the walls: all of them now show likenesses of MARLEY. SCROOGE blinks his eyes.]*

Gruel is a thin broth. The *hob* is a ledge in the fireplace. People would set a dish or cup of food on the hob to warm it up.

Bah! Humbug!

[SCROOGE walks in a circle about the room. The pictures change back into their natural images. He sits down at the table in front of the fire. A bell hangs overhead. It begins to ring, of its own accord. Slowly, surely, begins the ringing of every bell in the house. They continue ringing for nearly half a minute. SCROOGE is stunned by the ***phenomenon.*** *The bells cease their ringing all at once. Deep below SCROOGE, in the basement of the house, there is the sound of clanking, of some enormous chain being dragged across the floors; and now up the stairs. We hear doors flying open.]*

Bah still! Humbug still! This is not happening! I won't believe it!

[MARLEY'S GHOST enters the room. He is horrible to look at: pigtail, vest, suit as usual, but he drags an enormous chain now, to which is fastened cash-boxes, keys, padlocks, ledgers, deeds, and heavy purses fashioned of steel. He is ***transparent.*** *MARLEY stands opposite the stricken SCROOGE.]*

How now! What do you want of me?

Marley Much!

resounds echoes loudly throughout a space

various different from one another

phenomenon a happening, an event

transparent see-through

Scrooge Who are you?

Marley Ask me who I was.

Scrooge Who were you then?

Marley In life, I was your business partner: Jacob Marley.

Scrooge I see . . . can you sit down?

Marley I can.

Scrooge Do it then.

Marley I shall. *[MARLEY sits opposite SCROOGE, in the chair across the table, at the front of the fireplace.]* You don't believe in me.

Scrooge I don't.

Marley Why do you doubt your senses?

Scrooge Because every little thing affects them. A slight disorder of the stomach makes them cheat. You may be an undigested bit of beef, a blot of mustard, a crumb of cheese, a fragment of an underdone potato. There's more of gravy than of grave about you, whatever you are!

[There is a silence between them. SCROOGE is made nervous by it. He picks up a toothpick.]

Why do you think Scrooge is nervous?

Humbug! I tell you: humbug!

[MARLEY opens his mouth and screams a ghosty, fearful scream. The scream echoes about each room of the house. Bats fly, cats screech, lightning flashes. SCROOGE stands and walks backwards against the wall. MARLEY stands and screams again. This time, he takes his head and lifts it from his shoulders. His head continues to scream. MARLEY's face again appears on every picture in the room: all screaming. SCROOGE, on his knees before MARLEY.]

Mercy! Dreadful **apparition,** mercy! Why, O! why do you trouble me so?

Marley Man of the worldly mind, do you believe in me, or not?

Scrooge I do. I must. But why do spirits such as you walk the earth? And why do they come to me?

Marley It is **required** of every man that the spirit within him should walk abroad among his fellow-men, and travel far and wide; and if that spirit goes not forth in life, it is **condemned** to do so after death. *[MARLEY screams again; a tragic scream; from his ghosty bones.]* I wear the chain I **forged** in life. I made it link by link, and yard by yard. Is its pattern strange to you? Or would you know, you, Scrooge, the weight and length of the strong coil you bear yourself? It was full as heavy and long as this, seven Christmas Eves ago. You have labored on it, since. It is a **ponderous** chain.

apparition a ghost

required necessary

condemned judged as a criminal

forged made out of iron

ponderous large and heavy

[Terrified that a chain will appear about his body, SCROOGE spins and waves the unwanted chain away. None, of course, appears. Sees MARLEY watching him dance about the room. MARLEY watches SCROOGE; silently.]

There is no real chain on Scrooge. The chain is symbolic. Explain what you think the chain stands for. HINT: note what Marley's chain is made of.

Scrooge Jacob. Old Jacob Marley, tell me more. Speak comfort to me, Jacob . . .

Marley I have none to give. Comfort comes from other regions, Ebenezer Scrooge, and is **conveyed** by other **ministers,** to other kinds of men. A very little more, is all that is permitted to me. I cannot rest, I cannot stay, I cannot **linger** anywhere . . . *[He moans again.]* my spirit never walked beyond our countinghouse—mark me!—in life my spirit never **roved** beyond the narrow limits of our moneychanging hole; and weary journeys lie before me!

Mark me! is Marley's way of saying "Listen! Pay attention!"

Scrooge But you were always a good man of business, Jacob.

Marley *[Screams word "business"; a flash-pot explodes with him.]* BUSINESS!!! Mankind was my business. The common **welfare** was my business; charity, mercy, **forbearance, benevolence,** were, all, my business. *[SCROOGE is quaking.]* Hear me, Ebenezer Scrooge! My time is nearly gone.

Scrooge I will, but don't be hard upon me. And don't be flowery, Jacob! Pray!

Marley How is it that I appear before you in a shape that you can see, I may not tell. I have sat invisible beside you many and many a day. That is no light part of

conveyed sent

ministers those who care for others

linger to wait

roved wandered

welfare well-being

forbearance patience

benevolence goodness

my **penance.** I am here tonight to warn you that you have yet a chance and hope of escaping my fate. A chance and hope of my **procuring,** Ebenezer.

What does their conversation tell you about Scrooge and Marley's friendship during Marley's lifetime?

Scrooge You were always a good friend to me. Thank'ee!

Marley You will be haunted by Three Spirits.

Scrooge Would that be the chance and hope you mentioned, Jacob?

Marley It is.

Scrooge I think I'd rather not.

Marley Without their visits, you cannot hope to **shun** the path I **tread.** Expect the first one tomorrow, when the bell tolls one.

Scrooge Couldn't I take 'em all at once, and get it over, Jacob?

Marley Expect the second on the next night at the same hour. The third upon the next night when the last stroke of twelve has ceased to **vibrate.** Look to see me no more. Others may, but you may not. And look that, for your own sake, you remember what has passed between us!

[MARLEY places his head back upon his shoulders. He approaches the window and beckons to SCROOGE to watch. Outside the window, specters fly by, carrying money-boxes and chains. They make a confused sound of ***lamentation.*** *MARLEY, after listening a moment, joins into their mournful* ***dirge.*** *He leans to the window and floats out into the bleak, dark night. He is gone.]*

Scrooge *[Rushing to the window]* Jacob! No, Jacob! Don't leave me! I'm frightened!

penance a punishment

procuring getting hold of, acquiring

shun to avoid

tread to walk on

vibrate to move rapidly back and forth

lamentation sad cries or songs

dirge slow and sad music

[He sees that MARLEY has gone. He looks outside. He pulls the shutter closed, so that the scene is blocked from his view. All sound stops. After a pause, he re-opens the shutter and all is quiet, as it should be on Christmas Eve. ***Carolers*** *carol out of doors, in the distance. SCROOGE closes the shutter and walks down the stairs. He examines the door by which MARLEY first entered.]*

No one here at all! Did I imagine all that? Humbug! *[He looks about the room.]* I did imagine it. It only happened in my foulest dream-mind, didn't it? An undigested bit of . . . *[Thunder and lightning in the room; suddenly]* Sorry! Sorry!

[There is silence again. The lights fade out.]

Shutters are pieces of wood cut to fit over windows. In cold weather, people would close and lock their shutters at night. This helped to keep the room warmer. Because shutters blocked all light out, people would open them again during the day.

Scene 4

[Christmas music, choral, "Hark the Herald Angels Sing," sung by an onstage choir of children, spotlighted, D.C. Above, SCROOGE in his bed, dead to the world, asleep, in his darkened room. It should appear that the choir is singing somewhere outside of the house, of course, and a use of scrim is thus suggested. When the singing is ended, the choir should fade out of view and MARLEY should fade into view, in their place.]

Marley *[Directly to audience]* From this point forth . . . I shall be quite visible to you, but invisible to him. [Smiles] He will feel my presence, nevertheless, for, unless my senses fail me completely, we are—you and I—witness to the changing of a miser: that one, my partner in life, in business, and in **eternity:** that one: Scrooge. *[Moves to staircase, below SCROOGE]* See him now. He **endeavors** to **pierce** the darkness with his ferret eyes. *[To audience]* See him, now. He listens for the hour.

A *scrim* is a thin curtain used in theater. When strong light is shown on a scrim, it becomes transparent. The audience can then see what is happening behind it.

A *ferret* is a small rodent that looks something like a weasel. Ferrets have very good eyesight, even in dim light.

carolers people singing Christmas songs

eternity forever

endeavors tries

pierce to stab or cut through

[The bells toll. SCROOGE is awakened and ***quakes*** *as the hour approaches one o'clock, but the bells stop their sound at the hour of twelve.]*

Scrooge *[Astonished]* Midnight! Why this isn't possible. It was past two when I went to bed. An icicle must have gotten into the clock's works! I couldn't have slept through the whole day and far into another night. It isn't possible that anything has happened to the sun, and this is twelve at noon! [He runs to window; unshutters same; it is night.] Night, still. Quiet, normal for the season, cold. It is certainly not noon. I cannot in any way afford to lose my days. Securities come due, promissory notes, interest on investments: these are things that happen in the daylight! *[He returns to his bed.]* Was this a dream?

Promissory notes are legal IOUs. A person signs a promissory note stating that he will pay back money by a certain date.

[MARLEY appears in his room. He speaks to the audience.]

Marley You see? He does not, with faith, believe in me fully, even still! Whatever will it take to turn the faith of a miser from money to men?

Scrooge Another quarter and it'll be one and Marley's ghosty friends will come. *[Pauses; listens]* Where's the chime for one? *[Ding, dong]* A quarter past *[Repeats]* Half-past! *[Repeats]* A quarter to it! But where's the heavy bell of the hour one? This is a game in which I lose my senses! Perhaps, if I allowed myself another short doze . . .

Marley . . . Doze, Ebenezer, doze.

[A heavy bell thuds its one ring; dull and definitely one o'clock.

There is a flash of light. SCROOGE sits up, in a sudden. A hand draws back the curtains by his bed. He sees it.]

Heavy curtains around the bed kept the cold air out during the winter.

quakes shakes

Scrooge A hand! Who owns it! Hello!

[Ghosty music again, but of a new nature to the play. A strange figure stands before SCROOGE—like a child, yet at the same time like an old man: white hair, but unwrinkled skin, long, muscular arms, but delicate legs and feet. Wears white tunic; **lustrous** *belt cinches waist. Branch of fresh green holly in its hand, but has its dress trimmed with fresh summer flowers. Clear jets of light spring from the crown of its head. Holds cap in hand. The Spirit is called PAST.]*

A *tunic* is a piece of clothing. It is longer than a shirt but shorter than a dress.

Are you the Spirit, sir, whose coming was foretold to me?

Past I am.

Marley Does he take this to be a vision of his greengrocer?

Greengrocer is a British term for a grocer. A greengrocer sells fresh produce and other food in a small market.

Scrooge Who, and what are you?

Past I am the Ghost of Christmas Past.

Scrooge Long past?

Past Your past.

Scrooge May I ask, please, sir, what business you have here with me?

Past Your welfare.

Scrooge Not to sound ungrateful, sir, and really, please do understand that I am plenty **obliged** for your concern, but, really, kind spirit, it would have done all the better for my welfare to have been left alone altogether, to have slept peacefully through this night.

Past Your **reclamation,** then. Take heed!

Scrooge My what?

Past *[Motioning to SCROOGE and taking his arm]* Rise! Fly with me! *[He leads SCROOGE to the window.]*

lustrous full of light

obliged thankful

reclamation return to goodness; act of saving

What do you think Christmas Past means by this line of dialogue? What double meaning of *upheld* is suggested?

A *dissolve* is a lighting effect. Lights fade, making it appear that one scene melts away. They come up slowly on a new scene which was rapidly changed during the dimness.

Freezes is a theater word. It means that the actor stops all movement. Scrooge stands totally still through Marley's speech. The audience understands that a "frozen" actor cannot hear or see anything. The freeze ends with the puff of smoke and Marley's disappearance.

Scrooge *[Panicked]* Fly, but I am a **mortal** and cannot fly!

Past *[Pointing to his heart]* Bear but a touch of my hand here and you shall be upheld in more than this!

[SCROOGE touches the spirit's heart and the lights dissolve into sparkly flickers. Lovely crystals of music are heard. The scene dissolves into another. Christmas music again]

Scene 5

[SCROOGE and the GHOST OF CHRISTMAS PAST walk together across an open stage. In the background, we see a field that is open; covered by a soft, downy snow: a country road.]

Scrooge Good Heaven! I was **bred** in this place. I was a boy here!

[SCROOGE freezes, staring at the field beyond. MARLEY'S ghost appears beside him; takes SCROOGE'S face in his hands, and turns his face to the audience.]

Marley You see this Scrooge: stricken by feeling. **Conscious** of a thousand odors floating in the air, each one connected with a thousand thoughts, and hopes, and joys, and care long, long forgotten. [Pause] This one—this Scrooge—before your very eyes, returns to life, among the living. *[To audience, sternly]* You'd best pay your most careful attention. I would suggest **rapt.**

[There is a small flash and puff of smoke and MARLEY is gone again.]

Past Your lip is trembling, Mr. Scrooge. And what is that upon your cheek?

Scrooge Upon my cheek? Nothing . . . a **blemish** on the skin from the eating of overmuch grease . . . nothing . . . *[Suddenly]*

mortal a human

bred born

conscious aware

rapt deep

blemish mark or pimple

Kind Spirit of Christmas Past, lead me where you will, but quickly! To be **stagnant** in this place is, for me, **unbearable!**

Past You **recollect** the way?

Scrooge Remember it! I would know it blindfolded! My bridge, my church, my winding river! *[**Staggers** about, trying to see it all at once. He weeps again.]*

Past These are but shadows of things that have been. They have no consciousness of us.

[Four jocund travelers enter, singing a Christmas song in four-part harmony—"God Rest Ye Merry Gentlemen."]

Scrooge Listen! I know these men! I know them! I remember the beauty of their song!

Past But, why do you remember it so happily? It is Merry Christmas that they say to one another! What is Merry Christmas to you, Mr. Scrooge? Out upon Merry Christmas, right? What good has Merry Christmas ever done you, Mr. Scrooge? . . .

Scrooge *[After a long pause]* None. No good. None . . . *[He bows his head.]*

Past Look, you, sir, a school ahead. The schoolroom is not quite deserted. A solitary child, neglected by his friends, is left there still.

[SCROOGE falls to the ground; sobbing as he sees, and we see, a small boy, the young SCROOGE, sitting and weeping, bravely, alone at his desk: alone in a vast space, a void.]

Scrooge I cannot look on him!

Past You must, Mr. Scrooge, you must.

stagnant stuck

unbearable too unpleasant

recollect remember

staggers walks unsteadily

Scrooge It's me. *[Pauses; weeps]* Poor boy. He lived inside his head . . . alone . . . *[Pauses; weeps]* poor boy. *[Pauses; stops his weeping]* I wish . . . *[Dries his eyes on his cuff]* ah! it's too late!

Past What is the matter?

What change in Scrooge is shown by this dialogue?

Scrooge There was a boy singing a Christmas Carol outside my door last night. I should like to have given him something: that's all.

Past *[Smiles; waves his hand to SCROOGE]* Come. Let us see another Christmas.

[Lights out on little boy. A flash of light. A puff of smoke. Lights up on older boy]

Scrooge Look! Me, again! Older now! *[Realizes]* Oh, yes . . . still alone.

[The boy—a slightly older SCROOGE —sits alone in a chair, reading. The door to the room opens and a young girl enters. She is much, much younger than this slightly older SCROOGE. She is, say, six, and he is, say, twelve. Elder SCROOGE and the GHOST OF CHRISTMAS PAST stand watching the scene, unseen.]

Fan Dear, dear brother, I have come to bring you home.

Boy Home, little Fan?

What does Fan's speech suggest about young Scrooge's family life? How do you think he gets along with his father?

Fan Yes! Home, for good and all! Father is so much kinder than he ever used to be, and home's like heaven! He spoke so gently to me one dear night when I was going to bed that I was not afraid to ask him once more if you might come home; and he said "yes" . . . you should; and sent me in a coach to bring you. And you're to be a man and are never to come back here, but first, we're to be together all the Christmas long, and have the merriest time in the world.

Boy You are quite a woman, little Fan!

[Laughing; she drags at boy, causing him to stumble to the door with her. Suddenly we hear a mean and terrible voice in the hallway, Off. It is the SCHOOLMASTER.]

Schoolmaster Bring down Master Scrooge's travel box at once! He is to travel!

Scrooge's *travel box* is his trunk of clothes and personal belongings. *Master* was a title given to young boys.

Fan Who is that, Ebenezer?

Boy O! Quiet, Fan. It is the Schoolmaster, himself!

[The door bursts open and into the room bursts with it the SCHOOLMASTER.]

Schoolmaster Master Scrooge?

Boy Oh, Schoolmaster. I'd like you to meet my little sister, Fan, sir . . .

[Two boys struggle on with SCROOGE'S trunk.]

Fan Pleased, sir . . . *[She curtsies.]*

A *curtsy* is a polite show of respect. Fan would bend her knee, bend slightly at the waist, and lower her head. A boy like young Scrooge would bow instead. To bow, a boy bends forward at the waist and lowers his head.

Schoolmaster You are to travel, Master Scrooge.

Scrooge Yes, sir. I know sir . . .

[All start to exit, but FAN grabs the coattail of the mean old SCHOOLMASTER.]

Boy Fan!

Schoolmaster What's this?

Fan Pardon, sir, but I believe that you've forgotten to say your goodbye to my brother, Ebenezer, who stands still now awaiting it . . . *[She smiles, curtsies, lowers her eyes.]* pardon, sir.

Schoolmaster *[Amazed]* I . . . uh . . . harumph . . . uhh . . . well, then . . . *[Outstretches hand]* Goodbye, Scrooge.

What picture of the Schoolmaster does this dialogue give you? What do you think school was like for Scrooge and his classmates?

Boy Uh, well, goodbye, Schoolmaster . . .

[Lights fade out on all but BOY looking at FAN; and SCROOGE and PAST looking at them.]

Scrooge Oh, my dear, dear little sister, Fan . . . how I loved her.

Past Always a delicate creature, whom a breath might have **withered,** but she had a large heart . . .

Scrooge So she had.

How do you think Scrooge feels when he is reminded that his nephew is Fan's son?

Past She died a woman, and had, as I think, children.

Scrooge One child.

Past True. Your nephew.

Scrooge Yes.

An *apprentice* is a young person learning a trade or job. The apprentice would work for no wages for a certain number of years. An apprentice receives food, a place to live, and valuable work experience. This training helps young people to start in business on their own. The apprentice training plan began in ancient times. Today, it is not common in the U.S., but is still used in some other countries.

Past Fine, then. We move on, Mr. Scrooge. That warehouse, there? Do you know it?

Scrooge Know it? Wasn't I apprenticed there?

Past We'll have a look.

[They enter the warehouse. The lights crossfade with them, coming up on an old man in Welsh wig: FEZZIWIG.]

Scrooge Why, it's old Fezziwig! Bless his heart; it's Fezziwig, alive again!

[FEZZIWIG sits behind a large, high desk, counting. He lays down his pen; looks at the clock: seven bells sound.] Quittin' time . . .

Fezzwig Quittin' time . . . *[He takes off his waistcoat and laughs; calls off]* Yo ho, Ebenezer! Dick!

[DICK WILKINS and EBENEZER SCROOGE—a young man version—enter the room. DICK and EBENEZER are FEZZIWIG's apprentices.]

A *waistcoat* is a sleeveless vest worn over a shirt and under a coat. It is often made of fancier material than a man's coat and breeches (short pants).

Scrooge Dick Wilkins, to be sure! My fellow-'prentice! Bless my soul, yes. There he is. He was very much attached to me, was Dick. Poor Dick! Dear, dear!

Fezzwig Yo ho, my boys. No more work tonight. Christmas Eve, Dick. Christmas, Ebenezer!

withered crumbled

[They stand at attention in front of FEZZIWIG; laughing] Hilli-ho! Clear away, and let's have lots of room here! Hilli-ho, Dick! Chirrup, Ebenezer!

[The young men clear the room, sweep the floor, straighten the pictures, trim the lamps, etc. The space is clear now. A fiddler enters, fiddling.]

The lamps are oil-burning lamps. As their wicks burn down, the ends need to be "trimmed" so the light will not go out.

Hi-ho, Matthew! Fiddle away . . . where are my daughters?

[The fiddler plays. Three young daughters of FEZZIWIG enter followed by six young male **suitors.** *They are dancing to the music. All employees come in: workers, clerks, housemaids, cousins, the baker, etc. All dance. Full number wanted here.*

Throughout the dance, food is brought into the feast. It is "eaten" in dance, by the dancers. EBENEZER dances with all three of the daughters, as does DICK. They compete for the daughters, happily, in the dance. FEZZIWIG dances with his daughters. FEZZIWIG dances with DICK and EBENEZER. The music changes: MRS. FEZZIWIG enters. She lovingly scolds her husband. They dance. She dances with EBENEZER, lifting him and throwing him about. She is enormously fat. When the dance is ended, they all dance off, floating away, as does the music. SCROOGE and the GHOST OF CHRISTMAS PAST stand alone now. The music is gone.]

Past It was a small matter, that Fezziwig made those silly folks so full of gratitude.

Scrooge Small!

Past Shhh!

[Lights up on DICK and EBENEZER]

Dick We are blessed, Ebenezer, truly, to have such a master as Mr. Fezziwig!

suitors young men who want to marry particular girls

Young Scrooge He is the best, best, the very and absolute best! If ever I own a firm of my own, I shall treat my apprentices with the same dignity and the same grace. We have learned a wonderful lesson from the master, Dick!

Dick Ah, that's a fact, Ebenezer. That's a fact!

Past Was it not a small matter, really? He spent but a few pounds of his mortal money on your small party. Three or four pounds, perhaps. Is that so much that he deserves such praise as you and Dick so **lavish** now?

Scrooge It isn't that! It isn't that, Spirit. Fezziwig had the power to make us happy or unhappy; to make our service light or **burdensome;** a pleasure or a **toil.** The happiness he gave is quite as great as if it cost him a fortune.

Past What is the matter?

Scrooge Nothing particular.

lavish to give generously

burdensome heavy to carry

toil hard work

Past Something, I think.

Scrooge No, no. I should like to be able to say a word or two to my clerk just now! That's all!

What lesson do you think Scrooge has just learned?

[EBENEZER enters the room and shuts down all the lamps. He stretches and yawns. The GHOST OF CHRISTMAS PAST turns to SCROOGE all of a sudden.]

Past My time grows short! Quick!

[In a flash of light, EBENEZER is gone, and in his place stands an OLDER SCROOGE, this one a man in the prime of his life. Beside him stands a young woman in a mourning dress. She is crying. She speaks to the man, with ***hostility.****]*

Woman It matters little . . . to you, very little. Another **idol** has **displaced** me.

What is the relationship between young Scrooge and this woman? How can you tell?

Man What idol has displaced you?

Woman A golden one.

Man This is an even-handed dealing of the world. There is nothing on which it is so hard as poverty; and there is nothing it professes to condemn with such severity as the pursuit of wealth!

Woman You fear the world too much. Have I not seen your nobler **aspirations** fall off one by one, until the master-passion, Gain, **engrosses** you? Have I not?

Scrooge No!

Man What then? Even if I have grown so much wiser, what then? Have I changed towards you?

Woman No . . .

Man Am I?

hostility hatred and anger

idol an object of worship

displaced taken the place of something

aspirations goals

engrosses absorbs

Woman Our contract is an old one. It was made when we were both poor and content to be so. You are changed. When it was made, you were another man.

Man I was not another man: I was a boy.

Woman Your own feeling tells you that you were not what you are. I am. That which promised happiness when we were one in heart is **fraught** with misery now that we are two . . .

Scrooge No!

Woman How often and how keenly I have thought of this, I will not say. It is enough that I have thought of it, and can release you . . .

Scrooge *[Quietly]* Don't release me, madame . . .

Man Have I ever sought release?

Woman In words. No. Never.

Man In what then?

Woman In a changed nature; in an altered spirit. In everything that made my love of any worth or value in your sight. If this has never been between us, tell me, would you seek me out and try to win me now? Ah, no!

Scrooge Ah, yes!

Man You think not?

A dowry was the money and property a young woman owned. When she married, she brought her dowry with her. *Dowerless* means that Scrooge's young woman has no dowry. She has no money or property to bring to the marriage.

Woman I would gladly think otherwise if I could, heaven knows! But if you were free today, tomorrow, yesterday, can even I believe that you would choose a dowerless girl—you who in your very confidence with her weigh everything by Gain; or, choosing her, do I not know that your repentance and regret would surely follow? I do; and I release you. With a full heart, for the love of him you once were.

Scrooge Please, I . . . I . . .

fraught full of

Man Please, I . . . I . . .

Woman Please. You may—the memory of what is past half makes me hope you will—have pain in this. A very, very brief time, and you will dismiss the memory of it, as an unprofitable dream, from which it happened well that you awoke. May you be happy in the life that you have chosen for yourself . . .

Scrooge No!

Woman Yourself . . . alone . . .

Scrooge No!

Woman Goodbye, Ebenezer . . .

Scrooge Don't let her go!

Man Goodbye.

Scrooge No!

[She exits. SCROOGE goes to younger man: himself.] You fool! Mindless loon! You fool!

Why is the line "Fool. Mindless loon. Fool" repeated?

Man [To exited woman] Fool. Mindless loon. Fool . . .

Scrooge Don't say that! Spirit, remove me from this place.

Past I have told you these were shadows of the things that have been. They are what they are. Do not blame me, Mr. Scrooge.

Scrooge Remove me! I cannot bear it!

[The faces of all who appeared in this scene are now projected for a moment around the stage: enormous, ***flimsy,*** *silent.]*

Leave me! Take me back! Haunt me no longer!

[There is a sudden flash of light: a flare. The GHOST OF CHRISTMAS PAST is gone. SCROOGE is, for the moment, alone onstage. His bed is turned down, across the stage. A

flimsy not solid or sturdy

small candle burns now in SCROOGE'S hand. There is a child's cap in his other hand. He slowly crosses the stage to his bed, to sleep. MARLEY appears behind SCROOGE, who continues his long, elderly cross to bed. MARLEY speaks directly to the audience.]

Marley Scrooge must sleep now. He must **surrender** to the **irresistible drowsiness** caused by the recognition of what was. *[Pauses]* The cap he carries is from ten lives past: his boyhood cap . . . **donned** atop a hopeful hairy head . . . **askew,** perhaps, or at a **rakish** angle. **Doffed** now in honor of regret. Perhaps even too heavy to carry in his present state of weak remorse . . .

[SCROOGE drops the cap. He lies atop his bed. He sleeps. To audience]

He sleeps. For him, there's even more trouble ahead. *[Smiles]* For you? The play house tells me there's hot cider, as should be your anticipation for the specter Christmas Present and Future, for I promise you both. *[Smiles again]* So, I pray you hurry back to your seats refreshed and ready for a miser—to turn his coat of gray into a blazen Christmas holly-red. *[A flash of lightning. A clap of thunder. Bats fly. Ghosty music. MARLEY is gone.]*

surrender give in to

irresistible cannot be withstood

drowsiness sleepiness

donned put on

askew crooked

rakish dashing, jaunty

doffed took off

A Christmas Carol: Scrooge and Marley, Act I by Israel Horovitz

Directions Choose the letter of the best answer or write the answer using complete sentences.

Comprehension: Identifying Facts

1. Who is Bob Cratchit?
- **A** Scrooge's partner
- **B** Scrooge's clerk
- **C** Scrooge's nephew
- **D** Scrooge's brother

2. When does the first scene of the play take place?
- **A** in London
- **B** in Scrooge's office
- **C** on December 24
- **D** on December 25

3. Why does Scrooge's nephew come to the counting-house?

4. Where does Scrooge go when he closes the counting-house for the day?

5. What do the two gentlemen who visit Scrooge's office want from him?

6. Why does Jacob Marley's ghost visit Scrooge?

7. What does Marley tell Scrooge to expect on the next three nights?

8. What does the Spirit of Christmas Past look like?

9. Who is the young woman who speaks with Scrooge in the final scene?

10. What does Marley suggest to the audience about Act II?

Comprehension: Putting Ideas Together

11. Why does Jacob Marley wear a chain?
- **A** because he was a miser in his lifetime
- **B** because he was a criminal in his lifetime
- **C** to warn Scrooge what may happen to him
- **D** to force Scrooge to listen to what he says

12. Why does Scrooge refuse to give anything to help the poor?
- **A** He does not believe there are any poor people.
- **B** He has already given as much as he can afford.
- **C** He is very poor himself and cannot spare anything.
- **D** He feels no sympathy for the situation of the poor.

13. Scrooge often says "Bah. Humbug!" What exactly does he mean when he says this?

After Reading **continued on next page**

A Christmas Carol: Scrooge and Marley, Act I by Israel Horovitz

14. How does Scrooge treat Bob Cratchit?

15. What unusual things happen when Scrooge gets home that night?

16. What does Marley imply will happen to Scrooge if he does not change?

17. Which scenes from his past does Scrooge visit?

18. Why does Scrooge weep when he sees the place where he was a boy?

19. What kind of person is Fezziwig? Which details support your answer?

20. Why does the young woman break off her relationship with Scrooge?

Understanding Literature: Dialogue

To an audience in a theater, dialogue is the most important part of a play. Audiences do not have the chance to read any of the notes in the play. They can only hear dialogue. Actors use their faces, voices, and body language to show emotion through dialogue.

21. Describe the relationship between Scrooge and his nephew.

22. What kinds of things does Scrooge mutter during his walk home from the counting-house? What does this tell you about him?

23. Based on his dialogue, how does Scrooge feel during his conversation with Marley?

24. What does Fan's speech tell you about Scrooge's family life?

25. What can you tell about both Scrooge and his lost love from the final scene?

Critical Thinking

26. What is your overall feeling about Ebenezer Scrooge? Use details from the play to support your answer.

27. Do you believe that Scrooge will indeed change for the better? What hints in the play support your answer?

28. Between Fezziwig's Christmas party and parting with his lost love, Scrooge has changed a lot. What do you think brought about this change?

29. How have Scrooge's past experiences made him the person he has become? Does his past excuse his present behavior? Explain.

Thinking Creatively

30. Would you take your family to see this play at Christmastime? Why or why not?

Grammar Check

Interjections add expression to your writing. An interjection shows a feeling, such as pain or excitement. An interjection may be set off with a comma or an exclamation point. When writing dialogue, use interjections to make the language sound more real.

Pain: Ouch! I hit my toe.

Excitement: Wow, Melissa can certainly run fast!

Add an interjection to help express emotion in each sentence.

1 That violinist plays well!
2 We did not expect you today.
3 Jim, you almost fell!
4 The cake tastes burnt.
5 Gina, come here.

Vocabulary Builder

The suffix *-ment* means "the act or quality of." Adding *-ment* to a verb creates a noun.

Examples:
excite/excitement
arrange/arrangement

Add *-ment* to each word and use it correctly in a sentence.

1 amuse
2 encourage
3 measure
4 fulfill

Writing on Your Own

Pretend that you are Fred, Scrooge's nephew. Write to Scrooge, telling him what he is missing in life. Follow the correct form for a friendly letter. Include strong support for your opinions.

Listening and Speaking

Give an oral summary of the plot of Act I. Identify the setting and describe the main characters. Explain the conflicts and main events of the act. Identify questions that you expect to be answered in Act II.

Media and Viewing

Prepare costume designs for this play. Research the clothing worn during the Victorian period in England. Use the Internet and library to do your research. Use information, photos, sketches, and descriptions to plan costumes for two different characters in Act I. Show or describe the type of clothing, the color, and the fabric.

BEFORE READING THE SELECTION | **Build Understanding**

A Christmas Carol: Scrooge and Marley, Act II *by Israel Horovitz*

Charles Dickens
1812–1870

Israel Horovitz
1939–

Objectives

- To read and understand a play
- To identify and understand stage directions in a play

About the Authors

When he was a boy, Dickens's father went to debtor's prison. He owed money and had to stay in jail until the debts were paid. Young Charles had to work long hours in a factory. His job was to paste labels on bottles. Dickens never recovered from the shame he felt over the family debts. His novels contain many young boys struggling against poverty.

As a young man, Dickens taught himself shorthand. He soon took a job as a court reporter. In his early twenties, Dickens began to publish funny stories. Most of Dickens's novels came out in monthly parts in magazines. Each month, readers would eagerly wait for another chapter or two.

Playwright Israel Horovitz lives in New York. He has written more than 50 plays. Actors Al Pacino, Marsha Mason, and Jill Clayburgh began their careers in Horovitz plays. *A Christmas Carol: Scrooge and Marley* was first produced in Baltimore, Maryland, in 1978.

Shortly after the September 11, 2001, attacks, Horovitz wrote a play about the event. The play, *3 Weeks After Paradise*, tells about his experiences during the time.

About the Selection

Scrooge meets the Ghost of Christmas Present. He sees the Cratchits and his nephew celebrate Christmas. The Ghost of Christmas Future shows him his own lonely death. Scrooge awakens Christmas morning planning to be a better and kinder person. He sends the Cratchits a turkey and goes to his nephew's house for dinner. The next day, he gives Bob Cratchit a raise. He becomes a good master and a good friend.

Literary Terms **Stage directions** are the words in a script that are not spoken by characters. Audiences in a theater can see the set, characters, and movements, and hear sound effects. When you read a play, you see this information in the stage directions. Stage directions are usually written in italic type and set off by brackets or parentheses.

stage directions what tells the actors how to perform their parts of a play; they describe movements, tone, use of props, lighting, and other details

Reading on Your Own Setting a purpose for reading helps you determine and adjust your reading rate. If you are reading directions to perform a task, you should read slowly and carefully. Make sure you understand each step before you begin. If you are reading a play, here are some things to keep in mind:

- Read stage directions slowly and carefully. They may suggest action and mood that does not show in the dialogue.
- Read short lines of dialogue quickly. This helps you get the feeling of conversation.
- Read longer speeches more slowly. Think about the character's words and look for clues to the message.

Writing on Your Own Write a description of your favorite scene from *A Christmas Carol, Act I.* Use details so that someone might draw the scene from your description.

Vocabulary Focus Continue to go over boldfaced vocabulary words before you read. You might go through them one scene at a time. Use context clues and sound-alike words to help you define the new words.

Think Before You Read Would you be grateful to have a friend like Jacob Marley? Why or why not?

A Christmas Carol: Scrooge and Marley

From A Christmas Carol by Charles Dickens

Act II

Scene 1

[Lights. Choral music is sung. Curtain. SCROOGE, in bed, sleeping, in spotlight. We cannot yet see the ***interior*** *of his room. MARLEY, opposite, in spotlight equal to SCROOGE'S. MARLEY laughs. He tosses his hand in the air and a flame shoots from it, magically, into the air. There is a thunder clap, and then another; a lightning flash, and then another. Ghostly music plays under. Colors change. MARLEY'S spotlight has gone out and now reappears, with MARLEY in it, standing next to the bed and the sleeping SCROOGE. MARLEY addresses the audience directly.]*

Reading Strategy:
Text Structure

As you read, note the different kinds of text. How do they help you understand what you are reading?

Marley Hear this snoring Scrooge! Sleeping to escape the nightmare that is his waking day. What shall I bring to him now? I'm afraid nothing would astonish old Scrooge now. Not after what he's seen. Not a baby boy, not a rhinoceros, nor anything in between would astonish Ebenezer Scrooge just now. I can think of nothing . . . *[Suddenly]* that's it! Nothing! *[He speaks* ***confidentially.****]* I'll have the clock strike one and, when he awakes expecting my second messenger, there will be no one . . . nothing. Then I'll have the bell strike twelve. And then one again . . . and then nothing. Nothing . . . *[Laughs]* nothing will . . . astonish him. I think it will work.

[The bell tolls one. SCROOGE leaps awake.]

interior inside

confidentially as a secret

Scrooge One! One! This is it: time! *[Looks about the room]* Nothing!

[The bell tolls midnight.]

Midnight! How can this be? I'm sleeping backwards.

[One again]

Good heavens! One again! I'm sleeping back and forth! *[A pause. SCROOGE looks about.]* Nothing! Absolutely nothing!

[Suddenly, thunder and lightning. MARLEY laughs and disappears. The room shakes and glows. There is suddenly springlike music. SCROOGE makes a run for the door.]

Marley Scrooge!

Scrooge What?

Marley Stay you put!

Scrooge Just checking to see if anyone is in here.

[Lights and thunder again: more music. MARLEY is of a sudden gone. In his place sits the GHOST OF CHRISTMAS PRESENT—to be called in the stage directions of the play, PRESENT—center of room. Heaped up on the floor, to form a kind of throne, are turkeys, geese, game, poultry, brawn, great joints of meat, suckling pigs, long wreaths of sausages, mince-pies, plum puddings, barrels of oysters, red hot chestnuts, cherry-cheeked apples, juicy oranges, ***luscious*** *pears,* ***immense*** *twelfth cakes, and* ***seething*** *bowls of punch, that make the chamber dim with their delicious steam. Upon this throne sits PRESENT,* ***glorious*** *to see. He bears a torch, shaped as a Horn of Plenty. SCROOGE hops out of the door, and then peeks back again into his bedroom. PRESENT calls to SCROOGE.]*

Present Ebenezer Scrooge. Come in, come in! Come in and know me better!

Twelfthcakes are cakes made to eat on Twelfth Night, January 6. Twelfth Night is also called Epiphany or Three Kings' Day. Christians believe this is the date of the Magis' arrival at the site of Jesus' birth. A *Horn of Plenty* is also known as a cornucopia. It is shaped like a twisted cone. Its wide end flares open. A Horn of Plenty is filled with fruits of the harvest.

luscious tasty, juicy
immense huge
seething simmering, boiling
glorious wonderful

Scrooge Hello. How should I call you?

Present I am the Ghost of Christmas Present. Look upon me.

What do the stage directions tell you about Present? Would you know any of this from the dialogue?

[PRESENT is wearing a simple green robe. The walls around the room are now covered in greenery, as well. The room seems to be a perfect ***grove*** *now: leaves of holly, mistletoe and ivy reflect the stage lights. Suddenly, there is a mighty roar of flame in the fireplace and now the* ***hearth*** *burns with a* ***lavish,*** *warming fire. There is an ancient* ***scabbard girdling*** *the GHOST'S middle, but without sword. The* ***sheath*** *is gone to rust.]*

You have never seen the like of me before?

Scrooge Never.

Present You have never walked forth with younger members of my family; my elder brothers born on Christmases past.

Scrooge I don't think I have. I'm afraid I've not. Have you had many brothers, Spirit?

Present More than eighteen hundred.

The Ghost means that in every year, there has been a Christmas. This play takes place in 1834. Therefore this Ghost is the 1,834th Spirit of Christmas Present. Scrooge's response shows that he does not understand the joke.

Scrooge A tremendous family to provide for! *[PRESENT stands]* Spirit, conduct me where you will. I went forth last night

grove a small group of trees

hearth area in front of the fireplace

lavish generous, large in size

scabbard a loop from which a sword or dagger hangs

girdling wrapped around

sheath a cover for the blade of a sword or dagger

on **compulsion,** and learnt a lesson which is working now. Tonight, if you have aught to teach me, let me profit by it.

> How does Scrooge's dialogue show that he has already changed?

> *Aught* is a way of saying "anything." It is no longer in use.

Present Touch my robe.

[SCROOGE walks cautiously to PRESENT and touches his robe. When he does, lightning flashes, thunder claps, music plays. Blackout]

Scene 2

[PROLOGUE: MARLEY stands spotlit, L. He speaks directly to the audience.]

Marley My ghostly friend now leads my living partner through the city's streets.

> This line of dialogue tells the audience something that is happening before their eyes. Playwrights often write dialogue that serves this purpose. While sets are changed or when the stage is bare, audiences can get confused. They may not know where the characters are or what is happening. Dialogue like Marley's helps audiences know what is going on.

[Lights up on SCROOGE and PRESENT]

See them there and hear the music people make when the weather is **severe,** as it is now.

*[Winter music. Choral group behind scrim, sings. When the song is done and the stage is re-set, the lights will fade up on a row of shops, behind the singers. The choral group will hum the song they have just completed now and **mill** about the streets, carrying their dinners to the bakers' shops and restaurants. They will, perhaps, sing about being poor at Christmastime, whatever.]*

Present These **revelers,** Mr. Scrooge, carry their own dinners to their jobs, where they will work to bake the meals the rich men and women of this city will eat as their Christmas dinners. Generous people these . . . to care for the others, so . . .

*[PRESENT walks among the choral group and a sparkling **incense** falls from his torch on to their baskets, as he pulls*

> How do the stage directions help you understand and picture the scene?

compulsion force

severe harsh

mill to wander around

revelers people having fun

incense wood or spices that smell strong and sweet when burned *the covers off of the baskets. Some of the choral group become angry with each other.]*

Man #1 Hey, you, watch where you're going.

Man #2 Watch it yourself, mate!

[PRESENT sprinkles them directly, they change.]

Man #1 I pray go in ahead of me. It's Christmas. You be first!

Man #2 No, no, I must insist that YOU be first!

Man #1 All right, I shall be, and gratefully so.

Man #2 The pleasure is equally mine, for being able to watch you pass, smiling.

Man #1 I would find it a shame to quarrel on Christmas Day.

Man #2 As would I.

Man #1 Merry Christmas then, friend!

How did the incense from the torch change the two men?

Man #2 And a Merry Christmas straight back to you!

[Church bells toll. The choral group enter the buildings: the shops and restaurants; they exit the stage, shutting their doors closed behind them. All sound stops. SCROOGE and PRESENT are alone again.]

Scrooge What is it you sprinkle from your torch?

Present Kindness.

Scrooge Do you sprinkle your kindness on any particular people or on all people?

Present To any person kindly given. And to the very poor most of all.

Scrooge Why to the very poor most?

Present Because the very poor need it most. Touch my heart . . . here, Mr. Scrooge. We have another journey.

[SCROOGE touches the GHOST'S heart and music plays, lights change color, lightning flashes, thunder claps. A choral group appears on the street, singing Christmas carols.]

Scene 3

*[MARLEY stands spotlit in front of a scrim on which is painted the **exterior** of CRATCHIT'S four-roomed house. There is a flash and a clap and MARLEY is gone. The lights shift color again, the scrim flies away, and we are in the interior of the CRATCHIT family home. SCROOGE is there, with the SPIRIT (PRESENT), watching MRS. CRATCHIT set the table, with the help of BELINDA CRATCHIT and PETER CRATCHIT, a baby, pokes a fork into the mashed potatoes on his highchair's tray. He also chews on his shirt collar.]*

Scrooge What is this place, Spirit?

Present This is the home of your employee, Mr. Scrooge. Don't you know it?

Scrooge Do you mean Cratchit, Spirit? Do you mean this is Cratchit's home?

Present None other.

Scrooge These children are his?

Present There are more to come presently.

Scrooge On his **meager** earnings! What foolishness!

Present Foolishness, is it?

Scrooge Wouldn't you say so? Fifteen shillings a week's what he gets!

Present I would say that he gets the pleasure of his family, fifteen times a week times the number of hours a day! Wait, Mr. Scrooge. Wait, listen and watch. You might actually learn something . . .

exterior outside

meager very small amount

Warn't means "was not." Mrs. Cratchit does not always use proper English. You know from this that she is not an educated person.

Mrs. Cratchit What has ever got your precious father then? And your brother, Tiny Tim? And Martha warn't as late last Christmas by half an hour!

[MARTHA opens the door, speaking to her mother as she does.]

Martha Here's Martha, now, Mother! *[She laughs. The CRATCHIT CHILDREN squeal with delight.]*

Belinda It's Martha, Mother! Here's Martha!

Peter Marthmama, Marthmama! Hullo!

Belinda Hurrah! Martha! Martha! There's such an enormous goose for us, Martha!

Mrs. Cratchit Why, bless your heart alive, my dear, how late you are!

In Dickens's novel, readers learn that Martha works in a milliner's shop. A milliner makes ladies' hats. The milliner made Martha work into the night on Christmas Eve. She then had to work on Christmas morning before going to her parents' house. Scrooge is not the only mean employer in the city.

Martha We'd a great deal of work to finish up last night, and had to clear away this morning, Mother.

Mrs. Cratchit Well, never mind so long as you are come. Sit ye down before the fire, my dear, and have a warm, Lord bless ye!

Belinda No, no! There's Father coming. Hide, Martha, hide!

[MARTHA giggles and hides herself.]

Martha Where? Here?

Peter Hide, hide!

Belinda Not there! THERE!

[MARTHA is hidden. BOB CRATCHIT enters, carrying TINY TIM atop his shoulder. He wears a ***threadbare*** *and fringeless comforter hanging down in front of him. TINY TIM carries small crutches and his small legs are bound in an iron frame brace.]*

Bob and Tiny Tim Merry Christmas.

threadbare almost worn through

Bob Merry Christmas my love, Merry Christmas Peter, Merry Christmas Belinda. Why, where is Martha?

Mrs. Cratchit Not coming.

Bob Not coming: Not coming upon Christmas Day?

Martha *[Pokes head out]* Ohhh, poor Father. Don't be disappointed.

Bob What's this?

Martha 'Tis I!

Bob Martha! *[They embrace.]*

Tiny Tim Martha! Martha!

Martha Tiny Tim!

[TINY TIM is placed in MARTHA'S arms. BELINDA and PETER rush him offstage.]

Belinda Come, brother! You must come hear the pudding singing in the copper.

Tiny Tim The pudding? What flavor have we?

Peter Plum! Plum!

Tiny Tim Oh, Mother! I love plum!

[The children exit the stage, giggling.]

Mrs. Cratchit And how did little Tim behave?

Bob As good as gold, and even better. Somehow he gets thoughtful sitting by himself so much, and thinks the strangest things you ever heard. He told me, coming home, that he hoped people saw him in the church, because he was a **cripple,** and it might be pleasant to them to remember upon Christmas Day, who made lame beggars walk and blind men

What does this dialogue tell you about Tiny Tim?

cripple a disabled person who is unable to walk

see. *[Pauses]* He has the oddest ideas sometimes, but he seems all the while to be growing stronger and more **hearty** . . . one would never know. *[Hears TIM'S crutch on floor outside door]*

Peter The goose has arrived to be eaten!

Belinda Oh, mama, mama, it's beautiful.

Martha It's a perfect goose, Mother!

Tiny Tim To this Christmas goose, Mother and Father I say . . . *[Yells]* Hurrah! Hurrah!

Other Children *[Copying TIM]* Hurrah! Hurrah!

[The family sits round the table. BOB and MRS. CRATCHIT serve the trimmings, quickly. All sit; all bow heads; all pray.]

hearty strong

Bob Thank you, dear Lord, for your many gifts . . . our dear children; our wonderful meal; our love for one another; and the warmth of our small fire—*[Looks up at all]* A merry Christmas to us, my dear. God bless us!

All *[Except TIM]* Merry Christmas! God bless us!

Tiny Tim *[In a short silence]* God bless us every one.

[All freeze. Spotlight on PRESENT and SCROOGE]

Scrooge Spirit, tell me if Tiny Tim will live.

Present I see a **vacant** seat . . . in the poor chimney corner, and a crutch without an owner, carefully **preserved.** If these shadows remain **unaltered** by the future, the child will die.

Scrooge No, no, kind Spirit! Say he will be spared!

Scrooge means he wants Tiny Tim to live. To *be spared* is an old wording that is not often used anymore.

Present If these shadows remain unaltered by the future, none other of my race will find him here. What then? If he be like to die, he had better do it, and decrease the surplus population.

[SCROOGE bows his head. We hear BOB'S voice speak SCROOGE's name.]

Christmas Present repeats Scrooge's own words from Act I. What do the stage directions tell you about how Scrooge feels about hearing the words?

Bob Mr. Scrooge . . .

Scrooge Huh? What's that? Who calls?

Bob *[His glass raised in a toast]* I'll give you Mr. Scrooge, the Founder of the Feast!

Scrooge Me, Bob? You toast me?

Present Save your breath, Mr. Scrooge. You can't be seen or heard.

Mrs. Cratchit The Founder of the Feast, indeed! I wish I had him here, that miser Scrooge. I'd give him a piece of my mind to feast upon, and I hope he'd have a good appetite for it!

Bob My dear! Christmas Day!

vacant empty | **preserved** saved | **unaltered** not changed

Mrs. Cratchit It should be Christmas Day, I am sure, on which one drinks the health of such an **odious,** stingy, unfeeling man as Mr. Scrooge . . .

Scrooge Oh, Spirit, must I? . . .

Mrs. Cratchit You know he is, Robert! Nobody knows it better than you do, poor fellow!

Bob This is Christmas Day, and I should like to drink to the health of the man who employs me and allows me to earn my living and our support and that man is Ebenezer Scrooge . . .

What is the difference between Mr. and Mrs. Cratchit's feelings about Mr. Scrooge?

Mrs. Cratchit I'll drink to his health for your sake and the day's, but not for his sake . . . a Merry Christmas and a Happy New Year to you, Mr. Scrooge, wherever you may be this day!

Scrooge Just here, kind madam . . . out of sight, out of sight . . .

Bob Thank you, my dear. Thank you.

What do you think Scrooge has learned from this scene?

Scrooge Thank you, Bob . . . and Mrs. Cratchit, too. No one else is toasting me, . . . not now . . . not ever. Of that I am sure . . .

Bob Children . . .

All Merry Christmas to Mr. Scrooge.

Bob I'll pay you sixpence, Tim, for my favorite song.

Tiny Tim Oh, Father, I'd so love to sing it, but not for pay. This Christmas goose—this feast—you and Mother, my brother and sisters close with me: that's my pay—

A *lute* is a stringed instrument. It has a pear-shaped body and a long neck like that of a guitar. It is played by plucking, or pulling, the strings.

Bob Martha, will you play the notes on the lute, for Tiny Tim's song.

Belinda May I sing, too, Father?

Bob We'll all sing.

odious hateful

[They sing a song about a tiny child lost in the snow—probably from Wordsworth's poem. TIM sings the lead vocal; all chime in for the chorus. Their song fades under, as the GHOST OF CHRISTMAS PRESENT speaks.]

Present Mark my words, Ebenezer Scrooge. I do not present the Cratchits to you because they are a handsome, or brilliant family. They are not handsome. They are not brilliant. They are not well-dressed, or tasteful to the times. Their shoes are not even waterproofed by virtue of money or cleverness spent. So when the pavement is wet, so are the insides of their shoes and the tops of their toes. These are the Cratchits, Mr. Scrooge. They are not highly special. They are happy, grateful, pleased with one another, contented with the time and how it passes. They don't sing very well, do they? But, nonetheless, they do sing . . . *[Pauses]* think of that, Scrooge. Fifteen shillings a week and they do sing . . . hear their song until its end.

Scrooge I am listening. *[The chorus sings full volume now, until . . . the song ends here.]* Spirit, it must be time for us to take our leave. I feel in my heart that it is . . . that I must think on that which I have seen here . . .

Present Touch my robe again . . .

[SCROOGE touches PRESENT'S robe. The lights fade out on the CRATCHITS, who sit, frozen, at the table. SCROOGE and PRESENT in a spotlight now. Thunder, lightning, smoke. They are gone.]

William Wordsworth was one of the best-known poets in England. The stage direction is about a poem called "Lucy Gray, or Solitude." Lucy tries to light her mother's way home through the snow. She gets lost. Her parents follow her footprints over the snow until they disappear on a bridge.

Reading Strategy:
Text Structure

Name the kinds of text on this page. How do they help you understand and picture the action?

Scene 4

[MARLEY appears D.L.in single spotlight. A storm brews. Thunder and lightning. SCROOGE and PRESENT "fly" past, U. The storm continues, ***furiously,*** *and, now and again, SCROOGE and PRESENT will zip past in their travels. MARLEY will speak straight out to the audience.]*

Marley The Ghost of Christmas Present, my co-worker in this attempt to turn a miser, flies about now with that very miser, Scrooge, from street to street, and he points out partygoers on their way to Christmas parties. If one were to judge from the numbers of people on their way to friendly gatherings, one might think that no one was left at home to give anyone welcome . . . but that's not the case, is it? Every home is expecting company and . . . *[He laughs.]* Scrooge is amazed.

In Dickens's novel, Present took Scrooge to visit a mine. They watch as the miners celebrate Christmas. This is what Scrooge talks about in his last line of dialogue.

[SCROOGE and PRESENT zip past again. The lights fade up around them. We are in the NEPHEW'S home, in the living room. PRESENT and SCROOGE stand watching the NEPHEW: FRED and his wife, fixing the fire.]

Scrooge What is this place? We've moved from the mines!

Present You do not recognize them?

Scrooge It is my nephew! . . . and the one he married . . .

What does Scrooge's line "the one he married" tell you about him? Why would he not say "his wife" instead?

[MARLEY waves his hand and there is a lightning flash. He disappears.]

Fred It strikes me as sooooo funny, to think of what he said . . . that Christmas was a humbug, as I live! He believed it!

Wife More shame for him, Fred!

Fred Well, he's a comical old fellow, that's the truth.

Wife I have no patience with him.

furiously angrily

Fred Oh, I have! I am sorry for him; I couldn't be angry with him if I tried. Who suffers by his ill **whims?** Himself, always . . .

Scrooge It's me they talk of, isn't it, Spirit?

Fred Here, wife, consider this. Uncle Scrooge takes it into his head to dislike us, and he won't come and dine with us. What's the **consequence?**

Wife Oh . . . you're sweet to say what I think you're about to say, too, Fred . . .

Fred What's the consequence? He don't lose much of a dinner by it, I can tell you that!

Wife Ooooooo, Fred! Indeed, I think he loses a very good dinner . . . ask my sisters, or your **bachelor** friend, Topper . . . ask any of them. They'll tell you what old Scrooge, your uncle, missed: a dandy meal!

Fred Well, that's something of a relief, wife. Glad to hear it! *[He hugs his wife. They laugh. They kiss.]* The truth is, he misses much yet. I mean to give him the same chance every year, whether he likes it or not, for I pity him. Nay, he is my only uncle and I feel for the old miser . . . but, I tell you, wife: I see my dear and perfect mother's face on his own **wizened** cheeks and brow: brother and sister they were, and I cannot erase that from each view of him I take . . .

Wife I understand what you say, Fred, and I am with you in your yearly asking. But he never will accept, you know. He never will.

Fred Well, true, wife. Uncle may **rail** at Christmas till he dies. I think I shook him some with my visit yesterday . . . *[Laughing]* I refused to grow angry . . . no matter how nasty he became . . . *[Whoops]* It was HE who grew angry, wife! *[They both laugh now.]*

whims moods

consequence result

bachelor an unmarried man

wizened wrinkled and dried up

rail to yell at

Scrooge What he says is true, Spirit . . .

Fred and Wife Bah, humbug!

Fred *[Embracing his wife]* There is much laughter in our marriage, wife. It pleases me. You please me . . .

Wife And you please me, Fred. You are a good man . . . *[They embrace.]* Come now. We must have a look at the meal . . . our guests will soon arrive . . . my sisters, Topper . . .

Fred A toast first . . . *[He hands her a glass.]* A toast to Uncle Scrooge . . . *[Fills their glasses]*

Wife A toast to him?

Fred Uncle Scrooge has given us plenty of merriment, I am sure, and it would be ungrateful not to drink to his health. And I say . . . Uncle Scrooge!

What do you think Scrooge wants to say to Fred and his wife?

Wife *[Laughing]* You're a proper loon, Fred . . . and I'm a proper wife to you . . . *[She raises her glass.]* Uncle Scrooge! *[They drink. They embrace. They kiss.]*

Scrooge Spirit, please, make me visible! Make me **audible!** I want to talk with my nephew and my niece!

[Calls out to them. The lights that light the room and FRED and wife fade out. SCROOGE and PRESENT are alone, spotlit.]

Present These shadows are gone to you now, Mr. Scrooge. You may return to them later tonight in your dreams. *[Pauses]* My time grows short, Ebenezer Scrooge. Look you on me! Do you see how I've aged?

Scrooge Your hair has gone gray! Your skin, wrinkled! Are spirits' lives so short?

Present My stay upon this globe is very brief. It ends tonight.

Scrooge Tonight?

Present At midnight. The time is drawing near!

audible loud or clear enough to be heard

[Clock strikes 11:45.]

Hear those chimes? In a quarter hour, my life will have been spent! Look, Scrooge, man. Look you here. *[Two* ***gnarled*** *baby dolls are taken from PRESENT'S skirts.]*

Scrooge Who are they?

Present They are Man's children, and they cling to me, appealing from their fathers. The boy is Ignorance; the girl is Want. Beware them both, and all of their degree, but most of all beware this boy, for I see that written on his **brow** which is **doom,** unless the writing be erased. *[He stretches out his arm. His voice is now* ***amplified:*** *loudly and oddly.]*

In Dickens's novel, *Ignorance* and *Want* are live children, not dolls. Why do you think they are made into dolls in the play?

Scrooge Have they no **refuge** or resource?

Present Are there no prisons? Are there no workhouses? *[Twelve chimes]* Are there no prisons? Are there no workhouses?

[A PHANTOM, hooded, appears in dim light, D., opposite.] Are there no prisons? Are there no workhouses?

[PRESENT begins to deliquesce. SCROOGE calls after him.]

Scrooge Spirit, I'm frightened! Don't leave me! Spirit!

Present Prisons? Workhouses? Prisons? Workhouses . . .

gnarled twisted and bent

brow a forehead

doom death

amplified made louder

refuge a place of safety

[He is gone. SCROOGE is alone now with the PHANTOM, who is, of course, the GHOST OF CHRISTMAS FUTURE. The PHANTOM is ***shrouded*** *in black. Only its outstretched hand is visible from under his ghostly* ***garment.****]*

Scrooge Who are you, Phantom? Oh, yes, I think I know you! You are, are you not, the Spirit of Christmas Yet to Come? *[No reply]* And you are about to show me the shadows of the things that have not yet happened, but will happen in time before us. Is that not so, Spirit? *[The PHANTOM allows SCROOGE a look at his face. No other reply wanted here. A nervous giggle here.]* Oh, Ghost of the Future, I fear you more than any Specter I have seen! But, as I know that your purpose is to do me good and as I hope to live to be another man from what I was, I am prepared to bear you company. *[FUTURE does not reply, but for a stiff arm, hand and finger set, pointing forward.]* Lead on, then, lead on. The night is **waning** fast, and it is precious time to me. Lead on, Spirit!

What important information do you learn from the stage directions here?

[FUTURE moves away from SCROOGE in the same rhythm and motion employed at its arrival. SCROOGE falls into the same pattern, a considerable space apart from the SPIRIT. In the space between them, MARLEY appears. He looks to FUTURE and then to SCROOGE. He claps his hands. Thunder and lightning. Three BUSINESSMEN appear, spotlighted singularly: One is D.L.; one is D.R.; one is U.C. Thus, six points of the stage should now be spotted in light. MARLEY will watch this scene from his position, C. SCROOGE and FUTURE are R. and L. of C.]

First Businessman Oh, no, I don't know much about it either way, I only know he's dead.

Second Businessman When did he die?

First Businessman Last night, I believe.

shrouded wrapped up in

garment a piece of clothing

waning growing shorter or smaller; lessening

Second Businessman Why, what was the matter with him? I thought he'd never die, really . . .

First Businessman *[Yawning]* Goodness knows, goodness knows . . .

Third Businessman What has he done with his money?

Second Businessman I haven't heard. Have you?

First Businessman Left it to his Company, perhaps. Money to money; you know the expression . . .

Third Businessman He hasn't left it to me. That's all I know . . .

First Businessman *[Laughing]* Nor to me . . . *[Looks at SECOND BUSINESSMAN]* You, then? You got his money???

Second Businessman *[Laughing]* Me, me, his money? Nooooo! *[They all laugh.]*

Third Businessman It's likely to be a cheap funeral, for upon my life, I don't know of a living soul who'd care to **venture** to it. Suppose we make up a party and volunteer?

Second Businessman I don't mind going if a lunch is provided, but I must be fed, if I make one.

First Businessman Well, I am the most **disinterested** among you, for I never wear black gloves, and I never eat lunch. But I'll offer to go, if anybody else will. When I come to think of it, I'm not all sure that I wasn't his most **particular** friend; for we used to stop and speak whenever we met. Well, then . . . bye, bye!

Second Businessman Bye, bye . . .

Third Businessman Bye, bye . . .

[They glide offstage in three separate directions. Their lights follow them.]

To wear black gloves was a way to show respect when a person died. A close family member would dress entirely in black. A friend or distant cousin would wear black gloves. The people usually wore black for six months to a year.

venture to go out

disinterested indifferent

particular special

Whose death do you think the businessmen were talking about? Why do you think so?

Scrooge Spirit, why did you show me this? Why do you show me businessmen from my streets as they take the death of Jacob Marley. That is a thing past. You are future!

[JACOB MARLEY laughs a long, deep laugh. There is a thunder clap and lightning flash, and he is gone. SCROOGE faces FUTURE, alone on stage now. FUTURE wordlessly stretches out his arm-hand-and-finger-set, pointing into the distance, U. There, above them. Scoundrels "fly" by, half-dressed and ***slovenly.*** *When this scene has passed, a woman enters the playing area. She is almost at once followed by a second woman; and then a man in faded black; and then, suddenly, an old man, who smokes a pipe. The old man scares the other three. They laugh,* ***anxious.****]*

First Woman Look here, old Joe, here's a chance! If we haven't all three met here without meaning it!

Old Joe You couldn't have met in a better place. Come into the parlor. You were made free of it long ago, you know; and the other two an't strangers. *[He stands; shuts a door. Shrieking]* We're all **suitable** to our calling. We're well matched. Come into the parlor. Come into the parlor . . . *[They follow him D. SCROOGE and FUTURE are now in their midst, watching; silent. A truck comes in on which is set a small wall with fireplace and a screen of rags, etc. All props for the scene.]* Let me just rake this fire over a bit . . .

[He does. He trims his lamp with the stem of his pipe. The FIRST WOMAN throws a large bundle on to the floor. She sits beside it crosslegged, ***defiantly.****]*

What odds means "What difference does it make?"

First Woman What odds then? What odds, Mrs. Dilber? Every person has a right to take care of themselves. HE always did!

slovenly sloppy

anxious worried and scared

suitable acceptable

defiantly in a bold and challenging way

Mrs. Dilber That's true indeed! No man more so!

First Woman Why, then, don't stand staring as if you was afraid, woman! Who's the wiser? We're not going to pick holes in each other's coats, I suppose?

Mrs. Dilber No, indeed! We should hope not!

First Woman Very well, then! That's enough. Who's the worse for the loss of a few things like these? Not a dead man, I suppose?

Mrs. Dilber *[Laughing]* No, indeed!

First Woman If he wanted to keep 'em after he was dead, the wicked old screw, why wasn't he natural in his lifetime? If he had been, he'd have had somebody to look after him when he was struck with Death, instead of lying gasping out his last there, alone by himself.

A man has died. Mrs. Dilber and her friends have stolen some of his belongings. They have brought their bundles of stolen goods to sell to Joe. Read to see what things they stole.

Mrs. Dilber It's the truest word that was ever spoke. It's a judgment on him.

First Woman I wish it were a heavier one, and it should have been, you may depend on it, if I could have laid my hands on anything else. Open that bundle, old Joe, and let me know the value of it. Speak out plain. I'm not afraid to be the first, nor afraid for them to see it. We knew pretty well that we were helping ourselves, before we met here, I believe. It's no sin. Open the bundle, Joe.

First Man No, no, my dear! I won't think of letting you being the first to show what you've . . . earned . . . earned from this. I throw in mine.

[He takes a bundle from his shoulder, turns it upside down, and empties its contents out on to the floor.] It's not very extensive, see . . . seals . . . a pencil case . . . sleeve buttons . . .

Sleeve buttons are today called "cufflinks." They are usually made of gold or silver. Sometimes they are decorated with jewels. A *brooch* is a fancy pin.

Mrs. Dilber Nice sleeve buttons, though . . .

First Man Not bad, not bad . . . a brooch there . . .

Old Joe Not really valuable, I'm afraid . . .

First Man How much, old Joe?

Old Joe *[Writing on the wall with chalk]* A pitiful lot, really. Ten and six and not a sixpence more!

First Man You're not serious!

Ten and six means "ten shillings and sixpence." 12 pence, or pennies, = 1 shilling.

Old Joe That's your account and I wouldn't give another sixpence if I was to be boiled for not doing it. Who's next?

Mrs. Dilber Me! *[Dumps out contents of her bundle]* Sheets, towels, silver spoons, silver sugar-tongs . . . some boots . . .

Old Joe *[Writing on wall]* I always give too much to the ladies. It's a weakness of mine and that's the way I ruin myself. Here's your total comin' up . . . two pounds-ten . . . if you asked me for another penny, and made it an open question, I'd repent of being so liberal and knock off half-a-crown.

Most people think of robbing dead people as shocking and wrong. Mrs. Dilber and her friends defend themselves angrily because they feel ashamed. They insist "It's no sin" even though they feel it is. However, they are so poor that they overcome their shame for a little money.

First Woman And now do MY bundle, Joe.

Old Joe *[Kneeling to open knots on her bundle]* So many knots, madam . . . *[He drags out large curtains; dark]* What do you call this? Bed curtains!

First Woman *[Laughing]* Ah, yes, bed curtains!

Old Joe You don't mean to say you took 'em down, rings and all, with him lying there?

First Woman Yes, I did, why not?

Old Joe You were born to make your fortune and you'll certainly do it.

Hold my hand means "hesitate."

First Woman I certainly shan't hold my hand, when I can get anything in it by reaching it out, for the sake of such a man as he was, I promise you, Joe. Don't drop that lamp oil on those blankets, now!

Old Joe His blankets?

First Woman Whose else's do you think? He isn't likely to catch cold without 'em, I daresay.

Old Joe I hope that he didn't die of anything catching? Eh?

First Woman Don't you be afraid of that. I ain't so fond of his company that I'd **loiter** about him for such things if he did. Ah! You may look through that shirt till your eyes ache, but you won't find a hole in it, nor a threadbare place. It's the best he had, and a fine one, too. They'd have wasted it, if it hadn't been for me.

Old Joe What do you mean 'They'd have wasted it?'

First Woman Putting it on him to be buried in, to be sure. Somebody was fool enough to do it, but I took it off again . . .

[She laughs, as do they all, nervously.]

If calico ain't good enough for such a purpose, it isn't good enough then for anything. It's quite as becoming to the body. He can't look uglier than he did in that one!

> In the U.S., *calico* is cotton cloth with a print on it. But the British meaning is used here. The British meaning for calico is "plain, white cotton cloth."

Scrooge *[A low-pitched moan emits from his mouth; from the bones.]* OOOOOOOoooooOOOOOoooooOOOOOOOOooo ooOOOOOOoooooOO!

Old Joe One pound six for the lot. *[He produces a small flannel bag filled with money. He divvies it out. He continues to pass around the money as he speaks. All are laughing.]* That's the end of it, you see! He frightened every one away from him while he was alive, to profit us when he was dead! Hah ha ha!

All HAHAHAHAhahahahahahah!

Scrooge OOOoooOOOoooOOOoooOOOoooOOoooOOoo oOOOooo! *[He screams at them.]* **Obscene** demons! Why not market the corpse itself, as sell its trimming??? *[Suddenly]* Oh,

loiter to wait around without purpose

obscene disgusting

Spirit, I see it, I see it! This unhappy man—this stripped-bare corpse . . . could very well be my own. My life holds parallel! My life ends that way now!

[SCROOGE backs into something in the dark behind his spotlight. SCROOGE looks at FUTURE, who points to the corpse. SCROOGE pulls back the blanket. The corpse is, of course, SCROOGE, who screams. He falls aside the bed; weeping.]

Spirit, this is a fearful place. In leaving it, I shall not leave its lesson, trust me. Let us go!

[FUTURE points to the corpse.]

FUTURE spreads his robes for two reasons. One is to take Scrooge somewhere else. The other is as a smooth way to move from one scene to another.

Spirit, let me see some tenderness connected with a death, or that dark chamber, which we just left now, Spirit, will be forever present to me.

[FUTURE spreads his robes again. Thunder and lightning. Lights up, U., in the CRATCHIT home setting. MRS. CRATCHIT and her daughters, sewing]

Tiny Tim's Voice *[Off]* And He took a child and set him in the midst of them.

Scrooge *[Looking about the room; to FUTURE]* Huh? Who spoke? Who said that?

Mrs. Cratchit *[Puts down her sewing]* The color hurts my eyes. *[Rubs her eyes]* That's better. My eyes grow weak sewing by candlelight. I shouldn't want to show your father weak eyes when he comes home . . . not for the world! It must be near his time . . .

Peter *[In corner, reading. Looks up from book]* Past it, rather. But I think he's been walking a bit slower than usual these last few evenings, Mother.

Mrs. Cratchit I have known him walk with . . . *[Pauses]* I have know him walk with Tiny Tim upon his shoulder and very fast indeed.

Peter So have I, Mother! Often!

Daughter So have I.

Mrs. Cratchit But he was very light to carry and his father loved him so, that it was not trouble—no trouble.

[BOB, at door]

And there is your father at the door.

[BOB CRATCHIT enters. He wears a comforter. He is cold, ***forlorn.****]*

Peter Father!

Bob Hello, wife, children . . .

[The daughter weeps; turns away from CRATCHIT.]

Children! How good to see you all! And you, wife. And look at this sewing! I've no doubt, with all your ***industry,*** we'll have a quilt to set down upon our knees in church on Sunday!

Churches were not well-heated as they are today. People who had nice quilts might take them to church to stay warm.

forlorn unhappy   **industry** hard work

Mrs. Cratchit You made the arrangements today, then, Robert, for the . . . service . . . to be on Sunday.

Bob The funeral. Oh, well, yes, yes, I did. I wish you could have gone. It would have done you good to see how green a place it is. But you'll see it often. I promised him that I would walk there on Sunday, after the service. *[Suddenly]* My little, little child! My little child!

All Children *[Hugging him]* Oh, Father . . .

Bob *[He stands]* Forgive me. I saw Mr. Scrooge's nephew, who you know I'd just met once before, and he was so wonderful to me, wife . . . he is the most pleasant-spoken gentleman I've ever met . . . he said "I am heartily sorry for it and heartily sorry for your good wife. If I can be of service to you in any way, here's where I live." And he gave me this card.

Peter Let me see it!

Bob And he looked me straight in the eye, wife, and said, meaningfully, "I pray you'll come to me, Mr. Cratchit, if you need some help. I pray you do." Now it wasn't for the sake of anything that he might be able to do for us, so much as for his kind way. It seemed as if he had known our Tiny Tim and felt with us.

Mrs. Cratchit I'm sure that he's a good soul.

Bob You would be surer of it, my dear, if you saw and spoke to him. I shouldn't be at all surprised, if he got Peter a situation.

Mrs. Cratchit Only hear that, Peter!

Keeping company with means "going out with."

Martha And then, Peter will be keeping company with someone and setting up for himself!

Peter Get along with you!

Bob It's just as likely as not, one of these days, though there's plenty of time for that, my dear. But however and whenever we part from one another, I am sure we shall none of us forget poor Tiny Tim—shall we?—or this first parting that was among us?

All Children Never, Father, never!

Bob And when we recollect how patient and mild he was, we shall not quarrel easily among ourselves, and forget poor Tiny Tim in doing it.

All Children No, Father, never!

Little Bob I am very happy, I am, I am, I am very happy.

[BOB kisses his little son, as does MRS. CRATCHIT, as do the other children. The family is set now in one sculptural embrace. The lighting fades to a gentle pool of light, tight on them.]

Scrooge Specter, something informs me that our parting moment is at hand. I know it, but I know not how I know it.

[FUTURE points to the other side of the stage. Lights out on CRATCHITS. FUTURE moves slowing, gliding. SCROOGE follows. FUTURE points opposite. FUTURE leads SCROOGE to a wall and a tombstone. He points to the stone.]

Am I that man those **ghoulish parasites** so **gloated** over? *[Pauses]* Before I draw nearer to that stone to which you point, answer me one question. Are these the shadows of things that will be, or the shadows of things that MAY be, only?

[FUTURE points to the gravestone. MARLEY appears in light well U. He points to the grave as well. Gravestone turns front and grows to ten feet high. Words upon it: EBENEZER SCROOGE: Much smoke billows now from the grave. Choral music here. SCROOGE stands looking up at gravestone. FUTURE does not at all reply in mortals' words, but points once more to the gravestone. The stone undulates and glows. Music plays, beckoning SCROOGE. SCROOGE reeling in terror]

Sculptural embrace means the group is standing so still that it looks like a statue.

***Reading Strategy:* Text Structure**

Why would it be helpful to read this stage direction slowly?

Which character is speaking here? Why is there no name given before the dialogue?

ghoulish like a monster

parasites those who feed on living creatures

gloated felt satisfied at one's own good fortune

Oh, no. Spirit! Oh, no, no!

[FUTURE'S finger still pointing]

Spirit! Hear me! I am not the man I was. I will not be the man I would have been but for this **intercourse.** Why show me this, if I am past all hope?

[FUTURE considers SCROOGE'S logic. His hand wavers.]

Oh, Good Spirit, I see by your wavering hand that your good nature **intercedes** for me and pities me. Assure me that I yet may change these shadows that you have shown me by an altered life!

[FUTURE'S hand trembles; pointing has stopped.]

I will honor Christmas in my heart and try to keep it all the year. I will live in the Past, the Present, and the Future. The Spirits of all Three shall **strive** within me. I will not shut out the lessons that they teach. Oh, tell me that I may sponge away the writing that is upon this stone!

[SCROOGE makes a desperate stab at grabbing FUTURE'S hand. He holds firm for a moment, but FUTURE, stronger than SCROOGE, pulls away. SCROOGE is on his knees, praying.]

intercourse a meeting or experience

intercedes steps in to help someone

strive to make a great effort

Spirit, dear Spirit, I am praying before you. Give me a sign that all is possible. Give me a sign that all hope for me is not lost. Oh, Spirit, kind Spirit, I **beseech** thee: give me a sign . . .

[FUTURE deliquesces, slowly, gently. The PHANTOM'S hood and robe drop gracefully to the ground in a small heap. Music in. There is nothing in them. They are mortal cloth. The SPIRIT is elsewhere. SCROOGE has his sign. SCROOGE is alone. Tableau. The lights fade to black.]

Mortal cloths are things of Earth, not of the hereafter.

Scene 5

[The end of it. MARLEY, spotlighted, opposite SCROOGE, in his bed, spotlighted. MARLEY speaks to audience, directly.]

Marley *[He smiles at SCROOGE:]* The firm of Scrooge and Marley is doubly blessed; two misers turned; one, alas, in Death, too late; but the other miser turned in Time's **penultimate** nick. Look you on my friend, Ebenezer Scrooge . . .

Scrooge *[Scrambling out of bed; reeling in delight]* I will live in the Past, in the Present, and in the Future! The Spirits of all Three shall strive within me!

Marley *[He points and moves closer to SCROOGE'S bed.]* Yes, Ebenezer, the bedpost is your own. Believe it! Yes, Ebenezer, the room is your own. Believe it!

Scrooge Oh, Jacob Marley! Wherever you are, Jacob, know ye that I praise you for this! I praise you . . . and heaven . . . and Christmastime! *[Kneels facing away from MARLEY]* I say it to ye on my knees, old Jacob, on my knees! *[He touches his bed curtains.]* Not torn down. My bed curtains are not at all torn down! Rings and all, here they are! They are here: I am here: the shadows of things that would have been, may now be **dispelled.** They will be, Jacob! I know they will be!

beseech to plead, beg

penultimate next-to-last

dispelled scattered

[He chooses clothing for the day. He tries different pieces of clothing and settles, perhaps on a dress suit, plus a cape of the bed clothing: something of color.]

I am light as a feather, I am happy as an angel, I am as merry as a schoolboy. *[Yells out window and then out to audience]* Merry Christmas to everybody! Merry Christmas to everybody! A Happy New Year to all the world! Hallo here! Whoop! Whoop! Hallo! Hallo! I don't know what day of the month it is! I don't care! I don't know anything! I'm quite a baby! I don't care! I don't care a fig! I'd much rather be a baby than be an old wreck like me or Marley! (Sorry, Jacob, wherever ye be!) Hallo! Hallo there!

[Church bells chime in Christmas Day. A small boy, named ADAM, is seen now D.R., as a light fades up on him.]

Why does Scrooge not know what day of the month it is?

Hey, you boy! What's today? What day of the year is it?

Adam Today, sir? Why, it's Christmas Day!

Scrooge It's Christmas Day, is it? Whoop! Well, I haven't missed it after all, have I? The Spirits did all they did in one night. They can do anything they like, right? Of course they can! Of course they can!

Adam Excuse me, sir?

Scrooge Huh? Oh, yes, of course, what's your name, lad?

[SCROOGE and ADAM will play their scene from their own spotlights.]

Adam Adam, sir.

Scrooge Adam! What a fine, strong name! Do you know the poulterer's in the next street but one, at the corner?

Adam I certainly should hope I know him, sir!

Scrooge A remarkable boy! An intelligent boy! Do you know whether the poulterer's have sold the prize turkey that was hanging up there? I don't mean the little prize turkey, Adam. I mean the big one!

Adam What, do you mean the one they've got that's as big as me?

Scrooge I mean, the turkey the size of Adam: that's the bird!

Adam It's hanging there now, sir.

Scrooge It is? Go and buy it! No, no, I am absolutely **in earnest.** Go and buy it and tell 'em to bring it here, so that I may give them the directions to where I want it delivered, as a gift. Come back here with the man, Adam, and I'll give you a shilling. Come back here with him in less than five minutes, and I'll give you half-a-crown!

Adam Oh, my sir! Don't let my brother in on this.

[ADAM runs offstage. MARLEY smiles.]

Marley An act of kindness is like the first green grape of summer: one leads to another and another and another. It would take a **queer** man indeed to not follow an act of kindness with an act of kindness. One simply **whets** the tongue for more . . . the taste of kindness is too too sweet. Gifts—goods—are lifeless. But the gift of goodness one feels in the giving is full of life. It . . . is . . . a . . . wonder.

[Pauses; moves closer to SCROOGE, who is totally occupied with his dressing and arranging of his room and his day. He is making lists, etc. MARLEY reaches out to SCROOGE:]

Adam *[Calling, off]* I'm here! I'm here!

[ADAM runs on with a man, who carries an enormous turkey.]

in earnest serious **queer** strange **whets** sharpens

Adam says that his run was a world record. Do you think it really was a world record? Explain.

Here I am, sir. Three minutes flat! A world record! I've got the poultryman and he's got the poultry! *[He pants, out of breath.]* I have earned my prize, sir, if I live . . .

[He holds his heart, playacting. SCROOGE goes to him and embraces him.]

Scrooge You are truly a champion, Adam . . .

Man Here's the bird you ordered, sir . . .

Scrooge Oh, my, MY!!! look at the size of that turkey, will you! He never could have stood upon his legs, that bird! He would have snapped them off in a minute, like sticks of sealing wax! Why you'll never be able to carry that bird to Camden-Town. I'll give you money for a cab . . .

Sealing wax was used to seal envelopes. Although it held an envelope closed nicely, it was easily broken.

Man Camden-Town's where it's goin', sir?

Scrooge Oh, I didn't tell you? Yes, I've written the **precise** address down just here on this . . . *[Hands paper to him]* Bob Cratchit's house. Now he's not to know who sends him this. Do you understand me? Not a word . . . *[Handing out money and chuckling]*

Man I understand, sir, not a word.

***Reading Strategy:* Text Structure**

You can read these short lines of dialogue fast. Explain why you can read them faster than stage directions or long lines of dialogue.

Scrooge Good. There you go then . . . this is for the turkey . . . *[Chuckle]* and this is for the taxi. *[Chuckle]* . . . and this is for your world-record run, Adam . . .

Adam But I don't have change for that, sir.

Scrooge Then keep it, my lad. It's Christmas!

Adam *[He kisses SCROOGE'S cheek, quickly.]* Thank you, sir. Merry, Merry Christmas! *[He runs off.]*

Man And you've given me a bit overmuch here, too, sir . . .

Scrooge Of course I have, sir. It's Christmas!

precise exact

Man Oh, well, thanking you, sir. I'll have this bird to Mr. Cratchit and his family in no time, sir. Don't you worry none about that. Merry Christmas to you, sir, and a very happy New Year, too . . .

[The man exits. SCROOGE walks in a large circle about the stage, which is now gently lit. A chorus sings Christmas music far in the distance. Bells chime as well, far in the distance. A gentlewoman enters and passes. SCROOGE is on the streets now.]

Scrooge Merry Christmas, madam . . .

Woman Merry Christmas, sir . . .

[The portly businessman from the first act enters.]

Scrooge Merry Christmas, sir.

Portly Man Merry Christmas, sir.

Scrooge Oh, you! My dear sir! How do you do? I do hope that you succeeded yesterday! It was very kind of you. A Merry Christmas.

Portly Man Mr. Scrooge?

Explain how the question mark in "Mr. Scooge?" is a stage direction.

Scrooge Yes, Scrooge is my name though I'm afraid you may not find it very pleasant. Allow me to ask your pardon. And will you have the goodness to—*[He whispers into the man's ear.]*

Portly Man Lord bless me! My dear Mr. Scrooge, are you serious!?!

Scrooge If you please. Not a farthing less. A great many back payments are included in it, I assure you. Will you do me that favor?

Portly Man My dear sir, I don't know what to say to such munifi—

Scrooge *[Cutting him off]* Don't say anything, please. Come and see me. Will you?

Portly Man I will! I will! Oh I will, Mr. Scrooge! It will be my pleasure!

Scrooge Thank'ee, I am much obliged to you. I thank you fifty times. Bless you!

[Portly man passes offstage, perhaps by moving backwards. SCROOGE now comes to the room of his NEPHEW and NIECE. He stops at the door, begins to knock on it, loses his courage, tries again, loses his courage again, tries again, fails again, and then backs off and runs at the door, causing a tremendous bump against it. The NEPHEW and NIECE are startled.

Why does Scrooge have to work up courage to knock?

Scrooge *[poking head into room]* Fred!

Nephew Why, bless my soul! Who's that?

Nephew and Niece *[Together]* How now? Who goes?

Scrooge It's I. Your Uncle Scrooge.

Niece Dear heart alive!

Scrooge I have come to dinner. May I come in, Fred?

Nephew *May you come in???!!!* With such pleasure for me you may, Uncle!!! What a treat!

Niece What a treat, Uncle Scrooge! Come in, come in!

[They embrace a shocked and delighted SCROOGE: FRED calls into the other room.]

Nephew Come in here, everybody, and meet my Uncle Scrooge! He's come for our Christmas party!

[Music in. Lighting here ***indicates*** *that day has gone to night and gone to day again. It is early, early morning. SCROOGE walks alone from the party, exhausted, to his offices, opposite side of the stage. He opens his offices. The offices are as they were at the start of the play. SCROOGE seats himself with his door wide open so that he can see into the tank, as he awaits CRATCHIT, who enters, head down, full of guilt. CRATCHIT, starts writing almost before he sits.]*

Scrooge What do you mean by coming in here at this time of day, a full eighteen minutes late, Mr. Cratchit? Hallo, sir? Do you hear me?

BOB. I am very sorry, sir. I am behind my time.

Scrooge You are? Yes, I certainly think you are. Step this way, sir, if you please . . .

BOB. It's only but once a year, sir . . . it shall not be repeated. I was making rather merry yesterday and into the night . . .

Scrooge Now, I'll tell you what, Cratchit. I am not going to stand this sort of thing any longer. And therefore . . .

Scrooge says he is not going to stand for this and then pokes Bob's chest. Why did he say and do those things?

indicates points to

[He stands and pokes his finger into BOB'S chest.]

I am . . . about . . . to . . . raise . . . your salary.

Bob Oh, no, sir, I . . . *[Realizes]* what did you say, sir?

Smoking bishop is a hot punch with alcohol in it. A *coal scuttle* is an iron basket for storing extra coal by the fire.

Scrooge A Merry Christmas, Bob . . . *[He claps BOB'S back.]* A merrier Christmas, Bob, my good fellow! than I have given you for many a year. I'll raise your salary and endeavor to assist your struggling family and we will discuss your affairs this very afternoon over a bowl of smoking bishop. Bob! Make up the fires and buy another coal scuttle before you dot another i, Bob. It's too cold in this place! We need warmth and cheer, Bob Cratchit! Do you hear me? DO . . . YOU . . . HEAR . . . ME?

[BOB CRATCHIT stands, smiles at SCROOGE: BOB CRATCHIT faints. Blackout. As the main lights black out, a spotlight appears on SCROOGE: C. Another on MARLEY: He talks directly to the audience.]

Marley Scrooge was better than his word. He did it all and **infinitely** more; and to Tiny Tim, who did NOT die, he was a second father. He became as good a friend, as good a master, as good a man, as the good old city knew, or any other good old city, town, or borough in the good old world. And it was always said of him that he knew how to keep Christmas well,

infinitely much more

if any man alive possessed the knowledge. *[Pauses]* May that be truly said of us, and all of us. And so, as Tiny Tim observed . . .

Tiny Tim *[Atop SCROOGE'S shoulder]* God Bless Us, Every One . . .

[Lights up on chorus, singing final Christmas Song. SCROOGE and MARLEY and all spirits and other characters of the play join in. When the song is over, the lights fade to black.]

AFTER READING THE SELECTION | Apply the Skills

A Christmas Carol: Scrooge and Marley, Act II *by Israel Horovitz*

Directions Choose the letter of the best answer or write the answer using complete sentences.

Comprehension: Identifying Facts

1. Whom does Scrooge first meet in Act II, Scene 1?
- **A** the ghost of Jacob Marley
- **B** the ghost of Christmas Present
- **C** his nephew Fred and Fred's wife
- **D** Mrs. Cratchit and her children

2. What does Christmas Present sprinkle from his torch?
- **A** sugar
- **B** honesty
- **C** kindness
- **D** money

3. Why does Mrs. Cratchit object to toasting Scrooge's health?

4. Why does Christmas Present want Scrooge to observe the Cratchits?

5. Why does Fred always invite Scrooge for Christmas dinner?

6. What does Christmas Present show to Scrooge just before he disappears?

7. What does Christmas Future look like? What is his manner like?

8. What do the three businessmen discuss as Scrooge and Christmas Future listen?

9. Who are the three people who sell things to old Joe?

10. How well does Scrooge live up to his promise to learn the Spirits' lessons?

Comprehension: Putting Ideas Together

11. Which best describes the Ghost of Christmas Present?
- **A** cheerful
- **B** frightening
- **C** silent
- **D** solemn

12. What does Scrooge see happening at the Cratchits' house?
- **A** They are arguing about Martha.
- **B** They are making and then eating Christmas dinner.
- **C** They are mourning for Tiny Tim.
- **D** They are getting ready to go to church.

13. Why does Marley's Ghost want to surprise Scrooge at the start of Act II?

14. Why does Scrooge care about the fate of Tiny Tim?

15. What kind of people are Fred and his wife? How can you tell?

16. Where did Mrs. Dilber and the others get the things they sell to Joe?

17. What does Scrooge learn from his time with Christmas Future?

18. How does Scrooge spend his Christmas Day?

19. What happens when Bob Cratchit is late to work on December 26?

20. What is Scrooge's future like, after all?

Understanding Literature: Stage Directions

Dialogue and stage directions are the two parts of a play script. Dialogue is the words spoken by the actors. Stage directions give information. They tell the time and place of each scene. They describe scenery, lighting, and sound effects. They tell the actors where and how to move. They also include ideas about the characters' moods and the kinds of people they are.

21. What do the stage directions tell you about Christmas Present?

22. Scrooge asks whether Tiny Tim will live. Present repeats Scrooge's words about "the surplus population" back at him. The stage direction reads "Scrooge bows his head." What does Scrooge's bowed head tell you?

23. How do the stage directions help you to "hear" the sounds?

24. Reread the stage direction at the start of Scene 3. What do they suggest about Mrs. Cratchit?

25. There is a long stage direction just before Mrs. Dilber enters with her friends. What does this stage direction tell you?

Critical Thinking

26. How is the Ghost of Christmas Past like Fezziwig?

27. What does Christmas Present mean by telling Scrooge to beware of Ignorance and Want?

28. Why do you think Dickens and Horovitz decided to make Christmas Future silent?

29. Were you surprised that Cratchit, Fred, and the charity worker forgive Scrooge right away? Why or why not?

Thinking Creatively

30. Do you believe that people can actually change overnight, as Scrooge does? Explain your answer.

After Reading **continued on next page**

A Christmas Carol: Scrooge and Marley, Act II *by Israel Horovitz*

Grammar Check

Double negatives are two of these words used in one statement: *nothing, not, never, no.* Remember that the word "not" is in words like won't, can't, and shouldn't.

Examples:

Double Negative: Hilary **doesn't** have **no** cash

Corrected Sentence: Hilary doesn't have **any** cash.

Correct the double negative in each sentence. In each case, delete or change the second negative word.

1 We didn't want to bid on no items at the auction.

2 He couldn't do nothing to cheer her up.

Vocabulary Builder

Adding the suffix *-tion* to a verb makes it a noun. It also adds the meaning "quality, act, or result of."

Example:

verb: participate
noun: participation, "the act of participating"

Write the meanings of the *-tion* words and use them in sentences.

1 intention

2 accommodation

Writing on Your Own

Write a tribute, or words of praise, to the changed Scrooge. Your tribute may include short stories that show how Scrooge has changed.

Listening and Speaking

Write a monologue, which is a one-person dialogue. In it, have Scrooge think back on his experiences with a ghost from Act II. Speak as if you are Scrooge. Use the word *I.* Remember to talk loudly so that everyone can hear you. Present your monologue to the class.

Research and Technology

With a group of classmates, create a timeline of the life of Charles Dickens. Use the Internet and library to gather information about the following:

- main events in Dickens's life
- his most important works
- his travels and speaking jobs

Add pictures and drawings, such as of Dickens. Use some words from his works.

Literary Criticism: Reviews

A television or theater critic is a person who studies and makes judgments about performances. The word *criticism*, as used here, means *opinion*. It does not mean that the critic will say bad things about the work. The criticism could be either good or bad.

Most reviews have these parts:

- An overall idea what the story is about
- Ideas about how the work is like or different from another work
- An opinion about the work
- A suggestion about whether others should see or read the work

Reading Skill

The most common purpose for reading a review is to find out the critic's opinion. The critic's opinion should be the main idea of a review. Therefore, the main reading skill you need to use is finding the main idea.

You can often get an idea of the critic's opinion from the review's title. Sometimes, though, a review has no title. In that case, look at the first and last paragraphs. You will often find the main idea in one or both of these places.

Once you have identified the main idea, look for details that support it. When a critic gives an opinion, he or she must provide the reasons for it. Your job is to judge how well the details support the main idea. This will tell you whether or not to accept the critic's judgment.

The following details are examples that might support a critic's opinion:

Critic does not like a play:

> The lead actor is miscast. He does not seem like a king.

Critic likes a movie:

> It is funny and sad all at once.

As you read literary criticism, analyze the writer's response to the work. Use a graphic organzier like the one shown.

	TNT	Meadow Brook Theatre
Critic's summary		
Positive comments		
Negative comments		
Critic's overall opinion		

A Christmas Carol

The newspaper or magazine where a review appears tells you something about the audience of the criticism. In this case, the audience is TV viewers.

TNT

(Sun., Dec. 5, 8 p.m. ET)
Picks & Pans: Television

So you muttered "humbug" when you spied yet another version of A Christmas Carol on the TV schedule. Don't feel guilty. It doesn't take a spiritual descendant of Ebenezer Scrooge to notice that the Charles Dickens classic has been adapted nearly to death. (Two years ago, there was even a Ms. Scrooge.)

But TNT's Carol would be worth watching if only for the lead performance of Patrick Stewart. The ex-skipper of Star Trek: The Next Generation has been giving staged, one-man readings of A Christmas Carol for 10 years, and his approach to Scrooge is consistently interesting and intelligent. Early on, Stewart seems to be speaking on the misanthropic diatribes straight from Scrooge's flinty heart, rather than reciting thoroughly familiar quotations. And when Scrooge offers a boy a one-shilling tip, Stewart has the reformed miser feel a pang of the old parsimony.

. . . this Carol feels more like Masterpiece Theatre than seasonal merchandise . . .

Filmed in England with a solid supporting cast (including Richard E. Grant as Bob Cratchit and Joel Grey as the Spirit of Christmas Past), this Carol feels more like Masterpiece Theatre than seasonal merchandise–except when the filmmakers embellish Scrooge's nocturnal visions with gratuitous special effects.

The review ends with a summary of the critic's opinion.

Bottom line: Old story well told.
—*Terry Kelleher*

Toned-down *Christmas Carol* has more spirit

This review, published in a Michigan newspaper, evaluates a production of *A Christmas Carol* at a local theater called the Meadow Brook Theatre.

—by John Sousanis
Special to the Oakland Press

Director Debra Wicks has tinkered with Meadow Brook's recipe for *A Christmas Carol* just enough to make the old holiday fruitcake seem fresh. To be sure, Wicks's changes are subtle. Meadow Brook is still producing the Charles Nolte adaptation of Charles Dickens's Christmas classic that has been a mainstay of local theater for most of the last two decades.

The audience still is serenaded by a band of merry carolers in the lobby before the show. With its giant revolving set pieces and big bag of special effects, the production's script, set and costumes are unchanged from these many Christmases past.

But ironically, Wicks has infused the show with new energy by calming everything down a bit. In prior productions, the play's singing Londoners seemed positively hopped up on Christmas cheer to the point where one feared for the life of anyone not bubbling over with the spirit of the season.

Against this unebbing Yuletide, it was easy to forgive Scrooge of all his bah-hum-bugging. If only he had seen fit to give Tiny Tim a good spanking, we might all have enjoyed Christmas a little more. But Wicks has introduced a modicum of restraint into the Happy English populace, reducing the play's saccharine content considerably and making *A Christmas Carol* a more palatable holiday treat for adults and children.

Peter Hicks's set design for the show is, as always, enormous and gorgeous: Scrooge's storefront on a busy London street revolves to reveal the interior of the businessman's office and home, then opens on itself, providing the frame for scenes from Scrooge's boyhood, young adulthood and, of course, his potential end.

Meadow Brook's technical crew executes its stage magic without a hitch: Ghosts materialize and dematerialize in thick fogs and bolts of bright light, speaking to Scrooge in electronically altered voices and freezing the action onstage with a wave of their otherworldly hands.

The cast members take on multiple roles populating busy London in one scene, then visiting poor Scrooge in his dreams of Christmas Then, Now and Soon.

Standouts in the huge ensemble include John Biedenbach as Scrooge's put-upon assistant Bob Cratchit, Jodie Kuhn Ellison as Cratchit's fiercely loyal wife and Mark Rademacher, who pulls double duty as the Spirit of Christmas Present (the beefiest role in the play) and as a determined charity worker.

Scott Crownover, paying only passing attention to his English accent, takes an energetic turn as Scrooge's nephew, Fred, and Tom Mahard and Geoffrey Beauchamp have fun with a handful of roles they've been performing for years. Newcomer Sara Catheryn Wolf, fresh from three seasons at the Hilberry Theatre Company, provides an ethereal Spirit of Christmas Past.

Reviews of local productions often include judgments about all aspects of the production, including work by the director, set designer, and technical crew.

The biggest change for longtime fans of the spectacle, however, is the replacement of Booth Coleman as Scrooge. Dennis Robertson's

***Continued* on next page**

debut as the man in need of serious Christmas redemption is in perfect keeping with Wicks's toned-down production. If he's not quite as charismatic a miser as Coleman, Robertson is a much darker, even scarier Scrooge, which makes his ultimate transformation into an unabashed philanthropist that much more affecting.

All in all, *A Christmas Carol* is what it always has been: A well-produced, grand-scale event that is as much pageant as play. And like a beautifully wrapped gift under a well-decorated tree, it suits the season to a tee.

If you go, *A Christmas Carol* runs through December 24 at Meadow Brook Theatre, 127 Wilson Hall, Oakland University, Rochester Hills. Call 377-3300.

The critic summarizes his opinion.

Monitor Your Progress

Directions Choose the letter of the best answer or write the answer using complete sentences.

1. Which of the following purposes would not be supported by reading these reviews?

A To learn about different stage shows of *A Christmas Carol*

B To look at how two different stage shows are alike and different

C To learn how to bring a literary work to the stage

D To decide which stage show you would rather see

2. Which phrase from Sousanis's review best summarizes his opinion?

A Christmas Present is the beefiest role in the play.

B Hicks's set design is enormous and gorgeous.

C Robertson is not quite as charismatic as Coleman.

D It suits the season to a tee.

3. How does Kelleher generally feel about adaptations of *A Christmas Carol?*

A The story has been done too many times.

B The scriptwriter misunderstood the novel's message.

C *A Christmas Carol* should be done every year.

D Only the original play should ever be put on.

4. Name two details that support Sousanis's main idea.

5. Do you think Keller's review is probably correct? Why or why not?

Writing on Your Own

Write a review of your own. If possible, review a movie form of *A Christmas Carol*. If not, review any movie you have seen lately. Begin with a main idea. Give details that support the main idea. Remember to give your opinion of the movie.

COMPARING LITERARY WORKS | Build Understanding

A Christmas Carol: Scrooge and Marley by Israel Horovitz

About the Selections

This selection contains two scenes from *A Christmas Carol.* In the first one, Scrooge and Cratchit close the office on Christmas Eve. In the second scene, Fezziwig and all his employees have a festive Christmas party.

As you read, think about how the characters in the two scenes are alike and different.

Objectives

- To read and understand scenes from a play
- To compare and contrast characters and motivation

Literary Terms A character is a person who speaks and acts in a play. **Motivation** is the reason characters speak and act as they do. Motivation is the answer to the question "Why?" One character may be motivated by guilt due to things he has done wrong. Another may be motivated by nice things others have done for her. As you read, think about why the characters do and say certain things.

motivation a reason a character does something

Reading on Your Own Playwrights sometimes show character and motivation by using a foil. A foil is a character who behaves and speaks differently from another character. The foil gives the audience the chance to look at likenesses and differences. As you read these two scenes, notice differences between the characters. Ask how one character's actions reflect on another character.

Comparing continued on next page

A Christmas Carol: Scrooge and Marley by Israel Horovitz

Writing on Your Own These scenes show two employers who treat their workers very differently. Write a few sentences discussing why bosses treat their employees as they do.

Vocabulary Focus These scenes contain a number of multiple-meaning words.

Example: *The word fair*

Use in scenes: "It's not convenient, and it's not *fair.*"
Meaning: right or as it should be

Some other uses: We went to the *fair* this weekend.
Meaning: An event with farm goods and animals

Ella has fair skin.
Meaning: Light colored

Dane has a *fair* number of friends.
Meaning: a good amount; pretty many

Find at least two meanings for these words: *crown, bound, poor, will, clear, sweep, trim, firm.*

Think Before You Read What do you think employees want most from the people they work for?

from A Christmas Carol: *Scrooge and Marley, Act 1, Scene 2*

Cratchit I must be going home . . . *[He snuffs out his candle and puts on his hat.]* I hope you have a . . . very very lovely day tomorrow, sir . . .

Scrooge Hmmm. Oh, you'll be wanting the whole day tomorrow, I suppose?

Cratchit If quite convenient, sir.

Scrooge It's not convenient, and it's not fair. If I was to stop half-a-crown for it, you'd think yourself ill-used, I'll be bound?

[CRATCHIT smiles faintly.]

As you read, try to get an idea what each character is like.

Cratchit I don't know, sir . . .

Scrooge And yet, you don't think me ill-used when I pay a day's **wages** for no work . . .

Cratchit It's only but once a year . . .

Scrooge A poor excuse for picking a man's pocket every 25th of December! But I suppose you must have the whole day. Be here all the earlier the next morning!

The phrase picking a man's pocket is slang for "taking a person's money."

Cratchit Oh I will, sir. I will. I promise you. And, sir . . .

Scrooge Don't say it, Cratchit.

Cratchit But let me wish you a . . .

Scrooge Don't say it, Cratchit. I warn you . . .

Cratchit Sir!

Scrooge Cratchit!

[CRATCHIT opens the door.]

Cratchit All right, then, sir . . . well . . . *[Suddenly]* Merry Christmas, Mr. Scrooge!

[And he runs out the door, shutting same behind him.]

wages salary

Scrooge and Marley, Act 1, Scene 5

Fezziwig Yo ho, my boys. No more work tonight. Christmas Eve, Dick. Christmas, Ebenezer!

[They stand at attention in front of FEZZIWIG; laughing] Hilli-ho! Clear away, and let's have lots of room here! Hilli-ho, Dick! Chirrup, Ebenezer!

[The young men clear the room, sweep the floor, straighten the pictures, trim the lamps, etc. The space is clear now. A fiddler enters, fiddling.]

Hi-ho, Matthew! Fiddle away . . . where are my daughters?

[The fiddler plays. Three young daughters of FEZZIWIG enter followed by six young male **suitors.** *They are dancing to the music. All employees come in: workers, clerks, housemaids, cousins, the baker, etc. All dance. Full number wanted here. Throughout the dance, food is brought into the feast. It is "eaten" in dance, by the dancers. EBENEZER dances with all three of the daughters, as does DICK. They compete for the daughters, happily, in the dance. FEZZIWIG dances with the daughters. FEZZIWIG dances with DICK and EBENEZER. The music changes: MRS. FEZZIWIG enters. She lovingly scolds her husband. They dance. She dances with EBENEZER, lifting him and throwing him about. She is enormously fat. When the dance is ended, they all dance off, floating away, as does the music.]*

Past It was a small matter, that Fezziwig made those silly folks so full of gratitude.

Scrooge Small?

Past Shhh!?

[Lights up on DICK and EBENEZER.]

Dick We are blessed, Ebenezer, truly, to have such a master as Mr. Fezziwig!

Young Ebenezer He is the best, best, the very and absolute best! If ever I own a firm of my own, I shall treat my apprentices with the same dignity and the same grace. We have learned a wonderful lesson from the master, Dick!

Dick Ah, that's a fact, Ebenezer. That's a fact!

How do you think Scrooge felt as he heard his young self talk about how to treat employees?

suitors young men who want to marry particular girls

COMPARING LITERARY WORKS | Apply the Skills

A Christmas Carol: Scrooge and Marley by Israel Horovitz

Directions Choose the letter of the best answer or write the answer using complete sentences.

Comprehension: Identifying Facts

1. Who is Dick?

A Scrooge's old boss
B Scrooge's clerk
C Scrooge's old partner
D Scrooge's fellow-apprentice

2. Why does Scrooge object to paying Cratchit for December 25?

3. Why does Dick feel that he and Ebenezer are blessed?

Comprehension: Putting Ideas Together

4. Which best describes Fezziwig?

A kind and jolly
B mean and selfish
C careless and forgetful
D firm but fair

5. How is working for Fezziwig different from working for Scrooge? Which details support your answer?

6. How are Cratchit and Fezziwig alike? Give details that support your answer.

Understanding Literature: Motivation

7. What motivates Fezziwig and Scrooge to speak and act as they do in these scenes? Explain your answer.

8. In what way does Fezziwig serve as a foil for Scrooge?

Critical Thinking

9. Do you think Scrooge intends to work on Christmas Day? Why or why not?

Thinking Creatively

10. If you were Cratchit, would you continue to work for Scrooge? Why or why not?

Grammar Check

Commonly confused words sound or look alike. However, they often mean very different things. If you mix them up, you can confuse your readers.

Here are some commonly confused words and their definitions:

accept except	verb: to take what is offered preposition: other than
affect effect	verb: to change one's feelings noun: result
farther further	adjective: more distant adjective: more; to a greater degree

Use each commonly confused word correctly in a sentence.

Vocabulary Builder

Substitute a word from *A Christmas Carol* for the underlined word(s) in each sentence.

1 Cratchit <u>put out</u> his candle at the end of the day.

2 Fezziwig's pretty daughters danced with their <u>young men</u>.

3 Dick and Ebenezer felt great <u>thankfulness</u> toward Fezziwig.

Writing on Your Own

Choose two characters from these two scenes, or from the complete play. Write a short essay explaining how one character is a foil for the other. Use details in your essay to help make your ideas easier to understand.

Listening and Speaking

Choose one of these scenes, or a different two-person scene from the complete play. With a partner, perform a reading of the scene for the class. Make sure you both plan and practice before you perform.

Media and Viewing

Find pictures from the many movie versions of *A Christmas Carol*. Look online and in the library. Choose at least two characters and find several pictures of each of them. In a small group, discuss the different pictures of the characters. Look at the characters' clothes, hair, and faces. Think about which clothes, hair, and faces you think work best for the play. Exchange your ideas about them.

Reading Strategy:
Summarizing

You have learned about summarizing strategies in Unit 3. Continue to use those strategies as you read the selections in this unit. Ask yourself:

- Who or what is this about?
- What is the main thing being said about this topic?

If you are having trouble identifying the main idea, try rereading the text.

Literary Terms

science fiction fiction based on real or imagined facts of science

screenplay a play written to be filmed rather than performed live in a theater

comedy a play with a happy ending, intended to amuse its audience

anachronism a speech or event that could not actually have taken place at the time in which it happens in a literary work

The Monsters Are Due on Maple Street by Rod Serling

Rod Serling
1924–1975

About the Author

Rod Serling did not become serious about writing until college. At that time, he fell in love with radio drama. This sparked him to begin writing, and he won second prize in a script contest. Soon after, he landed his first job as a radio writer. Serling then branched out into something new—writing for television. He rocketed to fame writing scripts for the program *The Twilight Zone.*

The Twilight Zone was a science-fiction program. Serling's stories were more than simple stories. He also hid in them his opinions about the ways people behave.

Objectives

- To read and understand a science-fiction screenplay
- To identify and understand motivation

About the Selection

As the play opens, it is an ordinary pleasant evening on Maple Street. Suddenly there is a flash of light across the sky. All the power in the neighborhood goes out. Tommy tells his neighbors that there must be an alien family among them. This family looks human, he says, but is actually an alien family from outer space. Neighbors immediately look at one another, each thinking another must be the alien. The small crowd of neighbors turns into a mob.

When someone comes up in the darkness, Charlie shoots and kills him. The person turns out to be a neighbor. The crowd turns on Charlie. Charlie immediately accuses Tommy of being the alien. The neighbors turn on the boy, who begins to run from them.

Meanwhile, two enemy aliens watch from their spacecraft. One explains to the other how easy it is to take over these people: All you have to do is stop a few of their machines from working. Then, watch them destroy one another.

Before Reading continued on next page

The Monsters Are Due on Maple Street *by Rod Serling*

science fiction
fiction based on real or imagined facts of science

screenplay
a play written to be filmed rather than performed live in a theater

Literary Terms "The Monsters Are Due on Maple Street" is a **science-fiction screenplay**. A screenplay is written to be filmed with cameras, instead of acted on a stage. Science fiction is fiction based on real or imagined facts of science. Here are some common science-fiction parts:

- spaceships and aliens from other planets
- travel through space or time
- robots who can talk, act, and think on their own

Other than the science parts, science fiction is just like regular fiction. It has plots, characters, settings, and themes. As you read "The Monsters Are Due on Maple Street," try to think about the characters' motives. Remember that motives are the reasons characters speak and act as they do.

Reading on Your Own A summary is a short statement that gives a story's main ideas and important details. Summarizing helps you review and understand what you read. To summarize, you must first decide which details are important and which are not. As you read, pause to remember and put key details in your own words.

Writing on Your Own The characters in this play start rumors. In other words, they say things that they do not know are true. Write several sentences about the reasons people start rumors and the damage rumors can do.

Vocabulary Focus Look at the narrator's opening speech. Choose a partner. Make sure both of you know the meanings of all the words. Use a dictionary if necessary. Once you know the words, discuss the narrator's sentences. Work together to put the sentences in your own words.

Think Before You Read Think about when something goes wrong. Why do you think people commonly look for someone to blame?

The Monsters Are Due on Maple Street

CHARACTERS

Residents of Maple Street

Tommy	Woman
Narrator	Don Martin
Figure One	Sally (Tommy's Mother)
Figure Two	Steve Brand
Charlie's Wife	Man One
Mrs. Goodman	Man Two
Mrs. Brand	Pete Van Horn
Les Goodman	Charlie

Act 1

[Fade in on a shot of the night sky. The various ***nebulae*** *and planet bodies stand out in sharp, sparkling relief, and the camera begins a slow pan across the Heavens.]*

As you read, note the way the people behave. Think if you have seen people behave in the same ways.

Narrator's Voice There is a **fifth dimension** beyond that which is known to man. It is a dimension as vast as space, and as timeless as **infinity**. It is the middle ground between light and shadow—between science and **superstition**. And it lies between the pit of man's fears and the **summit** of his knowledge. This is the dimension of imagination. It is an area which we call The Twilight Zone.

To *pan* means to move across a space while still filming.

[The camera has begun to pan down until it passes the horizon and is on a sign which reads "Maple Street." Pan down until we are shooting down at an angle toward the street below. It's a tree-lined, quiet residential American street, very typical of the small town. The houses have front porches on which

nebulae clouds of gas in space

fifth dimension fiction idea or space outside of human understanding

infinity forever

superstition a belief in what does not really exist

summit top point

people sit and swing on gliders, ***conversing*** *across from house to house. STEVE BRAND polishes his car parked in front of his house. His neighbor, DON MARTIN, leans against the fender watching him. A Good Humor man rides a bicycle and is just in the process of stopping to sell some ice cream to a couple of kids. Two women gossip on the front lawn. Another man waters his lawn.]*

Narrator's Voice Maple Street, U.S.A., late summer. A tree-lined little world of front porch gliders, hop scotch, the laughter of children, and the bell of an ice cream **vendor**.

[There is a pause and the camera moves over to a shot of the Good Humor man and two small boys who are standing alongside, just buying ice cream.]

Narrator's Voice At the sound of the roar and the flash of light it will be precisely 6:43 P.M. on Maple Street.

[At this moment one of the little boys, TOMMY, looks up to listen to a sound of a tremendous screeching roar from overhead. A flash of light plays on both their faces and then it moves down the street past lawns and porches and rooftops and then disappears.

Various people leave their porches and stop what they're doing to stare up at the sky. STEVE BRAND, the man who's been polishing his car, now stands there ***transfixed****, staring upwards. He looks at DON MARTIN, his neighbor from across the street.]*

Steve What was that? A meteor?

Don *[Nods]* That's what it looked like. I didn't hear any crash though, did you?

Steve *[Shakes his head]* Nope. I didn't hear anything except a roar.

Mrs. Brand *[From her porch]* Steve? What was that?

Good Humor is a real ice-cream company. Good Humor workers drive their trucks through neighborhoods in warm weather. They sell ice-cream bars and other treats from the truck.

Which words in the stage directions tell you that this is a screenplay?

***Reading Strategy:* Summarizing**

Would you include the flash of light in a brief summary of the play? Why or why not?

Which parts of the play help you know it is science fiction?

A meteor is a large rock that flies through space. Sometimes meteors strike the Earth. They land with a hard crash, often making deep bowl-shaped holes called craters.

conversing talking; having conversations

vendor a seller

transfixed standing still in surprise

Steve *[Raising his voice and looking toward porch]* Guess it was a meteor, honey. Came awful close, didn't it?

Mrs. Brand Too close for my money! Much too close.

[The camera pans across the various porches to people who stand there watching and talking in low tones.]

Narrator's Voice Maple Street. Six-forty-four P.M. on a late September evening. *[A pause]* Maple Street in the last calm and **reflective** moment . . . before the monsters came!

[The camera slowly pans across the porches again. We see a man screwing a light bulb on a front porch, then getting down off the stool to flick the switch and finding that nothing happens.

Another man is working on an electric power mower. He plugs in the plug, flicks on the switch of the power mower, off and on, with nothing happening.

Through the window of a front porch, we see a woman pushing her finger back and forth on the dial hook. Her voice is ***indistinct*** *and distant, but* ***intelligible*** *and* ***repetitive****.]*

What do you think the flash of light was? Why do you think so?

Telephones used to have dials instead of push-buttons. The receiver rested on a hook. To call someone, you picked up the receiver. Then you pushed the hook down rapidly two or three times.

Woman Operator, operator, something's wrong on the phone, operator!

[MRS. BRAND comes out on the porch and calls to STEVE.]

Mrs. Brand *[Calling]* Steve, the power's off. I had the soup on the stove and the stove just stopped working.

reflective thoughtful

indistinct hard to see or hear

intelligible able to be understood

repetitive happens over and over again

Woman Same thing over here. I can't get anybody on the phone either. The phone seems to be dead.

[We look down on the street as we hear the voices creep up from below, small, mildly ***disturbed*** *voices highlighting these kinds of phrases:]*

VOICES

Electricity's off.

Phone won't work.

Can't get a thing on the radio.

My power mower won't move, won't work at all.

Radio's gone dead!

What do you think made the power go out?

[PETE VAN HORN, a tall, thin man, is seen standing in front of his house.]

Van Horn I'll cut through the back yard . . . See if the power's still on on Floral Street. I'll be right back!

[He walks past the side of his house and disappears into the back yard.

The camera pans down slowly until we're looking at ten or eleven people standing around the street and overflowing to the curb and sidewalk. In the background is STEVE BRAND'S car.]

Steve Doesn't make sense. Why should the power go off all of a sudden, and the phone line?

Don Maybe some sort of an electrical storm or something.

Charlie That don't seem likely. Sky's just as blue as anything. Not a cloud. No lightning. No thunder. No nothing. How could it be a storm?

Woman I can't get a thing on the radio. Not even the portable.

disturbed bothered; worried

[The people again ***murmur*** *softly in wonderment and question.]*

Charlie Well, why don't you go downtown and check with the police, though they'll probably think we're crazy or something. A little power failure and right away we get all **flustered** and everything.

A portable radio worked on batteries, not electricity. A power failure would not stop a portable radio from working.

Steve It isn't just the power failure, Charlie. If it was, we'd still be able to get a broadcast on the portable.

[There's a murmur of reaction to this. STEVE looks from face to face and then over to his car.]

Steve I'll run downtown. We'll get this all straightened out.

[He walks over to the car, gets in it, turns the key. Looking through the open car door, we see the crowd watching him from the other side. STEVE starts the engine. It turns over ***sluggishly*** *and then just stops dead. He tries it again and this time he can't get it to turn over. Then, very slowly and reflectively, he turns the key back to "off" and slowly gets out of the car.*

The people stare at STEVE. He stands for a moment by the car, then walks toward the group.]

Steve I don't understand it. It was working fine before . . .

Don Out of gas?

Steve *[Shakes his head]* I just had it filled up.

How does the power failure make the characters behave? Why do they behave this way?

Woman What's it mean?

Charlie It's just as if . . . as if everything had stopped. *[Then he turns toward STEVE.]* We'd better walk downtown.

[Another murmur of ***assent*** *at this.]*

Steve The two of us can go, Charlie. *[He turns to look back at the car.]* It couldn't be the meteor. A meteor couldn't do this.

murmur a soft flow of speech

flustered upset, bothered

sluggishly slowly and with difficulty

assent agreement

[He and CHARLIE exchange a look, then they start to walk away from the group.

We see TOMMY, a serious-faced fourteen-year-old in ***spectacles*** *who stands a few feet away from the group. He is halfway between them and the two men, who start to walk down the sidewalk.]*

Tommy Mr. Brand . . . you better not!

Steve Why not?

Tommy They don't want you to.

[STEVE and CHARLIE exchange a grin, and STEVE looks back toward the boy.]

Steve Who doesn't want us to?

Tommy *[Jerks his head in the general direction of the distant horizon]* Them!

Steve Them?

Charlie Who are them?

Tommy *[Very intently]* Whoever was in that thing that came by overhead.

[STEVE knits his brows for a moment, ***cocking*** *his head questioningly. His voice is* ***intense****.]*

Steve What?

Tommy Whoever was in that thing that came over. I don't think they want us to leave here.

[STEVE leaves CHARLIE and walks over to the boy. He kneels down in front of him. He forces his voice to remain gentle. He reaches out and holds the boy.]

Why does Steve have to "force" himself to speak gently?

Steve What do you mean? What are you talking about?

spectacles eyeglasses

cocking tilting

intense serious and forceful

Tommy They don't want us to leave. That's why they shut everything off.

Steve What makes you say that? Whatever gave you that idea?

Woman *[From the crowd]* Now isn't that the craziest thing you ever heard?

Tommy *[**Persistently** but a little **intimidated** by the crowd]* It's always that way, in every story I ever read about a ship landing from outer space.

Woman *[To the boy's mother, SALLY, who stands on the fringe of the crowd]* From outer space, yet! Sally, you better get that boy of yours up to bed. He's been reading too many comic books or seeing too many movies or something.

Sally Tommy, come over here and stop that kind of talk.

Steve Go ahead, Tommy. We'll be right back. And you'll see. That wasn't any ship or anything like it. That was just a . . . a meteor or something. Likely as not—*[He turns to the group, now trying to weight his words with an **optimism** he obviously doesn't feel but is desperately trying to **instill** in himself as well as the others.]* No doubt it did have something to do with all this power failure and the rest of it. Meteors can do some crazy things. Like sunspots.

Why do the adults half-believe what Tommy says about a spaceship?

persistently without giving up

intimidated frightened

optimism hopefulness

instill to fill with

Don *[Picking up the cue]* Sure. That's the kind of thing—like sunspots. They raise Cain with radio reception all over the world. And this thing being so close—why, there's no telling the sort of stuff it can do. *[He wets his lips, smiles nervously.]* Go ahead, Charlie. You and Steve go into town and see if that isn't what's causing it all.

[STEVE and CHARLIE again walk away from the group down the sidewalk. The people watch silently.

TOMMY stares at them, biting his lips, and finally calling out again.]

Tommy *Mr. Brand!*

[The two men stop again. TOMMY takes a step toward them.]

Tommy Mr. Brand . . . please don't leave here.

[STEVE and CHARLIE stop once again and turn toward the boy. There's a murmur in the crowd, a murmur of irritation and concern as if the boy were bringing up fears that shouldn't be brought up; words which carried with them a strange kind of ***validity*** *that came without logic but nonetheless* ***registered*** *and had meaning and effect. Again we hear a murmur of reaction from the crowd.*

TOMMY is partly frightened and partly ***defiant*** *as well.]*

Tommy You might not even be able to get to town. It was that way in the story. Nobody could leave. Nobody except—

Steve Except who?

Tommy Except the people they'd sent down ahead of them. They looked just like humans. And it wasn't until the ship landed that—

[The boy suddenly stops again, ***conscious*** *of the parents staring at them and of the sudden hush of the crowd.]*

Put the stage directions in your own words. How does Serling describe Tommy's words?

validity state of being sound or true

registered was understood

defiant bold and rude

conscious aware

Sally *[In a whisper, sensing the* ***antagonism*** *of the crowd]* Tommy, please son . . . honey, don't talk that way—

Man One That kid shouldn't talk that way . . . and we shouldn't stand here listening to him. Why this is the craziest thing I ever heard of. The kid tells us a comic book plot and here we stand listening—

[STEVE walks toward the camera, stops by the boy.]

Steve Go ahead, Tommy. What kind of story was this? What about the people that they sent out ahead?

Tommy That was the way they prepared things for the landing. They sent four people. A mother and a father and two kids who looked just like humans . . . but they weren't.

[There's another silence as STEVE looks toward the crowd and then toward TOMMY. He wears a tight grin.]

Steve Well, I guess what we'd better do then is to run a check on the neighborhood and see which ones of us are really human.

Reading Strategy:
Summarizing
How would you summarize the short scene with Tommy? Which details would you include?

Where do you think Pete is? Why do you think so?

[There's laughter at this, but it's a laughter that comes from a ***desperate*** *attempt to lighten the* ***atmosphere****. It's a release kind of laugh. The people look at one another in the middle of their laughter.]*

Charlie There must be somethin' better to do than stand around makin' bum jokes about it.

[Rubs his jaw nervously] I wonder if Floral Street's got the same deal we got. *[He looks past the houses.]* Where is Pete Van Horn anyway? Didn't he get back yet?

[Suddenly there's the sound of a car's engine starting to turn over. We look across the street toward the driveway of LES GOODMAN'S house. He's at the wheel trying to start the car.]

Sally Can you get it started, Les? *[He gets out of the car, shaking his head.]*

antagonism dislike

desperate without hope

atmosphere feelings of surroundings

Goodman No dice.

*[He walks toward the group. He stops suddenly as behind him, **inexplicably** and with a noise that inserts itself into the silence, the car engine starts up all by itself. GOODMAN whirls around to stare toward it.*

The car idles roughly, smoke coming from the exhaust, the frame shaking gently.

GOODMAN'S eyes go wide, and he runs over to his car.

The people stare toward the car.]

Man One He got the car started somehow. He got his car started!

*[The camera pans along the faces of the people as they stare, somehow caught up by this **revelation** and somehow, illogically, wildly, frightened.]*

Woman How come his car just up and started like that?

Sally All by itself. He wasn't anywheres near it. It started all by itself.

[DON approaches the group, stops a few feet away to look toward GOODMAN'S car and then back toward the group.]

Don And he never did come out to look at that thing that flew overhead. He wasn't even interested. *[He turns to the faces in the group, his face **taut** and serious.]* Why? Why didn't he come out with the rest of us to look?

What is Don suggesting about Goodman?

Charlie He always was an oddball. Him and his whole family. Real oddball.

Don What do you say we ask him?

[The group suddenly starts toward the house. In this brief fraction of a moment they take the first step toward performing

inexplicably in a way that cannot be explained

revelation a sudden understanding or explanation

taut tense and tight

*a **metamorphosis** that changes people from a group into a mob. They begin to head purposefully across the street toward the house at the end. STEVE stands in front of them. For a moment their fear almost turns their walk into a wild **stampede**, but STEVE'S voice, loud, **incisive**, and commanding, makes them stop.]*

Steve Wait a minute . . . wait a minute! Let's not be a mob!

[The people stop as a group, seem to pause for a moment, and then much more quietly and slowly start to walk across the street. GOODMAN stands alone facing the people.]

Goodman I just don't understand it. I tried to start it and it wouldn't start. You saw me. All of you saw me.

*[And now, just as suddenly as the engine started, it stops and there's a long silence that is gradually **intruded** upon by the frightened murmuring of the people.]*

Goodman I don't understand. I swear . . . I don't understand. What's happening?

Don Maybe you better tell us. Nothing's working on this street. Nothing. No lights, no power, no radio. *[And then meaningfully]* Nothing except one car—yours!

Why do you think the neighbors immediately blame Goodman? Why do they not look for an outside force to blame?

*[The people pick this up and now their murmuring becomes a loud **chant** filling the air with **accusations** and demands for action. Two of the men pass DON and head toward GOODMAN, who backs away, backing into his car and now at bay.]*

metamorphosis change into something else

stampede a hurried movement of many people together

incisive sharp and clear

intruded entered without being welcome or invited

chant words repeated with a rhythm

accusations statements of someone else's guilt or crime

Goodman Wait a minute now. You keep your distance—all of you. So I've got a car that starts by itself—well, that's a freak thing, I admit it. But does that make me some kind of a criminal or something? I don't know why the car works—it just does!

[This stops the crowd momentarily and now GOODMAN, still backing away, goes toward his front porch. He goes up the steps and then stops to stand facing the mob.

We see a long shot of STEVE as he comes through the crowd.]

Steve *[Quietly]* We're all on a monster kick, Les. Seems that the general impression holds that maybe one family isn't what we think they are. Monsters from outer space or something. Different than us. Fifth columnists from the **vast** beyond. *[He chuckles.]* You know anybody that might fit that description around here on Maple Street?

A *fifth columnist* was a spy—an enemy spy working in the United States.

Goodman What is this, a gag or something? This a practical joke or something?

[We see a close-up of the porch light as it suddenly goes out. There's a murmur from the group.]

Goodman Now I suppose that's supposed to **incriminate** me! The light goes on and off. That really does it, doesn't it? *[He looks around the faces of the people.]* I just don't understand this—*[He wets his lips, looking from face to face.]* Look, you all know me. We've lived here five years. Right in this house. We're no different from any of the rest of you! We're no different at all. Really . . . this whole thing is just . . . just weird—

Woman Well, if that's the case, Les Goodman, explain why—

[She stops suddenly, clamping her mouth shut.]

Goodman *[Softly]* Explain what?

vast huge, enormous

incriminate to make someone a criminal

Steve *[Interjecting]* Look, let's forget this—

Charlie *[Overlapping him]* Go ahead, let her talk. What about it? Explain what?

Woman *[A little* ***reluctantly****]* Well . . . sometimes I go to bed late at night. A couple of times . . . a couple of times I'd come out on the porch and I'd see Mr. Goodman here in the wee hours of the morning standing out in front of his house . . . looking up at the sky. *[She looks around the circle of faces.]* That's right, looking up at the sky as if . . . as if he were waiting for something. *[A pause]* As if he were looking for something.

A *cut* means that viewers are looking at a new shot. The camera has immediately switched its direction. A cut is different from a pan. In a pan, the camera sweeps across space, continuing the same shot.

[There's a murmur of reaction from the crowd again.

We cut suddenly to a group shot. As GOODMAN starts toward them, they back away frightened.]

Goodman You know really . . . this is for laughs. You know what I'm guilty of? *[He laughs.]* I'm guilty of **insomnia**. Now what's the **penalty** for insomnia? *[At this point the laugh, the humor, leaves his voice.]* Did you hear what I said? I said it was insomnia. *[A pause as he looks around, then shouts.]* I said it was insomnia! You fools. You scared, frightened rabbits, you. You're sick people, do you know that? You're sick people—all of you! And you don't even know what you're starting because let me tell you . . . let me tell you—this thing you're starting—that should frighten you. As God is my witness . . . you're letting something begin here that's a nightmare!

***Reading Strategy:* Summarizing**

Which details would you put in a summary of Act I? Why?

Act 2

[We see a medium shot of the GOODMAN entry hall at night. On the side table rests an unlit candle. MRS. GOODMAN walks into the scene, a glass of milk in hand. She sets the milk down on the table, lights the candle with a match from a box on the table, picks up the glass of milk, and starts out of scene.

interjecting interrupting

reluctantly without wanting to

insomnia state where one cannot sleep

penalty punishment

Mrs. Goodman comes through her porch door, glass of milk in hand. The entry hall, with table and lit candle, can be seen behind her.

Outside, the camera slowly pans down the sidewalk, taking in little knots of people who stand around talking in low voices. At the end of each conversation they look toward LES GOODMAN'S house. From the various houses we can see candlelight but no electricity, and there's an ***all-pervading*** *quiet that blankets the whole area, disturbed only by the almost whispered voices of the people as they stand around. The camera pans over to one group where CHARLIE stands. He stares across at GOODMAN'S house.*

We see a long shot of the house. Two men stand across the street in almost ***sentry****-like poses. Then we see a medium shot of a group of people.]*

A *long shot* means that the camera looks at the house from a great distance away. A *medium shot* is less far away.

Sally *[A little* ***timorously****]* It just doesn't seem right, though, keeping watch on them. Why . . . he was right when he said he was one of our neighbors. Why, I've known Ethel Goodman ever since they moved in. We've been good friends—

Charlie That don't prove a thing. Any guy who'd spend his time lookin' up at the sky early in the morning—well, there's something wrong with that kind of person. There's something that ain't legitimate. Maybe under normal **circumstances** we could let it go by, but these aren't normal circumstances. Why, look at this street! Nothin' but candles. Why, it's like goin' back into the dark ages or somethin'!

What do you think of Charlie's reasoning? Explain your opinion.

[STEVE walks down the steps of his porch, walks down the street over to LES GOODMAN'S house, and then stops at the foot of the steps. GOODMAN stands there, his wife behind him, very frightened.]

all-pervading spread through all parts

timorously in a frightened or timid way

circumstances situations

sentry guard

Goodman Just stay right where you are, Steve. We don't want any trouble, but this time if anybody sets foot on my porch, that's what they're going to get—trouble!

Steve Look, Les—

Goodman I've already explained to you people. I don't sleep very well at night sometimes. I get up and I take a walk and I look up at the sky. I look at the stars!

Mrs. Goodman That's exactly what he does. Why this whole thing, it's . . . it's some kind of madness or something.

Steve *[Nods **grimly**]* That's exactly what it is—some kind of madness.

Charlie's Voice *[Shrill, from across the street]* You best watch who you're seen with, Steve! Until we get this all straightened out, you ain't exactly above suspicion yourself.

Steve *[Whirling around toward him]* Or you, Charlie. Or any of us, it seems. From age eight on up!

Woman What I'd like to know is—what are we gonna do? Just stand around here all night?

Charlie There's nothin' else we can do! *[He turns back looking toward STEVE and GOODMAN again.]* One of 'em'll tip their hand. They got to.

A *hanging judge* is a judge known for sentencing people to death.

Steve *[Raising his voice]* There's something you can do, Charlie. You could go home and keep your mouth shut. You could quit strutting around like a self-appointed hanging judge and just climb into bed and forget it.

Charlie You sound real anxious to have that happen, Steve. I think we better keep our eye on you too!

Don *[As if he were taking the bit in his teeth, takes a hesitant step to the front]* I think everything might as well come out now. *[He turns toward STEVE.]* Your wife's done plenty of talking, Steve, about how odd you are!

grimly hopelessly, harshly

Charlie *[Picking this up, his eyes widening]* Go ahead, tell us what she's said.

[We see a long shot of STEVE as he walks toward them from across the street.]

Steve Go ahead, what's my wife said? Let's get it all out. Let's pick out every **idiosyncrasy** of every single man, woman, and child on the street. And then we might as well set up some kind of kangaroo court. How about a firing squad at dawn, Charlie, so we can get rid of all the suspects? Narrow them down. Make it easier for you.

Don There's no need gettin' so upset, Steve. It's just that . . . well . . . Myra's talked about how there's been plenty of nights you spent hours down in your basement workin' on some kind of radio or something. Well, none of us have ever seen that radio—

A *kangaroo court* is a special court that makes its own laws. It exists outside the law. A *firing squad* is a group of soldiers hired to shoot a prisoner. They all aim and shoot at once, so no one knows which bullet kills the person.

[By this time STEVE has reached the group. He stands there defiantly close to them.]

Charlie Go ahead, Steve. What kind of "radio set" you workin' on? I never seen it. Neither has anyone else. Who you talk to on that radio set? And who talks to you?

Steve I'm surprised at you, Charlie. How come you're so **dense** all of a sudden? *[A pause]* Who do I talk to? I talk to monsters from outer space. I talk to three-headed green men who fly over here in what look like meteors.

[STEVE'S wife steps down from the porch, bites her lip, calls out.]

idiosyncrasy unusual way to behave

dense stupid

A *ham radio* set is a kit for a beginning radio user. Ham radios had been popular since the early days of radios.

A *search warrant* is a paper signed by a judge. Any U.S. law person who wants to search private property must have a search warrant. To get one, he must prove that he will probably find proof of a crime. This law is clearly stated in the Fourth Amendment to the Constitution.

Who do you think the figure is? Why do you think so?

Mrs. Brand Steve! Steve, please. *[Then looking around, frightened, she walks toward the group.]* It's just a ham radio set, that's all. I bought him a book on it myself. It's just a ham radio set. A lot of people have them. I can show it to you. It's right down in the basement.

Steve *[Whirls around toward her]* Show them nothing! If they want to look inside our house—let them get a search warrant.

Charlie Look, buddy, you can't afford to—

Steve *[Interrupting]* Charlie, don't tell me what I can afford! And stop telling me who's dangerous and who isn't and who's safe and who's a **menace**. *[He turns to the group and shouts.]* And you're with him, too—all of you! You're standing here all set to **crucify**—all set to find a **scapegoat**—all desperate to point some kind of a finger at a neighbor! Well now look, friends, the only thing that's gonna happen is that we'll eat each other up alive—

*[He stops **abruptly** as CHARLIE suddenly grabs his arm.]*

Charlie *[In a hushed voice]* That's not the only thing that can happen to us.

*[Cut to a long shot looking down the street. A figure has suddenly **materialized** in the gloom and in the silence we can hear the clickety-clack of slow, **measured** footsteps on concrete as the figure walks slowly toward them. One of the women lets out a **stifled** cry. The young mother grabs her boy as do a couple of others.]*

Tommy *[Shouting, frightened]* It's the monster! It's the monster!

[Another woman lets out a wail and the people fall back in a group, staring toward the darkness and the approaching figure.

menace a danger

crucify to kill slowly and painfully

scapegoat someone to take the blame for a group

abruptly suddenly

materialized appeared

measured slow and steady

stifled made silent

We see a medium group shot of the people as they stand in the shadows watching. DON MARTIN joins them, carrying a shotgun. He holds it up.]

Don We may need this.

Steve A shotgun? *[He pulls it out of DON'S hand.]* Good Lord—will anybody think a thought around here? Will you people wise up? What good would a shotgun do against—

[Now CHARLIE pulls the gun from STEVE'S hand.]

Charlie No more talk, Steve. You're going to talk us into a grave! You'd let whatever's out there walk right over us, wouldn't yuh? Well, some of us won't!

[He swings the gun around to point it toward the sidewalk. The dark figure continues to walk toward them.

The group stands there, fearful, ***apprehensive****, mothers clutching children, men standing in front of wives. CHARLIE slowly raises the gun. As the figure gets closer and closer he suddenly pulls the trigger. The sound of it explodes in the stillness. There is a long angle shot looking down at the figure, who suddenly lets out a small cry, stumbles forward onto his knees and then falls forward on his face. DON, CHARLIE, and STEVE race forward over to him. STEVE is there first and turns the man over. Now the crowd gathers around them.]*

Steve *[Slowly looks up]* It's Pete Van Horn.

Don *[In a hushed voice]* Pete Van Horn! He was just gonna go over to the next block to see if the power was on—

Woman You killed him, Charlie. You shot him dead!

Charlie *[Looks around at the circle of faces, his eyes frightened, his face* ***contorted****]* But . . . but I didn't know who he was. I certainly didn't know who he was. He comes walkin' out of the darkness—how am I supposed to know who he was? *[He grabs STEVE.]* Steve—you know why I shot! How was

apprehensive frightened

contorted twisted out of shape

I supposed to know he wasn't a monster or something? *[He grabs DON now.]* We're all scared of the same thing. I was just tryin' to . . . tryin' to protect my home, that's all! Look, all of you, that's all I was tryin' to do. *[He looks down wildly at the body.]* I didn't know it was somebody we knew! I didn't know—

[There's a sudden hush and then an intake of breath. We see a medium shot of the living room window of CHARLIE'S house. The window is not lit, but suddenly the house lights come on behind it.]

Woman *[In a very hushed voice]* Charlie . . . Charlie . . . the lights just went on in your house. Why did the lights just go on?

Don What about it, Charlie? How come you're the only one with lights now?

How has Goodman's position with the group changed? Why?

Goodman That's what I'd like to know.

[A pause as they all stare toward CHARLIE.]

Goodman You were so quick to kill, Charlie, and you were so quick to tell us who we had to be careful of. Well, maybe you had to kill. Maybe Peter there was trying to tell us something. Maybe he'd found out something and came back to tell us who there was **amongst** us we should watch out for—

[CHARLIE backs away from the group, his eyes wide with fright.]

Charlie No . . . no . . . it's nothing of the sort! I don't know why the lights are on. I swear I don't. Somebody's pulling a gag or something.

[He bumps against STEVE, who grabs him and whirls him around.]

Steve A gag? A gag? Charlie, there's a dead man on the sidewalk and you killed him! Does this thing look like a gag to you?

amongst among

[CHARLIE breaks away and screams as he runs toward his house.]

Charlie No! No! Please!

[A man breaks away from the crowd to chase CHARLIE.

We see a long angle shot looking down as the man tackles CHARLIE and lands on top of him. The other people start to run toward them. CHARLIE is up on his feet, breaks away from the other man's grasp, lands a couple of desperate punches that push the man aside. Then he forces his way, fighting, through the crowd to once again break free, jumps up on his front porch. A rock thrown from the group smashes a window alongside of him, the broken glass flying past him. A couple of pieces cut him. He stands there ***perspiring****, rumpled, blood running down from a cut on the cheek. His wife breaks away from the group to throw herself into his arms. He buries his face against her. We can see the crowd* ***converging*** *on the porch now.]*

perspiring sweating

converging coming together

VOICES

It must have been him.

He's the one.

We got to get Charlie.

How is this group like a mob?

[Another rock lands on the porch. Now CHARLIE pushes his wife behind him, facing the group.]

Who do you think Charlie will name as the monster? Why?

Charlie Look, look I swear to you . . . it isn't me . . . but I do know who it is . . . I swear to you, I do know who it is. I know who the monster is here. I know who it is that doesn't belong. I swear to you I know.

Goodman *[Shouting]* What are you waiting for?

Woman *[Shouting]* Come on, Charlie, come on.

Man One *[Shouting]* Who is it, Charlie, tell us!

Don *[Pushing his way to the front of the crowd]* All right, Charlie, let's hear it!

[CHARLIE'S eyes dart around wildly.]

Charlie It's . . . it's . . .

Man Two *[Screaming]* Go ahead, Charlie, tell us.

Charlie It's . . . it's the kid. It's Tommy. He's the one!

Why does Tommy bury his face?

[There's a gasp from the crowd as we cut to a shot of SALLY holding her son TOMMY. The boy at first doesn't understand and then, realizing the eyes are all on him, buries his face against his mother.]

Sally *[Backs away]* That's crazy! That's crazy! He's a little boy.

Woman But he knew! He was the only one who knew! He told us all about it. Well, how did he know? How could he have known?

[The various people take this up and repeat the question aloud.]

VOICES
How could he know?

Who told him?

Make the kid answer.

Don It was Charlie who killed old man Van Horn.

Woman But it was the kid here who knew what was going to happen all the time. He was the one who knew!

[We see a close-up of STEVE.]

Steve Are you all gone crazy? *[Pause as he looks about]* Stop.

[A fist crashes at STEVE'S face, staggering him back out of the frame of the picture.

There are several close camera shots suggesting the coming of violence. A hand fires a rifle. A fist clenches. A hand grabs the hammer from VAN HORN'S body, etc. Meanwhile, we hear the following lines.]

Don Charlie has to be the one—Where's my rifle—

Woman Les Goodman's the one. His car started! Let's wreck it.

How will wrecking the car help?

Mrs. Goodman What about Steve's radio—He's the one that called them—

Mrs. Goodman Smash the radio. Get me a hammer. Get me something.

Steve Stop—Stop—

Charlie Where's that kid—Let's get him.

Man One Get Steve—Get Charlie—They're working together.

[The crowd starts to converge around the mother, who grabs the child and starts to run with him. The crowd starts to follow, at first walking fast, and then running after him.

We see a full shot of the street as suddenly CHARLIE'S lights go off and the lights in another house go on. They stay on for a moment, then from across the street other lights go on and then off again.]

Man One *[Shouting]* It isn't the kid . . . it's Bob Weaver's house.

Woman It isn't Bob Weaver's house. It's Don Martin's place.

Charlie I tell you it's the kid.

Don It's Charlie. He's the one.

> *Reading Strategy:* **Summarizing**
> Which details would you put in a summary of Act II? Why would you choose each detail?

[We move into a series of close-ups of various people as they shout, accuse, scream, ***interspersing*** *these shots with shots of houses as the lights go on and off, and then slowly in the middle of this nightmarish* ***morass*** *of sight and sound the camera starts to pull away, until once again we've reached the opening shot looking at the Maple Street sign from high above. The camera continues to move away until we dissolve to a shot looking toward the metal side of a space craft, which sits* ***shrouded*** *in darkness. An open door throws out a beam of light from the illuminated interior. Two figures* ***silhouetted*** *against the bright lights appear. We get only a vague feeling of form, but nothing more explicit than that.]*

Figure One Understand the ***procedure*** now? Just stop a few of their machines and radios and telephones and lawn mowers . . . throw them into darkness for a few hours, and then you just sit back and watch the pattern.

Figure Two And this pattern is always the same?

Figure One With few **variations**. They pick the most dangerous enemy they can find . . . and it's themselves. And all we need do is sit back . . . and watch.

interspersing switching between

morass a hard-to-understand situation

shrouded wrapped up in

silhouetted appearing as a shadow

procedure way something works

variations differences

Figure Two Then I take it this place . . . this Maple Street . . . is not **unique**.

Figure One *[Shaking his head]* By no means. Their world is full of Maple Streets. And we'll go from one to the other and let them destroy themselves. One to the other . . . one to the other . . . one to the other—

[Now the camera pans up for a shot of the starry sky and over this we hear the NARRATOR'S voice.]

Narrator's Voice The tools of **conquest** do not necessarily come with bombs and explosions and fallout. There are weapons that are simply thoughts, **attitudes**, **prejudices**—to be found only in the minds of men. For the record, prejudices can kill and suspicion can destroy and a thoughtless frightened search for a scapegoat has a fallout all its own for the children . . . and the children yet unborn. *[A pause]* And the pity of it is . . . that these things cannot be confined to . . . The Twilight Zone!

What is the fifth dimension?

unique one-of-a-kind

conquest a victory over an enemy

attitudes ways of looking at and thinking about things

prejudices unfair feelings and ideas

AFTER READING THE SELECTION | **Apply the Skills**

The Monsters Are Due on Maple Street *by Rod Serling*

Directions Choose the letter of the best answer or write the answer using complete sentences.

Comprehension: Identifying Facts

1. What do the characters see in the sky?
- **A** lightning
- **B** a flash of light
- **C** a meteor
- **D** a screeching roar

2. Which would not usually be bothered by power going off?
- **A** the telephone
- **B** the lights
- **C** the refrigerator
- **D** the stove

3. Why does Pete Van Horn leave Maple Street?

4. What does Tommy think he saw in the sky?

5. What happens when Les Goodman tries to start his car?

6. What are the neighbors doing at the start of Act II?

7. What does Don accuse Steve of?

8. What do the neighbors see coming toward them along the street?

9. What happens after everyone realizes whom Charlie has shot?

10. Who was responsible for the power failure?

Comprehension: Putting Ideas Together

11. Why does Tommy believe aliens have come to Maple Street?
- **A** He saw them.
- **B** He saw their spaceship.
- **C** He has read science-fiction stories.
- **D** He is an alien himself.

12. How do the neighbors react to Tommy's idea at first?
- **A** They half-believe him and are frightened.
- **B** They laugh at him for believing in aliens.
- **C** They accuse him of being responsible for the power failure.
- **D** They realize that he is a dangerous enemy.

13. What exactly is "the twilight zone"?

14. What unusual things happen at the start of the play?

15. Why do the neighbors single out Les Goodman for blame in Act I?

16. Why do the neighbors turn against Steve?

17. On what evidence do the neighbors accuse each other?

18. Who accuses Tommy after the shooting, and why?

19. What does Figure One explain to Figure Two?

20. What does the Narrator warn the audience about at the play's end?

Understanding Literature: Motivation

Motivation is the answer to the question "Why did he say or do that?" Characters are often motivated by their feelings. They may speak and act from anger, fear, jealousy, or love. Science-fiction writers usually write about motivations that humans might have. However, the characters often live through science-based events that could not really happen.

21. Which parts of this play tell you that it is science fiction?

22. The adults know that science fiction is not real. Why are they frightened by Tommy's idea about space aliens?

23. Why does Charlie shoot Pete Van Horn?

24. Why do the characters finally turn on Tommy?

25. Why is Steve less willing than the rest to accuse his neighbors?

Critical Thinking

26. Do you think the Narrator speaks for Rod Serling? Why or why not?

27. The play is set in a very ordinary neighborhood. What does the setting have to do with the tone of the play?

28. Who are "the monsters" on Maple Street? What makes them act like monsters?

29. Do you think the characters' fear and their attacks on each other could really happen? Why or why not?

Thinking Creatively

30. Say you lived on Maple Street. How would you have behaved while the power was out?

***After Reading* continued on next page**

The Monsters Are Due on Maple Street *by Rod Serling*

Grammar Check

There are four basic types of sentences.

Type	Function	Ends In	Example
Declarative	makes a statement	.	The cat is chasing a squirrel.
Interrogative	asks a question	?	Where is the cat?
Imperative	gives a command	. or !	Go rescue the cat! Keep the cat indoors.
Exclamatory	calls out or exclaims	!	Look, there's the cat!

Identify each type of sentence. Write a related sentence of a different type.

1 Did you read today's paper?

2 I have too much to read.

3 Watch out for that step!

4 I'm so pleased to see you!

Vocabulary Builder

Adding the suffix *–ize* to a noun makes a verb. *–Ize* means "to create or make."

Examples:

summary/summarize: "to create a summary"

critic/criticize "to make a criticism"

Convert each noun to an *–ize* verb. Check your spelling in the dictionary.

1 familiar

2 general

3 synthesis

4 character

5 analysis

Writing on Your Own

Write a report from the point of view of Figure One and Figure Two. Write what you learned from watching the events on Maple Street. Include these parts:

- facts about how the people behaved
- ideas for further action

Listening and Speaking

With a small group, stage a scene from the screenplay. Follow these steps:

- Choose a scene with enough roles for the students in the group.
- Choose a director.
- Practice the scene. Pay attention to stage directions.
- Present the scene to the class.

Media and Viewing

Make plans to film the scene you presented in the last activity. If you would rather, you can choose any other scene from the screenplay. Plan your camera angles. Consider special sound and lighting effects. Choose a place to film. If possible, film your scene and present it to the class.

Applications

An application gives certain information to a group or company. The group uses applications to help decide whom to accept. People fill out applications for the following reasons:

- to get a job
- to be admitted to a school
- to get a library card to open a savings account
- to join a club or sports league
- to get a driver's license

Read carefully to find out what information is needed. Note when and where the application should be turned in. Clip needed papers or payments to the application.

Reading Skill: Reading Closely

Read an application closely. In other words, carefully read every word. Follow each step on the application form. Start with the directions, and complete each one. If you have questions, ask. Do not leave any part blank, unless it is marked "optional." You can decide if you want to fill in "optional" parts or not. Read the fine print (small type at the bottom of the page) carefully. It often has facts you need to know.

Look over your application carefully. Make sure you have completed all parts. Make sure that your writing is easy to read. The checklist shown can help you.

Checklist for Filling Out an Application

Do I have the correct application?
Have I followed all the directions?
Have I written or typed clearly?
Have I signed the application?
Have I checked the application for mistakes?
Have I turned in the application by the deadline?
Do I have all needed papers or payments?
Have I read the fine print?
Are there any additional materials that must be sent with the application?

The Flat Rock Playhouse

The Flat Rock Playhouse has grown in recent years from a traditional summer theater to a regional powerhouse. It boasts one of the largest Resident Contract Agreements with Actors' Equity Association, the union of actors and stage managers, in the southern region. Flat Rock Playhouse unites its seasonal talent pool with its year-round administrative and artistic staff, 70% of whom were formerly apprentices and interns. The Playhouse proudly trains and educates to nurture its own future.

Do you have a reputable Equity Apprenticeship in your background?

Outside an education setting what steps have you taken to build a career? Have you begun professional networking?

- How are you going to make the contacts necessary to get the job?
- Do you have acting professionals on your reference list?
- What do you know about marketing yourself in the theater business? Do you have a professionally photographed head shot?
- Do you have a means to continually update your resume?
- Do you know how to find an agent? Do you know how to get call backs at a cattle-call audition?
- Would you feel comfortable in a professional environment?
- Are you ready to join a union? Are you a triple-threat talent?

We will be attending SETC in March and will be happy to contact all serious applicants who have already initiated contact regarding their audition numbers.

Applicants can, of course, call and set up personal auditions at the Playhouse if they are not attending SETC. However, if one's schedule or geographic distance from the Playhouse makes a personal audition impossible, one may send a videotaped audition consisting of two monologues and if applicable examples of singing and dance work. Also to expedite our selection and registration process, be sure to include two reference letters with the return correspondence. An application form and descriptive material about the program are subject to change due to variations in the talents and needs of each student class. Please complete and return the application at your earliest convenience if you wish to be considered among this year's candidates.

A photograph showing actors on stage with spotlights immediately conveys some of the activities at The Flat Rock Playhouse.

The questions imply that the program will teach these skills.

The directions tell you to submit the application promptly.

Read the title of the application to be sure it is the one you need.

Apprentice Application Form for the Vagabond School of the Drama

TO ENROLL: PLEASE **PRINT** THIS FORM, COMPLETE IT, AND RETURN IT WITH A HEADSHOT OR SNAP SHOT, as well as any other information you deem necessary. Videotapes are welcome. Auditions and/or interviews by the Executive Director or his appointee are required.

Read the directions closely to find out how to fill out the application. The directions may also describe other documents you have to provide.

Student Name ______________ Social Security ______

Address ______________

City ______________ State ________ Zip ______

Home Phone ________ Work Phone ________ E-mail ________

Age ______ Date of Birth / / Weight ____ Height _____ Hair Color _____

Instruction

Song ________ Dance ________ Instruments ________

Theater Training ______________

Parent/Guardian Name ______________

Address ______________

City ______________ State ________ Zip ______

Home Phone ________ Work Phone ________ E-mail ________

Please provide a character reference

Name ______________

Address ______________

City ______________ State ________ Zip ______

Home Phone ________ Work Phone ________ E-mail ________

The Vagabond School of the Drama, Inc. is a not-for-profit educational institution that admits students of any race, creed, sex, national, or ethnic origin.

Monitor Your Progress

Directions Choose the letter of the best answer or write the answer using complete sentences.

1. The Vagabond School of the Drama wants an application. What else does it ask for?
   A a check for $200
   B a headshot or snapshot
   C one letter of recommendation
   D the dates the applicant is available for an audition

2. Which part of the application asks about a person's experience?
   A "Videotapes are welcome."
   B "Return [this application] with a headshot or snap shot."
   C "Please provide a character reference."
   D "Instruction"

3. Which of the following is not necessary with the application?
   A videotapes
   B auditions
   C character references
   D headshots

4. Why do you think the application form says "PLEASE PRINT"?

5. Why is it good for a person to study at the Vagabond School of the Drama?

Writing on Your Own

Write a summary of the information about the Vagabond School of the Drama. Describe its mission or purpose, its history, its apprentice program, where it is, and other important things about the school.

COMPARING LITERARY WORKS | Build Understanding

A Loan for Columbus by Inez Carvalho

Inez Carvalho
1952–

About the Author

Inez Carvalho is the fictional name of former actress and theater director Christina Hamlett, an award-winning author, instructor, and professional script coverage consultant. Her credits include 25 books, 121 plays and musicals, five optioned features, and hundreds of articles on the performing arts, humor, health, and travel. Her work has appeared in magazines, newspapers, and Internet websites throughout the U.S., UK, Canada, Australia, and New Zealand.

About the Selection

"A Loan for Columbus" is based on two real characters and one real event. Christopher Columbus (1451–1506) was an explorer from Genoa, Italy. Isabella of Castile (1451–1504) became Queen Isabella I of Castile and Aragon in 1474. Columbus wanted money so he could sail to the West. He asked Isabella, who agreed to pay for the journey. Everything else in this play is made up by the author.

In the play, explorer Christopher Columbus asks for a loan. He wants to pay for a trip to the Indies. Columbus explains that he is sure he can find the Indies by going west. The vice-president of the First Bank of Castile will not give him the money. Her loan officer agrees. Columbus, disappointed, turns to leave. The loan officer then remembers that he is to meet the Queen for lunch. Since he has another date, he asks Columbus to dine with the Queen. "She will love to hear all about your voyage!" he tells Columbus.

As you read this selection, think of how it compares to "The Monsters Are Due on Maple Street." Although one story is a comedy and the other story is a dramatic play, they both have many similarities in style.

Objectives

- To read and understand a comedy
- To identify and understand anachronisms
- To compare and contrast a comedy and a dramatic play

***Comparing* continued on next page**

A Loan for Columbus *by Inez Carvalho*

comedy a play with a happy ending, intended to amuse its audience

anachronism a speech or event that could not actually have taken place at the time in which it happens in a literary work

Literary Terms A **comedy** is a play with a happy ending, intending to amuse its audience. It uses humor and jokes to make an audience laugh. Some comedies use real characters from history. In these comedies, the playwright may stretch facts to make jokes. In other words, the playwright will start with a fact and add made-up things to it. The playwright might also add characters that did not really live. To make the story funny, a playwright might also use **anachronisms**. This word means things that could not happen at that time of history. These out-of-place happenings can be very funny.

Reading on Your Own Think back to "Maple Street" and the things the people said and did. Decide how you would describe the mood of "Maple Street." As you read "A Loan for Columbus," think about what the people say and do. Try to get a feel for its mood. What important differences can you see between the moods in the two plays?

Writing on Your Own Both "The Monsters Are Due on Maple Street" and "A Loan for Columbus" are from certain periods in history. How does each writer make use of history in his or her play? Write a short paragraph telling how the authors' writing and results are alike and different.

Vocabulary Focus This selection has a number of slang idioms and expressions. Examples include: keep a straight face, cut straight to the chase, tide me over, packing very light, and tourist traps. Go over these phrases with a partner. Make sure both of you understand the meanings.

Think Before You Read Do you have a big dream that you would like to make come true? What can you do to make your dream come true?

A Loan for Columbus

Bold explorer's meeting with a loan officer goes poorly—but ends in a lunch date with a queen. . . .

Characters

Ms. Domingo, Vice President, First Bank of Castille

Mr. Santiago, loan officer

Donatella, Santiago's assistant

Christopher Columbus, a bold adventurer

TIME: 1492

Setting

*Mr. Santiago's office at First Bank of Castille, Spain. Desk and chair are left; two chairs face desk. Window upstage looks out on city. Door to bank **foyer** is down right.*

***AT RISE:** MR. SANTIAGO and MS. DOMINGO are sipping coffees and nibbling on **biscotti**. DOMINGO is in the middle of a humorous story.*

As you read, look for anachronisms, such as this one in the character list: No woman would have had a job in a bank in 1492. At that time, most women could not work. Only working-class women could work and those jobs were as servants or maids.

Domingo And so then I said, I really don't want to (*With **emphasis***) bore you with details, but pork futures are definitely the way to go! (*They both laugh.*)

Santiago By the by, did I tell you that DaVinci fellow dropped by last week?

Domingo Again? What was it this time?

Santiago talks about Leonardo da Vinci (1452–1519). Leonardo was an Italian artist, scientist, and inventor. Many people think he is history's greatest genius. Leonardo da Vinci experimented with ideas for human flight long before airplanes were invented.

foyer lobby

biscotti hard, crunchy Italian cookie

emphasis force

Which parts of the play make it a comedy?

Santiago He brought all kinds of **ludicrous** drawings for something he calls a human flying machine. Of course he wanted a loan to pay for it.

Domingo Flying out the window with our money, to say the least. I hope you told him no?

Santiago Absolutely! If there's one thing our bank has a **reputation** for, it's putting our funds behind projects that are well grounded!

Domingo So I hear you just got back from England. Any good gossip?

Henry VII's son grew up to be King Henry VIII. The joke of this speech is that Henry VIII was married six times.

Santiago Only that Henry the Seventh's got a new son—did I mention it? Quite the little flirt, too. Even at a few months, he was flirting with all the ladies at court. They were completely **besotted** with him.

Domingo Thank goodness the Church will only allow him to pick one for his wife when he's old enough! (*They chuckle. Knock on door is heard.*)

The Church refers to the Catholic Church. This was the only Christian church in 1492. The Protestant religions did not start until the 1500s. King Henry VIII (see above) started the Anglican Church when he was older.

Santiago (*Calling out*) Yes? (*DONATELLA enters.*)

Donatella Excuse me, Mr. Santiago, but your eleven o'clock is here.

Santiago Thanks, Donatella. Please show him in. (*She exits.*)

Domingo Seeing as how you're busy, I really should get going.

Santiago No, no. Not at all. I'd particularly like you to meet this one.

Domingo Oh?

Donatella's speech is another anachronism. "Your eleven o'clock" is a phrase that is common today, but did not exist in 1492.

Santiago (*Warning*) Although you have to promise to keep a straight face.

Domingo A new loan **applicant?**

ludicrous silly

reputation what people believe about one's character

besotted in love with

applicant a person making a request

Santiago I swear I don't know how these people keep managing to find us. Their chances of **acquiring** a large sum of money would be much better if they simply played the lottery! (*DONATELLA reenters with CHRISTOPHER COLUMBUS, who carries maps and a round gold ball.*)

Donatella Our loan officer, Mr. Santiago. (*COLUMBUS crosses the room to shake SANTIAGO'S hand, comically shifting his possessions to his left hand and arm to do so.*)

Santiago Ah, Mr. Columbus. I've been expecting you.

Columbus Please, call me Christopher.

Donatella Would you care for some coffee, sir?

Columbus No, thank you. You've been more than kind. (*DONATELLA exits.*)

Santiago (*Introducing DOMINGO*) Our vice president, Ms. Domingo. (*They shake hands.*)

Domingo So . . . what brings you to our sunny Bank of Castille?

acquiring obtaining

Columbus To cut straight to the chase, ma'am, I'm here for a loan.

Santiago A loan, you say?

Columbus Only a **modest** sum, you might say. Just to tide me over.

Domingo Tide you over?

Columbus Yes. Over the ocean. (*He* ***deposits*** *the maps and globe on the desk.*) I'm planning to take a very, very long trip.

Santiago Ah, yes—a vacation loan, is it? We've done quite a few of those recently.

Think about what you know about Christopher Columbus. What is funny in the difference between the facts of history and the dialogue?

Columbus Actually, sir, it's strictly business.

Domingo When were you planning to leave?

Columbus As soon as possible. I already have the ships picked out.

Santiago Ships plural, did you say? You need more than one?

Columbus Yes, sir. Three of them.

When Columbus says *the Indies,* he means India. In 1492, Europeans did not know about the Americas. Columbus thought he could reach India by sailing east. He did not know that the Americas and a second ocean were in between. His mistake is why the Caribbean Islands are called "the West Indies." It is also the reason for the term "American Indians."

Domingo (*Chuckling*) You must have a lot of luggage to need three ships for a **voyage.**

Columbus Actually, ma'am, I'm packing very light. I'm just planning to bring a lot back home with me.

Santiago Ah, yes! It's hard to resist those tourist traps.

Domingo And where are you planning to take these three ships of yours?

Columbus I'm sailing west . . . to the *Indies!*

Santiago (*Frowning*) The Indies?

Domingo (*Shaking head*) I don't believe I've ever heard of them.

modest small

deposits sets down

voyage a long trip, a journey

Columbus Of course not. That's because I'll be the first to ever go there!

Santiago And "there" is exactly where?

Columbus Allow me to demonstrate. (*He picks up ball and the pen plume from SANTIAGO's desk.*) As of this moment, we are here. (*He marks a big X on the ball and shows it to them.*)

Santiago Uh-huh.

Domingo Uh-huh.

Columbus What I intend to do is take my ships over to here. (*Turns ball to opposite side and makes another big X. DOMINGO and SANTIAGO look at the X, then at each other, then at COLUMBUS.*)

Santiago I don't think so.

Domingo I don't think so.

Columbus And why not?

Domingo Quite simply, sir, there's no "there" there. It doesn't exist.

Columbus Meaning what?

Santiago Meaning that banks deal in exact and absolute information.

Domingo Precisely! If you expect the First Bank of Castille to **finance** an **expedition,** it must be to a place that the mapmakers have actually put on a map.

Columbus But if they'd already put it on a map, then what would there be left to discover? (*SANTIAGO and DOMINGO look at each other, unsure of how to answer this.*) Let me put it this way: Have you ever stood on a beach and looked out to sea and noticed how everything seems to end at the **horizon?**

Until the late 19th century, pens were made from feathers. The center, straight part of a bird's feather is hollow and can hold ink. This is why a pen would have a plume.

Domingo quotes American writer Gertrude Stein (1874–1946). Stein once described Oakland, California, by saying "there is no there there." What makes this an anachronism?

finance to pay for

expedition journey with a specific purpose

horizon an imaginary line where the land appears to meet the sky

Domingo and Santiago (***In unison***) Uh-huh.

Columbus Well, my theory is that it doesn't.

Santiago Doesn't what?

Columbus Doesn't come to an end. (*He takes the ball and starts bouncing it around like a basketball.*) My theory is that there's a whole world on the other side of the horizon that's just waiting for someone to come along and discover it. A world that's ripe with opportunity, bursting with adventure, and **teeming** with more excitement than we could ever imagine. And I— (*He holds the ball as if aiming for a basket. He "shoots" it offstage.*) —want to be the one to prove that it's real.

What is funny about Domingo talking about a "financial institution"?

Domingo With money from our financial **institution?**

Columbus I certainly hope so.

Santiago Do you ever read the newspapers, Christopher?

Columbus Every morning. Why do you ask?

Santiago Then surely you've read the **commentaries** by some of the best minds in Spain who have declared that the world as we know it is as flat as a tortilla. What you see at the horizon is, quite frankly, all there is.

Columbus But how do they know? Have they ever taken a ship and sailed out as far as they could go?

Domingo Well, of course they have!

Columbus And?

Domingo And they had the good sense to turn around and come home just before they reached the edge and fell off.

Columbus But there's nothing to fall off into!

Domingo (*To SANTIAGO*) The poor man is obviously **delusional. . .**

in unison together

teeming full of

institution a business

commentaries articles giving opinions and supporting details

delusional crazy

Santiago (*To COLUMBUS*) You're obviously very passionate about your quest, sir. But you have to **appreciate** our position on the matter.

Domingo What my **associate** is trying to say is that eyebrows would be raised throughout all of Spain if we were to provide funds for **ventures** as ridiculously **foolhardy** as the one you've proposed.

Columbus But I could be blazing a trail for millions! I could be changing the course of history itself!

Santiago And at what cost?

Columbus I assure you that the price would be well worth the outcome. Not to mention the Nina, the Pinta and the Santa Maria could easily—

Domingo Excuse me, but who are they?

What do you know about *the Nina, the Pinta,* and *the Santa Maria?*

appreciate to understand

associate a person one works with

ventures risks

foolhardy foolish

Columbus They are the finest three ships in the world! They can also be outfitted for this entire journey for a little less than five thousand dollars.

Domingo (*To SANTIAGO*) Five thousand dollars we'll never see again.

Santiago Five thousand dollars is a **considerable** sum, especially considering that there's no **guarantee** you would ever be able to pay us back.

Columbus But when I return—

Santiago *If* you return—

Reading Strategy: **Summarizing**

What is Santiago's motivation for asking for collateral of $10,000?

Columbus Of course I will! (*SANTIAGO picks up loan* ***application*** *from desk.*)

Santiago On your loan application, you haven't mentioned any **collateral.**

Columbus Collateral?

Domingo You *do* have collateral, don't you?

Columbus Uh . . . how much collateral would you consider to be appropriate for an undertaking of this nature?

Santiago Well, in cases where such a high risk is involved, I'd say at least a **minimum** of ten thousand.

Columbus (*Puzzled*) If I had ten thousand in my pocket, why would I come to you for five?

Domingo What about **investments?** Do you have any of those?

Columbus I invest in dreams of the highest kind!

Santiago Yes, but dreams don't really pay the rent now, do they, sir?

considerable large

guarantee a promise

application a filled out form; a request

collateral money or goods that back up a loan

minimum smallest amount possible

investments monies paid out on the understanding that they will earn more money

Columbus (*Insistent*) But this dream is going to pay off! I can just feel it in my bones!

Santiago We admire your **conviction,** sir, but we at the First Bank of Castille hold a position of public trust. While we can't argue that you're certainly an **ambitious** young man who is going places—

Domingo —the Indies isn't going to be one of them, at least not with backing from our institution.

Columbus But you're closing your eyes to an incredible opportunity!

Santiago No, Christopher, Ms. Domingo and I are simply trying to open your eyes to the horrible dangers that would befall you if we allowed you to **proceed.**

Columbus What sort of dangers?

Domingo Huge, scaly monsters with yellow eyes and long tails and claws the size of a house that would reach out and grab you as soon as your ship **teetered precariously** on the brink of nothingness!

Why do Santiago and Domingo try to frighten Columbus with talk of monsters?

Santiago Your sails would catch fire from their hot breath!

Domingo And in a single crunch of their powerful **fangs,** you'd be gone forever!

Columbus (***Baffled***) Where are you getting this information? That's not true at all!

Domingo But it is!

Santiago You sail to the edge and *Pfffft!* It's all over!

Domingo And no repayment of the loan.

Santiago Not that we wouldn't feel badly about losing you.

conviction a strong opinion

ambitious eager to reach goals

proceed to go ahead

teetered rocked

precariously dangerously

fangs sharp teeth

baffled puzzled

Domingo It's just that we'd feel much worse about losing our money.

Santiago Certainly you can understand our position.

Columbus (*Sighing*) If only you'd try to see it my way just once. (*He spreads open the map, weights it at either end with their coffee cups and proceeds to dramatically describe the* ***scenario.***) You sail for months at a time on a shimmering blue-green sea. And then, all of a sudden, rising like a giant out of the water, you see it!

Santiago A sea monster!

Domingo A sea monster!

Columbus I'm talking about land!

Santiago Impossible!

Domingo Impossible!

Columbus is using words from the song "America the Beautiful." The song begins "Oh, beautiful, for spacious skies/For amber waves of grain..." Why is this an anachronism?

Columbus But it *is* possible! Along with **spacious** skies and purple mountains and **amber** fields of grain. And maybe—if I'm not mistaken—

Santiago Yes?

Columbus People. People very much like you and me. Why, they probably even have banks just like this one. Only instead of the Bank of Castille, it's probably called Bank of the New World. Who knows? Maybe even as we speak there's someone just like me sitting in an office just like this and asking for a loan to come and see if there's anything on this side of the ocean!

Domingo Well, perhaps after such a person makes such a voyage to our shores, you could ask to hitch a ride back with him! (*She and SANTIAGO laugh. They* ***simultaneously*** *pick up coffee cups, causing map to roll up.*)

scenario a story

spacious having plenty of room

amber gold-colored

simultaneously at the same time

Columbus (*Sadly*) So "no" is your final answer?

Santiago It's entirely for your own good, of course. We wouldn't want anything to happen to you.

Domingo Or to our money. (*DONATELLA enters.*)

Donatella Excuse me, Mr. Santiago—you asked me to let you know when your lunch date arrived. Her carriage just pulled up outside.

Santiago (*Groaning*) Oh, no! I totally forgot about her.

Domingo Who?

Santiago Queen Isabella. And I've already made other plans. (*Smacks himself in forehead*) How could I be so stupid?

What is funny about Santiago forgetting he had a lunch date with Queen Isabella?

Domingo She'll be upset if you cancel at the last minute.

Donatella Shall I send her up?

Santiago Not just yet. Try to delay her while I come up with a plan.

Donatella Whatever you say. (*She exits. As SANTIAGO and DOMINGO continue talking, a* ***disheartened*** *COLUMBUS rolls up his map.*)

Domingo I don't see how you can get out of it. She is the queen, you know.

Santiago Perhaps if I were to say I wasn't feeling well and sent someone else in my place . . . (*After a beat*) Did you have any plans today?

disheartened having lost hope

Domingo Sorry. I have a Board meeting.

Santiago But I can't just leave her without a lunch **companion.**

Columbus Since the two of you obviously have more important things to discuss, I'll just take my leave. (*He starts toward the door. SANTIAGO and DOMINGO exchange a look, simultaneously arriving at the same brainstorm.*)

Domingo Wait a minute! I just thought of something!

Santiago So did I!

What idea have Santiago and Domingo just had? What makes you think so?

Columbus What is it?

Santiago Are you doing anything for lunch?

Columbus (*With a shrug*) I thought I'd just grab a bite in the plaza.

Domingo Oh, but the plaza is so **pedestrian!** Wouldn't you rather have lunch with—oh, I don't know—maybe the Queen of Spain?

Columbus Why would the Queen of Spain want to have lunch with me?

Think about what you know of the history of Columbus and the Queen. What makes this part of the play funny?

Domingo Why not? You're bright, interesting, **articulate . . .**

Santiago And goodness knows, she can't resist bright, interesting, articulate chit-chat.

Domingo The two of you would hit it off splendidly!

Columbus Well . . .

Santiago You'd be doing me an enormous favor.

Columbus (*Suspiciously*) Hmm. Would this be a favor you'd possibly be interested in returning?

Santiago (*Equally suspicious*) In what way?

Columbus Perhaps a reconsideration of my loan application?

Santiago (*Hesitant*) Well . . .

companion a partner **pedestrian** ordinary **articulate** well-spoken

Domingo But of course! It's the least he can do!

Santiago (*Taking the hint*) Of course! Absolutely!

Domingo We'd have to get back to you, naturally.

Santiago Yes, yes, these things do take time.

Domingo But in the meantime—

Santiago In the meantime, you'll be having lunch with our beloved **monarch.** (*They start to rush him toward the door.*)

What do you think about the use of all the slang words? Do they fit in with the times?

Columbus But what will we talk about? What should I say?

Santiago Oh, I'm sure you'll think of something.

Columbus Maybe I could tell her about my voyage . . . ?

Domingo What a brilliant idea! I wish I'd thought of that myself.

Santiago I'm sure she'd love to hear all about it!

monarch a ruler; a king or queen

Columbus (*Just as he's about to exit*) And you won't forget about my application?

Santiago Not to worry!

Domingo It will be the bank's number-one priority! (*COLUMBUS exits. They close the door.*)

Santiago Are we completely out of our minds?

Domingo (*Shrugging*) It got you off the hook, didn't it? (*SANTIAGO crosses back to the desk, with DOMINGO following.*)

Santiago (*Picking up loan application from desk)* But we'll be the laughing stock of the entire Board if we even present this application to them, much less ask their approval. *(DOMINGO takes it from him.*)

Domingo The operative word being "if."

Santiago Meaning? (*DOMINGO tears it up and tosses it into the air like confetti.*)

Domingo Meaning that we won't.

Santiago That wasn't a very nice thing to do.

Domingo No harm done. He and Isabella will have a pleasant lunch, she'll think he's a nut, we'll tell him the Board denied his request for funds, and it's the last we'll ever hear of him.

Santiago (*Laughing*) I do believe you're right.

Domingo Change history, indeed! Discover new worlds! Where do people come up with these **outlandish** notions? How long would we stay in business if we said yes to such foolishness every time it comes along?

Santiago Not long at all. The First Bank of Castille is here to fund causes that are down-to-earth.

Domingo Instead of off the edge of it! (*They both laugh and toast each other with their coffee cups as curtain closes.*)

THE END

outlandish unusual and silly

A Loan for Columbus *by Inez Carvalho*

Directions Choose the letter of the best answer or write the answer using complete sentences.

Comprehension: Identifying Facts

1. Who is Mr. Santiago?
   A the owner of the bank
   B the vice-president of the bank
   C the loan officer
   D the secretary
2. With whom does Santiago have a lunch appointment?
   A Ms. Domingo
   B Queen Isabella
   C Christopher Columbus
   D Donatella
3. Who is Ms. Domingo?
4. Why did "that Da Vinci fellow" want to borrow money?
5. Why does Columbus need three ships for his voyage?
6. What does Columbus think is on the other side of the horizon?
7. Why will Santiago and Domingo not lend Columbus the money?
8. Why does Santiago not want to keep his lunch date?
9. What does Columbus want to trade for lunching with the Queen?
10. What trick do Santiago and Domingo play on Columbus?

Comprehension: Putting Ideas Together

11. Which person from history is not talked about in this play?
    A Queen Isabella
    B King Ferdinand
    C King Henry VII
    D King Henry VIII
12. Why does Columbus want to sail west?
    A He wants to get away from people to whom he owes money.
    B He wants to discover new worlds.
    C He wants to fall off the edge of the earth.
    D He wants to find a new trade route to Asia.
13. How do the bank officials think the people of Spain would react to Columbus's plans?
14. Why is Columbus reluctant to have lunch with the Queen?
15. Santiago and Domingo have ideas about what will happen to Columbus. The people on Maple Street have ideas about what will happen to them. How are these ideas alike?
16. What does Steve of "The Monsters Are Due on Maple Street" have in common with Columbus?

***Comparing* continued on next page**

A Loan for Columbus *by Inez Carvalho*

17. In what way do the two bank workers make decisions like the people of Maple Street?

18. Describe the ideal audiences for "A Loan for Columbus" and "The Monsters Are Due on Maple Street." Are they the same? Explain.

19. Describe the author's purpose for each play. Do you see anything in common between the two?

20. In "The Monsters Are Due on Maple Street," the group turns on the young boy when they have nowhere else to turn. What happens in "A Loan for Columbus" when Columbus has nowhere else to turn?

Understanding Literature: Comedy

A comedy is a funny play with a happy ending. Writers of comedies use many tools to make their audiences laugh. One such tool is the anachronism. This twisting of time can create humor.

21. What makes this play a comedy?

22. Identify three anachronisms in the play.

23. Summarize the mood of "A Loan for Columbus" and of "The Monsters Are Due on Maple Street" in one word each.

24. Think about how the anachronisms in each play make you feel. How are these feelings alike and different?

25. "A Loan for Columbus" is a stage play. "The Monsters Are Due on Maple Street" is a screenplay. What is the main difference between a stage play and a screenplay?

Critical Thinking

26. Why do you think the author twisted the facts of history in "A Loan for Columbus"?

27. Name one main common thing in "A Loan for Columbus" and "The Monsters Are Due on Maple Street." Explain the difference in the way each writer handles it.

28. Which do you think is a better play, "A Loan for Columbus" or "The Monsters Are Due on Maple Street"? Give reasons for your opinion.

29. What do you predict will happen after the end of each play? Support your predictions with details from the plays.

Thinking Creatively

30. Suggest one other way (besides asking the Queen) Columbus might pay for his voyage. Explain why this idea might work.

Grammar Check

A preposition tells the relationship between two people or things. If a sentence has a preposition, it must have at least two nouns or pronouns. Always use object pronouns as the objects of prepositions.

Common Prepositions

of	under	over
before	behind	beneath
on	in	off

Copy the sentences, choosing the correct pronouns. Circle the prepositions.

1 It was very kind of (he, him) to wait for (I, me).

2 She got behind (I, me) and caught the ball in her glove.

3 Before (I, me) could speak, the bridge was in front of (we, us).

Vocabulary Builder

Review each group of vocabulary words from "A Loan for Columbus." Give one synonym for each word and use it in a sentence.

1 ludicrous

2 delusional

3 expedition

4 pedestrian

Writing on Your Own

Write a short essay about the differences between comedy and drama. These ideas might help you:

- What is the basic difference between comedy and drama?
- Are they alike in any way? If so, how?
- Do you enjoy comedy or drama more? Why?

Listening and Speaking

"A Loan for Columbus." talks about Leonardo da Vinci and King Henry VIII of England. Choose one person and find out more about him. Plan a five-minute talk to share what you have learned with the class.

Research and Technology

Find information about Columbus's three voyages to the Americas. Look online and in the library. Work with a partner to write a narrative report about his voyages. Use information about his most important discoveries.

Unit 5 SPELLING WORKSHOP

Plurals

Most plurals in the English language follow spelling rules. You can easily spell most plural nouns correctly if you understand and use these rules.

Rules for Spelling Plurals

- Add *-s* to most nouns.

  novel/novels *poem/poems*
  dialogue/dialogues

- Add *-es* to nouns that end in *s, ss, sh, ch,* and *x.*

  pass/passes *dash/dashes*
  coach/coaches *tax/taxes*

- Change *y* to *i* and add *-es* to nouns that end in a consonant + *y.*

  memory/memories
  economy/economies

- Do not change the *y* and add *-s* to nouns that end in a vowel + *y.*

  play/plays *key/keys*

- For most nouns ending in *fe,* change the *fe* to *ve* and add *-s.*

  thief/thieves *wife/wives*

Irregular Plurals and Exceptions

- Some nouns have the same spelling in both forms.

  sheep *deer* *fish*

- Some nouns' base word spelling changes in the plural form.

  foot/feet *mouse/mice* *man/men*

- Nouns that you cannot count do not have plural forms.

  news *cash* *rice*

Use these steps with each word on the word list:

- Write the singular form.
- Write the plural form.
- Explain which rule applies.
- Add another example for each rule or each rule that is not followed.

Word List
biographies
boxes
characters
classes
countries
disks
envelopes
information
knives
plays

Unit 5 SUMMARY

In Unit 5, you read some different kinds of plays. There were dramatic, suspenseful, and funny plays. They all tell different stories and describe different ways characters get along.

Plays have different moods. A comedy is a funny play with a happy ending. A drama is a more serious play, which often has funny scenes or moments. A science-fiction play has scientific events that could not happen in real life. However, science fiction is just like any other drama or comedy in most ways. It tells stories about characters who speak and act in certain ways for special reasons.

All plays have certain things in common. They are made of dialogue and stage directions. Dialogue is the words the characters speak. Audiences must draw conclusions about motivation and attitude based on characters' words. Stage directions describe the scenery and tell the actors where and how to move. Screenplay stage directions also tell the camera how it should move.

Selections

- "A Christmas Carol: Scrooge and Marley," by Israel Horovitz, is a dramatic play. It tells the story of how a miser becomes kind and generous at Christmastime.
- "The Monsters Are Due on Maple Street," by Rod Serling, is a science-fiction screenplay. It describes what happens when a neighborhood suddenly loses power and no one knows why.
- "A Loan for Columbus," by Inez Carvalho, is a comedy. It tells about Christopher Columbus trying to pay for his trip to the New World.

Unit 5 REVIEW

Directions Choose the letter of the best answer or write the answer using complete sentences.

Comprehension: Identifying Facts

1. Who narrates "A Christmas Carol"?

A Marley's Ghost

B Ebenezer Scrooge

C Charles Dickens

D Israel Horovitz

2. Where does "A Christmas Carol" take place?

3. Who is the first person Scrooge speaks to on Christmas morning?

4. What kind of a place is Maple Street?

5. Why does Columbus go to the bank?

Comprehension: Putting Ideas Together

6. What does Scrooge do when Marley appears in his rooms?

A He refuses to believe what he sees.

B He pays no attention to him.

C He orders him to leave him alone.

D He is sorry for his miserly ways.

7. What does Marley's Ghost look like?

8. What does Fred do when he sees the death of Tiny Tim?

9. Why do Steve and Charlie decide not to walk downtown?

10. Summarize Columbus's idea about the earth.

Understanding Literature: Drama

Unlike other literature, drama is to be performed, not just read on the page. Plays can be funny, serious, scary, or show any other mood. They have characters, plots, settings, and themes, like other literature. And, as in other literature, the characters act from motivations.

11. What motivates Scrooge to growl and grumble about Christmas?

12. Why do Mrs. Dilber and her friends talk about how what they are doing is okay?

13. How is "The Monsters Are Due on Maple Street" like people really behave?

14. Are the people on Maple Street really "monsters"? Explain.

15. What makes "A Loan for Columbus" a comedy?

Critical Thinking

16. Do you believe that Scrooge really met Marley and the three other ghosts? Or did he dream the entire thing? Support your answer with ideas from the play.

17. Who is the Narrator in "The Monsters Are Due on Maple Street"? How does he know what is going on in the story? Explain your answer.

18. What kind of audience do you think would most enjoy "A Loan for Columbus"? Explain.

Thinking Creatively

19. Why do you think "A Christmas Carol" has always been so popular?

20. Would you lend money to Columbus for his voyage? Why or why not?

Speak and Listen

Find a long speech in a play from this unit. Memorize the speech and give a dramatic performance for the class. Remember to stay in character. Use your voice to show a mood. You may want to wear a costume.

Writing on Your Own

Write a short review of any of the three plays in this unit. Review the script rather than a performance. State your opinion of the script and support it with pieces from the play. Share your review with the class.

Beyond Words

Make a poster ad for a performance of any of the three plays in the unit. Show a key image or idea from the play. Hang your poster in the classroom.

Test-Taking Tip

When you are reading a test question, pay attention to words that are in bold type or capital letters. Those words will help you decide how to answer the question.

Exposition: Cause-and-Effect Essay

A cause-and-effect essay explains why something happens. It may also describe the results of certain events. A cause-and-effect essay might look at causes or it might look at effects.

Example of causes:

Example: Why do days get shorter in the fall?

Example of effects:

Example: What happens when people do not wear sunscreen?

Follow the steps in this workshop to write your own cause-and-effect essay.

Using the Form
You may use parts of this form in these types of writing:
- lab reports
- persuasive essays
- magazine articles
- speeches
- historical pieces

Assignment Write a cause-and-effect essay about a question or idea that interests you.

Your essay should have the following parts:

- a clear idea that can be covered in a few pages
- information from research
- facts about events and relationships
- a clear arrangement with transitions that show relationships among details
- writing without mistakes, including correct subject-verb agreement

Prewriting

Choosing Your Topic

To choose a good topic for your essay, use this strategy:

- **Brainstorming** Sometimes the best way to find a topic is to just start writing. Write for five minutes about whatever questions come to mind. Use phrases such as "What causes . . ." or "Why does . . ." to begin each question. Circle any questions that could make a good topic.

Narrowing Your Topic

A topic with many causes and effects may be far too wide. Narrow your topic to a single cause or a single effect. For example, the effects of a tornado—a single cause—would work. Use a word web to narrow your topic. Write your topic in the center and surround it with subtopics. Think of causes and effects for each subtopic. Decide which of the subtopics might make a good main point for your essay.

Ideas message, details, and purpose

Gathering Details

Conduct research. Do research to fill in any gaps in your knowledge. Use the library, go online, or interview experts. Use a two-column chart to gather details. In one column, list the causes for your event or situation. In the other column, list the effects.

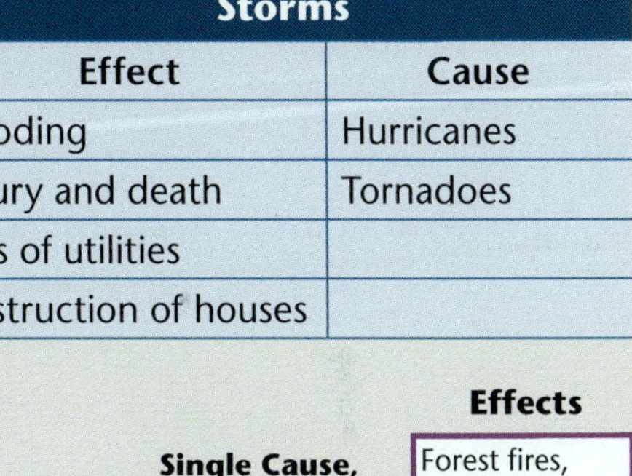

Storms	
Effect	**Cause**
flooding	Hurricanes
injury and death	Tornadoes
loss of utilities	
destruction of houses	

Writing Your Draft

Shaping Your Writing

Organize logically. Before you begin the body of your essay, decide how you want to arrange your details. Use these ideas:

- If you are writing about a single event with many causes:
  each cause: one paragraph
  each effect: one paragraph
- If you are writing about a single cause with many effects:
  each effect: one paragraph
- If you are writing about a series of causes and effects: arrange the events in the order they took place.

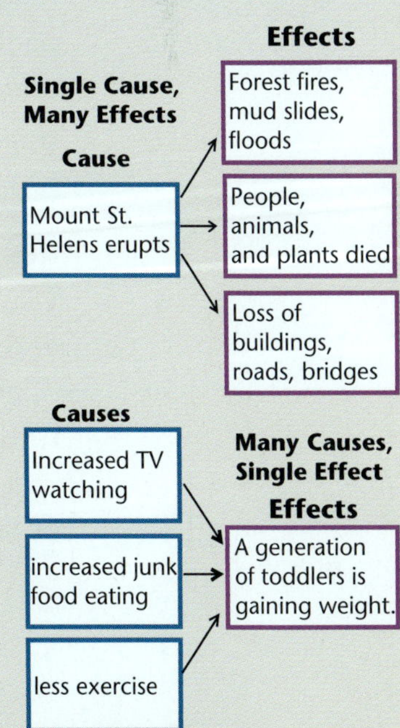

Write a strong introduction. Your introduction is the first thing your audience will read. Include a sentence or two explaining the importance of your topic. Then, tell the main points you will make in your essay.

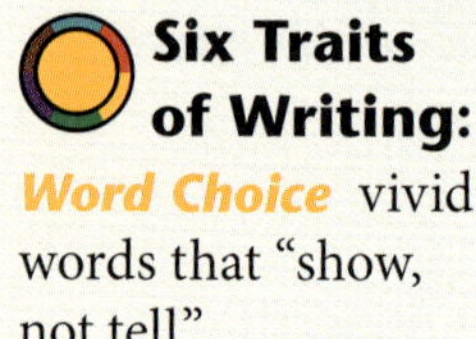
Six Traits of Writing:
Word Choice vivid words that "show, not tell"

Providing Elaboration

Explain causes and effects. Prove the cause-and-effect relationships you describe. As you draft, explain the logic of each cause-and-effect relationship you present. Use specific numbers, dates, names, or places whenever possible.

Use the SEE technique. For each main idea you identify, use the SEE plan to add depth to your essay. First, write a *Statement*. Next, write a sentence that *Extends* the idea. Finally, write a sentence that *Elaborates* on the extension.

Revising

Revising Your Paragraphs

Six Traits of Writing:
Organization order, ideas tied together

State main ideas clearly. By starting a new paragraph, you signal readers that a new idea is coming. Good writers state the main idea clearly in each paragraph. Use color coding to show how the other sentences fit together.

Reread each paragraph. Use two highlighters. In one color, mark phrases that show causes. In the other, mark those that discuss effects. Judge the connections between the two. Go back and add joining words to help readers see cause-and-effect connections.

Peer Review: Ask a classmate to review your draft. Ask him or her to judge whether you have logical cause-and-effect links.

Revising Your Sentences

Use the appropriate verb tense. Generally, you should use one verb tense throughout your paper. However, to show the order of events, you may need to shift tenses. Review your draft to find the tense of most of your verbs. Circle any verbs that are in a different tense. If these verbs are not about different times or repeating events, think about changing them.

Editing and Proofreading

Review your draft to fix mistakes.

Focus on Unnecessary Words: A few words work better than a lot of words. Review your work to cut out these types of unnecessary words:

Repetition: The hazy sky was **heavy and hazy.**

Filler Phrases: It is, **in fact,** a surprise.

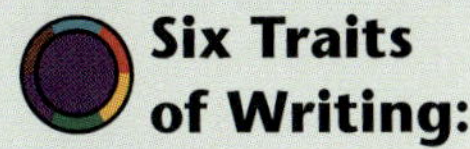

Conventions correct grammar, spelling, and mechanics

Publishing and Presenting

Consider one of the following ways to share your writing:

Present a diagram. Make a poster showing the cause-and-effect connections in your essay. Read your essay aloud, pointing out appropriate parts of the poster as you go.

Produce a talk show. Work with a partner. Take turns being a talk show host and a guest expert. Answer questions about your topic. Ask questions about your partner's topic.

Reflecting on Your Writing

Writer's Journal Write your thoughts on the experience of writing a cause-and-effect essay. Begin by answering these questions:

- Which prewriting plan was most useful for finding a topic?
- What was the most interesting thing you learned while writing?

Abstract Bird and Sun
José Ortega

Unit 6

Themes in the Oral Tradition

Myths, legends, folktales, and other stories have been passed down through generations. They tell of gods and goddesses, talking animals, and strange and exciting events. Most of these tales were first told long before reading and writing began. They have been told and retold through the ages by word of mouth. This is called the oral tradition. People used these traditional stories to communicate shared beliefs and to explain their world.

Unit 6 Selections **Page**

"Of course the greatest power Sara possessed . . . was her power of telling stories . . . . Any one who has been at school with a teller of stories knows what the wonder means."

—Frances Hodgson Burnett, ***A Little Princess***, 1905

Unit 6 About Themes in the Oral Tradition

Characteristics of Folk Literature

Gods and goddesses, talking animals, strange and amazing events—these are some of the parts of myths, legends, and folktales. Although writers retell these stories in print, most of these tales started long before reading and writing began. They have lasted so long because of the **oral tradition**—stories originally told at festivals and around campfires, rather than shared in print. Here are characteristics of the oral tradition:

Theme is the main idea of the story. Sometimes a theme is called universal, which means that the theme can be seen in stories in many different places around the world and throughout many different time periods.

A **moral** is a lesson about life that is taught by a story.

Heroes and **heroines** are the leading characters whose virtues and deeds are often celebrated in stories from the oral tradition.

Storytelling calls on the person who is talking to make the story exciting. Some stories in the oral tradition call on the storyteller to use these ways to make the story more interesting:

- **Hyperbole:** obvious and deliberate exaggeration not intended to be taken literally. Hyperboles are often used for dramatic or comic effect.
- **Personification:** giving characters such as animals or objects the characteristics or qualities of humans.
- **Allusion:** something referring to a historical event, a person, a place, or a work of literature.

"PEANUTS" reprinted by permission of United Feature Syndicate, Inc.

The Oral Tradition in Print

After years of sharing stories by word of mouth, many stories have been written down for readers. Here are the categories of those stories:

- A **myth** is an important story, often part of a culture's religion, that explains how the world came to be or why natural events happen, usually including gods, goddesses, or unusually powerful human beings. A **mythology** is a collection of a culture's myths.
- A **legend** is a traditional story that was at one time told orally and was handed down from one generation to another. They are based on real-life events but over time, legends often turn fact into fiction.
- A **folktale** is a story that has been handed down from one generation to another. The stories are about ordinary people.
- A **fable** is a short story or poem with a moral (lesson about life), often with animals who act like humans.
- An **epic** is a long story written in verse. There is often a larger-than-life hero that goes on a dangerous adventure.

***Reading Strategy:* Predicting**

When readers make predictions, they make guesses about what will happen next. The details in the text help readers make their predictions. In Part 1, you will read some selections that contain cause and effect.

- A **cause** is the reason something happens.
- An **effect** is what happens as a result.

As you read, make predictions based on the causes and effects of events. Remember, you can change your predictions as you learn more information.

Literary Terms

oral tradition stories originally told at festivals and around campfires, rather than shared in print

myth an important story, often part of a culture's religion, that explains how the world came to be or why natural events happen, usually including gods, goddesses, or unusually powerful human beings

theme the main idea of a literary work

mythology collection of myths

cause an event or situation that produces a result

effect the result produced

legend a traditional story that was at one time told orally and was handed down from one generation to another

hero the leading character in a story, novel, play, or film

BEFORE READING THE SELECTION | **Build Understanding**

Icarus and Daedalus *by Josephine Preston Peabody*

Josephine
Preston Peabody
1874–1922

About the Author

Josephine Preston Peabody was born in Brooklyn, New York. She moved with her family to Massachusetts when she was 10 years old. Both of her parents loved literature and the theater. Peabody learned to love reading and writing as a child. Her talent became obvious at an early age. She published a poem in *The Women's Journal* when she was 14. Her first book, *Old Greek Folk-Stories Told Anew* came out when she was 23 years old. "Icarus and Daedalus" is from this collection.

After attending Radcliffe College in Cambridge, Massachusetts, Peabody published her first book of poems. From 1901 to 1903, she taught English literature at Wellesley College. Peabody continued to write plays and poetry throughout her life.

Objectives

- To read and understand a myth
- To identify and understand themes in a myth

About the Selection

Myth is the foundation of Ancient Greek literature. Greek myths feature gods and goddesses with both magic powers and ordinary human failings. The gods would often fight. Sometimes a god would like a particular mortal and would bring this person luck. A jealous god or goddess might then harm this person on purpose.

Daedalus finds himself imprisoned on an island with his son, Icarus. In order to escape, Daedalus builds two pairs of wings. He warns Icarus not to fly too close to the sun. Icarus ignores the warning. The heat of the sun melts the wax of his wings. He falls to his death after landing in the sea.

***Before Reading* continued on next page**

BEFORE READING THE SELECTION *(cont.)* | **Build Skills**

Icarus and Daedalus *by Josephine Preston Peabody*

oral tradition stories originally told at festivals and around campfires, rather than shared in print

myth an important story, often part of a culture's religion, that explains how the world came to be or why natural events happen, usually including gods, goddesses, or unusually powerful human beings

theme the main idea of a literary work

mythology collection of myths

Literary Terms Since the beginning of time, people have passed down stories in the **oral tradition.** People in ancient times created **myths** to explain natural occurrences and to express beliefs about right and wrong. Myths are an attempt to explain the world in human terms. Many myths contain universal **themes** or important lessons about life. Every culture has its own collection of myths, or **mythology.** Many gods and goddesses in myths have human qualities. Some mortals have extraordinary strength and talent.

Reading on Your Own A *cause* is an event, action, or feeling that produces a result. That result is called an *effect.* Many story events have multiple causes and multiple effects. One event causes another, which in turn causes something else to happen. The linking of causes and effects moves the action forward.

As you read, analyze the cause-and-effect relationships. Ask yourself questions like these:

- What happened? Why did it happen?
- What will happen as a result of this?

Writing on Your Own Some myths teach lessons about right and wrong. Think of a lesson that taught you about the right way to live or act. Write three sentences that describe this lesson.

Vocabulary Focus Study the vocabulary words on the selection pages before you read the myth. Pronounce each word, find it in the story, and make sure you understand its meaning. This will make it easier for you to read and enjoy the myth.

Think Before You Read Have you ever been tempted to do something just because someone told you not to? What happened as a result?

Icarus and Daedalus

Among all those mortals who grew so wise that they learned the secrets of the gods, none was more **cunning** than Daedalus.

He once built, for King Minos of Crete, a wonderful Labyrinth of winding ways so cunningly tangled up and twisted around that, once inside, you could never find your way out again without a magic clue. But the king's favor **veered** with the wind, and one day he had his master **architect** imprisoned in a tower. Daedalus managed to escape from his cell; but it seemed impossible to leave the island, since every ship that came or went was well guarded by order of the king.

At length, watching the sea-gulls in the air—the only creatures that were sure of liberty—he thought of a plan for himself and his young son Icarus, who was **captive** with him.

As you read, look for characteristics of a myth. How does the first sentence tell you that this story is a myth?

King Minos was a son of Zeus, chief of the gods. *Crete* is an island in the Mediterranean Sea, southeast of Greece. The *Labyrinth* gave its name to a common everyday word for maze.

Reading Strategy: **Predicting**

How do you think Daedalus will try to escape the island?

cunning clever

veered changed direction

architect builder

captive prisoner

Little by little, he gathered a **store** of feathers great and small. He fastened these together with thread, molded them in with wax, and so fashioned two great wings like those of a bird. When they were done, Daedalus fitted them to his own shoulders, and after one or two efforts, he found that by waving his arms he could **winnow** the air and **cleave** it, as a swimmer does the sea. He held himself **aloft,** wavered this way and that with the wind, and at last, like a great **fledgling,** he learned to fly.

Without delay, he fell to work on a pair of wings for the boy Icarus, and taught him carefully how to use them, bidding him beware of **rash** adventures among the stars. "Remember," said the father, "never to fly very low or very high, for the fogs about the earth would weigh you down, but the blaze of the sun will surely melt your feathers apart if you go too near."

For Icarus, these cautions went in at one ear and out by the other. Who could remember to be careful when he was to fly for the first time? Are birds careful? Not they! And not an idea remained in the boy's head but the one joy of escape.

***Reading Strategy:* Predicting**

What do you think will happen to Icarus during the escape? Why do you think so?

The day came, and the fair wind that was to set them free. The father bird put on his wings, and, while the light urged them to be gone, he waited to see that all was well with Icarus, for the two could not fly hand in hand. Up they rose, the boy after his father. The hateful ground of Crete sank beneath them; and the country folk, who caught a **glimpse** of them when they were high above the treetops, took it for a vision of the gods—Apollo, perhaps, with Cupid after him.

Apollo was the god of music, poetry, and medicine. The Greeks believed that Apollo rode across the sky every day in a horse-drawn chariot. The chariot pulled the sun across the sky. *Cupid* was the Roman god of love. The Greeks called this god Eros.

store a pile built up little by little

winnow to dig grooves in, like a plow

cleave to separate

aloft in the air

fledgling baby bird

rash foolishly bold

glimpse a quick look

At first there was a terror in the joy. The wide **vacancy** of the air dazed them—a glance downward made their brains reel.

A *halcyon bird* is the Greek name for a kingfisher. The Greeks believed that kingfishers calmed the waves when they rested on the sea.

But when a great wind filled their wings, and Icarus felt himself **sustained,** like a halcyon bird in the hollow of a wave, like a child uplifted by his mother, he forgot everything in the world but joy. He forgot Crete and the other islands that he had passed over: he saw but vaguely that wingèd thing in the distance before him that was his father Daedalus. He longed for one draft of flight to **quench** the thirst of his captivity: he stretched out his arms to the sky and made towards the highest heavens.

Alas for him! Warmer and warmer grew the air. Those arms, that had seemed to uphold him, relaxed. His wings wavered, drooped. He fluttered his young hands **vainly**—he was falling—and in that terror he remembered. The heat of the sun had melted the wax from his wings; the feathers were falling, one by one, like snowflakes; and there was none to help.

He fell like a leaf tossed down the wind, down, down, with one cry that overtook Daedalus far away. When he returned, and **sought** high and low for his poor boy, he saw nothing but the birdlike feathers afloat on the water, and he knew that Icarus was drowned.

Sicily is a huge island in the Mediterranean Sea. It is just south of the "toe" of the boot-shaped country of Italy.

The nearest island he named Icaria, in memory of the child; but he, in heavy grief, went to the temple of Apollo in Sicily, and there hung up his wings as an offering. Never again did he attempt to fly.

vacancy emptiness

sustained held up, supported

quench satisfy

vainly uselessly

sought searched for

AFTER READING THE SELECTION | Apply the Skills

Icarus and Daedalus *by Josephine Preston Peabody*

Directions Choose the letter of the best answer or write the answer using complete sentences.

Comprehension: Identifying Facts

1. Who is Icarus?
- **A** a Greek architect
- **B** the king of Crete
- **C** the son of Daedalus
- **D** the father of Daedalus

2. Why does Minos imprison Daedalus?

3. What does Daedalus warn Icarus not to do?

Comprehension: Putting Ideas Together

4. Which word best describes Icarus?
- **A** rude
- **B** rash
- **C** curious
- **D** sneaky

5. What steps does Daedalus take to escape from the island?

6. How does Icarus feel while he is flying?

Understanding Literature: Mythology

A myth is an ancient story that forms part of the history of a people. Greek literature is based on dozens of Greek myths. In many myths, mortals clash with gods and goddesses. The gods would often punish mortals who became too strong or powerful.

7. What superhuman qualities does Daedalus possess?

8. What is the theme of "Daedalus and Icarus"?

Critical Thinking

9. Is Daedalus responsible for what happens to Icarus? Why or why not?

Thinking Creatively

10. If you were Daedalus, what would you have done differently during the escape from the tower?

After Reading **continued on next page**

Icarus and Daedalus *by Josephine Preston Peabody*

Grammar Check

Use a colon to introduce a list of items. Do not use a colon directly between a verb or preposition and its object.

Correct	Incorrect
The box contained many items: an alarm clock, a vase, and a book.	The box contained: an alarm clock, a vase, and a book.

Insert colons where needed.

1 I can travel on any of the following Mondays, Wednesdays, or Thursdays.

2 We want books, toys, and cookies.

3 I saw piles of paper, scattered pencils, and day-old pizza.

4 He found four things in the drawer two pens, a lock, and a nail.

Vocabulary Builder

A word's denotation is its dictionary definition. A word's connotations are the cultural meanings. Recognizing a word's connotations helps you understand its various meanings.

Example:
Word: *consequence*
Denotation: an effect; the result of an action
Connotation: punishment or other bad outcome

Explain the difference in connotation between the words in each pair.

1 antique/old

2 disagree/debate

Writing on Your Own

Do you believe that a single event can change a person's life? Think about what happens in "Icarus and Daedalus" and write a paragraph answering this question. Use evidence from the myth to support your ideas.

Listening and Speaking

With a small group, debate whether Daedalus shares any responsibility for Icarus's fall. Each side should prepare an argument and supporting evidence.

- Before the debate, think about what the other side may argue. Consider how your side will disprove their arguments.
- After the debate, poll your audience. Who was more convincing?

Media and Viewing

Use the Internet and library resources to find out how birds fly. Look at photographs and diagrams of their wing structure. Create a poster or three-dimensional model that explains how wings make flight possible.

Almanac

The word almanac comes from an old Spanish word for calendar. This word in turn comes from the Arabic word for climate. An almanac is a book of facts published once a year. There are two types of almanacs:

The original almanac is a one-year calendar called a farmer's almanac. The almanac forecasts the weather throughout the year and gives facts about astronomy. (Astronomy is the study of the stars, moons, and planets.) Farmers use the weather forecasts to make decisions about planting and harvesting crops. Sailors use the farmer's almanac to find out about high and low tides. You can see how the word almanac and the words calendar and climate are related.

Later, a new type of almanac called the general information almanac was made. A general information almanac provides a great variety of facts and figures. Most of these almanacs are published once every year. Here are just a few topics covered in the almanac:

- Biographies of U.S. presidents
- Facts and histories of nations
- Height of the world's tallest buildings
- Presidential elections since 1789
- Weights and measures
- Mass of the planets

An almanac usually appears very early in the year of its title. It includes information up to the start of that year. For example, the 2008 almanac comes out at the start of 2008. It is therefore a good source for facts about the year 2007.

Reading Skill: Using an Index

An almanac is a book you use to find specific information. When you are looking for information, it is quickest to start with the index. Look for a key word. Suppose you want to find the height of the world's tallest building. Look under BUILDINGS or SKYSCRAPERS to find the page.

Read the next pages to see information you would find in almanacs. Use that information to answer the questions on page 508.

Awards and Prizes

The Newbery Medal, 2000–2004

The Newbery Medal is awarded annually to the author of the year's outstanding children's book.

2000 Christopher Paul Curtis, *Bud, Not Buddy*

2001 Richard Peck, *A Year Down Yonder*

2002 Linda Sue Park, *A Single Shard*

2003 Avi, *Crispin: The Cross of Lead*

2004 Kate DiCamillo, *The Tale of Despereaux*

The National Book Awards, 2000–2004

The National Book Awards are given annually to the best books by American authors in several categories.

Fiction

2000 Susan Sontag, *In America*

2001 Jonathan Franzen, *The Corrections*

2002 Julia Glass, *Three Junes*

2003 Shirley Hazzard, *The Great Fire*

2004 Lily Tuck, *The News from Paraguay*

Nonfiction

2000 Nathaniel Philbrick, *In the Heart of the Sea: The Tragedy of the Whaleship Essex*

2001 Andrew Solomon, *The Noonday Demons: An Atlas of Depression*

2002 Robert A Caro, *Master of the Senate: The Years of Lyndon Johnson*

2003 Carlos Eire, *Waiting for Snow in Havana: Confessions of a Cuban Boy*

2004 Kevin Boyle, *Arc of Justice: A Saga of Race, Civil Rights, and Murder in the Jazz Age*

Young People's Literature

2000 Gloria Whelan, *Homeless Bird*

2001 Virginia Euwer Wolff, *True Believer*

2002 Nancy Farmer, *The House of the Scorpion*

2003 Polly Horvath, *The Canning Season*

2004 Pete Hautman, *Godless*

Phases of the Moon

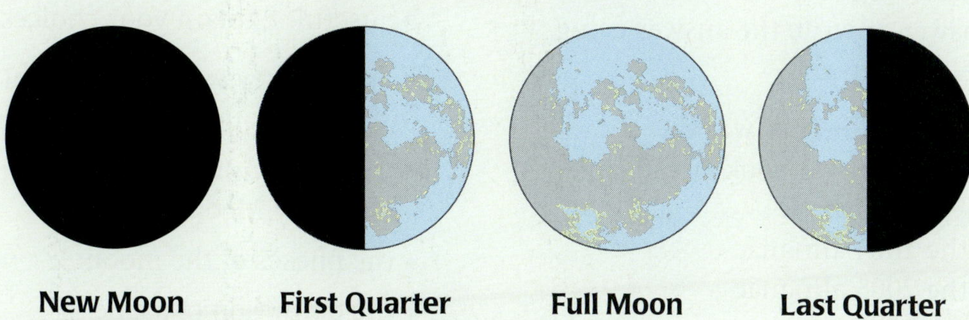

Beaufort Wind Scale

In 1806, Admiral Francis Beaufort created a scale that measured the force of winds against ships at sea. This scale has been used internationally since 1874 for measuring winds on land and at sea.

Force	Description of Wind	Mean Wind Speed in Knots[1]
Force 0	Calm	Less than 1
Force 1	Light air	1–3
Force 2	Light breeze	4–6
Force 3	Gentle breeze	7–10
Force 4	Moderate breeze	11–16
Force 5	Fresh breeze	17–21
Force 6	Strong breeze	22–27
Force 7	Moderate gale, near gale	28–33
Force 8	Fresh gale, gale	34–40
Force 9	Strong gale	41–47
Force 10	Whole gale, storm	48–55
Force 11	Storm, violent storm	56–63
Force 12	Hurricane	64 and above

[1] One knot = one nautical mile-per-hour, or 1.151 statute miles-per-hour.

Monitor Your Progress

Directions Choose the letter of the best answer or write the answer using complete sentences.

1. In which almanac was the information on book awards most likely published?
A the 2004 almanac
B the 2005 almanac
C the 2006 almanac
D the 2007 almanac

2. At how many knots per hour might the wind blow during a hurricane?
A 50 **C** 60
B 55 **D** 65

3. In which type of almanac would you find the lists of book awards? Explain.

4. List at least three jobs in which a general information almanac would be useful. Explain your choices.

5. List some key words you might use to find the following in the index:
- the winner of the 2003 Newbery Medal
- the phases of the moon
- the definition of a gale

Writing on Your Own

Think of a country you would like to learn more about. Read about this country in a current general information almanac. Use facts and statistics from the almanac to write a short report about the country.

BEFORE READING THE SELECTION | **Build Understanding**

Tenochtitlan: Inside the Aztec Capital by Jacqueline Dineen

About the Author

Jacqueline Dineen began her career as an editor for an educational publisher in London. Then she started writing children's books. She has written more than 100 books on a variety of subjects. Science, history, and geography are among her favorite topics. *Chocolate* is a history of chocolate for children. Another book on food is titled *Food from the Sea.* Other Dineen titles include *Lift the Lid on Mummies* and *The Early Inventions.* In "Tenochtitlan: Inside the Aztec Capital" Dineen shows readers how the ancient city was built. She uses description, eyewitness accounts, maps, photographs, and art.

Objectives

- To read and understand a nonfiction article
- To understand cause-and-effect relationships

About the Selection

Mexico City was built on the ruins of the ancient Aztec city of Tenochtitlan. Tenochtitlan sat on an island in the center of a Lake Texoco. Over the years, the lake was slowly drained to make room for the growing city. Mexico City is located on a drained lakebed, making the effects of earthquakes severe. The city is slowly sinking several inches a year.

"Tenochtitlan: Inside the Aztec Capital" tells about the people and activities of the original city. The Aztecs built their capital in the 1300s. It was a major city with palaces and temples. The Aztecs were skilled farmers, engineers, and craftsmen.

The Spaniards conquered the Aztecs in the early 1500s and destroyed Tenochtitlan. Most of its written records are lost. Archaeologists have studied the ruins of the city. They have also studied artifacts such as pottery and statues. They have arrived at many theories about everyday life in the Aztec capital.

***Before Reading* continued on next page**

Tenochtitlan: Inside the Aztec Capital by Jacqueline Dineen

cause an event or situation that produces a result

effect the result produced

Literary Terms A **cause** is an event or situation that produces a result. An **effect** is the result produced. In this nonfiction story, each effect may eventually become a cause for the next event. The result is a cause-and-effect chain, which propels action forward.

Reading on Your Own Many articles organize information in a certain way. The text structure can help you get the most out of the article. Look at features such as the title, the headings, and the subheads. Look at illustrations, maps, charts, and graphics to better understand information. All these features will help you locate information quickly while you are reading. Before reading the selection, fill in a KWL chart to help organize the information (described in Appendix A).

Writing on Your Own This article describes a city that was designed as it grew. You may have played games in which you designed a city or civilization. List some ideas that come to mind when you think about planning a city.

Vocabulary Focus This selection contains many words from the field of architecture, or building. Define each word and use it correctly in a sentence: *temple, hut, causeway, pillar, bridge, aqueduct,* and *courtyard.* Use a dictionary or context clues for help.

Think Before You Read How can we learn about ancient civilizations that left no written records?

Tenochtitlan:

Inside the Aztec Capital

The Lake City of Tenochtitlan

The city of Tenochtitlan began on an island in the middle of a swampy lake. There the Aztecs built their first temple to Huitzilopochtli. The place was given the name Tenochtitlan, which means "The Place of the Fruit of the Prickly Pear Cactus." Later on the name was given to the city that grew up around the temple. The Aztecs rebuilt their temples on the same site every 52 years, so the first temple eventually became the great Temple Mayor that stood at the center of the city.

The city started as a collection of huts. It began to grow after 1385, while Acamapichtli was king. The Aztecs were excellent engineers. They built three causeways over the swamp to link the city with the mainland. These were raised roads made of stone supported on wooden pillars. Parts of the causeways were bridges. These bridges could be removed to leave gaps and this prevented enemies from getting to the city. Fresh water was brought from the mainland to the city along stone **aqueducts.**

As you read, think about how text structure and features help you understand the article.

Tenochtitlan was located in what is now Mexico City. Lake Texcoco surrounded the island. It was gradually drained as the city grew larger.

Huitzilopochtli is the Aztec god of war and of the sun. His name means "Hummingbird of the South."

Mayor is a Spanish word for "greater, larger."

aqueducts bridge-like structures that carried water over long distances

Acamapichtli is known as the first ruler of Tenochtitlan. His name means "Handful of Arrows."

How can you tell that this is a nonfiction article?

The Spaniards were the first Europeans to explore the Americas. Hernan Cortés (1485–1547) led the men who discovered Tenochtitlan in 1519. The Spaniards conquered the Aztecs and settled the area.

Inside the City

The Spaniards' first view of Tenochtitlan was described by one of Cortés's soldiers, Bernal Diaz: "And when we saw all those towns and level causeway leading into Mexico, we were astounded. These great towns and buildings rising from the water, all made of stone, seemed like an enchanted vision."

By that time Tenochtitlan was the largest city in Mexico. About 200,000 people lived there. The houses were one story high and had flat roofs. In the center of the city was a large square. The twin temple stood on one side, and the king's palace on another. Officials' houses made of white stone also lined the square. There were few roads. People traveled in canoes along canals.

Floating Gardens

Tenochtitlan was built in a huge valley, the Valley of Mexico, which was surrounded by mountains. Rivers flowed from the mountains into Lake Texcoco, where Tenochtitlan stood. The lake was linked to four other shallow, swampy lakes. The land around the lakes was dry because there was very little rain. The Aztecs dug ditches and piled up the earth to make islands in the shallow parts of the lake. These chinampas, or swamp gardens, could be farmed. The ditches carried water into larger canals that were used for **irrigation** and as waterways to the city.

Texcoco and the lake to the south contained fresh water, but the northern lakes contained salt water, which was no good for irrigation. The Aztecs built an embankment 10 miles long to keep out the salt water and also to protect the city from flooding.

irrigation using ditches or other methods to water crops during the dry season

Feeding the People

Archaeologists think that when Tenochtitlan was at its greatest, about one million people lived in the Valley of Mexico. That included Tenochtitlan and the 50 or 60 city-states on the mainland surrounding the lakes. Food for all these people had to come from farming.

Historians are not sure how many people in Tenochtitlan were farmers, but they think it may have been between one third and one half of the population. The rest were the nobility, craftspeople, and others. Each chinampa was only big enough to grow food for one family. Most people in Tenochtitlan depended on food from outside the city.

As the city grew, more and more land was drained for farming and for building. Farmers had no tools except simple hoes and digging sticks, but the loose soil was fertile and easy to turn. The main crop was corn, but farmers also grew tomatoes, beans, chili peppers, and prickly pears. They grew maguey cactus for its fibers and to make a drink called pulque. Cacao trees were grown in the hottest areas. The seeds were used for trading and to make a chocolate drink.

***Reading Strategy:* Predicting**

How do you think the Aztecs managed to feed the city's population?

Aztec society was divided into several social classes.

Until the Europeans arrived in the 1500s, the Aztecs had never tasted sugar. Nor had the Europeans ever tasted chocolate. It was travel across the Atlantic that brought these two ingredients together. No one knows who first combined Eastern sugar with Western chocolate. The combination has been popular ever since.

Why do you think the author wrote this article? Explain your thinking.

Inside an Aztec Home

There were big differences between a rich Aztec home and a poor one. The nobles' houses were like palaces. They were one story high and built around a courtyard. Each of the four sides contained four or five large rooms. The courtyards were planted with flower and vegetable gardens. Some houses on the island in the center of the city were built of adobe—bricks made from mud and dried in the sun. Adobe is still used for building in Mexico today. These grand houses and palaces were whitewashed so that they shone in the sun. The Spanish soldier Bernal Diaz described buildings that looked like "gleaming white towers and castles: a marvelous sight."

There is very little evidence about the buildings in Tenochtitlan and hardly any about the poor people's houses. What we do know has been pieced together from scattered historical records such as documents that record the sale of building sites on the chinampa gardens. All of the poorer people's homes were built on the chinampas on the outskirts of the city. Because the chinampas would not take the weight of stone, houses had to be built of lighter materials such as wattle-and-daub. This was made by weaving reeds together and then plastering them with mud. We know that the outskirts of the city were divided into groups of houses inside walled areas, or compounds. A whole family lived in each compound. The family consisted of a couple, their married children, and their grandchildren. Every married couple in the family had a separate house of one or two rooms. All the houses opened onto an outdoor patio that belonged to the whole family.

Outside the house, the families often kept turkeys in pens. The turkeys provided eggs and meat. There was also a beehive for honey. Most families had a bathhouse in the garden.

Furniture and Decoration

Aztec houses were very plain inside. Everyone slept on mats of reeds that were spread on the dirt floor at night. Families had cooking pots and **utensils** made of clay. There were **goblets** for pulque and other drinks, graters for grinding chilis, and storage pots of various designs. Reed baskets were also used for storage. Households had grinding stones for grinding corn into flour. There was also a household **shrine** with statues of the gods.

The houses had no windows or chimneys, so they must have been dark and smoky from the cooking fire. There were no doors, just an open doorway. Even the palaces had open doorways with cloths hanging over them.

utensils forks, knives, and spoons

goblets large drinking glasses or bowls

shrine a holy place

AFTER READING THE SELECTION | Apply the Skills

Tenochtitlan: Inside the Aztec Capital *by Jacqueline Dineen*

Directions Choose the letter of the best answer or write the answer using complete sentences.

Comprehension: Identifying Facts

1. Who built the city of Tenochtitlan?
   A the Aztecs
   B the Spaniards
   C the Mexicans
   D the Indians
2. Why did the engineers build so many bridges and causeways?
3. What are chinampas?

Comprehension: Putting Ideas Together

4. What were the Aztecs especially skilled at?
   A poetry
   B architecture
   C engineering
   D fighting
5. What were the houses in the city made of?
6. How was a nobleman's house different from that of a farmer?

Understanding Literature: Cause and Effect

Cause-and-effect relationships happen many times in this article. The cause is the event that produced the result. The effect is the result produced.

7. Identify one cause-and-effect relationship in the article. Was the effect positive or negative? Explain.
8. How is the article different from a myth? How is it alike? Do myths also contain cause-and-effect relationships?

Critical Thinking

9. What is your overall impression of the Aztecs? Think about what you have learned about the city. What do the facts you have read tell you about their civilization?

Thinking Creatively

10. Why do you think the Spaniards were so impressed with Tenochtitlan?

Grammar Check

A comma signals a brief pause. The chart shows several uses of the comma.

Before a conjunction joining independent clauses
John thought he was late, so he rushed through the parking lot.
After an introductory phrase or clause
If you go to the play, when will you get home?
Between items in a series
It was a dark, cold, windy night.

Insert commas where needed.

1 The semifinalists in the spelling bee are Joseph Omar Sara and Lorna.

2 In the distance the child played with her toys.

3 The flight lasted twelve seconds and the plane traveled 120 feet.

Vocabulary Builder

Use your knowledge of words from the selection to answer the following questions.

1 What might you do with a set of **goblets?**

2 Why did the city of Tenochtitlan need **aqueducts?**

3 What were **utensils** used for?

4 Why might people go to a **shrine?**

Writing on Your Own

Write a short description of the city of Tenochtitlan.

- Write details about the time, place, and surroundings.
- List vivid verbs and adjectives that will appeal to the five senses.

Listening and Speaking

Deliver a persuasive speech. Convince the authorities to build a city on a small island in a lake.

- Use note cards. Write a short statement explaining your position.
- Write key words and supporting evidence.
- Refer to your note cards as you deliver your speech.

Research and Technology

The city of Tenochtitlan changed over time. Write a brief report on how Tenochtitlan developed. Explain what became of the city and what is there today. Mention how the city was planned, and describe the engineering used to build it. Share your finished report with the class.

COMPARING LITERARY WORKS | **Build Understanding**

Uniaí's Son and the Guaraná *retold by Mercedes Dorson*

Objectives

- To read and understand a legend
- To read about the birth of an epic hero
- To compare and contrast a legend with a myth

About the Oral Tradition

This story is an example of how the oral tradition has changed in modern times. In the past, people told stories aloud. They told stories to entertain one another. They retold myths and legends to recall the past and make it seem very exciting. They passed down folktales that taught children important lessons.

Today, writers like Mercedes Dorson are capturing the oral tradition in print. They collect folktales, myths, and legends and write them. This is a new way of passing on the oral tradition. People read these stories and share them with their children by reading them aloud. This means that the oral tradition is alive and well.

About the Selection

"Uniaí's Son and the Guaraná" is a legend of the Amazon rain forest. The Amazon River runs from the Andes Mountains of Peru through Brazil to the Atlantic. The rain forest is a dense jungle of lush tropical plants. It is home to many different types of birds and animals, as well as people. Rain forests grow in areas that get more than 70 inches of rain every year.

This legend tells about Uniaí, a beautiful woman of the Brazilian rain forest. She lives with her brothers in an enchanted garden. When Uniaí marries and has a baby, her brothers stop speaking to her. She leaves the garden with her son. Uniaí's son wants to see her old home. When he goes there, his uncles have him killed. He is reborn and becomes the father of the Maué tribe.

As you read the selection, compare it to "Icarus and Daedalus." The stories have many similarities and differences.

Literary Terms A **legend** is a special kind of folktale. It recounts something that a culture believes about its own early history. Legends often tell about **heroes.** The legend "Uniaí's Son and the Guaraná" tells about the birth of an epic hero. An epic hero is a person who embodies all the qualities his or her culture most admires. Epic heroes may or may not have been real people. To their own cultures, they are always real. Legends, like myths, often contain universal themes that apply to all times and places.

legend a traditional story that was at one time told orally and was handed down from one generation to another

hero the leading character in a story, novel, play, or film

Reading on Your Own Think about the major theme or themes you found in "Icarus and Daedalus." As you read "Uniaí's Son and the Guaraná," look for its theme. Do the two selections share any major themes?

Writing on Your Own "Uniaí's Son and the Guaraná" is a legend. "Icarus and Daedalus" is a myth. Compare these two tales. Write a short paragraph explaining how they are alike and different.

Vocabulary Focus This selection contains a number of vivid verbs. Define each one and use it correctly in a sentence: *maneuver, weave, pluck, sprinkle, attract, bask, refuse, beg, warn, relent.* Use the dictionary or context clues for help.

Think Before You Read What heroes exist in your culture? Were they real people or imaginary characters?

Uniaí's Son and the Guaraná

As you read, look for clues that help you understand the theme or themes.

Which aspects of the story's opening help you identify it as a legend?

Lianas are woody vines that grow roots in the ground.

It is said that in the beginning there were three **siblings,** two brothers and a sister. The brothers were strong and handsome, and their agile bodies were skillfully decorated with designs made from both the red dye of the *urucu* seed and the black dye of the *genipapo* seed. The sister's name was Uniaí.

Uniaí was a tall, black-haired woman who owned an enchanted place named Noçoquém. The giant trees, all the jungle animals, and exotic plants **coexisted** happily in this place. Its beauty was beyond compare. Uniaí knew the secrets of the forest. She understood that the manioc root, the sweet potato, and the *pupunha* nut were for eating. She was aware that certain lianas that hung on the biggest trees could be made into the deadly poison *curare*. She knew coconuts and calabashes made the best drinking **vessels** and that **intricate**

siblings children of the same parents

coexisted lived together

vessels bowls or cups for drinking

intricate complex

necklaces could be fashioned from the seeds of the açaí palm tree. Everything the brothers needed, Uniaí could provide from the surrounding jungle.

Uniaí did not have a husband. In those days animals were also people, and they all wanted to marry her. Uniaí's brothers did not want their sister to marry. They wanted her to stay with them forever, taking care of all their selfish demands. It was she who prepared the pancakes made from the manioc root to eat with the fish they caught in the river. It was she who wove the beautiful baskets out of palm leaves in which they stored the berries they collected. It was her **nimble** fingers that plucked the colorful feathers from the toucan to make the **adornments** the brothers wore on feast days. And it was Uniaí who planted the **majestic** nutmeat tree that dominated Noçoquém.

The snake was the first to express his interest in capturing the love of Uniaí. Every day he sprinkled a magic perfume in the path of Uniaí. If someone made a wish in the presence of the enchanted perfume, the wish would come true. Whenever Uniaí crossed the path she would exclaim, "What a lovely scent there is here!"

***Reading Strategy:* Predicting**

What do you predict will happen between Uniaí and the snake?

Each day, the little snake **maneuvered** himself closer to Uniaí to attract her attention. Finally, one day he stretched himself out in the middle of the path. When Uniaí stopped to bask in the wonderful scent of the sweet perfume, the snake looked straight into her eyes. He wished that she were his wife, and at that moment she became instantly married to the snake and heavy with child.

Her brothers did not like this new state of affairs at all. "Now she will only take care of the child and will not do anything for us!"

They were furious! They refused to see their sister, and once she had the baby, they refused to see her newborn son. Saddened, Uniaí left Noçoquém.

nimble quick and clever

adornments ornaments, decorations

majestic royal

maneuvered changed position

During this time, Uniaí's majestic nut tree was growing. Its limbs spread so far, it appeared to be a mass of green sky. From the tree's branches hung fruits with delicious nuts hidden inside.

Uniaí built her house far away, next to the Tapajós River. Her child was born strong and beautiful. She would bathe him in the midst of the bright blue and black morpho butterflies that hovered near the water like multicolored clouds. The boy grew taller and more handsome every day.

Uniaí would tell him stories of Noçoquém. She would tell him of the plants that grew there, of the sweet nectar from the *miriti* palm tree, of his uncles' great skill when they fished for the giant *pirarucu* fish, and of the special tree and its nutmeats.

As soon as he learned how to speak, the boy expressed his wish: "I would also like to eat the nuts. I want to taste the fruit that my uncles like so much."

"It is difficult, my son," replied Uniaí. "Now your uncles are the keepers of Noçoquém, and we cannot enter."

The boy nonetheless continued begging for the nuts that were so good to eat. His mother warned him, "It is dangerous, my son. Your uncles have placed a macaw, a parakeet, and an armadillo, whose bony-plated skin is like an armor, as guards in Noçoquém."

A *macaw* is a type of parrot. An *armadillo* is an animal whose head and body are covered in bony plates.

The boy did not **relent.** He insisted, "But I still want to go."

He wanted to go because he wanted to go. Uniaí knew there was no way to **deter** him, so she finally accompanied him to Noçoquém rather than risk his going alone. With her special knowledge of Noçoquém, Uniaí was able to sneak around the guards. The boy was so taken by the sweet fragrance of the nuts that he did not want to wait to eat them. His mother agreed to roast them right there under the tremendous tree, despite the danger of getting caught by the armadillo.

It happened that the armadillo, walking through Noçoquém later that day, saw the ashes of the fire under the tree where Uniaí and her son had roasted the nutmeats. He ran to report to the brothers what he had seen. One of the brothers was doubtful. He **queried** his brother, "Could it be? The armadillo may be mistaken."

The parakeet also saw the ashes and came to tell the brothers. And the macaw flew in later and **confirmed** the existence of the ashes as well. The brothers decided to send the fierce purple-mouthed howler monkey to guard the nut tree. They suspected that Uniaí and her son were the

relent give in

deter to turn aside

queried asked

confirmed stated to be true

Reading Strategy: **Predicting**

What do you think will happen to the boy? Why do you think this?

What universal theme do you recognize in this sequence of events?

intruders, and they instructed the monkey to capture any creature that might appear.

The day after Uniaí took her son to Noçoquém, the boy decided to return to the enchanted place because he could not resist the **delectable** nuts. He knew his mother would not want him to return, so he went by himself.

The monkey saw the boy climb up the nutmeat tree. Well-hidden from the boy by the other trees, the monkey armed his bow. He shot arrows with razor-sharp edges carved out of fish bones. Many nuts fell to the ground, and the boy fell with them.

When night descended and Uniaí realized that her son was missing, she ran to Noçoquém. She ran as fast as she could. Uniaí found her son lifeless under the majestic tree. She tried to breathe life back into him, but to no **avail.**

She cried so hard she could not stop. She was **inconsolable.** In her despair she threw herself on her son. As she lay over his body, a lightning bolt struck next to them, followed immediately by an explosion of thunder. Uniaí took this to be a sign.

With new strength she spoke to her **inanimate** son. "Your uncles are responsible. They wanted you like this. Without life. But it will not be! From you I

intruders those who go where they are not invited or welcome

delectable tasty

avail help, use

inconsolable unable to be comforted

inanimate motionless

will make the seed of the most powerful plant ever to be seen!" As Uniaí planted the body of her child in the earth she sang:

"Large you will be, healer of men!
All will have to appeal to you
to put an end to illness,
to have strength in war
to have strength in love.
Large you will be."

She willed that from the boy's eyes the *guaraná* plant would be born. The fruit of the *guaraná* plant would look exactly like the human eye. The outer shell of the fruit would resemble the eyelids. When the fruit ripened, it would reveal a large black seed surrounded by the white flesh of the fruit.

The *guaraná* fruit really does look like a human eye. People of the Amazon region grind it to powder and make it into a tea. They also use guaraná seeds to cure fevers and stomach aches.

Days afterward, when Uniaí went to see the plant she had created from the pain of her son's death, she was astonished by how much the fruit of the *guaraná* reminded her of her lost son's eyes. She wanted to cry again, missing her boy, when suddenly she saw her son hidden behind the dense leaves of the *guaraná*. He looked happy, strong, and beautiful. She was **gratified** that her strength and **persistence** was matched by her son's, and that he had been born twice, once of her and now of the *guaraná*.

Uniaí's reborn son would **originate** the Maué tribe. It would be the Maué Indians who would discover the **stimulant** qualities of the *guaraná:* vigor and persistence. The seeds of this powerful plant would be used to make the tonic that gives these Indians the strength in love and war that they are known for throughout the Amazon region.

How does Uniaí's son fit the definition of an epic hero?

gratified pleased

persistence stubborn will

originate be the founder of

stimulant to refresh

Uniaí's Son and the Guaraná *retold by Mercedes Dorson*

Directions Choose the letter of the best answer or write the answer using complete sentences.

Comprehension: Identifying Facts

1. Who is the father of Uniaí's son?

A her brother
B the great nutmeat tree
C the monkey
D the snake

2. Why do Uniaí's brothers not want her to marry?

3. How does Uniaí's son die?

Comprehension: Putting Ideas Together

4. What do Icarus and Uniaí's son have in common?

A They both disobey warnings.
B They are both clever and brave.
C They are both careless and forgetful.
D They are both heroic warriors.

5. Describe the main challenges Daedalus and Uniaí face. How are they alike? How are they different?

6. Why does Uniaí's son insist on going back to Noçoquém in spite of her warnings?

Understanding Literature: Universal Theme

A universal theme is a main idea of a literary work that can be understood by people of all different cultures. Examples of universal themes include friendship, peace, and happiness.

7. What is the theme of "Icarus and Daedalus"? What is the theme of "Uniaí's Son"? How are they alike and different?

8. Explain why Uniaí's son can be called an epic hero.

Critical Thinking

9. Would you describe Uniaí as a hero? Why or why not?

Thinking Creatively

10. What do you think became of Uniaí's two brothers? Explain your reasoning.

Grammar Check

A subject pronoun is used as the subject of a sentence. An object pronoun is used as the direct or indirect object of a verb. It is also used as the object of a preposition.

Subject Pronouns	Object Pronouns
I, he, she, they, we	me, him, her, them, us

Choose the correct pronoun in each pair.

1 (He, Him) and (I, me) agreed to weed the garden.

2 (She, Her) gave the book to (I, me) so that (we, us) could read the story.

3 (They, Them) and their uncle visited (we, us) last week.

Vocabulary Builder

Review each group of words. Decide whether the boldfaced word from "Uniaí's Son and the Guaraná" belongs with the other two words. Explain.

1 **siblings,** brothers, sisters

2 **nimble,** slow, uncomfortable

3 **confirmed,** true, prove

4 **originate,** copy, destroy

Writing on Your Own

Write a short essay comparing and contrasting Icarus and Uniaí's son. Consider these questions:

- How does each story show the son's act of disobedience?
- What are the consequences of the son's action?
- Do the storytellers want you to admire either character? Explain your thinking.

Listening and Speaking

Retell either "Icarus and Daedalus" or "Uniaí's Son and the Guaraná" to someone. Don't memorize the story you choose. Instead, retell it in your own way. Try to maintain the tone of the original myth/legend.

Media and Viewing

Look online and in the library for photographs of the plants mentioned in the story. Put together an illustrated dictionary of the plants. Include the plants' names, pictures, and brief definitions. Share your dictionary with the class.

Reading Strategy:
Questioning

Asking questions as you read will help you understand and remember more of the information. Questioning the text will also help you to be a more active reader. As you read, ask yourself:

- What is my reason for reading this text?
- What decisions can I make about the facts and details in this text?
- What connections can I make between this text and my own life?

Literary Terms

trickster a character who uses cleverness and quick thinking to outsmart enemies, sometimes by playing tricks on them

folktale a story that has been handed down from one generation to another

Sun and Moon in a Box *retold by Richard Erdoes and Alfonso Ortiz*

About the Authors

Richard Erdoes
1912–

Richard Erdoes was born in Frankfurt, Germany. He studied art and later worked as a cartoonist. He sketched funny portraits for several German daily newspapers.

In 1939, when the Nazis occupied Austria, Erdoes went to France. He moved to New York in 1940. He found work as an illustrator for newspapers and magazines. While working at *Life* magazine, Erdoes took photographs for an article on a Sioux reservation. His eyes were opened to the conditions there. Since then, he has written more than 20 books on the American West.

Alfonso Ortiz
1939–1997

Alfonso Ortiz was born in San Juan, a Tewa pueblo in northern New Mexico. He earned degrees in sociology and anthropology. He spent many years of his life as a university professor. Ortiz brought many scholars from the community to the university. He encouraged them to share their knowledge with students and teachers. He also worked with the Association on American Indian Affairs. Ortiz was president of that organization for 15 years.

About the Selection

"Sun and Moon in a Box" is a Zuñi myth. The Zuñi are Southwestern Indians. As this story begins, the sun and moon are not yet in the sky. Eagle and Coyote find the box in which the Kachinas keep the sun and the moon. They steal the box and take it away with them. When Coyote opens the box, the sun and moon escape.

Objectives

- To read and understand a myth

***Before Reading* continued on next page**

Sun and Moon in a Box *retold by Richard Erdoes and Alfonso Ortiz*

trickster a character who uses cleverness and quick thinking to outsmart enemies, sometimes by playing tricks on them

Literary Terms Myths are products of the background, customs, and beliefs of the people who created them. This background is called the cultural context of a myth. In "Sun and Moon in a Box," the cultural context is Zuñi or Southwestern American Indian. One element of this myth is the **trickster**. A trickster is a character who influences others and plays jokes on them. Tricksters occur in the mythology of many cultures.

Reading on Your Own A comparison tells how two or more things are alike. A contrast tells how they are different. You can compare and contrast an ancient culture with your own culture. You can find similarities and differences between an ancient myth and a modern story. Comparing and contrasting helps you understand new ideas.

Writing on Your Own You may have read a story about a character like Coyote who plays tricks on others. Write a paragraph about a trickster you have read about. Describe what you would expect a trickster to say and do.

Vocabulary Focus As you read the myth, keep track of new words. Write them in your notebook. Use context clues to help you define each one. Once you have finished reading, look the words up in a dictionary. Make sure your definitions are correct.

Think Before You Read How might stealing the sun and moon benefit a person? Why would anyone want to do this? How might stealing the sun and moon be hurtful? Who would be most affected? Why?

Sun and Moon in a Box

Zuñi Folk Tale

Coyote and Eagle were hunting. Eagle caught rabbits. Coyote caught nothing but grasshoppers. Coyote said: "Friend Eagle, my chief, we make a great hunting pair."

"Good, let us stay together," said Eagle.

They went toward the west. They came to a deep canyon. "Let us fly over it," said Eagle.

"My chief, I cannot fly," said Coyote. "You must carry me across."

"Yes, I see that I have to," said Eagle. He took Coyote on his back and flew across the canyon. They came to a river. "Well," said Eagle, "you cannot fly, but you certainly can swim. This time I do not have to carry you."

As you read, think about how Eagle's personality compares to that of Coyote.

***Reading Strategy:* Questioning**

What question or questions might you ask of Eagle and Coyote?

What does Coyote do that makes him a trickster?

Eagle flew over the stream, and Coyote swam across. He was a bad swimmer. He almost drowned. He coughed up a lot of water. "My chief," he said, "when we come to another river, you must carry me." Eagle regretted to have Coyote for a companion.

They came to Kachina Pueblo. The Kachinas were dancing. Now, at this time, the earth was still soft and new. There was as yet no sun and no moon. Eagle and Coyote sat down and watched the dance. They saw that the Kachinas had a square box. In it they kept the sun and the moon. Whenever they wanted light they opened the lid and let the sun peek out. Then it was day. When they wanted less light, they opened the box just a little for the moon to look out.

"This is something wonderful," Coyote whispered to Eagle.

"This must be the sun and the moon they are keeping in that box," said Eagle. "I have heard about these two wonderful beings."

"Let us steal the box," said Coyote.

"No, that would be wrong," said Eagle. "Let us just borrow it."

When the Kachinas were not looking, Eagle grabbed the box and flew off. Coyote ran after him on the ground. After a while Coyote called Eagle: "My chief, let me have the box. I am ashamed to let you do all the carrying."

"No," said Eagle, "you are not **reliable**. You might be curious and open the box and then we could lose the wonderful things we borrowed."

For some time they went on as before—Eagle flying above with the box, Coyote running below, trying to keep up. Then once again Coyote called Eagle: "My chief, I am ashamed to let you carry the box. I should do this for you. People will talk badly about me, letting you carry this **burden**."

"No, I don't trust you," Eagle repeated. "You won't be able to **refrain** from opening the box. Curiosity will get the better of you."

"No," cried Coyote, "do not fear, my chief, I won't even think of opening the box." Still, Eagle would not give it to him, continuing to fly above, holding the box in his **talons**. But Coyote went on **pestering** Eagle: "My chief, I am really embarrassed. People will say: 'That lazy, disrespectful Coyote lets his chief do all the carrying.'"

"No, I won't give this box to you," Eagle objected. "It is too precious to **entrust** to somebody like you."

Kachinas are religious spirits of the Zuni and Hopi nations. They link Earth and the spirit world. Colorful Kachina dances take place every year. Dancers wear masks that represent the different Kachinas. *Pueblo* is a Spanish word for town. When the Spaniards came to North America, they called the small Indian towns pueblos. This was because the Indian towns looked exactly like small Spanish pueblos.

Many American Indian myths tell of a time when the world was still unfinished. In this myth, the sun and moon are not yet in the sky. This is part of the cultural context of this myth.

***Reading Strategy:* Questioning**

What questions might you ask about Eagle's and Coyote's actions?

reliable trustworthy

refrain to hold back

pestering annoying

burden something that is carried

talons long claws

entrust to give trust to

They continued as before, Eagle flying, Coyote running. Then Coyote begged for the fourth time: "My chief, let me carry the box for a while. My wife will scold me, and my children will no longer respect me, when they find out that I did not help you carry this load."

Then Eagle **relented**, saying: "Will you promise not to drop the box and under no **circumstances** to open it?"

"I promise, my chief, I promise," cried Coyote. "You can rely upon me. I shall not betray your trust."

Then Eagle allowed Coyote to carry the box. They went on as before, Eagle flying, Coyote running, carrying the box in his mouth. They came to a wooded area, full of trees and bushes. Coyote pretended to lag behind, hiding himself behind some bushes where Eagle could not see him. He could not **curb** his curiosity. Quickly he sat down and opened the

relented gave in

circumstances situations

curb to control or suppress

box. In a flash, Sun came out of the box and flew away, to the very edge of the sky, and at once the world grew cold, the leaves fell from the tree branches, the grass turned brown, and icy winds made all living things shiver.

Then, before Coyote could put the lid back on the box, Moon jumped out and flew away to the outer rim of the sky, and at once snow fell down from heaven and covered the plains and the mountains.

Eagle said: "I should have known better. I should not have let you persuade me. I knew what kind of low, cunning, stupid creature you are. I should have remembered that you never keep a promise. Now we have winter. If you had not opened the box, then we could have kept Sun and Moon always close to us. Then there would be no winter. Then we would have summer all the time."

AFTER READING THE SELECTION | Apply the Skills

Sun and Moon in a Box *retold by Richard Erdoes and Alfonso Ortiz*

Directions Choose the letter of the best answer or write the answer using complete sentences.

Comprehension: Identifying Facts

1. Why does Coyote want to hunt with Eagle?
- **A** Coyote cannot find food on his own.
- **B** Coyote wants to steal the sun and moon.
- **C** Coyote wants to learn to fly.
- **D** Coyote wants to find the Kachinas.

2. Why do Eagle and Coyote travel to the West?

3. Where do Coyote and Eagle first see the sun and moon?

Comprehension: Putting Ideas Together

4. Which word best describes Coyote?

A sulky	**C** clumsy
B clever	**D** mean

5. Why does Eagle refuse to give Coyote the box at first?

6. Why does Coyote want to carry the box for Eagle?

Understanding Literature: Trickster

A trickster is a character who resembles his name. He plays jokes on other characters. He tricks other characters into doing his work for him. The popularity of trickster tales reflects on the cultures the tales come from.

7. What makes Coyote a trickster?

8. Coyote is featured in many American Indian tales. What does his popularity tell you about Zuñi culture?

Critical Thinking

9. Do you think Eagle is at all responsible for the coming of winter? Explain your thinking.

Thinking Creatively

10. What might have become of the world if Coyote had not opened the box? What would the world be like without winter? Explain your thinking.

Grammar Check

Capital letters signal the beginning of a sentence or quotation. They identify proper nouns and adjectives.

Sentence beginning
My dog ran away.
Quotation
I yelled, "Come back!"
Proper nouns
Mexico, Jefferson, Ireland
Proper adjectives
Mexican, Jeffersonian, Irish

Add the missing capitals letters.

1 did you last visit cleveland in april or may?

2 we visited the cayman islands after the meeting of the women's sports foundation.

3 my brother charles, who lives in new zealand, visited us on thanksgiving.

Vocabulary Builder

Idioms do not mean what the words literally say. Instead, they are examples of figurative language. Example: "He can't carry a tune in a bucket," means "He can't sing in tune."

Create a class list of idioms and idiomatic expressions. Compare their literal and figurative meanings.

Writing on Your Own

Write a plot summary of "Sun and Moon in a Box."

- Take notes on the setting, major characters, main events, and final outcome.
- Include one major event each from the beginning, the middle, and the end.

Listening and Speaking

With a partner, find five unusual facts about an animal. Include these facts in a story about the animal. Do not reveal the animal's name. Tell the story to your classmates and have them guess the animal. Use facial expressions and body movements to help the other students with their guesses.

Research and Technology

Use Internet and library resources to research Zuñi culture. Choose one aspect of the culture that interests you. Write a feature article. Here are some tips to help you:

- Start with a fact or detail that will grab the reader's attention.
- Use headings to emphasize main ideas.

Food Label

The federal government requires that all packaged foods have labels. These labels must list the ingredients in order of quantity. They must specify the serving size. They must list nutrition information per serving.

Reading Skill

To read food labels, you need the skill of understanding a graphic organizer. Food labels all follow a standard format. They all include the same types of information. They all use certain abbreviations. To read graphic organizers, you need to look at the way they are set up. To read a chart, you must look at the heads of the columns. This tells you what information is in the rows below.

Common abbreviations used in food labels are g and mg. "G" stands for gram, a unit of mass. A raisin weighs about one gram. "Mg" means milligram, or one-thousandth of a gram.

Food labels measure in percents. "Percent" means "part of 100" and % is a symbol for percent. The percents in a food label are based on a 2,000-calorie diet. This means that the numbers are percents of 2,000 rather than 100. 10% of 2,000 = 200, 25% of 2,000 = 500, and so on.

Nutrition Facts

Serving Size 1/2 cup (75g)
Servings Per Container 4

Amount Per Serving	
Calories	170
Calories from Fat	90
	% Daily Value**
Total Fat 10g	15%
Saturated Fat 25g	25%
Cholesterol 30mg	10%
Sodium 110mg	5%
Total Carbohydrate 18g	6%
Dietary Fiber 0g	0%
Sugars 15g	
Protein 3g	
Vitamin A	6%
Vitamin C	2%
Calcium	8%
Vitamin D	7%
Iron	2%

**Percent Daily Values are based on a 2,000 calorie diet. Your daily values may be higher or lower depending on your calorie needs.

Fun Time Banana Nut Ice Cream

INGREDIENTS:
MILK, CREAM, SKIM MILK, SUGAR, BANANAS, ROASTED CASHEWS (CASHEWS, SALT), CORN SYRUP, VEGETABLE GUMS, BANANA FLAVOR, VANILLA, LEMON JUICE, CARROT JUICE (COLOR), YELLOW COLOR #5.

Fruit Bars

Nutrition Facts

Serving Size 1 bar (125g)
Servings Per Container 4

Amount Per Serving	
Calories	110
Calories from Fat	0
	% Daily Value**
Total Fat 0g	0%
Saturated Fat 0g	0%
Cholesterol 0mg	0%
Sodium 20mg	1%
Total Carbohydrate 28g	9%
Dietary Fiber 0g	0%
Sugars 25g	
Protein 0g	
Vitamin A	0%
Vitamin C	8%
Calcium	2%
Vitamin D	0%
Iron	0%

**Percent Daily Values are based on a 2,000 calorie diet. Your daily values may be higher or lower depending on your calorie needs.

INGREDIENTS: WATER, STRAWBERRY PIECES, SUGAR, CITRIC ACID, VEGETABLE GUM, LEMON JUICE, BEET JUICE (COLOR), BLACK CURRANT (COLOR).

Monitor Your Progress

Directions Choose the letter of the best answer or write the answer using complete sentences.

1. Which of these nutrients does the ice cream have the highest percentage of?
   A fiber
   B carbohydrates
   C calcium
   D sodium

2. What is the main ingredient in the fruit bars?
   A strawberries
   B sugar
   C water
   D milk

3. About what percentage of your daily calories does one serving of ice cream have?
   A about 5 percent
   B about 10 percent
   C about 20 percent
   D about 50 percent

4. Which is more nutritious, one serving of ice cream or one fruit bar? Explain your answer.

5. Why do you think food labels all follow the same format?

Writing on Your Own

Look through the cupboards in your kitchen. Find a packaged food with a nutrition-facts label. Write a brief analysis of how healthy this food is. Use facts and percents from the label in your analysis.

BEFORE READING THE SELECTION | Build Understanding

The People Could Fly by *Virginia Hamilton*

Virginia Hamilton
1936–2002

Objective

- To read and understand a folktale

About the Author

"I started writing as a kid," Virginia Hamilton once said. "It was always something I was going to do." Hamilton has written novels, stories, and collections of African-American folktales. She has been called "America's most honored writer of books for children."

Hamilton grew up listening to tales told by her parents, aunts, and uncles. She remembers her childhood by saying "heard 'tells' every day of my life from parents and relatives." Some of those stories were about slavery, and most were about the past. As a result, the past came to play an important role in Hamilton's writing. She first encountered traditional African folktales on a visit to Africa. These tales also influenced Hamilton's own writing.

Hamilton's writing combines elements of history, myth, legend, and dream. Her book *M.C. Higgins, the Great* won the Newbery Medal in 1975. This award recognizes the outstanding children's book of the year.

About the Selection

"The People Could Fly" is a freedom tale. It is a kind of folktale that enslaved Africans told to keep their hopes alive, despite the hardships they faced. Like many freedom tales, "The People Could Fly" contains images of freedom and escape. There are also many references to the original storytellers' native Africa.

In "The People Could Fly," the slave Toby whispers magic words that help people escape in flight. In the end, he flies away himself.

Literary Terms A **folktale** is a story that is told and retold by word of mouth. Folktales are passed down through families and cultures. They began as a part of the oral tradition.

folktale a story that has been handed down from one generation to another

Similar folktales are told by different cultures throughout the world. They feature common character types, plot elements, and themes. Folktales often teach lessons about life. They present a clear difference between good and evil.

Reading on Your Own When you compare and contrast, you recognize similarities and differences. Use a Venn diagram to compare and contrast character traits, situations, and ideas.

- Reread the text to locate the details you will compare.
- Write the details on a diagram like this one. Shared qualities belong in the overlapping area. Qualities not shared go in the circles outside the overlapping area.

Comparing and contrasting helps you understand the structure and meaning of a literary work.

Writing on Your Own Folktales have been told to families and passed from one generation to the next. List three reasons that families tell stories to each other.

Vocabulary Focus Like all folktales, this story was told before it was written. Casual and local expressions, called idioms, reflect the story's place in the oral tradition. As you read, pay attention to ways of saying things that are not proper English. Work with a partner to make sure you understand what they mean.

Think Before You Read In what way do real people "fly"?

the People Could Fly

African American Folk Tale

As you read, think about how this story would sound if you were listening to it.

Which expressions tell you that this story is part of the oral tradition?

Reading Strategy: **Questioning**

What questions do you have at this point in the story?

They say the people could fly. Say that long ago in Africa, some of the people knew magic. And they would walk up on the air like climbin up on a gate. And they flew like blackbirds over the fields. Black, shiny wings flappin against the blue up there.

Then, many of the people were captured for Slavery. The ones that could fly shed their wings. They couldn't take their wings across the water on the slave ships. Too crowded, don't you know.

The folks were full of **misery**, then. Got sick with the up and down of the sea. So they forgot about flyin when they could no longer breathe the sweet scent of Africa.

Say the people who could fly kept their power, although they **shed** their wings. They kept their secret magic in the land of slavery. They looked the same as the other people from Africa who had been coming over, who had dark skin. Say you couldn't tell anymore one who could fly from one who couldn't.

One such who could was an old man, call him Toby. And standin tall, yet afraid, was a young woman who once had wings. Call her Sarah. Now Sarah carried a babe tied to her back. She trembled to be so hard worked and scorned.

The slaves labored in the fields from sunup to sundown. The owner of the slaves callin himself their Master. Say he was a hard lump of clay. A hard, **glinty** coal. A hard rock pile,

misery sadness **shed** dropped **glinty** catching the light wouldn't be moved. His Overseer on horseback pointed out the slaves who were slowin down. So the one called Driver cracked his whip over the slow ones to make them move faster. That whip was a slice-open cut of pain. So they did move faster. Had to.

Sarah hoed and chopped the row as the babe on her back slept.

Say the child grew hungry. That babe started up **bawling** too loud. Sarah couldn't stop to feed it. Couldn't stop to soothe and quiet it down. She let it cry. She didn't want to. She had no heart to **croon** to it.

"Keep that thing quiet," called the Overseer. He pointed his finger at the babe. The woman **scrunched** low. The Driver cracked his whip across the babe anyhow. The babe hollered like any hurt child, and the woman fell to the earth.

The old man that was there, Toby, came and helped her to her feet.

"I must go soon," she told him.

"Soon," he said.

Sarah couldn't stand up straight any longer. She was too weak. The sun burned her face. The babe cried and cried, "Pity me, oh, pity me," say it sounded like. Sarah was so sad and starvin, she sat down in the row.

"Get up, you black cow," called the Overseer. He pointed his hand, and the Driver's whip snarled around Sarah's legs. Her sack dress tore into rags. Her legs bled onto the earth. She couldn't get up.

Toby was there where there was no one to help her and the babe.

"Now, before it's too late," panted Sarah. "Now, Father!"

"Yes, Daughter, the time is come," Toby answered. "Go, as you know how to go!"

An *overseer* was a man who supervised the slaves in the fields. He made sure they stuck to their jobs and did not waste time. The overseer was a white man who was paid a salary. Overseers were often cruel. Most slaves hated and feared them.

bawling crying

croon to sing softly

scrunched squeezed together tightly

Reading Strategy: Questioning

What questions do you have about what happens here?

Which aspects of this story show that it is a folktale?

He raised his arms, holding them out to her. "*Kum . . . yali, kum buba tambe,*" and more magic words, said so quickly, they sounded like whispers and sighs.

The young woman lifted one foot on the air. Then the other. She flew clumsily at first, with the child now held tightly in her arms. Then she felt the magic, the African mystery. Say she rose just as free as a bird. As light as a feather.

The Overseer rode after her, hollerin. Sarah flew over the fences. She flew over the woods. Tall trees could not **snag** her. Nor could the Overseer. She flew like an eagle now, until she was gone from sight. No one dared speak about it. Couldn't believe it. But it was, because they that was there saw that it was.

Say the next day was dead hot in the fields. A young man slave fell from the heat. The Driver come and whipped him. Toby come over and spoke words to the fallen one. The words of ancient Africa once heard are never remembered completely. The young man forgot them as soon as he heard them. They went way inside him. He got up and rolled over on the air. He rode it awhile. And he flew away.

Another and another fell from the heat. Toby was there. He cried out to the fallen and reached his arms out to them. "*Kum kunka yali, kum . . . tambe!*" Whispers and sighs. And they too rose on the air. They rode the hot breezes. The ones flyin were black and shinin sticks, wheelin above the head of the Overseer. They crossed the rows, the fields, the fences, the streams, and were away.

"**Seize** the old man!" cried the Overseer. "I heard him say the magic words. Seize him!"

The one callin himself Master come runnin. The Driver got his whip ready to curl around old Toby and tie him up. The slaveowner took his hip gun from its place. He meant to kill old, black Toby.

snag to catch

seize to grab and hold

But Toby just laughed. Say he threw back his head and said, "Hee, hee! Don't you know who I am? Don't you know some of us in this field?" He said it to their faces. "We are ones who fly!"

Why is Toby not afraid of the Driver or the Master?

And he sighed the ancient words that were a dark promise. He said them all around to the others in the field under the whip,

"*. . . buba yali . . . buba tambe. . . .*"

There was a great outcryin. The bent backs straightened up. Old and young who were called slaves and could fly joined hands. Say like they would ring-sing. But they didn't shuffle in a circle. They didn't sing. They rose on the air. They flew in a flock that was black against the heavenly blue. Black crows or black shadows. It didn't matter, they went so high. Way above the plantation, way over the slavery land. Say they flew away to *Free-dom.*

To *ring-sing* means to stand in a circle holding hands to sing and dance. To *shuffle* means to dance with your feet dragging along the ground.

And the old man, old Toby, flew behind them, takin care of them. He wasn't cryin. He wasn't laughin. He was the **seer.** His gaze fell on the plantation where the slaves who could not fly waited.

"*Take us with you!*" Their looks spoke it but they were afraid to shout it. Toby couldn't take them with him. Hadn't the time to teach them to fly. They must wait for a chance to run.

"Goodie-bye!" The old man called Toby spoke to them, poor souls! And he was flyin gone.

So they say. The Overseer told it. The one called Master said it was a lie, a trick of the light. The Driver kept his mouth shut.

The slaves who could not fly told about the people who could fly to their children. When they were free. When they sat close before the fire in the free land, they told it. They did so love firelight and *Free-dom*, and tellin.

They say that the children of the ones who could not fly told their children. And now, me, I have told it to you.

A plantation was a large farm. 250–300 slaves might live and work on a plantation. They tended crops of cotton, tobacco, or sugarcane. They lived in small cabins and had their own gardens. The white owner and his family lived in a huge house. Some slaves cooked, cleaned, and served in the house instead of outdoors in the fields. Slaves had to obey strict rules, such as not gathering in large groups. They were on call to work at all times, every day.

seer a person with great power

AFTER READING THE SELECTION | Apply the Skills

The People Could Fly *by Virginia Hamilton*

Directions Choose the letter of the best answer or write the answer using complete sentences.

Comprehension: Identifying Facts

1. Why did the captured Africans shed their wings?

A They forgot how to fly.
B The ship was too crowded.
C Their wings had been stolen.
D Their wings were not real.

2. What does Driver do in the fields?

3. Why does Sarah's baby cry?

Comprehension: Putting Ideas Together

4. Which word best describes the Overseer?

A cruel
B cunning
C kind
D heroic

5. What does Toby do to help Sarah?

6. What happens after Toby flies away?

Understanding Literature: Folktale

Folktales are stories of the people. They are often told in casual everyday speech or dialect. This reflects their connection to the oral tradition. Many folktales describe magical things that could not really happen. Sometimes the magical events symbolize, or stand for, something else.

7. Identify elements in this story that make it a folktale.

8. Are the characters in this story realistic? Could there really have been people who do and say these things? Why or why not?

Critical Thinking

9. Why does Toby decide to leave when he does? Explain your thinking.

Thinking Creatively

10. What do you think this story meant to African Americans? Explain your answer.

Grammar Check

An abbreviation is a shortened form of a word or phrase. Most abbreviations end with a period. Abbreviations are useful when taking notes or writing lists.

Instance	Example	Abbreviation
Common Titles	Doctor	Dr.
Academic Degrees	Master of Arts	M.A.
Addresses	Avenue	Ave.
Measurements	centimeter	cm

Match each abbreviation with its long form.

1 qt. **a** ounce
2 blvd. **b** quart
3 oz. **c** boulevard
4 ml **d** milliliter

Vocabulary Builder

This selection is filled with informal words from casual speech. This helps identify it as part of the oral tradition. Define these words from the selection: *babe, bawling, hollered, awhile, shuffle,* and *tellin.* Give a "proper" English equivalent for each word and use it correctly in a sentence. Use context clues to help understand each word.

Writing on Your Own

People read reviews to find out if they will like a book, play, or movie. Write a review of "The People Could Fly."

- Give your opinions about the characters, the use of description and dialogue, and the plot.
- Support your opinions with specific details from the story.

Listening and Speaking

With a partner, prepare a television news report on the amazing events of the story. Include facts about when and where the events took place. Have a pretend interview with an "eyewitness" of the event. When you are ready, present your news report to a small group.

Research and Technology

Slave songs are part of the African-American oral tradition. They were often coded to give slaves directions to help them escape to the north. Conduct research on coded slave songs, such as "Wade in the Water" or "Follow the Drinking Gourd." Present the lyrics of the song with an explanation of the coded words.

The Coming of Asin *collected by The United Nations Women's Guild*

Objectives

- To read and understand a legend
- To compare and contrast a legend and a folktale

About the Author and Selection

This story is part of a collection of stories written by different authors collected by The United Nations Women's Guild. The collection of stories is called an anthology. For more information on anthologies, look at the How to Use This Book section in the front pages of this book.

This legend originally comes from Bolivia. Bolivia is a South American country bordering on Brazil and Chile. During the 1200s, Bolivia was the center of the Incan empire. The Spaniards defeated the Incas and took over the area in the 1500s. Today, Quechua and Aymara Indians make up over half of Bolivia's population. They still speak their traditional languages.

This legend tells the story of the stranger Asin. He is ugly and bent. When he appears among the Pilagá tribe, they make fun of him. The chief's daughter, however, is kind to him. She discovers that he can change his shape and is really a handsome young man. They marry.

When the chief of the village goes to war, Asin offers to go along with the army. The chief rudely refuses his services. Asin appears among the chief's army as a fierce warrior on an iron horse. He defeats the enemy in battle. Many of the villagers follow Asin as their new chief.

The old chief plots to kill Asin, but Asin prevents him. Asin casts spells on the old village to punish everyone for their treatment of him.

As you read this selection, compare this story to "The People Could Fly." How are the stories alike and how are they different?

Literary Terms The story of Asin is a legend. It was told and retold many times before it was written down. Like many legends, it tells about a hero. The hero in this case is an outsider. He comes into a place where he is not welcomed because he is different. However, he soon shows qualities that the people admire. He becomes the leader of the people.

Reading on Your Own Both legends and folktales feature heroes. Think about the character of Toby in "The People Could Fly." List the qualities that make him a hero. Read "The Coming of Asin" to see how its hero compares to Toby.

Writing on Your Own "The People Could Fly" is told in informal language that reflects the oral tradition. "Asin," in contrast, is written in a very "literary" style. Write a brief essay explaining which style you prefer reading, and why.

Vocabulary Focus "Asin" uses very simple adjectives to describe people and things. Find one or two exact, vivid synonyms for each adjective from the story: crooked, handsome, ugly, long, beautiful, grateful, young.

Think Before You Read Why do people make fun of and mistreat strangers? Why are people who are different often the targets of this type of treatment?

THE Coming OF Asin

Traditional Bolivian Folktale

As you read, think about the characteristics that make this story a legend.

There was once a chief among the Pilagá people by the name of Nalaraté. Nalaraté was known for his victories in war, and the men who followed him were battle-hardened warriors. Into Nalaraté's village one day there came a curious stranger. When the people saw him they laughed, for he was **grotesque** and ugly. Whereas other men were lean and straight, the stranger was crooked, with a large **paunch**. And whereas other men had long black hair, the stranger had none at all. Other men wore loincloths, but as for the stranger, he wore a fox-skin cloak over his shoulders.

A *loincloth* is a long strip of fabric. Men wrap the fabric several times around their hips and between their legs. Loincloths were commonly worn long ago in hot-weather countries.

"What kind of creature is this?" Nalaraté's people asked each other. "He is not of the Toba tribe, nor of the Matacao, nor the Tereno. He must be a tribe all by himself, for where could there be other people like him?" They **mocked** him this way, but the stranger simply listened and made no answer. Finally one of the Pilagá asked him. "Who are you?"

"My name is Asin," the stranger answered quietly.

He remained in the village and built himself a small shelter of boughs and grass. The people **tolerated** him as a curiosity, and they treated him as a beggar. If a man caught a fish that was too small to cook, he might toss it to Asin, and Asin would take it humbly and express his thanks. But though the people didn't send Asin out of the village they **abused** him in many ways. Sometimes, for sport, the men would wipe

Does Asin seem heroic to you so far in the story? Why or why not?

grotesque very disgusting

paunch belly

mocked made fun of

tolerated put up with

abused mistreated

their hands on Asin's fox-skin cloak and make a great joke of it when he complained.

One day Asin went to the house of the chief. Nalaraté said, "Do not enter here. What is in my house that you want to steal?"

Asin answered, "I only want to borrow a comb from your daughter."

Nalaraté laughed. "Since you have no hair on your head, what could you do with a comb?"

But Nalaraté's daughter overheard them talking, and she said to Asin, "Here, I will lend you the comb."

Asin took it and thanked her and went down to the river. The girl picked up her water jars and followed him, curious as to what he would do with a comb. When she came near the river, she hid among the trees and watched Asin. She saw him remove his fox-skin cloak. As Asin stood there in the water he changed instantly into a handsome young warrior with long black hair, which he combed with the comb the girl had lent him.

Reading Strategy: **Questioning**

What questions do you have about Asin at this point in the story?

"He is handsome and he has great powers!" the girl said to herself. "I will have him for my husband."

Asin finished combing his hair. Then he transformed himself again into the ugly stranger, and put the fox-skin cloak back on his shoulders. After he had left, the girl filled her water jars and carried them home.

What aspects of the story show that it is a legend? Does it remind you of other legends you have read?

When Asin came to Nalaraté's house to return the comb, the girl said, "sit down with me here."

Asin replied, "Why do you want me to sit with you? I am ugly."

The girl said, "Even though my father will object, I will have you for my husband."

Asin answered, "Very well, then. Let us sit where people can see."

The girl put a skin on the ground in front of the house and they sat on it together, **signifying** that they were married.

signifying showing, symbolizing

When people saw them sitting there, they said, "The chief's daughter has lost her mind. She is married to Asin."

When Nalaraté came he was angry. He ordered his daughter to leave Asin and choose another man of the village, but she refused, saying, "He is my husband now."

That night, Asin **demonstrated** his magic powers. From under the fox-skin cloak he brought out a mosquito netting to protect them from insects. He brought out food, and they ate. He brought out a beautiful red skirt-cloth and gave it to his wife.

When the girl's mother saw what Asin could do, she said, "I didn't protest when you married Asin. What can he bring out from under the fox skin for me?"

The girl said, "Ask for whatever you want, he will give it to you."

The mother said, "It is the beautiful red skirt-cloth that I want."

"Take it," Asin said, and she took it. Then Asin reached under the fox-skin cloak and brought out a yellow skirt-cloth for his wife. He brought out ears of corn and a honeycomb full of honey and gave them to the girl's mother, and she was grateful. She said again, "I wasn't one of those who objected to Asin's living here."

Nalaraté was at a drinking party with the warriors of the village. When he returned early in the morning he said, "Get my things ready, we are going on an **expedition** against the Matacao tribe."

Asin said, "I will come with you."

demonstrated showed

expedition journey with a specific purpose

The chief replied **scornfully**, "No, how could I take you? You would be a **hindrance**. You are no warrior. You don't even have a horse. If you had a horse, could you even make it go in the right direction? And if you arrived at the place of battle, what could you do but cause us shame and **misery**? No, stay here with the women. As for my daughter, she chose a beggar instead of a warrior. She will starve. I will give her nothing."

Nalaraté and his warriors mounted their horses and rode away. When they were out of sight, Asin said, "Now I will go."

Why does Asin decide to fight for people who mistreat him?

He mounted his donkey and followed the war party. When he had left the village behind, he clapped his hands together, *tao,* and his donkey changed into a fiery iron horse. He clapped his hands again, *tao,* and changed himself into a handsome young man as his wife had seen him at the river. When night came, Nalaraté's warriors made camp. Before Asin entered the camp, he changed his iron horse back into a donkey, and himself into an ugly man without hair.

The war party saw him then, and they made jokes and asked, "Why did you come?" They threw him some scraps of food, which he took. After a while he mounted his donkey and rode on ahead of the war party. He spent the night alone at a watering place. He brought out food from under his fox skin and he ate until he was satisfied.

In the morning he again joined the warriors, and he rode at a distance behind them. The men joked about Asin. Then they sighted the camp of the enemy. Nalaraté ordered Asin to return to the village. He said, "Go back at once before you cause us trouble and shame."

Asin stopped and waited, as the Pilagá men went cautiously forward. Then he changed himself into the warrior with the flowing black hair, and he changed his donkey into the fiery iron horse. He rode fiercely past the Pilagá men into the camp of the enemy and fought with them. Nalaraté's warriors stopped and watched the battle, asking each other, "Who is this man? Who is this man?"

scornfully with anger **hindrance** obstacle **misery** sadness

One of them cried out, “It is Asin! He changed his donkey into a fiery iron horse!”

Then the Pilagá went forward to join the battle, but by the time they arrived Asin had scattered the enemy and rounded up all the horses. They met him coming back, driving the horses before him. He did not speak to the Pilagá, but went on and left them behind.

Asin returned to the village. He said to his wife, “Let us leave this village where I have been mistreated.” His wife agreed. Her mother said, “I will come too.” So Asin took them and his horses to a new place on the edge of a river and made a new house.

When Nalaraté arrived home he found his house empty. The women of the village told him how Asin had gone away with his household.

The men blamed Nalaraté, saying, “It is your fault, you abused him. And he is the greatest of warriors.”

Nalaraté was angry. He said, “If you want him for your chief, follow him.”

Many of the men did. They took their families and went to the place where Asin had built his house. There they built a new village. And Asin was the chief.

Nalaraté decided he would destroy Asin for the grief he had caused him. But Asin learned of the plot, and he called all the men of the village together and spoke to them. He said, "There is a wind coming. It will be cold. Go and brace your houses, and put heavy thatch on the roof." They went and prepared their houses. Then Asin clapped his hands, *tao,* and the cold wind came. It swept across the country. People became cold and sought refuge inside their houses. But the wind blew away the thatch from the roofs. Only in Asin's village did the roofs remain. Everywhere else people were punished by the cold and the wind. In his own house Asin clapped his hands, *tao,* and made a fire. People came to him begging for an **ember** so that they could have a fire in their houses too. To those people who were his friends, Asin gave firebrands. When his enemies came and begged for fire, he turned them away. Nalaraté himself came, but Asin said, "First you merely abused me; then you planned to kill me. Why should I give you fire?" Nalaraté went away and was cold.

All those who hadn't abused Asin had fire and were warm, but the others suffered and died. The rivers froze, and snow covered the land.

At last the wind stopped, and the ice and snow melted, and Asin came out of his house. He went to Nalaraté's village and found the people dead. He changed the old men into yulo birds and mazamorras birds, and they flew away. He changed the old women into chaja birds, and they flew away. He changed the middle-aged people into hawks and vultures, and they flew away. And the children he changed into ducks and herons, and they flew away. Asin found Nalaraté where he had taken refuge from the cold in a well, and he changed him into an alligator.

This is the legend of Asin, who was abused because of his appearance.

***Reading Strategy:* Questioning**

What questions do you have about Nalaraté at this point in the story?

Thatch is dried hay. People use thick bundles of thatch to make roofs. Thatch roofs keep out the rain and cold very well. You can still see thatched-roof buildings today in the United Kingdom. One of the most famous is the Globe Theater in London.

ember a bit of burning wood from a fire

COMPARING LITERARY WORKS | **Apply the Skills**

The Coming of Asin *collected by The United Nations Women's Guild*

Directions Choose the letter of the best answer or write the answer using complete sentences.

Comprehension: Identifying Facts

1. Why do the villagers mock and abuse Asin?

A They do not like his looks.

B They do not understand his language.

C They are afraid of his powers.

D They admire his strength and courage.

2. Why does the chief's daughter want to marry Asin?

3. What does Asin do in the battle with the Matacao?

Comprehension: Putting Ideas Together

4. What do the Master in "The People Could Fly" and Nalaraté have in common?

A They both own many slaves.

B They are both cruel chiefs.

C They both promise to destroy the hero.

D They both learn an important lesson.

5. How is Toby's situation in "The People Could Fly" like Asin's?

6. What do you think is the most important difference between Toby and Asin?

Understanding Literature: Hero

A hero is the leading character in a story, novel, play, or film. In this unit, a hero also means a character with great strength, courage, and power. These heroes are also admired for their noble qualities.

7. Which of Asin's qualities and actions make him a hero?

8. Who do you think is a greater hero, Asin or Toby? Explain the reasons for your opinion.

Critical Thinking

9. Why did Toby and Asin choose to remain in places where they were abused? Explain your thinking.

Thinking Creatively

10. How would you have reacted if Asin had arrived in your hometown one day? Explain your answer.

Grammar Check

There are several rules for the titles of artistic and literary works.

- Capitalize the first word of a title.
- Capitalize all important words in a title. Do not capitalize articles, or conjunctions of less than four letters.
- Titles of short poems, songs, articles, and short stories are written in italics.
- Titles of books, plays, movies, paintings, epic poems, and periodicals are written inside quotation marks.

Make any necessary changes to each title.

1 war and peace (novel)

2 jingle bells (song)

3 beowulf (epic poem)

4 singin' in the rain (movie)

Vocabulary Builder

Each of these past-tense verbs appears in the story: *mocked, tolerated, punished, abused, blamed, clapped,* and *demonstrated*. Use each verb correctly in a sentence.

Writing on Your Own

Write a short essay comparing the importance of the setting in "The People Could Fly" and "The Coming of Asin." Consider these questions:

- Where and when does each tale take place?
- Could the same story have happened in a different setting? Why or why not?
- How does the setting affect the characters and events?

Listening and Speaking

Write and deliver a monologue. Choose one of the following:

- Asin speaks to the people after they choose him as their chief.
- Nalaraté tells his friends how and why he will destroy Asin.

Your monologue should include specific details from the story. Use your voice dramatically to deliver your monologue to the class.

Media and Viewing

Work with a partner to design a comic strip based on "The Coming of Asin." Share the tasks of writing the dialogue and drawing the pictures. Study comic strips online or in the daily newspapers for models. Each strip should include four panels.

Unit 6 SPELLING WORKSHOP

Vowel Sounds in Unstressed Syllables

In many words, the vowel sound in certain syllables is not clear. These indistinct vowel sounds come in unstressed syllables. The sound "uh," for example, provides a spelling challenge.

That Troublesome "Uh" Sound

Most people can easily spell words like "reward" or "inherit," because each vowel sounds clear. Many words, though, have at least one syllable with an unclear vowel sound. The *e* in *category*, for example, sounds like the first *i* in *medicine*. This "uh" sound may be spelled by any vowel. It may also occur in more than one syllable, as in <u>a</u>band<u>o</u>n. Study the word list, noting the spelling of vowels in unstressed syllables.

Practice

Each scrambled Word List word includes one additional vowel. Unscramble the letters. Remove the extra vowel to spell the word correctly.

1. ygertocai
2. aygexon
3. iclatere
4. ndaoaabn
5. cndeeiiam
6. pimlltuay
7. disapeeo
8. deeevince
9. sciidlpneii
10. eeceytrm

Word List
- abandon
- article
- category
- cemetery
- discipline
- episode
- evidence
- medicine
- multiply
- oxygen

WORD FACTORY

Unit 6 SUMMARY

In Unit 6, you read a number of stories from the oral tradition. The oral tradition is the literature of the people. "Oral" refers to speech; these stories were told and retold through the generations. They were never written down until modern times. Each time the story is told, it changes just a little. This is an important part of the oral tradition. The oral tradition includes myths, folktales, and legends.

Recently, people have begun collecting these tales and writing them down. This is why you see the words "retold by" next to some of the author's names. These people are keeping the oral tradition alive for new generations. People of today can read the tales, even if there is no one to tell them.

Storytellers want their stories to be entertaining. Therefore they often give their heroes magical powers. They describe events that could not take place in the real world. These might include talking animals or flying people. For ordinary people, the real world was often a place of hard work and hard luck. Stories provided an escape from tough realities.

Selections

- "Icarus and Daedalus," by Josephine Preston Peabody, is a Greek myth. It warns mortals not to show off as if they were gods.
- "Tenochtitlan: Inside the Aztec Capital" by Jacqueline Dineen is a nonfiction article. It describes the Aztec capital city and the customs of the people.
- "Uniaí's Son and the Guaraná," retold by Mercedes Dorson, is a legend of the Amazon River people. It tells of the birth of an epic hero.
- "Sun and Moon in a Box" retold by Richard Erdoes and Alfonso Ortiz is a Zuñi myth. It gives an explanation as to why we have winter weather.
- "The People Could Fly" by Virginia Hamilton is an African-American folktale. It describes the magical escape of slaves who are being whipped and beaten.
- "The Coming of Asin," collected by The United Nations Women's Guild, is a Bolivian legend. It describes the arrival of a stranger and his effect on a tribe of people.

Unit 6 REVIEW

Directions Choose the letter of the best answer or write the answer using complete sentences.

Comprehension: Identifying Facts

1. Which selection is a myth?
   - **A** "Tenochtitlan: Inside the Aztec Capital"
   - **B** "Icarus and Daedalus"
   - **C** "The People Could Fly"
   - **D** "The Coming of Asin"
2. Where was the city of Tenochtitlan built?
3. What does Eagle tell Coyote when he gives him the box to carry?
4. Why does Sarah get whipped in "The People Could Fly"?
5. What does Asin look like when he arrives in the village?

Comprehension: Putting Ideas Together

6. Why does Icarus disobey Daedalus?
   - **A** He does not want to leave Crete.
   - **B** He hates Daedalus.
   - **C** He forgets what Daedalus told him.
   - **D** He is afraid to fly.
7. What was it like to be an Aztec farmer in Tenochtitlan?
8. How do Uniaí's brothers guess that she has returned to Noçoquem?
9. How are Coyote and Eagle alike? How are they different?
10. What magic powers does Asin have?

Understanding Literature: The Oral Tradition

The oral tradition includes works that were told and retold before being written. These stories often tell about heroes with magic powers. They feature animals that talk and act like people. They include mischievous tricksters that entertain listeners.

Tales from the oral tradition often teach important lessons about a culture. Some explain a natural feature like the seasons. These are called myths. Some tell stories of heroes who are larger than life. These can be folktales, epics, or legends.

11. How is a written myth like "Icarus and Daedalus" part of the oral tradition?
12. Uniaí's son is only a baby in the story. However, he is already heroic in some ways. Describe what makes him a hero at his very young age.
13. What human traits do you recognize in Coyote and Eagle?

14. What is the theme of "The People Could Fly"?

15. Can Asin be described as an epic hero? Why or why not?

Critical Thinking

16. What kind of legend might someone write about the city of Tenochtitlan? Explain your answer.

17. Can the people in "The People Could Fly" really fly? If not, what does flight mean in the story? Explain your answer.

18. Why do you think Asin changed the dead Pilagá people into birds?

Thinking Creatively

19. Which character in this unit did you admire the most? Which did you like the least? Why?

20. Which story did you most enjoy reading? Why was this one your favorite?

Speak and Listen

Choose a main character from one of the selections in this unit. Make a new tale about this character. Make sure that the events of your tale fit the character's personality. For example, any tale about Coyote should present him as a trickster. Tell your tale to the class.

Writing on Your Own

Write a research report about one of the cultures represented in this unit. Find out more about the culture's tradition of storytelling. Identify other tales from this culture. Share your report with the class.

Beyond Words

Create a bulletin board display for younger students about any one of the selections. Go online to find images, or look through collections in the library for ideas. You may draw your own pictures or take your own photographs. Make your display vivid and colorful. Make sure that it gives a sense of the story.

Test-Taking Tip

When you reread a written answer, imagine that you are someone reading it for the first time. Ask yourself if the ideas and information make sense. Revise your answer to make it clearer and more organized.

Research: Research Report

A research report analyzes information. It presents a clear and accurate picture of a topic or answers questions. Follow the steps outlined in this workshop to write your own research report.

Assignment Write a research report about an issue that interests or affects you in some way.

Using the Form
You may use elements of this form in these types of writing:
- news articles
- lab reports
- persuasive essays
- biographies

What to Include Your research report should feature the following elements:

- an overall focus or main idea to be analyzed
- information gathered from multiple sources
- a thesis statement giving your viewpoint or perspective
- a clear organization and smooth transitions
- facts and details to support each main point
- visuals to support key ideas
- accurate, complete citations identifying sources according to an accepted format
- error-free writing, including the correct use of personal pronouns

Prewriting

Choosing Your Topic

To choose the right topic to research, use this strategy:

Newswatch and Notebook Browse Look through recent magazines or newspapers, listen to the news, and review your notebooks. List current events, issues, and subjects of interest. Write questions about them. Choose your topic from one of these ideas.

Narrowing Your Topic

Make sure your topic is narrow enough to cover in a short report. For example, "illiteracy" is too big of a topic for a research paper. You can narrow the topic by asking focused questions. Example: "How serious a problem has illiteracy become in America?"

Six Traits of Writing:
Ideas message, details, and purpose

Gathering Details

Use a variety of primary and secondary sources. Primary sources are firsthand or original accounts. They include eyewitness statements and interviews. Secondary sources are written by people who did not witness events firsthand. They include newspaper and encyclopedia articles and reference books. Fact-check information from a reliable Internet source whenever possible against printed sources.

Take notes. Use one or more of these strategies to take notes:

- Use index cards. Write one note per card and note the source and page number. It is very helpful to be able to find things again when you want to.
- Photocopy articles and copyright pages. Highlight important information such as acknowledgments.
- Print articles from the Internet. Make sure to print the URL so you can find the page again. You can also copy Internet articles directly into a "notes" folder.

You will use these notes to help you write your report. Copying directly from sources without citing them is called plagiarism. Plagiarism means the theft of someone's words and ideas. It is very easy for teachers to notice plagiarism from Internet sources.

Source Card

Papp, Joseph and Kirkland,
Elizabeth
Shakespeare Alive!
New York: Bantam Books, 1998

Note Card

Education
Papp, p. 5
Most of the common people in
Shakespeare's time could not read.

Writing Your Draft

Shaping Your Writing

Develop a main idea or thesis. Review your prewriting notes to determine the overall focus of your report. Write a single sentence expressing your main idea. This sentence is called a thesis statement.

Example:
Whales are among the most intelligent mammals on Earth.

As you draft, refer to your thesis statement to help keep your report focused.

Outline Format
Thesis Statement
I. First main point
A. First supporting detail
B. Second supporting detail
II. Second main point
A. First supporting detail
B. Second supporting detail

Make an outline. Group your prewriting notes by category. Use Roman numerals (I, II, III) to number your most important points. Under each Roman numeral, use capital letters (A, B, C) for the supporting details. Develop your draft by turning the notes from your outline into complete sentences.

Providing Elaboration

Include visuals that will support your main ideas. Charts and visual aids help give detailed information without interrupting the flow of the text. Explain what each visual proves. Direct readers to refer to these graphic aids as needed.

Six Traits of Writing:
Organization order, ideas tied together

Find points for clarification. When you use new words you learned during the research stage, define them for readers. Explain and give examples when you write about facts that readers might not understand.

Revising

Revising Your Overall Structure

Analyze your organization. After drafting, look over your draft. Look at your organization to see if it matches your outline. Stop at the end of each paragraph and refer to your outline. Follow these steps:

1. Mark each paragraph with the Roman numeral and capital letter from your outline. Write a word or phrase to identify the subject of the paragraph.
2. All paragraphs with the same Roman numeral should appear together. If they do not, decide whether the new order of ideas is an improvement. If it is not, correct it.

Six Traits of Writing:
Sentence Fluency smooth rhythm and flow

Revising Your Sentences

Vary sentence length. To add interest to your writing, vary the length of your sentences. Underline your sentences in alternating colors so you can easily see differences in length.

Editing and Proofreading

Review your draft for errors in grammar, spelling, and punctuation. Correct the mistakes. You may want to ask a classmate to proofread your report for these errors.

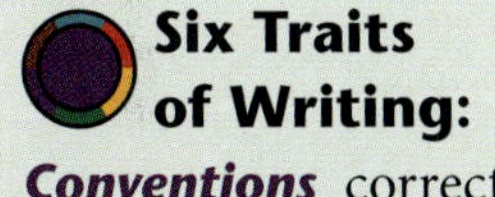

Six Traits of Writing:
Conventions correct grammar, spelling, and mechanics

Focus on citations: Cite the sources for quotations, facts, and ideas that are not your own. Citations appear in parentheses directly after the information cited. Include the author's last name and the page number.

Publishing and Presenting

Create a reference list. Create a bibliography or works cited list of your sources. Check with your teacher to find out which format he or she prefers.

Give an oral presentation. Use your research report as the basis for an oral presentation on your topic. Keep your audience in mind. Prepare your presentation and revise accordingly.

Reflecting on Your Writing

Writer's Journal Write your thoughts on the experience of writing a research report. Begin by answering these questions:

- Which revising strategy did you find most effective? Explain.
- What did you learn about the topic you chose?

Appendix A: Graphic Organizers

Graphic organizers are like maps. They help guide you through literature. They can also help you plan or "map out" your own stories, research, or presentations.

1. Character Analysis Guide

This graphic organizer helps you learn more about a character in a selection.

To use: Choose a character. List four traits of that character. Write down an event from the selection that shows each character trait.

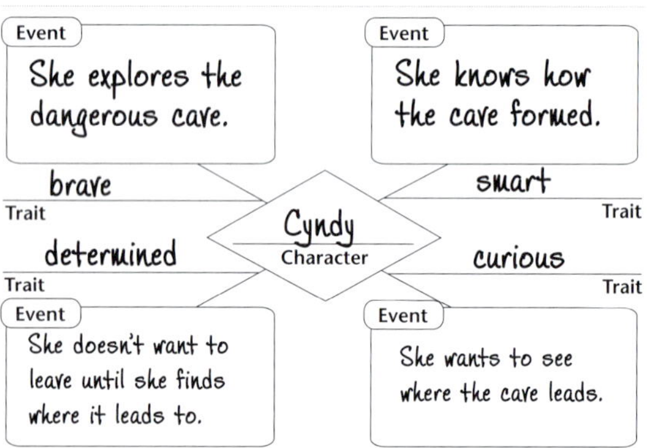

2. Story Map

This graphic organizer helps you summarize a story that you have read or plan your own story.

To use: List the title, setting, and characters. Describe the main problem of the story and the events that explain the problem. Then write how the problem is solved.

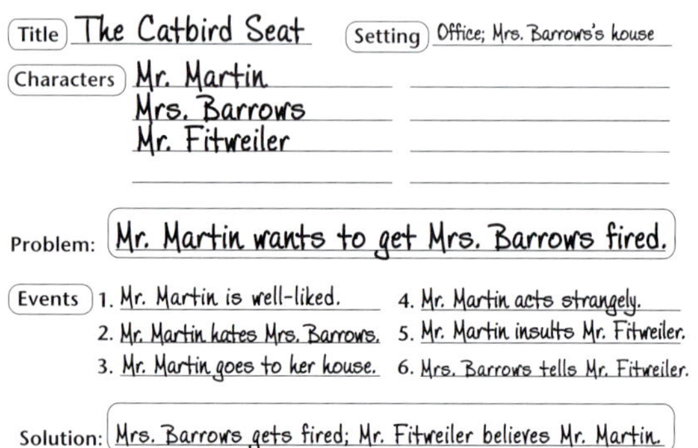

3. Main Idea Graphic (Umbrella)

This graphic organizer helps you determine the main idea of a selection or of a paragraph in the selection.

To use: List the main idea of a selection. Then, write the details that show or support the main idea of the story.

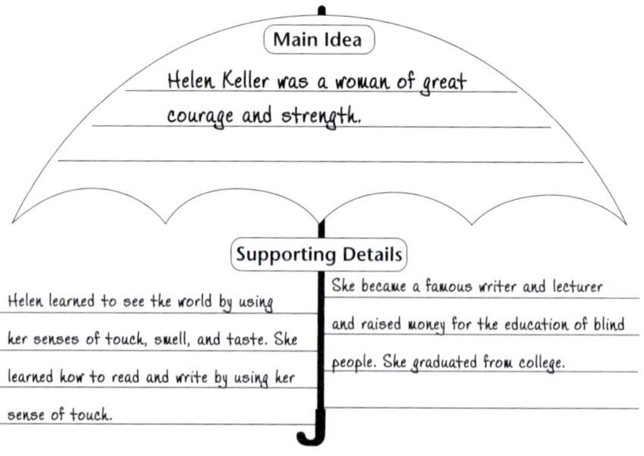

4. Main Idea Graphic (Table)

This graphic organizer is another way to determine the main idea of a selection or of a paragraph in the selection. Just like a table is held up by four strong legs, a main idea is held up or supported by many details.

To use: Write the main idea of a selection or paragraph on the tabletop. Then, write the details that show or support the main idea of the selection or paragraph on the table legs.

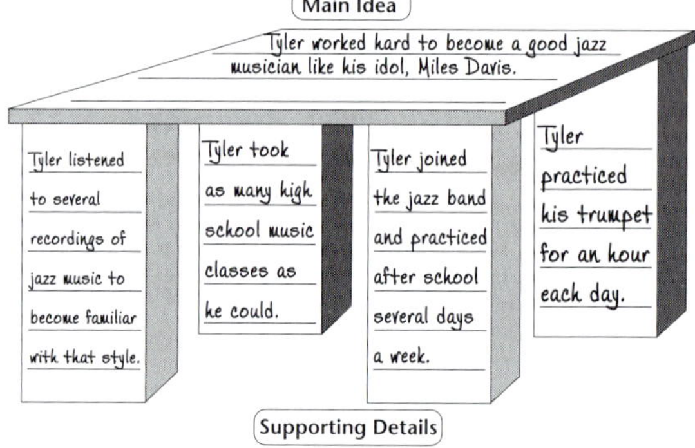

5. Main Idea Graphic (Details)

This graphic organizer is also a way to determine the main idea of a selection or of a paragraph in the selection. If the main idea of a selection or paragraph is not clear, add the details together to find it.

To use: First, list the supporting details of the selection or paragraph. Then, write one sentence that summarizes all the events. That is the main idea of the story.

6. Venn Diagram

This graphic organizer can help you compare and contrast two stories, characters, events, or topics.

To use: List the things that are common to both stories, events, characters, and so on in the "similarities" area between the circles. List the differences on the parts that do not overlap.

What is being compared? ______________

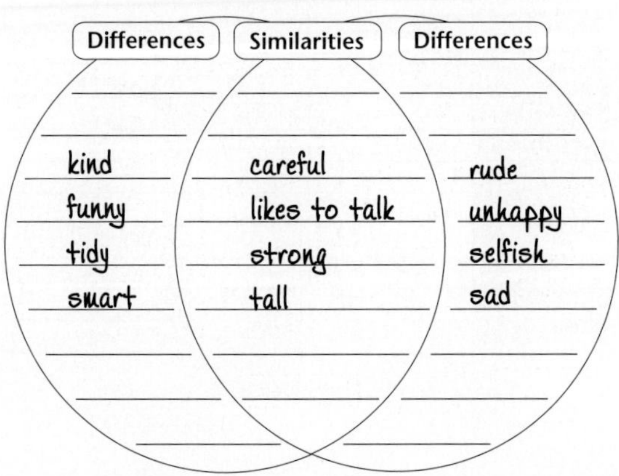

7. Sequence Chain

This graphic organizer outlines a series of events in the order in which they happen. This is helpful when summarizing the plot of a story. This graphic organizer may also help you plan your own story.

To use: Fill in the box at the top with the title of the story. Then, in the boxes below, record the events in the order in which they happen in the story. Write a short sentence in each box and only include the major events of the story.

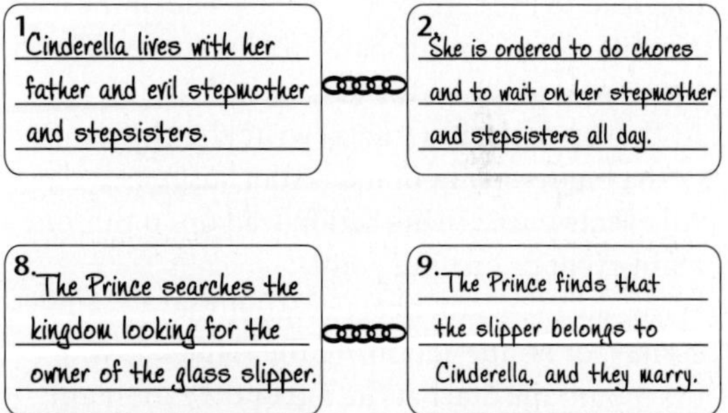

8. Concept Map

This graphic organizer helps you to organize supporting details for a story or research topic.

To use: Write the topic in the center of the graphic organizer. List ideas that support the topic on the lines. Group similar ideas and details together.

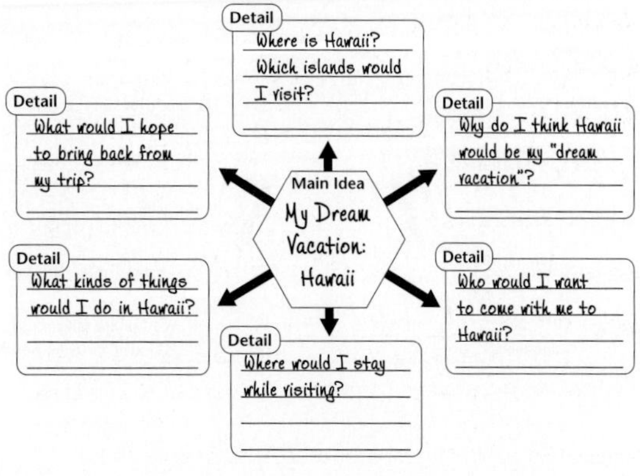

9. Plot Mountain

This graphic organizer helps you organize the events of a story or plot. There are five parts in a story's plot: the exposition, the rising action, the climax, the falling action, and the resolution (or denouement). These parts represent the beginning, middle, and end of the selection.

To use:

- Write the exposition, or how the selection starts, at the left base of the mountain. What is the setting? Who are the characters?
- Then, write the rising action, or the events that lead to the climax, on the left side of the mountain. Start at the base and list the events in time order going up the left side.
- At the top of the mountain, write the climax, or the highest point of interest or suspense. All events in the rising action lead up to this one main event or turning point.
- Write the events that happen after the climax, or falling action, on the right side of the mountain. Start at the top of the mountain, or climax, and put the events in time order going down the right-hand side.
- Finally, write the resolution, or denouement, at the right base of the mountain. The resolution explains how the problem, or conflict, in the story is solved or how the story ends.

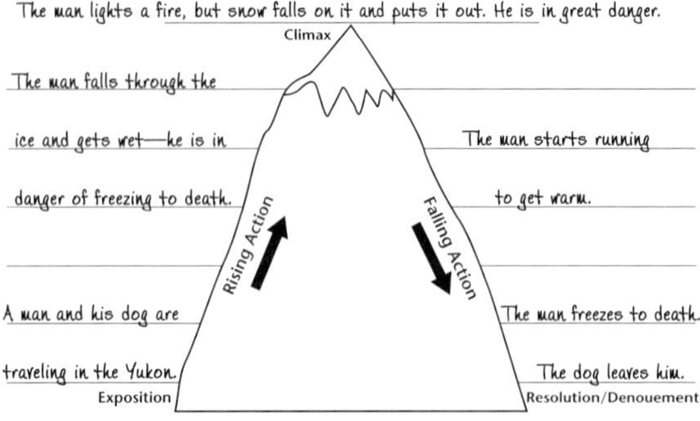

10. Structured Overview

This graphic organizer shows you how a main idea branches out in a selection.

To use: Write the main idea of a selection in the top box. Then, branch out and list events and details that support the main idea. Continue to branch off more boxes as needed to fill in the details of the story.

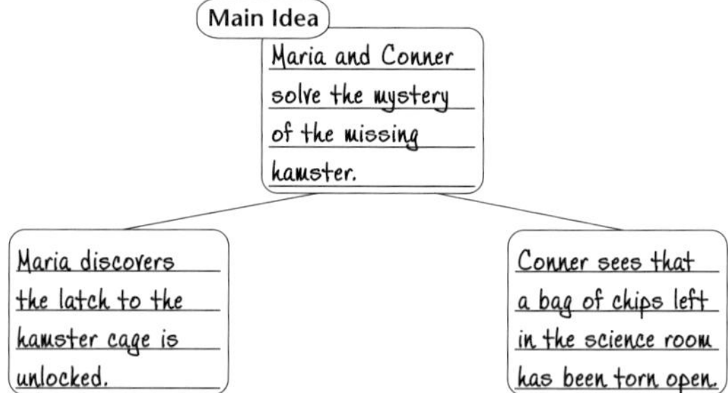

11. Semantic Table

This graphic organizer can help you understand the differences among words that have similar meanings.

To use: Choose a topic. List nouns for that topic in the top row. Put adjectives that describe your topic in the first column. Then, fill in the rest of the grid by checking those adjectives that are appropriate for the nouns. That way, in your writing, you can use words that make sense for your story.

Topic: Homes

Adjectives ↓ Nouns →	apartment	4-bedroom home	cabin
large	—	✔	—
expensive	—	✔	—
quiet	—	✔	✔

12. Prediction Guide

This graphic organizer can be used to predict, or try to figure out, how a selection might end. Before finishing a selection, fill in this guide.

To use: List the time, place, and characters in the selection. Write what the problem, or conflict, is in the story. Then, try to predict possible endings or solutions. Compare your predictions with others.

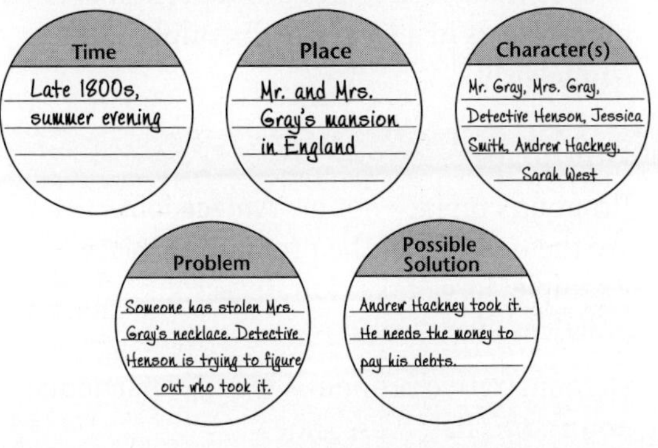

13. Semantic Line

This graphic organizer can help you think of synonyms for words that are used too often in writing.

To use: At the end of each line, write two overused words that mean the opposite. Then, fill in the lines with words of similar meaning. In the example below, the opposite words are *beautiful* and *ugly.* Words that are closer in meaning to beautiful are at the top. Words that are closer in meaning to ugly are at the bottom. The word *plain* falls in the middle.

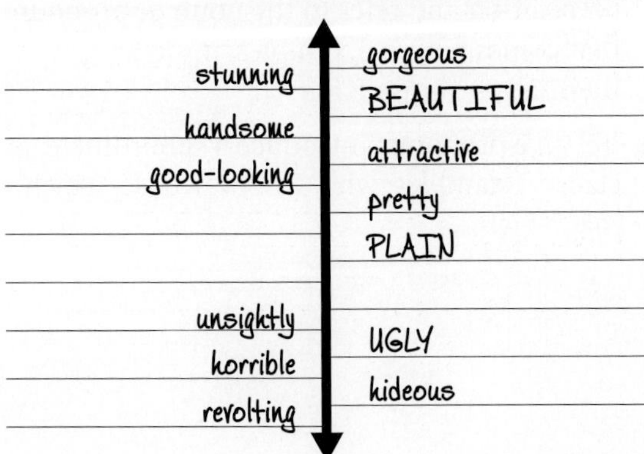

14. KWL Chart

This graphic organizer can help you learn about a topic before you start reading a selection or conducting research.

To use: Before you start reading a selection or conducting research, fill in the organizer. Write the topic on the line. In the first column, write what you already *know* (K) about your topic. Next, list what you *want* (W) to know about your topic in the next column. Then, as you start reading a selection or conducting research, write down what you *learn* (L) in the last column.

Topic: Mount Everest

K What I Know	W What I Want to Know	L What I Have Learned
It's a tall mountain in Asia. People may have tried to climb it. It's part of a larger mountain chain. It's one of the most famous mountains in the world.	How tall is it? Is it the tallest? What mountain chain is it part of?	It is the tallest in the world. It is part of the Himalayas. People have climbed it before. Some people have died trying.

Appendix B: Grammar

Parts of Speech

Adjectives

- Adjectives describe nouns and pronouns. They answer *What kind? Which one? How many?* or *How much*? Example: The *new* book costs *five* dollars.
- Comparative adjectives compare two nouns and usually end in *–er.* Example: *newer*
- Superlative adjectives compare three or more nouns and usually end in *–est.* Example: *newest*

Adverbs

- Adverbs modify verbs, adjectives, and other adverbs. They answer *When? How? How often?* and *How long?* Many adverbs end in *–ly.* Example: She laughed *loudly.*

Conjunctions

- Conjunctions connect parts of a sentence.
- Coordinating conjunctions connect two equal parts of a sentence using words like *and, but, nor, or, for, yet, so,* and *as well as.* Example: Do you want milk *or* water?
- Correlative conjunctions are used in pairs and connect equal parts of a sentence. Correlative conjunctions are *both/and, neither/nor, either/or, but/also.* Example: The teenagers had *neither* the time *nor* the money.
- Subordinating conjunctions connect two unequal parts of a sentence using words like *after, although, before, because, since, if, unless, while.* Example: *Since* you are arriving late, we will eat dinner at 7 p.m.

Interjections

- Interjections are words or phrases that show strong feeling, often followed by exclamation points. Examples: Wow! Ouch! Oops!

Nouns

- A noun names a person, place, thing, or idea.
- Proper nouns are names that are capitalized. Examples: Susan, New York

Prepositions

- Prepositions relate nouns and pronouns to other words in a sentence. Examples: above, from, with

Pronouns

- Pronouns replace nouns. Antecedents are the nouns that the pronouns replace. Example: Jorge takes karate lessons, and *he* practices every week.
- Demonstrative pronouns identify particular nouns: *this* hat, *those* shoes
- Indefinite pronouns do not refer to particular nouns. Examples: all, everyone, none
- Interrogative pronouns begin questions. Examples: who, which, what
- Personal pronouns refer to people or things. Examples: I, me, you, it, he, she, we, us, they, him, her, them
- Possessive pronouns show ownership. Examples: my, mine, his, hers, its, our, yours, their, ours, theirs
- Reflexive pronouns follow a verb or preposition and refer to the noun or pronoun that comes before. Examples: myself, themselves, himself, herself
- Relative pronouns introduce a subordinate clause. Examples: who, whom, whose, which, that, what

Verbs

- Verbs show action or express states of being.
- If the verbs are *transitive*, they link the action to something or someone. Example: John *hit* the ball. Action verbs that are *intransitive* do not link the action to something or someone. Example: The ball *flew*.
- Linking verbs connect a subject with a word or words that describe it. Some linking verbs are *am, are, was, were, is,* and *be*. Example: Susan *is* student council president.

Grammar Glossary

Active and Passive Voice

- Active voice is when the subject is *doing* the action. A sentence written in active voice is often shorter and easier to understand. Example: Jane drove the car to school.
- Passive voice is when the subject *receives* the action. A sentence written in passive voice can be awkward. Use a passive sentence only when the doer is unknown or unnecessary. Example: The car was driven by Jane.

Antecedent

- An antecedent is the noun or pronoun that a pronoun refers to in a sentence. Example: *Kevin* ran for Student Council so that *he* could help improve the school. *Kevin* is the antecedent for the pronoun *he*.

Appositives

- An appositive is a noun or pronoun that follows another noun or pronoun. An appositive renames or adds detail about the word. Example: Mr. Smith, *our principal*, is a great leader.

Clauses

- A clause is a group of words that contains a subject and a verb. There are independent and dependent clauses.
- An independent clause can stand alone because it expresses a complete thought. Example: Our dog eats twice a day. She also walks two miles a day. Two independent clauses can also be joined to form one sentence by using a comma and a coordinating conjunction, such as *and, but, nor, or, for, yet, so,* and *as well as*. Example: Our dog eats twice a day, *and* she walks two miles a day.
- A dependent clause cannot stand alone because it does not express a complete thought. Example: Because exercise is good for pets. This is a fragment or incomplete sentence. To fix this, combine a dependent clause with an independent clause. Example: Our dog walks two miles a day because exercise is good for pets.

Complements

- A complement completes the meaning of a verb. There are three types of complements: direct objects, indirect objects, and subject complements.
- A direct object is a word or group of words that receives the action of the verb. Example: Jane set the table. (*The table* is the complement or direct object of the verb *set*.)
- An indirect object is a word or group of words that follow the verb and tell for whom or what the action is done. An indirect object always comes before a direct object in a sentence. Example: Setting the table saved her mother some time. (*Her mother* is the complement or indirect object of the verb *saved*.)
- A subject complement is a word or group of words that further identify the subject of a sentence. A subject complement always follows a linking verb. Example: Buddy is the best dog. (The word *dog* is the complement of the subject *Buddy*.)

Contractions

- A contraction is two words made into one by replacing one or more letters with an apostrophe. Examples: *didn't* (did not), *you're* (you are)

Double Negatives

- A double negative is the use of two negative words, such as *no* or *not*, in a sentence. To fix a double negative, make one word positive. Incorrect: She *did not* get *no* dessert after dinner. Correct: She did not get *any* dessert after dinner.

Fragments

- A fragment is not a complete sentence. It may have a subject and verb, but it does not express a complete thought. Incorrect: The leaves that fell in the yard. Correct: The leaves that fell in the yard needed to be raked.

Gerunds

- A gerund is a verb with an *–ing* ending. It is used as a noun. Example: *Golfing* is fun! Here, *golfing* is a noun and the subject of the sentence.

Infinitives

- An infinitive is the word *to* plus the present tense of a verb. An infinitive can be a noun, adjective, or adverb in a sentence. Example: *To write* was her dream job. Here, *To write* is the infinitive, and it serves as a noun.

Modifiers

- A modifier is a word or group of words that change the meanings of other words in the sentence. Adjectives and adverbs are modifiers.
- A dangling or misplaced modifier is a group of descriptive words that is not near the word it modifies. This confuses the reader. Incorrect: Tucked up in the closet, Sarah found her grandma's photographs. *Tucked up in the closet* modifies Sarah. However, the photographs, not Sarah, are tucked up in the closet! Correct: Sarah found her grandma's photographs tucked up in the closet.

Parallel Structure

- Parallel structure is the use of words to balance ideas that are equally important. Incorrect: In the winter, I love to skate, snowmen, and to ski. Correct: In the winter, I love *to skate, to make* snowmen, and *to ski*.

Phrases

- A phrase is a group of words that does not have both a subject and a verb. Types of phrases include gerund phrases, infinitive phrases, and participial phrases.
- A gerund phrase has a gerund plus any modifiers and complements. The entire phrase serves as a noun. Example: Playing basketball with his friends was Trevor's favorite pastime. *Playing basketball with his friends* is the gerund phrase.
- An infinitive phrase has an infinitive plus any modifiers and complements. The entire phrase serves as a noun, adjective, or adverb in a sentence. Example: My mother liked to bake cookies on the weekend. *To bake cookies on the weekend* is the infinitive phrase.
- A participial phrase has a participle (a verb in its present form *[–ing]* or past form *[–ed or –en]*) plus all of its modifiers and complements. The entire phrase serves as an adjective in a sentence. Example: Wearing the robes of a king, Luis read his lines perfectly during play tryouts. *Wearing the robes of a king* is the participial phrase, and it modifies or describes the subject, Luis.

Plural Nouns

- A plural shows more than one of a particular noun. Use the following rules to create the plural form. Remember that there are exceptions to many spelling rules that you must simply memorize.
- Add *–s* to most singular nouns. Example: table/tables
- Add *–es* to a noun if it ends in *–ch, –sh, –s, –x,* and *–z.* Example: church/churches
- If a noun ends with a vowel and a *–y,* add an *–s* to make the plural. Example: donkey/donkeys
- If a noun ends with a consonant and a *–y,* drop the *–y* and add an *–ies* to make the plural. Example: puppy/puppies
- If a noun ends in an *–f* or *–fe,* change the *–f* or *–fe* to a *v* and add *–es.* Example: knife/knives
- If a noun ends in an *–o,* sometimes you add *–es* and sometimes you add *–s.* Look in a dictionary to find out. Examples: potato/potatoes, radio/radios

Possessives

- A possessive noun shows ownership of an object, action, or idea. A possessive noun ends in *'s.* Example: Susan's book
- A possessive pronoun also shows ownership of an object, action, or idea. Example: his glove

Pronoun–Antecedent Agreement

- Pronoun-antecedent agreement occurs when the pronoun matches the antecedent (the word it refers to) in gender and number.
- To agree in gender:
  –Replace the name of a male person with a masculine pronoun. Example: *Jake* ran down the field, and *he* scored.

  –Replace the name of a female person with a feminine pronoun. Example: *Ana* read "The Most Dangerous Game," and *she* loved it.

  –Replace singular names with *it* or *its.* Example: The *kitten* ran through the room, and *it* pounced on the ball.

  –Replace plural names with *they, them,* or *their.* Example: The *tenth graders* came into the gym, and *they* played volleyball.
- To agree in number:
  –Make the pronoun singular if its antecedent is singular. Example: *Michael* told *himself* that he did the right thing.

  –Make the pronoun plural if its antecedent is plural. Example: The hungry *teenagers* ordered sandwiches for *themselves.*

Run-on Sentences

- A run-on sentence is the combination of two or more sentences without proper punctuation.
- To correct a run-on sentence, you can break it into two or more sentences by using capital letters and periods. Incorrect: The house was built in 1960 it needs new windows. Correct: The house was built in 1960. It needs new windows.
- You can also correct a run-on sentence by adding a comma and a coordinating conjunction to separate the sentences. Correct: The house was built in 1960, *so* it needs new windows.
- Another way to correct a run-on sentence is by adding a semicolon between the sentences. A semicolon should stand alone and should not have a coordinating conjunction after it. Correct: The house was built in 1960; it needs new windows.

Sentence Construction

- A simple sentence has one independent clause that includes a subject and a predicate. Example: The afternoon was warm and sunny.
- A compound sentence has two or more independent clauses joined by a comma and a coordinating conjunction or joined by a semicolon. Example: The afternoon was warm and sunny, so we decided to drive to the beach.
- A complex sentence has one independent clause and one or more dependent clauses. Example: We are going to the beach if you want to come along.
- A compound–complex sentence has two or more independent clauses joined by a comma and a coordinating conjunction. It has at least one dependent clause. Example: Although the morning was cold and damp, the afternoon was warm and sunny, so we decided to drive to the beach.

Sentence Types

- You can use a declarative sentence, an exclamatory sentence, an imperative sentence, or an interrogative sentence in writing.
- A declarative sentence tells us something about a person, place, or thing. This type of sentence ends with a period. Example: Martin Luther King Jr. fought for civil rights.
- An exclamatory sentence shows strong feeling or surprise. This type of sentence ends with an exclamation point. Example: I can't believe the price of gasoline!
- An imperative sentence gives commands. This type of sentence ends with a period. (Note: The subject of an imperative sentence is the implied "you.") Example: Please read chapter two by next Monday.
- An interrogative sentence asks a question. This type of sentence ends with a question mark. Example: Will you join us for dinner?

Subjects and Predicates

- The subject of a sentence names the person or thing doing the action. The subject contains a noun or a pronoun. Example: The students created posters and brochures. The subject of this sentence is *The students*. The predicate of this sentence (see definition below) is *created posters and brochures*.
- The predicate of a sentence tells what the person or thing is doing. The predicate contains a verb. Example: The fans waited for the hockey game to begin. The predicate of this sentence is *waited for the hockey game to begin*. The subject of this sentence is *The fans*.

Punctuation Guidelines

Apostrophe

- Shows ownership (possessive nouns): Kelly's backpack
- Shows plural possessive nouns: The five students' success was due to hard work.
- Shows missing letters in contractions: that's (that is)

Colon

- Introduces a list after a complete sentence: We learned about planets: Mars, Venus, and Jupiter.
- Adds or explains more about a complete sentence: Lunch was one option: pizza.

- Follows the salutation in a formal letter or in a business letter: Dear Mr. Jackson:
- Separates the hour and the minute: 2:15
- Introduces a long quotation: Lincoln wrote: "Four score and seven years ago . . ."

Comma

- Separates three or more items in a series: We planted corn, squash, and tomatoes.
- Joins two independent clauses when used with a coordinating conjunction: Sam and Raul did their homework, and then they left.
- Separates a city and state: Los Angeles, California
- Separates a day and year: October 15, 2006
- Follows the salutation and closing in a friendly letter: Dear Shanice, Love always,
- Follows the closing in a business letter: Sincerely,
- Sets off a restrictive phrase clause: Angela, the youngest runner, won the race.
- Sets off an introductory phrase or clause: Before he started the experiment, Jason put on safety glasses.

Dash

- Sets off an explanation in a sentence: The three poets—Langston Hughes, Robert Frost, and William Carlos Williams—are modernist poets.
- Shows a pause or break in thought: After years away, I returned—and found lots had changed.

Ellipses

- Show that words have been left out of a text: Our dog dove into the lake . . . and swam to shore.

Exclamation Point

- Shows emotion: Our team won!

Hyphen

- Divides a word at the end of a line: We en-joyed the beaches.
- Separates a compound adjective before a noun to make its meaning clearer: much-loved book
- Separates a compound number: thirty-three.
- Separates a fraction when used as an adjective: two-thirds full

Period

- Marks the end of a statement or command: July is the warmest month.
- Follows most abbreviations: Mrs., Dr., Inc., Jr.

Question Mark

- Marks the end of a question: How many eggs are left?

Quotation Marks

- Enclose the exact words of a speaker: He said, "I'll buy that book."
- Enclose the titles of short works: "Dover Beach," "America the Beautiful"

Semicolon

- Separates items in a series when commas are within the items: We went to Sioux Falls, South Dakota; Des Moines, Iowa; and Kansas City, Kansas.
- Joins two independent clauses that are closely related: We went to the movie; they came with us.

Capitalization Guidelines

Capitalize:

- the first word of a sentence: The teacher asked her students to read.
- the first word and any important words in a title: *To Kill a Mockingbird*
- all proper nouns: Marlon Smith, Atlanta, March
- the pronoun *I*
- languages: English, French
- abbreviations: Mrs., Sgt., FDR, EST

Commonly Confused Words

accept, except

- *Accept* (verb) means "to receive." Example: The children will *accept* ice cream.
- *Except* (preposition) means "leaving out." Example: The children enjoyed all flavors *except* strawberry.

affect, effect

- *Affect* (verb) means "to have an effect on." Example: This storm will *affect* our town.
- *Effect* (noun) means "a result or an outcome." Example: The *effect* was a struggling local economy.

its, it's

- *Its* (adjective) is the possessive form of "it." Example: Our hamster liked to run on the wheel inside *its* cage.
- *It's* is a contraction for "it is." Example: *It's* a long time before lunch.

lie, lay

- *Lie* (verb) means "to rest." Example: Jenny had a headache, so she needed to *lie* down.
- *Lay* (verb) means "to place." Example: Jamal went to *lay* his baseball glove on the bench.

lose, loose

- *Lose* (verb) means "to misplace or not find something." Example: I always *lose* my sunglasses when I go to the beach.
- *Loose* (adjective) means "free or without limits." Example: Someone let Sparky *loose* from his leash.

than, then

- *Than* (conjunction) shows a comparison. Example: You are older *than* I am.
- *Then* (adverb) means "at that time." Example: Will turned the doorknob and *then* slowly opened the door.

their, there, they're

- *Their* (pronoun) shows possession. Example: This is *their* house.
- *There* (adverb) means "place." Example: Sit over *there*.
- *They're* is a contraction for "they are." Example: *They're* coming over for dinner.

to, too, two

- *To* (preposition) shows purpose, movement, or connection. Example: We drove *to* the store.
- *Too* (adverb) means "also or more than wanted." Example: I, *too*, felt it was *too* hot to go outside.
- *Two* is a number. Example: Ava has *two* more years of high school.

your, you're

- *Your* (adjective) shows possession and means "belonging to you." Example: Take off *your* hat, please.
- *You're* is a contraction for "you are." Example: *You're* the best artist in the school.

Appendix C: Writing

Types of Writing

Before you can begin the writing process, you need to understand the types, purposes, and formats of different types of writing.

Descriptive Writing

Descriptive writing covers all writing genres. Description can be used to tell a story, to analyze and explain research, or to persuade. Descriptive writing uses images and colorful details to "paint a picture" for the reader.

Five Senses in Descriptive Writing

Consider the five senses in your descriptive writing: sight, smell, touch, sound, and taste. Using your senses to help describe an object, place, or person makes your writing more interesting. Before you begin, ask yourself the following:

- How does something look? Describe the color, size, and/or shape. What is it like?
- What smell or smells are present? Describe any pleasant or unpleasant smells. Compare the smells to other smells you know.
- How does something feel? Think about textures. Also think about emotions or feelings that result from the touching.
- What sounds do you hear? Describe the volume and the pitch. Are the sounds loud and shrill, or quiet and peaceful? What do the sounds remind you of?
- What does something taste like? Compare it to a taste you know, good or bad.

Expository Writing

Expository writing explains and informs through essays, articles, reports, and instructions. Like descriptive writing, it covers all writing genres. The purpose of this type of writing is to give more information about a subject. This can be done in many ways. The two most common formats in the study of literature are the compare and contrast paper and the cause and effect paper.

- Compare and Contrast Paper—This paper shows the similarities and differences of two or more characters, objects, settings, situations, writing styles, problems, or ideas.
- Cause and Effect Paper—This paper explains why certain things happen or how specific actions led to a result. A cause and effect paper can be set up by writing about the result (effect) first, followed by the events that led up to it (causes). Or, the paper can trace the events (causes), in order, that lead up to the result (effect).

Narrative Writing

Narrative writing tells a story. The story can be true (nonfiction) or made up (fiction). Narratives entertain or inform readers about a series of events. Poetry, stories, diaries, letters, biographies, and autobiographies are all types of narrative writing.

Key Elements in Narrative Writing

Think about the type of narrative you want to write and these key elements of your story:

- Characters: Who are the major and minor characters in the story? What do they look like? How do they act?

- Dialogue: What conversations take place among the characters? How does the dialogue show the reader something about the personalities of the characters?
- Setting: Where and when do the events take place? How does the setting affect the plot?
- Plot: What events happen in the story? In what order do the events occur? What is the problem that the main character is struggling with? How is the problem solved?

There are two common ways to set up your narrative paper. You can start at the beginning and tell your story in chronological order, or in the order in which the events happened. Or, you can start at the ending of your story and, through a flashback, tell what events led up to the present time.

Persuasive Writing

Persuasive writing is used when you want to convince your reader that your opinion on a topic is the right one. The goal of this paper is to have your reader agree with what you say. To do this, you need to know your topic well, and you need to give lots of reasons and supporting details. Editorials (opinion writing) in the newspaper, advertisements, and book reviews are all types of persuasive writing.

Key Elements of Persuasive Writing

Choosing a topic that you know well and that you feel strongly about is important for persuasive writing. The feelings or emotions that you have about the topic will come through in your paper and make a stronger argument. Also, be sure that you have a good balance between appealing to the reader's mind (using facts, statistics, experts, and so on) and appealing to the reader's heart (using words that make them feel angry, sad, and so on). Think about these key elements:

- Topic: Is your topic a good one for your audience? Do you know a lot about your topic? Is your topic narrow enough so that you can cover it in a paper?
- Opinion: Is your opinion clear? Do you know enough about the opposite side of your opinion to get rid of those arguments in your paper?
- Reasons: Do you have at least three reasons that explain why you feel the way you do? Are these reasons logical?
- Supporting details or evidence: Do you have facts, statistics, experts, or personal experience that can support each reason?
- Opposing arguments: Can you address the opposite side and get rid of their arguments?
- Conclusion: Can you offer a solution or recommendation to the reader?
- Word choice: Can you find words that set the tone for your opinion? Will these words affect your readers emotionally?

There are two common ways to set up this paper. The first format is a six-paragraph paper: one paragraph for your introduction, three paragraphs for each of your three reasons, one paragraph for the opposing arguments and your responses to them, and one paragraph for your conclusion. Or you can write a five-paragraph paper where you place the opposing arguments and responses to each of your three reasons within the same paragraphs.

Research Report

A research report is an in-depth study of a topic. This type of writing has many uses in all subjects. It involves digging for information in many sources, including books, magazines, newspapers, the Internet, almanacs, encyclopedias, and other places of data. There are many key elements in writing a research report. Choosing a thesis statement, finding support or evidence for that thesis, and citing where you found your information are all important.

There are several uses of a research report in literature. You can explore a writer's life, a particular writing movement, or a certain writer's style. You could also write about a selection.

Business Writing

Business writing has many forms: memos, meeting minutes, brochures, manuals, reports, job applications, contracts, college essays. No matter what the format, the goal of business writing is clear communication. Keep the following key elements in mind when you are doing business writing:

- Format: What type of writing are you doing?
- Purpose: What is the purpose of your writing? Is the purpose clear in your introduction?
- Audience: Are your words and ideas appropriate for your audience?
- Organization: Are your ideas well-organized and easy to follow?
- Style: Are your ideas clearly written and to the point?

The Writing Process

The writing process is a little different for each writer and for each writing assignment. However, the goals of writing never change: Writers want to:

- have a purpose for their writing
- get their readers' attention and keep it
- present their ideas clearly
- choose their words carefully

To meet these goals, writers need to move through a writing process. This process allows them to explore, organize, write, revise, and share their ideas. There are five steps to this writing process: prewriting; drafting; revising; editing and proofreading; and publishing and evaluating.

Use the following steps for any writing assignment:

Step 1: Prewriting

Prewriting is where you explore ideas and decide what to write about. Here are some approaches.

Brainstorming

Brainstorming is fast, fun, and full of ideas. Start by stating a topic. Then write down everything you can think of about that topic. Ask questions about the topic. If you are in a group, have one person write everything down. Think of as many words and ideas as you can in a short time. Don't worry about neatness, spelling, or grammar. When you are finished, group words that are similar. These groups may become your supporting ideas.

Graphic Organizers

Graphic organizers are maps that can lead you through your prewriting. They provide pictures or charts that you fill in. Read the descriptions of these organizers in Appendix A, and choose the ones that will help you organize your ideas.

Outline

An outline can help you organize your information. Write your main ideas next to each Roman numeral. Write your supporting details next to the letters under each Roman numeral. Keep your ideas brief and to the point. Here's an example to follow:

Topic for persuasive paper: Lincoln High School should have a swimming pool.

I. Health benefits for students
  A. Weight control
  B. Good exercise
II. Water safety benefits for students
  A. Learn-to-swim programs
  B. Water safety measures to help others
III. School benefits
  A. Swim team
  B. Added rotation for gym class
IV. Community benefits
  A. More physically fit community members
  B. More jobs for community members

Narrowing Your Topic

Narrowing your topic means to focus your ideas on a specific area. You may be interested in writing about Edgar Allan Poe, but that is a broad topic. What about Poe interests you? Think about your purpose for writing. Is your goal to persuade, to explain, or to compare? Narrowing your scope and knowing your purpose will keep you focused.

Note-Taking and Research

Refer to the "How to Use This Book" section at the beginning of this textbook and Appendix D for help with note-taking and research skills.

Planning Your Voice

Your voice is your special way of using language in your writing. Readers can get to know your personality and thoughts by your sentence structure, word choice, and tone. How will your writing tell what you want to say in your own way? How will it be different from the way others write?

Step 2: Drafting

In the drafting step, you will write your paper. Use your brainstorming notes, outline, and graphic organizers from your prewriting stage as your guide. Your paper will need to include an introduction, a body, and a conclusion.

Introduction

The introduction states your topic and purpose. It includes a *thesis statement,* which is a sentence that tells the main idea of your entire paper. The last line of your introduction is a good place for your thesis statement. That way, your reader has a clear idea of the purpose of your paper before starting to read your points.

Your introduction should make people want to read more. Think about what your audience might like. Try one of these methods:

- asking a question
- sharing a brief story
- describing something
- giving a surprising fact
- using an important quotation

When you begin drafting, just write your introduction. Do not try to make it perfect the first time. You can always change it later.

Body

The body of your paper is made up of several paragraphs. Each paragraph also has a topic sentence, supporting details, and a concluding statement or summary. Remember, too, that each paragraph needs to support your thesis statement in your introduction.

- The topic sentence is usually the first sentence of a paragraph. It lets the reader know what your paragraph is going to be about.
- The supporting details of a paragraph are the sentences that support or tell more about your topic sentence. They can include facts, explanations, examples, statistics, and/or experts' ideas.
- The last sentence of your paragraph is a concluding statement or summary. A concluding statement is a judgment. It is based on the facts that you presented in your paragraph. A summary briefly repeats the main ideas of your paragraph. It repeats your idea or ideas in slightly different words. It does not add new information.

Conclusion

The conclusion ties together the main ideas of the paper. If you asked a question in your introduction, the conclusion answers it. If you outlined a problem, your conclusion offers solutions. The conclusion should not simply restate your thesis and supporting points.

Title of the Paper

Make sure to title your paper. Use a title that is interesting, but relates well to your topic.

Step 3: Revising

Now that you've explored ideas and put them into a draft, it's time to revise. During this step, you will rewrite parts or sections of your paper. All good writing goes through many drafts. To help you make the necessary changes, use the checklists below to review your paper.

Overall Paper

- ☑ Do I have an interesting title that draws readers in?
- ☑ Does the title tell my audience what my paper is about?
- ☑ Do I have an introduction, body, and conclusion?
- ☑ Is my paper the correct length?

Introduction

- ☑ Have I used a method to interest my readers?
- ☑ Do I have a thesis statement that tells the main idea of my paper?
- ☑ Is my thesis statement clearly stated?

Body

- ☑ Do I start every paragraph on a new line?
- ☑ Is the first line of every paragraph indented?
- ☑ Does the first sentence (topic sentence) in every paragraph explain the main idea of the paragraph? Does it attract my readers' attention?
- ☑ Do I include facts, explanations, examples, statistics, and/or experts' ideas that support the topic sentence?
- ☑ Do I need to take out any sentences that do not relate to the topic sentence?
- ☑ Do the paragraphs flow in a logical order? Does each point build on the last one?
- ☑ Do good transition words lead readers from one paragraph to the next?

Conclusion

- ☑ Does the conclusion tie together the main ideas of my paper?
- ☑ Does it offer a solution, make a suggestion, or answer any questions that the readers might have?

Writing Style

- ☑ Do I use words and concepts that my audience understands?
- ☑ Is the tone too formal or informal for my audience?
- ☑ Are my sentences the right length for my audience?
- ☑ Do I have good sentence variety and word choice?

Step 4: Editing and Proofreading

During the editing and proofreading step, check your paper or another student's paper for errors in grammar, punctuation, capitalization, and spelling. Use the following checklists to help guide you. Read and focus on one sentence at a time. Cover up everything but the sentence you are reading. Reading from the end of the paper backward also works for some students. Note changes using the proofreader marks shown on the following page. Check a dictionary or style manual when you're not sure about something.

Grammar

- ☑ Is there a subject and a verb in every sentence?
- ☑ Do the subject and verb agree in every sentence?
- ☑ Is the verb tense logical in every sentence?
- ☑ Is the verb tense consistent in every sentence?
- ☑ Have you used interesting, lively verbs?
- ☑ Do all pronouns have clear antecedents?
- ☑ Can repeated or unnecessary words be left out?
- ☑ Are there any run-on sentences that need to be corrected?
- ☑ Does sentence length vary with long and short sentences?

Punctuation

☑ Does every sentence end with the correct punctuation mark?

☑ Are all direct quotations punctuated correctly?

☑ Do commas separate words in a series?

☑ Is there a comma and a coordinating conjunction separating each compound sentence?

☑ Is there a comma after an introductory phrase or clause?

☑ Are apostrophes used correctly in contractions and possessive nouns?

Capitalization

☑ Is the first word of every sentence capitalized?

☑ Are all proper nouns and adjectives capitalized?

☑ Are the important words in the title of the paper capitalized?

Spelling

☑ Are words that sound alike spelled correctly (such as *to, too,* and *two*)?

☑ Is every plural noun spelled correctly?

☑ Are words with *ie* or *ei* spelled correctly?

☑ Is the silent *e* dropped before adding an ending that starts with a vowel?

☑ Is the consonant doubling rule used correctly?

If the paper was typed, make any necessary changes and run the spell-check and grammar-check programs one more time.

Proofreading Marks

Below are some common proofreading marks. Print out your paper and use these marks to correct errors.

Symbol	Meaning
¶	Start new paragraph
⁀	Close up
#	Add a space
∩∪	Switch words or letters
≡	Capitalize this letter
/	Lowercase this letter
ℯ	Omit space, letter, mark, or word
^	Insert space, mark, or word
⊙	Insert a period
^,	Insert a comma
⬭ sp	Spell out
. . . . (stet)	Leave as is (write dots under words)

Step 5: Publishing and Presenting

Once you have made the final text changes, make sure that the overall format of your paper is correct. Follow the guidelines that were set up by your teacher. Here are some general guidelines that are commonly used.

Readability

- Double space all text.
- Use an easy-to-read font such as Times Roman, Comic Sans, Ariel, or New York.
- Use a 12-point type size.
- Make sure that you have met any word, paragraph, or page count guidelines.

Format

- Make at least a one-inch margin around each page.
- Place the title of the paper, your name, your class period, and the date according to your teacher's guidelines. If you need a title page, make sure that you have a separate page with this information. If you do not need a title page, place your name, class period, and date in the upper right-hand corner of the first page. Center the title below that.
- Check to see if your pages need to be numbered. If so, number them in the upper right-hand corner or according to your teacher's guidelines.
- Label any charts and graphics as needed.
- Check that your title and any subheads are in boldface print.
- Check that your paragraphs are indented.

Citations

- Cite direct quotations, paraphrases, and summaries properly. Refer to the Modern Language Association (MLA) or American Psychological Association (APA) rules.
- Punctuate all citations properly. Refer to MLA or APA rules.

Bibliographies

- Include a list of books and other materials you reviewed during your research. This is a reference list only. Below are examples of how you would list a book, magazine article, and Web site using MLA style:

Book:
Author's Last Name, Author's First Name. *Book Title.* Publisher's City: Publisher's Name, Year.

London, Jack. *The Call of the Wild.* New York: Scholastic, 2001.

Magazine:
Author's Last Name, Author's First Name. "Article Title." Magazine Title. Volume Date: Page numbers.

Young, Diane. "At the High End of the River." *Southern Living.* June 2000: 126–131.

Web Site:
Article Title. Date accessed. URL

Circle of Stories. 25 Jan. 2006. <http://www.pbs.org/circleofstories/>

Six Traits of Writing

Good writing is not a miracle. It is not an accident either. Good writing is part science and part art. It is the result of careful thinking and choices. To write well, you need to know about six different traits that determine the quality of writing.

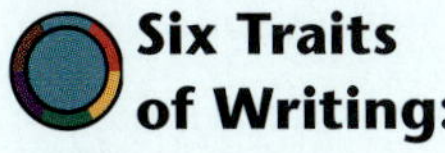

Six Traits of Writing:

Ideas message, details, and purpose

What message do you want to get across? What details are important to get your message across clearly? Ideas are the heart of any writing. So begin the writing process by developing strong, clear ideas. Set off your ideas with details that stand out and catch attention.

Six Traits of Writing:

Organization order, ideas tied together

A piece of writing has a structure or pattern, just like a building. Organize your ideas into a structure that makes sense and fits the ideas well. For example, you may tell about events or steps in order. You may compare two things or explain a solution or an effect. Organization holds writing together and gives shape to ideas.

Six Traits of Writing:

Voice the writer's own language

Your writing should "sound like you." It should capture your thoughts and your point of view. This is your "voice." In writing, your voice shows that you are interested in and understand the subject. Your voice also gives a personal tone to your writing that is yours alone.

Six Traits of Writing:

Word Choice vivid words that "show, not tell"

Choose your words so that they are clear and interesting. Name things exactly. Use strong action verbs and specific adjectives. Good word choice helps you say exactly what you want to say. It helps your readers create a mental picture of what you want them to understand.

Six Traits of Writing:

Sentence Fluency smooth rhythm and flow

Well-made sentences make your writing easy to read. Aim for sentences that have the natural rhythms of speech. Vary sentence length and style. Then your sentences will flow. They will move your readers through your writing with ease.

Six Traits of Writing:

Conventions correct grammar, spelling, and mechanics

Once you have written something, ask yourself: Could this be published in a newspaper? Make sure your writing is free from mistakes in spelling, grammar, and mechanics. Mechanics includes things such as correct capitalization and punctuation.

Appendix D: Research

Planning and Writing a Research Report

Use the following steps to guide you in writing a research report.

Step 1: Planning the Report

Choose a subject. Then narrow your topic. You may be interested in the poetry of Robert Frost, but that subject is too broad. Narrow your focus. The graphic organizers in Appendix A may help you narrow your topic and identify supporting details.

Step 2: Finding Useful Information

Go to the library and browse the card catalog for books. Check almanacs, encyclopedias, atlases, and other sources in the reference section. Also review *The Reader's Guide to Periodical Literature* for magazines.

Draw from primary sources. Primary sources are first-hand accounts of information, such as speeches, observations, research results, and interviews. Secondary sources interpret and analyze primary sources.

Use the Internet to further explore your topic. Be careful; some Internet sources are not reliable. Avoid chat rooms, news groups, and personal Web sites. Check the credibility of sites by reviewing the site name and sponsor. Web sites whose URL ends with .org, .gov, and .edu are typically good sources.

Step 3: Logging Information

Use index cards to take notes. Include this information for each source:

- name of author or editor
- title of book or title of article and magazine
- page numbers
- volume numbers
- date of publication
- name of publishing company
- Web site information for Internet sources
- relevant information or direct quotations

Step 4: Getting Organized

Group your cards by similar details and organize them into categories. Find a system that works for you in organizing your cards. You can color-code them, use different-colored index cards for different sections, label them, and so on. Do not use any note cards that do not fit the categories that you have set up. Make conclusions about your research. Write a final topic outline.

Step 5: Writing Your Report

Follow the writing process in Appendix C to write your report. Use your own words to write the ideas you found in your sources (paraphrase). Do not plagiarize—steal and pass off another's words as your own. Write an author's exact words for direct quotations, and name the author or source.

Step 6: Preparing a Bibliography or Works Cited Page

Use the information on your note cards to write a bibliography or works cited page. If you are writing a bibliography, put your note cards in alphabetical order by *title*. If you are writing a works cited page, put your note cards in alphabetical order by *author*.

See *Bibliographies* in Appendix C.

Research Tools

Almanac
An annual publication containing data and tables on politics, religion, education, sports, and more

American Psychological Association (APA) Style
A guide to proper citation to avoid plagiarism in research papers for the social sciences

Atlas
A bound collection of maps of cities, states, regions, and countries including statistics and illustrations

Audio Recording
Recordings of speeches, debates, public proceedings, interviews, etc.

The Chicago Manual of Style
Writing, editing, proofreading, and revising guidelines for the publishing industry

Database
A large collection of data stored electronically and able to be searched

Dictionary
A reference book of words, spellings, pronunciations, meanings, parts of speech, and word origins

Experiment
A series of tests to prove or disprove something

Field Study
Observation, data collection, and interpretation done outside of a laboratory

Glossary
A collection of terms and their meanings

Government Publications
A report of a government action, bill, handbook, or census data usually provided by the Government Printing Office

Grammar Reference
Explanation and examples of parts of speech, sentence structure, and word usage

History
A chronological record that explains past events

Information Services
A stored collection of information organized for easy searching

Internet/World Wide Web
A worldwide network of connected computers that share information

Interview
A dialogue between a subject and a reporter or investigator to gather information

Journal
A type of magazine offering current information on certain subjects such as medicine, the economy, and current events

Microfiche
Historical, printed materials saved to small, thin sheets of film for organization, storage, and use

Modern Language Association (MLA) Handbook
A guide to proper citation to avoid plagiarism in research papers for the humanities

News Source
A newspaper or a radio, television, satellite, or World Wide Web sending of current events and issues presented in a timely manner

Periodical
A magazine, newspaper, or journal

The Reader's Guide to Periodical Literature
A searchable, organized database of magazines, newspapers, and journals used for research

Speech
A public address to inform and to explain

Technical Document
A proposal, instruction manual, training manual, report, chart, table, or other document that provides information

Thesaurus
A book of words and their synonyms, or words that have almost the same meanings

Vertical File
A storage file of original documents or copies of original documents

Appendix E: Speaking

Types of Public Speaking

Public speaking offers a way to inform, to explain, and to entertain. Here are some common types of public speaking:

Debate

A debate is a formal event where two or more people share opposing arguments in response to questions. Often, someone wins by answering questions with solid information.

Descriptive Speech

A descriptive speech uses the five senses of sight, smell, touch, taste, and sound to give vivid details.

Entertaining Speech

An entertaining speech relies on humor through jokes, stories, wit, or making fun of oneself. The humor must be appropriate for the audience and purpose of the speech.

Expository Speech

An expository speech provides more detailed information about a subject. This can be done through classification, analysis, definition, cause and effect, or compare and contrast.

Group Discussion

A group discussion allows the sharing of ideas among three or more people. A group discussion may be impromptu (without being planned) or may include a set topic and list of questions.

Impromptu Speech

An impromptu speech happens at a moment's notice without being planned. The speaker is given a random topic to discuss within a given time period.

Interview

An interview is a dialogue between a subject and a reporter or investigator. An interview draws out information using a question-and-answer format.

Literature Recitation

A literature recitation is the act of presenting a memorized speech, poem, story, or scene in its entire form or with chosen excerpts.

Literature Response

A literature response can serve many purposes. A speaker can compare and contrast plots or characters. An analysis of the work of one author can be presented. Writing style, genre, or period can also be shared.

Narrative

A narrative is a fiction or nonfiction story told with descriptive detail. The speaker also must use voice variation if acting out character dialogue.

Reflective Speech

A reflective speech provides thoughtful analysis of ideas, current events, and processes.

Role Playing

Role playing is when two or more people act out roles to show an idea or practice a character in a story. Role playing can be an effective tool for learning.

Preparing Your Speech

Use the following steps to prepare your speech:

Step 1: Defining Your Purpose

Ask yourself:

- Do I want to inform?
- Do I want to explain something?
- Do I want to entertain?
- Do I want to involve the audience through group discussion, role playing, or debate?
- Do I want to get the audience to act on a subject or an issue?

Step 2: Knowing Your Audience

Ask yourself:

- What information does my audience already know about the topic?
- What questions, concerns, or opinions do they have about the topic?
- How formal or informal does my presentation need to be?
- What words are familiar to my audience? What needs explanation?
- How does my audience prefer to get information? Do they like visuals, audience participation, or lecture?

Step 3: Knowing Your Setting

Ask yourself:

- Who is my audience?
- Is the room large enough to need a microphone and a projector?
- How is the room set up? Am I on stage with a podium or can I interact with the audience?
- Will other noises or activity distract the audience?

Step 4: Narrowing Your Topic

Ask yourself:

- What topic is right for the event? Is it timely? Will it match the mood of the event?
- Is there enough time to share it?
- What topic is right for me to present? Is it something I know and enjoy? Is it something people want to hear from me?

Step 5: Prewriting

Ask yourself:

- What examples, statistics, stories, or descriptions will help me get across my point?
- If telling a story, do I have a sequence of events that includes a beginning, middle, and end?

Step 6: Drafting Your Speech

Your speech will include an introduction, a body, and a conclusion.

The introduction states your topic and purpose. It includes a thesis statement that tells your position. Your introduction should also establish your credibility. Share why you are the right person to give that speech based on your experiences. Lastly, your introduction needs to get people's attention so they want to listen. At the top of the next page are some possible ways to start your speech.

- Ask a question.
- Share a story.
- Describe something.
- Give a surprising fact.
- Share a meaningful quotation.
- Make a memorable, purposeful entrance.

The body of your speech tells more about your main idea and tries to prevent listener misunderstandings. It should include any of the following supporting evidence:

- facts
- details
- explanations
- reasons
- examples
- personal stories or experiences
- experts
- literary devices and images

The conclusion of your speech ties your speech together. If you asked a question in your introduction, the conclusion answers it. If you outlined a problem, your conclusion offers solutions. If you told a story, revisit that story. You may even want to ask your audience to get involved, take action, or become more informed on your topic.

Step 7: Selecting Visuals

Ask yourself:

- Is a visual aid needed for the audience to better understand my topic?
- What visual aids work best for my topic?
- Do I have access to the right technology?

The size of your audience and the setting for your speech will also impact what you select. Remember that a projection screen and overhead speakers are necessary for large groups. If you plan on giving handouts to audience members, have handouts ready for pickup by the entrance of the room. A slide show or a video presentation will need a darkened room. Be sure that you have someone available to help you with the lights.

Practicing and Delivering Your Speech

Giving a speech is about more than simply talking. You want to look comfortable and confident.

Practice how you move, how you sound, and how you work with visuals and the audience.

Know Your Script

Every speaker is afraid of forgetting his or her speech. Each handles this fear in a different way. Choose the device that works for you.

- Memorization: Know your speech by heart. Say it often so you sound natural.
- Word-for-word scripts: Highlight key phrases to keep you on track. Keep the script on a podium, so you are not waving sheets of paper around as you talk. Be careful not to read from your script. The audience wants to see your eyes.
- Outlines: Write a sentence outline of your main points and supporting details that you want to say in a specific way. Transitions and other words can be spoken impromptu (without being planned).

- Key words: Write down key words that will remind you what to say, like "Tell story about the dog."
- Put your entire speech, outline, or key words on note cards to stay on track. They are small and not as obvious as paper. Number them in case they get out of order.

Know Yourself

Your voice and appearance are the two most powerful things you bring to a speech. Practice the following, so you are comfortable, confident, and convincing:

- Body language: Stand tall. Keep your feet shoulder-width apart. Don't cross your arms or bury your hands in your pockets. Use gestures to make a point. For example, hold up two fingers when you say, "My second point is . . ." Try to relax; that way, you will be in better control of your body.
- Eye contact: Look at your audience. Spend a minute or two looking at every side of the room and not just the front row. The audience will feel as if you are talking to them.
- Voice strategies: Clearly pronounce your words. Speak at a comfortable rate and loud enough for everyone to hear you. Vary your volume, rate, and pitch when you are trying to emphasize something. For example, you could say, "I have a secret. . . ." Then, you could lean toward the audience and speak in a loud, clear whisper as if you are telling them a secret. This adds dramatic effect and engages the audience.
- Repetition of key phrases or words: Repetition is one way to help people remember your point. If something is important, say it twice. Use transitions such as, "This is so important it is worth repeating" or "As I said before, we must act now."

Appendix F: Listening

Listening Strategy Checklist

Here are some ways you can ensure that you are a good listener.

Be an Active Listener

- ☑ Complete reading assignments that are due prior to the presentation.
- ☑ Focus on what is being said.
- ☑ Ask for definitions of unfamiliar terms.
- ☑ Ask questions to clarify what you heard.
- ☑ Ask the speaker to recommend other readings or resources.

Be a Critical Listener

- ☑ Identify the thesis or main idea of the speech.
- ☑ Try to predict what the speaker is going to say based on what you already know.
- ☑ Determine the speaker's purpose of the speech.
- ☑ Note supporting facts, statistics, examples, and other details.
- ☑ Determine if supporting detail is relevant, factual, and appropriate.
- ☑ Form your conclusions about the presentation.

Be an Appreciative Listener

- ☑ Relax.
- ☑ Enjoy the listening experience.
- ☑ Welcome the opportunity to laugh and learn.

Be a Thoughtful and Feeling Listener

- ☑ Understand the experiences of the speaker.
- ☑ Value the emotion he or she brings to the subject.
- ☑ Summarize or paraphrase what you believe the speaker just said.
- ☑ Tell the speaker that you understand his or her feelings.

Be an Alert Listener

- ☑ Sit up straight.
- ☑ Sit near the speaker and face the speaker directly.
- ☑ Make eye contact and nod to show you are listening.
- ☑ Open your arms so you are open to receiving information.

Analyze the Speaker

- ☑ Does the speaker have the experiences and knowledge to speak on the topic?
- ☑ Is the speaker prepared?
- ☑ Does the speaker appear confident?
- ☑ Is the speaker's body language appropriate?
- ☑ What do the speaker's tone, volume, and word choices show?

Identify the Details

- ☑ Listen for the tendency of the speaker to favor or oppose something without real cause.
- ☑ Be aware of propaganda—someone forcing an opinion on you.
- ☑ Don't be swayed by the clever way the speaker presents something.
- ☑ After the speech ask about words that you don't know.

Identify Fallacies of Logic

A fallacy is a false idea intended to trick someone. Here are some common fallacies:

- *Ad hominem*: This type of fallacy attacks a person's character, lifestyle, or beliefs. Example: Joe should not be on the school board because he skipped classes in college.
- False causality: This type of fallacy gives a cause–effect relationship that is not logical. This fallacy assumes that something caused something else only because it came before the consequence. Example: Ever since that new family moved into the neighborhood, our kids are getting into trouble.
- Red herring: This type of fallacy uses distractions to take attention away from the main issue. Example: Since more than half of our nation's people are overweight, we should not open a fast-food restaurant in our town.
- Overgeneralization: This type of fallacy uses words such as *every*, *always*, or *never*. Claims do not allow for exceptions to be made. Example: People who make more than a million dollars a year never pay their fair share of taxes.
- Bandwagon effect: This type of fallacy appeals to one's desire to be a part of the crowd. It is based on popular opinion and not on evidence. Example: Anyone who believes that our town is a great place to live should vote for the local tax increase.

Take Notes

- Write down key messages and phrases, not everything that is said.
- Abbreviate words.
- Listen for cues that identify important details, like "Here's an example" or "To illustrate what I mean."
- Draw graphs, charts, and diagrams for future reference.
- Draw arrows, stars, and circles to highlight information or group information.
- Highlight or circle anything that needs to be clarified or explained.
- Use the note-taking strategies explained in "How to Use This Book" at the beginning of this textbook.

Appendix G: Viewing

Visual aids can help communicate information and ideas. The following checklist gives pointers for viewing and interpreting visual aids.

Design Elements

Colors

- ☑ What colors stand out?
- ☑ What feelings do they make you think of?
- ☑ What do they symbolize or represent?
- ☑ Are colors used realistically or for emphasis?

Shapes

- ☑ What shapes are created by space or enclosed in lines?
- ☑ What is important about the shapes? What are they meant to symbolize or represent?

Lines

- ☑ What direction do the lines lead you?
- ☑ Which objects are you meant to focus on?
- ☑ What is the importance of the lines?
- ☑ Do lines divide or segment areas? Why do you think this is?

Textures

- ☑ What textures are used?
- ☑ What emotions or moods are they meant to affect?

Point of View

Point of view shows the artist's feelings toward the subject. Analyze this point of view:

- ☑ What point of view is the artist taking?
- ☑ Do you agree with this point of view?
- ☑ Is the artist successful in communicating this point of view?

Graphics

Line Graphs

Line graphs show changes in numbers over time.

- ☑ What numbers and time frame are represented?
- ☑ Does the information represent appropriate changes?

Pie Graphs

Pie graphs represent parts of a whole.

- ☑ What total number does the pie represent?
- ☑ Do the numbers represent an appropriate-sized sample?

Bar Graphs

Bar graphs compare amounts.

- ☑ What amounts are represented?
- ☑ Are the amounts appropriate?

Charts and Tables

Charts and tables organize information for easy comparison.

- ☑ What is being presented?
- ☑ Do columns and rows give equal data to compare and contrast?

Maps

- ☑ What land formations are shown?
- ☑ What boundaries are shown?
- ☑ Are there any keys or symbols on the map? What do they mean?

Appendix H: Media and Technology

Forms of Media

Television, movies, and music are some common forms of media that you know a lot about. Here are some others.

Advertisement

An advertisement selling a product or a service can be placed in a newspaper or magazine, on the Internet, or on television or radio.

Broadcast News

Broadcast news is offered on a 24-hour cycle through nightly newscasts, all-day news channels, and the Internet.

Documentary

A documentary shares information about people's lives, historic events, objects, or places. It is based on facts and evidence.

Internet and World Wide Web

This worldwide computer network offers audio and video clips, news, reference materials, research, and graphics.

Journal

A journal records experiences, current research, or ideas about a topic for a target audience.

Magazine

A magazine includes articles, stories, photos, and graphics of general interest.

Newspaper

A newspaper most often is printed daily or weekly.

Photography

Traditionally, photography has been the art or process of producing images on a film surface using light. Today, digital images are often used.

The Media and You

The media's role is to entertain, to inform, and to advertise. Media can help raise people's awareness about current issues. Media also can give clues about the needs and beliefs of the people.

Use a critical eye and ear to sort through the thousands of messages presented to you daily. Be aware of the media's use of oversimplified ideas about people, decent and acceptable language, and appropriate messages. Consider these questions:

- Who is being shown and why?
- What is being said? Is it based on fact?
- How do I feel about what and how it is said?

Technology and You

Technology can improve communication. Consider the following when selecting technology for research or presentations:

Audio/Sound

Speeches, music, sound effects, and other elements can set a mood or reinforce an idea.

Computers

- Desktop publishing programs offer tools for making newsletters and posters.
- Software programs are available for designing publications, Web sites, databases, and more.
- Word processing programs feature dictionaries, grammar-check and spell-check programs, and templates for memos, reports, letters, and more.

Multimedia

Slide shows, movies, and other electronic media can help the learning process.

Visual Aids

Charts, tables, maps, props, drawings, and graphs provide visual representation of information.

Handbook of Literary Terms

A

act (akt) the major unit of action in a play (p. 342)

alliteration (ə lit ə rā´ shən) repeating sounds by using words whose beginning sounds are the same (p. 304)

anachronism (ə nak´ rə niz əm) a speech or event that could not actually have taken place at the time in which it happens in a literary work (p. 466)

author's purpose (ȯ´ thərs pėr´ pəs) the reason(s) for which the author writes: to entertain, to inform, to express opinions, or to persuade (p. 42)

autobiography (ȯ tə bī og´ rə fē) a person's life story, written by that person (pp. 19, 224)

B

biography (bī og´ rə fē) a person's life story, written by someone else (p. 224)

C

cause (kôz) an event or situation that produces a result (p. 510)

character (kar´ ik tər) a person or animal in a story, poem, or play (pp. 224, 342)

character analysis (kar´ ik tər ə nal´ ə sis) thinking carefully about a character's traits (p. 224)

character traits (kar´ ik tər trātz) a character's way of thinking, behaving, or speaking (pp. 145, 224)

characterization (kar ik tər ə zā´ shən) the way a writer develops character qualities and personality traits (p. 73)

characters (kar´ ik tərz) the people or animals in a story (p. 98)

chronological order (kron´ ə loj´ ə kəl ôr´dər) a plot that moves forward in order of time (p. 6)

climax (klī´ maks) the high point of interest or suspense in a story (p. 98)

comedy (kom´ ə dē) a play with a happy ending, intended to amuse its audience (p. 466)

concrete poem (kon´ krēt pō´ əm) a poem shaped to look like its subject (p. 278)

conflict (kon´ flikt) the struggle of the main character against himself or herself, another person, or nature (p. 98)

D

dialogue (dī´ ə lôg) the conversation among characters in a story; the words that characters in a play speak (p. 342)

diction (dik´ shən) the proper choice of words, or saying words correctly (p. 243)

drama (drä´ mə) a story told through the words and actions of a character, written to be performed as well as read (p. 342)

E

effect (ə fekt´) the result produced (p. 510)

essay (es´ ā) a written work that shows a writer's opinions on some basic or current issue (pp. 53, 204)

exposition (ek spə zish´ ən) the part of the story that introduces the setting, characters, and conflict (p. 98)

expository essay (ek spoz´ ə tôr ē es´ ā) an essay that informs or explains (p. 204)

external conflict (ek stėr´ nl) a character's struggle against an outside force such as another character or nature (p. 158)

F

fact (fakt) something that actually happened or can be proven (p. 236)

fairy tale (fer´ ē tāl) an imaginary story with magical deeds and characters such as fairies, elves, and giants (p. 158)

falling action (fȯl´ ing ak´ shən) the events following the climax (p. 98)

fiction (fik´ shən) writing that is imaginative and designed to entertain; the author creates the events and characters (p. 30)

figurative language (fig´ yər ə tiv lang´ gwij) writing or speech not meant to be understood exactly as it is written (p. 285)

first person (fėrst pėr´ sən) a point of view where the narrator is also a character, using the pronouns *I* and *we* (p. 19)

flashback (flash´ bak) a look into the past at some point in a story (pp. 42, 133)

folktale (fōk´ tāl) a story that has been handed down from one generation to another (p. 543)

foreshadowing (fôr shad´ ō ing) the clues or hints that a writer gives about something that has not yet happened (p. 133)

H

haiku (hī kü) a form of Japanese poetry having three lines with five syllables in the first, seven in the second, and five in the third (p. 278)

hero (hir´ ō) the leading character in a story, novel, play, or film (p. 519)

I

idiom (id´ ē əm) a phrase that has a different meaning that its words really mean (p. 224)

idolized character (ī´ dl īzd kar´ ik tər) a character that stands for a trait, such as honor or courage (p. 224)

imagery (im´ ij rē) the use of words that appeal to the five senses (p. 323)

internal conflict (in tėr´ nl kon´ flikt) a character's struggle against himself or herself to overcome opposing feelings, beliefs, needs, or desires (p. 158)

irony (ī rə nē) the difference between what is expected to happen in a story and what does happen (p. 180)

L

legend (lej´ ənd) a traditional story that was at one time told orally and was handed down from one generation to another (p. 519)

lyric poem (lir´ ik pō´ əm) a short poem that expresses a person's emotions or feelings (p. 278)

M

main idea (mān ī dē´ ə) the most important thought or message in a written work (p. 204)

metaphor (met´ ə fôr) a figure of speech that makes a comparison but does not use *like* or *as* (p. 285)

meter (mē´ tər) the repetition of stressed and unstressed syllables (p. 311)

a	hat	e	let	ī	ice	ô	order	u̇	put	sh	she	ə	a in about
ā	age	ē	equal	o	hot	oi	oil	ü	rule	th	thin		e in taken
ä	far	ėr	term	ō	open	ou	out	ch	child	ᴛʜ	then		i in pencil
â	care	i	it	ȯ	saw	u	cup	ng	long	zh	measure		o in lemon
													u in circus

mood (müd) the feeling that writing creates (pp. 42, 133)

motivation (mō tə vā′ shən) a reason a character does something (p. 424)

motive (mō′ tiv) a reason a character does something (p. 145)

myth (mith) an important story, often part of a culture's religion, that explains how the world came to be or why natural events happen, usually including gods, goddesses, or unusually powerful human beings (p. 498)

mythology (mi thol′ ə jē) collection of myths (p. 498)

N

narration (na rā′ shən) the act of telling a story or giving an account of something (p. 6)

narrative (nar′ ə tiv) a story, usually told in chronological order (p. 6)

narrative poem (nar′ ə tiv pō′ əm) a poem that tells a story (p. 297)

narrator (nar′ ā tər) one who tells a story (p. 6)

nonfiction (non′ fik′ shən) writing about real people and events (p. 30)

O

onomatopoeia (on ə mat ə pē′ ə) using words that sound like their meaning (p. 304)

opinion (ə pin′ yən) a belief or judgment (p. 236)

oral tradition (ôr′ əl trə dish′ ən) stories originally told at festivals and around campfires, rather than shared in print (p. 498)

P

personification (pər son ə fə kā′ shən) giving characters such as animals or objects the characteristics or qualities of humans (p. 285)

persuasive essay (pər swā siv es′ ā) an essay meant to influence (p. 236)

playwright (plā′ rīt) an author of the play (p. 342)

plot (plot) the series of events in a story (p. 98)

poetry (pō′ i trē) literature in verse form that usually has rhythm and paints powerful or beautiful impressions with words (p. 278)

point of view (point ov vyü) the position from which the author or storyteller tells the story (p. 19)

R

reflective essay (ri flek′ tiv es′ ā) a personal essay that explores an author's feelings (p. 212)

repetition (rep ə tish′ ən) using a word, phrase, or image more than once, for emphasis (p. 304)

resolution (rez ə lü′ shən) the act of solving the conflict in a story (p. 98)

rhyme (rim) words that end with the same or similar sounds (p. 311)

rhythm (riᴛʜ′ əm) a pattern created by the stressed and unstressed syllables in a line of poetry (p. 311)

rising action (rīz′ ing ak′ shən) the buildup of excitement in a story (p. 98)

S

satire (sat´ īr) humorous writing that makes fun of foolishness or evil (p. 73)

scene (sēn) a unit of action in a play that takes place in one setting (p. 342)

science fiction (sī´ əns fik´ shən) fiction based on real or imagined facts of science (p. 432)

screenplay (skrēn´ plā) a play written to be filmed rather than performed live in a theater (p. 432)

setting (set´ ing) the time and place in a story (pp. 42, 98)

short story (shôrt stôr´ ē) a brief work of prose fiction that includes plot, setting, characters, point of view, and theme (p. 98)

simile (sim´ ə lē) a figure of speech in which two things are compared using a phrase that includes the words *like* or *as* (p. 285)

stage directions (stāj də rek´ shəns) what tells the actors how to perform their parts of a play; they describe movements, tone, use of props, lighting, and other details (p. 379)

style (stīl) an author's way of writing (p. 6)

suspense (sə spens´) a quality that makes a reader uncertain or nervous about what will happen next (pp. 106, 297)

symbol (sim´ bəl) something that represents something else (p. 285)

T

theme (thēm) the main idea of a literary work (pp. 174, 498)

third person (thėrd pėr´ sən) a point of view where the narrator is not a character, and refers to characters as *he* or *she* (p. 19)

trickster (trik´ stər) a character who uses cleverness and quick thinking to outsmart enemies, sometimes by playing tricks on them (p. 530)

W

word choice (wėrd chois) words a writer uses and how they are put together (p. 243)

a	hat	e	let	ī	ice	ô	order	u̇	put	sh	she	ə	a in about
ā	age	ē	equal	o	hot	oi	oil	ü	rule	th	thin		e in taken
ä	far	ėr	term	ō	open	ou	out	ch	child	ᴛʜ	then		i in pencil
â	care	i	it	ȯ	saw	u	cup	ng	long	zh	measure		o in lemon
													u in circus

Glossary

A

abruptly (ə brupt´ lē) suddenly (pp. 62, 450)

abused (ə byüzd´) mistreated (p. 552)

acceptance (ak sep´ təns) thinking of something as good or right (p. 213)

accompanying (ə kum´pə nē) traveling with (p. 228)

accusations (ak yə zā´ shənz) statements of someone else's guilt or crime (p. 444)

acquiring (ə kwīr´ ing) obtaining (p. 469)

adornments (ə dôrn´ məntz) ornaments, decorations (p. 521)

Agency (ā´ jən sē) a tribal office (p. 136)

agitated (aj´ ə tātd) angry (p. 62)

aides (ādz) assistants (p. 228)

Alice blue (al´ is blü) a steel blue color favored by Theodore Roosevelt's daughter Alice (p. 305)

alien (ā´ lyən) very different or strange (p. 205)

all-pervading (ôl´ pər vād´ ing) spread through all parts (p. 447)

aloft (ə lôft´) in the air (p. 501)

amber (am´ bər) gold-colored (p. 476)

ambitious (am bish´ əs) eager to reach goals (p. 475)

amid (ə mid´) with (p. 60)

amongst (ə mungst´) among (p. 452)

amplified (am´ plə fīd) made louder (p. 395)

ancestral (an ses´ trəl) having to do with ancestors (p. 46)

anonymous (ə non´ ə məs) nameless (p. 352)

antagonism (an tag´ ə niz əm) dislike (p. 442)

anxious (angk´ shəs) worried and scared (p. 398)

aphids (ā´ fidz) tiny garden bugs (p. 256)

apparent (ə par´ ənt) easy to understand (p. 136)

apparition (ap ə rish´ ən) a ghost (p. 358)

applicant (ap´ lə kənt) a person making a request (p. 468)

application (ap lə kā´ shən) a filled out form; a request (p. 474)

appreciate (ə prē´ shē āt) to understand (p. 473)

apprehensive (ap ri hen´ siv) frightened (p. 451)

aqueducts (ak´ wə dukt) bridge-like structures that carried water over long distances (p. 511)

arc (ärk) a curved section of a circle (p. 299)

architect (är´ kə tekt) builder (p. 499)

archives (är´ kivz) old records and files (p. 228)

articulate (är tik´ yə lit) well-spoken (p. 478)

askew (ə skyü´) crooked (p. 374)

asperity (a sper´ ə tē) anger (p. 183)

aspirations (as pə rā´ shənz) goals (p. 371)

assassination (ə sas´ n āt shən) having to do with a planned murder (p. 230)

assent (ə sent´) agreement (p. 438)

associate (ə sō´ shē āt) a person one works with (p. 473)

assortment (ə sôrt´ mənt) variety (p. 36)

asthmatic (az mat´ ik) gasping (p. 136)

atmosphere (at´ mə sfir) feelings of surroundings (p. 442)

attitudes (at´ ə tüdz) ways of looking at and thinking about things (p. 457)

audible (ô´ də bəl) loud or clear enough to be heard (pp. 259, 394)

auditorium (ô də tôr´ ē əm) a theater (p. 344)

avail (ə vāl´) help, use (p. 524)

awe (ô) mixed feelings of fear and wonder (p. 175)

azaleas (ə zā´ lyəz) flowering shrubs or their flowers (p. 279)

B

bachelor (bach′ ə lər) an unmarried man (p. 393)

baffled (baf′ əld) puzzled (p. 475)

banished (ban′ ishd) sent away (p. 299)

bantam's eggs (ban′ təmz egz) eggs of a small chicken (p. 119)

barbell (bär′ bel) an exercise weight (p. 208)

barren (bar′ ən) boring (p. 74)

battalions (bə tal′ yənz) groups of soldiers (p. 225)

bawling (bôling) crying (p. 545)

bellowing (bel′ ō ing) roaring (p. 134)

benevolence (bə nev′ ə ləns) goodness (p. 359)

beseech (bi sēch′) to plead, beg (p. 407)

beset (bi set′) attacked from all sides (p. 314)

besotted (bi sot′ təd) in love with (p. 468)

bestow (bi stō′) to give (p. 345)

biscotti (bi′ skät ē) hard, crunchy Italian cookie (p. 467)

blander (bland ər) less tasty (p. 207)

bleak (blēk) gray and cheerless (p. 346)

blemish (blem′ ish) mark or pimple (p. 364)

bloodhound (blud′ hound) a dog with a keen sense of smell (p. 109)

blotting (blot′ ing) remove (p. 214)

boarders (bôr′ dərz) people who live in a rooming-house (p. 184)

bodily (bod′ l ē) physically (p. 165)

bore (bôr) carried (p. 313)

bosom (bu̇z′ əm) a woman's chest (p. 214); breast (p. 315)

bred (bred) born (p. 364)

brooch (brōch) a large pin worn as jewelry (p. 287)

brooded (brü′ dəd) worried (p. 25)

brow (brou) a forehead (p. 395)

buckskin (buk′ skin) yellowish-gray leather made from the hide of a deer (p. 298)

bungalow (bung′ gə lō) a cottage (p. 107)

bungalows (bung′ gə lōz) houses (p. 76)

burden (bėrd′ n) something that is carried (p. 533)

burdensome (bėrd′ n səm) heavy to carry (p. 370)

buttes (byützs) steep hills standing alone in flat land (p. 288)

C

cacophony (kə kof′ ə nē) noise (p. 63)

camaraderie (kä mə rä′ dər ē) friendship (p. 229)

captive (kap′ tiv) prisoner (p. 499)

carolers (kar′ əl ərz) people singing Christmas songs (p. 361)

chalice (chal′ is) a large cup (p. 315)

chamber (chām′ bər) an enclosed space (p. 44)

chant (chant) words repeated with a rhythm (p. 444)

chi-chi (kī kī) trendy (p. 182)

circumstances (sėr′ kəm stans əz) situations (pp. 447, 534)

cirrus (sir′ əs) high, thin clouds (p. 298)

clamoring (klam′ ər ing) crying out (p. 77)

clause (klôz) a part of a law or contract (p. 245)

cleave (klēv) to separate (p. 501)

clung (klung) held on tightly (p. 11)

a	hat	e	let	ī	ice	ô	order	u̇	put	sh	she	ə: a	in about
ā	age	ē	equal	o	hot	oi	oil	ü	rule	th	thin	e	in taken
ä	far	ėr	term	ō	open	ou	out	ch	child	ꟺ	then	i	in pencil
â	care	i	it	ȯ	saw	u	cup	ng	long	zh	measure	o	in lemon
												u	in circus

coalesced (kō ə lesd´) grew together (p. 182)

cocking (kok ing) tilting (p. 439)

coexisted (kō ig zis´ təd) lived together (p. 520)

collateral (kə lat´ ər əl) money or goods that back up a loan (p. 474)

commentaries (kom´ ən ter ēz) articles giving opinions and supporting details (p. 472)

communal (kə myü´ nl) shared (p. 213)

companion (kəm pan´ yən) a partner (p. 478)

companionship (kəm pan´ yən ship) the company of others (p. 216)

compassion (kəm pash´ ən) feelings of love and understanding (p. 238)

compelled (kəm peld´) forced (p. 23)

composure (kəm pō´ zhər) calmness (p. 160)

compulsion (kəm pul´ shən) force (p. 383)

conceivably (kən sē´ və bəl ē) understandably (p. 75)

conceived (kən sēvd´) created (a baby) (p. 228)

conclusion (kən klü zhən) an ending (p. 347)

condemned (kən demd´) judged as a criminal (p. 358)

confidentially (kon fə dən´ shəl lē) in a secretive manner (p. 182); as a secret (p. 380)

confirmed (kən fėrmd´) stated to be true (p. 523)

conquest (kon´ kwest) a victory over an enemy (p. 457)

conscious (kon´ shəs) aware (pp. 364, 441)

consequence (kon´ sə kwens) result (p. 393)

considerable (kən sid´ ər ə bəl) large (p. 474)

consolation (kən sol ə dā´ shən) something that comforts a disappointed person (p. 119)

contemplation (kon təm plā´ shən) deep thought (p. 181)

contentment (kən tent´ mənt) calm happiness (p. 165)

contorted (kən tôrtd´) twisted out of shape (p. 451)

contraption (kən trap´ shən) machine (p. 31)

converging (kən vėrj´ ing) coming together (p. 453)

conversing (kən vėrs´ ing) talking; having conversations (p. 435)

conveyed (kən vād´) sent (p. 359)

conviction (kən vik´ shən) a strong opinion (p. 475)

corralling (kə ral´ ling) gathering (p. 134)

corridor (kôr´ ə dər) a long hall (p. 46)

coveted (kuv´ it əd) wanted; desired (p. 312)

covetous (kuv´ ə təs) greedy (p. 344)

cowered (kou´ ərd) crouched fearfully (p. 110)

creation (krē ā´ shən) life on Earth (p. 215)

cripple (krip´ əl) a disabled person who is unable to walk (p. 387)

croon (krün) to sing softly (p. 545)

croquet (krō kā´) a game using wooden balls and mallets (p. 147)

croupy (krü´ pē) hoarse (p. 137)

crucify (krü´ sə fī) to kill slowly and painfully (p. 450)

culminated (kul´ mə nātd) had its greatest moment (p. 238)

cultivated (kul´ tə vā tid) planted by man (p. 110)

cultures (kul´ chərz) organized societies (p. 213)

cumulative (kyü´ myə lə tiv) collection (p. 61)

cunning (kun´ ing) clever (p. 499)

curb (kėrb) to control or suppress (p. 534)

cussing (kus ing) swearing (p. 246)

D

defiant (di fī´ ənt) bold and rude (p. 441)

defiantly (di fī´ ənt lē) in a bold and challenging way (p. 398)

delectable (di lek´ tə bəl) tasty (p. 524)

deliquesce (del ə kwes´) to melt away; disappear (p. 355)

delusional (di lü´ zhən əl) crazy (p. 472)

demonstrated (dem´ ən strātd) showed (p. 554)

dense (dens) stupid (p. 449)

deposits (di poz´ itz) sets down (p. 470)

derived (di rīvd´) gotten (p. 348)

desirable (di zī´ rə bəl) attractive (p. 351)

desperate (des´ pər it) without hope (p. 442)

destitute (des´ tə tüt) people who have nothing (p. 351)

deter (di tėr´) to turn aside (p. 523)

devastated (dev´ ə stāt əd) ruined (p. 246)

dictating (dik´ tāt ing) speaking something to be written down by others (p. 226)

dirge (dėrj) slow and sad music (p. 360)

discipline (dis´ ə plin) order and control (p. 244)

discomforts (dis kum´ fərtz) difficulties (p. 208)

discrimination (dis krim ə nā´ shən) unfair treatment and opinions (p. 226)

disembarking (dis em bärk´ ing) getting off a ship or train (p. 77)

disheartened (dis härt´nd) having lost hope (p. 477)

disinterested (dis in´ tər ə stid) indifferent (p. 397)

dislodge (dis loj´) to come loose (p. 289)

dismal (diz´ məl) bare and ugly (p. 347)

dismayed (dis mād´) troubled (p. 24)

dispatched (dis pachd´) sent off (p. 63)

dispelled (dis peld´) scattered (p. 407)

displaced (dis peld´) taken the place of something (p. 371)

dissever (di sev´ ər) to separate; divide (p. 313)

distinct (dis tingkt´) different (p. 325)

disturbed (dis tėrbd´) bothered; worried (p. 437)

diverse (dī´ vərz) varied (p. 257)

diversions (də vėr´ zhənz) ways to have fun (p. 246)

diverted (də vėrtd´) caused to change direction (p. 54)

doffed (dofd) took off (p. 374)

domestic (də mes´ tik) made of use to people (p. 246)

donned (dond) put on (p. 374)

doom (düm) death (p. 395)

draggled (drag´ əld) wet and dirty (p. 108)

drowsiness (drou´ zē nəss) sleepiness (p. 374)

dusky (dus´ kē) dark (p. 161)

E

eldest (el´ dist) oldest (p. 61)

elemental (el ə mən´ tl) made of the elements (p. 256)

eliminate (i lim´ ə nāt) to get rid of (p. 245)

elite (i lēt) members of the leading class (p. 227)

elixir (i lik´ sər) a magic potion (p. 183)

emanating (em´ ə nāt ing) coming out from a place (p. 259)

ember (em´ bər) a bit of burning wood from a fire (p. 557)

a hat	e let	ī ice	ô order	ů put	sh she	ə { a in about
ā age	ē equal	o hot	oi oil	ü rule	th thin	e in taken
ä far	ėr term	ō open	ou out	ch child	ᴛʜ then	i in pencil
â care	i it	ȯ saw	u cup	ng long	zh measure	o in lemon
						u in circus

embroidery (em broi′ dər ē) a design made on fabric with needlework (p. 48)

eminent (em′ ə nənt) outstanding (p. 57)

emphasis (em′ fə sis) force (p. 467)

emphatic (em fat′ ik) forceful (p. 245)

employ (em ploi′) a job (p. 347)

encounter (en koun′ tər) to meet or find (p. 355)

endeavoring (en dev′ ər) trying (p. 351)

endeavors (en dev′ ərz) tries (p. 361)

enforce (en fôrs′) to put into effect (p. 246)

engrosses (en grōs′ əz) absorbs (p. 371)

enlarge (en lärj′) to make larger (p. 184)

entangled (en tang′ gəld) tangled up (p. 159)

entrust (en trust′) to give trust to (p. 533)

establishments (e stab′ lish mənt) companies, organizations, or businesses (p. 352)

eternal (i tėr′ nl) everlasting (p. 183)

eternity (i tėr′ nə tē) forever (p. 361)

evade (i vād′) to avoid or escape (p. 258)

exalting (eg zôlt ing) joyful (p. 25)

exasperated (eg zas′ pə rātd) extremely annoyed (p. 134)

exceptional (ek sep′ shə nəl) unusual (p. 75)

exhilarated (eg zil′ ə rātd) excited (p. 24)

exile (eg′ zīl) being sent away from one's country or home (p. 230)

expectancy (ek spek′ tən sē) a hopeful eagerness (p. 307)

expedition (ek spə dish′ ən) journey with a specific purpose (pp. 471, 554)

exquisite (ek′ skwi zit) beautiful in a delicate way (pp. 229, 325)

exterior (ek stir′ ē ər) outside (p. 385)

extricate (ek′ strə kāt) to untangle (p. 159)

exulted (eg zul′ təd) rejoiced (p. 77)

F

faltered (fôl′ tərd) stumbled (p. 136)

fangs (fangz) sharp teeth (p. 475)

fatigue (fə tēg′) tiredness (p. 238)

federal (fed′ ər əl) national (p. 225)

feeble (fē′ bəl) weak (p. 206)

feisty (fī′ stē) lively (p. 226)

feminist (fem′ ə nist) a person who fights for women's rights (p. 225)

fervor (fėr′ vər) great feeling (p. 225)

festive (fes′ tiv) cheerful; like a party (p. 351)

fifth dimension (fifth də men′ shən) fiction idea or space outside of human understanding (p. 434)

finance (fə nans′) to pay for (p. 471)

fixity (fik′ sə tē) steadiness (p. 75)

flanked (flangkd) situated on both sides of (p. 32)

fledgling (flej′ ling) baby bird (p. 501)

fledglings (flej′ lingz) baby birds (p. 111)

flimsy (flim′ zē) not solid or sturdy (p. 373)

flue (flü) a shaft for the passage of hot air (p. 43)

flustered (flus′ tərd) upset, bothered (p. 438)

foolhardy (fül′ här dē) foolish (p. 473)

forbearance (fôr′ ber əns) patience (p. 359)

forebears (fôr′ berz) ancestors (p. 54)

forenoon (fôr′ nün) late morning (p. 325)

forester (fôr′ ə stər) someone who works in a forest (p. 161)

forged (fôrjd) made out of iron (p. 358)

forlorn (fôr lôrn′) unhappy (p. 403)

formidable (fôr′ mə də bəl) amazing (p. 32)

foyer (foi′ ər) lobby (p. 467)

fraught (frôt) full of (p. 372)

fumes (fyüm) gases (p. 214)

fundamental (fun də men′ tl) basic (p. 238)

furious (fyu̇r′ ē əs) very angry (p. 348)

furiously (fyu̇r′ ē əs lē) angrily (p. 392)

fuzzier (fuz ē ər) less clear (p. 298)

G

gait (gāt) pace of walking (pp. 113, 345)

galvanized (gal′ və nīzd) excited (p. 58)

garment (gär′ mənt) a piece of clothing (p. 396)

gauge (gāj) to measure (p. 244)

gaunt (gônt) thin and bony (p. 76)

gene (jēn) the part of living things that passes along traits (p. 258)

ghoulish (gü′ lish) like a monster (p. 405)

gingham (ging′ əm) a cotton fabric (p. 305)

girdling (gėr′ dl ing) wrapped around (p. 382)

glimpse (glimps) a quick look (p. 501)

glinty (glint′ ē) catching the light (p. 544)

gloated (glōtd) observed with glee (p. 75); felt satisfied at one's own good fortune (p. 405)

globules (glob′ yülz) small, round drops (p. 207)

glorious (glôr′ ē əs) wonderful (p. 381)

gnarled (närld) twisted and bent (p. 395)

goblets (gob′ litz) large drinking glasses or bowls (p. 515)

gooey (gü′ ē) sticky and soft (p. 208)

gratified (grat′ ə fīd) pleased (p. 525)

grimaces (grə mās′ əz) twisting of the face in pain or disgust (p. 44)

grimly (grim′ lē) hopelessly, harshly (p. 448)

grotesque (grō tesk′) very disgusting (p. 552)

grove (grōv) a small group of trees (p. 382)

guarantee (gar ən tē′) a promise (p. 474)

gully (gul′ ē) a ditch (p. 256)

H

harmonious (här mō′ nē əs) in agreement (p. 237)

hearth (härth) area in front of the fireplace (p. 382)

hearty (här′ tē) strong (p. 388)

heyday (hā′ dā) the best time for someone or something (p. 237)

hindrance (hin′ drəns) obstacle (p. 555)

hoarding (hôr′ ding) keeping too much (p. 216)

homage (hom′ ij) respect (p. 349)

honed (hōnd) sharpened by scraping (p. 305)

honeysuckle (hun′ ē suk əl) a climbing shrub with sweet-smelling flowers (p. 298)

horizon (hə rī′zn) an imaginary line where the land appears to meet the sky (p. 471)

hostility (ho stil′ ə tē) not friendly (p. 246); hatred and anger (p. 371)

huckleberry (huk′ əl ber ē) a low bush bearing small blue-black berries (p. 288)

humanity (hyü man′ ə tē) all people (p. 239)

hyacinths (hī′ ə sinthz) fragrant flowers (p. 162)

a	hat	e	let	ī	ice	ô	order	u̇	put	sh	she	ə	a in about
ā	age	ē	equal	o	hot	oi	oil	ü	rule	th	thin		e in taken
ä	far	ėr	term	ō	open	ou	out	ch	child	ŦH	then		i in pencil
â	care	i	it	ȯ	saw	u	cup	ng	long	zh	measure		o in lemon
													u in circus

I

idiosyncrasy (id ē ō sing´ krə sē) unusual way to behave (p. 449)

idol (ī´ dl) an object of worship (p. 371)

ignored (ig nôrd´) paid no attention to (p. 8)

immense (i mens´) huge (pp. 23, 381)

imminent (im´ ə nənt) about to happen (p. 182)

immortal (i môr´ tl) never dying (p. 259)

implored (im plôrd´) begged (p. 345)

impressionable (im presh´ ə nə bəl) easily influenced (p. 151)

impropriety (im prə prī´ ə tē) bad behavior (p. 348)

improvising (im´ prə vīz ing) making up on the spot (p. 24)

in earnest (in ėr´ nist) serious (p. 409)

in unison (in yü´ nə sən) together (p. 472)

inanimate (in an´ ə mit) motionless (p. 524)

incense (in´ sens) wood or spices that smell strong and sweet when burned (p. 383)

incisive (in sī´ siv) sharp and clear (p. 444)

incoherent (in kō hir´ ənt) rambling (p. 181)

inconsolable (in kən sō´ lə bəl) unable to be comforted (p. 524)

incriminate (in krim´ ə nāt) to make someone a criminal (p. 445)

incurable (in kyůr´ ə bəl) unable to change (p. 239)

indebted (in det´ id) owing money (p. 343)

indelibly (in del´ ə bəl ē) unable to be erased (p. 61)

indicates (in´ də kātz) points to (p. 413)

indifferent (in dif´ ər ənt) not caring (p. 214)

indigenous (in dij´ ə nəs) native-born (p. 229)

indispensable (in dis pen´ sə bəl) absolutely necessary (p. 238)

indistinct (in dis tingkt´) hard to see or hear (p. 436)

induce (in düs´) persuade (p. 346)

industry (in´ də strē) hard work (p. 403)

inescapably (in ə skā´ pə bəl ē) to not escape (p. 74)

inexplicably (in ik splik´ ə bəl ē) in a way that cannot be explained (pp. 137, 443)

infancy (in´ fən sē) babyhood (p. 213)

infinitely (in´ fə nit lē) much more (p. 414)

infinity (in fin´ ə tē) forever (p. 434)

initiation (i nish ē ā´ shən) process by which one becomes a member of a group (p. 99)

inlet (in´ let) a narrow strip of water (p. 213)

insignificant (in sig nif´ ə kənt) not important (p. 152)

insomnia (in som´ nē ə) state where one cannot sleep (p. 446)

insomniac (in som´ nē ak) one who has trouble sleeping (p. 355)

installed (in stôld´) put into place (p. 207)

instill (in stil´) to fill with (p. 440)

institution (in stə tü´ shən) a business (p. 472)

intact (in takt´) whole (p. 349)

integration (in tə grā´ shən) the mixing of people and ideas (p. 216)

intellect (in´ tə lekt) the ability to think (p. 229)

intelligible (in tel´ ə je bəl) able to be understood (p. 436)

intense (in tens´) serious and forceful (p. 439)

intention (in ten´ shən) plan (p. 161)

intercedes (in tər sēdz´) steps in to help someone (p. 406)

intercourse (in´ tər kôrs) a meeting or experience (p. 406)

interfere (in tər fir´) to involve oneself in (p. 352)

interim (in´ tər im) time between (p. 54)

interior (in tir´ ē ər) inside (p. 380)

interjecting (in tər jekt′ ing) interrupting (p. 446)

interplanetary (in tər plan′ ə ter ē) between planets (p. 175)

interspersing (in tər spėrs′ ing) switching between (p. 456)

intimacies (in′ tə mə sēz) personal items; secrets (p. 305)

intimidated (in tim′ ə dātd) frightened (p. 440)

intoned (in tōnd′) said in a monotone or singsong voice (p. 183)

intricate (in′ trə kit) complex (p. 520)

intrigue (in trēg′) great interest (p. 54)

intruded (in trüd′ əd) entered without being welcome or invited (p. 444)

intruders (in trüd′ ərz) those who go where they are not invited or welcome (p. 524)

intuition (in tü ish′ ən) knowledge that comes from feeling and sensing (p. 258)

investments (in vest′ məntz) monies paid out on the understanding that they will earn more money (p. 474)

irresistible (ir i zis′ tə bəl) cannot be withstood (p. 374)

irrigation (ir ə gā′ shən) using ditches or other methods to water crops during the dry season (p. 512)

J

jittery (jit′ ər ē) nervous (p. 244)

jocund (jok′ ənd) cheerful (p. 343)

jumble (jum′ bəl) a mixture or confused heap (pp. 47, 186)

justifies (jus′ tə fīz) tries to prove that something is right (p. 214)

K

kerosene lamps (ker′ ə sēn lampz) oil-burning lamps (p. 109)

L

laboring (lā′ bər ing) moving with great effort (p. 136)

lamentation (lam ən tā′ shən) sad cries or songs (p. 360)

lavish (lav′ ish) to give generously (p. 370); generous, large in size (p. 382)

lavishly (lav′ ish lē) generously (p. 78)

legislation (lej ə slā′ shən) the making of laws (p. 237)

liberality (lib ə ral′ ə tē) generosity (p. 350)

lightning bugs (līt′ ning bugz) fireflies (p. 147)

linger (ling′ gər) to wait (p. 359)

literally (lit′ ər ə lē) actually (p. 184)

litter (lit′ ər) a straw covering (p. 119)

loiter (loi′ tər) to wait around without purpose (p. 401)

longevity (lon jev′ ə tē) long life (p. 46)

lopsided (lop′ sī′ did) crooked (p. 152)

ludicrous (lü′ də krəs) silly (p. 468)

lumbered (lum′ bərd) moved slowly and heavily (p. 186)

luminous (lü′ mə nəs) giving off light (p. 279)

luscious (lush′ əs) tasty, juicy (p. 381)

luster bowl (lus′ tər bōl) a low vase for flowers (p. 162)

lustrous (lus′ trəs) full of light (p. 363)

a	hat	e	let	ī	ice	ô	order	u̇	put	sh	she	ə { a	in about
ā	age	ē	equal	o	hot	oi	oil	ü	rule	th	thin	e	in taken
ä	far	ėr	term	ō	open	ou	out	ch	child	ᴛʜ	then	i	in pencil
â	care	i	it	ȯ	saw	u	cup	ng	long	zh	measure	o	in lemon
												u	in circus

M

majestic (mə jes´ tik) royal (p. 521)

malcontent (mal´ kən tent) an unhappy person (p. 355)

malicious (mə lish´ əs) hateful (p. 164)

mallet (mal´ it) a long-handled wooden hammer (p. 147)

maneuvered (mə nü´ vərd) changed position (p. 521)

manned (mand) operated by astronauts (p. 205)

masonry (mā´ sn rē) stonework (p. 115)

mastery (mas´ tər ē) great skill (p. 228)

materialized (mə tir´ ē ə līzd) appeared (p. 450)

meager (mē´ gər) very small amount (p. 385)

measured (mezh´ ərd) slow and steady (p. 450)

menace (men´ is) a danger (pp. 32, 450)

mercenary (mėr´ sə ner ē) interested only in money (p. 181)

merely (mir´ lē) only (p. 7)

metamorphosis (met ə môr´ fə sis) change into something else (p. 444)

microgravity (mī krō grav´ ə tē) very little gravity (p. 206)

mill (mil) to wander around (p. 383)

mimic (mim´ ik) to copy (p. 307)

minimum (min´ ə məm) smallest amount possible (p. 474)

ministers (min´ ə stərz) those who care for others (p. 359)

minnow (min´ ō) a small fish (p. 280)

misanthrope (mis´ ən thrōp) someone who hates mankind (p. 355)

miser (mī´ zər) one who hates to spend money (p. 355)

misery (miz´ ər ē) sadness (pp. 544, 555)

mocked (mokd) made fun of (p. 552)

modest (mod´ ist) small (p. 470)

momentarily (mō´ mən ter ə lē) briefly (p. 141)

momentum (mō men´ təm) the energy to move forward (p. 238)

monarch (mon´ ərk) a ruler; a king or queen (p. 479)

morass (mə ras´) a hard to understand situation (p. 456)

morose (mə rōs´) gloomy and unhappy (p. 347)

mortal (môr´ tl) a human (p. 364)

mourner (môr´ nər) one who grieves for a dead person (p. 344)

multitude (mul´ tə tüd) the masses; the population (p. 351)

murmur (mėr´ mər) a soft flow of speech (p. 438)

mute (myüt) silent (p. 343)

N

nauseous (nô´ shəs) sick to the stomach (p. 206)

nebulae (neb´ yə lē) clouds of gas in space (p. 434)

negligee (neg lə zhā´) a sheer nightgown (p. 182)

negotiations (ni gō´ shē āt shənz) bargaining (p. 228)

nimble (nim´ bəl) quick and clever (p. 521)

nurture (nėr´ chər) to care for (p. 239)

nurtured (nėr´ chərd) took care of (p. 229)

O

obliged (ə blījd´) thankful (p. 363)

obscene (əb sēn´) disgusting (p. 401)

odious (ō´ dē əs) hateful (p. 390)

ominously (om´ ə nəs lē) menacingly (p. 184)

onset (ôn´ set) beginning (p. 225)

opes (ōpz) opens (p. 315)

optimism (op´ tə miz əm) hopefulness (p. 440)

optimist (op´ tə mist) a very hopeful person (p. 239)

originate (ə rij´ ə nāt) be the founder of (p. 525)

outlandish (out lan´ dish) unusual and silly (p. 480)

overcome (ō vər kum´) to defeat (p. 206)

overlapping (ō vər lap´ ing) extending over a part of something so as to coincide with that part (p. 46)

P

paralyzed (par´ ə līzd) made unable to move (p. 113)

parasites (par´ ə sītz) those who feed on living creatures (p. 405)

parched (pärchd) dried out (p. 45)

particular (pər tik´ yə lər) special (p. 397)

passion (pash´ ən) strong feeling (p. 314)

passionate (pash´ ə nit) having strong feelings (p. 226)

paunch (pônch) belly (p. 552)

pedestrian (pə des´ trē ən) ordinary (p. 478)

penalty (pen´ l tē) punishment (p. 446)

penance (pen´ əns) a punishment (p. 360)

penultimate (pi nul´ tə mit) next-to-last (p. 407)

perfunctorily (pər fungk´ tər ē) without interest (p. 25)

persistence (per sis´ təns) stubborn will (p. 525)

persistently (per sis´ tənt lē) without giving up (p. 440)

perspiring (pər spīr´ ing) sweating (p. 454)

pervasive (pər vā´ siv) spread all over (p. 182)

pestering (pes´ ter ing) annoying (p. 533)

petals (pet´ lz) colored parts of a flower (p. 279)

phantom (fan´ təm) a ghost (p. 343)

phenomenon (fe nom´ ə non) a happening, an event (p. 356)

phonetic (fə net´ ik) having to do with sounds (p. 35)

pierce (pirs) to stab or cut through (p. 361)

piping (pīp ing) singing (p. 119)

pitifully (pit´ i fəl lē) in a way that causes others to feel pity (p. 344)

plight (plīt) a bad situation (p. 137)

pneumonia (nü mō´ nyə) a lung disease (p. 137)

point of ethics (point ov eth´ ikz) a matter of right and wrong (p. 183)

ponderous (pon´ dər əs) large and heavy (pp. 136, 358)

portly (pôrt´ lē) heavily built (p. 343)

precariously (pri ker´ ē əs lē) dangerously (p. 475)

precise (pri sīs´) exact (p. 410)

predominantly (pri dom´ ə nənt lē) mostly (p. 60)

preening (prēn ing) cleaning by licking (p. 160)

prejudices (prej´ ə dis ez) unfair feelings and ideas (pp. 239, 457)

presently (pri zent´ lē) right away (p. 120)

a	hat	e	let	ī	ice	ô	order	u̇	put	sh	she	ə { a	in about
ā	age	ē	equal	o	hot	oi	oil	ü	rule	th	thin	e	in taken
ä	far	ėr	term	ō	open	ou	out	ch	child	ᴛʜ	then	i	in pencil
â	care	i	it	ȯ	saw	u	cup	ng	long	zh	measure	o	in lemon
												u	in circus

preserved (pri zėrvd´) saved (p. 389)

presumptuous (pri zump´ chü əs) overconfident (p. 160)

primroses (prim´ rōz əz) small flowers (p. 159)

privacy (prī´ və sē) secrecy or being alone (p. 216)

procedure (prə sē´ jər) way something works (p. 456)

proceed (prə sēd´) to go ahead (p. 475)

procuring (prə kyůr ing) getting hold of, acquiring (p. 360)

profited (prof´ it əd) made money on (p. 348)

profound (prə found´) deeply felt (p. 314)

prohibited (prō hib´ it əd) refused to allow (p. 246)

prosaic (prō zā´ ik) ordinary (p. 80)

providence (prov´ ə dəns) a valuable gift (p. 114)

provision (prə vish´ ən) a gift (p. 351)

purchase (pėr´ chəs) a firm hold (p. 117)

Q

quakes (kwākz) shakes (p. 362)

quarried (kwôr´ ē) carved out of the ground (p. 287)

queer (kwir) strange (p. 409)

quench (kwench) satisfy (p. 502)

queried (kwir´ ēd) asked (pp. 56, 523)

quicksilver (kwik´ sil vər) a silver metal (p. 280)

quota (kwō´ tə) a group (p. 139)

R

radiant (rā´ dē ənt) shining (p. 34)

rail (rāl) to yell at (p. 393)

rakish (rā´ kish) dashing, jaunty (p. 374)

rallied (ral´ ēd) came together (p. 225)

rapt (rapt) deep (p. 364)

rash (rash) foolishly bold (pp. 161, 501)

readapted (re ə daptd´) got used to again (p. 208)

reassuring (re ə shůr´ ing) comforting (p. 31)

rebellion (ri bel´ yən) a revolution (p. 227)

recitations (res ə tā´ shənz) oral presentations given from memory (p. 34)

reclamation (rek lə mā´ shən) return to goodness; act of saving (p. 363)

recollect (rēk ə lekt´) remember (p. 365)

referring (ri fėr´ ing) connecting (p. 325)

reflective (ri flek´ tiv) thoughtful (p. 436)

refrain (ri frān´) to hold back (p. 533)

refuge (ref´ yüj) a place of safety (p. 395)

regal (rē´ gəl) royal (p. 225)

register (rej´ ə stər) a book of signatures (p. 344)

registered (rej´ ə stər) was understood (p. 441)

relent (ri lent´) give in (p. 523)

relented (ri lentd´) gave in (p. 534)

reliable (ri lī´ ə bəl) trustworthy (p. 533)

reluctantly (ri luk´ tənt lē) without wanting to (p. 446)

repetitive (ri pet´ ə tiv) happens over and over again (p. 436)

replenish (ri plen´ ish) to refill (p. 347)

reputation (rep yə tā´ shən) what people believe about one's character (p. 468)

required (ri kwīrd´) necessary (p. 358)

rerouted (rē rüt´ əd) sent in a different way (p. 206)

Reservation (rez ər vā´ shən) tribal land (p. 135)

resignation (rez ig nā´ shən) acceptance (p. 226)

resolute (rez´ ə lüt) determined, not to be moved (p. 349)

resounds (ri zoundz´) echoes loudly throughout a space (p. 356)

resumed (ri zümd´) began again (p. 10)

revelation (rev ə lā´ shən) a sudden understanding or explanation (p. 443)

revelers (rev´ əl ərz) people having fun (p. 383)

reverted (ri vėrtd´) went back (p. 21)

revived (ri vīvd´) came back to consciousness (p. 108)

rheumatism (rü´ mə tiz əm) a painful disease of the muscles, joints, and nerves (pp. 136, 165)

ridicule (rid´ ə kyül) making fun of something (p. 216)

routine (rü tēn´) regular (p. 139)

routinely (rü tēn´ lē) naturally (p. 206)

roved (rōvd) wandered (p. 359)

ruse (rüz) a plan to fool someone (p. 229)

S

sardonically (sär don´ i kəl lē) mockingly (p. 181)

scabbard (skab´ ərd) a loop from which a sword or dagger hangs (p. 382)

scapegoat (skāp´ gōt) someone to take the blame for a group (p. 450)

scarcely (skers´ lē) hardly (p. 75)

scenario (si ner´ ē ō) a story (p. 476)

scornfully (skôrn´ fəl lē) with anger (p. 555)

scoundrels (skoun´ drəlz) criminals (p. 343)

scrunched (skrunchd) squeezed together tightly (p. 545)

seamstress (sēm´ stris) a woman who sews (p. 227)

seer (sir) a person with great power (p. 547)

seething (sēᴛʜ ing) simmering, boiling (p. 381)

segregation (seg rə gā´ shən) the forced separation of racial groups (p. 238)

seize (sēz) to grab and hold (p. 546)

self-esteem (self e stēm´) a sense of worth (pp. 151, 215)

sentry (sen´ trē) guard (p. 447)

seraphs (ser´ əfz) angels (p. 312)

severe (sə vir´) harsh (p. 383)

sheath (shēth) a cover for the blade of a sword or dagger (p. 382)

shed (shed) dropped (p. 544)

shirking (shėrk´ ing) avoiding (p. 138)

shrewd (shrüd) clever (p. 228)

shrine (shrīn) a holy place (pp. 80, 515)

a hat	e let	ī ice	ô order	ů put	sh she	ə: a in about
ā age	ē equal	o hot	oi oil	ü rule	th thin	e in taken
ä far	ėr term	ō open	ou out	ch child	ᴛʜ then	i in pencil
â care	i it	ȯ saw	u cup	ng long	zh measure	o in lemon
						u in circus

shrouded (shroud əd) wrapped up in (pp. 396, 456)

shun (shun) to avoid (pp. 78, 360)

sibilantly (sib´ ə lənt lē) with a hissing sound (p. 182)

siblings (sib´ lingz) children of the same parents (p. 520)

signifying (sig´ nə fī ing) showing, symbolizing (p. 553)

silhouetted (sil ü et´ təd) appearing as a shadow (p. 456)

simultaneously (sī məl tā´ nē əs lē) at the same time (pp. 24, 476)

skittering (skit´ ər ing) skipping lightly (p. 75)

slovenly (sluv´ ən lē) sloppy (p. 398)

sluggishly (slug´ ish lē) slowly and with difficulty (p. 438)

sluice (slüs) a drain (p. 115)

smolder (smōl´ dər) smoke (p. 47)

snag (snag) to catch (p. 546)

solemnized (sol´ əm nīzd) honored or remembered (p. 345)

solitary (sol´ ə ter ē) alone, lonely (p. 344)

solitude (sol´ ə tüd) being alone (p. 21)

sought (sôt) searched for (p. 502)

spacious (spā´ shəs) having plenty of room (p. 476)

spectacles (spek´ tə kəlz) eyeglasses (p. 439)

specter (spek´ tər) a ghost (p. 434)

staccato (stə kä´ tō) short, quick beat (p. 63)

staggers (stag´ ərz) walks unsteadily (p. 365)

stagnant (stag´ nənt) stuck (p. 365)

stampede (stam pəd´) a hurried movement of many people together (p. 444)

statesman (stāts´ mən) a person in politics (p. 230)

stifled (stī´ fəld) made silent (p. 450)

stifling (stī´ fəl ing) smothering (p. 135)

stimulant (stim´ yə lənt) to refresh (p. 525)

stipulated (stip´ yə lāt əd) stated as a rule (p. 245)

store (stôr) a pile built up little by little (p. 501)

strategy (strat´ ə jē) plan (p. 20)

strive (strīv) to make a great effort (p. 406)

stung (stung) hit hard (p. 299)

stutter (stut´ ər) to hesitate or stumble over words (p. 307)

sublime (sə blīm´) wonderful (p. 226)

subtle (sut´ l) hard to detect (p. 256)

suitable (sü´ tə bəl) acceptable (p. 398)

suitors (sü´ tərz) young men who want to marry particular girls (pp. 369, 427)

summit (sum´ it) top point (p. 434)

summons (sum´ ənz) a notice to appear in court (p. 258)

superstition (sü pər stish´ ən) a belief in what does not really exist (p. 434)

surplus (sėr´ pləs) extra (p. 352)

surrender (sə ren´ dər) give in to (p. 374)

sustained (sə stānd´) held up, supported (p. 502)

sustenance (sus´ tə nəns) aid (p. 137)

swerve (swėrv) to turn quickly (p. 280)

T

talons (tal´ ənz) long claws (p. 533)

tamales (tə mä´ lēz) Latin American food made of meat wrapped in cornmeal (p. 227)

taut (tôt) tense and tight (p. 443)

teeming (tē´ ming) full of (p. 472)

teetered (tē´ tərd) rocked (p. 475)

temperament (tem´ pər ə mənt) mood (p. 244)

thickets (thik′ itz) dense bushes (p. 110)

threadbare (thred′ ber) almost worn through (p. 386)

threshold (thresh′ ōld) a length of wood, stone, etc., along the bottom of a doorway (p. 47)

thronged (thrôngd) circled around (p. 60)

thronging (thrông′ ing) rushing (p. 63)

thrusting (thrust′ ing) pushing (p. 62)

tightfisted (tīt′ fis′ tid) tight with money (p. 344)

timorously (tim′ ər əs lē) in a frightened or timid way (p. 447)

toil (toil) hard work (p. 370)

tolerance (tol′ ər əns) respect for other people (p. 239)

tolerant (tol′ ər ənt) accepting (p. 237)

tolerated (tol′ ə rāt əd) put up with (p. 552)

tolls (tōlz) rings (p. 346)

tranquil (trang′ kwəl) peaceful (p. 226)

transfixed (tran sfiksd′) standing still in surprise (p. 435)

transparent (tran sper′ ənt) see-through (p. 356)

tread (tred) to walk on (p. 360)

trifle (trī′ fəl) a little (p. 346)

trousseau (trü′ sō) a bride's clothes and linens (p. 183)

tuft (tuft) a tiny bunch (p. 110)

turquoise (tėr′ koiz) a greenish-blue gemstone (p. 102)

U

ultimate (ul′ tə mit) final (p. 245)

ultimately (ul′ tə mit lē) finally (p. 229)

unaltered (un ôl′ tərd) not changed (p. 389)

unbearable (un ber′ ə bəl) too unpleasant (p. 365)

uncanny (un kan′ ē) strange (p. 54)

unified (yü′ nə fīd) joined (p. 230)

unique (yü nēk′) one-of-a-kind (p. 457)

upland (up′ lənd) high ground (p. 315)

utensils (yü ten′ səlz) forks, knives, and spoons (p. 515)

utter (ut′ ər) to say (p. 280)

uttering (ut′ ər ing) saying (p. 227)

V

vacancy (vā′ kən sē) emptiness (p. 502)

vacant (vā′ kənt) empty (p. 389)

vainly (vān′ lē) uselessly (p. 502)

valiant (val′ yənt) brave (p. 123)

validity (və lid′ ə tē) state of being sound or true (p. 441)

variations (ver ē ā′ shənz) differences (p. 456)

various (ver′ ē əs) different from one another (p. 356)

vast (vast) huge, enormous (p. 445)

veered (vird) changed direction (p. 499)

vendor (ven′ dər) a seller (p. 435)

venture (ven′ chər) to go out (p. 397)

ventures (ven′ chərz) risks (p. 473)

a hat	e let	ī ice	ô order	u̇ put	sh she	ə { a in about
ā age	ē equal	o hot	oi oil	ü rule	th thin	e in taken
ä far	ėr term	ō open	ou out	ch child	ᴛʜ then	i in pencil
â care	i it	ȯ saw	u cup	ng long	zh measure	o in lemon
						u in circus

veranda (və ran´ də) an open porch (p. 109)

verge (vėrj) edge (p. 160)

vessels (ves´ əlz) bowls or cups for drinking (p. 520)

vibrate (vī´ brāt) to move rapidly back and forth (p. 360)

vigor (vig´ ər) strength (p. 351)

visualizing (vizh´ ü ´ līz ing) seeing or forming a mental vision of (p. 186)

vital (vī´ tl) very important (p. 141)

vivify (viv´ ə fī) to bring to life (p. 135)

vocabulary (vō kab´ yə ler ē) a group of words (p. 148)

void (void) emptiness (p. 346)

voyage (voi´ ij) a long trip, a journey (p. 470)

vulgar (vul´ gər) tasteless (p. 181)

W

wager (wāj) to bet (p. 350)

wages (wā´ jər) salary (pp. 353, 425)

waning (wān´ ing) growing shorter or smaller; lessening (p. 396)

weasel (wē´ zəl) a small mammal that eats rats, mice, birds, and eggs (p. 281)

weightlessness (wāt´ lis nəss) being without weight (p. 205)

welfare (wel´ fer) support, especially for the poor (p. 214); well-being (p. 359)

Welsh rarebit (welsh rer´ bit) a dish of melted cheese served on crackers or toast (p. 162)

whack (hwak) a sharp hit (p. 121)

wheezes (hwēz´ əz) hard, whistling breathing sounds (p. 44)

wheezing (hwēz´ ing) breathing heavily (p. 346)

whets (hwetz) sharpens (p. 409)

whiffed (hwifd) struck out (p. 298)

whims (hwimz) moods (p. 393)

wholeheartedly (hōl´ här´ tid lē) with all one's energy, enthusiasm, etc. (p. 32)

winnow (win´ ō) to dig grooves in, like a plow (p. 501)

withered (wiᴛʜ´ ərd) crumbled (p. 368)

wizened (wiz´ nd) wrinkled and dried up (p. 393)

wonderment (wun´ dər mənt) astonishment (p. 175)

writhing (rīᴛʜ´ ing) twisting and turning, as if in pain (p. 299)

Y

yew (yü) an evergreen (p. 305)

Index of Fine Art

Index of Authors and Titles

Index

D

E

F

G

M

N

O

P

Q

R

S

T

Z

Acknowledgments

Grateful acknowledgment is made to the following for copyrighted material:

Pages 7–11: "Papa's Parrot" by Cynthia Rylant from *Every Living Thing.* Copyright © 1985 by Cynthia Rylant. Reprinted with the permission of Atheneum Books for Young Readers, an imprint of Simon & Schuster Children's Publishing Division.

Pages 20–25: From *An American Childhood* by Annie Dillard. Copyright © 1987 by Annie Dillard. Reprinted by permission of HarperCollins Publishers, Inc.

Pages 31–36: From *Barrio Boy* by Ernesto Galarza. Copyright © 1971 by the University of Notre Dame. Used with permission.

Pages 43–48: From *The Bonesetter's Daughter* by Amy Tan, copyright © 2001 by Amy Tan. Used by permission of G.P. Putnam's Sons, a division of Penguin Group (USA) Inc.

Pages 54–64: "My Furthest-Back Person–The African" by Alex Haley, published July 16, 1972, by *The New York Times Magazine.* Copyright © 1972 by Alex Haley. Reprinted by permission of John Hawkins & Associates, Inc.

Pages 99–102: "The Bear Boy" by Joseph Bruchac from *Flying with the Eagle, Racing the Great Bear.* Copyright © 1993 by Joseph Bruchac. Reprinted by permission.

Pages 129–130: "Mongoose on the Loose" reprinted from *Americas*, a bimonthly magazine published by the General Secretariat of the Organization of American States (OAS) in English and Spanish. Reprinted by permission.

Pages 134–141: From *Train Time* by D'Arcy McNickle, copyright © 1936 by D'Arcy McNickle. Reprinted by permission.

Pages 146–152: "My Self, Myself" from *Finding Our Way* by René Saldaña, Jr. Copyright © 2003 by René Saldaña, Jr. Used by permission of Random House Children's Books, a division of Random House, Inc.

Pages 159–165: "The Third Wish" from *Not What You Expected: A Collection of Short Stories* by Joan Aiken. Copyright © 1974, 2002 by Joan Aiken. Used by permission of Brandt & Hochman Literary Agents, Inc.

Pages 175–176: "Zoo" by Edward D. Hoch, copyright © 1958, 1986 by Edward D. Hoch. Reprinted by permission of the author.

Pages 181–186: "A Dozen of Everything" by Marion Zimmer Bradley, copyright © 1959 by Ziff-Davis Publications, Inc. Reprinted by permission of the author and the author's agents, Scovil Chichak Galen Literary Agency, Inc.

Pages 205–208: "Life Without Gravity" by Robert Zimmerman originally published in *Muse Magazine, April 2002.* © 2002 Carus Publishing Company. All rights reserved. Author Zimmerman owns the rights. Reprinted by permission of the author.

Pages 213–216: "I Am a Native of North America" by Chief Dan George from *My Heart Soars.* Copyright © 1974 by Clarke Irwin. Used by permission.

Pages 220–221: "Keeping It Quiet" from *Prentice Hall Science Explorer Sound and Light.* Copyright © 2005 by Pearson Education, Inc., publishing as Pearson Prentice Hall. Used by permission.

Pages 225–230: "For the Love of Country" by Emma Trelles from *Latina Magazine September 2004.* Copyright © 2004 by Latina Magazine. Reprinted with permission from Latina Media Ventures LLC.

Pages 237–239: "All Together Now" by Barbara Jordan from *Sesame Street Parents.* Reprinted by permission of Hilgers Bell & Richards Attorneys at Law for the Estate of Barbara Jordan.

Pages 244–247: "The Real Story of a Cowboy's Life" from *The West: An Illustrated History* by Geoffrey C. Ward. Copyright © 1996 by The West Book Project, Inc. By permission of Little, Brown and Company. Pages 256–260: "Walking" by Linda Hogan. Reprinted from *Parabola, The Magazine of Myth and Tradition, vol. 15.2 (Summer 1990).* Copyright © 1990 by Linda Hogan. Reprinted by permission of the author.

Page 279: "The Rider" by Naomi Shihab Nye from *Invisible.* Reprinted by permission of the author, Naomi Shihab Nye, 2006.

Page 280: "Seal" from *Laughing Time: Collected Nonsense* by William Jay Smith. Copyright © 1990 by William Jay Smith. Reprinted by permission.

Page 281: "Two Haiku" ("O foolish ducklings . . ." and "After the moon sets . . .") and "Haiku" ("Deep in a windless . . .") first appeared in *Cricket Songs: Japanese Haiku*, published by Harcourt. Copyright © 1964 by Harry Behn. Reprinted by permission of Curtis Brown, Ltd. All rights reserved.

Page 286: "Life" from *Remembrances of Spring: Collected Early Poems* by Naomi Long Madgett. Used by permission of the author.

Page 287: "The Courage That My Mother Had" by Edna St. Vincent Millay from *Collected Poems*, HarperCollins. Copyright © 1954, 1982 by Norma Millay Ellis. All rights reserved. Used by permission of Elizabeth Barnett, literary executor.

Pages 288–289: "Loo-Wit" by Wendy Rose from *The Halfbreed Chronicles and Other Poems.* Copyright © 1985 by Wendy Rose. Reprinted by permission.

Pages 298–299: "How I Learned English" by Gregory Djanikian from *Falling Deeply Into America* Carnegie Mellon University. Copyright © 1989 by Gregory Djanikian. Reprinted by permission of the author.

Page 305: From *In an Iridescent Time* by Ruth S. Stone. Copyright © 1959 by Ruth S. Stone. Reprinted by permission of the author.

Page 306: "Weather" by Eve Merriam from *Catch A Little Rhyme*. Copyright © 1966 by Eve Merriam. Copyright © renewed 1994 by Dee Michel and Guy Michel. All rights reserved. Used by permission of Marian Reiner.

Page 307: "One" by James Berry from *When I Dance*. Copyright © 1990 by James Berry. Reproduced by permission of PFD (www.pfd.co.uk) on behalf of James Berry. All rights reserved.

Page 314: "Martin Luther King" by Raymond Richard Patterson. Used by permission of The Estate of Raymond R. Patterson.

Pages 343–374 and Pages 380–415 and Pages 425–427: "A Christmas Carol: Scrooge and Marley" by Israel Horovitz. Copyright © 1994 by Fountain Pen, LLC. All rights reserved. Reprinted by permission of William Morris Agency, LLC on behalf of the Author. CAUTION: Professionals and amateurs are hereby warned that *A Christmas Carol: Scrooge and Marley* is subject to a royalty. It is fully protected under the copyright Laws of the United States of America and all of the countries covered by the International Copyright Union (including the Dominion of Canada and rest of the British Commonwealth), the Berne Convention, the Pan-American Copyright Convention and the Universal Copyright Convention as well as all countries with which the United States has reciprocal copyright relations. All rights, including professional/amateur stage rights, motion picture, recitation, lecturing, public reading, radio broadcasting, television, video or sound recording, all other forms of mechanical or electronic reproduction, such as CD-ROM, CD-I, information storage and retrieval systems and photocopying, and the rights of translation into foreign languages, are strictly reserved. Particular emphasis is laid upon the matter of readings, permission for which must be secured from the Author's agent in writing. Inquiries concerning rights should be addressed to: William Morris Agency, LLC, 1325 Avenue of the Americas, New York, N.Y. 10019.

Page 420: "Picks & Pans: A Christmas Carol (TNT)" by Terry Kelleher from *People Weekly, December 6th, 1999, Vol.52.* Copyright © 1999 by People Weekly. Registered trademarks of Time, Inc. All rights reserved Time Inc. Reprinted by permission.

Pages 421–422: "Toned-down 'Christmas Carol' has more spirit" by John Sousanis, from *The Oakland Press, November 29, 2000, Vol. 156, No. 280.* John Sousanis is a Detroit, MI based writer, playwright and director, and former theater critic for The Oakland Press. Copyright © 2000 The Oakland Press. Reprinted by permission of the author.

Pages 433–457: From "The Monsters Are Due on Maple Street" by Rod Serling. Copyright © 1960 by Rod Serling; Copyright © 1988 by Carolyn Serling, Jodi Serling and Anne Serling. Reprinted by permission.

Pages 462–463: "The Flat Rock Playhouse Apprentice Showcase ad Apprentice Application Form" by Staff. www.flatrockplayhouse.org. Reprinted by permission.

Pages 467–480: "A Loan for Columbus" by Inez Carvalho in Plays, The Drama Magazine for Young People, October 2005. Copyright © PLAYS/Sterling Partners, Inc. 2005. Reprinted with the permission of the publisher PLAYS/Sterling Partners, Inc., PO Box 600160, Newton, MA 02460. Performance rights must be obtained from the publisher.

Pages 511–515: "Tenochtitlan: Inside the Aztec Capital" by Jacqueline Dineen from *The Aztecs.* Copyright © 1992 by Heinemann Educational Publishers. Reprinted by permission of Harcourt Education.

Pages 520–525: "Uniai's Son and the Guaraná" from *Tales from the Rain Forest–Myths and Legends from the Amazonian Indians of Brazil.* Edited by Mercedes Dorson and Jeanne Wilmot. Copyright © 1997 by Mercedes Dorson and Jeanne Wilmot. Foreword copyright © 1997 by Barry Lopez. Reprinted by permission of The Ecco Press, an imprint of HarperCollins Publishers, Inc.

Pages 531–535: "Sun and Moon in a Box (Zuni)", from *American Indian Trickster Tales* by Richard Erdoes and Alphonso Ortiz, copyright (c) 1998 by Richard Erdoes & The Estate of Alphonso Ortiz. Used by permission of Viking Penguin, a division of Penguin Group (USA) Inc. All rights reserved.

Pages 544–547: "The People Could Fly" from *The People Could Fly: American Black Folktales* by Virginia Hamilton, copyright © 1985 by Virginia Hamilton. Used by permission of Alfred A. Knopf, an imprint of Random House Children's Books, a division of Random House, Inc.

Pages 552–557: "The Coming of Asin" from *Ride with the Sun II: An Anthology of Folk Tales and Stories from Countries of the United Nations*, compiled by the United Nations Women's Guild. Copyright © 1955, 2005 by the United Nations Women's Guild. Reprinted by permission.

Note: Every effort has been made to locate the copyright owner of material reproduced in this component. Omissions brought to our attention will be corrected in subsequent editions.

Photo Credits

Cover image © Digital Vision/Getty Images; page x middle © Andres Rodriguez/Shutterstock; page x bottom © Anna Chelnokova/Shutterstock; page xx top © PhotoDisc Volumes Education 2 41307; page xx middle © Blend Images/SuperStock; page xxiv © Images.com/CORBIS; page 3 © PEANUTS reprinted by permission of United Features Syndicate, Inc.; page 5 Courtesy of Cynthia Rylant; page 9 © James Gritz/Robert Harding Picture Library Ltd/Alamy; page 11 © Vstock/Alamy; page 18 © Time Life Pictures/Getty Images; page 21 © PhotoCreate/Shutterstock; page 23 © Image Bank/Getty Images; pages 24–25 © Annie Griffiths/DRK Photo; page 29 Courtesy of the Library of Congress; page 33 © John Lei/Omni-Photo Communications, Inc.; page 35 © Richard Hutchings/PhotoEdit, Inc.; page 41 © Marc Brasz/CORBIS All Rights Reserved; page 44 © Jon Arnold Images/Alamy; page 47 © Bob Krist/CORBIS All Rights Reserved; page 52 © Alex Gotfryd/Corbis/Bettman; page 55 © Betty Press/Panos Pictures; page 57 © Map Resources; page 59 © Images & Stories/Alamy; page 62 © PhotoDisc Nature, Wildlife and the Environment Volume 006 6118; page 72 © Bettman/CORBIS; page 76 © Richard T. Nowitz/CORBIS All Rights Reserved; page 79 © PhotoDisc U.S. Landmarks and Travel Volume 16 16236; page 92 © Nicholas Wilton/Images.com; page 95 © PEANUTS reprinted by permission of United Features Syndicate, Inc.; page 97 © Prentice Hall School Division; page 99 © Jack Parsons/Omni-Photo Communications, Inc.; page 101 © PhotoDisc Nature, Wildlife and the Environment Volume 006 6303; page 102 Copyright President and Fellows of Harvard College 1995. All rights reserved. © 2006 Harvard University Peabody Museum-Harvard University, 26-7-10/95879 T85. Photograph by Hillel Burger.; page 105 © Underwood & Underwood/CORBIS; page 107 © Clem Haagner/Photo Researchers, Inc.; page 111 © E. Hanumantha Rao/Photo Researchers, Inc.; page 118 © Dinodia Images/Alamy; page 122 © Paolo Koch/Photo Researchers, Inc.; page 129 © Gunter Ziesler/Peter Arnold, Inc.; page 130 © Larry Luxner 2001; page 132 © The Newberry Library; page 135 © Photo Collection Alexander Alland, Sr./CORBIS All Rights Reserved; page 139 © CORBIS All Rights Reserved; page 140 © CORBIS All Rights Reserved; page 144 © Tina Saldana/Random House; page 147 © Awilli/Zefa/CORBIS; page 149 © Ajax/Zefa/CORBIS; page 150 © Comstock/Jupiter Images; page 157 © Prentice Hall School Division; page 159 © Pal Hermansen/Getty Images Inc.-Stone Allstock; page 162 © Alan Briere/SuperStock, Inc.; page 164 © Hideki Fujii/Getty Images Inc.-Image Bank; page 170 © Ingram Publishing Animals (colourful bird),(hens); page 170 © AGS Globe Royalty-free: PhotoDisc Nature, Wildlife and the Environment Volume 006 6059 (goat), 6325 (flamingo); page 170 © PhotoDisc Nature, Wildlife and the Environment Volume 044 44002 (lion), 44025 (giraffe), 44057 (chimpanzee), 44058 (orangutan), 44096 (cow), 44090 (sheep), 44189 (snake), 44121 (bear), 44129 (eagle); page 173 © Matthew Peyton/Getty Images, Inc.; page 179 © Marion Zimmer Bradley/Scovil Chichak Galen Literary Agency, Inc.; page 181 Igor Oleynikov; page 185 Igor Oleynikov; page 198 © Isy Ochoa/SuperStock; page 201 © PEANUTS reprinted by permission of United Feature Syndicate, Inc.; page 203 © Robert Zimmerman; page 205 © NASA/Johnson Space Center; page 206 © Brand X Pictures BXP46153h; page 207 © NASA/Johnson Space Center; page 211 © Corbis/Bettmann; page 213 © PhotoDisc U.S. Landmarks and Travel Volume 16 16329; page 215 © Jaune Quick-to-See-Smith, "Buffalo", 1992, oil, collage, mixed media on canvas, Diptyph 66 x 96"/Flomenhaft Gallery; page 220 © Ted Streshinsky/Corbis/Bettmann; page 221 © Mark Peterson/Corbis/Bettmann; page 223 © Emma Trelles; page 227 © Archivo Iconografico/CORBIS All Rights Reserved; page 228 The Granger Collection, New York; page 229 © Penny Slinger; page 235 © Getty Images; page 237 ©Hulton-Deutsch Collection/Corbis/Bettmann; page 242 © Seth Resnick/Corbis/Bettmann; page 245 © Hisom Silviu/Shutterstock; page 247 © Kansas State Historical Society, Topeka, Kansas; page 252 Stephanie Pershing and Kathy Kruger; page 254 © Christopher Felver/CORBIS All Rights Reserved; page 257 PhotoDisc U.S. Landmarks and Travel Volume 16 A0003284; page 259 © Bruce Wheadon/Shutterstock; page 272 © Peter Sickles/SuperStock; page 275 CALVIN AND HOBBES © 1992 Watterson. Reprinted with permission of UNIVERSAL PRESS SYNDICATE. All rights reserved.; page 277 top left © 1998 James McGoon; page 277 top right © Oscar White/Corbis/Bettmann; page 277 middle © Hiebonsha/Pacific Press Service; page 279 © Ed Kashi/CORBIS; page 280 © Martin Harvey/Peter Arnold, Inc.; page 281 © Christie's Images/CORBIS; page 284 top left © Detroit Free Press; 284 top right © Christie's Images/CORBIS; page 284 middle © Patricia Allen-Wolk; page 286 © Royalty-Free/CORBIS; page 287 © The Newark Museum/Art Resource, NY; pages 288–289 © PhotoDisc Nature, Wildlife and the Environment 2 Volume 044 44328; page 296 © Gregory Djanikian; page 298 © Patrik Giardino/CORBIS; page 303 top left © Ruth Stone/Binghamton University, New York; page 303 top right © Photo by Bachrach. Used by permission of Marian Reiner.; page 303 middle © Gezette de Buro fur Fotografie; page 305 © Swim Ink 2, LLC/

CORBIS All Rights Reserved; page 306 © Robert Venn/ Shutterstock; page 307 © Bruno Budrovic/Images.com; page 310 top left © Corbis/Bettmann; page 310 top right © William E. Stafford; page 310 middle © The Ohio Historical Society; page 312 © PhotoDisc Nature, Wildlife and the Environment Volume 006 6263; page 314 © Time Life Pictures/Getty Images; page 315 © Nadia Richie/Images.com; page 322 © Bettmann/CORBIS; page 324 © Robert Whitman/Images.com; page 336 © Lou Wall/CORBIS All Rights Reserved; page 339 © PEANUTS reprinted by permission of United Feature Syndicate, Inc.; page 341 top © Time & Life Pictures/Getty Images; page 341 middle © AP Wide World Photos; page 345 © CBS/The Kobal Collection; page 346 Charles Janasz as Bob Cratchit in the Guthrie Theater's 1992 production of A Christmas Carol adapted by Barbara Field. Photo credit: Michal Daniel.; page 351 © Jeffrey Coolidge/Getty Images Inc.-Image Bank; page 353 Bob Davis as Bob Cratchit, Kevin James Kelly as Charles Dickens and Richard Ooms as Ebneezer Scrooge in the Guthrie Theater's 1994 production of A Christmas Carol adapted by Barbara Field. Photo credit: Michal Daniel.; page 357 Bob Davis as Bob Cratchit and Nathaniel Fuller in the Guthrie Theater's 1994 production of A Christmas Carol adapted by Barbara Field. Photo credit: Michal Daniel.; page 358 © Michal Daniel; page 359 © David Buffington/Getty Images, Inc.- Photodisc; page 362 © C Squared Studios/Getty Images, Inc.- Photodisc; page 370 © Michal Daniel; page 378 top © Time & Life Pictures/ Getty Images; page 378 middle © AP Wide World Photos; page 382 Jim Baker as Ghost of Christmas Present in the Guthrie Theater's 1975 production of A Christmas Carol adapted by Barbara Field. Photo credit: Michal Daniel.; page 385 © Michal Daniel; page 388 © Michal Daniel; page 391 © David Toase/Getty Images, Inc.– Photodisc; page 395 © Michal Daniel, 2000; page 403 The Cratchit family and Ebenezer Scrooge in the Guthrie Theater's 1994 production of A Christmas Carol adapted by Barbara Field. Photo credit: Michal Daniel; page 406 © Gary Braasch/CORBIS; page 412 Ebenezer Scrooge celebrating in the Guthrie Theater's 1994 production of A Christmas Carol adapted by Barbara Field. Photo credit: Michal Daniel; page 415 © Michal Daniel; page 420 © Photofest; page 425 © CBS/The Kobal Collection; page 426 © Michal Daniel; page 431 © Bettmann/CORBIS; page 433 © Dhoxax/Shutterstock; page 436 © William Low, "Woman on telephone as seen through window," oil on paper. Courtesy of the artist.; page 440 © William Low, "Overview of Family Walking Dog on the Street", oil on paper. Courtesy of the artist.; page 444 © Constance Coleman Richardson, American (1905-2002), "Streetlight", 1930, oil on canvas, 28 x 36 inches. © Indianapolis Museum of Art, Gift of Mrs. James W. Fesler; page 449 © Peter Willi/SuperStock; page 453 © David Tipling/Alamy; page 462 © Flat Rock Playhouse, The State Theatre of North Carolina, You Theatre production of Alice's Adventures In Wonderland; page 465 © Inez Carvalho/Sterling Partners, Inc.; page 469 Jim Haynes; page 473 Jim Haynes; page 477 Jim Haynes; page 479 Jim Haynes; page 492 © Jose Ortega/Images.com; page 495 PEANUTS © 2003, reprinted by permission of United Feature Syndicate, Inc.; page 497 Library of Congress; page 500 The Granger Collection, New York; page 520 © Galen Rowell/CORBIS All Rights Reserved; page 522 © William Coupon/CORBIS All Rights Reserved; page 523 © Warren Morgan/CORBIS All Rights Reserved; page 524© Theo Allofs/CORBIS All Rights Reserved; page 529 top © Bassouls Sophie/CORBIS Sygma; page 529 middle © AP/ Wide World Photos; page 532 © Ron Sanford/CORBIS; page 534 © Darren Bennett/Animals Animals; page 540 © Ingram Publishing Food and Beverage mixed fruit; page 542 © Prentice Hall School Division; page 554 © Edward S. Curtis/CORBIS All Rights Reserved; page 556 © Christie's Images/CORBIS All Rights Reserved

Staff Credits

Rosalyn Arcilla, Melania Benzinger, Carol Bowling, Laura Chadwick, Kazuko Collins, Nancy Condon, Barbara Drewlo, Kerry Dunn, Marti Erding, Sara Freund, Sue Gulsvig, Daren Hastings, Laura Henrichsen, Brian Holl, Bev Johnson, Julie Johnston, Patrick Keithahn, Marie Mattson, Daniel Milowski, Stephanie Morstad, Carrie O'Connor, Jeffrey Sculthorp, Julie Theisen, LeAnn Velde, Daniela Velez, Amber Wegwerth, Charmaine Whitman, Sue Will